Juvenile Justice

An Introduction

Third Edition

John T. Whitehead
East Tennessee State University

Steven P. Lab
Bowling Green State University

anderson publishing co.
2035 Reading Road
Cincinnati, OH 45202
800-582-7295

Juvenile Justice: An Introduction, Third Edition

Copyright © 1990, 1996, 1999
Anderson Publishing Co.
2035 Reading Rd.
Cincinnati, OH 45202

Phone 800.582.7295 or 513.421.4142
Web Site www.andersonpublishing.com

Library of Congress Cataloging-in-Publication Data

Whitehead, John T.
    Juvenile justice : an introduction / John T. Whitehead , Steven P. Lab. -- 3rd ed.
        p.   cm.
    Includes bibliographical references (p.   ) and indexes.
    ISBN 0-87084-904-2 (pbk.)
    1. Juvenile delinquency. 2. Juvenile justice, Administration of.
    3. Juvenile justice, Administration of--United States. I. Lab, Steven P.   II. Title.
    HV9069.W46   1998
    364.36--dc21   98-40326
                                                                    CIP

Cover design by Tin Box Studio/Cincinnati, OH   EDITOR Ellen S. Boyne
Cover photo credit: © David Young-Wolff/Tony Stone Images   ACQUISITIONS EDITOR Michael C. Braswell

Dedication

to

Pat, Danny & Timmy Whitehead

and

Danielle Lab

FOREWORD

In this Third Edition of *Juvenile Justice: An Introduction* we have done two things. First, we have updated all of the materials throughout to make the book as current as possible. Second, we have deleted some older material and added new information, especially in a number of the supplementary boxes. We think that this edition offers a comprehensive and current discussion of juvenile justice and juvenile delinquency and can meet the needs of anyone teaching juvenile justice or juvenile delinquency courses.

As was true of the first edition, we have tried to set the stage for discussion and debate in the classroom. Thus, we have included material on many current issues in juvenile justice, including the death penalty for juveniles, the extent of racism in the system, the question of what to do with violent juveniles including such options as blended sentencing and increased use of the adult court, the effectiveness of DARE programs, corporal punishment, school crime, and discussion of the various delinquency theories. There are questions at the end of each chapter to help stimulate discussion of these issues.

An Instructor's Guide is available. It contains chapter summaries, test bank questions, suggestions for classroom activities and videos to supplement the text.

We thank all of the people at Anderson for their support of the book. We especially thank Ellen Boyne for her excellent work in editing and producing the final product, including her work on the glossary. We are grateful to Bill Simon (now retired), Mickey Braswell and Susan Braswell, and all of the others at Anderson for their professional and personal dedication and effort.

JTW
SPL

TABLE OF CONTENTS

Chapter 4
Sociological Explanations for Delinquency   77

Chapter 5
Gang Delinquency

113

Chapter 6
Drugs and Delinquency

147

Chapter 13
The Victimization of Juveniles

345

Chapter 14
The Future of the Juvenile Justice System

369

CHAPTER 1

The Definition and Extent of Delinquency

Key Terms and Phrases

dark figure of crime
delinquency
Index offenses
juvenile
Monitoring the Future (MTF)
    Survey
National Youth Survey (NYS)
National Crime Victimization
    Survey (NCVS)

offense rate
panel design
self-report measures
Short-Nye instrument
status offenses
transfer
Uniform Crime Reports (UCR)
victim surveys
waiver

Efforts to deal with and correct the deviant behavior of young people appear throughout history. At the same time, the problem of "delinquency" is a relatively new development. The reason for this seeming contradiction lies in the changing mechanisms of social control that have developed over the past two centuries. Throughout most of history the young and old alike were subjected to the same systems of justice and could receive the same punishments for their behavior. There was little distinction made between offenders of different ages. This is not to suggest that the judges and administrators could not or would not make allowances for youthful offenders. Indeed, although many juveniles were sentenced to the same harsh sentences as adults, including the death penalty, often these penalties were not carried out by the system (Platt, 1977).

It has only been in the last 100 years that different systems of dealing with problem youths have emerged. Separate institutions for housing juveniles have been around only since the mid- to late-1800s and the juvenile court has not yet reached its 100th birthday. In the relatively short time period since these changes were initiated, society has introduced different standards of justice for juveniles and a separate system for handling youthful offenders. As a result, youthful offenders who used to be seen as simply young "criminals" have been transformed into "delinquents." This label was set aside to denote those juve-

1

niles who, for one reason or another, have come to the attention of the juvenile justice system. This label of "delinquent," however, represents a variety of different behaviors and means different things at different places and points in time. It is important to understand the diversity in definitions of delinquency in order to examine adequately the workings of the juvenile justice system.

Defining Delinquency

As already noted, delinquency has a number of different meanings. These various interpretations appear both in state statutes and criminological discussions of juvenile behavior. As a result, it is possible to delineate three types of definitions corresponding to the behavior of the juvenile and the intended use of the definition. The three types of definitions are: (1) criminal law definitions, (2) status offense definitions, and (3) social/criminological definitions.

Criminal Law Definitions

The criminal law reflects activities that society has defined as unacceptable and takes steps to sanction. A criminal law definition of delinquency, therefore, delineates activity that is illegal regardless of the age of the offender. That is, delinquency is simply a substitute label for criminal behavior by a juvenile. The only distinction between being a delinquent and being a criminal is the age of the individual.

Criminal law definitions of delinquency often define a delinquent as someone who violates the criminal laws of the jurisdiction (see Figure 1.1). The key to these statutes is the idea that the juvenile violated the criminal law. There is no distinction made in terms of the age of the offender, except for the label that will be imposed (delinquent versus criminal) and the system that will handle the individual (juvenile versus adult). A criminal law definition explicitly extends the criminal statutes to the juvenile population.

Figure 1.1   Sample State Code Definitions

Section 602 of the California Welfare and Institutions Code defines a "delinquent" as "any person who is under the age of 18 years when he violates any law of this state or of the United States or any ordinance of any city or county of this state defining crime other than an ordinance establishing a curfew based solely on age . . ." (West's Annotated California Codes, 1984).

Similarly, Ohio's Chapter 2151.02 states that a "delinquent child" includes any child:

    a)   Who violates any law of this state, the United States, or any ordinance or regulation of a political subdivision of the state, which would be a crime if committed by an adult . . . [or]

    b)   Who violates any lawful order of the court . . .
          (Page's Ohio Revised Code Annotated, 1994).

Status Offense Definitions

Besides the criminal actions that can be committed by a juvenile that trigger involvement with the juvenile justice system, there are a variety of specific actions for which only juveniles can be held accountable. These behaviors are usually referred to as **status offenses** because they can be committed only by persons of a particular "status." These actions are illegal only for persons of that particular status. Thus, juvenile status offenses represent acts that are illegal only for juveniles. Adults who take part in these acts are not subject to sanctioning by the formal justice system.

While the term "status offender" is the most common term for those who violate these acts, a variety of other names have been given to these individuals. Among the more common names are "unruly," "dependent," "incorrigible" and acronyms such as PINS (person in need of supervision) or CHINS (child in need of supervision). Section 601 of the California Welfare and Institutions Code of the 1960s is often used as an example of an ambiguous status offense definition. This section defined a status offender as:

> Any person under the age of eighteen who persistently or habitually refuses to obey the reasonable and proper orders or directions of his parents, guardian, custodian, or school authorities who is beyond the control of such person, or . . . who from any cause is in danger of leading an idle, dissolute, lewd, or immoral life . . . (West's Annotated California Codes, 1972).

This section gained notoriety when the 1967 President's Commission on Law Enforcement and the Administration of Justice used it to point out problems with juvenile justice. The wording of such statutes is sufficiently vague to allow wide latitude in interpretation. Indeed, the second part of California's definition dealing with "an idle, dissolute, lewd, or immoral life" was declared unconstitutionally vague (*Gonzalez v. Mailliard*, 1971).

Many states provide more detailed status offense definitions that outline specific behaviors (see Figure 1.2). The terminology of these statutes, however, typically maintains the vagueness and latitude that appeared in the California definition. These statutes allow the juvenile justice system to intervene in the life of almost any youth. The behaviors outlined by these and other similar statutes make virtually any behavior of a juvenile sanctionable by the state. The definitions are all-encompassing.

Actions that typically fall under the heading of status offenses include truancy, smoking, drinking, curfew violations, disobeying the orders of parents, teachers or other adults, swearing, running away, and other acts that are allowable for adults. All juveniles violate these statutes at one time or another. Normal youthful behavior includes many of these activities. It is possible that all youths could be subjected to system intervention under these types of "status" definitions.

Figure 1.2   Ohio's Definition of an "Unruly" Child

An unruly child is:

a) Any child who does not subject himself or herself to the reasonable control of his or her parents, teachers, guardian, or custodian, by reason of being wayward or habitually disobedient;

b) Any child who is an habitual truant from home or school;

c) Any child who so deports himself or herself as to injure or endanger his or her health or morals or the health or morals of others;

d) Any child who attempts to enter the marriage relation in any state without the consent of his or her parents, custodian or legal guardian, or other legal authority;

e) Any child who is found in a disreputable place, visits or patronizes a place prohibited by law, or associates with vagrant, vicious, criminal, notorious, or immoral persons;

f) Any child who engages in an occupation prohibited by law or is in a situation dangerous to life or limb or injurious to his or her health or morals or the health or morals of others;

g) Any child who violates a law . . . applicable only to a child (*Page's Ohio Revised Code Annotated*, 1997: Chapter 2151.022).

Social/Criminological Definitions

The study of delinquency and juvenile justice often relies on definitions of delinquency that do not conform precisely to the legal definitions of "delinquent" or "status offense." The definition of delinquency often takes on a specific meaning depending on the interests of the group or individual dealing with juvenile misconduct at any given time or place. As a result, no single definition is used by all individuals. For example, the 1967 President's Commission on Law Enforcement and the Administration of Justice took a very broad view of delinquency by combining the elements of delinquent and status offense statutes:

> Delinquency comprises cases of children alleged to have committed an offense that if committed by an adult would be a crime. It also comprises cases of children alleged to have violated specific ordinances or regulatory laws that apply only to children . . . (President's Commission, 1967b:4).

Cloward and Ohlin (1960) provide a definition of delinquency that is dependent upon the response of the justice system. Delinquent acts are characterized "by the fact that officials engaged in the administration of criminal justice select them, from among many deviant acts, as forms of behavior proscribed by the approved norms of society" (Cloward & Ohlin, 1960: 2-3). This definition relies on the criminal and juvenile justice systems to determine which actions are to be considered delinquent. It does, however, recognize that these social control agents are (or should be) responsive to the views and needs of the larger society. That is, the actions chosen for intervention by the formal justice systems are to be determined by the sentiments of society. Such a definition limits the discussion of delinquency to those actions that are handled by the justice system. Juvenile behavior that is ignored by the system is not to be considered delinquent.

The use of any of the above definitions of delinquency—criminal law, status offense or criminological—presents a view of juvenile behavior as either delinquent or nondelinquent, with no middle ground within which the individual can fall. An alternative means of looking at delinquency would be to consider a continuum of juvenile conduct ranging from extreme delinquency at one end to extreme conforming behavior at the other end. Such a depiction of delinquency is provided by Cavan and Ferdinand (1981). Figure 1.3 shows a continuum of delinquency that depicts the extreme behavior patterns and various gradations between them. The shape of the continuum, a bell curve, represents the proportional distribution of juveniles along the continuum. It is assumed that the largest group of youths would fall into the middle category of "normal conformity." The left-hand portion of the curve represent youths who run the risk of being apprehended and labeled delinquent. These juveniles are involved, to varying degrees, in delinquent behavior. Minor underconformity may include such acts as status and victimless offenses, while the delinquent contraculture category includes serious acts such as murder and rape and suggests organized involvement in deviance. The right side of the curve represents individuals who do not become involved in delinquency. Few juveniles appear in either of the contraculture categories of extreme delinquency or extreme goodness.

Figure 1.3   Behavior Continuum

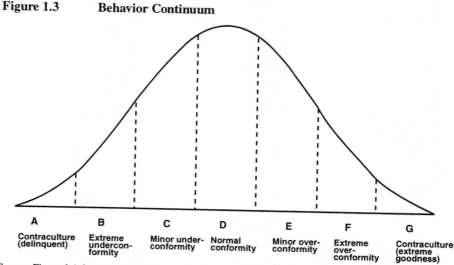

A	B	C	D	E	F	G
Contraculture (delinquent)	Extreme underconformity	Minor underconformity	Normal conformity	Minor overconformity	Extreme overconformity	Contraculture (extreme goodness)

Source: Figure 2.1 from *Juvenile Delinquency*, 4th ed. by Ruth Shonle Cavan and Theodore N. Ferdinand. Copyright © 1981 by Ruth Shonle Cavan and Theodore N. Ferdinand. Reprinted by permission.

This last view of delinquency more closely represents the type of definition emerging in criminological study. It does not limit the researcher to a simple legal definition or an either/or dichotomy. Instead, it allows the inspection of various types of delinquent activity as well as activity that is highly overconforming. Seen as a continuum, juvenile activity can be subdivided into various parts and phases that change over time and can be compared to one another.

What is a Juvenile?

In every definition of delinquency there is an implicit assumption of what constitutes a **juvenile**. Interestingly, the legal definition of a juvenile varies from jurisdiction to jurisdiction. This means that persons subject to the juvenile statutes in one location may not be subject to them in another place. Table 1.1 presents the age at which the adult court assumes responsibility for the actions of individuals in different jurisdictions. Individuals who are under these ages are considered juveniles and are handled in the juvenile justice system. The majority of states (37), the District of Columbia and the federal courts recognize juveniles as individuals below the age of 18. Three states define juveniles as those age 15 or younger, and 10 states define juveniles as those under 17 years old.

Table 1.1   Ages at Which Criminal Courts Gain Jurisdiction over Young Offenders

Age 16	Age 18	
Connecticut	Alabama	Nevada
New York	Alaska	New Jersey
North Carolina	Arizona	New Mexico
	Arkansas	North Dakota
	California	Ohio
	Colorado	Oklahoma
Age 17	Delaware	Oregon
	District of	Pennsylvania
Georgia	Columbia	Rhode Island
Illinois	Florida	South Dakota
Louisiana	Hawaii	Tennessee
Massachusetts	Idaho	Utah
Michigan	Indiana	Vermont
Missouri	Iowa	Virginia
New Hampshire	Kansas	Washington
South Carolina	Kentucky	West Virginia
Texas	Maine	Federal Districts
Wisconsin	Maryland	
	Minnesota	
	Mississippi	
	Montana	
	Nebraska	

Source: Sickmund, Snyder & Poe-Yamagata (1997).

Besides setting an upper age for juvenile status, other factors influence whether an individual can be handled in the juvenile justice system. First, some states set a lower age limit in outlining who can be treated by the juvenile justice process. These ages typically range from age six to age 10. In those states with a lower age level, any juvenile below the minimum age who exhibits deviant behavior is simply returned to his or her parents or guardian for handling. A second age consideration is the termination of the juvenile system's intervention with an individual. Some state statutes allow the juvenile system to continue supervision and intervention with individuals who have passed the maximum age limit. This occurs mainly when that person committed his or her act as a juvenile and/or is being handled as an extension of intervention begun when he or she was a juvenile. These provisions typically set an absolute maximum age, such as age 21.

A final provision that intercedes in the determination of age for juvenile justice system intervention deals with the **waiver** or **transfer** of an individual to adult court. Waiver is a process by which an individual who is legally a juvenile is sent to the adult criminal system for disposition and handling. While ages 15 and 16 have traditionally constituted the youngest ages at which waiver could occur, recent years have seen a move toward waiving younger individuals to the adult system. The age of the individual is only one factor that must be considered in transferring a juvenile (other factors will be discussed in a later chapter). Juveniles who are handled by the adult system comprise a special category of delinquents (or criminals) with which a discussion of juvenile justice must deal.

The varying definitions of delinquency and considerations of what constitutes delinquent behavior have a major impact on any study of juvenile justice. The definition alters the type of behavior with which we are concerned, the practices and interventions used in the treatment of delinquency, and the number of problems and youths who are subjected to intervention and study. It is the effect of the definition of delinquency on the measurement of delinquency to which we now turn.

Measuring the Extent of Delinquency

There are a number of different ways to measure delinquency, each of which produces a different picture of the delinquency problem. The various methods for measuring delinquency result in different absolute levels of delinquency as well as different information on the offense, the offender and the victim. The three basic approaches to measuring delinquency are the use of official records, the administration of self-report surveys and the use of victimization surveys.

Official Measures of Delinquency

Official measures of delinquency are based on the records of various justice system agencies. Consequently, the level of delinquency reflects both the activity of juveniles and the activity of the agency that is dealing with the youths. The degree of detail in the records also varies by agency. The police, courts and corrections each have different sets of priorities and mandates under which they operate. As a result, the data compiled by the agencies differ from one another. The following pages will consider data from each of these official sources.

UNIFORM CRIME REPORTS

The **Uniform Crime Reports (UCR)** provide information on the number of offenses coming to the attention of the police, the number of arrests police make and the number of referrals by the police to the juvenile court. This data is collected yearly by the Federal Bureau of Investigation and provides information on 29 categories of offenses. These counts reflect only those crimes known to the police. Actions that are not reported to the police are not included in the yearly crime figures. The UCR is comprised of two offense subgroups. The first eight offenses are known as the Part I or **Index offenses**. Included in this group are the more serious crimes (as delineated by the FBI) of murder, rape, robbery, aggravated assault, burglary, larceny, motor vehicle theft and arson. All remaining offenses fall within the Part II category. Extensive information, including demographic data on the victim and offender (if known), circumstances of the offense, the use of a weapon, and the time and place of the offense, is gathered for the Part I offenses. For Part II offenses, only information on offenses for which a suspect has been arrested are tabulated.

Age Distribution. Due to the fact that only about 20 percent of all crimes are cleared by an arrest each year, little information is known about the offender in most crimes. Some idea about the participation of juveniles in delinquent/criminal behavior, however, can be gathered from an inspection of those cases for which an offender can be identified and/or arrested. Table 1.2 presents arrest data by age for 1996. A total of 11,093,211 arrests were reported to the FBI. Of these arrests, 2,103,658 or 18.9 percent of the total were of juveniles under the age of 18.

A closer inspection of the arrest data reveals the extent to which youths were involved in serious offending. For the violent crimes of murder, rape, robbery and aggravated assault, youths comprised 18.7 percent of the total arrests. This represents almost 102,000 offenses. More striking is the fact that youths were arrested for more than 530,000 property offenses. This reflects more than one-third of all property offense arrests in 1996. These figures show that juveniles made up 30.8 percent of all arrests for Part I Index offenses. Taken by themselves, these figures are large. The problem is exacerbated, however, when you consider that youths between the ages of 10 and 17 (inclusive) make up

Table 1.2   Age Distribution of Juvenile Arrests, 1996

Offense Charged	All ages	Under age 18	Under 10	10-12	13-14	15	16	17
Total	11,093,211	2,103,658	32,450	151,551	495,448	418,656	494,000	511,553
Murder and nonnegligent manslaughter	14,447	2,172	17	16	224	359	651	905
Forcible rape	24,347	4,128	61	346	1,016	751	888	1,066
Robbery	121,781	39,037	266	1,882	8,377	8,100	9,883	10,529
Aggravated assault	387,571	56,894	1,000	4,366	12,756	10,626	13,358	14,788
Burglary	264,193	97,809	2,487	9,110	25,262	19,548	20,896	20,506
Larceny-theft	1,096,488	370,607	7,749	43,132	104,406	70,042	74,988	70,290
Motor vehicle theft	132,023	54,813	199	1,706	12,568	13,403	14,190	12,747
Arson	13,755	7,302	9,221,623	2,342	965	797	653	
Violent crimes	548,146	102,231	1,344	6,610	22,373	19,836	24,780	27,288
Percent distribution	100.0	18.7	.2	1.2	4.1	3.6	4.5	5.0
Property crimes	1,506,459	530,531	11,357	55,571	144,578	103,958	110,871	104,196
Percent distribution	100.0	35.2	.8	3.7	9.6	6.9	7.4	6.9
Other assaults	972,984	171,366	3,791	19,502	46,982	32,258	34,417	34,415
Forgery and counterfeiting	88,355	6,238	28	115	612	905	1,780	2,798
Fraud	324,776	18,872	95	799	4,558	4,964	3,416	5,040
Embezzlement	11,449	958	4	11	48	57	326	512
Stolen property	111,066	30,189	187	1,439	6,473	6,214	7,504	8,372
Vandalism	234,215	103,333	4,660	13,595	28,098	18,616	20,332	18,032
Weapons; carrying, possessing, etc.	161,158	39,363	600	2,542	8,542	7,646	9,485	10,548
Prostitution and commercialized vice	81,036	1,104	10	16	114	153	263	548
Sex offenses (except forcible rape)	70,619	12,660	589	1,811	3,943	2,188	1,999	2,130
Drug abuse violations	1,128,647	158,447	296	2,951	23,458	29,232	44,199	58,311
Gambling	16,984	2,263	5	34	258	422	678	866
Offenses against family and children	103,800	5,850	165	369	1,345	1,191	1,385	1,395
Driving under the influence	1,013,932	12,814	120	34	187	459	3,481	8,443
Liquor laws	491,176	112,553	194	994	11,175	17,787	33,088	49,315
Drunkenness	522,869	17,111	103	216	2,095	2,768	4,313	7,616
Disorderly conduct	626,918	159,951	1,766	11,887	40,073	32,114	36,642	37,469
Vagrancy	21,735	2,873	15	92	515	568	721	962
All other offenses	2,767,751	329,070	4,791	17,544	69,905	65,774	80,702	90,354
Suspicion	4,859	1,604	18	82	336	339	391	438
Curfew and loitering law violations	142,433	142,433	940	5,927	32,448	33,302	40,132	29,684
Runaways	141,844	141,844	1,372	9,409	47,332	37,815	33,095	12,821

Source: Federal Bureau of Investigation (1997). Adapted by authors.

roughly 11 percent of the total United States population (U.S. Bureau of the Census, 1992). Youthful offenders are contributing more than their fair share to the level of arrests in the nation.

Race Distribution. The UCR also provides information on the race of juvenile arrestees. Table 1.3 presents data on arrests for whites, blacks, Native American and Asian/Pacific island youths. White youths make up the vast majority of all arrestees (69.7%) and account for two-thirds of the Part I property offenses. Black youths, however, are greatly overrepresented in violent personal offenses (murder, rape, robbery and aggravated assault). This overrepresentation of blacks in the violent offense category (47.2%) is even more dramatic in light of the fact that blacks comprise only about 15 percent of the youthful United States population (U.S. Bureau of the Census, 1992).

An examination of individual Part I offenses provides a more detailed look at the data. While white youths and black youths commit roughly the same number of violent offenses, blacks commit 50 percent more murders and robberies than whites. Conversely, white youths dominate in all other offense categories. Based on population figures, however, offending by black youths far surpasses their population percentages in all Part I offenses except arson.

Residence Distribution. One of the traditional methods for investigating crime and delinquency has involved the use of the offender's place of residence. Often this has been used as a proxy measure for the social class background of the individual. Unfortunately, the UCR does not gather detailed enough information on arrested offenders for an inspection of social class issues. Instead, the reports include basic information on the arrest rates by city size. Information on offenses cleared by arrest of juveniles according to various city sizes is found in Table 1.4.

The figures in Table 1.4 reflect the percent of all offenses that were cleared with the arrest of a juvenile. The trend in the figures is for the proportion of youths arrested to decrease as the size of the city increases. Juveniles account for only 16 percent of the cleared Index offenses in cities of more than one million population (figures not shown). In comparison, arrests of youths make up roughly one-quarter of the cleared Index offenses in cities of less than 100,000 population. Regardless of the city size, arrest rates for property offenses are significantly higher than the figures for personal crimes.

Sex Distribution. Interest in the deviant behavior of females has flourished in recent years. The number of studies and books written about delinquent and criminal females has greatly increased since the early 1970s. The UCR routinely presents breakdowns of crime by sex of the offender. The 1996 UCR figures (Table 1.5) show that juvenile females made up 25 percent of all juvenile arrests. Adult females, however, constitute only 19 percent of adult arrests. While males may be more active, the relative seriousness of the offending for the two sexes is the same, with 30 percent of the arrests for both groups being in the Index category.

Table 1.3   Race Distribution of Juvenile Arrests, 1996

Offense Charged	Arrests Under 18					Percent Distribution			
	Total	White	Black	American Indian or Alaskan Native	Asian or Pacific Islander	White	Black	American Indian or Alaskan Native	Asian or Pacific Islander
Total	2,099,997	1,462,863	573,498	25,515	38,121	69.7	27.3	1.2	1.8
Murder and nonnegligent manslaughter	2,171	848	1,248	14	60	39.1	57.5	.6	2.8
Forcible rape	4,123	2,279	1,772	38	34	55.3	43.0	.9	.8
Robbery	39,012	15,432	22,578	193	809	39.6	57.9	.5	2.1
Aggravated assault	56,791	32,775	22,594	576	846	57.7	39.8	1.0	1.5
Burglary	97,634	71,885	22,861	1,305	1,583	73.6	23.4	1.3	1.6
Larceny-theft	369,771	260,972	94,522	5,371	8,906	70.6	25.6	1.5	2.4
Motor vehicle theft	54,775	31,647	20,876	815	1,417	57.8	38.1	1.5	2.6
Arson	7,289	5,836	1,290	81	82	80.1	17.7	1.1	1.1
Violent crimes	102,097	51,335	48,192	821	1,749	50.3	47.2	.8	1.7
Property crimes	529,449	370,340	139,549	7,572	11,988	69.9	26.4	1.4	2.3
Other assaults	171,111	106,615	59,906	1,942	2,648	62.3	35.0	1.1	1.5
Forgery and counterfeiting	6,255	4,829	1,242	63	91	77.6	20.0	1.0	1.5
Fraud	18,864	9,940	8,238	82	604	52.7	43.7	.4	3.2
Embezzlement	957	599	344	2	12	62.6	35.9	.2	1.3
Stolen property	30,127	18,179	11,111	306	531	60.3	36.9	1.0	1.8
Vandalism	103,207	82,357	18,057	1,272	1,521	79.8	17.5	1.2	1.5
Weapons; carrying, possessing, etc.	39,331	24,877	13,480	356	618	63.3	34.3	.9	1.6
Prostitution and commercialized vice	1,104	650	412	25	17	58.9	37.3	2.3	1.5
Sex offenses (except forcible rape)	12,644	8,812	3,589	112	131	69.7	28.4	.9	1.0
Drug abuse violations	158,161	98,396	57,221	1,093	1,451	62.2	36.2	.7	.9
Gambling	2,263	334	1,916	1	12	14.8	84.7	.1	.5
Offenses against family and children	5,796	4,344	1,253	50	149	74.9	21.6	.9	2.6
Driving under the influence	12,775	11,651	725	251	148	91.2	5.7	2.0	1.2
Liquor laws	112,191	101,943	6,284	2,989	975	90.9	5.6	2.7	.9
Drunkenness	17,098	15,066	1,557	366	109	88.1	9.1	2.1	.6
Disorderly conduct	159,814	100,900	56,113	1,429	1,372	63.1	35.1	.9	.9
Vagrancy	2,869	1,823	1,002	21	23	63.5	34.9	.7	.8
All other offenses	328,465	234,209	84,564	3,450	6,242	71.3	25.7	1.1	1.9
Suspicion	1,604	1,220	367	8	9	76.1	22.9	.5	.6
Curfew and loitering law violations	142,135	103,664	34,756	1,655	2,060	72.9	24.5	1.2	1.4
Runaways	141,710	110,780	23,620	1,649	5,661	78.2	16.7	1.2	4.0

Source: Federal Bureau of Investigation (1997). Adapted by authors.

Table 1.4   Residential Distribution of Juvenile Arrests, 1996

City size	Crime Index total	Violent crime	Property crime	Murder and non-negligent homicide	Forcible rape	Robbery	Aggravated assault	Burglary	Larceny-theft	Vehicle theft	Arson
Total cities	1,749,610	454,488	1,295,122	7,427	27,486	88,064	331,511	182,893	993,519	118,710	10,038
% under 18	21.1	13.1	24.0	8.7	11.5	18.5	11.9	20.2	24.8	22.9	48.2
Over 250,000											
Population	538,287	188,197	350,090	3,731	11,056	43,502	129,908	54,547	248,935	46,608	3,441
% under 18	17.2	11.8	20.2	8.6	10.4	17.7	10.1	16.1	20.3	24.8	44.1
100,000-249,999											
Population	271,132	75,574	195,558	1,335	4,347	15,739	54,153	31,312	145,912	18,334	1,606
% under 18	18.9	12.0	21.6	8.9	9.3	16.9	10.8	16.6	22.7	21.3	48.0
50,000-99,999											
Population	256,918	61,122	195,796	833	3,787	11,291	45,211	26,037	154,631	15,128	1,322
% under 18	23.5	14.2	26.4	9.7	11.1	20.5	13.0	21.2	27.6	23.2	48.3
25,000-49,999											
Population	221,681	45,479	176,202	558	2,953	7,573	34,395	22,534	142,085	11,583	1,177
% under 18	24.2	14.8	26.6	7.7	13.6	20.7	13.7	22.0	27.8	20.8	51.5
10,000-24,999											
Population	256,701	45,277	211,424	539	3,002	6,420	35,316	26,049	170,664	14,711	1,291
% under 18	23.8	15.0	25.7	7.4	13.9	21.0	14.2	23.5	26.5	20.2	52.0
Under 10,000											
Population	204,891	38,839	166,052	431	2,341	3,539	35,528	22,414	131,292	12,346	1,201
% under 18	24.7	15.2	26.9	10.0	15.5	19.1	14.8	28.1	27.1	22.5	53.2

Source: Federal Bureau of Investigation (1997). Adapted by authors.

Table 1.5   **Sex Distribution of Arrests, 1996**

Offense Charged	Males		Females	
	Total	Under age 18	Total	Under age 18
Total	7,918,554	1,411,148	2,056,390	481,164
Murder and nonnegligent manslaughter	12,062	1,907	1,384	132
Forcible rape	21,505	3,689	247	55
Robbery	101,998	33,001	11,091	3,568
Aggravated assault	284,004	40,320	61,640	10,240
Burglary	209,076	78,327	27,190	8,906
Larceny-theft	655,775	222,730	337,434	114,044
Motor vehicle theft	104,562	42,634	16,427	7,578
Arson	10,431	4,334	1,860	753
Violent crime	419,569	78,853	74,362	13,995
Property crime	979,844	349,491	382,911	131,281
Other assaults	695,386	111,388	177,644	43,374
Forgery and counterfeiting	51,372	3,551	28,105	2,093
Fraud	168,385	13,696	116,746	4,491
Embezzlement	5,633	477	4,619	389
Stolen property	84,867	23,395	14,435	3,378
Vandalism	182,709	82,856	29,336	10,283
Weapons	135,565	32,621	11,637	3,049
Prostitution and commercialized vice	30,657	496	46,097	552
Sex offenses	59,062	10,589	5,324	904
Drug abuse violations	857,057	124,758	173,831	18,164
Gambling	13,834	2,059	2,206	62
Offenses against family and children	61,308	2,753	19,263	1,647
Driving under the influence	756,935	9,490	130,246	1,828
Liquor laws	352,456	68,908	83,737	29,059
Drunkenness	422,605	12,998	57,656	2,639
Disorderly conduct	437,824	106,269	116,257	33,512
Vagrancy	16,168	1,791	4,135	368
All other offenses	2,039,086	226,087	465,210	67,463
Suspicion	2,941	1,097	827	343
Curfew and loitering law violations	93,756	93,756	38,991	38,991
Runaways	54,476	54,476	73,642	73,642

Source: Federal Bureau of Investigation (1997). Adapted by authors.

Trends in Delinquency. The trend in youthful crime has changed in recent years. The best way of examining change over time is to consider the **offense rate** (typically the number of offenses per 100,000), which eliminates the influence of any changes in the number of potential offenders on the delinquency data. Juvenile arrest rates showed a steady increase throughout the 1960s and mid-1970s, leveled off and showed some decline in the late-1970s and 1980s, and have increased in recent years. Total arrest rates of juveniles increased by 33 percent from 1965 to 1970 and 29 percent from 1970 to 1975 (Federal Bureau of Investigation, 1993). While decreases of 7 percent and 14 percent appeared in data for 1975 to 1980 and 1980 to 1985, the data from 1987 to

1996 show juvenile arrests increasing by 35 percent (Federal Bureau of Investigation, 1997). Clearly, the increases have outpaced the decreases over the past 30 years.

A Critique of the UCR. The UCR is the longest-running and most widely known and cited method of collecting information on crime in the United States. It began in 1931 and has continued on a yearly basis since that time. Despite this longevity and notoriety, the UCR has a number of flaws that must be considered when using the data (see O'Brien, 1985). The most frequent notation made about the data is the fact that it reflects only those offenses known to the police. Critics of the UCR point out that many individuals, for whatever reason, opt not to contact the police when they are a victim or a witness to a crime. This failure to bring crimes to the attention of the police results in an undercount of crime in the United States The unreported crimes are typically referred to as the **dark figure of crime**.

A second common criticism of UCR data is that they are subject to the needs and mandates of the reporting agencies. Police agencies who report to the FBI do so on a voluntary basis. Each agency collects the data themselves and forwards the information to the FBI. Political and economic pressures have been known to influence the amount and accuracy of counts sent to the UCR system. For example, changes in police procedure due to political decisions can alter the amount of attention a police department pays to a certain form of crime. Similarly, an emphasis on reducing the level of a certain crime can be accomplished through the simple reclassification of an offense from one category to another (e.g., listing rapes as "other sex offenses" or aggravated assaults as "simple assaults"). Decisions like these by police departments can greatly alter the yearly offense counts and the computations of trends in the data over time.

A further concern in using the UCR in studies of deviance is the lack of information on offenders in much of the data. Information about offenders in the UCR reflects only those offenders who were caught in the course of the crime or ensuing investigation. With a total clearance rate of about 20 percent, little is known about the offenders in most crimes. It is possible that these official figures are distorted in terms of the age, race, sex and residential distribution of the total offending population. The UCR provides no information about the offender in roughly 80 percent of the crimes committed each year.

Another serious problem entails the fact that the UCR counts offenses and not offenders. It would be easy to claim that the number of offenders is equal to the number of reported offenses. Unfortunately, this would provide a highly inaccurate picture. Many offenders commit more than one offense over a period of time. Alternatively, some individuals may commit a single act (such as bank robbery) that legally constitutes more than one offense (robbery, assault and possibly kidnapping). These problems make it difficult to estimate the number of offenders over any period of time using the UCR. The number of offenders is clearly not equal to the number of offenses.

A variety of other concerns must be considered in using the UCR data. Among these are the differences in legal definitions of offenses, which change over time and from place to place, as well as alterations in the methods of data collection over time (such as the move from hand tabulation to computer tabulation). A further concern is the possible bias in enforcement of the law. One potential outcome of enforcement bias could be the overrepresentation of lower-class youths in the UCR figures. The most problematic aspect of the UCR for the study of delinquency entails the combined issues of the dark figure of crime and the failure to identify offenders in the vast majority of all cases. It is due to these problems that alternative methods of unofficial crime and delinquency data have been developed. Before turning to these types of data collection, we will look at two additional official measures of delinquency.

JUVENILE COURT STATISTICS

Juvenile court data present a picture of the cases and the juveniles who reach the adjudication stage of the system. The numbers of juveniles who appear in these records are smaller than those found in the UCR police data. This is due primarily to the fact that most juveniles reach the court through contact with the police, who filter and screen cases. Relatively few youths are referred to court directly by their families, schools or other associates. In 1991, the police referred 85 percent of the cases in juvenile court (Butts et al., 1994). Estimated numbers of delinquency cases from 1960 to 1994 are found in Table 1.6. Similar to the UCR figures, the number of cases rose steadily into the 1970s, leveled off and dropped somewhat throughout the 1970s and 1980s, and have increased again in the 1990s.

Table 1.6   **Estimated Number and Rate of Delinquency Cases in Juvenile Court, 1960-1994**

Year	Estimated Number of Delinquency Cases	Child Population 10-17 Years of Age	Rate
1960	510,000	25,368,000	20.1
1965	697,000	29,536,000	23.6
1970	1,052,000	33,141,000	31.7
1975	1,317,000	33,960,000	38.8
1980	1,445,400	31,171,000	46.4
1985	1,114,000	26,400,000	42.2
1990	1,273,700	25,484,400	50.0
1994	1,555,300	27,730,200	56.1
1995	1,714,300	28,242,000	60.7

Source: Nimick et al. (1987), Snyder et al. (1987), Snyder et al. (1990), Butts et al. (1994), Butts (1996), Sickmund (1997).

The column labeled "rate" in Table 1.6 reflects the number of cases each year in relation to the size of the juvenile population. Where the absolute number of cases could reflect a larger pool of youths in society who could have court contact, the rate standardizes the number of cases according to the available youths. Interpretation of the rate figures is straightforward. For example, the 1960 rate of 20.1 means that there were 20.1 delinquency cases in juvenile court for every 1,000 youths in the population. The trend in the rate data roughly approximates that of the absolute numbers. The rate steadily increased starting in 1961, peaked in 1980, fell in the early 1980s and has risen since 1985.

Information on sex, race, offender and residence is also available in the court statistics. Like the UCR data, males dominate throughout the juvenile court statistics. The male rate in 1987 was 70.3 per 100,000 population and has steadily risen to a rate of 81.3 in 1991. In contrast, the female rate has remained relatively stable over the same time period, ranging from 17.4 in 1987 to 19.8 in 1991 (Butts et al., 1994).

Similar to UCR figures, court data show that property offenses dominate at more than one-half (51.7%) of all petitions. Public order offenses (such as disorderly conduct and liquor violations) and offenses against persons each contribute approximately 20 percent to the juvenile court caseload. Not surprisingly, the courts handle more older youths than are found in police figures. The modal age is 16, followed by age 17. It would appear that older youths may have more extensive prior problems or are involved in more serious offending.

In terms of race, raw court numbers are dominated by white youths (roughly one-half of all petitions). Despite the fact that more white youths appear in juvenile court, blacks are overrepresented given their proportion in the population. The 1994 rate for white youths is 45.2 per 1,000, while the rate for black youths is more than double that at 119.4 (Butts, 1996). Finally, court statistics mirror UCR figures in terms of residence, with urban youths being the most prevalent.

JUVENILE CORRECTIONS STATISTICS

A third official source of information on juveniles coming into contact with the juvenile justice system is records kept on juvenile correctional facilities. The U.S. Justice Department routinely conducts a census of the population of juvenile facilities. As with juvenile court statistics, the numbers of youths who appear in these statistics are smaller than the UCR and court figures. This is due to the funneling process of the juvenile system whereby fewer and fewer youths are subjected to intervention the further one looks into the system. In addition, the juvenile court may handle youths in a variety of ways that do not involve institutionalization. Figure 1.4 provides a view of how petitions coming to juvenile court in 1995 were handled. Almost one-half (45%) of the cases that came to the juvenile court were handled without a formal petition being made. Of those petitioned, 43 percent were not adjudicated as a delinquent, although 41 percent of those received some form of intervention (Sickmund, 1997).

Clearly, juvenile facilities rely heavily upon the juvenile court for their clients, and few of the youths coming into contact with the court are sentenced to confinement. Therefore, the figures found in data from juvenile facilities represent only a fraction of all the youths having contact with the juvenile system.

Figure 1.4   Juvenile Court Processing of Delinquency Cases, 1995

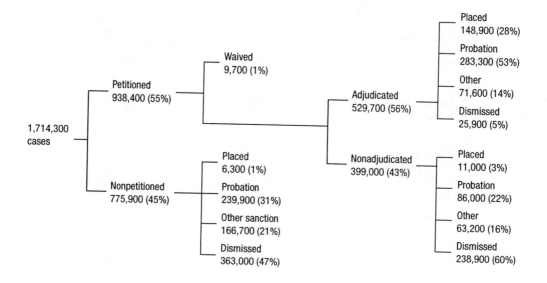

Source: Sickmund, Snyder & Poe-Yamagata (1997).

Note: Detail may not add to totals because of rounding.

Table 1.7 presents data on youths in public and private juvenile facilities in 1993. The data in the table represent a one-day count and the daily totals would vary around these figures. For 1993, public facilities handled almost 63,000 youths, while private institutions dealt with an additional 36,000 (Austin et al., 1995). Information on the age, race, sex and type of offense is also provided in correctional data. Not unlike UCR or court statistics, correctional figures show that most offenders are male. Table 1.7 shows that females make up roughly 30 percent of the private and 11 percent of the public institutions' clients.

Great differences appear in the institutional populations when you look at the racial composition of the juveniles. Sixty-five percent of the juveniles in public institutions are nonwhite, while only 44 percent of the private facilities' clients are nonwhite. The racial discrepancy may be due to various factors. First, private institutions can select the youths they wish to admit. Second, wealthier white families can better afford the treatment costs imposed by many private institutions. A final possibility may entail a bias on the part of the court to send black youths to (more punitive) public facilities. The age makeup of the institutions also differs, with the private institutions handling a younger clientele than the public facilities. Unfortunately, the data does not provide a clear basis for determining the reasons for various differences between the public and private populations.

Table 1.7   **Characteristics of Juveniles in Correctional Facilities: Average One Day Counts—1993**

Characteristic	Public Facility	Private Facility
Number of Juveniles	62,818	36,190
Sex:		
Male	51,511	25,795
Female	11,307	10,395
Age:		
9 and under	0	724
10-13 years	3,769	5,429
14-17 years	50,254	28,228
18-21 years	8,795	1,810
Race/Ethnicity:		
White	21,986	20,266
Black	27,640	11,581
Hispanic	11,307	3,257
Other	1,885	1,086
Reason for Admission:		
Delinquent acts	59,677	14,476
Status offenses	1,185	5,429
Nonoffenders	628	9,771
Voluntary	628	6,514

Source: Austin et al. (1995).

Similarly, differences in the reason for admission appear when comparing public and private institutions. The vast majority of the youths in public facilities are there because of committing delinquent offenses (95%). Conversely, youths in private facilities are there as status offenders (15%), as nonoffenders, such as dependent, abused or neglected (27%) or as voluntary admittees (18%).

The trend in correctional figures is somewhat interesting. Figures tend to indicate that the number of incarcerated youths has been steadily increasing. The total number of admissions increased from 638,000 in 1978 to 823,000 in 1991. From 1983 to 1993, the one-day count of youths in public and private facilities increased from 80,091 to 99,008—a 24 percent increase. These increases are due to two factors. The first involves longer stays by youths. That is, youths are staying longer in the institutions; thus, there is greater overlap in the institutional stays, which inflates the daily head count. Second, increasing violence and drug problems in the late 1980s led to larger numbers of youths being incarcerated.

Summary of Official Statistics

Each of the various official measures of delinquency presents a slightly different view of juvenile offending. In terms of numbers of offenses, the UCR presents the most disturbing picture due to the large numbers of offenses it reflects. In addition to the number of offenses, the UCR provides detailed information on a variety of demographic and crime-related characteristics. Unfortunately, as noted earlier, this source of data has a number of inherent defects that limit its usefulness, in particular its reliance upon offenses known to the police.

Juvenile court statistics and correctional facility data also present a somewhat narrow picture of juvenile misconduct. A large part of the problem with these figures lies in the fact that they are greatly dependent on the productivity of the police. Most youths entering the courts and institutions initiate their journey by way of police contact. Any failure at the police level, therefore, carries over to these other counts. The increased levels of status offenses in court and correctional data is one point at which discrepancy with the arrest data appears. This is probably due to court referrals from sources other than the police. The problems and differences do not make the information useless. Rather, the data can be used to assess the workings of the institutions over time and provide insight to the juvenile system. However, they cannot be used to give an accurate portrayal of the extent of the juvenile crime problem.

Self-Report Measures of Delinquency

Self-report measures attempt to gauge the level of delinquency by asking individuals to tell of their participation in deviant activity. This approach has a number of advantages. First, actions besides just those "known to the police" are considered. Second, it becomes possible to gather information on all offenders and not just those few who are arrested for an offense. Where the UCR data mainly reflect information on those offenses for which an individual has been arrested, self-reports do not need an arrest in order to have information on the perpetrator. Third, self-report surveys can ask a variety of questions designed to elicit information useful in understanding why an individual violates the law. Information routinely collected includes data on family background (such as broken home, parental affection), economic status (occupation, income), education, attitudes (toward school, family or work), friends' behavior, and other topics, as well as direct questions about the deviant behavior. This type of information is not available from most official delinquency measures. For these and other reasons, self-report methods have proliferated in recent years.

Self-report surveys have a fairly long history in juvenile justice. One of the earliest surveys was developed by James Short and Ivan Nye (see Figure 1.5). This survey asked youths to note the frequency with which they committed each of 23 items. The items in the scale are dominated by status and minor offenses. The few serious crimes included in the original list (such as stealing over $50) were deleted in subsequent versions of the scales, which included only the seven starred items. Dentler and Monroe (1961) offer a similar self-report survey that focuses on minor delinquent offenses.

Figure 1.5   Short and Nye Self-Reported Delinquency Items

Defied parents' authority*
Driven too fast or recklessly
Taken little things (worth less than $2) that did not belong to you*
Taken things of medium value ($2-$50)
Taken things of large value ($50)
Used force (strong-arm methods) to get money from another person
Taken part in "gang fights"
Taken a car for a ride without the owner's knowledge
Bought or drank beer, wine, or liquor (including drinking at home)*
Bought or drank beer, wine, or liquor (outside your home)
Drank beer, wine, or liquor in your own home
Deliberate property damage*
Used or sold narcotic drugs
Had sex relations with another person of the same sex (not masturbation)*
Had sex relations with a person of the opposite sex
Gone hunting or fishing without a license (or violated other game laws)
Taken things you didn't want
"Beat up" on kids who hadn't done anything to you
Hurt someone to see them squirm

---

*Commonly used items in subsequent self-report studies.

Source: Short and Nye (1958).

Self-report scales like the **Short-Nye instrument** invariably uncover a great deal of delinquent activity. Indeed, various studies using these types of scales show that virtually every person is a delinquent. This is due to the type of questions asked in the scale. It is hard to conceive of anyone saying they never committed any of the behaviors asked. Defying parental authority or trying alcohol at some time are rather universal activities by juveniles. Asking if the individual has "ever" committed an act contributes to the high levels of positive responses. Compared to official counts of delinquency, such self-reports show a great deal more deviance.

More recent self-report surveys, such as the **Monitoring the Future (MTF) survey** (see Table 1.8), include many more serious offenses and elicit significantly fewer positive responses. The MTF project includes questions on hitting teachers, group fighting, weapon use, robbery and aggravated assault. The data in Table 1.8 show the great differences in response rates between less serious and more serious offenses. For example, arguing or fighting with parents is reported by 85 percent or more of the respondents, while fewer than 10 percent report using a weapon in the commission of a theft. Although many persons commit various deviant acts, the majority of subjects confine their activity to minor offenses. Indeed, when major, serious offenses are included in the scales there is a great decrease in the level of reported offending. The figures become much more similar to those in official statistics. Hindelang, Hirschi and Weis (1981) report similar results in a survey of Seattle youths covering 69 offenses ranging from grand theft and aggravated assault to minor theft, vandalism and simple assault to defying one's parents. These authors found that minor offenses elicited high rates of positive responses while more serious crimes showed much lower levels of offending.

Table 1.8.   **Percent Reporting One or More Delinquent Acts in Last 12 Months—Monitoring the Future Survey**

Delinquent Activity	Class of											
	1985		1987		1989		1991		1993		1995	
	Males	Females	Males	Females	Males	Females	Males	Females	Males	Females	Males	Females
Argued or had fight with either of your parents	86.0	91.8	88.3	94.5	87.2	93.2	87.8	93.0	84.5	92.0	86.9	94.1
Hit an instructor or supervisor	5.1	1.0	3.9	1.1	5.7	0.9	4.7	1.1	5.7	1.7	4.2	1.7
Gotten into a serious fight in school or at work	23.7	12.7	21.8	13.9	23.7	15.7	23.4	11.9	21.6	13.0	17.9	11.4
Taken part in a fight where a group of your friends were against another group	26.1	14.9	23.7	15.7	27.8	12.6	26.2	13.6	29.0	14.5	23.3	13.9
Hurt someone badly enough to need bandages or a doctor	19.0	13.0	17.5	3.4	21.0	3.4	20.1	4.0	21.4	5.0	20.4	4.1
Used a knife or gun or some other thing (like a club) to get something from a person	5.3	1.3	5.1	1.5	6.5	1.0	5.3	1.2	8.1	1.0	5.4	1.4
Taken something not belonging to you worth under $50	38.6	21.5	40.8	27.9	38.7	24.5	41.8	21.7	40.1	23.5	40.4	23.1
Taken something not belonging to you worth over $50	11.9	2.1	13.6	3.8	12.5	3.4	15.0	4.4	17.5	4.4	14.4	4.5
Taken something from a store without paying for it	31.8	20.8	36.0	23.6	34.7	23.2	39.6	22.0	37.6	23.3	35.7	24.0
Taken a car that didn't belong to someone in your family without permission of the owner	7.8	3.4	8.1	3.1	7.0	3.7	8.3	3.9	8.2	3.8	6.6	3.0
Taken part of a car without permission of the owner	11.1	2.3	11.2	2.4	10.5	3.0	10.6	1.7	12.5	2.1	8.1	2.3
Gone into some house or building when you weren't supposed to be there	34.5	18.0	33.1	21.2	30.6	20.8	30.7	17.3	34.1	17.5	29.6	17.1
Set fire to someone's property on purpose	2.9	0.6	2.7	0.5	4.3	0.7	3.6	0.6	5.9	0.9	3.7	1.2
Damaged school property on purpose	18.9	8.5	21.4	9.2	19.3	7.5	18.8	6.5	22.3	7.2	21.4	7.4
Damaged property at work on purpose	9.9	1.0	9.3	1.7	10.3	2.9	10.8	1.8	10.5	2.0	10.2	2.4

Source: Maguire & Pastore (1996). Adapted by the authors.

One problem with many self-report surveys is the fact that they are one-shot studies. That is, they take a single measurement on one sample of youths. There is no second sample to which to compare the results and no repeat measurement taken on the same or similar persons at a later point in time. One exception is the Monitoring the Future project, which surveys a national sample of youths each year. While different respondents participate each year, it is possible to examine general trends and changes over time. A more involved design was used by the **National Youth Survey (NYS)**. Through the use of a **panel design**, the NYS interviewed the same set of individuals repeatedly over an extended period of time. The NYS began with a group of 11- to 17-year-olds from across the United States and reinterviewed them over a period of years. The NYS data also allow for comparisons in numbers of offenses and changes over time, with the added feature that changes are not due to differences in the groups being interviewed each year.

AGE DISTRIBUTION

The age distribution of offending is greatly dependent on the items included in the survey. Self-report surveys using minor and status offenses reveal that criminal activity is largely a juvenile problem. Indeed, if questions were posed to probe behavior over the past year, adults could hardly be expected to report status offense violations. Similarly, juveniles tend to report less involvement in serious offenses (such as aggravated assault and felony theft). Older youths also tend to report more drug and alcohol use, possibly due to easier availability of these substances as one grows older. While offending may occur throughout one's life, the trend is for offending to increase in frequency as one reaches the later teen and early adult years. After that point in time, there is movement toward the commission of fewer offenses. The variety of offenses also increases throughout the juvenile years.

RACE DISTRIBUTION

Unlike in official data, the distribution of offenses by race does not show great differences. Data from the NYS and MTF show only minor variation between black respondents and white respondents. In the NYS, a greater percentage of blacks report involvement in felony assaults, some minor assaults, and robbery, while white percentages exceed black figures for hitting parents, minor theft offenses, damage offenses, and most other categories of crime (Elliott et al., 1983). These differences, however, are generally very small and range in the area of one to five percentage points. Differences in the MTF data also tend to be very small.

SOCIAL CLASS DISTRIBUTION

Social class is often considered in studies of self-report delinquency. This is possible because the researcher can either ask the respondent questions about his or her social class or can discreetly gather data about each individual who answers the survey. According to the NYS, a slightly greater number of lower-

and working-class youths report involvement in most crime categories. Only for some minor offenses do the figures for middle-class youths exceed the figures for the other social classes (Elliott et al., 1983). As with race, the differences between the social classes are minimal and amount to a few percentage points. The Seattle self-report data also show little discrepancy in delinquency according to the social class of the individual regardless of the seriousness of the offense (Hindelang, Hirschi & Weis, 1981).

SEX DISTRIBUTION

Self-report surveys display sex differences similar to those found in official data. Almost without exception, males report higher involvement in offending than females, although the differences are dependent on the type of behavior. Table 1.8 includes data on the sex differential in the MTF. Like the race and social class findings, many of the differences are small. There are some instances of great discrepancy, however, between the data for males and the data for females. These differences appear mainly in the more serious offenses (such as serious assaults and fights) and some public disorder and minor property offenses. Similarly, Hindelang, Hirschi and Weis (1981) report that the differences between male and female participation in delinquency increase as the seriousness of the behavior increases.

CRITIQUE OF SELF-REPORT DATA

Self-report studies paint a different picture of offending compared to official figures and pose separate problems for researchers. The most common concern with self-report data involves the truthfulness of the respondents. Interestingly, most investigations into the validity of the data show that self-report figures are fairly accurate. This assessment is based on various studies that compare self-report results to lie-detector tests, repeated measures and cross-checks with other forms of data (Clarke & Tifft, 1966; Gold, 1970; Hardt & Peterson-Hardt, 1977; Hindelang, Hirschi & Weis, 1981; Lab & Allen, 1984). The greatest discrepancies between self-report and official figures can be attributed to the different domains of behavior that are tapped by the two methods. Official records focus more on serious offenses, while self-reports often look for minor offending. An additional shortcoming of self-report data is the focus on juveniles. Due to the problems of locating accessible groups of adults, most self-report research has been carried out on juveniles. Although the data are rich with information on kids, there is little opportunity to compare the findings to those found on adults. Typical adult samples found in self-report surveys deal with institutionalized adults or young adults in college settings. Neither of these groups are representative of the general adult population. The method of selecting youths for self-report surveys may also bias the results. The typical use of school students in surveys may inadvertently miss high-rate offenders who are truants or dropouts and not present at the time of data collection.

There are great advantages to using self-report data. First, these data provide information on offenses not known to the police. Second, the method is able to probe the number of times each individual commits an offense. Much official data (especially police records) are not readily set up to track an individual over time. Self-reports, however, can simply ask about the number and frequency of offending. Third, self-report surveys often ask a variety of questions about the individual's background that provide a rich base of information on the demographic and social factors related to delinquent activity. Finally, the richness of the data allows for a more complete discussion of the reasons why an individual acts in a certain way than the data found in official records.

Victimization Measures of Delinquency

A third source of information on deviant activity is found in **victim surveys**. Like self-reports, victim surveys question the general population about their experiences with deviance. Instead of asking which actions the individual has committed, however, these surveys ask whether the individual has been the *victim* of a deviant act. Such surveys were developed as a direct result of criticisms about underreporting in official crime measures.

Victim surveys uncover a great deal of activity unknown to the police. This fact has been demonstrated time and again in different surveys and locations. Ennis (1967), reporting on one of the early victim surveys, showed that victimization data uncover roughly twice as much crime as official police records. This increase over official records has been used by many writers to justify the criticisms of official data. Many people simply do not report their victimization to the police. As a result, those criminal actions are not reflected in the official measures of crime.

While victimization data uncover greater amounts of deviance, this type of measurement has little utility for the study of who is delinquent and why individuals become deviant. The only time a victim can provide information about a perpetrator is when the act is a personal offense or when an individual has been identified or caught for the offense. The **National Crime Victimization Survey (NCVS)** asks respondents to estimate the age of the offender in those instances in which there was contact between the parties or in which the offender was caught. More than 22 percent of the violent crime victims in 1993 reported that their offender was under age 18 (U.S. Department of Justice, 1995). This represents 11.5 percent for rape, 21.9 percent for robbery and 23.2 percent for assault. These estimates are based on the perception of the victim and not on the perpetrator's actual age (which is usually unknown).

Although victimization data is very useful in the study of crime, it has limited usefulness for the study of delinquency. It tells little about the age of the offender, the demographic characteristics of the perpetrator or the reasons for the action. Most of the time when victimization data are presented in terms of juveniles, they deal with the juvenile victim and not the juvenile offender. Victimization data tell us something about the relative size of the crime problem and about the needs and feelings of the victim, but little about the offender or the reasons for delinquent behavior.

The Escalation of Violence by Youths

Violence committed by juveniles has become a topic of major concern in recent years. The perception held by many people and the image portrayed by the media is one of rapid increases in the occurrence and seriousness of youthful violent behavior. An examination of official crime statistics bears this out. The Uniform Crime Reports (Federal Bureau of Investigation, 1997) reveals that arrests of juveniles for homicide increased by 50 percent from 1987 to 1996. In comparison, homicide arrests remained relatively stable for adults. Table 1.9 presents changes in murder and aggravated assault arrest rates since 1987. Over the 10-year period, arrests of males for murder increased by more than 50 percent, while female arrests increased by about 19 percent. The increasingly violent nature of juvenile behavior also can be seen in aggravated assault figures, which often differ from homicide only in the outcome of the action. That is, a homicide victim is simply an aggravated assault victim who dies. According to UCR arrest data, juvenile arrests for aggravated assault increased 70 percent from 1987 to 1996 (Federal Bureau of Investigation, 1997). The increase in arrests for adults over the same time period was 39 percent. While the aggravated assault arrest rate has increased for both adults and juveniles, the youthful arrest rate is increasing at a faster pace.

Table 1.9   **Changes in Murder and Aggravated Assault Arrest Rates for Juveniles**

	1987-96	1992-96	1995-96
Males			
Murder	+53.3%	−19.0%	−15.3%
Aggravated Assault	+60.4	−3.3	−5.6
Females			
Murder	+18.9	−7.6	0.0
Aggravated Assault	+124.1	+28.0	+2.9

Despite the great increases since the mid-1980s, the data is beginning to show a rollback in youthful violence. The homicide arrest rate for juvenile males has dropped since 1991, with a substantial decline from 1994-1995. Similarly, arrests of males for aggravated assault dropped 4.5 percent, and female homicide arrests fell almost 12 percent. Data from the NCVS shows drops in juvenile violent crimes since 1993, with a 32 percent drop in aggravated assaults (Sickmund, Snyder & Poe-Yamagata, 1997). While the absolute number of arrests for homicide and aggravated assault may remain high (2,039 and 50,560 in 1996, respectively), the direction of change is promising.

A key question arising from the changes in violence among juveniles asks what caused the increases. While it is not possible for us to address the issue fully at this point, one key consideration is the availability of firearms among youths. This is especially appropriate in light of the greater increases in homicides compared to aggravated assaults. According to the FBI (1997), 84 percent of murder victims aged 13-19 were killed with a firearm in 1996. Non-gun homicides have remained relatively stable since the mid-1970s, while homicides involving a gun have significantly increased from a low in the early 1980s to a peak in the most recent figures. While these data cannot prove that gun availability is a cause of increasing homicide, they strongly suggest that firearms are a major contributor to the changes.

There is no doubt that juveniles have become more violent. Both official and self-report data provide evidence of this fact. The general public has become aware of this shift through media depictions and personal experiences. A common depiction in television shows and the movies, as well as the daily news, is a drive-by shooting attributed to juvenile gang members. This increase in violence has engendered changes ranging from legislation mandating the waiver of younger youths to adult court, to calls for increased early intervention and prevention programs. These various approaches will be addressed throughout this text.

Comparing the Delinquency Measures

The three types of delinquency measures (official, self-report and victimization) show both similarities and differences. In general, all three show that delinquency is a widespread problem. It is not restricted to any one group, area or type of offense. The level of offending increased throughout the 1960s and early 1970s, leveled off and showed some decreases in the late 1970s and 1980s, increased in the late 1980s and early 1990s (particularly in serious personal offenses) and is starting to decrease in recent years. There is a clear diversity in offending. Youths are involved in all types of behavior from status offenses to serious personal crimes. Property crimes dominate in all measures and personal offenses are the least common. Males dominate in all but a couple of delinquency categories, such as prostitution and running away. All of the measures show that offending is greater in urban areas.

Most differences in the measures appear in the relative magnitude of offending and by offending subgroups in the population. Both victimization and self-report measures uncover more offending than do official measures. Official measures themselves differ in magnitude, with police figures leading court and correctional data. In terms of demographics, official figures show a much larger number of black offenders than self-report measures. Self-report statistics find little racial difference in offending. Social class differences also tend to disappear when most self-report data are considered. Similar discrepancies emerge when considering the sex of the offenders. While males dominate in magnitude of offending (by any measure), official figures show the sexes committing different types of offenses. Self-report data, however, tend to portray the sexes as participating in the same types of behavior.

The differences between the measures are a result of measurement techniques. Official records provide an ongoing look at the level and change in delinquency from year to year according to the formal justice system. These records reflect offenses that are brought to the attention of the authorities. Actions that are not reported but are withheld from public officials are lost to these records. Self-reports typically portray a larger delinquency problem than official figures. The cause of this is the type of activities that are probed in the survey. Surveys that inquire about minor status offenses will always find high delinquency levels. When more serious offenses form the core of the questionnaire, however, the number of delinquents falls to lower levels. Victim surveys also tend to show a greater level of deviant activity than official records. This is true for juveniles as well as adults. Unfortunately, little more can be said about delinquent behavior from victimization reports due to victims' lack of knowledge about offenders.

No single method of measuring delinquency should be considered better than the others. The usefulness of the measures depends entirely on the question that is being answered. Each method provides a different set of information about delinquency. Official records are useful in noting change in official processing and handling of youths over time. They also provide a long-term set of data that allows the inspection of changes over time. These official data are also rich in information about various demographic and offense factors not found in other measures. Self-reports provide a measure of delinquency based on the offender's viewpoint. They are capable of addressing behaviors that may not result in arrests and lead to official records. These measures are rich in data on minor crimes, the number of offenses an individual commits, demographics on offenders, and why an individual acts in a certain way. Finally, victimization data are useful in probing the actual level of crime and gaining some basic information on delinquents. More important, however, is the usefulness in probing the reactions and decision-making processes of victims. Victimization data are more limited for the study of delinquent behavior than the other two types of measures.

Summary

The study of delinquency depends heavily on the definition of delinquency and the measurement of the problem. The definition is not clear-cut and varies greatly from one study to another. Delinquency can be limited to those acts that are violations of the criminal code, can signify those actions that are illegal only for juveniles, can represent some combination of both criminal and status offenses, or can be molded to fit the criminological question of each researcher.

The outcome of this search for a definition of delinquency is a vast array of different measures of delinquency and resultant claims about the level of delinquent activity. The major methods of measuring crime and delinquency—official, self-report and victimization—all rely on somewhat different conceptions of what constitutes delinquency. The UCR, for example, is oriented more toward a criminal law point of view and considers only two very broad status offense categories (runaway; curfew and loitering) among the 29 offense categories. Conversely, self-reports often rely heavily on status offenses in their surveys and include only a few (mostly property) criminal offenses. The interest in victimization surveys for the extent of the crime problem and the concerns of the victim results in information on delinquency almost exclusively geared toward serious personal offenses. Throughout this great confusion of definitions and measures there is no clear sign of arriving at a consensus on the issues.

Perhaps the reason behind the great discrepancies in definitions and measures can be found in the history of juvenile justice. The juvenile system has grown quickly over the past century and has seen many changes. Part of this is due to changes in the view society holds of youthful offenders. It may also be attributable to changes in the field of criminology and corrections. The changes in the juvenile system and the impact of various factors on the definition and extent of delinquency make up the substance for the next chapter on the history of juvenile justice.

DISCUSSION QUESTIONS

1. You have been appointed to write a definition of delinquency for the state legislature. You can either propose a new definition or rely on the existing definition. What is your definition? Why is it best and why should it be accepted?

2. You have been asked to research each of the following questions or issues. What type of delinquency measure(s) will you use and why?
    —How much delinquency is there in the country?
    —What characterizes the typical juvenile offender?
    —What are some of the causes for delinquency?
    —Has the delinquency rate increased or decreased over the past 15 years?

3. A discussion has arisen over the best measure of delinquency. As an expert on such matters, you are asked to present an unbiased view of the strengths and weaknesses of official, self-report and victimization measures. Be as thorough as possible.

4. You have been asked to comment on media reports of increasing delinquency. What statistics will you use in your response and why? Has delinquency been increasing? Are the increases restricted to any one group of offenders or offenses?

CHAPTER 2

The History of Juvenile Justice

Key Terms and Phrases

abandonment
apprenticeship
Chancery Court
child savers
Commonwealth v. Fisher
dowry
Ex parte Crouse

houses of refuge
infanticide
involuntary servitude
Kent v. United States
nullification
parens patriae
wet-nursing

There is no question that juvenile misbehavior is a major concern in modern American society. No matter which definition of delinquency or which form of measurement is used, the level of delinquent activity is high. Any understanding of the juvenile justice system must begin with an analysis of delinquency in a historical framework. Interestingly, the history of juvenile delinquency and juvenile justice is a relatively short one. While deviance on the part of young persons has always been a fact of life, societal intervention and participation in the handling of juvenile transgressors has gained most of its momentum in the last 100-150 years. This chapter will discuss the state of affairs leading to the development of a juvenile justice system and briefly examine the early workings of that system.

Property and Person

An understanding of the development of juvenile justice must begin with an understanding of the place of children in society. Throughout most of history, there was no such status as "child." Youthful members of society did not enjoy a separate status that brought with it a distinct set of expectations, behaviors and/or privileges. Rather, the young were either property or people. The very young, from birth to age five or six, held much the same status as any other property in society. They were subject to the same dictates as other property—they were bought, sold and disposed of according to the needs of the owner. Once the individual reached the age of five or six, he or she became a full-fledged member of society and was expected to act according to the same mandates placed on all "adult" members of society (Aries, 1962).

The state of indifference toward the young and the absence of any separate status are easy to understand within a historical setting. First, the life expectancy of the average person was short. More importantly, the infant mortality rate exceeded 50 percent. The failure to develop a personal, caring attitude for infants, therefore, can be viewed as a defense mechanism. Indifference reduced or eliminated the pain and sorrow that would accompany the loss of the infant. A second explanation for the lack of concern over the young entailed the inability of many families to provide for the young. Families lived from day to day on what they could produce. Each child represented an increased burden to the already overburdened family.

The inability to provide economically for a child led to a variety of practices. **Infanticide**, or the killing of young children, was a common response to the appearance of an unwanted and demanding child prior to the fourth century (and continued in some places into the fourteenth century) (Mause, 1974). Mothers would kill their young in order to alleviate the future needs of providing for the child. The great chances that the infant would die anyway from disease or illness made this practice easier for the parents.

The killing of female offspring was especially prominent. Females were considered more burdensome than males. This was because they would not be as productive as a male if they lived and because of the **dowry** practice. The marriage of a daughter often necessitated the provision of goods by the female's family to the groom. The basic rationale was that the groom and his family were assuming the burden of caring for a marginally productive female. The dowry practice was especially problematic for the poor, who could not provide a sufficient enticement for a prospective husband. The killing of a female infant, therefore, not only removed the immediate needs of caring for the infant but also eliminated the future need of a dowry.

A practice similar to infanticide was **abandonment**. Parents would abandon their children to die for the same reasons underlying infanticide. Abandonment grew to be the more acceptable practice in the fourth to thirteenth centuries and appeared as late as the seventeenth and eighteenth centuries. Infanticide and abandonment were not restricted to the poor members of society. Historical records show that even the affluent accepted the killing of infants. One prime example of this is the story of Oedipus the king. Oedipus, the son of the Greek king and queen, was destined to kill his father and marry his mother. In order to avoid this fate, the parents had the infant Oedipus bound at the ankles, taken to the mountains, and abandoned.

Another method that appeared for handling youths was **wet-nursing**. A wet-nurse was a surrogate mother paid to care for a child (Mause, 1974).

Wealthy families would hire other women to raise their children until the off-spring had reached the stage of "adulthood," at which time the children would return and assume a productive role in the family. Poor women, who assumed the role of wet nurses, would kill their natural offspring in order to save their mother's milk for the "paying" youths. The arrangement served a monetary purpose for the poor while relieving the wealthy of an unwanted responsibility.

Children who survived the first few years of life became subjected to a new set of activities. These new actions, however, retained the economic concerns that allowed for infanticide and other practices. The inability to provide for the needs of the family prompted the development of **involuntary servitude** and **apprenticeship** for the young. In essence, these actions were nothing more than the sale of youths by the family. The father, by selling the children, accomplished two things. First, he alleviated the burden of having to feed and clothe the person. Second, he gained something of "greater" value in return—money, a farm animal, food or some other necessity of life. Such practices also were promoted as a means of providing labor for those in need. The rise of industrialization created a need for labor skills that could be learned by children through apprenticeships.

A second set of reasons behind the apprenticeship and servitude of youths was the general view that individuals who survived the years of infancy were simply "little adults." Indeed, children participated in the same activities as adults. Children worked at trades, drank alcohol, dueled, and participated in sex with adults and other young people. Part of this can be attributed to the lack of distinct expectations for youth. There was no period of schooling or education that separated the young from the actions of adults. Additionally, the living conditions of the family placed all ages within the same set of social conditions. The family home was typically a single room used for all activities. Eating, sleeping and entertaining occurred in the same place and in view of everyone. The youthful members of society, therefore, learned and participated early in life.

The general view that children were the same as adults extended to the realm of legal sanctioning. Children were viewed as adults and were subject to the same rules and regulations as adults (Empey, 1982). There did not exist a separate system for dealing with youthful offenders. At best, the father was responsible for controlling the child—and his choices for punishment had no bounds. Additionally, society could sanction youths in the same way as adults. The law made no distinction based on the age of the offender. In fact, youths could be (and were) sentenced to death for various deviant actions. While the law allowed for and prescribed harsh punishments, there is some question regarding how frequently the more serious actions were actually used. Platt (1977) suggested that while many youths could be sentenced to death, few received such a sentence and most of those who did were never put to death. Similarly, Faust and Brantingham (1979) claimed that a process of **nullification**, or refusal to enforce the law against children, took place because of the lack of penalties geared specifically for juvenile offenders.

Throughout most of history, children held no special status in society. They did not receive any special, protected treatment. If anything, they were subjected to harsher treatment than adults. In terms of legal proscriptions, children could be held liable for the same actions and in the same fashion as adults. There was no legal term of "delinquency" under which the state could intervene with youths. Youths fell under the same statutes and guidelines that were used with adult offenders.

The concept of childhood began to emerge in the sixteenth and seventeenth centuries. It was during this time that medical advancements brought about a lengthening of the life expectancy of youths. Youths also began to be viewed as different from adults. They were in need of protection, assistance and guidance in order to grow up uncorrupted by the world. This movement was led by clergy and scholars of the time. These leaders saw the young as a source of attack on the immoral and sinful aspects of society. Youths, who were not yet corrupted, had to be shielded from society and trained for their future role in the world. Children were seen as a catalyst for general social change. Childhood came to be seen as a period of time during which the young could receive an education and moral training without the pressures of adulthood.

Table 2.1   Highlights in the Development of Juvenile Justice

16th-17 century	concept of "childhood" begins to emerge
1825	first House of Refuge opened in New York
1838	*Ex parte Crouse* established *parens patriae* as basis for state intervention with youths
1841	probation started in Boston by John Augustus
mid-1800s	development of cottage reformatories for juveniles
1892	New York legislation enacted, providing for separate trials for youthful offenders
1899	first juvenile court in Cook County (Chicago), Illinois
1905	*Commonwealth v. Fisher*—reaffirmation of *parens patriae* philosophy for juvenile court
1912	U.S. Children's Bureau established to oversee juvenile justice
1920	all but three states with juvenile court 320 separate juvenile courts in the United States
1920-1960	growth of juvenile justice system—separate institutions, few legal challenges, new agencies and treatments
1966	*Kent v. United States*—beginning of legal challenges to *parens patriae* and juvenile justice processing

Accompanying these changes were alterations in how youthful offenders should be disciplined. Responses to misbehavior began to be tailored to fit the age of the offender. In England, youths under the age of seven could not be held responsible for their actions, individuals between eight and 14 could be held responsible only when it could be shown they understood the consequences of their actions, and youths age 14 and over were considered adults (Empey, 1982). While these types of changes began to recognize the difference between juveniles and adults, the actions taken against offenders remained the same, regardless of the age of the offender.

The Rise of Juvenile Institutions

Changes in the methods of dealing with problem youths corresponded to the changes occurring in American society during the early 1800s. During this time, there was a great movement toward the cities. Industrialization was drawing families out of the countryside and to the cities. The cities were growing in both size and density. In addition, the individuals moving to the cities brought with them a variety of outlooks and ideas. This growing diversity in the population was especially true of the cities in the United States, which were attracting immigrants from a wide range of European countries. The promise of a better life in the new world also brought with it a great deal of poverty.

Methods for dealing with problem youths grew out of the establishment of ways to handle poor people in the cities (see Rothman, 1971; 1980). The poor were seen both as a threat to society and in need of help. The primary response to dealing with the poor entailed the training of the poor. It was assumed that these people could be made into productive members of society. Unfortunately, there was little that could be done with the adult poor. They were beyond the training stage and were set in their ways. The children of the poor, however, were viewed as trainable. A key aspect of this training was the removal of the child from the bad influences and substandard training of the poor parents. While this view became prominent in the 1800s, Krisberg and Austin (1978) noted that as early as 1555 the English established the Bridewell Institution in London to handle youthful beggars. The primary emphasis of the institution was the handling of poor and destitute youths, although in practice the institution handled all problem youths, including delinquents. The Bridewell institution was envisioned as a place where the youths would be trained in a skill that they could use after they were released.

The establishment of institutions in the early 1800s in the United States closely followed the ideas of the Bridewell Institution. The institutions were viewed as places for training those individuals who were not productive and who seemed to pose a threat to society. There was a heavy emphasis on the problems of the poor. The establishment of institutions for the poor and delinquent also reflected a shift in the view of causes of deviance. Throughout most of history, deviance was viewed as a result of problems inherent in the individual. The 1800s, meanwhile, witnessed a growth in the belief that deviance was a result of poor environmental conditions. A change in the environment, therefore, should result in changed behavior. The earlier the individual was placed into a new environment, the better the chances of having a positive impact on the person's actions. The establishment of new institutions also provided the court with an alternative to doing nothing with juveniles or placing them in adult institutions.

Houses of Refuge

The establishment of institutions for children in the 1800s clearly conformed to these ideas. These early institutions were called **houses of refuge** and were envisioned as a place for separating the youth from the detrimental environment of the city. The first house of refuge was established in New York in 1825 and was followed by institutions in Boston (1826) and Philadelphia (1828). The rationale and set-up of the houses of refuge closely followed the concern for the poor and the need for training discussed above.

Central aspects in the handling of youths were indeterminate sentences, education, skills training, hard work, religious training, parental discipline, and apprenticeships (Pisciotta, 1983). The use of education, skills training, hard work and apprenticeships were clear indications that the goal was to produce a productive member of society. Indeterminate sentences allowed the institution to work with each person on an individual basis. Where one youth may benefit from a short period of intervention, another child may require extended work and assistance. The interest in religious training and parental discipline carried over the historical ideas that the best methods of training lay in the realm of the family and the church. The families of the youths in the institution were considered to be lacking in the ability to provide these basic needs. The houses of refuge were envisioned as shelters and sanctuaries that would protect and nurture their wards away from the corrupting influences of the city and the poor family (Rothman, 1971).

The establishment of the houses of refuge also was seen as a means of removing children from the criminogenic influences of the workhouses and adult jails (Krisberg & Austin, 1978). Reformers saw the prior methods of handling youths through the adult system as nothing more than placing poor and problem juveniles in contact with adult criminal offenders. The natural outcome would be "schools for crime" that produced more problems than they solved. The houses of refuge supposedly differed by offering education and training in useful skills within a setting that allowed for control and discipline of the children.

While the rationale and the goals of the houses of refuge were laudable, the daily operations and the impact of the institutions were questionable. Many of the activities were far removed from the real world. Inmates had little, if any, contact with members of the opposite sex. Military behavior was the norm. This included enforced silence, marching to and from different activities, the wearing of uniforms, and swift and habitual corporal punishment (Rothman, 1971). Apprenticeships often failed to be more than simple slave labor. Many of the apprenticeships were on farms in the country. Problem youths were apprenticed to ship captains and sent to sea. In general, there was no quality control or oversight for the apprenticeships. The institutional labor was often dictated by contractual obligations that led to exploitation of the youths by the institutional masters. Children were bribed, beaten and even subjected to extended incarceration if the monetary interests of the administrators were at stake (Pisciotta, 1982).

In addition to failing to provide the basic tools that they promised, the houses of refuge also failed in other respects. For the most part, these institutions were nothing but new prisons. They were tremendously overcrowded. This overcrowding was partly due to the admission of persons not suited for the goals of the institutions. The houses of refuge served the poor, destitute and delinquent youths. At the same time, they handled poverty-stricken adults and adult offenders. The overcrowding of the facilities by such diverse groups of inmates changed the focus of daily operations from the goals of education and training to that of simple custody and discipline. The establishment of institutions like the Lyman School for Boys in 1848 by the state of Massachusetts eliminated the housing of adult and juvenile offenders in the same facility but carried on the tradition of overcrowding and related problems. In general, the early houses of refuge failed to provide their stated goals and settled into a process very reminiscent of that of the adult prisons and jails that had previously been the norm for handling youths.

New Reformatories

The failure of the early houses of refuge did not lead to the end of juvenile institutions. While the problems of the houses of refuge were well known by the mid-1800s, proponents argued that the principles underlying intervention were correct. The issue, therefore, was in proper implementation of intervention. Emphasis on education, training and parental discipline led to the establishment of "cottage" reformatories.

The cottage setup was intended to parallel a family closely. Concerned surrogate parents would oversee the training and education of a small number of problem youths. Discipline would be intermixed with the care and concern typical of family life. Most of the cottages were located in the country and emphasized work on the farm. This was supposed to separate the youths from the criminogenic features of the urban environment and to instill a sense of hard, honest work in the charges. The idea of indeterminate sentencing carried over to the cottage approach.

Other changes in the handling of youths accompanied the growth of these cottage reformatories. Foremost among these features was the development of probation in 1841 by John Augustus. While the early use of probation was centered on adult offenders, by 1869 the state of Massachusetts dictated that the State Board of Charities would participate in, and take charge of, court cases involving youthful offenders (Krisberg & Austin, 1978). Probation officers would assist in the gathering of information on the youths, suggest alternative means of intervention and oversee the placement of juveniles in reformatories

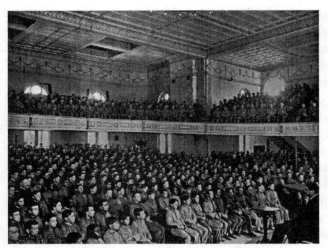

Inmates attend a presentation at Elmira State Prison. Elmira Reformatory was established in 1876 for handling youthful offenders, but accepted both juveniles and young adults. *Photo: Library of Congress/Corbis*

and apprenticeships. Another method of dealing with youths, in accordance with the cottage idea, entailed the "placing out" of juveniles into foster homes. For the most part, these placements were the same as apprenticeships. Such placements were seen as an alternative to institutionalization and allowed for the training of youth in a worthwhile occupation.

Unfortunately, these new alternatives for handling youths faced many of the same problems as the earlier houses of refuge. The institutions and cottages became overcrowded to the point that custody became the primary concern. Apprenticeships proved to be little more than slave labor and youths often fled at the first opportunity. One analysis of 210 apprenticed individuals found that 72 percent of the youths either ran away or returned to the institution (Pisciotta, 1979). The harsh treatment of the youths in the institutions led to running away, the setting of fires, and various sexual problems (Pisciotta, 1982). The inability to handle some youths prompted the establishment of special facilities such as the Elmira Reformatory in 1876. Unfortunately, Elmira accepted both juveniles and young adults, negating the premise of separating youths from criminogenic older offenders. A final problem with the institutions was the continued mixing of both deviant and destitute youths in the same facilities. The institutions considered that being poor was closely tied to deviant activity and, as a result, intervened in the lives of lower-class individuals regardless of the existence (or lack) of a delinquent or criminal act.

Institutions for Females

Throughout the development of alternatives for handling males, little attention was paid to females. Problem girls were dealt with in the same institutions as males and adults. Part of the reason for this was the relatively small number of females officially handled by agents of social control. Exceptions to this situation began to appear in the mid-1800s with the establishment of separate institutions for girls. One of the most well known facilities for females was the Lancaster State Industrial School for Girls in Massachusetts. The girls committed to Lancaster had the same basic backgrounds as boys found in other institutions. They were mostly from poor, immigrant families who were faced with the vagaries and problems of the urban environment (Brenzel, 1983). The institutions were set up as family cottages in order to deal with these problems.

The hoped-for end product of the institutions for girls was the production of females capable of fulfilling their place in society. Where boys were to become productive laborers, females were to learn how to be good housewives and mothers (Brenzel, 1983). Success with the girls was gauged by successful marriage and parenthood. Much of the concern centered on the plight of future generations who were to be raised by the problem girls rather than on the girls themselves. Unfortunately, these institutions fared no better than those handling boys. While some girls successfully graduated from the institutions, married and became mothers, others did not realize the goals set by the institutions. In addition, Lancaster and similar institutions tended to be little more than prisons for youths. They were characterized by overcrowding, lack of treatment, and strict discipline. The different focus from male institutions did not result in different outcomes.

The Establishment of the Juvenile Court

The juvenile court arose in response to the failure of the earlier interventions with juveniles and attempted to address the issues of the era. The late 1800s continued to experience great levels of immigration by lower-class Europeans to the industrial cities of the United States. Environmental factors remained at the head of the list of causes for deviant behavior. In addition, the emergence of psychological and sociological explanations for behavior suggested that the problems of society could be fixed. Finally, middle- and upper-class individuals (primarily women) were interested in doing something to help the poor and destitute. The new court system utilized many of the earlier intervention ideas. Consequently, the expansion of juvenile justice was subjected to many of the same problems as the earlier interventions, as well as new concerns.

The Growth of the Juvenile Court

The first recognized individual juvenile court was established in Cook County, Illinois, in 1899. While this represented the first official juvenile court, a variety of jurisdictions implemented and experimented with similar institutions. Between 1870 and 1877, the state of Massachusetts established separate court dockets, separate hearings and separate record keeping for cases involving juveniles under the age of 16 (Ryerson, 1978). New York passed legislation in 1892 that provided for separate trials for juvenile offenders, although they continued to be held in the adult system (Platt, 1977). Similarly, Judge Ben Lindsey of Colorado, a leading advocate of juvenile court, operated a quasi-juvenile court for a number of years prior to the establishment of the court in Illinois (Parsloe, 1978). Regardless of the initial beginnings, by 1920 all but three states had juvenile courts, and there were more than 320 separate juvenile courts in the United States (Ryerson, 1978).

The legislation that established the Illinois court reflected the general belief in the ability to alter youthful behavior. First, the court was to operate in a highly informal manner without any of the trappings of the adult court. Lawyers and other adversarial features of the adult system (such as rules of evidence and testimony under oath) were discouraged. The judge was to take a paternal stance toward the juvenile and provide whatever help and assistance was needed. The emphasis was on assisting the youth rather than on punishing an offense. Second, all juveniles under the age of 16 could be handled by the new court. The court was not restricted to dealing with youths who committed criminal acts. Rather, the court could intervene in any situation in which a youth was in need of help. In practical terms, this allowed intervention into the lives of the poor and immigrants, whose child-raising practices did not conform to the ideas of the court. Third, the new court relied extensively on the use of probation. Probation continued to serve both administrative functions for the court as well as supervisory actions with adjudicated youths.

While no two juvenile courts could claim to have the same program, the courts all held the same general principles of providing assistance for the juveniles. Julian W. Mack of the Chicago juvenile court aptly portrayed the role and methods of the court when he stated:

> Most of the children who come before the court are, naturally, the children of the poor. In many cases the parents are foreigners, frequently unable to speak English, and without an understanding of American methods and views. What they need, more than anything else, is kindly assistance; and the aim of the court, in appointing a probation officer for the child, is to have the child and the parents feel, not so much the power, as the friendly interest of the state; to show them that the object of the court is to help them to train the child right . . . (Mack, 1909).

Within this statement, Mack noted the minor concern over the deviant act in the court, the goal of providing assistance to both the youth and the family, the place of probation in the court, and the typical youth who was subjected to court intervention.

The progressive reforms that led to the establishment of the juvenile courts also had other influences. One of the impacts was a gradual widening of the juvenile court's mandate. The original Illinois statute allowed intervention for criminal activity, dependency and neglect. In 1903, Illinois added such actions as curfew violation and incorrigibility (status offenses) to the situations allowing intervention. A second area of change involved the development of new institutions for handling youths who needed to be removed from their families. One of the first new institutions was the Illinois State School at St. Charles, Illinois, which was funded in 1901 and opened in 1905 (Platt, 1977). These institutions closely followed the family/cottage model used throughout the late

1800s. The greatest distinction was in the administrative unit (the juvenile court vs. the adult court) and not in orientation. A move toward using full-time, paid probation officers also occurred shortly after the court's beginnings. By 1912, the federal government established the U.S. Children's Bureau to oversee the expanding realm of juvenile justice (Ryerson, 1978).

A final major movement coming from the progressive reforms was the institution of court-affiliated guidance clinics. The first of these was established in Chicago by William Healy, a leading proponent of the juvenile court, in 1909. These clinics relied on the new psychological and sociological explanations emerging during this time. Central to these explanations was the need for the expert analysis of each juvenile in order to identify the unique factors contributing to the individual's behavior. Following Healy's example, 232 clinics were established by 1931 (Krisberg & Austin, 1978).

The Legal Philosophy of the Court

Perhaps the greatest challenge to the growth of the juvenile system entailed debate over the philosophy of the court and the question of a juvenile's constitutional rights. Critics of the court and earlier interventions often claimed that the state was subjecting juveniles to intervention without regard to their rights and those of the family. In many instances the state was forcibly removing a youth from his parents' custody. These new interventions were viewed as an abrogation of the family's position in society. The problems of constitutional rights and the new juvenile justice system were deemed inconsequential compared to the possible benefits that could accrue from intervention. Indeed, the state relied on the doctrine of *parens patriae* for justification of its position. Table 2.1 presents key factors in the growth of *parens patriae* and its application to the juvenile court.

Parens patriae, or the state as parent, was based on the actions of the English **Chancery Court**. The Chancery Court was primarily concerned with property matters in feudal England. One aspect of the court's function was to oversee the financial affairs of juveniles whose parents had died, and who were not yet capable of handling their own matters. The court acted as a guardian until such time that the youth could assume responsibility. In practice, the court dealt only with matters involving more well-to-do families. The offspring of the poor did not have any property to protect. As an arm of the state, the Chancery Court often converted much of the property to the ownership of the state. There would be little to gain in overseeing the needs of the poor. However, regardless of the intention of the Chancery Court, the precedent was set for intervention into the lives of children.

Movements to intervene into the lives of children in the United States were quick to rely on *parens patriae* for justification. The earliest example of this involved the case ***Ex parte Crouse***. Mary Ann Crouse was incarcerated upon her mother's request but against her father's wishes. Her father argued that it was illegal to incarcerate a child without the benefit of a jury trial. In rejecting the father's argument, the court denied that the Bill of Rights applied to youths. The Pennsylvania Supreme Court ruled in 1838:

> May not the natural parents, when unequal to the task of education, or unworthy of it, be superseded by the *parens patriae*, or common guardian of the community? It is to be remembered that the public has a paramount interest in the virtue and knowledge of its members, and that of strict right the business of education belongs to it. That parents are ordinarily entrusted with it, is because it can seldom be put in better hands; but where they are incompetent or corrupt, what is there to prevent the public from withdrawing their faculties, held as they obviously are, at its sufferance? The right of parental control is a natural, but not an inalienable one. It is not excepted by the declaration of rights out of the subject of ordinary legislation (*Ex parte Crouse*, 1838).

The *Crouse* opinion set the tone for intervention with juveniles in the United States. In essence, the state could intervene, regardless of the reason, if it found that the child was in need of help or assistance that the parents and family could not provide. The decision relied solely on the good intentions of the state and the need to provide the proper training for the child.

Intervention based on *parens patriae* did not go completely unchallenged. Critics charged that the state was overextending its rights by intervening in many minor matters that should simply be ignored. More importantly, the argument was made that the state provided little more than incarceration and was not providing the education, training and benevolent care that was required under the *parens patriae* doctrine. In *People v. Turner* (1870), the Illinois Supreme Court stated:

> In our solicitude to form youths for the duties of civil life, we should not forget the rights which inhere both in parents and children. The principle of the absorption of the child in, and its complete subjection to the despotism of, the State, is wholly inadmissible in the modern civilized world.
>
> The parent has the right to the care, custody, and assistance of his child. The duty to maintain and protect it, is a principle of a natural law.

In this instance, the court affirmed the rights of the parent to care for the child. The intervention of the state was to be reserved for instances in which the youth had violated a criminal law and after the application of due process concerns. The good intentions of the state and the needs of the youth were not enough to warrant unfettered intervention into the family unit. Despite this apparent shift in legal concerns, most jurisdictions ignored the opinion and continued to follow the general guidelines set forth in the *Crouse* decision.

The issues of a child's and parent's rights were largely settled in the 1905 case, **Commonwealth v. Fisher**. In this case, the Pennsylvania Supreme Court directly addressed the question of a juvenile's behavior, his or her constitutional rights and the intent of the juvenile system in intervention. The court said:

> The design is not punishment, nor the restraint imprisonment, any more than is the wholesome restraint which a parent exercises over his child. The severity in either case must necessarily be tempered to meet the necessities of the particular situation. There is no probability, in the proper administration of the law, of the child's liberty being unduly invaded. Every statute which is designed to give protection, care, and training to children, as a needed substitute for parental authority, and performance of parental duty, is but a recognition of the duty of the state, as the legitimate guardian and protector of children where other guardianship fails. No constitutional right is violated (*Commonwealth v. Fisher*, 1905).

The key concern was with regard to the intent of the intervention and not the rights of the juvenile, the parents or the effectiveness of the system. In essence, the child had a right to intervention and not a right to freedom. Moreover, the parents had little, if any, rights in the disposition of the child. The juvenile court was viewed as providing help in the most benevolent fashion possible. The Pennsylvania Supreme Court was granting the juvenile system a free hand in dealing with youths.

The basic constitutionality of the juvenile system went largely unchallenged after the *Fisher* decision. Those cases that did arise were met with the same rationale and outcome of the earlier case. It was not until the mid-1960s that the courts began to alter their views and grant some constitutional rights to juveniles. Indeed, not until 1966 was the benevolent premise of the juvenile system adequately challenged. In the U.S. Supreme Court case of **Kent v. United States**, Justice Abe Fortas said:

> There is evidence, in fact, that there may be grounds for concern that the child receives the worst of both worlds: that he gets neither the protections accorded to adults nor the solicitous care and regenerative treatment postulated for children (*Kent v. United States*, 1966).

As will be seen in Chapter 8, the constitutional rights provided to juveniles in the last two decades are not equal to those provided to adults. The courts have continued to reserve various powers for the state and to treat juveniles as a separate class of citizens with different rights and expectations.

Problems of the Court

Despite the swift adoption of the juvenile court and its related components, the new system was faced with a number of problems and failures. A major problem involved the extent to which the various operations were initiated. Many of the courts and agencies relied solely on untrained volunteers. The number of full-time, paid juvenile court judges, probation officers and trained clinicians was small. Ryerson (1978) cited one survey (Beldon, 1920) that found that only 55 percent of the courts provided regular probation services and, of those with probation, less than 50 percent of the officers were full-time employees. The same survey reported that there were only 23 full-time juvenile court judges in the United States in 1918 (Beldon, 1920). The child guidance clinics experienced the same shortage of trained professionals. As a result, most youths did not receive any evaluation. Most evaluations that occurred took place after a child was incarcerated (Ryerson, 1978). This lack of adequate staff was accompanied by inadequate facilities and resources. While the juvenile court retained the use of institutionalization, the choice of placement usually rested with those institutions that had existed prior to the court's establishment. The problems of these institutions were the same as before. Harsh treatment, military regimentation, lack of training and education, high recidivism, and running away all continued. The new agencies, such as the child guidance clinics, similarly failed to provide the treatment and supervision they promised.

Criticism of the court also focused on its expanded jurisdiction. As noted above, new statutes outlined juvenile behavior that had previously been left to the family for correction. The expanded jurisdiction of the court, which was based on *parens patriae,* also led to an increase in unofficial dispositions and handling of youths. There is evidence that many proceedings took place without the presence of a judge or the keeping of records. Such actions were justified on the basis of relieving the burden of the court and the desire to avoid the stigma of a more formal procedure. While these reasons may have been laudatory, they encouraged the handling of more juveniles with very minor transgressions. Many trivial actions, such as making noise, sledding in the street, playing in the street, riding bicycles on the sidewalk and throwing paper into the sewers, became the subject of these unofficial cases (Rothman, 1980).

Benevolence or Self-Interest?

The institution of the juvenile court has generally been held as a progressive, humanitarian development. Most historians refer to the time period from about 1880 to the 1920s as the Progressive Era. It was during this time that many laws were passed mandating apparent humanitarian reforms. Actions such as mandatory schooling, regulations on working conditions for both adults and juveniles, concern over the plight of the poor and immigrants, the growth of agencies dealing with health concerns, and the establishment of the juvenile court were listed as examples of the benevolent actions of the reformers and society. Coercion within the juvenile justice system, and other forms of intervention, were considered a necessary evil for improving the lot of those who did not know any better (Rothman, 1980). Schlossman (1977) went so far as to label the benevolent movement in juvenile justice to be an exercise in love. He plainly stated that institutions and the court needed to provide the type of love, affection and concern found in the family setting.

Benevolence, however, was not the driving factor, according to other writers. Anthony Platt (1977) referred to the persons involved in the development of the juvenile court as **child savers**. The issue he addressed was the rationale for saving the youths. Platt viewed the growth of juvenile justice as a part of a larger social movement that attempted to solidify the position of corporate capitalism in the United States. Rather than being a humanistic endeavor to help the less fortunate members of society, intervention through the courts allowed the powerful classes of society to mold a disciplined, complacent labor force. The juvenile court was a means of preserving the existing class system in the United States (Platt, 1977). Krisberg and Austin (1978) essentially made the same argument. They saw the system as a vehicle of the upper classes for controlling the "dangerous" (lower) classes in society.

Both Platt (1977) and Krisberg and Austin (1978) pointed to a variety of factors in support of their contentions. First, the driving force behind the growth of the juvenile system, especially the juvenile court, were middle- and upper-class individuals. Middle-class women formed one key group in the system's development (Platt, 1977). These women were the wives and daughters of the industrialists and landed gentry who controlled production and had the greatest say in government. A second form of support rested on the fact that the system grew during the time when the lower-class ranks were swelling with new, poor immigrants. In essence, the lower class was growing to a point where it could pose a threat to the status quo. Third, and related to the second, was the establishment of new laws that addressed the activity of the lower classes. Statutes governing youthful behavior primarily addressed the actions of the poor and immigrants. The government extended control over entirely new classes of behaviors in the juvenile justice statutes. A fourth indication of the juvenile system's inherent bias was the exploitative use of children who were incarcerated or under the care of the system. Youths were placed in involuntary servitude, indentured and apprenticed, all under the argument that they would benefit from learning a trade. Realistically, according to Platt (1977) and Krisberg and Austin (1978), these actions supplied immediate cheap labor and indoctrinated the youths in the capitalistic ideology of the upper classes. It is upon these and similar arguments that various writers have questioned the benevolent intentions of those individuals involved in the juvenile justice system movement.

Additional support for the argument that the system lacked the benevolence purported in many studies comes from an evaluation of the treatment of females and blacks. Pisciotta (1983) offered evidence that the juvenile justice system had been both racist and sexist. The author noted that most residential institutions in the early 1800s refused to admit blacks. Instead, black youths were subjected to continued incarceration in adult facilities until special institutions for blacks could be built. One of the earliest separate black institutions was opened in Philadelphia in 1848. Exceptions to the rule of separating whites and blacks were restricted to instances in which the admittance of blacks was economically advantageous to those in charge. Once admitted to an institution, little education was supplied. Intervention with blacks revolved around training them to perform menial labor and to learn their "proper place" in society. Females were handled in a similar fashion (Pisciotta, 1983). Academic education was minimized, while religious, moral and domestic training was emphasized. This view of proper training for women rested on the expectation that females were to stay in the home and raise the next generation of children (Brenzel, 1983; Pisciotta, 1983).

One possible problem with the proposal that the juvenile court was a self-serving invention of the powerful involves the place of the new professionals in the growth of the system. As noted earlier, the emergence of the new psychological and sociological explanations for behavior played a major role in the direction of the juvenile institutions and court. Why did these professionals not criticize the growth of juvenile justice if, indeed, it was simply a means for the powerful to control the masses? Platt (1977) addressed this issue by pointing out that the professionals received a great deal of benefit from juvenile justice, regardless of the driving forces. These individuals gained a reputation as experts, secured employment as either full-time employees or paid consultants, gained access to data and information otherwise denied, and found a forum willing to let them advance their theories and ideas. It was not that these professionals may not have objected to the biased premise of the system, they simply found more personal benefits in allowing the system to be instituted and advanced.

The debate over the intent of those forming the juvenile court has not been resolved. The usefulness of recognizing the difference in opinion is in opening the way for varied suggestions about dealing with problem youths. Individuals who assume the benevolence point of view turn to a variety of theoretical explanations and accompanying forms of intervention. Advocates of the self-interest perspective focus on the actions of society and not the individual offender. Instead of looking for ways to help the youth, these writers suggest that changes in the social structure account for variation in the levels of deviance. This approach will be further explored in Chapter 4.

Juvenile Justice: 1920s-1960s

Most of the great movements and changes in juvenile justice were completed by the early 1920s. By this time, the juvenile court was solidly entrenched as the proper institution for dealing with problem youths. The problems and criticisms directed at the court and its institutions were passed off as the failure to implement the programs properly. The shortcomings were not inherent features of the system. Advocates called for increased resources, time and patience. Society and the legal system were content to leave the juvenile justice system alone to search for effective interventions, provided the system continued to act in the best interests of its youthful clients. Changes in the handling of youths over the next few decades, therefore, were restricted to generating new theories of behavior, attempting new types of treatment and evaluating their efforts.

Various new institutions were established for handling problem youths. These were necessitated both by increased numbers of youths entering the system and differing approaches to treating youths. Psychological explanations and perspectives led to the growth of various training and counseling (group and individual) programs. Psychotherapeutic interventions gained prominence in the 1940s and led to private and public institutions based on these ideas. The use of such interventions as guided group interaction and peer pressure formed the basis of programs such as the Highfields Project in 1950. Highfields was a short-term, residential facility that allowed the youths to visit their families and remain a part of the community. This type of program helped form the basis for halfway houses and other community interventions. Chapter 12 will address such actions in more detail.

One of the best known of the experimental interventions of this time period was the Chicago Area Project (CAP). Based on the ecological analysis of crime and delinquency (see Chapter 4), the CAP viewed deviance as being a result of the community environment. The project had three distinct aspects: recreation programs for youths, vigilance and community self-renewal, and mediation. Work with juveniles primarily fell under the first and third of these ideas. The basic intent of the CAP was to involve youths in nondeviant activities; provide outlets for youthful exuberance; guide youths to finding proper, acceptable solutions for problems; assist the youths with school and jobs; and work with youths who had been released back into the community after institutional stays. While the impact of the program on delinquency has never been clearly demonstrated, recent analyses (Schlossman & Sedlak, 1983; Schlossman, Zellman and Shavelson, 1984) have indicated some success with individual problems. The scope of the CAP prompted the adoption of various parts of its program in other cities.

Summary

The growth of juvenile justice from the 1920s to the early 1960s followed a pattern of new programs—all within the original mandate and scope of the early reformers. The issues that fueled debate in the early years have returned to be debated in recent years. Many of the ideas are being retried, adapted and subjected to new scrutiny. The remainder of the text will look at the varied issues and the operation of the juvenile system, primarily since the early 1960s. Questions of theory, implementation, practice and evaluation form the core of the discussion.

DISCUSSION QUESTIONS

1. Concern over child abuse has greatly increased over the past two decades. Many people argue that society's young are treated worse today than at any time in history. Based on your knowledge, place this view within a historical framework. That is, outline the historical view of children and some of the major practices for handling kids.

2. You are an administrator of an early house of refuge and are asked to give a dispassionate view of your institution. What are the strengths and weaknesses of this type of institution? What problems do you face and how can you correct them?

3. The legislature is proposing to abolish the juvenile court. Argue in favor of the legal philosophy that is the basis for the court. What is the philosophy, why has it been legally upheld throughout the years, and why should it be maintained?

CHAPTER 3

Explaining Delinquency:
Biological and Psychological Approaches

Key Terms and Phrases

atavistic
biosociology
cerebrotonic
classicism
concordance
determinism
dizygotic
ectomorph
endomorph
free will
hedonism
hypoglycemia
id-ego-superego
interpersonal maturity levels
   (I-levels)
intelligence quotient (IQ)
medical model/medical
   analogy
mesomorph
Minnesota Multiphasic
   Personality Inventory
   (MMPI)
modeling

monozygotic
moral development
multiple causation
nature-nurture controversy
neoclassicism
neurotransmitters
operant conditioning
orthomolecular factors
personality classifications
phrenology
physiognomy
positivism
premenstrual syndrome
psychoanalysis
reactive hypoglycemia
soft determinism
somatotypes
somotonic
spiritualistic explanations
theory
viscerotonic
XYY chromosomal pattern

Throughout the history of juvenile justice, criminologists and others interested in deviant behavior have sought to explain why certain individuals act in certain ways at certain times. The number of theories for deviant behavior has grown considerably over the past 100 years as the field of criminology has progressed and the level of research has improved. A **theory** can be described as an attempt to answer the question "Why?" Why does an individual violate the norms of society? Why do certain conditions seem to accompany deviant behavior? Why does deviance occur when it does? These and other "why" questions form the basis for the theories that have been proposed for explaining delinquent behavior.

The types of factors that have been used to explain delinquency take a wide variety of forms. Early **spiritualistic explanations** or demonologic explanations reflected the belief that deviant acts were the result of the battle between good and evil, God and the Devil. Individuals who committed crimes were possessed by the Devil. Consequently, the solution to deviance involved exorcising the Devil and delivering the individual back to God. Oftentimes this could only be accomplished through the death of the Devil's vessel—the individual. The soul would then be freed to join God.

These nonscientific explanations gave way in the 1700s with the advent of classicism and the movement into positivistic approaches in the later 1800s. Classicism and positivism are "schools of thought" rather than specific theories of behavior. These schools lay out general beliefs about people and the world that shape the form that individual theories will take.

Theoretical Schools of Thought

Every explanation of behavior, whether it be conventional or deviant behavior, rests on a number of implicit assumptions about individuals and the world within which they operate. These beliefs form the core of many arguments about the causes of crime and how to deal with offenders. For example, differences in opinions about the death penalty often boil down to different beliefs about whether punishment can deter people. Every science has schools of thought that organize its ideas. In criminology, the two schools are classicism and positivism.

The Classical School

Classicism finds its roots in the writings of Cesare Bonesana Marchese de Beccaria (1738-1794) and Jeremy Bentham (1748-1832). Beccaria was an Italian aristocrat who broke with the ruling classes to condemn the methods of dealing with crime and morals in society. In outlining a new set of criminal and penal practices, he set forth a number of beliefs about humankind and the function of society in dealing with deviance.

Under classicism, humans are viewed as being free-willed. That is, individuals choose to act the way that they do after calculating the pros and cons of an activity. Coupled with the idea of **free will** is the belief that humans are **hedonistic**. Under the "hedonistic calculus," individuals seek to maximize pleasure and minimize pain (Bentham, 1948). Individuals, therefore, choose activities and behaviors based on their calculation of the amount of pleasure and pain that will result. Pleasurable behaviors will be undertaken and repeated, while painful activities will cease. Under classicism, individuals make a conscious, rational decision to commit crime based on the expectation of a pleasurable outcome.

These beliefs about free will and **hedonism** had a great influence on the type of law and criminal justice system proposed by the early classicists. Clearly, the solution to crime was to alter the outcome of the hedonistic calculation. That is, if you can increase the pain and reduce the pleasure, you can reduce, and possibly eliminate, deviant behavior. Beccaria used this rationale and focused his efforts on defining a set of laws and punishments that would alter the choices of individuals. Because it was the crime that would bring the pleasure, Beccaria emphasized the offense and the legal system, not the offender, in his work. He felt that individu-

Jeremy Bentham (1748-1832), a proponent of Cesare Beccaria's ideas, was a major contributor to classical thought and reform with regard to criminal law. *Photo: Archive Photos*

als could not make an informed decision to avoid deviance unless they were presented with a clear set of laws and punishments. Consequently, classicism argues that there must be a set punishment for each crime and the level of punishment must be sufficient to offset any pleasurable consequence of an individual's behavior.

The most important goal for classicism is the prevention and deterrence of crime through the use of punishment. Sanctions were meant to keep crime and deviance from occurring in the first place. Ideally, individuals would be deterred from crime by the knowledge of the pain that would come from being caught and punished. Punishment was not meant to be a form of retribution or retaliation by society. Indeed, it was the indiscriminate use of the law and punishment during his time that prompted Beccaria to propose these changes. Punishment was solely for the purpose of altering the outcome of the "hedonistic calculus."

Classicism dominated discussions of crime, deviance and the law in the 1800s. Indeed, changes in laws reflected the general belief in free will and attempts to deter individuals from becoming involved in crime. Unfortunately, crime did not disappear and new ideas about behavior began to emerge in the late 1800s. Much of this movement toward a new "school of thought" grew out of the developing medical sciences.

Table 3.1   **Major Elements of Classicism and Positivism**

Classicism	Positivism
Free Will	Determinism
Hedonism	Multiple Causation
Rational Offender	Emphasize Offender/
Emphasis on Offense	Situation Differences
Legal Responses—	Medical Model—
Clear laws and procedures	Crime as "symptom"
Punishment for Prevention	Individualized response
and Deterrence	Rehabilitation and Treatment

Neoclassicism

Soft Determinism
Free Will with Limited Choices
Punishment or Treatment
The Positivistic School

The Positivistic School

Positivism takes an approach that is diametrically opposed to that outlined in classicism. Rather than place the responsibility for deviance on the individual, positivists absolve the doer of guilt and place the blame on a wide array of potential causes. The key idea for positivism is **determinism**. Everything that any individual does, both deviant and conventional, is determined (caused) by factors beyond the control of the individual. Altering behavior, therefore, cannot be brought about through simply raising the amount of pain a person will receive if caught and punished. Rather, changing behavior can be accomplished only by identifying and eliminating the factors that are causing the individual to act in a certain way.

While some positivists have attempted to identify a single causal factor for deviance, positivism typically recognizes the **multiple causation** of behavior. A deviant act may be the result of many different things occurring at the same time or a series of events or factors occurring over a period of time. Likewise, the same deviant act committed by different people may be the outcome of totally different causes. Both the diversity and simultaneity of causes require looking at each individual case for reasons behind behavior. The approach used by positivists to identify causes is typically referred to as a **medical model** or **medical analogy**.

Using a medical model, the scientist approaches deviance the same way that a doctor approaches a sickness. Just like a doctor considers coughs and fevers as symptoms of larger problems, the positivist views deviant acts, like burglary and rape, as symptoms of other underlying causes or conditions. Doctors do not simply seek to eliminate the cough or fever. Instead, they work to eliminate the cause(s) of those symptoms. The positivist deals with crime in much the same manner. Positivism does not treat every individual who commits the same deviant act in the same fashion. For example, two people with a fever may be suffering from two different medical conditions, requiring two totally different treatments. Similarly, two burglars may have committed their acts for different reasons, thus necessitating totally different interventions. In essence, the positivist must consider each deviant act as a symptom and, like a doctor, diagnose the underlying cause and prescribe an appropriate treatment. The emphasis in positivism, therefore, is not on the offense. Rather, the emphasis is on the offender and the unique situation, and the various factors causing the individual to be an offender.

The logical extension of the focus on determinism and multiple causation is the belief in rehabilitation and treatment. Instead of punishing an individual for his or her actions, positivism seeks to remove the root causes of the deviant behavior. The proper rehabilitation or treatment strategies may be as diverse as the number of clients. For example, one burglar may need financial assistance for his family when the offense was committed in order to provide food for his family, while another burglar may need group counseling to address the specific animosity she had toward the victim that led to the action. Treatment and rehabilitation need to be tailored to the circumstances of the individual. This does not mean that similar responses cannot be used for similar offenders. Rather, positivism argues that uniqueness must be recognized and addressed in all responses to deviance.

Positivism emerged from the 1800s as the dominant school of thought. Advances in the medical fields and the development of psychology and sociology presaged a more scientific approach to explaining and understanding deviance. Particularly in terms of juveniles, the growth of juvenile justice blamed underlying causes for deviant behavior and sought to find ways to protect juveniles and correct any inadequacies that led to delinquency. While the criminal justice system retained vestiges of classicism and deterrence, the juvenile justice system and the emerging field of criminology embraced the ideas of positivism.

Neoclassicism and a Summary

Today, the overwhelming belief in positivism has given way to a compromise position with classicism. **Neoclassicism** takes the position that an individual exercises some degree of free will. The choices, however, are limited by a large number of factors both within and outside the individual. Sometimes referred to as **soft determinism**, this approach holds that an individual can only make decisions based on the available choices. The available options determine the extent to which the person can exercise his or her free will. This compromise gives both the classicist and positivist a stake in the criminal and juvenile justice systems.

The balance of this chapter and the entire next chapter discuss a wide range of theories. The biological and psychological theories appearing in this chapter are primarily positivistic in orientation. For the most part, they approach deviance as the outcome of forces beyond the control of the individual. The sociological theories appearing in Chapter 4, however, more often incorporate elements of free will in their arguments.

Biological and Sociobiological Theories

Explanations of deviance based on biological factors are among the earliest as well as the most recent theories in criminology. Medical advances, particularly in the 1800s, led to explanations of behavior that focused on the biological makeup of the individual. The underlying assumption made by the early biological theorists was that, if the biological makeup of the individual dictated his or her physical capabilities, these characteristics could also contribute to the type of behavior exhibited by the person.

Physical Appearance

Early biological explanations focused almost exclusively on observable physical features of offenders (see Table 3.2). One approach, **physiognomy**, suggested that facial features were related to behavior. Typical features associated with criminals included shifty and beady eyes, a weak chin and facial hair characteristic of the opposite sex. Interest in physical appearance and the lack of any scientific basis for physiognomy led to the introduction of **phrenology**, which concerned itself with both the shape of the skull and facial features. The phrenologist's true interest, however, was in the brain that was housed in the skull. The absence of the ability to examine and study the brain directly simply led them to find a proxy for the brain. Phrenologists believed that any abnormalities—bumps or crevices—in the skull would be repeated in the shape of the brain. Assuming that different areas of the brain handled different dispositions (e.g., aggressiveness, friendliness), it would be possible to identify those persons who would be more aggressive by inspecting the shape of their skulls. While phrenology had a more scientific argument than physiognomy, it too suffered from the lack of scientific proof.

Table 3.2   **Physical Appearance Explanations**

Physiognomy	Focus on facial features
Phrenology	Focus on shape of skull and implications for the brain
Atavism	General "ape-like" appearance; earlier stage of evolution; advocates included Lombroso, Hooten
Somatotypes	Body types/physiques related to behavior; often related to different temperaments; advocates included Sheldon, Glueck and Glueck

LOMBROSO'S ATAVISM

Physical appearance theories received their greatest support from the work of Cesare Lombroso, considered the father of modern criminology. Lombroso, basing his ideas on Charles Darwin's theory of the survival of the species, viewed criminals as throwbacks to an earlier state of human existence. These individuals were not as physically or mentally advanced as the rest of society. Lombroso (1876) identified a number of **atavistic** qualities that were indicative of the individual's developmental state. These atavistic, or ape-like, qualities generally reflected the physical features of the apes from whom humans had descended (see Table 3.3). In addition to these physical features, Lombroso identified a second set of nonphysical atavistic qualities in response to criticism that the physical features alone could be found in both deviants and nondeviants.

Table 3.3   Lombrosian Atavistic Characteristics

Physical Characteristics	Nonphysical characteristics
Protruding jaw	Sensitivity to temperature changes
High forehead	Agility
Asymmetrical face	Lacking a sense of right or wrong
Bad teeth	Fondness for animals
Deep, close-set eyes	Tolerance of pain
Excessively long arms or legs	
Abnormal nasal features	
Exaggerated sex organs	

Specific tests of Lombroso's theory were undertaken by a number of researchers. In his own study of incarcerated offenders, Lombroso (1876) noted that more than 40 percent of the criminals had five or more atavistic traits. These "born criminals" were a direct result of the lack of evolutionary progression found in the person. The remaining criminals fell into categories of "criminaloids," "insane" criminals and criminals of "passion." Criminaloids were composed of individuals who entered criminal activity due to a variety of factors including mental, physical and social conditions that, when occurring at the same time, would trigger deviant behavior (Vold & Bernard, 1986). Insane criminals included idiots and mentally deranged individuals, while criminals of "passion" acted out of anger, hate, love or other—generally spontaneous—emotion.

Lombroso's early research failed to meet a critical methodological requirement. Many of his early findings were based on studies restricted exclusively to incarcerated criminals. The failure to include a control group of noncriminals (or even nonincarcerated criminals) meant that he was unable to state whether the results would be different if he studied people in the general public. Indeed, subsequent research by Lombroso, which added control groups, pointed out this weakness and led him to consider environmental, social and other nonphysical factors in explaining deviance.

Cesare Lombroso (1836-1909), often considered the father of modern criminology, maintained that a number of physical as well as nonphysical atavistic characteristics were related to criminal tendencies. *Photo: Corbis-Bettman*

Lombroso's pathbreaking work on physical appearance and criminality led to a great deal of controversy. Goring (1913) provided one of the earliest scientific critiques of Lombroso's ideas. Comparing convicts to a control group of noncriminal citizens, Goring found only minor differences in the physical makeup of the two groups. Conversely, Hooton (1931) claimed to find a great deal of physical difference between 14,000 convicts and 3,000 noncriminal subjects. Hooton also found differences between different types of offenders. He claimed that various physical features could be used to identify persons participating in different deviant acts. A number of criticisms, however, have been leveled at Hooton's work (Vold & Bernard, 1986). Among these criticisms are the facts that Hooton did not consider past offense history of his subjects and he ignored information that clearly contradicted his conclusions.

SOMATOTYPES

Despite the early criticisms of appearance theories, the basic idea of physical appearance has been used in subsequent research into **somatotypes**, or body types. Perhaps the best known of these studies was that by Sheldon (1949). Building on the work of Kretschmer (1925), Sheldon identified three basic somatotypes. He then extended the argument by outlining a specific temperament corresponding to each type. The physiques and corresponding temperaments appear in Table 3.4.

Table 3.4   Sheldon's Physiques and Temperaments

Physique	Temperament
Endomorph: short, fat, round, soft	**Viscerotonic:** soft, easygoing, extrovert
Mesomorph: muscular, large, barrel chested, thick, hard	**Somotonic:** dynamic, active, athletic, aggressive, talkative
Ectomorph: bony, thin, skinny, small, delicate	**Cerebrotonic:** nervous, complainer, introvert

Source: Constructed from Sheldon (1949).

While Sheldon's categories were not pure types and there may have been a degree of crossover between these categories for most people, Sheldon believed that it was possible to classify individuals according to their dominant tendencies. Classifying delinquents being treated in a residential facility, Sheldon (1949) found that mesomorphic characteristics were more prevalent, with ectomorphic features least common. He concluded that mesomorphic individuals were more likely to commit delinquent acts.

Support for the relationship between mesomorphy and delinquency was evident in the studies of Sheldon Glueck and Eleanor Glueck (1956) and Juan Cortés (1972). Glueck and Glueck (1956) compared 500 delinquents to 500 nondelinquents and found twice as many mesomorphs in the delinquent group. Similarly, Cortes (1972) reported a greater tendency for delinquents than nondelinquents to be mesomorphic. Unfortunately, both studies shared similar methodological problems with Sheldon's work. First, much of the research was based on subjective determinations of body type, often by simply looking at photographs of the youths, and tended to ignore changes in body type as the youths grew older. Second, the researchers ignored the possibility that mesomorphic youths were more often recruited into delinquency than other youths, and not due to any natural propensity that accompanied their physical makeup. Third, the identification of delinquents through the simple use of incarcerated youths may reflect the institutionalization of mesomorphic delinquents because of a perceived threat from larger, more imposing offenders. Finally, the determination of mesomorphs as being somotonic (aggressive, active, etc.) often rested on the finding that many delinquents were mesomorphs and that delinquent behavior, by its nature, is somotonic. It would appear that the usefulness of physical-type theories for contemporary juvenile justice is somewhat limited.

Genetic-Inheritance Studies

The possibility that criminality may be inherited can be found in many of the early writings of those interested in physical appearance (see Goring, 1913). Physical features are clearly passed on from generation to generation. A logical extension is that nonphysical factors, such as behavioral tendencies, are also passed on from parents to offspring. Two basic methods for studying this question are the comparison of the behavior of twins and comparing the behavior of offspring to their biological parents.

Table 3.5   Traditional Genetic Explanations

Twin Studies	Assume greater similarity in behavior for monozygotic twins (identical) than for dizygotic twins (fraternal) or normal siblings
Adoption Studies	Assume similar behavior between offspring and biological parents even when reared in another environment
XYY Chromosome	Abnormality of the sex chromosome pair; "supermale" is more aggressive and more criminal

TWIN STUDIES

Studying twins for the genetic propensity to be deviant requires the identification of different types of twins. **Monozygotic** (MZ), or identical, twins are the product of a single fertilized egg that separates into two developing individuals. This process guarantees that the two individuals will have an identical genetic makeup. The second type of twins are known as **dizygotic** (DZ) or fraternal twins. In this case, the two offspring are the result of two separate eggs fertilized by separate sperm. The result will be genetically similar offspring (due to the common parents) but the two offspring will not be genetically identical. Dizygotic twins are no more genetically similar than any two siblings born at different points in time. An examination of the genetic propensity for deviant behavior rests on finding greater **concordance**, or similarity, in behavior for MZ twins than for DZ twins or common siblings.

Several studies claim to find a genetic component to behavior. In one early study, Newman and associates (1937) found that in 93 percent of the cases in which one MZ twin was delinquent the other twin was also delinquent. The corresponding result for DZ twins was only 20 percent. The higher concordance in behavior for the MZ twins was interpreted as evidence of a genetic factor in delinquency. Similarly, using a registry of 6,000 pairs of twins in Denmark, Christiansen (1974) found that, for MZ twins, 36 percent of those who had a criminal record also had a brother with a criminal record. Criminal DZ twins had a criminal brother only 12 percent of the time.

More recently, Lyons (1996) and Silberg et al. (1996) have reported on two large-scale twin studies. The Harvard Twin Study drew subjects from a registry of Vietnam era veterans who were born between 1939 and 1957 (Lyons, 1996). Based on phone interviews with 3,226 pairs of men covering adult and juvenile behavior, the analysis found higher concordance for MZ twins than DZ twins, especially in adult criminality. Lyons (1996) concluded that genetic factors help dispose individuals to act in certain ways. Silberg and associates (1996) have used a prospective research design to examine psychopathology in the Virginia Twin Study of Adolescent Behavioral Development. While not focused exclusively on delinquency, the authors reported evidence of genetic influences for MZ subject pairs. This is particularly true for individuals with multiple psychological problems. It is important to note that both of these studies find strong environmental, as well as genetic, influences on behavior.

While other reviews find support for a genetic component to behavior (see, for example, Ellis, 1982; Wilson & Herrnstein, 1985), a number of problems plague the studies. First, most of the observed relationships are small and insignificant (Reiss & Roth, 1993). Second, several studies show that DZ twins are more concordant than normal siblings, which would not be expected from a genetic argument (Rutter, 1996). Similarly, cross-sex correlations are lower than within-sex correlations, raising questions about the magnitude of a genetic influence (Rutter, 1996). Third, most studies lack control over the environmental influences impacting on the individuals (Katz & Chamblis, 1995; Reiss & Roth, 1993). The levels of concordance may be due to similarity in rearing practices or imitation between siblings. Identical twins may be expected to act more similarly by family and friends as a result of the "identical" label. Fraternal twins may be expected to be more individual and not so similar. Finally, distinguishing between MZ and DZ twins can be done only by using laboratory tests. Unfortunately, in most studies the determination is based on how similar the siblings look, what they have been told throughout their lives, or the visual determination of a doctor (often at the time of birth). The failure to distinguish the two types of twins adequately could greatly affect the study results. Despite these problems, there is the possibility that at least some of the cause of deviant behavior is due to genetic influences.

ADOPTION STUDIES

A second method of investigating the genetic contribution to deviance is through the comparison of the behavior of adopted offspring and their biological parents. Adoption studies improve on those of twins by attempting to remove the youths from the environment of the real parents. Any resultant similarity between the offspring and the biological parent can then be attributed to the genetic similarity between the subjects rather than to environmental influences.

The results of various adoption studies lend support for genetic arguments similar to those found in twin studies. Schulsinger (1972), comparing psychopaths and nonpsychopaths to their biological relatives, found a greater number of psychopathic biological relatives for the psychopathic subjects. The difference, however, was not great (7%) and was based on a total of only 114 observations. Equally qualified support was found in Crowe's (1972) analysis of 104 females and their offspring. Crowe reported a 13 percent difference in the arrests of offspring of offending and nonoffending mothers. The difference, however, reflects a total difference of only six fewer offenders in the nonoffending mother group. The results tend to support a genetic argument, but the support is, at best, weak. Greater support comes from a study by Hutchings and Mednick (1977), which involved a much larger sample. These authors reported that more biological fathers of criminal boys are criminal (49%) than are fathers of noncriminal boys (31%). Introduction of the adoptive father's criminality does not eliminate this relationship, although it does temper the results.

One important qualifier that must be considered in adoption studies involves the separation of the genetic and environmental influences on the individuals. The assumption throughout the research is that the simple fact of adoption is enough to guarantee that the environment of the biological parents is being controlled. Ellis (1982) points out, however, that one overwhelming consideration in many adoptions is the matching of the adopting environment to that from which the individual is being taken. This would seriously impair a study's ability to distinguish the effects of genetics and environment. A related factor deals with the point of the adoption. Few studies can substantiate when the adoptions actually took place. Adoptions close to birth would have the best chance of eliminating the environmental influence of the biological parents. Adoptions after that point in time could involve a good deal of environmental impact carried to the new environment. Additionally, some (see, for example,

Kopp & Parmelee, 1979; Sameroff & Chandler, 1975) would argue that the environment can play a significant part even when the child is still in the womb. This could be accomplished through trauma to the mother, nutrition or other environmental factors. While each of these qualify and temper the results of adoption studies, they do not negate the fact that most such studies show a tendency toward a genetic component in behavior.

In an attempt to clarify the varied findings from past studies, Walters (1992) undertook a meta-analysis of family, twin and adoption studies. Included in the analysis were 38 studies dating from 1930 to 1989. In a meta-analysis, the researcher uses the reported data from past studies and computes a common statistic for all studies, thereby allowing a direct comparison of the different results. Walters (1992) reports that there is a "low-moderate" correlation between heredity and crime. The significance of this finding, however, is problematic because the more methodologically rigorous studies provided less support for the relationship. This was especially true for the adoption studies, which have the best chance of separating genetics from the environment (Walters, 1992).

CHROMOSOMAL EXPLANATIONS

Where the prior studies of genetic factors have focused on inheritance, genetics can also be investigated through abnormalities that appear in the genetic makeup of the individual. Foremost among the genetic problems that have been related to deviance is the appearance of the **XYY chromosomal pattern** among males. XYY is a characteristic of the sex chromosome in which the presence of a Y dictates that the individual is a male. The appearance of a double Y in the sex chromosome leads some to refer to these individuals as "super males." Among the first to study the possibility that XYY males are overly aggressive and more criminal, Jacobs, Brunton and Melville (1965) reported finding a greater proportion of abnormal males with XYY in a prison hospital than among males in the general population. While the XYY theory had many proponents in the 1950s and 1960s, Witken and associates (1976) provided perhaps the most realistic assessment of its impact on criminality. Starting with all men born in Copenhagen, Denmark, from 1944 to 1947, the authors eliminated all those who were less than roughly six feet tall (XYY individuals are generally taller than normal). The remaining sample of 4,139 men were subjected to chromosomal analysis, yielding a final sample of 12 XYY men (roughly one-quarter of 1 percent of the men tested). Examination of official records, however, revealed that only one of the 12 XYY men had a conviction. The authors concluded that there was little evidence that these men were more aggressive than normal individuals (Witken et al., 1976). The Witken et al. study and others have failed to show a greater number of XYY males among the criminal population or a greater propensity for aggression among such men in the general population.

To date, theorists have not provided strong support for their genetic arguments. This is not to say that genetics hold no influence on behavior. Genetic research is still in its infancy and future advances may reveal contributors to a wide range of behaviors. Nevertheless, the problem of separating the environmental influences from a genetic component will remain as a serious concern.

Biosocial Factors

The recent trend in biological theories of behavior falls within the realm of what are known as biosocial approaches. **Biosociology**, or sociobiology, refers to the idea that the biological makeup of the organism and the surrounding environment are intimately related. The environment plays a part in shaping the organism and the organism, through its daily activity and interpretation of the world, shapes the environment. In terms of deviant behavior, the old belief that deviance is a direct result of a biological condition is no longer tenable. Instead, biosociology sees deviance occurring when specific biological conditions coincide with appropriate sociological or environmental factors. For example, an individual with a congenital hormonal defect may be overly aggressive in situations that force him or her into a choice between fight and flight. This individual, however, does not seek out such situations or become aggressive without the external stimulus. The more modern biological explanations of behavior, therefore, accommodate both biological and sociological factors. Among the biosocial factors that receive the most attention are endocrine/hormonal influences and orthomolecular/chemical imbalances in the body.

Table 3.6   Biosocial Influences

Endocrine/hormonal factors—natural bodily chemicals; key targets in past research include testosterone, menstruation

Orthomolecular/chemical factors—substances introduced to the body that may alter behavior; key targets include sugar, alcohol, drugs

Neurotransmitters—impact of interrupting, enhancing or hindering the transmission of information in the brain; key targets include dopamine, serotonin, norepinephrine

---

ENDOCRINE/HORMONE INFLUENCES

Among the normal functions of the body are the production and secretion of various hormones. These natural chemicals control many of the basic bodily functions including growth, reproduction and the functioning of the central nervous system. In terms of deviant behavior, most attention has been focused on reproductive hormones (Shah & Roth, 1974). One such area of study probes the relationship between testosterone level and aggressive behavior. Androgen, the male sex hormone present in testosterone, has been found to be related to aggressive behavior, particularly in animal studies (see, for example, Brennan, 1947). Studies on human subjects, typically of incarcerated offenders, have found higher testosterone levels among more aggressive and more serious offenders (Booth & Osgood, 1993; Ehrnkranz et al., 1974; Kreuz & Rose,

1972; Rada et al., 1976). While such studies suggest that testosterone leads to greater levels of aggression, the evidence is not totally convincing. Among the problems are conflicting findings in the research (Shah & Roth, 1974), the fact that testosterone levels vary over even short time periods, and the fact that testosterone is affected by diet, stress, exercise and social factors (Booth & Osgood, 1993; Katz & Chamblis, 1995; Nassi & Abramowitz, 1976; Reiss & Roth, 1993). The minimal correlation revealed in the research is further tempered by these problems.

A second examination of hormonal influences on behavior involves the female menstrual cycle. A variety of changes and hormonal imbalances may occur during premenstrual days and the days of menstruation. These physical changes, referred to as **premenstrual syndrome**, may prompt various changes in mood and behavior, including possible deviant activity. In an early study, Morton and associates (1953) reported that more than three-quarters of the violent female offenders committed their crimes during the menstrual and premenstrual days. Dalton (1964), based on prisoner self-reports concerning their menstrual cycles, claimed that 49 percent of the women committed their offenses during the premenstrual or menstrual days. Despite these results, there are a number of problems in the analyses. First, Horney (1978) notes that menstrual cycles experience a great deal of variability over time and ages, which makes the determination of past cycles based solely on recall almost impossible. Second, other factors besides menstruation could account for the relationship. Horney (1978) provides a variety of rival explanations for the menstruation-aggression relationship, including psychological and emotional factors that could induce menstruation at times other than in the normal cycle. The evidence, therefore, suggests a weak relationship between menstruation and crime.

ORTHOMOLECULAR/CHEMICAL IMBALANCES

While endocrine factors deal with naturally produced bodily chemicals, **orthomolecular factors** refer to chemicals that are introduced to the body or altered through diet or other influences. One commonly discussed potential problem is the influence of sugar on behavior. **Hypoglycemia** is the term most often used in these discussions. However, hypoglycemia, a condition of *low* blood sugar, manifests itself in a lack of energy, lethargy, nervousness and, in the extreme, coma. It is difficult to imagine hypoglycemic individuals taking aggressive deviant actions against anyone or anything. The proper term for the relationship between blood sugar levels and criminal activity is **reactive hypoglycemia**, which refers to changes in the blood sugar level, both higher and lower, as a result of dietary intake.

While various researchers claim to have found support for a relationship between hypoglycemia and crime (Bonnett & Pfeiffer, 1978; Geary, 1983; Hippchen, 1978; Hippchen, 1981; Podolsky, 1964; Schauss, 1980), their conclusions rest upon suspect research methodology (Gray & Gray, 1983). Much of the support comes from anecdotal accounts of physicians and psychologists who have simply compared a person's diet to his or her behavior without establishing the different bodily needs or processes of the different individuals. What constitutes an overconsumption of sugar by one individual may be minor for another individual. Also, most studies using the oral glucose tolerance test to screen for blood sugar problems fail to recognize that this test is not a definitive measure of blood sugar (Gray & Gray, 1983). When more in-depth measures are used, the studies fail to support reactive hypoglycemia as an explanation for deviance. Most studies also fail to note that nutrition and diet are highly related to social class, which may be the operant factor in the relationship with deviance (Katz & Chamblis, 1995). Given the state of the evidence, reactive hypoglycemia appears to be a minor cause of deviance (American Dietetics Association, 1984; Gray & Gray, 1983; National Dairy Council, 1985).

Alcohol is another substance linked to deviant behavior. That alcohol correlates with delinquency and criminality is indisputable. What is questionable is the mechanism at work. Many would argue that alcohol is a disinhibitor, thus allowing for normally avoided behavior to become manifest. Reiss and Roth (1993) suggest a more biological connection in which alcohol alters the processing of information and, depending on the dosage, may prompt aggression and irritability, or more passivity and sluggishness. Similar arguments can be made for the impact of other legal and illegal drugs on the body.

ADDITIONAL BIOSOCIAL APPROACHES

A wide range of additional factors have been considered as potential influences of deviant behavior. One area of study deals with whether different **neurotransmitters** (chemicals involved in the transmission of electrical impulses through the nervous system) are capable of altering an individual's behavior. Among the neurotransmitters that have been investigated are dopamine, norepinephrine and serotonin. Goldman, Lappalainen and Ozaki (1996) report that dopamine is directly related to aggressive behavior. Similarly, Virkkunen, Goldman and Linnoila (1996) note that serotonin levels influence impulse control, hyperactivity and other behavior related to deviance. Research has shown that it is possible to alter various neurotransmitters, both purposefully and inadvertently through the use of drugs, alcohol and other substances. Such changes can alter social behavior (Brunner, 1996). While still in its early stages, this research suggests that there is a relationship between different neurotransmitters and deviance (Brennan, Mednick and Volavka, 1995; Reiss & Roth, 1993). Most of the research is based on small samples and the degree of the relationship remains questionable.

Most of the recent biosocial approaches suffer from similar problems. First, the identification of correlations is often touted as clear evidence of a causal relationship. Second, there may be reversed time order in many of the relationships (Reiss & Roth, 1993). For example, aggressive behavior may lead to physical confrontations that involve head injuries and alterations in the functioning of the brain. Third, the ability to generalize results of studies based on animals to human beings is questionable. Finally, the studies typically fail to consider other spurious factors—such as social status, diet and the environment—in the consideration of biosocial influences. It is possible that these other factors are influencing both deviance and neurological functioning.

Box 3.1   Biosocial Arguments in Court

The "Twinkie Defense"

On November 27, 1978, Dan White shot and killed San Francisco Mayor George Moscone and City Supervisor Harvey Milk in a job dispute. After resigning his post as city supervisor on November 10, Dan White asked Mayor Moscone to reappoint him to his vacant, former position. The mayor refused and appointed Harvey Milk, a prominent leader in the homosexual community of San Francisco, to the position.

On the morning of November 27, Dan White, avoiding metal detectors, entered City Hall, shot Mayor Moscone five times, reloaded the gun, crossed the hall to Harvey Milk's office and shot Supervisor Milk four times. At trial, defense psychologists successfully argued "diminished mental capacity" as a result of long-term psychological depression, exacerbated by a craving for junk food that drove him into a deeper depression. The high sugar content of the junk food, particularly Twinkies, Coke and candy bars, aggravated the depression. Rather than being convicted of first-degree murder, Dan White was convicted of voluntary manslaughter and received a sentence of 5 to 7 years, 8 months in prison. He was released on one year's parole on January 6, 1984, having served less than five years in prison for two murders.

Genetic Disposition—An Unsuccessful Attempt

In 1991, Stephen Mobley robbed a Pizza Hut in Georgia, killing a store manager in the process. After confessing to the crime, Mobley's lawyers attempted to introduce genetic evidence as mitigating factors during the sentencing stage of the trial. At issue was whether a family history, which included several generations of violence and aggression among male family members, could be used in court. More specifically, the defense asked the court to order neurological testing to help establish such a genetic predisposition. In support of their request, the defense pointed to prior research on genetic disposition for violence and aggression in another family. The court ultimately rejected the argument (see Denno, 1996).

Implications for Juvenile Justice

At the present time there is still relatively little known about the relationships between biological influences and deviant behavior. Despite methodological problems, studies have provided qualified support for biosocial explanations. At the same time, they raise many more questions.

Early biological explanations of delinquency had only minor impact on juvenile justice due to the great shift toward psychological and sociological explanations in the early 1900s. The new biosocial approaches, however, have engendered renewed interest in biological influences on behavior. Conditions with a genetic component, such as schizophrenia, can be modified or controlled by drugs. Behaviors related to hormonal or orthomolecular problems also can be altered through changes in diet or drug therapy. As biosocial research progresses, additional practical uses for curbing deviance will emerge. Already, the formal justice system has begun to consider biological factors in its daily decisionmaking.

The courts have been asked to recognize the influence of biological factors in different cases, with varying degrees of success (see Box 3.1). Additionally, various courts have begun to offer sentence alternatives that require medical/drug treatment as a condition of release. For example, Depo-Provera, a drug that inhibits the production of testosterone, has been used with sex offenders. Similarly, correctional agencies have removed "junk food" machines from their institutions as a means of limiting the amount of sugar and food additives that their charges consume.

While biological explanations have yet to gain prominence in juvenile justice, there is reason to believe that they will continue to draw increased attention in the future. As Brennan and associates note:

> Understanding of the interaction of genetic and environmental factors in the causes of crime may lead to the improvement of treatment and prevention. Partial genetic etiology does not in the least imply pessimism regarding treatment or prevention. Quite the contrary! Several genetically based conditions are treated very successfully by environmental intervention (Brennan, Mednick & Volavka, 1995: 90).

At the same time, caution must be taken when implementing programs based on biosocial research. These activities may also bring about more harm than good. For example, altering a diet to do away with "problem" foods may inadvertently damage an otherwise good diet. The most prudent direction for biosocial advocates to pursue at the present time would be expanded research.

Psychological Explanations

A second general area of explanations for delinquency entails psychological theories. As with other types of theories, psychological explanations take a variety of forms and include a wide range of factors. Early psychological theories were based on biological/physical factors. Indeed, psychiatry, which is usually seen as a part of the general psychological field, is distinguished by its strong commitment to finding physiological bases for aberrant behavior. Psychiatrists are medical doctors who specialize in the general area of mental disorders. Many psychological explanations, however, do not look for a physical explanation. Instead, the psychological orientation can be seen as having a few distinctive characteristics. First and foremost, these approaches generally view problems as arising out of early life experiences. Deviance is seen as a result of problems and flaws that were not recognized and corrected during the adolescent years. Second, psychological explanations are highly individualistic. Deviance results from adverse social situations, incomplete socialization, poor development of personality, or a variety of other factors. While many individuals may display the same or similar behavior, different explanations may be necessary for each person. Finally, because of the individualistic orientation, psychological explanations lend themselves to a treatment orientation. Rather than focus on who will become deviant, emphasis is on working with individuals who are already having problems and assisting them to overcome the problem. The following discussion will deal with a few of the more well-known explanations for delinquency and deviance—psychoanalytic, developmental, personality and mental deficiency explanations.

Psychoanalytic Explanations

The psychoanalytic approach owes its prominence to Sigmund Freud (1856-1939). The major premise of **psychoanalysis** is that unconscious, and perhaps instinctual, factors account for much of the deviant behavior that is displayed by an individual. Deviance is seen as the outward manifestation of the unconscious desires and drives of the individual. Problems arise from the individual's inability to exert personal control over his or her desires due to faulty or incomplete training during the early years of life. The goal of psychoanalysis is the identification of unconscious, precipitating factors and the development of conscious methods for dealing with them.

Table 3.7	**The Freudian Personality**
Id	Unconscious desires, drives, instincts
Superego	Learned values, behaviors; moral character of the individual; outlines the acceptable and unacceptable; may be conscious or unconscious
Ego	Social identity of individual; actual behavior; conscious activity

Freudian psychoanalysis outlines three distinct parts to the personality that are involved in behavior. The **id** reflects the unconscious desires, drives and instincts within the individual. In simple terms, the id can be seen as the selfish, "I want" part of the individual. The **superego** entails values that the individual learns from those around him or her. These values form the moral character of the individual and help dictate what the person considers acceptable or unacceptable behavior. It is in the superego where self-criticism and positive self-image resides. The superego is a result of early moral training and provides the rationale for refraining from various types of behavior. Where the id looks for satisfaction of desires, the superego responds with either a "can't have" orientation or a "must do" response. That is, the superego helps orient the individual's behavior away from simple desires and toward the value system that the person has incorporated. The actions of the superego may be both conscious and unconscious depending on the type of behavior in question and the degree of moral training involved. The final part of the personality, the **ego**, is the social identity that is exhibited through behavior. It is often the manifestation of the conflict between the id and the superego. The ego is the conscious attempt to satisfy the needs of the id while continuing to abide by the mandates of the superego. This aspect is always conscious because it is the solution to the question of whether the individual follows his or her drives or the morally correct line of activity.

The key to the conflict between the id and the superego is found in the unconscious of the individual. Psychoanalysis seeks to uncover the causes of behavior by bringing the unconscious conflict to consciousness. Often, psychoanalysis is undertaken only when the conflict between the id and the superego appears as criminally deviant behavior. The conflict, however, will not always appear in this way. There are various methods by which the individual can handle the internal conflict. As illustrated in Table 3.8, deviance may appear in some mechanisms such as repression, rationalization or displacement. At the same time, these and other mechanisms can lead to socially acceptable behaviors.

Table 3.8   Psychoanalytic Defense Mechanisms

REPRESSION—An active attempt to push desires and thoughts out of one's consciousness or to keep material from reaching consciousness. Example: You forget that you owned a pet which was run over by a car when you were a child.

DISPLACEMENT—A change in the primary object of a feeling or desire to a secondary one that is less threatening. Example: You are angry at your boss but you yell at your husband or wife instead.

SUBLIMATION—Here the displacement is more long-term and the object chosen is socially acceptable. Example: You want to hit and hurt your father, but you become a professional boxer or football player.

DENIAL—The truth of certain facts or experiences is denied, rather than forgotten as in repression. Example: Your daughter dies, but you act as if she is alive, keeping a bed made up for her.

REACTION FORMATION—A desire is changed or transformed into the opposite feeling or desire. Example: You hate or deeply resent your father, but you tell everyone how much you love him and act toward him in a loving manner.

PROJECTION—You have an unconscious desire or thought, but you attribute it to someone else instead of acknowledging it in yourself. Example: You no longer love someone but accuse him or her of no longer loving you instead.

RATIONALIZATION—The process of finding an acceptable reason for doing something unacceptable. Example: You punish your child harshly, but say "I'm doing this for your own good."

REGRESSION—You replace your desires or thoughts with those from an earlier stage of your development. Example: You are under stress and get angry at someone who works for you, so you throw a temper tantrum.

Source: Van Voorhis, Braswell & Lester (1997).

Sigmund Freud (1856-1939) was the developer of the psychoanalytic approach to explaining delinquency. Freud's impact on the study of delinquency has been monumental. *Photo: Leo Baeck Institute/ Archive Photos*

A large number of researchers have further developed the psychoanalytic approach and applied it to delinquent behavior. Erikson (1968) suggests that some youths fail to develop an identity (or ego) of their own. Instead, they gather much of their self-image from those with whom they associate, particularly their peers. Delinquent peers inevitably lead the individual to delinquency. Where Erikson (1968) focuses on the failure to develop an ego, Abrahamson (1944) and Aichhorn (1963) target the poor development of a superego. The absence of an adequate superego leaves the id unchecked. As a result, the individual responds with behavior that reflects his or her uncontrolled instincts, drives and desires.

Despite the development of a large body of literature, the psychoanalytic approach continues to be subjected to strong criticism. One of the most problematic concerns is the lack of empirical referents for the theory. Psychoanalysis relies on vaguely defined terms and constructs to represent its key concepts. Consequently, it is very difficult to subject the theory to empirical testing. There is no clear method for measuring the id, ego or superego. These terms are open to a broad degree of subjective interpretation. A second major criticism involves the fact that psychoanalysis is totally retrospective. That is, it is useful only for looking at what has already happened. It is geared toward uncovering the reasons why something happened and working to correct those reasons. A third area of concern deals with the emphasis on early childhood. With few exceptions (such as Erickson), it is assumed that little change occurs after adolescence. Adult behavior is viewed only as a result of poor childhood socialization and not from factors appearing in adult life. Finally, psychoanalysis is criticized for ignoring social-structural factors in the determination of behavior. Indeed, with the heavy emphasis on the unconscious, psychoanalysis examines the social setting of the individual only to the extent that it failed to provide the necessary moral atmosphere during early adolescence.

Developmental Approaches

A number of writers identify the source of deviance in interrupted or arrested developmental patterns during childhood. The basic assumption behind these explanations is that all individuals develop through a number of stages. Each stage provides an integral part of the total knowledge and understanding that a person needs to operate in society. The failure of an individual to complete any one of these stages or steps successfully may lead to some form of socially unacceptable behavior. This basic argument can be seen in Freud's psychoanalytic explanation, in which the failure to develop appropriate super-ego and ego responses to the id takes place in early childhood. The child is born with the id but must learn to internalize the moral dictates of society as he or she grows.

Table 3.9   Developmental Perspectives

Interpersonal Maturity Levels—progressive development of social skills; seven stages; deviance from interrupted development

Moral Development—three moral levels with six stages; progressive change; deviance from incomplete development; key author: Kohlberg

Learning Theories—deviance is learned; modeling; operant conditioning; key authors: Bandura and Walters

---

DEVELOPMENTAL VIEWS

Perhaps one of the most well-known developmental approaches in delinquency research is the scale of **interpersonal maturity levels** (I-levels). The various I-levels reflect the progressive development of social and interpersonal skills. The I-levels represent a continuum from the most basic stage of development through the most advanced stage (see Table 3.10). The interruption of any stage makes the attainment of later stages difficult, if not impossible.

Table 3.10   Interpersonal Maturity Levels

Level 1:	The individual learns to discriminate between himself/herself and others.
Level 2:	The individual starts to separate things into persons and objects, partly on the basis of his/her own needs and what he/she can control.
Level 3:	At this level the individual begins to learn rules and can start to manipulate the environment for his/her own benefit.
Level 4:	The individual begins to perceive things from the standpoint of others. He/she sees conflicts between expectations of others and his/her own needs.
Level 5:	Here the individual becomes aware of patterns of behavior and relationships. There becomes an awareness of distinctions made between events, objects and roles in society.
Level 6:	The individual is able to distinguish between himself/herself and the roles he/she plays. These are not one and the same and can accommodate one another.
Level 7:	At this level the individual begins to perceive a variety of methods for dealing with the world and makes choices based on his/her and other's past experiences and for the benefit of everyone.

Source: Compiled from Sullivan, Grant & Grant (1957).

While delinquency and deviance can occur at any I-level, most occurs in conjunction with levels 2, 3 and 4. Level 2 individuals operate primarily on the basis of their own need. Other persons and objects are seen as providing the individual with enjoyment or everyday needs. Level 3 individuals begin to integrate rules, but are still oriented toward their own needs. As a result, they may realize what they are doing is wrong but cannot justify the rules with their desires. Finally, persons in level 4 may resort to delinquent behavior as a means of striking out against what they perceive as contradictory demands. These individuals maintain personal desires while also responding to the demands and needs of others. The inability to cope with competing demands may release the individual to delinquent activity. Individuals at any level try to balance their own needs against the expectations and needs of others. Operating at the lower maturity levels, however, leads to behavior that is counter to societal demands, with or without the cognizant understanding of those demands.

Kohlberg's (1981) developmental model notes that individuals progress through various stages of **moral development** that outline right and wrong. Kohlberg offers six stages arranged into three moral levels (see Table 3.11). The Preconventional Level is characteristic of young children, while most adults fall into the Conventional Level. Only a small proportion of adults reach the Postconventional or Principled Level. Deviant individuals typically fail to display the same level of moral development as noncriminals with the same or similar characteristics. As in the I-level classification scheme, Kohlberg views deviance as a result of interrupted or incomplete development.

Table 3.11   **Kohlberg's Moral Development**

Level I.   Preconventional Level

Stage 1   Right is obedience to authority and rules, and avoiding punishment. There is clear concern for one's own physical well-being.

Stage 2   Right corresponds to seeing one's own needs, taking responsibility for one's self, and allowing others to do the same. At issue is a fair exchange with others.

Level II.   Conventional Level

Stage 3   Right is avoiding the disapproval of others, having good intentions and motives, and being concerned for others. Individuals are aware of others and their needs.

Stage 4   Right is doing one's duty to society and others, and upholding the social order. The individual is capable of looking at things from society's viewpoint.

Level III.   Postconventional or Principled Level

Stage 5   Right is based on upholding the rules and values agreed upon by society. The individual feels obligated to society. There is a recognized social contract between the individual and society that outlines acceptable behavior.

Stage 6   Right is a reflection of universal ethical principles. The individual recognizes the moral rightness of behavior and acts accordingly.

Source: Compiled from Kohlberg (1981).

The usefulness of the developmental perspective is limited primarily to treatment. As with psychoanalytic ideas, the identification of developmental stages and problems typically occurs *after* deviance has been manifested. The individual then undergoes a one-on-one evaluation in which the potential for subjective evaluation becomes a problem. In instances in which developmental typologies have been used for prediction (such as with I-levels), the predictive capacity of the tools has been found to be weak. Further, developmental approaches have been criticized as imprecise, contradictory and not necessarily sequential (see, for example, Rich & DeVitis, 1985; Simpson, 1974; Williams & Williams, 1970). In general, developmental arguments have proved much more useful in the treatment of deviant individuals.

LEARNING THEORIES

Implicit in developmental discussions is the idea that people learn right from wrong. In learning theories, the emphasis is on how an individual learns and what factors are effective in promoting learning. The failure of an individual to complete a developmental stage successfully, therefore, may be due to a problem in the learning process. **Modeling** is perhaps the simplest form of learning. According to Bandura and Walters (1963), children learn by copying the behavior of others. Most modeling follows the behavior of significant others, particularly parents, siblings, peers and other individuals close to the child. Modeling, however, is not limited to the people around the youth. Children also can learn from characters, both real and fictional. At this level, the modeling is of the character being portrayed and not an actual individual. The process, however, remains roughly the same. (Further discussion of modeling and identification will be taken up under the heading of sociological learning theories.)

A more classical psychological learning theory is that of **operant conditioning**. Operant conditioning deals with the reinforcement of behavior through a complex system of rewards. Skinner (1953) and others view subsequent behavior as a consequence of past responses to behavior. Specifically, an individual repeats (or does not repeat) a behavior based on what happened when the behavior in question appeared in the past. For example, a child who does as he or she is told by his or her parents is given a treat for being good. The treat becomes a reinforcer for future good behavior. In operant conditioning, the reinforcement comes after the behavior or action of the individual. Actions that result in a pleasurable response (positive reinforcers) or that eliminate painful or unpleasant situations (negative reinforcers) will be repeated. Learning, therefore, becomes an ongoing process, with every choice made by the individual resulting in some form of response. Future actions are based on the reinforcement (or lack thereof) of past behavior.

Bandura and Walters (1963) combined conditioning and modeling in a general discussion of learning. They noted that the degree to which a child models his or her behavior is mitigated by the level of reward or punishment that the model receives. For example, a child observing an act of aggression by another person or a fictional character is more likely to copy that act if the aggressive person is rewarded or not punished. Therefore, the process of learning through operant conditioning can take a vicarious route through observation of the experiences of others.

Psychological learning theories have not gone without criticism. Among the concerns is a relative lack of rigorous empirical study using human subjects. Modeling and operant conditioning both receive a good deal of support from simple intuitive assessments of behavior. Additionally, operant conditioning has been observed in laboratory settings using various animals. Correlational studies provide the greatest deal of support. Unfortunately, most of these supportive studies have serious methodological flaws and provide only tentative conclusions. A second concern is that modeling and operant conditioning approaches also ignore the contribution of the individual to behavior. The basic assumption is that the individual is a product of the environment and has little influence in his or her choice of activity. A final consideration involves the use of conditioning to alter delinquent behavior. While it may be possible to influence an individual's behavior, is such action ethical or legal? This is a question faced by any attempt to alter behavior. The practical use of knowledge becomes an issue in this context.

Personality and Delinquency

Various researchers have proposed that deviants display certain personality characteristics that can be used to explain the behavior and identify the individuals. Psychologists have developed a wide array of personality classifications and measures for uncovering personality traits. Early classifications were the direct result of clinical evaluations of individuals. "Deviant" and "normal" individuals were compared in an attempt to identify deviant personality factors.

Table 3.12   Personality Explanations

Glueck and Glueck's Delinquent Personality—extroverted, impulsive, hostile, resentful, defiant, less fearful of failure

Quay's Personality Types—neurotic-disturbed, unsocialized-psychopathic, subcultural-socialized, inadequate-immature

The Minnesota Multiphasic Personality Inventory—standardized test based on 10 clinical personality scales

GLUECK AND GLUECK'S STUDY

One of the early attempts to distinguish delinquents from nondelinquents using personality factors was conducted by Sheldon Glueck and Eleanor Glueck (1950). Glueck and Glueck compared 500 delinquents to 500 nondelinquents along a wide range of factors. The two groups were matched on age, ethnicity, residence and intelligence. The results produced fairly similar results for the two groups when individual personality traits were examined. Consideration of the entire range of personality features, however, led Glueck and Glueck to claim that delinquents are more extroverted, vivacious, impulsive, . . . less self-controlled . . . are more hostile, resentful, defiant, suspicious, . . . destructive . . . and are less fearful of failure or defeat than the non-delinquents. They are less concerned about meeting conventional expectations and are more ambivalent toward or far less submissive to authority. They are, as a group, more socially assertive (Glueck & Glueck, 1950: 275).

This picture of delinquents was meant to summarize their overall personality pattern and indicate differences from conventional youths.

A number of concerns can be raised about Glueck and Glueck's results. First, the individuals who evaluated the youths were aware of which youths were delinquent and which were not delinquent. It is possible that this knowledge biased the evaluators and contributed to finding negative or preconceived delinquent traits. Second, not all the traits associated with the delinquents are undesirable. For example, being extroverted, assertive, less fearful of failure and less submissive are traits that many individuals would find valuable. The portrayal of delinquents in these terms could be considered counter to what is expected from deviant individuals. Third, there is concern with the time order in the variables. The presentation of data assumes that the individuals had these traits before they exhibited delinquent behavior and suggests a possible causal connection. It could be argued, however, that offenders are hostile, resentful, defiant and ambivalent to authority due to their contact with the justice system. These feelings come after contact with the system, not before the delinquent act.

THE QUAY TYPOLOGY

Herbert Quay (1965) identifies four personality types among delinquent youths. Each of the types includes different underlying reasons for delinquent behavior. The "neurotic-disturbed" youth is basically introverted and displays clear feelings of inferiority. Delinquent behavior by these youths is accompanied by guilt and further feelings of inadequacy and failure. "Unsocialized-psychopathic" youths, on the other hand, are overtly aggressive and malicious, and do not view their behavior as wrong. The "subcultural-socialized" delinquent acts in accordance with the behavior of his or her peers. This individual joins a group and operates in such a fashion as to remain an accepted member of that group. Deviance is simply a means to retaining group status. The final personality type, "inadequate-immature," appears to be opposite to the subcultural-socialized youth. This individual is immature and lacks direction. Delinquency is something the youth drifts in and out of as situations arise. There appears to be little or no motivation or rational explanation for the behavior.

Perhaps the major problem with the Quay typology is its lack of exhaustive categories. The four identified personality types do not represent all possible variations. The use of any typology is questionable when it leaves many individuals unclassified. This state of affairs is due, to a large extent, to identification of personality types using institutionalized youths. While it may be useful for identifying factors that may be of help in the treatment of offenders, the Quay system is not as helpful in the prediction of future delinquency.

A STANDARDIZED PERSONALITY MEASURE—THE MMPI

The **Minnesota Multiphasic Personality Inventory (MMPI)** provides a standardized method for uncovering personality traits in individuals. The MMPI is an inventory of 556 true/false questions that are designed to tap 10 personality dimensions identified in past clinical analyses (Megargee & Bohn, 1979). It is an attempt to arrive at the same clinical conclusions without the need for extended clinical observation. No single scale question is associated with deviant behavior. Rather, everyone is assumed to answer some questions in a deviant manner. Deviance is more likely as the individual answers in a deviant fashion on a number of questions. The key, therefore, is the overall tendency in the scales.

While the MMPI has been used extensively, it has been challenged on a number of grounds. First, to the extent that the prior clinical evaluations are in error, poorly conceived or invalid, the MMPI results also are questionable. The results are only as good and useful as the underlying clinical factors. Second, MMPI results have been found to be somewhat determined by demographic variability (Hathaway & Monachesi, 1953). Third, the MMPI is useful primarily in the treatment of offenders, and not for predicting or explaining deviance prior to its occurrence. Finally, because the MMPI has been refined using institutionalized subjects, it is possible that it reflects factors related to institutional life and experiences, rather than to a deviant personality. The inventory has been subjected to relatively few tests outside of the institutional setting.

EVALUATING PERSONALITY FACTORS

Besides the evaluation of individual personality approaches, like those discussed above, different researchers have attempted to make summary evaluations of the strength and usefulness of personality information. In an early analysis, Schuessler and Cressey (1950) were unable to find clear personality differences between criminals and noncriminals. Conversely, Waldo and Dinitz (1967), evaluating personality studies appearing between 1950 and 1967, noted that 80 percent of the studies were able to show statistically significant differences between criminals and noncriminals using personality factors. A similar result was reported in a study that updates Waldo and Dinitz's study through 1975 (Tennenbaum, 1977).

While these results favor personality tests, the authors (Tennenbaum, 1977; Waldo & Dinitz, 1967) present a number of problems with studies of personality. Perhaps the most damaging problem entails the time-order of the relationship between personality and deviance. Many studies fail to probe whether personality leads to delinquency or if delinquency and system processing produces the observed personalities. A second problem is the fact that personality scores and studies often rely on subjective evaluations by clinical workers. Knowledge that the incarcerated subjects have committed certain types of actions may lead to identifying personality traits that fit that behavior. The explanation, therefore, becomes a circular one—the behavior determines the personality and the personality explains the behavior. A final concern reflects the general failure of many studies to observe proper research methodology. The studies fail to draw adequate (or random) samples, do not use control groups for comparison and do not consider other variables that may be more important in explaining the phenomenon under question. While these criticisms make the results problematic for the identification and prediction of behavior, they do not negate the potential usefulness of the techniques in the rehabilitative setting.

Mental Deficiency and Delinquency

Mental deficiency has been considered a prime correlate of deviance for many years. The debate concerning the mental capacity of deviant individuals has a long history that was energized by the development of IQ testing. The **IQ**, or **intelligence quotient**, was developed by Alfred Binet in the early 1900s as a numerical representation of the mental ability of the individual. The formula for IQ is rather simple:

$$IQ = (mental\ age/chronological\ age) \times 100$$

The mental age of an individual is determined by performance on a standardized test. The test consists of questions geared toward individuals of different ages. A 10-year-old is expected to be able to answer a certain level of questioning as well as all those from the easier levels. More difficult questions are assumed to be beyond the ability of the average 10-year-old. Once an individual's mental age is determined, the researcher simply divides that figure by the respondent's actual age and multiplies by 100.

Since the development of the IQ test, many researchers have attempted to show that delinquency and deviance are related to low intelligence. The assumption that IQ is related to crime is not a surprising one, given the knowledge that most incarcerated offenders tend to be less educated and display below-average scores on academic achievement tests. The major source of debate concerning IQ revolves around the question of whether IQ is due to nature or nurture.

The **nature-nurture controversy** refers to the question of whether intelligence is inherited and, therefore, determined at conception (nature), or whether intelligence is an outcome of growth in the environment (nurture). The nature argument views IQ as set at birth and not subject to outside influences. The social and physical environment, including education, has little or no influence on a person's IQ. Conversely, the nurture side of the debate proposes that an individual's IQ is the outcome of complex interactions between the genetic makeup of the person and the environment to which the individual is exposed. This view suggests that IQ can be altered through education and other environmental interventions.

The view that intelligence is genetically determined received a great deal of support in the early days of IQ testing. Goddard (1920) found that most criminals were "feebleminded." A feebleminded person was defined as any adult with a mental age of 12 (IQ of 75) or less. Unfortunately, Goddard (1920) relied solely on incarcerated individuals for his group of "criminals" and did not use a comparison group in the analysis. More recently, Wilson and Herrnstein (1985) and Herrnstein and Murray (1994) have argued that IQ is substantially due to genetics and that IQ is a strong predictor of criminal activity. Wilson and Herrnstein (1985) claim that IQ is a stronger predictor of deviance than is social class. Unfortunately, the authors also assert that minorities, particularly blacks, score lower on IQ. Tied to the genetic argument, this opens the door for claims of racism and obscures the rest of their argument.

Other researchers have also taken up the genetic/racial/IQ argument. William Shockley (1967) speculates that low IQ scores among blacks are due to their genetic inferiority. Jensen (1969), subjecting this position to empirical test, claims that 80 percent of the differences in IQ scores between blacks and whites is due to genetic factors. Using this line of reasoning, Gordon (1976) suggests that lower IQ among blacks, along with the corresponding high delinquency in black areas, indicates a positive causal relationship between IQ and delinquency. Unfortunately, the data are capable of showing only a correlation and fall far short of proving any causation.

Hirschi and Hindelang (1977) provide the most widely cited argument in the IQ-delinquency literature. Moving away from the racial component, the authors report that IQ is at least as important in predicting delinquency as social class or race. In addition, IQ is related to delinquency regardless of the race or social class of the individual.

Except for the controversy stirred by Wilson and Herrnstein (1985) and Herrnstein and Murray (1994), the recent IQ-delinquency debate looks at the relative influence of nature and nurture, rather than an either/or situation. Both genetic and environmental factors are at work. The only question involves the relative contribution of genetics and the environment. The major issue concerning IQ has become whether IQ is a direct or indirect cause of delinquent behavior. The leading opinion is that IQ is an indirect cause of delinquency (Hirschi & Hindelang, 1977; Menard & Morse, 1984; Moffitt et al., 1981). Far from causing an individual to be deviant, many theorists hold that low IQ leads to poor school performance, which prompts a lack of concern for education, a rebellious attitude toward the school and societal demands and, eventually, a heightened chance of deviant behavior. Consequently, individuals with a low IQ who can be encouraged to stay in school through special help or innovative educational practices may not experience the problems and frustrations that precipitate deviant activity.

Implications for Juvenile Justice

Before addressing the impact of psychological theories, it is important to point out some of the criticisms leveled at the area. As has been noted throughout the above discussions, psychologically oriented explanations are not particularly helpful for the prediction of behavior. Many are formulated after the fact, and seek primarily to explain the observed behavior retrospectively. The emphasis is on why something happened and not on predicting what will happen in the future. A second concern with psychological studies is the reliance on subjective interpretations. Most psychological endeavors rest on the opinion of individuals who have been trained in the field of psychology. Unfortunately, there is no single orientation or perspective that drives the entire field (or even subfields) of psychology. The subjective nature of psychology, therefore, often leads to conflicting opinions, even when individuals are looking at the exact same information.

Some commentators criticize what they see as the individualistic nature of psychological explanations. Indeed, many psychological endeavors examine individual subjects, so the precise explanation for deviance could vary from subject to subject. This criticism may be shortsighted, however, given the fact that these individualistic approaches form the basis of other, more general theories. For example, operant conditioning is a key component of differential association-reinforcement theory, while hedonism is at the heart of Gottfredson and Hirschi's general theory of crime (see Chapter 4 for discussions of both of these theories).

Psychological explanations have their greatest impact on the correctional end of the juvenile justice system. Psychology's emphasis on identifying the cause of an individual's behavior fits the general treatment orientation of juvenile justice. As a result, juvenile corrections places heavy emphasis on counseling, education and other rehabilitative methods. Techniques such as I-level classifications and the MMPI are used to gain insight into a juvenile's problems and subsequently design a response to those problems. Additionally, behavior modification techniques are used to set up token economies in detention centers and training schools (see Chapters 8 and 11). Psychology will more than likely remain primarily a correctional tool in juvenile justice until such time that more precise methods of evaluation are generated or the predictive ability of psychological findings are enhanced.

Summary

The biological and psychological explanations discussed in this chapter represent theories and perspectives developed over many decades. While some have been discounted because of their lack of rigor and relevance, they have engendered discussions that may lead to more applicable and useful theories. Psychological explanations have found a clear place in the juvenile justice system. This is particularly true in the juvenile court and in the correctional phase of processing. Biological explanations have not fared so well. This is due mainly to the poor quality of the early explanations and the current lack of expertise in the physical sciences held by criminologists and criminal justicians. The next chapter turns to a discussion of the sociological explanations that hold the dominant position in modern discussions of delinquency and criminality.

DISCUSSION QUESTIONS

1. Compare and contrast the classical and positivist schools of thought. What are the basic assumptions each holds about the individual and behavior? What implications does each have for the juvenile justice system?

2. There is a movement to shift the emphasis in the juvenile justice system from sociological theories and explanations for delinquency to the biosocial perspective. Point out and explain what you see as the more promising biosocial approaches. Also, project the problems or shortcomings that will result if the emphasis is shifted (that is, what are the problems with the biosocial approach?).

3. Identifying a "criminal or delinquent personality" has proved to be quite difficult. Outline some of the more well-known methods for isolating this personality and what problems exist with these approaches. Which method would you use if you had to pick one, and why?

4. Psychological theories are common in correctional practice. Pick two specific psychological approaches and illustrate their usefulness and shortcomings for use in correcting juvenile delinquents (i.e., critique the approaches).

CHAPTER 4

Sociological Explanations of Delinquency

Key Terms and Phrases

anomie
bond to society
Chicago School
concentric zone theory
conflict theory
containment theory
culture conflict
developmental theories
differential association
differential identification
differential opportunity
differential reinforcement
division of labor
dramatization of evil
drift
ecological fallacy
elaboration model
focal concerns
gemeinschaft society
General Strain Theory (GST)
generic control theory
gesselschaft society
inner containment
invasion, domination and
    succession
labeling perspective
looking-glass self
mechanical solidarity

modes of adaptation
natural areas
organic solidarity
outer containment
pluralistic conflict
primary deviance
private, parochial and public
    sources of control
radical conflict
rational choice theory
reintegrative shaming
role-taking
routine activities perspective
secondary deviance
self-control theory
social area analysis
social control theories
social disorganization
social reality of crime
strain theory
subculture
subculture of violence
successful status degradation
    ceremony
symbolic interaction
techniques of neutralization
transfer of evil
vertical integration

The most prevalent explanations of delinquent behavior are sociologically oriented theories. Indeed, criminology, criminal justice and juvenile justice in the twentieth century have grown around sociological perspectives. The reasons for this are understandable. First, the great changes in society during and after the Industrial Revolution were accompanied by increased levels of deviant behavior. This behavior, however, was more prevalent in the cities. This led to a natural view that deviant behavior was an outgrowth of social relationships, especially those in urban areas. Second, sociological theories hold a great deal of intuitive appeal. Many of the ideas, as will be seen, are based on common sense and do not require a great deal of education or training for simple understanding. A third reason behind the dominance of sociological explanations involves the ability to test such theories. While tests of biologically oriented theories fail to provide empirical support and psychological theories often defy empirical testing or are restricted to individuals, most sociological explanations are accompanied by attempts at empirical research and often find some degree of support.

Sociological theories and perspectives reflect elements of both classicism and positivism. From the positivistic view, sociological theories consider a wide array of social and environmental factors as explanations of deviant behavior. Delinquency is a response to the setting in which the individual finds himself or herself. The neighborhood in which an individual grows up, one's peers, the views of others, social and moral training, the organization of society, economic conditions and the effect of being processed in the criminal justice system are among the many factors considered in sociological theories. Classical elements appear in discussions of deterrence, control and routine activity theories, in which the individual is presumed to have some degree of choice in his or her behavior. This chapter attempts to outline the major points of each theory or view and draw out similarities and differences in the sociological explanations for deviance.

The Ecological Perspective

As perhaps the earliest sociological explanation to gain importance in criminology, the ecological perspective sought to explain deviance as a natural outgrowth of the location in which it occurs. This perspective is often referred to as the **Chicago School** because it arose out of the work done by social scientists at the University of Chicago using the city of Chicago as a research site. Research in the early twentieth century recognized the great growth in the number and size of large cities. European immigrants and southern blacks were flocking to the industrial cities of the north and northeast. For the first time, there were cities that were home to thousands of people. These new urban areas were densely populated and many of the new residents were uneducated, unemployed and could not speak English. Along with this great influx of people came increases in various social problems—including criminal activity.

Table 4.1   **The Ecology of Crime**

Concentric Zones	"Natural areas"; city growth as expanding circles from the city center; central business district and zone in transition are key for deviance; key author: Burgess
Delinquency Areas	Delinquency concentrates in the same area over time, despite changing population makeup; "social disorganization" is the cause; key authors: Shaw and McKay
Social Areas	Focus on similarities in social characteristics rather than geographical location; social disorganization argument; "vertical integration"; private, parochial and public control; key authors: Lander, Bordua, Chilton, Bursik and Grasmick

Concentric Zones

Researchers of the Chicago School utilized what is known as the **concentric zone theory** to study the growth of the city and its accompanying social problems. The ideas of the concentric zone theory were borrowed from plant ecology where the proliferation of plant life follows a natural progression. Plants take root and prosper in areas that provide the needed requirements for growth. There are various **natural areas** for different plants. Ferns and moss grow in the valleys between hills because these spots provide the shade and moisture necessary for such plant life—they are natural areas. A natural area for cacti is the desert. In an analogous fashion, ecological researchers saw the establishment and growth of cities following a similar pattern of natural progression. Concentric zone theory viewed city growth as following a natural progression of increasingly larger circles around the original city center.

Ernest Burgess (1925) presented a simple graphic display of the various zones or concentric circles that the theory entailed. Zone 1, the "Central Business District" (CBD), was the original core of the city. Using the ecological or natural area analogy, the city was originally established in a certain spot because of the features of the location. For example, crossroads of major trade routes, locations providing water transportation or water power, and the availability of natural resources would all be factors making the establishment of a city in that place a "natural" choice. Zone 1, therefore, represented the earliest settlement of business in the city. Zone 2 was considered the "zone in transition." This area had traditionally been residential but was becoming more industrialized. As new industry was established and moved to the city, it was only natural for business leaders to seek locations that provided the same advantages that prompted the original establishment of the city. These businesses wished to settle in and around the CBD. In turn, the residents living around the CBD desired to move away from the new industrial factories. Those individuals who could not afford to move were forced to stay in zone 2. The homes in this zone were mostly rental property and were left in disrepair. It was not a desirable area in which to live.

Figure 4.1   Concentric View of the City

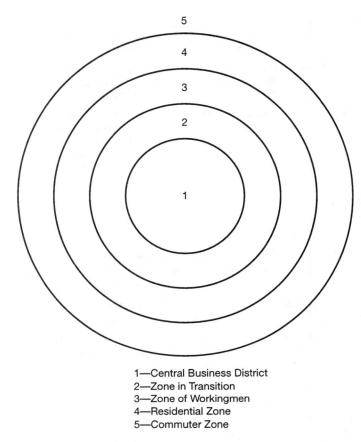

1—Central Business District
2—Zone in Transition
3—Zone of Workingmen
4—Residential Zone
5—Commuter Zone

The remaining zones represented areas of generally increasing affluence. The "zone of working men," zone 3, was populated by lower-class and lower-middle-class factory workers. These families had the resources to move out of zone 2 but had to remain within close proximity to the employment and retail establishments of the inner zones. During the early years of the twentieth century, there was little or no public transportation; most people moved around the city on foot. In addition, many individuals worked long hours throughout the day and night, making close living accommodations to work a necessity. Zones 4 and 5, the residential and commuter zones, were populated by more wealthy middle- and upper-class families.

Shaw and McKay: Delinquency Areas

Using the concentric zone theory, Clifford Shaw and Henry McKay (1942) analyzed the occurrence of delinquency in Chicago. While their approach was sophisticated for the 1920s and 1930s, their methods were rudimentary by today's standards. The researchers took a map of Chicago, plotted concentric circles on it and placed pins in the map to represent each delinquent act. Assessing the occurrence of delinquency in terms of where it occurred, Shaw and McKay (1942) reported that delinquency was concentrated in the CBD and the zone in transition, and decreased as the distance from the center of the city increased. It was the city center where economic conditions were poorest and new arrivals were able to find affordable housing.

Table 4.2   Shaw and McKay's Delinquency Areas

1)	Crime and delinquency rates are highest in and around the "central business district" (the CBD and the zone in transition)
2)	Crime and delinquency are highest in areas of low economic resources, as measured by levels of public assistance received, the rental value of housing units and the level of owner-occupied housing
3)	Crime and delinquency rates are highest in areas dominated by foreign-born and Negro heads of households

Source: Shaw & McKay (1942).

While these were interesting findings, they did not explain why this pattern occurred. The deviance in these areas was not due to the groups inhabiting the areas. If the delinquency was racially or ethnically determined, it would have been expected that the delinquency rates would follow those groups as they moved to other areas of the city. This did not occur.

Examining the changes in Chicago for 1900-1920, the time period of the study, Shaw and McKay (1942) noted a process of **invasion, domination and succession** taking place. They saw that, over a period of time, poor foreign-born and Southern immigrants would invade the central city areas due to their economic situation and the availability of inexpensive living conditions in the areas. Over time, one group would gain some degree of dominance in the area. As the residents gained employment and were assimilated into American society, however, they would leave these inner-city areas for the more desirable outer zones. Meanwhile, new groups of poor people would take their place in zones 1 and 2. The delinquency problem was a result not of specific people, but of the constant turnover of people in the area. This turnover caused a problem referred to as **social disorganization** (Shaw & McKay, 1942). The people in these core areas were unable to exert any control over the behavior of those living there. The major concern for the people was to better themselves and move on to other areas. Life in zones 1 and 2 was seen as a temporary state. As a result, people did not concern themselves with improving the area, getting to know one another or taking control of conditions. There was a lack of social organization that could bring about improvements.

Social Areas

Research conducted since Shaw and McKay's study has shown that many cities do not follow the concentric zone form of growth. As a consequence, ecological theorists have shifted to **social area analysis**. Where natural area analysis emphasized a strict ecological analogy and physical geographic approach, social area analysis identifies areas in terms of their social characteristics. Where common distance from the CBD defined a natural area in the concentric zonal approach, similarities in average income, education, population density and other variables are used to identify areas in social area analysis. A single social area may consist of two geographically separate land areas. They are considered the same social area due to their similar makeup in terms of the social factors under observation. This move to social area analysis held more intuitive appeal for social scientists.

Rather than look at concentric circles, Lander (1954) examined differences in census tracts in Baltimore. He found that racially heterogeneous areas (areas with similar levels of blacks and whites) experienced more trouble at exerting social control over the behavior of individuals in the area. Census tracts that were racially homogeneous (dominated either by blacks or by whites) were able to marshall the population to make changes and exert control in the areas. He interpreted this as support for social disorganization theory. Lander (1954), Bordua (1958) and Chilton (1964), conducting similar analyses in Baltimore, Indianapolis and Detroit, all found that poor economic conditions and anomic factors (lack of control, concern, conformity or direction among area residents) were related to delinquency in much the same fashion.

Recent ecological analyses have uncovered similar concentrations of crime and delinquency in certain residential areas. Bursik and Grasmick (1993) argue that many neighborhoods display high levels of crime and delinquency due to their inability to marshall the necessary resources for control. The authors claim that neighborhood control requires input from **private, parochial and public sources of control** (see Table 4.3). Bursik and Grasmick point out that lower-class, transient, high-crime neighborhoods have trouble developing these sources of control. Areas undergoing a great deal of change will have an unstable base for private and parochial control mechanisms, while even in stable neighborhoods with strong private and parochial networks the residents may not be able to marshall the public support needed for effective delinquency control. Hope (1997) refers to this as a problem of **vertical integration**. That is, some neighborhoods are left out when it comes to working with those in power.

Table 4.3   Sources of Neighborhood Control

Private	interpersonal relationships: family, friends and close associates
Parochial	neighborhood networks and institutions: schools, churches, businesses, social organizations/groups
Public	agencies and institutions of the city, state or other governmental unit

See Hunter (1985); Bursik & Grasmick (1993).

Critique of the Ecological Approach

While the ecological approach and the Chicago School shifted attention away from the biological views of Lombroso to a more sociological orientation, these new ideas also suffered from various problems. First, the ecological approach did not have any one theoretical argument that gave it direction. Despite the fact that Shaw and McKay (1942) proposed social disorganization as a theoretical argument, the ecological perspective borrowed various theories and themes (such as anomie) when the occasion arose. This lack of a single coherent theory hampered the growth and use of the ecological approach.

Second, many researchers fell into the trap of invoking the **ecological fallacy**. The ecological fallacy refers to attributing results based on grouped data to an individual. For example, a researcher would find that delinquency was highest in areas of low income, low average education and high density. He or she would then state that an uneducated individual from a poor family living in a two-bedroom home with nine people would be delinquent. In doing so, the researcher commits an ecological fallacy. The fact that an area with certain characteristics has a high rate of delinquency does not mean that an individual exhibiting similar personal characteristics will be delinquent. In fact, many of the delinquents in the identified area may exhibit the exact opposite traits. Knowledge about an area would not tell anything about a specific individual.

A third area of concern dealt with the heavy reliance on official records of delinquency. The finding that delinquency was highest in low socioeconomic areas found a great deal of support in official records. Various examinations using self-report studies (Dentler & Monroe, 1961; Hindelang, Hirschi & Weis, 1981; Short & Nye, 1958; Tittle, Villemez & Smith, 1978), however, found little difference in delinquency between the social classes. The findings of many ecological studies, therefore, could have been attributable to biased official records.

Despite these and other problems with the ecological approach, the early work of the Chicago School brought crime and delinquency theory squarely into the sociological tradition. For the most part, these early sociological explanations provided a clean break from the biological work of Lombroso and his followers. The ecological studies also provided much of the framework for subsequent theoretical advances.

Learning Theory

Sutherland: Differential Association

While there are a number of different learning theories, the most prominent for the study of delinquency is that of Edwin Sutherland. Sutherland's (1939) **differential association** theory views learning as the culmination of various social inputs faced by individuals throughout their lives. Sutherland observed, as did Shaw and McKay, that delinquency was concentrated in the inner-city areas. Instead of attributing this to the area and the problem of social disorganization, Sutherland proposed that deviance was more easily learned in these areas. The disorganization of the area provided a degree of instability, which led to the growth of deviant lifestyles and points of view. Juveniles came into daily contact with both deviant and conventional ideas. As a result, children could learn to accept deviance just as easily as they could conventional behavior.

Table 4.4   Sociological Learning Theories

Differential Association—learning comes from direct social contact with others; family and peers most important; contacts vary in importance by frequency, duration, priority and intensity; deviance results from greater input favoring deviance; key author: Sutherland

Differential Identification—learning can come from the mass media and non-face-to-face interaction; "role taking"; key author: Glaser

Differential Reinforcement—learning from both social and nonsocial inputs; operant conditioning argument; key authors: Jeffery, Burgess and Akers

---

Edwin Sutherland (1883-1950) proposed the theory of differential association, a learning theory of delinquency. Sutherland's theory can be considered the first truly sociological effort to explain crime. *Photo: Indiana University Archives*

In explaining his views, Sutherland proposed nine specific points to differential association (see Table 4.5). Underlying these nine points is the idea that deviance is learned in the same fashion as conforming behavior. The major sources of that learning are the people with whom an individual comes in contact, particularly family, peers and religious institutions. Explicit in the theory is the idea that everyone is exposed to both deviant and conforming information. The choice of activity depends on the relative amount of influence favoring either deviant or conventional behavior.

The basic formula for differential association has been criticized from a variety of perspectives. One of the criticisms revolves around Sutherland's failure to define or operationalize his terms. For example, he states that associations vary in frequency, duration, priority and intensity.

In failing to define what each of these means, he left them open to interpretation. The common definitions of frequency (number of contacts), duration (length of a contact), priority (temporal order of the contacts) and intensity (significance of the contact) have been supplied by other researchers. Sutherland also fails to define explicitly "an excess of definitions." A second problem, stemming from the first, entails the lack of convincing empirical support for the theory. Although there have been a large number of studies focusing on differential association (for example, Adams, 1974; DeFleur & Quinney, 1966; Reiss & Rhodes, 1964; Short, 1960), most of the empirical support is indirect and highly qualified. The fact that Sutherland assumes that deviance is a rational decision is a further possible problem. Many researchers and theorists would argue that choosing deviant behavior is irrational. A final problem deals with the fact that Sutherland explicitly discounted the influence of factors other than social, face-to-face contacts. While reasonable for the early 1900s, changes in the modern world have prompted researchers to modify and extend the original ideas of differential association.

Table 4.5   Sutherland's Differential Association Theory

1. Criminal behavior is learned.

2. Criminal behavior is learned in interaction with other persons in a process of communication.

3. The principal part of the learning of criminal behavior occurs within intimate personal groups.

4. When criminal behavior is learned, the learning includes (a) techniques of the crime, which are sometimes very complicated, sometimes very simple; (b) the specification of motives, drives, rationalizations and attitudes.

5. The specific direction of motives and drives is learned from definitions of the legal codes as favorable or unfavorable.

6. A person becomes delinquent because of an excess of definitions favorable to violation of law over definitions unfavorable to violation of law.

7. Differential associations may vary in frequency, duration, priority and intensity.

8. The process of learning criminal behavior by association with criminal and anti-criminal patterns involves all of the mechanisms that are involved in any other learning.

9. While criminal behavior is an expression of general needs and values, it is not explained by those general needs and values, since noncriminal behavior is an expression of the same needs and values.

Source: Compiled from Sutherland & Cressey (1974:75-76).

Modifications to Differential Association

One of the most logical modifications to make to differential association is the inclusion of the mass media and non–face-to-face communication in the theory. Glaser's (1956) **differential identification** proposes that personal association is not always necessary for the transmission of behavioral guidelines. He sees real and fictional presentations on television and other forms of the mass media as providing information concerning acceptable behavior, especially to children. The basic idea is one of imitation or modeling. An individual observes the activity of a character and begins to copy that character. Another term for this is **role-taking**. The child assumes the role that is portrayed. This is especially problematic for children because of their inability to recognize that the media portrayals are in themselves roles and not the actual behavior of the actor playing the role. Youthful observers see the behavior as life-like and do not recognize the fictional nature of the material. A youth might observe a glorified version of crime from a desirable fictional character and, thus, act in accordance with that portrayal.

A second set of modifications of differential association revolves, at least loosely, around the ideas of operant conditioning. **Differential reinforcement** (Jeffery, 1965) and differential association-reinforcement (Burgess & Akers, 1968) theories propose that an individual can learn from a variety of sources, both social and nonsocial. Social factors include the ideas of both differential association and differential identification. Nonsocial factors, on the other hand, can refer to the outcome of the behavior. If the behavior results in a pleasurable payoff (e.g., useful stolen goods), the behavior will be repeated. The absence of an acceptable return on the behavior or the receipt of an adverse stimuli (an undesirable outcome such as being caught and imprisoned) would prompt avoidance of the activity in the future. Burgess and Akers (1968) rewrote differential association using operant conditioning terminology.

Subcultural Theories

The work of the Chicago School also provided the basis for various subcultural explanations. A key to the discussions of Shaw and McKay (1942), Sutherland (1939) and others was the diversity of people in the cities. It was this cultural diversity that prompted the idea of social disorganization and that provided different inputs to the learning process. Subcultural theorists took these ideas and focused directly on the fact of diversity in the population.

Defining **subculture** is not an easy task. In the simplest sense, a subculture is a smaller part of a larger culture. While it must vary to some degree from the larger culture, it is not totally different. The subculture exists within and is part of the larger culture. More detailed definitions typically refer to a set of values, beliefs, ideas, views and/or meanings that a group of individuals hold and that are to some degree different from those of the larger culture.

Table 4.6   Subcultural Explanations

Lower-Class Gangs Delinquency—problems meeting middle-class goals and aspirations cause low self-esteem; culture conflict; subcultural characteristics—malicious, negativistic and nonutilitarian; key author: Cohen

Lower-Class Focal Concerns—identifiable lower-class cultural values (trouble, toughness, smartness, excitement, fate, autonomy); conflict with middle-class values; deviance is by-product of following subcultural values; key author: Miller

Subculture of Violence—violence is accepted as legitimate method for problem solution; regional (Southern U.S.); racial orientation; key authors: Wolfgang and Ferracuti; Curtis

Techniques of Neutralization—methods for accommodating subcultural activity within larger cultural norms; drift; key authors: Sykes and Matza

From a subcultural perspective, delinquency and criminality are the result of individuals attempting to act in accordance with subcultural norms. This can occur in two ways. First, an individual acts according to subcultural mandates that may be considered deviant by the larger cultural mandates of society. This problem could be common for new immigrants who have traditionally acted according to one set of cultural proscriptions and are now faced with a different set of expectations in a new cultural setting. Second, deviance may result from the inability to join or be assimilated adequately into a new culture. Consequently, the individual may strike out against society because of the frustration faced in attempting to live according to the new cultural expectations.

Cohen: Delinquent Boys

Albert Cohen (1955), recognizing the concentration of delinquency among lower-class boys, proposed that these youths feel ill-equipped to compete in and deal with a middle-class society. The middle-class orientation of society is set up in such a fashion that lower-class youths cannot succeed. This is compounded by the fact that they are expected to follow the goals and aspirations of the middle class. All youths are measured against a middle-class measuring rod. A key component to this problem is the failure of lower-class families to assimilate their young into the middle-class value system.

The failure to succeed in terms of middle-class values leads to feelings of failure and diminished self-worth among the lower-class youths. As a result, these boys join together in groups and act in concert with the group (subcultural) norms instead of with the mandates of the larger culture. While this provides the youths with some degree of self-worth, status and success, it also leads to **culture conflict**. That is, by following one set of cultural (or subcultural) practices, the individual is violating the prescriptions of another culture. In the case of the boys in Cohen's study, adherence to the subcultural group's mandates means violating the laws of middle-class society.

Cohen (1955) identifies three aspects of the emergent "lower-class gang delinquency." He claims that the subculture is *malicious, negativistic* and *nonutilitarian*. In support of this contention, he points out that the youths often steal items with the intent of causing trouble and harm for another person, not because they want the item. He sees much of the deviant activity as a means of tormenting others. The behavior brings about an immediate "hedonistic" pleasure instead of supplying any long-term need or solution to a problem. In general, there appears to be little point in the behavior, aside from causing trouble for the larger middle-class culture.

Cohen's conception of subcultural deviance has not gone unchallenged. First, he fails to provide any empirical support for his assertions. Indeed, self-report studies show a more even distribution of offending in society than is assumed by Cohen. Second, he is unable to identify explicitly the elements that make up the lower-class subculture. His discussion of youths being malicious, negativistic and nonutilitarian is a tautological (circular) explanation. That is, these three key features define the subculture, which, in turn, is used to explain the existence of these three features. A third concern involves the possible middle-class bias that the author brings to his analysis. Cohen develops his argument by observing the behavior of the youths under question. He then imputes values and beliefs (the core ideas for a subculture) to those behaviors. From a middle-class point of view, the behaviors of the lower-class youths may appear as malicious, negativistic and nonutilitarian. Lower-class youths, however, may be acting as they do for reasons entirely different from those Cohen assumes. In addition, Kitsuse and Dietrick (1959) note that Cohen fails to present evidence that lower-class youths actually aspire to middle-class measures of success. The absence of such aspirations would negate the very basis of reaction formation and the theory itself.

Miller: Lower-Class Focal Concerns

Walter Miller (1958) proposes a subcultural explanation of deviance that goes beyond the behavior of juveniles to include lower-class males of all ages. Miller views the lower class as operating under a distinct set of cultural values, which he refers to as **focal concerns** (see Table 4.7). These are: trouble, toughness, smartness, excitement, fate and autonomy. Adherence to these lower-class focal concerns or values provides status, acceptance and feelings of belonging for the lower-class individual (Miller, 1958).

At the same time that these values provide positive reinforcement in the lower-class world, they bring about a natural conflict with middle-class values. The goal of the lower-class individual is not to violate the law or the middle-class norms. Instead, the goal is to follow the focal concerns of his or her class and peers. Deviant behavior, therefore, is a by-product of following the subcultural focal concerns (Miller, 1958). This is different from the view of Cohen (1955), in which deviance is a conscious method of striking out against the middle-class society and value system. Where Cohen (1955) sees the origins of the subcultural behaviors in the reaction of lower-class individuals faced with a middle-class world, Miller (1958) views the focal concerns as an integral part of the lower class.

Table 4.7	**Miller's Lower-Class Focal Concerns**
Trouble	Refers to the fact that lower-class males spend a large amount of time preoccupied with getting into and out of trouble. Trouble may bring about desired outcomes such as attention and prestige.
Toughness	Emphasis on physical prowess, athletic skill, masculinity and bravery. Partly a response of lower-class males raised in single-female–headed households.
Smartness	Basically the idea of being "streetwise." The concern is on how to manipulate the environment and others to your own benefit without being subjected to sanctions of any kind.
Excitement	Refers to the idea that lower-class individuals are oriented around short-term hedonistic desires. Activities, such as gambling and drug use, are undertaken for the immediate excitement or gratification that is generated.
Fate	The belief that, in the long run, individuals have little control over their lives. Luck and fortune dictate the outcome of behavior. Whatever is supposed to happen will happen regardless of the individual's wishes. This allows for a wide latitude in behavior.
Autonomy	While the individual believes in fate, there is a strong desire to resist outside control imposed by other persons. Individuals want total control over themselves until fate intervenes.

The criticisms leveled against Miller's presentation are similar to those found in relation to Cohen. First, there is a clear possibility of a middle-class bias on the part of Miller. The author is observing lower-class behavior and passing judgments from a middle-class orientation. Second, the explanation is circular. The behavior of the lower class is used to identify the value system, which, in turn, is used to explain the behavior. Finally, Miller ignores factors such as female and middle-class deviance.

The Subculture of Violence

Wolfgang and Ferracuti (1967) propose that there exists a **subculture of violence**. The subculture of violence reflects a value system that accepts the use of violence to solve problems. This basic idea has found support in studies of regional homicide rates and violence among blacks.

Various authors (Doerner, 1978; Erlanger, 1974; Gastil, 1971; Hackney, 1969; Loftin & Hill, 1974; Smith & Parker, 1980) have debated the existence of a Southern culture of violence. Historically, official data have shown that the South leads the nation in homicides. Attempting to explain this dominance in violence, researchers propose that the South has distinctive cultural values and attitudes that predispose or allow the use of physical force. Much of the Southern subculture is viewed as a result of socialization, including emphases on honor, self-defense and protection; the use of firearms; and military training; among others. Recent data, however, have shown that the South is no longer the dominant region in terms of violence (Kowalski & Petee, 1991; Nelson, Corzine & Huff-Corzine, 1994; O'Carroll & Mercy, 1989).

Curtis (1975), noting high levels of violence among blacks, offers a similar subcultural explanation. The author claims that there is an emphasis on manliness in the black community that prompts the use of force and violence. According to this theory, instead of backing down and looking for alternative solutions for problems, black males typically resort to force in settling disputes. Part of the origin of this black subculture is the movement of blacks from the South to the major industrialized cities of the North (Curtis, 1975). The Southern subculture of violence and the ecology of crime both play a role in Curtis's discussion.

Sykes and Matza: Techniques of Neutralization

Throughout the discussion of subcultural explanations there is a subtle failure to address the fact that no individual operates in just the subculture. Rather, every individual must deal with both the subcultural and the larger cultural expectations. Indeed, many individuals attempt to abide by both sets of values—those of the subculture and those of the larger culture. Juveniles, in particular, often act in accordance with one set of values or rules and still maintain a self-image that places them in the realm of acceptable behavior of the larger culture.

Matza (1964) attempts to explain how this can happen by discussing the amount of **drift** that occurs throughout an individual's life. He states that individuals are pushed and pulled at different times in their lives into various modes of activity. A deviant at one point in time may be a model citizen at another time. People drift between different modes of behavior throughout their lives and are never completely deviant or completely conforming. Behavior depends on the different circumstances confronting the person.

Accommodating different lifestyles and behaviors, however, requires individuals to find justifications for the discrepancies. For example, juveniles who commit delinquent acts often see themselves as no better and no worse than anyone else, despite recognizing their deviant activity. Sykes and Matza (1957) outline five **techniques of neutralization** that allow the juvenile to accommodate the deviant behavior while maintaining a self-image as a conformist (see Table 4.8). Each technique requires the individual to admit to the behavior under question. The youth invokes one of the techniques in order to justify his or her behavior in light of confrontation with conventional cultural values. These techniques allow the individual to reconcile both subcultural and cultural values at the same time. While there is not yet an exact understanding of how, when and by whom neutralization techniques are used, evidence does show that such techniques are used in various settings (Agnew, 1994; Agnew & Peters, 1986; Minor, 1981; Thurman, 1984).

Table 4.8   **Sykes and Matza's Techniques of Neutralization**

Denial of Responsibility—the youth may claim that the action was an accident or, more likely, assert that he or she was forced into the action by circumstances beyond his or her control.

Denial of Injury—focuses on the amount of harm caused regardless of violating the law. The absence of harm to an individual may involve pointing to a lack of physical injury, that the action was a prank or that the person or business could afford the loss.

Denial of the Victim—the juvenile can deny the existence of a victim by claiming self-defense or retaliation, the absence of a victim (such as when it involves a business and not a person) and/or that characteristics of the victim brought the harm on himself or herself (such as hazing a homosexual).

Condemnation of the Condemnors—the youth turns the tables on those individuals who condemn his or her behavior by pointing out that the condemnors are no better than he or she. In essence, the condemnors are also deviant.

Appeal to Higher Loyalties—conflict between the dictates of two groups will be resolved through adherence to the ideas of one group. The juvenile may see greater reward and more loyalty to the subcultural group on some issues, which, in turn, lead to deviant behavior.

Source: Constructed from Sykes & Matza (1957).

Critique of the Subcultural Approach

The attempt to explain deviance through the use of subcultures faces a number of problems. The greatest problem entails identifying a subculture. The typical process of identifying subcultures through the behavior of the individuals leads to a good deal of circular reasoning. For example, violent behavior is used to identify a subculture of violence, which, in turn, is used to explain the commission of violence. The use of behaviors for identifying subcultures also faces the problem of substituting behaviors for values. A subculture entails a difference in values, beliefs and norms from those held by the larger culture. It is questionable to what extent you can impute values from behaviors. Two separate forms of activity may reflect the same basic value. For example, in order to feed their families (basic value), one individual takes a low-paying job while another robs the local grocery store (different behaviors).

A second problem entails finding ways of identifying which set of values (subcultural or cultural) is being followed at different times. This becomes especially problematic when the values are similar to one another. Assuming that there is variability in values and beliefs from group to group, how many values and how great a difference must exist in order to consider the group a subculture? Additionally, not all values can have the same degree of importance. Further, to what extent can an individual be deviant without belonging to a subculture? There is ample evidence that middle- and upper-class individuals also partake in deviance. Subcultural theorists have spent little, if any, time addressing the behavior of these individuals. Clearly, subcultural explanations require a good deal of additional research before they can be accepted or rejected.

Routine Activities and Rational Choice

Yet another theoretical area with ties to the ecological school is one dealing with routine activities and rational choice. While the two areas have developed out of different backgrounds, they both accept the basic premise that the movement of offenders and victims over space and time places them in varying situations in which criminal activity will be more or less possible. Within these different situations, individuals will make choices about what to do and what not to do (see Clarke & Felson, 1993). Routine activities and rational choice arguments, therefore, rest in the arena of neoclassicism, in which there is an element of choice.

The **routine activities perspective** assumes that the normal behavior of individuals contributes to deviant events. Cohen and Felson (1979) outline three criteria necessary for the commission of a crime: (1) the presence of a suitable target; (2) a motivated offender; and (3) an absence of guardians. The possibility for deviance is enhanced when these three elements coincide. Cohen and Felson (1979) demonstrate their position by pointing out that since World War II people spend more time away from home, society has become more mobile, and marketable, portable goods have become more available. As a consequence, crime has significantly increased. The changes in the routines of people and society have increased the opportunities for crime. The routine activities of individuals have been found to be related to a wide array of both personal and property offenses (Belknap, 1987; Kennedy & Forde, 1990; Miethe, Stafford & Long, 1987; Roncek & Maier, 1991).

Closely tied to routine activities is rational choice theory. **Rational choice theory** assumes that potential offenders make choices based on various factors in the physical and social environments. Among the factors influencing choices are the payoff, effort, support and risks involved in the potential behavior (Cornish & Clarke, 1986). In essence, the individual chooses if, when and where to commit a crime based on the opportunities that are presented to him or her. There is ample evidence that offenders do make choices. Studies of burglars demonstrate that these offenders consider an array of factors when deciding to commit a crime, including the financial or emotional need, the availability of concealment, the effort needed to gain entry, the presence of potential observers, the anticipated payoff and the offender's familiarity with the area (Bennett, 1986; Bennett & Wright, 1984a; Cromwell, Olson & Avery, 1991; Decker, Wright & Logie, 1993; Rengert & Wasilchick, 1985; Reppetto, 1974; Taylor & Nee, 1988; Wright & Decker, 1994). This does not mean that offenders do not act spontaneously to opportunities. Such unplanned behavior, however, does not reflect irrationality. Rather, the actions may rest on past observations and experiences in such a way as to suggest unconscious decisionmaking.

The support for rational choice, however, is not without qualification. The factors identified as important vary from study to study. For example, Tunnell (1992) and Piliavin and associates (1986) both report that offenders focus on the rewards in their decisionmaking and often discount factors related to risk and potential punishment. Rational choice theory is also criticized for its inability to explain impulsive acts and actions that clearly take place in high-risk settings. What must be considered is the fact that an individual can make choices only from the alternatives available. It is possible that some individuals will make what appears to be an irrational choice because of limited choices or an inability to identify other options. The neoclassical nature of the theory does not assume total volition by the individual. Finally, Akers (1990) argues that rational choice is little more than an extension of a learning theory in which individuals respond to rewards and punishments. Rather than argue its uniqueness, most researchers see rational choice as an extension of and complement to various ideas, including learning theories (see, for example, Fattah, 1993; Harding, 1993; Trasler, 1993).

Social Control Theory

While most theories look to identify factors that lead or push a juvenile into delinquency, **social control theories** seek to find factors that keep an individual from becoming deviant. Control theorists ask why many people refrain from violating the law even though they are presented with ample opportunity to commit crimes. Reckless (1967) views the main issue being addressed by control theories in terms of explaining why one individual becomes deviant and another does not when they are both faced with the same situations. The explanations offered deal with the degree of control exerted on the individual.

Table 4.9   Social Control Explanations

Hirschi's Social Control Theory—bond to society; attachment, commitment, involvement, belief; weak bond allows deviance, but does not cause deviance

Containment Theory—internal and external influence on behavior; inner containment, outer containment, pushes, pulls, pressures; key author: Reckless

Self-Control Theory—internalized self-control key to behavior; deviance from being impulsive, insensitive, short-sighted, physical, etc.; good parenting leads to self-control; key authors: Gottfredson and Hirschi

---

Hirschi: Control Theory

Hirschi's (1969) theory states that "delinquent acts result when an individual's bond to society is weak or broken" (Hirschi, 1969: 16). The underlying assumption is that the individual's behavior is controlled by the connections the person has to the conventional social order. Deviance shows up when the level of control over an individual disappears or diminishes to a point at which he or she is free to choose prohibited lines of activity.

A key question for social control theory becomes the basis for the **bond to society**. Bond is primarily a result of socialization that takes place during childhood. Hirschi (1969) outlines four elements of bond: attachment, commitment, involvement and belief (see Table 4.10). The failure of an individual to care about what others think about his or her behavior and views (attachment), to work toward acceptable goals (commitment), to use one's energies and time in socially acceptable behaviors (involvement) and/or to accept the common value system in society (belief) opens the door for deviant and delinquent behavior. The weak or broken bond does not *cause* deviance. Rather, it *allows for* deviance. In other words, weak or broken bonds could be viewed as necessary for deviance, but not sufficient. An individual with weak bonds may or may not choose to commit deviant acts.

Table 4.10   Elements of Hirschi's Bond

Attachment	"sensitivity to the opinion of others" (p. 16)
	The more an individual cares about what others think of himself/ herself, the less likely they will choose behavior that brings about negative input.
Commitment	a "person invests time, energy, himself, in a certain line of activity" (p. 20)
	As a person builds an investment in conventional endeavors, any choice of deviant behavior will place that investment at risk.
Involvement	"engrossment in conventional activities" (p. 22)
	Because time and energy are limited, once they are used in the pursuit of conventional activities there is no time or energy left for deviant behavior.
Belief	"the existence of a common value system within the society or group" (p. 23)
	As a person is socialized into and accepts the common belief system, he/she will be less likely to violate those beliefs through deviant activity.

Source: Constructed by authors from Hirschi (1969).

Numerous tests of Hirschi's social control theory have been undertaken. Hirschi's (1969) own analysis involved surveying more than 4,000 high school boys about their delinquent activity and elements of bond. He found that delinquency was related to weaker attachment to parents, education and school, lower aspirations (i.e., lacking commitment), more time spent "joyriding" in cars or being bored (involvement) and less respect for the police and the law (belief). These findings, along with many others, provided empirical support for the theory. Various studies (Hindelang, 1973; Krohn & Massey, 1980; Poole & Regoli, 1979; Wiatrowski, Griswold & Roberts, 1981) report findings consistent with Hirschi's control theory.

Despite the support for the theory, a number of problematic issues remain. First, the theory does not adequately explain how the bond of an individual becomes weak or broken. The theory tries to explain why an individual is deviant and not how they became that way. While poor socialization is the easiest explanation, the theory fails to demonstrate how this occurs. Second, the relative impact of the four elements of bond is left unresolved. For example, if attachment is strong and commitment is moderate but involvement and belief are weak, will this permit deviance or not? As a result of this problem, the theory cannot directly offer suggestions on how to avoid the weakening of bond or how to repair bond.

Another area of concern deals with episodic deviance. Many youths vacillate between delinquent and conventional behavior. This "drift" cannot be explained using control theory. While an individual chooses to commit deviance, the theory does not explain the vacillation in choices over time and place. Such drift can only be adequately explained by proposing that the bond is strengthened and weakened both easily and often. A final concern is that the theory assumes all bonding is to conventional, nondeviant lifestyles. It may be possible that a juvenile is raised in a household in which the parents are deviant and espouse nontraditional behaviors. According to the theory, a juvenile in these circumstances should be bonded to deviance. Indeed, Jensen and Brownfield (1983) report that juveniles will follow the deviant behaviors of their parents as well as the nondeviant themes.

Reckless: Containment Theory

Containment theory (Reckless, 1962) represents another variation on the idea of social control. While Hirschi's bond relies mainly on influences and control imposed on an individual by others around him or her, containment proposes that the individual may have some control over his or her own behavior. In an early discussion of his theory, Reckless (1962) outlines two types of containment: **outer containment** and **inner containment** (Table 4.11). "The assumption is that there is a containing external structure which holds individuals in line and that there is also an internal buffer which protects people against deviation of the social and legal norms" (Reckless, 1962). Outer containment offers direct control over the individual from outside sources. The elements of inner containment are necessary due to the fact that an individual is not always under the direct control of outer containment. Thus, internalized moral codes, tolerance of frustration, and other factors help the individual refrain from deviance. The combination of these two factors should provide an effective means of avoiding deviant behavior.

Table 4.11   Elements of Reckless's Containment Theory

Forces promoting conformity:

Outer Containment	the influence of family, peers and environment on behavior; social pressure, supervision, training and group membership
Inner Containment	individual factors such as self-concept, tolerance of frustration, goal-directedness, internalized moral codes

Forces promoting deviance:

Internal Pushes	restlessness, discontent, anxiety, hostility
External Pressures	poverty, unemployment, minority status, social inequality
External Pulls	deviant peers, subcultures, media presentations

Source: Compiled from Reckless (1962).

Besides offering factors that work in opposition to deviance, Reckless (1962) outlines factors that promote deviant behavior. These are *internal pushes, external pressures* and *external pulls*. Each of these influence an individual's activity. Poverty, unemployment, discontent, anxiety, deviant peers and other factors may lead or push people into deviant activity as a viable form of behavioral response. These three factors make deviance an acceptable alternative, while inner and outer containment work to offset their influence.

Containment theory has received both support and criticism. Much of the support revolves around the fact that the theory includes factors related to both society and the individual. Additional support comes from the fact that Reckless proposes a theory to explain conforming behavior occurring amidst great amounts of deviance. Most of the empirical support comes from studies conducted by Reckless and his colleagues (Dinitz, Kay & Reckless, 1958; Reckless, Dinitz & Murray, 1956; Scarpitti et al., 1960), who have reported that a good self-concept (inner containment) can insulate a youth against deviance despite living in a high-delinquency area.

The major criticism against containment theory has come in the form of methodological critiques centering on the ability to operationalize the key ideas. Schrag (1971) argues that many of the terms are vague and fall within more than one category. For example, peers work as both constraining forces in outer containment and deviant producing features of external pulls. Such inconsistency makes the theory hard to test empirically. This may be one cause of the lack of empirical support uncovered by other researchers (Schwartz & Tangri, 1965; Tangri & Schwartz, 1967). Another criticism of containment theory centers around the idea of positive self-concept as an "insulator" against deviance. Indeed, research has failed to find an empirical connection between self-concept and deviance.

Self-Control Theory

Control theory has undergone its greatest change with the introduction of **self-control theory** by Gottfredson and Hirschi (1990). Rather than assume that behavior is controlled by outside forces throughout an individual's life, Gottfredson and Hirschi argue that self-control, internalized early in life, can serve to keep a person from involvement in deviant behavior. Self-control serves as a restraint from choosing the short-term gratification endemic to most criminal behavior. Gottfredson and Hirschi (1990: 90) claim that

> people who lack self-control will tend to be impulsive, insensitive, physical (as opposed to mental), risk-taking, short-sighted, and non-verbal, and they will tend therefore to engage in criminal and analogous acts.

Self-control theory assumes that humankind is hedonistic and makes choices emphasizing immediate, short-term pleasure.

According to Gottfredson and Hirschi (1990), the primary source of self-control is good parenting. Poor self-control is the result of ineffective child-rearing practices by the parents. Good parenting entails exhibiting concern for the child, consistent monitoring of the child's behavior, the ability to identify problematic behaviors, appropriate reactions to inappropriate behavior, and the time and energy to carry through with parental responsibilities. Should the parents fail to build self-control, other social institutions, such as schools, may influence its formation, but they are typically poor substitutes for the family (Gottfredson & Hirschi, 1990). Once self-control is internalized, it serves to modify an individual's behavior throughout his or her life.

Self-control theory has received both support and criticism. A number of studies have found evidence that a lack of self-control is related to deviant behavior (Grasmick et al., 1993; Keane, Maxim & Teevan, 1993; Wood, Pfefferbaum & Arneklev, 1993). Indeed, both a global measure of self-control as well as individual components (such as risk-taking, self-centeredness and immediate gratification) exert strong influence on various forms of deviance, with the more global measure having the greatest consistency and impact (Wood, Pfefferbaum & Arneklev, 1993). At the same time, the theory has been criticized for its inability to explain significant changes in behavior later in life and to consider the basic social structure as a contributor to parenting and self-control (Lilly, Cullen & Ball, 1995). In addition, Akers (1991) argues that the theory is tautological. That is, low self-control is determined by the commission of deviant acts, and the deviant acts are the result of low self-control.

Strain Theory

Strain theory views deviance as a direct result of the existing social structure. The very form of society causes an individual to act in a deviant fashion.

Unlike other theories, strain theory moves the onus for deviance from the individual and places it on society. Unacceptable behavior by an individual is seen as a natural (and expected) response to the problems posed by the social structure.

Anomie and the Form of Society

An understanding of strain theory begins with an examination of changes in the form of society. Two primary forms of society have been identified by Toennies (1957). These are *gemeinschaft* and *gesselschaft* societies (see Table 4.12). The most common form throughout history has been the **gemeinschaft society**, which is characterized by small, rural, agrarian cities and towns. People in these homogenous communities knew each other very well and interacted with one another on an almost continual basis. In some respects, the entire community formed a large extended family. At the same time, families and individuals could function independently from one another and provide for all their own needs. Durkheim (1933) termed this **mechanical solidarity**. The absence of an individual through death, migration or ostracism simply resulted in the remaining members assuming the role and obligations of the departed person.

Table 4.12   The Changing Society

Gemeinschaft Society	Gesselschaft Society
rural, agrarian	urban, technocratic
small, homogeneous communities	large, heterogeneous communities
primary relationships	secondary relationships
mechanical solidarity—	organic solidarity—
functional independence	functional interdependence
	division of labor

Toennies (1957) points out, however, that society has evolved into a **gesselschaft society**, which is more urbanized, technocratic and diverse. The growth of large cities has prompted more impersonal relationships. Under such secondary relationships, a person is an acquaintance to many others but is close to only a select few (such as their immediate family and close friends). Secondary relationships dominate in the workforce and in most daily interaction. Production is dominated by an **organic solidarity** by which tasks have become specialized and complex (Durkheim, 1933). This newer society requires a great deal of interdependency (organic solidarity). Every person supplies something to the overall societal needs, and the increased level of specialization in jobs does not allow for the easy movement of one individual into a role filled by another person. In essence, there is a **division of labor** by which everyone has a specific job that must be done for the good of society.

Changes in society have led people to expect different things out of life. In gemeinschaft society, individuals expected very little from their labors except daily subsistence. Acquiring wealth to provide for a good retirement, to buy comforts or to go on a vacation were luxuries alien to most people. As a result, most people did not look upon one another as competitors. The move to a ges-selschaft society with its organic solidarity, however, led to such competition. The increasing industrialization and division of labor provided for specialized jobs and the ability to accumulate extras. Each individual supplied some element to a larger end product. Different input to that product, however, received different rewards. Each level of the division of labor was compensated at different levels of return.

The problem with this type of social setup is the fact that humankind is inherently egoistic (Durkheim, 1933). Everybody aspires to the top and desires the best. Happiness is the result of realizing one's expectations. Unfortunately, modern society, with its specialized jobs, means that one person runs the company while another sweeps the floor. Each job is important to the whole but the compensation for different jobs is not the same. As a result, some individuals receive more than others while everyone aspires to reach the top. The inability of individuals to recognize the necessity of different jobs and payoffs and the inability to control the egoistic urges within themselves was what Durkheim called **anomie**. Loosely translated, anomie refers to a state of normlessness or inadequate regulation. More specifically, it is the inability of the individual to regulate his or her expectations in accordance with changes in society and what is possible under the prevailing social situations. Anomie results in various forms of deviant behavior, including crime. According to Durkheim, the solution to the problem of anomie is for society to provide regulation and realistic expectations for each individual. It is incumbent on society to provide the regulation because egoistic individuals are incapable of providing it for themselves.

Merton: Modes of Adaptation

In 1938, Robert Merton took the basic ideas of anomie and the changes in society and expanded the discussion to what is known as **strain theory**. Merton (1938) saw anomie as the lack of correspondence between culturally accepted *goals* and socially institutionalized *means* to achieve those goals. The problem is that American society presents everyone with the goals of achieving material success and reaching the top. At the same time, however, society limits access to the means for achieving those goals. For example, higher education is a necessary prerequisite for entrance into many professions. Not all individuals, however, have the money or opportunity to gain this needed schooling. Thus, the means to succeed have been blocked for some societal members. The disjuncture between goals and means is a property of the social structure. Merton argues that what is needed is equal access to the means of achieving the goals.

Merton (1938) outlines five **modes of adaptation** used by individuals to cope with the strain between goals and means (see Table 4.13). Each mode of adaptation reflects an individual's acceptance or rejection of culturally prescribed goals and socially institutionalized means of achieving those goals. *Conformity* represents the acceptance of both the goals and means, regardless of whether he or she succeeds. *Innovation* reflects acceptance of the prescribed goals but the resort to unacceptable or illegitimate methods of achieving success when faced with an inability to succeed via acceptable means. In *ritualism* the exact opposite occurs. While the individual gives up on achieving the goals, he or she continues to act in a socially acceptable fashion. A *retreatist* rejects both the goals and the means. This individual retreats from society through such means as drug or alcohol use, vagrancy or psychological withdrawal. The final mode of adaptation, *rebellion*, reflects an attempt to replace the existing societal goals and means with a new set that provides more opportunity for everyone in society.

Table 4.13   **Merton's Modes of Adaptation**

Mode of Adaptation	Cultural Goals	Institutionalized Means
Conformity	+	+
Innovation	+	−
Ritualism	−	+
Retreatism	−	−
Rebellion	±	±

+ means acceptance, − means rejection, ± means rejection and substitution

Source: Merton (1938).

The choice of adaptation varies from individual to individual. The most common response, according to Merton (1938), is conformity. This line of action presents the individual with the least amount of resistance and does not add the problems of deviance to the problem of not succeeding. In the remaining modes, individuals can be considered deviant either in their outlook or in their actions. Delinquency appears in innovation, retreatism and rebellion, in which accepted modes of behavior (means) are replaced by unacceptable actions. While the root problem of anomie is structurally determined, the choice of adaptation can be understood only in light of individual circumstances.

Cloward and Ohlin: Differential Opportunity

Structural limitations on success have prompted many writers to view deviant behavior as a natural response to blocked opportunities. The **differential opportunity** argument rests on the assumption that illegitimate opportunities are available when legitimate opportunities are blocked. Cloward and Ohlin (1960), however, point out that illegitimate opportunities to succeed also may be limited. The ability to follow illegitimate activities to material success is subject to various social and environmental conditions in much the same fashion as legitimate endeavors. For example, youths who find that educational opportunities and good-paying jobs are not available to them may opt to pursue delinquent activities. The ability to pursue such illegitimate activities successfully, however, may be contingent upon the availability of training in criminal activity, the presence of fencing operations or social support systems for such behavior. In essence, there are structural determinants of criminal behavior that are similar to those affecting conventional activity.

Cloward and Ohlin (1960) discuss blocked illegitimate opportunity in terms of three subcultural responses. The first, a "criminal" subculture, entails opportunities for monetary success. Here success requires access to various structural necessities, such as the presence of an established, adult criminal population from which juveniles can be introduced to deviance. The absence of such opportunities may result in the formation of a "conflict" subculture. Conflict will appear when opportunities to succeed illegitimately are blocked and there is a lack of social control in an area, thereby allowing for more destructive activity. Finally, the "retreatist" subculture includes individuals who fail in both legitimate and illegitimate lines of behavior and simply withdraw from society.

General Strain Theory

Agnew (1992) has proposed an alternative version of strain that he calls **General Strain Theory (GST)**. Rather than focusing only on the inability to achieve societally prescribed goals, Agnew suggests that strain can arise from two other sources. The first entails the removal of desired or valued stimuli. Examples may include restricting a youth's normal activities, moving to another city away from friends, canceling a long-planned trip or being forced to quit a sports team. A second source of strain may be the presentation of negative stimuli that may cause an individual to become angry or frustrated. Having to walk to school through a dangerous neighborhood, be bused to a distant school, live in an abusive household or be harassed by other youths are all potential forms of negative stimuli. These two sources of strain prompt individuals to respond, possibly with delinquent or criminal behavior (Agnew, 1992). There are also many nondeviant coping mechanisms that an individual can utilize (Agnew, 1997). Agnew and White (1992) provide empirical support for General Strain Theory. They report finding a positive relationship between measures of generalized strain and delinquent behavior.

Assessing Strain Theory

The practical implication of traditional strain theory (Merton's view) would appear to be changing the structural barriers to success that underlie deviant activity. Unfortunately, problems with strain theory suggest that such activity would be premature. One major issue entails the problem of operationalizing the key concepts, such as anomie, aspirations, opportunity and perceptions. Differing definitions of these terms lead to conflicting empirical support for the theory.

Studies by Kornhauser (1978), Kitsuse and Dietrick (1959), Quicker (1974), Agnew (1984) and others have noted that the assumed relationship between strain and deviant behavior is not clear. Kornhauser's (1978) review of the literature found that, in some instances, deviance appears to be related to low aspirations, while in others, deviance may actually cause changes in aspirations instead of the reverse. For example, some individuals may substitute immediate gratification and goals in place of long-term, societal goals. This may be a direct result of the recognized inability to achieve the societal goal.

A second problem stems from the fact that many studies focus on middle- and upper-class youths while the Mertonian strain theory appears more applicable to lower-class and gang activity. Third, strain theory fails to present any explanation for the choice of adaptation. Little attention is directed to why one person chooses deviance and another does not. Finally, Mertonian strain assumes that all deviance is a result of unfulfilled aspirations. Agnew's (1992) theory addresses some of these issues. It appears that future research should take the broader approach offered by Agnew.

The Labeling Perspective

Another approach that places the blame for much deviance on society is the **labeling perspective**. The basic assumption of labeling is that being labeled as deviant by social control agents forces a person to act according to the label. Further deviance is a result of being contacted and sanctioned by the system. Consequently, continued deviance is a response to the actions of society. For example, being labeled a "delinquent" may lead to exclusion from participation in extracurricular school activities. This inability to participate in conforming activities may prompt further deviant behavior.

Table 4.14   The Labeling Perspective

Symbolic Interaction—the creation of meaning through interaction; "self" as socially defined; looking-glass self; key authors: Mead, Cooley

Dramatization of Evil—early term for labeling; emphasizing label of delinquent; transfer of evil from act to actor; key author: Tannenbaum

Primary and Secondary Deviance—rationalized deviance versus using deviance as response to societal action; mentalistic constructs; key author: Lemert

Status Degradation—the process of labeling; ritualistic, ceremonial imposition of new label; key author: Garfinkel

The Construction of Self-Image

The labeling perspective owes much to the ideas of **symbolic interactionism**. Symbolic interactionism proposes that every individual develops his or her self-image through a process of interaction with the surrounding world (Mead,

1934). An individual responds to the environment based on his or her interpretation of the environment. The meaning of the environment comes out of interaction with other people and the environment. For example, the color red is red because people have agreed that it is red. Its meaning arises out of interaction.

The same process applies to an individual's self-concept. Interaction with other people provides an individual with input about his or her own self. If an individual perceives a positive image of himself or herself from others, the person will hold a positive self-image. A simple way of viewing this process is through what Cooley (1902) calls the **looking-glass self**. The idea is that the individual views himself or herself the way that other people look at him or her. The individual attempts to see what other people see and acts accordingly. The same way a person looks in a mirror to see what others see, he or she tries to examine his or her total self to see what others see.

Labeling takes these ideas and proposes that individuals mold their behavior in accordance with the perception of others. Tannenbaum (1938) saw sanctioning of deviant behavior as a step in altering a juvenile's self-image from that of a normal, conventional youth to that of being a delinquent. System processing identifies a youth as delinquent, emphasizes the label and ultimately segregates the youth from normal juvenile behavior. This **dramatization of evil** results in juveniles viewing themselves as deviant, which leads to actions consistent with the self-image. Basically, the process of labeling entails a **transfer of evil** from the act to the actor (Tannenbaum, 1938). Instead of viewing the act as deviant and bad, the actor becomes bad and the focus for social action. No longer is the individual someone who committed a crime, the individual is a criminal.

Lemert: Primary and Secondary Deviance

Perhaps the most noted spokesperson for labeling, Edwin Lemert (1951), distinguishes between two types of deviance. **Primary deviance** comprises those actions that "are rationalized or otherwise dealt with as functions of a socially acceptable role" (Lemert, 1951). These deviant acts are common and garner minimal attention and mild sanctions. As a result, the individual is not labeled and his or her self-image is not altered. **Secondary deviance**, however, occurs when an individual "begins to employ his deviant behavior or a role based upon it as a means of defense, attack, or adjustment to the overt and covert problems created by the consequent societal reaction to him" (Lemert, 1951). This means that society has successfully labeled the individual as deviant. The individual now views himself or herself as different and deviant, and will act accordingly. It is important to note that primary and secondary deviant acts entail the same types of behavior. What distinguishes secondary deviance from primary deviance is the reason behind the action. The behavior is secondary if the act cannot be rationalized as the outcome of a nondeviant social role *and* it is committed as an attack or defense against societal reaction. Secondary deviance, therefore, is a mentalistic construct. That is, it relies on the mind-set and attitude of the individual involved.

The reasons for conforming to the label are simple. First, a deviant label makes participation in conventional activity difficult. Societal members expect deviance and react to the individual as a deviant, regardless of whether specific behavior is deviant or conforming. Second, by accepting the label, the individual blunts the impact of any negative feedback provided by society. For example, young children cry when told they are bad because the information is counter to their beliefs. Children would not be affected, however, if they saw themselves as bad. Negative input would simply point out what they already knew and accepted. Finally, individuals conform to labels as a means of striking out against those who are condemning them. Using a kind of "if that is what you think" attitude, individuals decide to show society just how bad they can really be if that is what society wants.

The process by which an individual assumes a negative label is not simple. A single deviant act generally will not lead to the successful application of a label. Lemert (1951) proposes an outline of the process that culminates in secondary deviance:

> (1) primary deviation; (2) social penalties; (3) further primary deviation; (4) stronger penalties and rejections; (5) further deviation, perhaps with hostilities and resentment beginning to focus upon those doing the penalizing; (6) crisis reached in the tolerance quotient . . .; (7) strengthening of the deviant conduct as a reaction to the stigmatizing and penalties; (8) ultimate acceptance of deviant social status and efforts at adjustment on the basis of the associated role (p. 77).

Lemert notes that this process is not set with any definite number of steps or a particular sequence of events. Rather, the process is an illustration of the types of factors that occur.

Status Degradation

Garfinkel (1956) expands on the "process" of labeling in his discussion of successful status degradation ceremonies. A **successful status degradation ceremony** is one that moves a person to a lower social status (for example, from "conforming individual" to "deviant"). Table 4.15 outlines the requirements for a successful degradation ceremony. The eight requirements can be classified into three types of factors. First, the individual and his or her behavior must be seen as different and unacceptable compared to what is socially approved. Second, the individual or agency that is doing the denouncing must be given the power to denounce on behalf of society. Finally, there must be some sort of ritualistic separation of the denounced individual from the rest of society. This could take the form of actual physical separation (incarceration) or proclamation to society (court proceedings). The successful application of a label requires that all three of these factors take place. An individual who is not labeled after multiple acts of primary deviance has not been subjected to a "successful" degradation ceremony.

Table 4.15   Garfinkel's Successful Status Degredation Ceremonies

1. "Both event and perpetrators must be . . . made to stand out as 'out of the ordinary.'"

2. "Both event and perpetrator must be placed within a scheme of preferences that show" that the behavior is ordinary for the individual and is in opposition to the desired behavior.

3. "The denouncer must so identify himself to the witnesses that during the denunciation they regard him not as a private person but as a publically known person."

4. The denouncer must make the denunciation in the name of the larger group.

5. "The denouncer must arrange to be vested with the right to speak in the name of [the group's] ultimate values."

6. "The denouncer must get himself so defined by the witnesses that they locate him as a supporter of these values."

7. Both the denouncer and witnesses "must be made to experience their distance from" the denounced.

8. "The denounced person must be ritually separated from a place in the legitimate order."

Source: Compiled from Garfinkel (1956).

The Impact of Labeling on Juveniles

The assumptions of the labeling perspective suggest that youths who have contact with the juvenile justice system are successfully labeled and act accordingly. Unfortunately, empirical research presents conflicting evidence on this point. Most support for labeling stems from studies that report higher recidivism for youths with prior system contact. They assume that the later deviance is due to successful labeling. The flaw in this argument is that there is no measure of the individual's self-concept in these studies. It is impossible, therefore, to identify the recidivistic behavior as secondary deviance (the result of labeling) or as further primary deviance. Studies that directly examine changes in self-concept after system intervention present conflicting results. Various studies (Foster, Dinitz & Reckless, 1972; Lipsett, 1968; Snyder, 1971) report little or no effect of system contact on self-image, while others uncover lower self-concept (Ageton & Elliott, 1973; Jensen, 1972; Street, Vinter & Perrow, 1966). Any inability to find changes in a person's self-image would interrupt the proposed causal chain and raise doubt about labeling's impact.

Part of the failure of the labeling perspective may be due to the lack of attention paid to the impact of family, friends and peer groups. For example, a youth may report no change in self-concept after contact with the formal justice system because he or she actually aspires to gain the label of "gang member." The youth pursues system contact in order to legitimize his or her gang affiliation. Formal system labeling also may fail if the individual receives accolades from family and friends. Conversely, a youth may be labeled by peers even if the system decides not to act. Each of these cases demonstrates that system intervention may not be necessary or sufficient for imposing a label. Most evaluations of labeling ignore the many potential confounding factors that may be at work (see Palamara, Cullen & Gersten, 1986).

Conflict Theories

Theories of social conflict represent the most clear case of deviance caused by the social structure. In contrast to most theories, which focus on the breaking of laws, **conflict theory** addresses the making and enforcing of laws. Violations of the legal codes are only manifestations of the conflict inherent in the establishment of those codes. While conflict theories can be divided into a wide range of specific views, these various ideas can be subsumed (loosely) under the headings of pluralistic conflict and radical conflict.

Table 4.16	**Conflict Theories**
Pluralistic	diverse groups pursue power; power varies by issue; people may belong to numerous groups; conflict is normal outcome of competition; key authors: Vold, Dahrendorf
Radical	Marxist, critical; two primary groups—"haves" and "have nots"; economic basis of power; haves criminalize the behavior of the have nots to maintain the status quo; key authors: Marx and Engels; Taylor, Walton and Young; Quinney

Pluralistic Conflict

Pluralistic conflict is closely associated with the writings of George Vold (1958; 1979) and Ralf Dahrendorf (1959). Under this view, society is composed of a great number of diverse groups that compete for power. These groups represent differing interests in societal affairs. Groups wield varying amounts of power depending upon the issue and the degree of support they can engender. Using their power, each group attempts to coerce social control agents into taking action consistent with the group's desires. Conflict, therefore, is a normal outcome of competition between groups.

The number of groups and the power of each group varies over time and issue. Additionally, each individual may be a member (whether active or passive) of many groups. Individuals choose to support and participate in a group depending on the issue at hand (Turk, 1972; 1980). For example, individuals who support efforts to decriminalize drug laws while they are in college may work with groups advocating drug education and enforcement once they have children of their own.

Criminal behavior reflects the interests of one group being imposed on individuals from a competing group. In essence, when one group wins the battle to influence the legal system and fashion legislation, the other group is the most likely to be criminalized. Unless the losing group modifies its behavior in light of the new legal codes, it will violate the new social norms and possibly be considered criminal. According to pluralistic conflict, therefore, deviance is an inevitable outcome of normal competition for power and influence in society. Those groups who can marshal the most support have the greatest chance of determining what is considered deviant.

Radical Conflict

The ideas comprising **radical conflict** fall under various headings, including Marxist conflict, critical conflict and the new criminology. Central to the radical conflict approach is the focus of attention on two societal groups—the "haves" and the "have nots." Where pluralistic conflict sees interaction between many competing forces, the radical view proposes conflict between groups determined solely by economic position. The basic cause of deviance and other social ills is the capitalistic system that places people into competing groups.

Marx and Engels (1906) saw the rise of capitalism resulting in the exploitation of the working class (the proletariat) by those who own the means of production (the bourgeoisie). In essence, a few capitalists hold most of society's private property and they work to solidify their position of economic and social control. The capitalist uses the proletariat to increase his or her wealth while paying the minimal amount for the efforts of the workers. In turn, the lower classes act out against the capitalist and threaten the status quo. The capitalists institute laws and methods of social control to preserve their societal position. For radical theorists, the criminal and juvenile justice systems are tools of the bourgeois class for maintaining capitalism. Crime is simply a reaction of the lower classes to the prevailing economic system (Taylor, Walton & Young, 1973).

Richard Quinney, one of the most well known modern radical theorists, sees the competition for wealth as the key to conflict. The economically powerful use the law and the criminal justice system to maintain their dominance. In his writings, Quinney (1970) proposes a **social reality of crime**, which explains, from a conflict perspective, the formation and application of law. Quinney argues that law is made by the powerful, in the interests of the powerful, and serves to keep the powerful in power. The state represents the interests of those in power.

Radical theorists see the deindustrialization of the United States as a key causal factor in crime. The underlying argument is that as industrial jobs have disappeared in favor of the most cost-efficient methods of production, the lower classes have become increasingly disenfranchised (Young & Matthews, 1992). Accompanying the loss of jobs in heavy industry has been a corresponding increase in lower-paying service jobs that are insufficient to maintain a reasonable standard of living. This deindustrialization has widened the gap between the haves and have nots and caused the growth of a large "underclass" in society (Hagedorn, 1988; Vigil, 1988). Underclass individuals can either do their best in the available employment or they can strike out against society. The deindustrialization/underclass argument has been applied to gang participation and behavior by several authors (Hagedorn, 1988; Jackson, 1991; Knox, 1991; Moore, 1993; Vigil, 1988).

Conflict Theory and Juvenile Justice

Besides its recent application to the growth of juvenile gangs, conflict theory has been applied to discussions of the formation of the juvenile justice system. Platt (1977) argues that the development of juvenile justice was a means for the economically advantaged to extend their control over the lower classes. The lower classes held the greatest potential threat for capitalism because they had the least to lose and the most to gain should capitalism be abolished. Similarly, Herman Schwendinger and Julia Schwendinger (1979) place the advent of the juvenile court within the larger framework of a capitalist system that did not need child labor and needed a means of socializing the lower classes to the capitalist system. The juvenile justice system can provide control over the idle youth of the lower class.

Most criticisms of conflict theory focus on radical conflict. One concern questions the failure of radical conflict to account for the role of the middle class (and other classes). Sykes (1974) addresses this issue by claiming that the middle class is duped into working for the status quo through a misguided feeling that they have a stake in capitalism. Such an explanation, however, ignores the size and diversity of the middle class in American society. Another problem arises in the proposed solution to capitalism. Marx, Quinney, Bonger and others see the establishment of a socialistic state as the answer. Klockars (1979), however, points out that existing socialist states experience many problems similar to those found in capitalist societies. A third problem is the lack of empirical research and support for conflict theory. Radical theory rests primarily on historical interpretations and rhetorical discussions and is resistant to empirical conceptualization and measurement. As a result, radical conflict has had minimal impact on juvenile justice. (See Chapter 14 for a discussion of radical theory and the future of juvenile justice.)

The Integration and Elaboration of Theories

One trend in criminological theorizing is the attempt to integrate various theories into more unified, coherent explanations of deviance. Many writers feel that, rather than attempt to show that any single theory is appropriate in all situations, each theory should be viewed as applicable to different domains of behavior. A number of authors have experimented with linking different explanations into an integrated theory of deviance. This process, also referred to as an **elaboration model**, attempts to take components of various theories and construct a single explanation that incorporates the best parts of the individual theories. Delbert Elliott and his colleagues (Elliott, 1985; Elliott, Ageton & Canter, 1979; Elliott, Huizinga & Ageton, 1985), working with extensive longitudinal data, have constructed and tested a model that includes elements of social control, strain and differential association theories. In their studies, the authors provide a rough sequential process leading to deviance. Strain is seen as leading to a weakened bond to conventional society that, in turn, leads to increased bonding with deviants and subsequent deviant behavior. Mediating this entire process is the influence of learning.

Other authors also report on attempts at linking social control (bond) and differential association theories (see Marcos, Bahr & Johnson, 1986; Massey & Krohn, 1986; Thornberry, 1987; Thornberry et al., 1994) and control and subcultural theories (Giordano, Cernkovich & Pugh, 1986). In general, these investigations uncover a dynamic process in which different effects influence deviance at various points in the process. These attempts at building more elaborate explanations have not gone unchallenged (see, for example, Hirschi, 1987). The challenges, however, are not widespread and often appear to reflect rhetorical positions based on defense of favored theories that may not fare well in the new models.

Recent interest in **developmental theories** generally reflect efforts that incorporate ideas from several theories and perspectives. Conger and Simmons (1997), for example, point out that biological factors play a role in cognitive ability, which impacts on how family, friends and schools may treat the person, which may then impact on an individual's success in school or in making choices. Throughout this process, the individual faces different demands and opportunities for which he or she may or may not be adequately prepared. Similarly, Moffitt (1997) offers a sequence in which neuropsychological deficits alter an individual's temperament, speech, learning ability and other factors, which may cause withdrawal, rejection by others, poor self-concept, failure at school and a host of other problems. Each of these problems appear as key factors in several theories. The key for Moffitt (1997) is the sequential and cumulative nature of the various factors. Several authors start with a single perspective and proceed to point out or build an elaboration of the theory. Sampson and Laub (1997) and Matsueda and Heimer (1997) begin with labeling ideas, especially symbolic interaction, and point out that early problems may lead to labeling, which blocks opportunities, which causes strain, which may result in deviance.

LeBlanc (1997) offers a **generic control theory** that draws on ideas from a variety of perspectives. He claims that

> in a favorable environment and setting, control mechanisms operate efficiently and change in harmony with social expectations, and as a consequence, conformity results and maintains itself over time (p. 234).

In essence, he proposes that control can come from several sources that vary over time and situation. He offers four primary categories of control mechanisms. The first, "bonding," deals with how individuals are integrated to and act as part of the community. A second source is "unfolding." This control reflects the growth and development of individuals, especially in terms of internalizing values. "Modeling," the third type, incorporates patterns that the person can emulate in order to conform. Finally, "constraining" refers to regulation imposed by others. Each of these mechanisms interact to enhance the level of control. In support of his propositions, LeBlanc (1997) offers a multilayered model that simultaneously discusses criminal acts, the criminal and criminality. LeBlanc notes, however, that the model requires more work before it can be operationalized for testing. For our purposes, the value of the theory is in its use of concepts and ideas from a wide range of individual theories.

A final example of the integration/elaboration approach involves the idea of **reintegrative shaming**. Braithwaite (1989) offers shaming as a key mechanism for showing societal disapproval. The shaming, however, needs to be imposed in such a fashion as to draw the offending party into conforming society. Elements of several theories are incorporated in Braithwaite's argument. Labeling and symbolic interaction are important for understanding the risk in shaming someone without concern for reintegration. Social control elements appear in the need to bond the person to society. Additionally, the family is a key actor in teaching proper behavior (learning theory). Braithwaite (1989) also argues that a great deal of shaming takes place vicariously through stories and examples (modeling and imitation ideas).

Many of these "new" theories have yet to undergo rigorous testing. The advantages of the elaboration/integration approach appears in the attempt to draw together long theoretical traditions, each of which has demonstrated some empirical support. The fact that no single theory has adequately explained deviance suggests that this new direction should be continued.

The Impact of Theories on Juvenile Justice

While a good deal of theorizing has been devoted to the causes of delinquent activity, the extent to which these explanations have an impact on the daily operations of the juvenile justice system is highly variable. Some theories have found their way into the mainstream of justice system activity at one point in time or another. Others have had little, if any, impact on societal action. Many times the impact of an explanation falls within the realm of rhetoric, in cases in which the theory is given as a rationale for system activity when little is actually done in compliance with the theoretical suggestions.

Court dispositions and correctional treatments display the closest relationships between theories and justice system action. As noted in Chapter 2, the rhetoric of the juvenile court has consistently emphasized the importance of learning and benevolent care of youths. Social learning theory provides support for interventions that focus on providing proper role models and environments conducive to conforming behavior. Trends toward deinstitutionalization and diversion (see Chapters 10 and 11) rely on the arguments of labeling theory as well as learning principles. Thus, the past 20 years have experienced movements to community corrections and less restrictive interventions (see Chapter 12). Recent movements toward incarceration and deterrence of juveniles clearly rely on classical and neoclassical assumptions of free will and hedonistic choice.

On a larger scale, various theoretical perspectives have helped influence general social movements. The Great Society reforms, which began in the mid-1960s, attempted to address the social inequities that lead to deviance. Educational programs, economic assistance, vocational training, physical improvement of inner cities, and other efforts can be traced to strain, subcultural, learning and ecological explanations of social ills. In many of these social actions, delinquency and criminality were only two of many social problems being addressed. The impact of these specific programs is a matter of debate. The consistency in crime, delinquency and recidivism rates suggests that there was little impact on these problems. Why they did not have an impact is not clear. Some authors argue that the interventions were too short-lived to alter long-standing social problems. Others claim that the implementation of the programs was incomplete or inappropriate. Still others deny the adequacy of the theoretical explanations being utilized. Regardless of past failures, the various theories continue to find their way into the policies and procedures of the juvenile justice system.

Summary

Explanations of delinquent and criminal behavior, whether biological, psychological or sociological in nature, provide some insight into the reasons for deviance. The diversity in perspectives, however, illustrates the lack of understanding that still exists. Indeed, the search for a single theory that explains all—or almost all—deviance appears to be an effort in futility. The most reasonable consideration is to view deviance as multifaceted. The explanation, therefore, must consider a wide range of variables and influences. Juvenile justice must not ignore theory simply because until this point in time it has failed to arrive at a totally adequate explanation. Rather, the system must take care to select, implement and evaluate ideas in light of expanding knowledge and research. While the remainder of the text deals with various interventions and system actions, theory forms an implicit base for all discussions.

DISCUSSION QUESTIONS

1. Sociological explanations for deviance are currently the most well known. Pick any sociological theory, outline the argument and translate those ideas into practical applications for dealing with juveniles.

2. The President has called for a study that will set the tone for future directions in juvenile justice. As a member of that commission, you have the opportunity to advocate an underlying theory. Which sociological theory will you fight for and why is it the best possible approach for guiding the juvenile justice system? Present both strengths and weaknesses of your choice.

3. A recent trend in delinquency explanations is the integration or elaboration model. Discuss how you can integrate subculture, learning and control theories. How are they related and what will the new explanation provide that any single theory cannot?

CHAPTER 5

Gang Delinquency

The study of juvenile misbehavior consistently portrays delinquency as a group phenomenon. Research shows that juveniles commit more deviant acts while in the company of other youths than when they are alone. Hindelang (1971) notes that 62 percent of all delinquent activity is group-related. Similarly, Erickson (1971) finds that between 60 and 93 percent of official delinquent acts occur in group settings. Self-report studies reveal that 65 percent of delinquency is group-related (Erickson, 1971). While agreeing with the general argument of a group component in delinquency, Erickson and Jensen (1977) suggest that the level of group violation may be exaggerated by ignoring differences in types of offenses. The authors, studying 1,700 high school students, show that group participation in delinquency varies according to the type of activity being considered. Drug use, alcohol use, burglary and vandalism are all found to be highly group-oriented. Conversely, assaults, fights and status offenses tend to be more individual offenses (Erickson & Jensen, 1977). These differences in group activity according to offense are the same for males and females and across time and place.

While these and other studies illustrate a propensity for juveniles to act in groups, there is some question as to the mechanism at work in the findings. The clear implication of the findings of group activity is that the group experience includes the commission of delinquency. Alternatively, Erickson (1973) and Feyerherm (1980) suggest that much of the group dimension in offending is due to differential response by society. These authors suggest a **group hazard hypothesis**, which proposes that delinquency committed in groups has a greater chance of being detected and acted upon by the juvenile and criminal justice systems. Erickson (1973), in a study of 336 youths, reports that the group hazard hypothesis holds for select types of delinquent acts, especially the more serious offenses. Surveying 562 high school youths, Feyerherm (1980) reports that group involvement has a greater impact on apprehension than on arrest. This is true primarily for theft offenses. Group behavior simply may make recognition of a problem easier, thus more youths involved in group delinquency become involved with the juvenile justice system. The finding of high levels of group behavior in self-report surveys, however, suggests that the group hazard hypothesis is not a complete explanation of the group nature of delinquent activity.

Interest in group behavior is far from new. Early delinquency research often focused on the idea that youthful misconduct was a result of peer influences. Differential association theory (Sutherland, 1939) proposed that much delinquent activity was the result of learning that took place in interactions between youths. Shaw and associates (Shaw et al., 1929; Shaw & McKay, 1942) focused heavily on the idea that juvenile misbehavior took place in groups. This theme of group behavior has persisted throughout the study of delinquency. Many of the theoretical orientations (especially those presented in Chapter 4) either explicitly or implicitly consider youthful companions as a source of deviant ideas and behavior. Discussions of Cohen (1955), Miller (1958) and Hirschi (1969) are only a few of those that recognize the influence of peers on deviance.

Much of the interest in group delinquency revolves around the idea of juvenile gangs. Popular concern about gangs can be attributed to the finding that many youthful offenses are committed in concert with other juveniles. Another source for the public's concern may be the portrayal of gang behavior in the mass media. Movies and plays such as *The Blackboard Jungle, West Side Story* and *Colors* dramatize the lure of gangs for youths and the aggressive nature of these groups of youths.

While there was a great deal of interest in gangs during the 1950s and early 1960s, the late 1960s and early 1970s saw a general lack of attention paid to the problem of juvenile gangs. This was not related to any decline in the activity or existence of gangs (Bookin-Weiner & Horowitz, 1983). Rather, a shift to interest in labeling theory and a broader concern over the social order made gangs a minor problem. No longer was the emphasis in juvenile justice placed on the activity of the offender. The new theoretical orientations focused on the problems of deviance in the structure of society and its systems of social control. As a result, gang problems did not retain their priority as research issues. Not until the late 1980s did we see a renewed interest in gangs and gang behavior. Gang researchers attribute the renewed interest to the escalation of gang violence and the belief that gangs are the driving force behind growing drug problems, particularly crack cocaine. Consequently, the past decade has seen an explosion of gang research.

Gangs Defined

While there has been a great deal of interest and research in gang activity, no single definition of a gang has developed. In general, the term "gang" has referred to groups that exhibit characteristics setting them apart from other affiliations of juveniles. Various researchers have proposed different definitions of a gang.

In one of the earliest gang definitions, Thrasher (1936) defined a gang as:

> an interstitial group originally formed spontaneously, and then integrated through conflict. It is characterized by the following types of behavior: meeting face to face, milling, movement through space as a unit, conflict, and planning. The result of this collective behavior is the development of tradition, unreflective internal structure, *esprit de corps*, solidarity, morale, group awareness, and attachment to a local territory (p. 57).

This definition introduced a number of key ideas. First, a gang was a specific form of a group. Second, what made these groups different from others was a system of activity and behavior that included conflict and mutual support of members. Finally, gangs were found in those areas of a city that were deteriorating and in a state of disorganization (**interstitial areas**). Gangs, therefore, were seen by Thrasher as a unique phenomenon of the poor, inner-city, immigrant areas of the early twentieth century.

A number of researchers have built on Thrasher's definition. The key change to the definition is the need for society to recognize the group as a threat. Under such a definition, the absence of social recognition would negate the consideration of a group as a gang. Exactly what constitutes recognition and who has to do the recognizing is not clear. Klein and associates (Klein, Gordon & Maxson, 1986; Klein, Maxson & Gordon, 1984; Maxson, Gordon & Klein, 1985) note that the delineation of a gang often relies on the activity of the criminal justice system. Unfortunately, the authors find differing criteria constituting gang behavior in different jurisdictions.

Beyond simple recognition as a gang, most definitions now require some degree of criminal/delinquent activity. Klein (1971), offering perhaps the most widely accepted definition, claims that a gang refers

to any denotable adolescent group of youngsters who (a) are generally perceived as a distinct aggregation by others in their neighborhood, (b) recognize themselves as a denotable group (almost invariably with a group name) and (c) have been involved in a sufficient
number of delinquent incidents to call forth a consistent negative
response from neighborhood residents and/or enforcement agencies
(p. 13).

The degree to which a group must be deviant before being considered a gang,
however, is not clear-cut. Where Klein requires "a sufficient number of delinquent incidents," Huff (1993) needs "frequent and deliberate" illegal activities.
A more extreme view posits that "violence" is the key element denoting a gang
(Yablonsky, 1962). Recently, Sanders (1994) takes up the violence theme in
defining a gang as

any transpersonal group of youths that shows a willingness to use
deadly violence to claim and defend territory, attack rival gangs, . . .
or engage in other criminal behavior . . . (p.20).

Violence, however, is not universally accepted as critical to defining a gang.
In the National Youth Gang Survey, Spergel and Curry (1990) reveal that only
23 percent of the respondents listed violence as a part of their agency's working definition. More common criteria includes some degree of organization
(47%), identifying symbols (68%) and general criminal or antisocial activities
(59%), among others. For more than 40 percent of the respondents, criminal
behavior is not a key to the definition. What this demonstrates is that there still
does not exist any single, accepted definition of what constitutes a gang.
    Curry and Decker (1998) identify six elements typical in most gang defini-
tions: (1) group, (2) symbols, (3) communication, (4) permanence, (5) turf, and
(6) crime (see Table 5.1). Being a group is perhaps the easiest of the elements
to understand, although most definitions require a minimum number of members. Symbols serve to provide the group with an identity. These elements often
are developed for internal use and may not convey meaning outside the group.
The symbols also may be used in communication between and among gangs,
their members and others. The development of symbols and unique forms of
communication can contribute to the longevity or permanence of the gang. As
groups gain permanence they become harder to combat and dismantle. The element of turf, while common, is not as universal as the other elements because
there are many examples of gangs that do not claim a physical territory. The
final element, crime, is the most important, because group involvement in
criminal activities is key to distinguishing a gang from other groups of people
who may use the other elements, such as college fraternities and the Boy Scouts
(Curry & Decker, 1998).

Table 5.1   **Typical Elements of a "Gang" Definition**

Group	a specified minimum number of members, certainly more than two
Symbols	clothes, hand signs, colors, etc., which serve to indicate membership
Communication	verbal and nonverbal forms, such as made-up words, graffiti, hand signals, etc.
Permanence	gangs must persist over time, generally at least one year or more
Turf	territory claimed and/or controlled by the gang (not as common in many definitions)
Crime	involvement in criminal behavior

Source: Compiled from Curry & Decker (1998).

Rather than attempt to arrive at a single definition for gangs, some authors opt to identify different types of gangs. Table 5.2 presents four different typologies. Huff (1989) and Taylor (1990) offer types based on the motivation or outcome of the gang behavior. Knox (1991) classifies gangs into four different levels based on formality, development and sophistication. Finally, Spergel and Curry (1993) outline three types that correspond to common terminology used by law enforcement agencies. Using an approach to gangs like that taken by Huff, Taylor and Knox, Spergel and Curry negate the need for a single definition and suggest that there are different degrees or types of gangs.

That a single definition of a **gang** has not been agreed upon should be clear to the reader. The term has different meanings to different individuals, in different locations, at different times. What is common about gangs is the perception that they pose some form of threat to the safety of others.

Early Gang Research

Interest in gangs formed a good portion of the empirical and theoretical research prior to the mid-1960s. Much of the early research on gangs focused on describing the gangs and examining the daily workings of these groups. The research relied to a great extent on participant observation techniques. This research approach involved going out and observing the gangs on a daily basis.

Members of the Crips gang in Los Angeles' Compton district demonstrate signs used by their gang. *Photo: Daniel Lainé/Corbis*

Such analysis provided a first-hand look at the structure and behavior of the gangs under study.

Thrasher: Gangs

Perhaps the most noted of the early studies of gangs was that of Frederick Thrasher. Thrasher (1936) studied 1,313 gangs with roughly 25,000 members in Chicago. He noted that the beginnings of gangs were found in spontaneous play groups within the interstitial areas of the city. Two key ideas appeared in this view of gang origins. First, gangs were primarily a result of the areas of town that were characterized by a large amount of transiency, great numbers of immigrant youths, poor living conditions and a state of social disorganization. These ideas were simple extensions of the early work of Shaw et al. (1929), Shaw and McKay (1942) and the Chicago School. The social conditions of the area were unable to provide alternative modes of interaction for the juveniles. The gangs supplied needed interaction and social contact for the youths.

Table 5.2   **Gang Typologies**

Huff (1989)	Hedonistic Gang: emphasize getting high and having a good time, minor property crime Instrumental Gang: economic concerns, high level of property crimes, individual drug sales Predatory Gang: crimes of opportunity (robbery, mugging), use of addictive drugs, use of weapons
Taylor (1990)	Scavenger Gang: lacks set goals, no structure, provides members with sense of belonging Territorial Gang: centers on defense of turf, clear leader and identity Corporate Gang: purpose is to make money, very formal structure, well organized
Knox (1991)	Pre-Gang: small, loose-knit, lacks label, no criminal activity, unstable leadership Emergent Gang: informal organization, small group, recognized as gang, developing leadership, minor offending Crystallized Gang: larger group, formal leadership and rules, community recognition as gang, active criminal involvement, gun use Formalized Gang: large, interstate, use of automatic weapons, stable leadership, organized crime, formal rules and regulations
Spergel and Curry (1993)	Street Gang: common identity, regular interaction, significant illegal behavior, violence Traditional Youth Gang: mainly adolescent, concern with status and turf, identifiable leaders, colors, signs, symbols, persists over time Posse/Crew: crime for economic gain, usually drug involvement, loose internal organization, connected adult criminals

Second, Thrasher viewed gangs as an outgrowth of innocent, everyday behavior. Spontaneous play groups provided the basis and possibility for conflict. The groups provided a feeling of belonging and togetherness for the participants. The development of leadership, cohesion and conflict served to strengthen the spontaneous groups and the establishment of a gang.

Gangs were comprised mostly of adolescent members. The size of the gangs varied greatly. Thrasher (1936) noted that 455 gangs were comprised of juveniles between the ages of 11 and 17, while an additional 305 had members between the ages of 16 and 25. Few members remained in gangs very long past the young adult ages due to movement into marriage and legitimate employment. Most gangs (60%) consisted of six to 20 youths. Others, however, were as small as two to three members and a few numbered more than 100.

Box 5.1   The Roots of Gangs Remain in Casual Association

Recent research portrays the beginnings of gangs in casual groupings of youths involved in everyday behavior, similar to the work of Thrasher (1936). The following quotes from Hagedorn (1988) illustrate this process.

It was a lotta us. 'Cause it was like so many people living in Hillside (Housing Project). And we used to help each other, you know, hang together. We really wasn't about fighting people. It was just about kicking it, you know, having fun. And we really didn't ever run in packs. It was just two, three fellas. And we used to go places and people used to jump us. (Clay, Hillside Boys) (pp. 60-61)

You know we were just standing on the corner, then we got to just getting together every day, and then we came up with something called the 34th Street Players. And as we kept going north, the gangs got to coming around and they got to have gang fights and they got to robbing and just carrying on. (Rick, 3-4 Mob) (p. 61)

In the summertime, when school was out, we'll come loiter on the corners, you know, nothing wild. Its just we'd use to hang there and drink some beer and play basketball on the Clarke playground. You know we'd use to get together and ante up out little money. So the 1-9s use to be with us and we use to all get together and just play basketball until like six or seven o'clock. And then the police saw that we were having fun, they use to come up on the playground and chase us away. And then where did that left us? We couldn't play basketball. What else to do? So we started stealing. I ain't saying that's why we started stealing because we were stealing then. But I'm saying that if we couldn't play basketball in our own backyards, what else to do but catch the bus and go out stealing? (David, 2-7s) (p. 64)

Source: Hagedorn (1998). Reprinted with permission.

Thrasher did not see gangs as a stable or permanent entity. The development of gangs, or **ganging**, was a continuous process. The fact that ganging was primarily an adolescent activity accounted for the fluidity of the gangs. Change was due to the maturing of individual members, the movement of members out of the immediate community and the ability of the gang to provide meaningful activity for its members. While the specific makeup of the gang changed, many gangs would survive by replacing old members with new recruits. The recruits would come from those youths residing in the territory controlled by the gang.

Gang activity very often centered on conflict. This conflict occurred both within the individual gang and between different gangs. According to Thrasher (1936), conflict helped build *esprit de corps* and unity among the gang's members. Disputes within the group were settled through conflict and thus provided a basis for common values, loyalty and cohesion among the membership. Successful conflict also provided the individual group member with prestige and status. Indeed, leadership was often determined by physical prowess as displayed in conflict situations. Conflict with other gangs brought about increased cohesion among group members and helped to draw the gang into a more formal, organized and long-term system of interaction.

The gang, therefore, was a means for youths in disorganized, inner-city areas to gain acceptance and exert some power over their situation. The lack of social control and organization found in these areas led to the formation of gangs. Gangs were not a planned response by the youths. Instead, gangs were formed from the spontaneous play groups in which the youths found themselves.

Bloch and Niederhoffer: Gangs as a Natural Response

Twenty years after Thrasher's (1936) monumental work, Bloch and Niederhoffer (1958) expanded on many of his ideas. Where Thrasher viewed gangs as primarily a lower-class juvenile phenomenon, Bloch and Niederhoffer proposed that gangs were different from other juvenile groups simply by a matter of degree. The gang provided its members with status, success and feelings of belonging that they were not being provided by the larger society (Bloch & Niederhoffer, 1958). Lower-class youths, who made up most gangs, were simply striving to succeed in the same sense as middle- and upper-class youths. Their social position, however, led them into situations that made gang behavior an acceptable alternative.

More specifically, Bloch and Niederhoffer (1958) noted that society had worked to prolong the period of adolescence while demanding adult behavior of the juveniles. The youths were asked to comport themselves as adults while being barred from participation in the adult world. The gang provided the youths with an outlet for behavior that built feelings of self-worth. Gang youths were simply seeking the security, recognition and acceptance that was not forthcoming from larger society. In the course of this search, gang members found that conflict, defiance of authority, aggression and other actions received approval from other youths. Thus, the gang became an alternative source of social support and approval. Gangs were more recognizable in lower-class areas due to the greater incidence of aggression and conflict as compared to middle-class groups of youths.

The organization of the gang was not greatly different from that portrayed by Thrasher (1939). Gangs developed leadership, cohesion, loyalty and support through their daily activities. Bloch and Niederhoffer (1958), however, saw gangs as somewhat more fragile in terms of their longevity. The loss of a leader was seen as bringing about the dissolution of the gang. They viewed the gang as having less permanence than the gangs studied by Thrasher. Despite this departure in views, both studies saw the gang as providing needed social support and status for participating youths.

Yablonsky: Near Groups

A different view of gangs is found in Yablonsky's (1962) explanation of gang formation and participation. First, Yablonsky concentrates mainly on violent gangs, whose activity focuses on violence and aggression. The violent gang strives for emotional gratification through hostile actions toward gang members and nonmembers. It also provides a sense of power for the participating individuals. Most of the youths are sociopathic individuals who lack compassion and feeling for others.

> He (the gang member) is characteristically unable to experience the pain of the violence he may inflict on another, since he does not have the ability to identify or empathize with any others (Yablonsky, 1962: 198). Incapable of ego achievement through normal channels, the sociopathic youth selects or helps to construct in the violent-gang role patterns in which he is a "successful" person (Yablonsky, 1962: 201).

According to this perspective, violent gang youths are different from those individuals discussed by other authors.

A second major departure from other explanations is the repudiation of the gang as a well-organized group. Yablonsky (1962) sees the violent gang as a **near group**. A near group is characterized by a relatively short lifetime, little formal organization, lack of consensus between members, a small core of continuous participants, self-appointed leadership (as opposed to group-approved) and limited cohesion. Most "members" of the gang participate on the fringe and become involved only when individual or group violence is indicated. Besides participating in violence, there are few demands placed on the youths. The gang simply provides an outlet for violence. The gang leader holds little allegiance from the membership and looks to the members for status and reputation. Self-aggrandizement, not group issues, is the major concern for gang members. This near group view is restricted only to the violent gangs in Yablonsky's (1962) discussion. Other gangs may reflect the more classic portrayal found in other writings, although Yablonsky would argue that the violent near group is the dominant form of gang in society.

Characteristics of Gangs

Research over the past 20 years has provided a great deal of information on gangs. Unfortunately, there is as much disagreement as agreement on many issues. As with the definition of a gang, questions still exist concerning issues such as the extent of gang membership, the migration of gangs, member characteristics and gang organizational structure. The following pages attempt to synthesize the diverse literature and provide a general view of gangs in today's society.

The Extent of Gang Membership

The modern benchmark for assessing the extent of gang membership is Miller's (1975; 1980) national survey research. The initial research surveyed 159 professionals from 81 agencies in 12 major United States cities (New York, Chicago, Los Angeles, Philadelphia, Houston, Detroit, Baltimore, Washington, Cleveland, San Francisco, St. Louis and New Orleans). The survey was unique in that it was conducted during the lull in high interest in gangs and the fact that it was national in scope. An expanded version of this survey was conducted in 24 cities using information from 445 respondents representing 160 agencies (Miller, 1980). Using a very strict definition of gangs, Miller (1975) reported an estimated 760 gangs with more than 28,000 members. Using a more liberal definition of gangs, which includes simple group behavior, the estimates jumped to 2,700 gangs with 81,500 members. While these numbers appear high, Miller contends that his figures probably underrepresent the actual number of gangs in the target cities. It is also important to note that these figures are only for six United States cities and do not include the number of gangs and members found in other American cities.

Recently, the National Youth Gang Center (NYGC) conducted a large-scale national survey of police and sheriff's departments on the extent of gangs and gang membership. The Center surveyed 4,120 agencies (in 2,821 cities and 1,300 counties) and received 3,440 responses (an 83% response rate). The selection of agencies was determined by past survey results indicating the existence of gangs, as well as the inclusion of cities with no prior evidence of gang activity. Based on law enforcement responses, 2,007 jurisdictions claimed they had a gang problem in 1995; the presence of gangs was reported in all 50 states. A total of 23,388 gangs was reported by 1,741 agencies, although not all agencies provided estimates of the number of gangs or number of gang members (Office of Juvenile Justice and Delinquency Prevention, 1997). The top 10 states in terms of the reported number of gangs are listed in Table 5.3. These 10 states contain two-thirds of the reported number of gangs. Three-quarters of the respondents provided estimates on the number of gang members in their jurisdiction. These agencies reported almost 665,000 members, with 58 percent of the members appearing in California, Illinois and Texas (Office of Juvenile Justice and Delinquency Prevention, 1997). One-quarter of all gang members are found in Los Angeles, Los Angeles County and Chicago. Table 5.4 presents data on the top 10 states and top 10 jurisdictions as determined by the reported number of gangs and gang members. It is important to note that since many agencies did not respond to the survey, these figures represent a lower boundary for the number of gangs and gang members.

Table 5.3   **Top Ten States by Number of Gangs**

	No. Gangs
California	4,927
Texas	3,276
Illinois	1,363
Colorado	1,304
Arizona	974
Florida	793
Missouri	740
Washington	668
Oregon	653
Utah	598

Source: Office of Juvenile Justice and Delinquency Prevention (1997).

The NYGC figures present the largest estimates of the gang problem to date. Indeed, each successive study adds to the estimates. Spergel et al. (1990) reported 1,400 gangs with 121,000 members in 45 cities. Curry et al. (1993) found 4,881 gangs with 250,000 members in 79 cities. As already noted, the NYGC survey uncovered at least 23,388 gangs with 665,000 members in 2,007 jurisdictions. One factor to note in this trend is the steady increase in the number of cities included in the surveys. It could be argued that the increasing scope of the problem is solely due to the expansion of the number of respondents. Howell (1997a), however, notes that this expansion is due to the emergence of gangs in new cities. Indeed, cities that did not report gangs in earlier studies have done so in more recent efforts.

While national surveys provide global estimates, they typically fail to put the problem into any context. That is, what proportion of the juvenile population participates in gangs? More localized examinations of the gang problem provide some insight to this question. Mays, Fuller and Winfree (1994), surveying junior and senior high school students in southeast New Mexico, report that 20 percent claim gang membership and an additional 25 percent can be classified as gang **wannabes**. More than one-half of the youths express no interest in ever joining a gang. Thornberry and Burch (1997) find that 30 percent of the youths in the Rochester (NY) Youth Development Study claim gang membership at some point prior to high school graduation. Fewer students report gang membership in other studies. Based on a five-year panel study of Denver youth, Esbensen and Huizinga (1993) report that less than 7 percent of the respondents in any given year could be classified as gang members. The fact that the key determinant for gang membership was actual participation in illegal behavior may have suppressed the level of reported gang membership. Similarly, Esbensen and Osgood (1997) found that less than 11 percent of the eighth grade respondents in the GREAT (Gang Resistance Education and Training) evaluation (see discussion later in this chapter) claimed past membership in gangs committing illegal behavior. Finally, in a survey of junior and senior high students in one midwestern urban area, Lab and Clark (1994) found that slightly more than 10 percent of the respondents claim to be gang members.

Table 5.4 **Top Ten States and Top Ten Jurisdictions by Number of Gang Members**

State	No. Members
California	254,618
Illinois	75,226
Texas	57,060
Ohio	17,025
Indiana	17,005
New Mexico	16,910
Arizona	16,291
Florida	15,247
Nevada	12,525
Minnesota	12,382
Jurisdiction	
Los Angeles County, CA	60,000
Los Angeles, CA	58,197
Chicago, IL	33,000
Santa Ana, CA	11,000
Cleveland, OH	10,000
Long Beach, CA	10,000
San Antonio, TX	7,000
Gary, IN	7,000
Bernalillo, NM	7,000
East St. Louis, IL	6,500

Source: Office of Juvenile Justice and Delinquency Prevention (1997).

Three clear results emerge from attempts to measure gang participation. First, gangs are found throughout the United States, in both large and small cities, and in both urban and rural areas. Second, the scope of the gang problem is growing. Finally, the majority of youths do not belong to gangs and probably never will. While the proportion claiming membership varies from one site to another, a small but significant percent of youths do claim gang membership.

Gang Migration

One of the oft-mentioned "facts" about recent gang behavior is that of gangs migrating from place to place. Typically, this discussion centers around the idea that gangs are deliberately moving and setting up chapters in other places for the purpose of selling drugs. Support for this assertion is most often anecdotal and relies on the simple observation of the same or similar gang names, colors, graffiti or behavior from place to place. Solid proof of gang migration, however, is not available.

For the most part, the apparent migration is more accidental than planned. Skolnick, Bluthenthal and Correl (1993) note that most gang travel and migration begins with nongang, non–crime-related activities. Visits to family members in other places or the relocation of a family are typical means by which gang members find themselves in a new environment. In essence, the gang migration is an unintended consequence of normal family behavior. The connection between gangs in different cities, usually considered a result of planned migration, is also more illusory than real (Huff, 1993; Spergel et al., 1990). Survey respondents note that most cities experience gang problems before any significant level of migration is apparent (Maxson, Woods & Klein, 1996). While gangs in different cities may have the same name, colors and symbols, these are borrowed from other places. The appearance of established gangs, such as the Crips and Bloods, in cities with no history of gang problems can often be attributed to the arrival of a single gang member who is displaced through family migration.

However, that there may be gang "chapters" in different cities cannot be totally discounted. Indeed, as competition for drug territory has increased, some gangs have attempted to move operations into smaller cities. This movement, however, is typically limited and does not indicate state-wide or country-wide organizations of juvenile gangs. One possible—and plausible—explanation for the apparent "franchising" of gangs in different cities is that more sophisticated drug dealers and organizations recruit youths and emerging gangs as local "employees" in the drug trade. Migration for drug selling, therefore, is more an illusion than a reality. Indeed, low migration levels result in relatively small impacts on a city's existing drug problems (Maxson, Woods & Klein, 1996). For the most part, juvenile gangs are not as entrepreneurial as the public likes to think.

Age

Most research portrays the typical gang member as an adolescent (Cooper, 1967; Kanter & Bennett; 1968; Klein, 1971; Miller, 1975; Robin, 1967; Short

& Strodbeck, 1965). Miller's (1975) national survey showed that the peak age years tend to fall in the mid-teen age group. The fact that gangs often use schools as a recruiting grounds (Hutchinson & Kyle, 1993) adds to the youthful dominance in most gangs. However, this does not mean that younger or older individuals are excluded from gang membership. Indeed, many studies (see, for example, Hagedorn, 1988; Horowitz, 1983; Howell, 1997a; Klein & Maxson, 1989; Moore, 1993; Spergel et al., 1990; Toy, 1992) report that the age range of gang members has expanded in recent years, particularly at the older end. Gangs often include younger youths as wannabes. These wannabes typically undergo socialization into the gang akin to a period of apprenticeship, during which time they may be utilized to distribute drugs or commit criminal acts for older members. While past research suggested that older members gravitated away from the gang and into more mainstream social activities and behavior, more recent analyses suggest that many members remain in the gang for extended periods of time. The lack of meaningful employment opportunities, coupled with potentially lucrative gang behavior, entices some individuals to retain their membership into their twenties and thirties (Moore, 1991).

Social Class

Most studies find that the vast majority of gangs are found in lower-class areas and are comprised of lower-class juveniles. The predominantly lower-class nature of gangs finds a great deal of support in the early examinations and explanations of ganging behavior. Thrasher's (1936) definition of gangs relies heavily on the physical location of the groups in the lower-class, deteriorating areas of the city. Subsequent analyses paint a similar picture of gang behavior through explanations of deviance that are heavily reliant on the conflict between lower-class individuals and dominant middle-class society (Cloward & Ohlin, 1960; Cohen, 1955; Miller, 1958). More recent studies suggest that gang delinquency is no longer restricted to the inner city (Johnstone, 1981; Spergel, 1984). Gangs, however, are still concentrated in lower-class areas. These areas are simply no longer restricted to the center of the city.

A separate phenomenon appearing in the literature involves middle-class gangs. Such gangs are in opposition to the usual view of gang membership and causes of ganging. Middle-class youths are not faced with the same degree of blocked success as lower-class juveniles. Lowney (1984) views the middle-class gang more as a near group along the lines of Yablonsky (1958). **Wilding gangs** fit this near group image. While not as disadvantaged as other youths, these groups strike out at what they perceive as inequalities and infringements on their rights by other ethnic groups (Cummings, 1993). Such middle-class gangs typically do not have well-defined roles, they lack cohesion, and much of the group activity revolves around casual interaction. While many middle-class groups do not fit the traditional image of a gang, the similarity between members and the participation in group organized behavior leads some to conclude that the youths are a gang (Lowney, 1984). These gangs tend to be less numerous and they are typically centered around less violent behavior than their lower-class counterparts.

Race and Ethnicity

Gangs do not appear to be reserved for any particular ethnic or racial groups. Virtually all races and ethnic groups have provided gang delinquents over the years. Most of Thrasher's (1936) gangs consisted of white youths of European descent. Evaluations in the 1950s and 1960s tended to report greater numbers of black gangs, while more recent studies have found significant numbers of Hispanic gang members. Curry (1996) reports that, based on law enforcement estimates, African-Americans and Hispanics constitute the largest portions of gang membership (see Table 5.5). This change over time appears to be related more to the economic and social standing of the larger cultural groups than to any other factor.

Table 5.5   Law Enforcement Estimates of Gang Ethnic Makeup

African-American	48%
Hispanic	43%
White	5%
Asian	4%

Source: Compiled from Curry (1996).

One clear finding of many studies involves the makeup of the individual gangs. Typically, gangs tend to be homogeneous in terms of race and ethnicity (Klein, 1971; Short & Strodbeck, 1965; Spergel, 1966; Thrasher, 1936). That is, there are relatively few gangs that include white, black, Hispanic and Asian members together. Part of the reason for this is that it is the similarity between youths that prompts them to come together as a group in the first place. If, as some theorists suggest, gangs are an outgrowth of spontaneous play groups, it is natural for like individuals to join together and participate in joint activities. Gang delinquency is a simple extension of other daily activities.

While participation in gangs has never been closed to any group of individuals, most traditional gang studies did not draw any great attention to any single type of gang. Few studies attempted to distinguish between gangs from different ethnic backgrounds. Indeed, most research through the 1960s ignored the issue of race/ethnicity. Recent research on gangs has taken more interest in gangs from specific ethnic backgrounds. Indeed, the racial/ethnic makeup of a gang is a prime consideration in the discussion of ganging behavior.

Recent studies have focused on Chicano (Horowitz, 1983; Moore, 1991, 1993; Sanders, 1994; Vigil, 1993, 1997; Zatz, 1985) and Asian (Chin, 1990; Chin, Fagan & Kelly, 1992; Huff, 1993; Joe & Robinson, 1980; Sanders, 1994; Toy, 1992) gangs. Each of these studies portrays gang membership and activity as being a result of life in lower-class communities. Many gang members are recent immigrants or first-generation Americans. The youths often face problems with success in the schools and other social situations. Gang behavior is seen as an alternative to the lack of success and status faced by youths. Lower-class youths, regardless of ethnic or racial background, spend a good deal of time on the streets, where they meet and interact with other youths. Education is provided through daily street activity.

The gang provides marginal youths with many of the same things desired by other youths. The gang offers its members a sense of belonging, self-esteem and status, which may not be forthcoming at home (Moore, 1991; Vigil, 1993, 1997). Brown (1978) portrays gangs as a form of extended family. This view of gangs is not unlike the explanations for gang behavior set forth in earlier analyses.

Females and Gangs

Research on gangs has been devoted almost exclusively to the role of males. This is due primarily to the fact that females do not contribute to gang membership or activity to any large extent. Thrasher's (1936) pathbreaking study of 1,313 gangs found only five or six female gangs over the course of the study. Most other research or theories on gangs (e.g., Bloch & Niederhoffer, 1958; Cohen, 1955; Miller, 1958; Yablonsky, 1962) ignored the participation of females. Miller (1975) found that less than 10 percent of all gangs were female-based. Individual female gangs, with separate membership and leadership, usually were adjuncts to male gangs and responded to the mandates and activities of their male counterparts (Campbell, 1984, 1990; Miller, 1975). This auxiliary status of female gangs was most clearly seen in the adoption of similar names to the dominant male gangs (e.g., Disciples and Lady Disciples).

Although explanations for female ganging have been rare, they generally follow the same pattern of logic found for male gangs. Brown (1978), Short and Strodbeck (1965) and others have pointed to many of the same social factors associated with male gangs. Blocked opportunity, lack of success at school and home, lack of status, desire for belonging, and community disorganization were among the cited reasons for female gang participation (Bowker & Klein, 1983; Campbell, 1990; Moore, 1988). While female ganging may be due to the same factors as male involvement, the failure to delineate factors specific to females may have been due to the lack of research directed at female gang activity.

Female gangs have received increased attention in recent years. Esbensen and Huizinga (1993) report that at least 20 percent of the gang membership in Denver is female. Data from the Rochester Youth Development Study show a higher prevalence of gang membership among females than males (Bjerregaard & Smith, 1993). Fagan (1990), Campbell (1990) and Esbensen and Osgood (1997) claim that females comprise roughly one-third of gang members. Curry et al. (1993) uncovered more than 7,000 female gang members in 27 cities. While in many cases the females are still part of auxiliary groups (Monti, 1993), there are indications of growing numbers of autonomous female gangs with their own leadership and separate meetings, which operate independently from the male gang in many instances (Campbell, 1984; Fishman, 1988; Moore, 1991). Female gang members are known to act as lookouts and to carry weapons for male members, as well as to participate in their own deviant activities (Fishman, 1988). Indeed, female gang members tend to participate in many of the same forms of deviance as males, including drug use and violence (Bjerregaard & Smith, 1993; Campbell, 1990; Decker & Van Winkle, 1996; Fishman, 1988).

Organization and Size

Gangs tend to have some type of internal organization that affects the activities of its members, the status of those members and the decision-making processes of the group (Bloch & Niederhoffer, 1958; Curry & Decker, 1998; Thrasher, 1936; Yablonsky, 1962). The degree of formality and control exercised by the gang varies greatly from gang to gang. Gangs that are more entrepreneurial tend to have a more formal hierarchical structure. Territorial gangs are more loosely organized and have an informal structure (see, e.g., Sanders, 1994).

Table 5.6   Law Enforcement Estimates of the Average Size of the Total Gang

	N	%
Up to 50	18	47.4
51 to 100	7	18.4
100 to 1,000	13	34.2
Total	52	100.0
Mean = 144.4 Median = 60.0		

Source: Spergel et al. (1990).

At the heart of most gangs is a single core of devoted members. This core may vary in size but it is always much smaller than the size of the entire gang. The majority of the gang usually reflects a large body of fringe members who rarely take part in decisionmaking and participate in gang activities only at selected times. Gangs that claim memberships of 100 and greater are probably counting a large number of fringe members.

The core of the gang provides the leadership and decision-making body of the group. Not all gangs, however, have the same leadership structure (Kelling, 1975). In some groups, leadership is provided by a single individual determined according to the talents of the core members. Physical prowess usually determines the leader of the gang, but this is only a general statement. Some gangs have highly differentiated leadership roles in which different talents call for varied leadership according to the present needs of the group. Fights and violence will call on the best fighter. Criminal activity for profit may require the efforts of another youth who knows more about committing the crime and fencing the goods. Internal conflict may necessitate the efforts of someone who can negotiate and come up with alternative solutions. The extent of such specialization is determined by the abilities of the core members and the needs of the group. Still other gangs may vest leadership in different individuals for each subgroup of the gang or may have a very informal leadership structure in which no clear leaders can be identified (Sanders, 1994).

Besides the core group, many gangs include a range of different subgroups (Miller, Geertz & Cutter, 1961). This is especially true in recent years, as we have seen gang members from different age groups, and more intergenerational gangs (Hutchinson & Kyle, 1993; Moore, 1991, 1993). Often, the subgroups are based on the age of the gang members. A simple form of organization may have only three membership groups—young "wannabes," the core of the gang and "old guard" members. The different subgroups of a gang may be identified by various names or labels, such as PeeWees, Juniors, Seniors or Old Heads. It is important to note that this tripartite view of a gang is only a simple presentation. Some gangs may have a more complicated system of subgroups, including female auxiliaries or affiliations with gang chapters in other areas of a city. The actual organizational structure varies greatly from gang to gang and from place to place.

Cohesion

A major factor in most discussions of gang behavior is the degree of group cohesion. Typically, gangs are viewed as having a strong, cohesive core membership with varying numbers of fringe members. Terms frequently associated with gangs include solidarity, *esprit de corps* and mutual support. Gang members come together and associate with one another because of the support and status they receive from other group members. While many scholars view cohesion as an essential element of gangs (e.g., Bloch & Niederhoffer, 1958; Thrasher, 1936; Vigil, 1993; Zevitz, 1993), others claim that gangs lack cohesion and are only loose gatherings of youths (Cummings, 1993; Sanders, 1994; Yablonsky, 1962) that fail to supply the support and satisfaction found in other groups (Short & Strodbeck, 1965).

Box 5.2   The Desire to Belong

The desire for belonging, support and a sense of self-worth are all common elements cited in gang membership. This attitude is easily expressed by youthful delinquents in the following statements:

A kid wants to be accepted, so he will do what the other kids are doing even if he knows it's wrong. He doesn't want to be embarrassed or disrespected by refusing to do something. On the other hand, he doesn't want to be seen doing something good or positive, then he'll get ridiculed for it. The people I knew and hung out with would really disrespect you and sometimes hurt you if you didn't do what they wanted you to. There's a code among friends, and if you want to be with them, then you do *everything* they say and you cover up and look out for each other. This means lying and doing a lot of illegal stuff. If you don't they will hurt you and disrespect you, ridicule you and use you in any way they can. It's unbelievable pressure. You have to work your way up within a gang. You do this by doing everything they want. This means dressing like them, acting like them, and looking like them. (p. 46)

Even me myself. A lot of my peers made me feel that I was wanted more than I felt at home. The littlest thing could happen at home that made me feel that my friends liked me better than my own family. And I would just turn to them. And you turn to them more and more. You become bad. (p. 48)

Source: Goldstein (1990). Reprinted with permission.

Cohesion may arise out of different factors and activities of the gangs. Klein and Crawford (1968) suggest that cohesion develops out of factors external to the group but common to the group members. Juveniles who find themselves faced with inadequate opportunities for advancement, poverty, poor school performance, lack of familial support, or other factors may find support and acceptance in the gang. These situations help to explain both group cohesion and gang formation. The increased intergenerational nature of gang membership also contributes to the sense of cohesion. Younger members are often siblings or offspring of current or past gang members. "Apprenticeship" periods for wannabes and initiation rituals help build the sense of cohesion. Cohesion also results from gang behavior, particularly conflict activity. Fights in defense of territory, a gang's honor or an individual member can serve to strengthen a gang's organization and resolve.

The extent of gang cohesion can be found in the names, territory and other identifiers associated with different gangs. Many gangs choose identifying names for themselves that reflect their ethnic or racial backgrounds. Examples of such names include the Black Assassins and the Latin Kings. Names can also reflect the territory claimed by different gangs. Many gangs award the right to wear distinctive clothing to their members. This clothing typically includes the wearing of "colors," that is, jackets emblazoned with the group name or symbol. Graffiti is used for a variety of reasons, ranging from promoting an individual gang member's reputation to demarcating the territory controlled by a gang. It must be recognized, however, that these outward symbols do not in themselves guarantee cohesion. Indeed, the use of names, colors or graffiti only provides an indicator of cohesion.

The Variability of Gang Characteristics

Attempts to delineate what a gang looks like are doomed to failure. We must recognize that gangs, like any other collective of individuals, will take on different characteristics based on the desires of the members and the underlying goals of the group. Some gangs may be highly structured with many members, clear leadership and set agendas. Other gangs may be loose confederations of a few individuals who interact on a sporadic basis. Names, colors, territory, leadership and other components of gangs are in themselves only potential indicators of ganging. Just as the general characteristics of gangs vary, so do the behavioral tendencies of these groups.

Gang Behavior

The typical view of gang activity, especially as it has been portrayed in the media, has not changed much over the years. Gangs are portrayed as in constant violent confrontation with one another and with the general public. Contrary to this media portrayal, gangs participate in a variety of different behaviors. This does not mean that the gang fights and drive-by shootings are fictional. Such confrontations have taken place in the past and continue to occur today. The image, however, is distorted. Past and present research suggests that such violent confrontations are rare relative to other gang behavior. Indeed, gangs are involved in many nonviolent activities. Thrasher (1936) noted that many gangs supplied leisure activities, a forum for talk and play, and even gambling. Yablonsky's (1962) study explicitly excluded delinquent (property offending) and social (neither violent nor delinquent) gangs and focused only on those gangs that did participate in violence.

Much gang aggression does not necessarily involve physical conflict. In one early analysis (Miller, Geertz & Cutter, 1961), less than 7 percent of one gang's aggressive acts involved physical attacks, and none of those actions involved a weapon. Almost 94 percent of the aggression was verbal and most did not contain anger (Miller et al., 1961). The verbal aggression mainly served as a means of handling violations of group norms and providing commentary on member's actions. Indeed, the authors noted that this aggression was used to ensure group cohesion. Miller (1966) reported that sentiments in favor of violence rarely were manifested in actual physical expression. One study of black gang members (Robin, 1967) reported similar findings. Only 13 percent of the deviant acts involved violent offenses, while the majority (37%) reflected disorderly conduct. An additional 25 percent of the offenses were against property (Robin, 1967).

Box 5.3 Typical Gang Behavior

While gang behavior includes conflict and violence, most of the activity does not involve serious physical aggression. Violence, however, does occur and has changed in recent years. The following quotes illustrate both the nonviolent nature of most gang behavior and the typical form of past gang violence.

Well, in the summertime, we'd come loiter on the corners, you know, and not anything wild. It's just we use to hang there and get everybody together so we can go drink some beer and play basketball on the Clarke playground. (David, 2-7s) (Hagedorn, 1988:94)

On Fridays we'd all meet up on Reservoir Park, sit down, get high, talk. See if anybody know any good, you know, good ways to make any money. That was it. (Ben, Vicelords) (Hagedorn, 1988:94)

Getting high. Getting high, and the higher you got the more devilish things got on your mind. If we could work we would, but whenever we got off work and got paid we would always come back there and do what we had to do, you know, let each other know we was OK. (Dan, Castlefolks) (Hagedorn, 1988:94-95)

There were some weapons used during my time, but not like now, in comparison to when I was growing up [in El Hoyo Maravilla]. It was mostly fighting—fair fights. Square off with a guy. [Fistfights?] Fistfights. If you lost, you just shook hands and that was it. [No weapons at all?] No, I wouldn't say no weapons at all. There were some weapons. Some knives, a few guns. But there was hardly any weapons showing when we used to fight. (Moore, 1991:60)

While physical aggression may not dominate gang behavior, gangs are involved in significant numbers of crimes. One source of information involves surveys of law enforcement agencies. Estimates from law enforcement reports reveal large numbers of offenses (Curry et al., 1996). Table 5.7 indicates that gangs were responsible for more than 580,000 offenses in 122 cities and eight counties in 1992.

Table 5.7   Law Enforcement Estimates of the Number of Crimes Committed by Youth Gangs by City Size, 1992

	Number of Gangs	Number of Crimes
Cities over 200,000 (population)	4,722	51,155
Cities 150,000-200,000	788	46,616
Cities 25,000-150,000	8,964	89,232
Smaller Cities	251	3,156
Counties	1,918	390,172
Total	16,643	580,331

Source: Curry et al. (1996).

The extent of criminal behavior by gang members also can be addressed through self-report surveys. According to the Rochester Youth Development Survey, the 30 percent of respondents who claim gang membership also report committing 65 percent of the delinquent acts (Thornberry & Burch, 1997). More specifically, they report committing 69 percent of the violent acts and 68 percent of the property offenses. This criminal activity, therefore, more than doubles their representation in the survey (Thornberry & Burch, 1997). Finally, Spergel et al. (1990) point out that gang members are more criminally active than nonmembers, and commit three times the level of violence.

Based on the level of gang member delinquency, one could argue that the elimination of gangs would significantly reduce the level of youthful deviance. An alternative possibility, however, is that gangs simply attract already delinquent youths, rather than causing increased deviance. The delinquency, therefore, is independent of gang membership. Following this argument, Thornberry et al. (1993) identify three possible models of the delinquency-gang relationship—selection, social facilitation and enhancement. The selection model maintains that gangs recruit or attract already delinquent youths. In this model, the level of delinquency would be independent of gang status. Under social facilitation, belonging to a gang is the cause of increased deviance. Periods of gang membership, therefore, will result in delinquent activity not found during nonmembership. Finally, the enhancement model strikes a middle ground in which gangs recruit delinquency-prone youths and enhance their deviance.

Two recent studies have sought to test these models of gang influence directly. Using panel data from the Denver Youth Survey, Esbensen and Huizinga (1993) report that gang members are indeed more delinquent while they are actively involved in the gang. At the same time, however, these youths also report higher levels of offending both before and after active gang participation. Thornberry et al. (1993) find that the gang-delinquency relationship varies according to the type of offense and the level of commitment to the gang. The social facilitation model fits for personal and drug-related offenses, while none of the models fits well for property offenses. In addition, youths who remain in gangs for a longer period of time tend to increase their offending (the enhancement model) more than do transient gang members (Thornberry et al., 1993). What these two studies suggest is that the gang is not necessarily the cause of delinquent behavior. Rather, gang membership appears to add to an already established level of deviance by participating youths.

Gang Violence

One clear trend in gang behavior has been an increase in the level of violence and physical aggression in recent years. Where much of the early research attempted to dispel the dominant myth of the centrality of violence in the gangs, more recent studies note that violence is on the rise. Miller (1975, 1982) notes that as early as the late 1970s there was a clear increase in the use of weapons and participation in physical confrontation. While confrontations appeared in the past, they were not a dominant activity and often occurred within the confines of the gang. Miller and associates (1961) noted that 70 percent of all aggressive gang activity was against members of the same gang. Recent research suggests that violence is now a more open activity directed at a greater array of targets, both inside and outside the immediate gang. The seriousness of the violence is also high, as demonstrated by the number of gang-related killings. According to Miller (1975), Chicago and Los Angeles had a combined average of 81 gang-related killings in the early 1970s. By the late 1980s, this average climbed to 187 (Block & Block, 1992; Meehan & O'Carroll, 1992). In 1994, however, these cities combined for a total of more than 1,000 gang-related homicides (Howell, 1997). Curry and Decker (1998) point out that the level of gang homicides increased fivefold between 1987 and 1992.

Gang violence no longer conforms to the typical image of a **rumble** or gang fight. Rather, most violence appears in the form of forays. A **foray** typically entails an attack by two or three youths upon a single member (or possibly a few members) of a rival gang. A typical form of attack is a drive-by shooting. For example, three members of the Bloods drive around a corner where a member of the Crips lives, they shoot from the car and then speed away from the scene. A similar retaliatory foray by the Crips would be the consequence of the Bloods' action. The foray becomes a self-perpetuating activity. This modern gang violence differs from the rumble in a number of ways. First, gangs use lethal weapons, especially guns, more often. Second, the violence appears to be more random, partly due to the use of automobiles and the willingness to attack when innocent bystanders are present. Third, the violence occurs more frequently through the constant small forays rather than in the occasional large rumble. Finally, the hit-and-run tactics of the foray make the violence appear more impersonal. Nongang peers and other individuals who become victims may often be injured as a result of a foray that occurs on the street.

The greatest similarity with earlier images of gang violence is the fact that most violence occurs between gang members and other youths and is not directed against the general public. Indeed, both Cohen (1969) and Miller (1975) find that roughly 60 percent of gang victims are themselves members of gangs. An additional 12 percent of the victims are nongang peers. Decker and Van Winkle (1996) report that, out of 99 St. Louis gang members interviewed in the early 1990s, 16 had been killed by the middle of the decade.

Drug Activity

A second major topic of discussion concerning gang behavior involves drug activity. There is no doubt that many gang members use and sell drugs, and that drug sales are an integral part of some organized gangs. The degree to which gangs are involved in drugs, however, is highly variable. For example, drug sales in one gang may involve sales only among its own members, while another gang may be deeply involved in the drug trade throughout the community. Fagan (1990), in a survey of Los Angeles, San Diego and Chicago gang members, finds that roughly 28 percent are rarely involved in drug use, while 35 percent are seriously involved in both drug use and sales. In addition, he uncovers little support for the claim that drug sales were integrally related to the formal organization of the gang. Similarly, Klein et al. (1991) note that drug sales are not dominated by gangs in Los Angeles County. While these findings argue that gangs are not the most important component of the drug trade, they do show that some gangs and some gang members are involved. Others also show that while there is a great deal of drug use, the sale of drugs for profit is highly variable (Decker & Van Winkle, 1994; Hagedorn, 1994; Mays et al., 1994; Padilla, 1993). Perhaps the prime example of gang involvement in drug marketing is the growth of Jamaican posses (although primarily an adult operation) as an organized force for the distribution and sale of marijuana and cocaine in the United States (Gay & Marquart, 1993).

Drugs and gang violence are typically portrayed as going hand in hand. Whether drug involvement is a driving force behind gang violence, however, is not clear. Klein et al. (1991) report little evidence that drugs are more prevalent in gang homicides than nongang homicides, and violence is rare in both gang and nongang drug arrests. Similarly, Maxson (1995) notes that violence in drug sales is rare, occurring in roughly 5 percent of the cases. A recent review of studies also finds little support for a drug-homicide connection in gang behavior (Howell, 1997b). Despite these findings, there is no doubt that conflicts over drugs and sales territories do escalate to violence. It is the extent to which such instances occur that needs further exploration.

Types of Gangs

Not all gangs participate in the same types of deviant behavior as other gangs. Indeed, recent research shows that some gangs tend to specialize in particular forms of criminal activity. That same research even suggests that a few gangs exist primarily as a forum for criminal behavior, as opposed to a forum for more generalized group behavior. The identification of specific types of offending by gangs, however, is as elusive as identifying a single gang definition. Each gang may do something slightly different from every other gang.

Asian gangs, for example, often appear to serve a definitive purpose for their members, and do so through a more narrow selection of criminal acts. A number of studies (Chin et al., 1992; Huff, 1993; Toy, 1992) report that Asian gangs appear to be very profit-oriented and tend to restrict their deviant activities to those that bring a monetary return. Chin et al. (1992) show how extortion, primarily from Asian businesses, is a central focus of Asian youth gangs. Violence for these gangs is used only as a means to maintain financial control over an area and is not an end in itself (Chin et al., 1992; Toy, 1992). Both Huff (1993) and Chin et al. (1992) claim that these gangs often have strong ties to organized crime, which directs both the financial dealings and the use of violence in the Asian communities.

Analyses of Chicano gangs portray a somewhat different picture. While these gangs are strongly territorial (Moore, 1991; Sanders, 1994; Vigil, 1993, 1997), there does not appear to be a strong entrepreneurial reason for control of the territory. Rather, control over territory or turf provides the youths with a sense of control. The territory also provides the gang with a delineated area from which it has almost exclusive rights to gang recruitment. Besides the territorial nature of Chicano gangs, these groups tend to be more heavily involved in drug use (Moore, 1991, 1993) and general deviance (Vigil, 1993).

Explaining Gang Behavior

The reasons behind gang behavior and violence are varied. An examination of different research studies provides different insights. The most prevalent reasons appear to be status, control of turf or territory, and financial gain. Each of these factors are interrelated. As noted earlier, most gang members are from the lower classes. Opportunities for legitimate success and for gaining status in the community are limited by the realities of the world—among other factors, jobs are few, education seems irrelevant, many must quit school before graduation to help support the family, and male role models are missing due to the absence of fathers in the home. The gang serves to provide a means of gaining status. Gang members can prove themselves on the street and are accepted for their contributions to the gang. They can gain honor through their allegiance to other gang members. They are provided with a sense of family and belonging that does not come from the broken, "female-headed" household. The need for belonging and status also appears in "wilding" gang activity, in which youths randomly attack individuals from a different ethnic background as a form of retaliation for reduced opportunities and perceived injustice (Cummings, 1993; Pinderhughes, 1993). Often, wilding gangs are composed of nonminority youths striking out at minorities.

Turf or territory, a second reason for violence, provides the sense of ownership and control often denied to gang youths (Vigil, 1993). Overcrowded living conditions, frequent movement from place to place, lack of finances to purchase personal property, and other factors lead youths to feel a lack of control. The defense of turf is a means of exerting control and ownership. While it is not ownership in the legal sense of the term, such control helps provide the feelings of status desired by the gang youth. Attacks on the turf are seen as an attack on the property, honor and status of the individual gang members, and violence is used to protect the turf (Hutchinson & Kyle, 1993).

Financial gain is a third major reason for gang membership and activity. The lower-class gang youth is faced with a lack of legitimate job opportunities. The gang can provide training in criminal activity (such as robbery and burglary), the opportunity for such criminal actions, and support for this behavior. Trafficking in illegal drugs is a lucrative activity for the gangs. It also brings about contact and opportunities with organized crime and a means of increasing status in the gang and community. At the same time that the drug trade has opened new doors for the gang members, it has also added to the stakes in control of turf and the level of violence between gangs.

While the outward appearance of gang behavior is different from socially acceptable activity, the reasons for the behavior are not much different from that of most other persons. The gang youth values status, belonging, ownership, control and financial gain. These are major reasons behind the behavior of nondeviant youths and adults as well. The gang has simply supplied alternative methods for achieving its ends.

Intervention with Gangs

Responding to gangs and gang problems is an area in which much work remains to be done. Unfortunately, the first response by many cities to an emerging gang problem is one of denial (Hagedorn, 1988). Cities often do not want to admit that they have gangs. The outcome of such denial is the emergence of a full-blown problem before the authorities are prepared to deal with it. Once the problem is identified, a number of different responses have been used to address the problem.

Spergel and Curry (1993), in the **National Youth Gang Survey**, identified five common intervention strategies (see Table 5.8). The approach listed by 44 percent of the respondents as their primary form of response is *suppression*, or the use of arrest, prosecution, incarceration and other criminal justice system procedures. The intervention ranked second in primacy is *social interventions*

(31.5%), followed by *organizational change and development* (10.9%) and *community organization* (8.9%). The approach listed as having the lowest rank is *opportunities provision*. These results indicate that traditional criminal justice system responses are the most common responses to gang problems, while efforts to alter the social conditions that cause ganging are addressed the least. Interestingly, in an analysis of the perceived effectiveness of the five types of intervention strategies, Spergel and Curry (1993) report that opportunities provision is viewed as the most effective/promising approach, while suppression is seen as the least effective.

Table 5.8   Gang Intervention Strategies

Suppression	Includes any form of social control in which the criminal justice system (police, courts or corrections) or society attempt to impose formal or informal limits on behavior.
Social Intervention	Basically a "social work" approach to working with gangs in the neighborhoods (such as detached worker programs).
Organizational Change and Development	Deals with altering the organization(s) responding to gang problems, such as through the establishment of gang units or specialized training of its personnel.
Community Organization	Efforts aimed at mobilizing the community toward self-improvement and change, including both physical and social alterations.
Opportunities Provision	Recognizing the lack of meaningful jobs and the training needed to succeed, and taking steps to change the problems. Education, vocational training and job placement are elements.

Source: Spergel & Curry (1993).

Historically, criminal and juvenile justice system personnel have had the primary responsibility for addressing gang behavior. At one extreme, this has been done through the simple application of the criminal code against offending youths. At the other end of the spectrum, law enforcement agencies have involved themselves in functions more akin to social work, such as midnight basketball leagues and youth clubs. In between these extremes fall specialized gang units, conflict resolution/response teams and similar activities. The following pages will address four approaches to gang problems: (1) new legal/law enforcement avenues, (2) detached worker programs, (3) the GREAT Program, and (4) Aggression Replacement Training.

Legal/Law Enforcement Changes

Increased concern about gangs has prompted the development of new organizational structures and the passage of new legislation as means of combating gang problems. Many police departments, particularly in large cities, have established specialized gang crime units (Curry et al., 1992). One of the most notable is the Los Angeles Police Department's Community Resources Against Street Hoodlums program (referred to as the **CRASH program**), which targets gangs and gang behavior for suppression. In support of such efforts, many states have passed legislation making gang affiliation a crime or increasing penalties for gang-related criminal behavior. California's Street Terrorism Enforcement and Prevention Act of 1988 (referred to as the **STEP Act**) effectively criminalizes membership in a street gang. Under the STEP Act, the police can invoke civil penalties against gang members for associating with one another in public, promoting their gang, displaying gang symbols and being involved in other similar gang behavior. Many states have enhanced the penalties for crimes committed as a result of or in connection to gang membership. Statutes such as those in Florida (Florida Statutes 874.01) and Georgia (Georgia Code 16-16-3) require harsher penalties for gang-related crimes. Despite such efforts, ganging has not abated. Indeed, the gang problem has continued to grow in the Los Angeles area even in the face of the STEP Act.

Detached Worker Programs

Detached workers have been an integral part of many programs dealing with youths over the years (for example, the Chicago Area Project and Mobilization For Youth). **Detached worker programs** place gang workers into the community and free the workers from heavy paperwork and administrative requirements (Klein, 1969). The workers are expected to spend considerable time in the neighborhoods, maintain more consistent contact with gangs and provide immediate assistance and input to youths. Many programs rely on past gang members for workers. Klein (1971) notes that the strengths of the program include the ability to reach youths who normally are not contacted, the flexibility of workers to handle situations in unique ways and the ability to establish confidential relationships with youths.

Unfortunately, many of these strengths also provide the basic weaknesses of the program (Klein, 1969). First, the flexibility of the workers may result in inconsistency among workers and a lack of clear focus. A more important problem is that close work with the groups may lead to increased gang cohesion through the provision of directed group activities and interaction. Third, the use of former gang members as workers provides mixed messages. While these individuals should have a good rapport with and have intimate knowledge of gangs, contact with former rival gangs and gang members could cause friction and pose a danger to the worker. Finally, intensive contact with gangs often results in high turnover among the workers.

The impact of detached workers on gang behavior can be observed in the Group Guidance Project in Los Angeles. In terms of activities, Klein (1969) noted that the detached workers organized 113 sporting events, 90 outings, 16 service projects and 14 self-help programs, among other activities. However, in assisting the groups in finding alternative behaviors, the project inadvertently caused greater cohesiveness and, indirectly, delinquent behavior (Klein, 1969). Gangs contacted by the same worker throughout the evaluation became closer and were more successful at recruiting new members. Additionally, these groups participated in greater numbers of delinquent acts after the intervention of the detached workers. The end result suggested that detached worker programs caused more harm than good. Lundman (1993), reviewing the use of detached workers in various locations, also pointed out the failure of this approach to reduce delinquency.

Recent proposals for intervention with gangs typically include a heavy detached worker component, although they may not use that terminology. Spergel's (1984; 1986) and Fox's (1985) discussions of gang interventions reveal a striking similarity with detached worker programs. Emphasis is placed on intimate contact with gang members, providing alternative lines of behavior and serving as a resource for gangs. Based on Klein's earlier work, it could be argued that this approach is ill-fated. Goldstein (1993), however, argues that detached worker programs are not a failure. Instead, he claims that the programs failed due to problems with program implementation, inadequate identification of the basic problem and the appropriate subjects, and the lack of intensity in the intervention. He claims, therefore, that detached worker programs will work if they are implemented appropriately.

The GREAT Program

The Gang Resistance Education and Training Program (referred to as the **GREAT Program**) began in 1991 under a grant from the Bureau of Alcohol, Tobacco and Firearms (ATF) to the Phoenix, Arizona, Police Department. Not unlike the Drug Abuse Resistance Education (DARE) program, GREAT is taught by local police officers in middle schools. The curriculum is presented in the schools over nine weeks (one class meeting per week). The thrust of the program is to provide youths with the necessary skills for identifying high-risk situations and how to resist the pressure/allure of taking part in gangs and gang activity. Beyond targeting just ganging, program curricula are geared toward increasing self-esteem, changing attitudes and eliminating participation in violent behavior. A key component of GREAT is to teach nonviolent conflict resolution techniques to the youths. While still relatively new, the program has been adopted by schools throughout the United States. There is also a four-week program for third- and fourth-grade students. A summer component is available to reinforce the materials learned in school and to provide alternative activities to gang participants.

Figure 5.1   GREAT Program Components

	Lesson	Purpose
1.	Introduction	To acquaint students with the GREAT program and their officers.
2.	Crimes/Victims and Your Rights	To familiarize students with the concepts of crimes, their victims and their impact on the neighborhood.
3.	Cultural Sensitivity/ Prejudice	To familiarize students with the concept of differences and their impact on the neighborhood.
4a&b.	Conflict Resolution	To create an atmosphere of understanding that would enable all parties to better address problems and work on solutions together.
5.	Meeting Basic Needs	Students will be better equiped to meet their basic needs without joining gangs.
6.	Drugs/Neighborhoods	Students will understand the correlation between drugs and their effects on the neighborhood.
7.	Responsibility	To understand the diverse responsibilities of people within their community.
8.	Goal Setting	Understanding the need for goal setting and how to establish long-term goals in life.

Source: Bureau of Alcohol, Tobacco and Firearms (n.d.), *GREAT Program Manual*. Washington, DC: author. Reprinted with permission.

The newness of GREAT means that a definitive evaluation of its impact has not yet been undertaken. An early national evaluation, using a pretest and posttest survey of participating students, reports that resistance skills increased, fewer students reported wanting to be gang members, and the number of students getting into trouble decreased after program participation. In addition, students retained the information they were taught in the program (Arizona Prevention Resource Center, 1994). While the results are positive, there are three major caveats to consider. First, the evaluation did not include any non-participating youths as a control group. Second, the changes are modest and may not be large enough to have a substantive impact on the number of gang members or the level of gang behavior in the area. Finally, because the posttest was conducted immediately after the provision of the GREAT curriculum, it is possible that the results were only short-term.

Currently, a more in-depth evaluation of GREAT is underway at 13 sites, using both cross-sectional and longitudinal designs. Esbensen and Osgood (1997) report promising findings from the initial cross-sectional survey. The longitudinal design will not be completed until 1999. Based on survey results from 5,836 eighth-grade students in 11 school districts, students who completed the GREAT curriculum report lower delinquency rates, lower gang membership and more negative attitudes about gangs (Esbensen & Osgood, 1997). Program participants also display "more prosocial behaviors and attitudes" toward police, the school, family and peers. While from only a one-year follow-up, the results suggest that the program has an impact on ganging activity. The longitudinal results will further clarify this position.

Aggression Replacement Training

Another intervention receiving attention in recent years is the idea of **Aggression Replacement Training (ART)**. Goldstein (1993) points out that gang members simply do not know how to deal with everyday situations. They tend to be deficient at handling interpersonal relationships, aggression management and planning. Given these problems, Goldstein (1993) argues that any successful intervention will have to deal with these deficiencies. ART incorporates three main components aimed at such problems: (1) skillstreaming, (2) anger control, and (3) moral education (see Table 5.9). **Skillstreaming** focuses on teaching the proper behavioral responses to various situations. The **anger control** component deals with recognizing and controlling anger. Finally, **moral education** attempts to teach moral values and lead individuals to choose socially acceptable solutions to problem situations.

Table 5.9   **Components of Aggression Replacement Training**

Skillstreaming	teaching the proper behavioral responses to various situations using modeling, role-playing and group feedback
Anger Control	how to recognize the onset of anger, how to control anger, the proper outlet for emotions, and alternative responses to arousing situations
Moral Education	enhancing the cognitive development of the individual and teaching moral values (parallels Kohlberg's Moral Development)

Source: Goldstein & Glick (1994).

Evaluations of ART show that the technique can be effective. Goldstein and Glick (1994), reviewing past studies with nongang populations, illustrate the impact of ART on improved anger control, decreased acting out and increased prosocial behavior. Based on initial research with gangs, Goldstein and Glick claim that ART is effective at improving interpersonal skills and attitudes toward work, as well as reducing recidivism. The evaluation, however, does not find better anger control or community adjustment, although the tendency is in favor of ART. Goldstein and Glick (1994) claim that ART is most effective when dealing with entire gangs, because it is the gang that is supporting the inappropriate responses to anger and conflict situations. Further evaluations of ART with gangs will be necessary before its efficacy can be fully established.

Overview of Interventions

Evidence concerning the effectiveness of dealing with gangs mirrors the research concerning interventions with individual offenders. The basic conclusion is that most methods of intervention have had little impact on deviant activity. Indeed, some evaluations suggest that intervention exacerbates the problem. A large part of past failures may be due to what Klein (1995) refers to as "conceptually misguided, poorly implemented, half-heartedly pursued" responses and programs.

We must recognize that most programs do not address the major underlying cause of ganging and gang behavior: the lack of social opportunities. Despite the recognition that opportunity provision has the most promise, there are few programs that target this area. The lack of education, training and jobs is an issue that receives little attention in gang interventions. Rather, arrest, prosecution and incarceration remain the mainstay of society's response. Many authors (see, e.g., Cummings & Monti, 1993; Goldstein, 1993; Hagedorn, 1988; Huff, 1990, 1993; Moore, 1991) claim that until major changes are made in the basic social structure, gangs will persist and thrive.

There is room for some hope in dealing with gangs, largely due to recent initiatives that transcend the typical, narrowly focused, local programs. The establishment in 1994 of the National Youth Gang Center should help to coordinate research and knowledge about gangs. Similarly, programs such as the Chicago Gang Violence Reduction Project and the Comprehensive Community-Wide Approach to Gang Prevention are relying on multiple interventions to address gangs and ganging. These programs incorporate elements of suppression, community organization, social interventions, and others into a unified approach to the problem (Thornberry & Burch, 1997). Finally, programs such as GREAT and ART, as well as appropriately implemented detached worker programs, are receiving attention and being evaluated for their effectiveness.

Summary

Interest in gang activity has a long history in juvenile justice and appears to have engendered renewed interest in the last few years. The research efforts to date provide striking similarities to one another. The form and explanations for ganging have changed little since Thrasher's (1936) early work. The most clear difference in recent work has been concerned with the finding of more serious violence directed against a wider range of victims. Despite this persistent and increasingly dangerous problem, there do not appear to be any clearly successful methods for dealing with gangs.

DISCUSSION QUESTIONS

1. Gang delinquency is apparently on the rise and you are called on to explain to the public about gangs and gang behavior. How would you define a gang? What is the typical gang like? How much danger do gangs pose to the average citizen?

2. Gangs are typically accused of dominating violence and drug use/sales. What can you tell about gang involvement in these actions? How does this compare to the general impression about gangs? What is the GREAT Program and how does it relate to these problems?

3. Due to the apparent increase in gang violence, the police are called on to do something about the problem. As a member of the police department, what programs, interventions or actions would you suggest for dealing with gangs and/or the public's perception? Be as specific as possible. If past programs form the basis of your suggestions, provide information on the strengths and weaknesses of those programs and how you would improve on them.

CHAPTER 6

Drugs and Delinquency

Key Terms and Phrases

affective approaches
DARE program
detoxification
Drug Use Forecasting (DUF)
    program
"Just Say No" campaign
knowledge approach
maintenance programs
Monitoring the Future (MTF)
    Project

outpatient drug-free programs
psychopharmacological
    explanations
reciprocal relationship
skills training
spurious
systemic violence
therapeutic communities
Toughlove
use, abuse and addiction

For many parents, the war on delinquency has become the war on drugs (Vito, 1989). Often, there has been a perception that drug use is epidemic in the United States, especially among our youth. A team of drug use experts contends that our high school students report "a level of involvement in illicit drugs which is greater than has been documented in any other industrialized nation in the world" (Johnston, O'Malley & Bachman, 1996). Media coverage greatly influenced this perception by their almost daily reports of drug-related homicides in major cities in the late 1980s. Much of this concern has been directed at cocaine in its various forms. Beyond the fact that drug use (from alcohol and tobacco to heroin and cocaine) is illegal for juveniles, there is evidence that many youths are under the influence of drugs or alcohol at the time they commit delinquent acts (Beck, Kline & Greenfeld, 1988). While the causal relationship between drugs and delinquency is the matter of some debate, the indisputable correlation between the two (Huizinga, Loeber & Thornberry, 1995) raises a variety of issues for the juvenile justice system. This chapter will examine the various issues involved in the drugs-delinquency connection—the extent of drug use, the evidence on the causal relationship, and ways to combat the problem. Before examining these topics, however, it is necessary to define some key terms involved in drug research.

Three common terms used in any discussion of the drug problem are **use, abuse and addiction**. While definitions for these ideas vary from source to source, we can identify some uniform components in most definitions. Use and abuse are considered to be synonomous by most authors when juveniles are considered. This is true because juveniles are legally barred from the use of any drug, including alcohol. Indeed, even medically prescribed drugs are supposed to be administered by an adult following strict guidelines. Abuse generally refers to the use of any drug beyond that legally prescribed for a medical condition. For juveniles, therefore, any use constitutes abuse. According to the World Health Organization (1964), addiction refers to chronic use of a drug to the point at which the individual develops a need to continue use of the drug, increases the amount used over time and develops a psychological or physical dependence on the drug. The following pages will deal mainly with references to simple use and abuse of drugs by juveniles, regardless of whether addiction is present. Addiction becomes an issue at the treatment stage, at which different approaches are needed for addicted individuals.

Gauging the Extent of Drug Use

Measuring the extent of drug use is somewhat difficult due to the private nature of the behavior. The only individual involved is the user. There is no victim who calls the police and files a complaint. In essence, the victim and offender are the same person. Consequently, the primary source of information on drug use (the extent of it and changes in it) is individual self-reports of behavior. Such self-report surveys have been conducted on both the general population and groups of known offenders. Data from both sources are considered below.

Drug Use Among Adolescents

Drug availability is one factor that makes drug use understandable. In 1995, 65 percent of students age 12 to 19 reported that drugs were available at school. This percentage increased to almost 80 percent (79.5%) if a student reported that street gangs were present at his or her school. Marijuana was the easiest drug to obtain; 36.4 percent of the students surveyed reported that it was easy to obtain (Chandler et al., 1998).

Drug use in the general population has been measured on a yearly basis since the 1970s by the **Monitoring the Future (MTF) Project**, carried out by Johnston and associates at the University of Michigan. The MTF Project surveys representative samples of high school seniors during the spring of their senior year and in follow-up surveys in college and beyond (Johnston, O'Malley

& Bachman, 1996). In recent years, eighth- and tenth-grade samples have been added to the survey. The project gathers information on a wide variety of behaviors, including levels and types of drug use. In addition, MTF presents drug use information for different time frames, ranging from "ever" using a drug to "daily use" in the past 30 days.

Table 6.1 presents information on daily drug use for high school seniors graduating in the years from 1975 to 1995. A number of key observations can be made from this information. First, drug use varies greatly by type of drug. Second, only a small fraction of respondents use any drug other than alcohol or tobacco on a regular basis. This table clearly supports arguments that much drug use—other than marijuana, alcohol or cigarettes—is experimental. Third, the overall trend in the statistics is that illegal drug use among high school seniors is increasing slightly. For example, Table 6.2 shows that, in 1995, 23.8 percent of the seniors reported having used any illicit drug in the past month, compared to 14.4 percent in 1992. Similarly, 21.2 percent of the seniors reported having used marijuana in the last 30 days, compared to 11.9 percent in 1992 and 19 percent in 1994 (for 1996 statistics, see Table 6.3). Almost 2 percent (1.8%) of the 1995 seniors reported use of cocaine in the last month, compared to 1.3 percent in 1992. However, these figures are still below the statistics for 1985, when 29.7 percent of the seniors reported use of any drug in the last 30 days, 25.7 percent reported use of marijuana and 6.7 percent reported use of cocaine.

The data still suggest, however, that drug use is not the rampant problem portrayed by the media or assumed by the public (see Table 6.2). Fewer than 5 percent of high school seniors used any one drug other than marijuana, alcohol or tobacco at least once in the last 30 days in 1995 (and this also held true for 1996; see Table 6.3). Interestingly, 30-day percentages increased from 1992 to 1995 for most drug categories, particularly marijuana and tobacco. Examination of the annual prevalence of drug usage (not shown) revealed higher incidences of use as well as the same increase in use from 1992 to 1996. The increases in the most recent data are counter to prevalent decreases through the period of 1986 to 1992, except for isolated new drugs, such as crack cocaine.

The most prevalent drug, regardless of the time frame used, is alcohol. Indeed, 51.3 percent of the respondents report using alcohol in the last 30 days (see Table 6.2). Cigarettes and marijuana/hashish are the next most prominent drugs at 33.5 percent and 21.2 percent, respectively. The remainder of the drugs are used by very few of the high school seniors. Less than 5 percent of the students report using any other drug in the last month. The drugs that are of the most concern to society are used by very few individuals. Cocaine (including crack cocaine), heroin and the other "harder" drugs are not the most prevalent drugs in use. Alcohol and tobacco, both legal drugs for adults, are the most commonly used drugs. Stephens (1987) argues that simple use in the past year should not be used as an indicator of a drug "problem" because such use may simply reflect simple experimentation. He argues that much drug use is "experimental or occasional recreational use" and that "other than alcohol and cigarettes, marijuana is clearly the most abused . . . psychoactive drug in American

Table 6.1   **Long-Term Trends in Thirty-Day Prevalence of *Daily* Use of Various Types of Drugs for Twelfth Graders**

	Percent who used daily in last thirty days									
	Class of 1975	Class of 1976	Class of 1977	Class of 1978	Class of 1979	Class of 1980	Class of 1981	Class of 1982	Class of 1983	Class of 1984
Approx. N =	*9,400*	*15,400*	*17,100*	*17,800*	*15,500*	*15,900*	*17,500*	*17,700*	*16,300*	*15,900*
Marijuana/Hashish	6.0	8.2	9.1	10.7	10.3	9.1	7.0	6.3	5.5	5.0
Inhalants	—	*	*	0.1	*	0.1	0.1	0.1	0.1	0.1
Inhalants, Adjusted	—	—	—	—	0.1	0.2	0.2	0.2	0.2	0.2
Amyl & Butyl Nitrites	—	—	—	—	*	0.1	0.1	0.0	0.2	0.1
Hallucinogens	0.1	0.1	0.1	0.1	0.1	0.1	0.1	0.1	0.1	0.1
Hallucinogens, Adjusted	—	—	—	—	0.2	0.2	0.1	0.2	0.2	0.2
LSD	*	*	*	*	*	*	0.1	*	0.1	0.1
PCP	—	—	—	—	0.1	0.1	0.1	0.1	0.1	0.1
Cocaine	0.1	0.1	0.1	0.1	0.2	0.2	0.3	0.2	0.2	0.2
Crack	—	—	—	—	—	—	—	—	—	—
Other Cocaine	—	—	—	—	—	—	—	—	—	—
Heroin	0.1	*	*	*	*	*	*	*	0.1	*
Other Opiates	0.1	0.1	0.2	0.1	*	0.1	0.1	0.1	0.1	0.1
Stimulants	0.5	0.4	0.5	0.5	0.6	0.7	1.2	0.7	0.8	0.6
Crystal Meth. (Ice)	—	—	—	—	—	—	—	—	—	—
Sedatives	0.3	0.2	0.2	0.2	0.1	0.2	0.2	0.2	0.2	0.1
Barbiturates	0.1	0.1	0.2	0.1	*	0.1	0.1	0.1	0.1	*
Methaqualone	*	*	*	*	*	0.1	0.1	0.1	*	*
Tranquilizers	0.1	0.2	0.3	0.1	0.1	0.1	0.1	0.1	0.1	0.1
Alcohol										
Daily	5.7	5.6	6.1	5.7	6.9	6.0	6.0	5.7	5.5	4.8
Been drunk daily	—	—	—	—	—	—	—	—	—	—
5+ drinks in a row/ in last 2 weeks	36.8	37.1	39.4	40.3	41.2	41.2	41.4	40.5	40.8	38.7
Cigarettes										
Daily	26.9	28.8	28.8	27.5	25.4	21.3	20.3	21.1	21.2	18.7
Half-pack or more per day	17.9	19.2	19.4	18.8	16.5	14.3	13.5	14.2	13.8	12.3
Smokeless Tobacco	—	—	—	—	—	—	—	—	—	—
Steroids	—	—	—	—	—	—	—	—	—	—

NOTES: Level of significance of difference between the two most recent classes: s = .05, ss = .01, sss = .001. '—' indicates data not available. '*' indicates less than .05 percent. Any apparent inconsistency between the change estimate and the prevalence estimates for the two most recent classes is due to rounding error.

Source: Johnston, O'Malley & Bachman (1996: 90).

Table 6.1 (*continued*)

				Percent who used daily in last thirty days							
Class of 1985	Class of 1986	Class of 1987	Class of 1988	Class of 1989	Class of 1990	Class of 1991	Class of 1992	Class of 1993	Class of 1994	Class of 1995	'94–'95 change
16,000	15,200	16,300	16,300	16,700	15,200	15,000	15,800	16,300	15,400	15,400	
4.9	4.0	3.3	2.7	2.9	2.2	2.0	1.9	2.4	3.6	4.6	+1.0ss
0.2	0.2	0.1	0.2	0.2	0.3	0.2	0.1	0.1	0.1	0.1	+0.1
0.4	0.4	0.4	0.3	0.3	0.3	0.5	0.2	0.2	—	—	—
0.3	0.5	0.3	0.1	0.3	0.1	0.2	0.1	0.1	0.2	0.2	−0.1
0.1	0.1	0.1	*	0.1	0.1	0.1	0.1	0.1	0.1	0.1	0.0
0.3	0.3	0.2	*	0.3	0.3	0.1	0.1	0.1	—	—	—
0.1	*	0.1	*	*	0.1	0.1	0.1	0.1	0.1	0.1	0.0
0.3	0.2	0.3	0.1	0.2	0.1	0.1	0.1	0.1	0.3	0.3	0.0
0.4	0.4	0.3	0.2	0.3	0.1	0.1	0.1	0.1	0.1	0.2	+0.1
—	—	0.1	0.1	0.2	0.1	0.1	0.1	0.1	0.1	0.1	0.0
—	—	0.2	0.2	0.1	0.1	0.1	*	0.1	0.1	0.1	+0.1
*	*	*	*	0.1	*	*	*	*	*	0.1	0.0
0.1	0.1	0.1	0.1	0.2	0.1	0.1	*	*	0.1	0.1	0.0
0.4	0.3	0.3	0.3	0.3	0.2	0.2	0.2	0.2	0.2	0.3	+0.1
—	—	—	—	—	0.1	0.1	0.1	0.1	*	0.1	0.0
0.1	0.1	0.1	0.1	0.1	0.1	0.1	0.1	0.1	*	0.1	+0.1
0.1	0.1	0.1	*	0.1	0.1	0.1	*	0.1	*	0.1	+0.1
*	*	*	0.1	*	*	*	0.1	0.0	0.1	0.1	0.0
*	*	0.1	*	0.1	0.1	0.1	*	*	0.1	0.1	0.0
5.0	4.8	4.8	4.2	4.2	3.7	3.6	3.4	2.5	—	—	—
								3.4	2.9	3.5	+0.6ss
—	—	—	—	—	—	0.9	0.8	0.9	1.2	1.3	+0.1
36.7	36.8	37.5	34.7	33.0	32.2	29.8	27.9	27.5	28.2	29.8	+1.6
19.5	18.7	18.7	18.1	18.9	19.1	18.5	17.2	19.0	19.4	21.6	+2.2s
12.5	11.4	11.4	10.6	11.2	11.3	10.7	10.0	10.9	11.2	12.4	+1.2
—	4.7	5.1	4.3	3.3	—	—	4.3	3.3	3.9	3.6	−0.4
—	—	—	—	0.1	0.2	0.1	0.1	0.1	0.4	0.2	−0.2

Table 6.2   **Long-Term Trends in *Thirty-Day* Prevalence of Various Types of Drugs for Twelfth Graders**

	Class of 1975	Class of 1976	Class of 1977	Class of 1978	Class of 1979	Class of 1980	Class of 1981	Class of 1982	Class of 1983	Class of 1984
				Percent who used in last thirty days						
Approx. N =	9,400	15,400	17,100	17,800	15,500	15,900	17,500	17,700	16,300	15,900
Any Illicit Drug	30.7	34.2	37.6	38.9	38.9	37.2	36.9	32.5	30.5	29.2
Any Illicit Drug Other Than Marijuana	15.4	13.9	15.2	15.1	16.8	18.4	21.7	17.0	15.4	15.1
Marijuana/Hashish	27.1	32.2	35.4	37.1	36.5	33.7	31.6	28.5	27.0	25.2
Inhalants	—	0.9	1.3	1.5	1.7	1.4	1.5	1.5	1.7	1.9
Inhalants, Adjusted	—	—	—	—	3.2	2.7	2.5	2.5	2.5	2.6
Amyl/Butyl Nitrites	—	—	—	—	2.4	1.8	1.4	1.1	1.4	1.4
Hallucinogens	4.7	3.4	4.1	3.9	4.0	3.7	3.7	3.4	2.8	2.6
Hallucinogens, Adjusted	—	—	—	—	5.3	4.4	4.5	4.1	3.5	3.2
LSD	2.3	1.9	2.1	2.1	2.4	2.3	2.5	2.4	1.9	1.5
PCP	—	—	—	—	2.4	1.4	1.4	1.0	1.3	1.0
Cocaine	1.9	2.0	2.9	3.9	5.7	5.2	5.8	5.0	4.9	5.8
Crack	—	—	—	—	—	—	—	—	—	—
Other Cocaine	—	—	—	—	—	—	—	—	—	—
Heroin	0.4	0.2	0.3	0.3	0.2	0.2	0.2	0.2	0.2	0.3
Other Opiates	2.1	2.0	2.8	2.1	2.4	2.4	2.1	1.8	1.8	1.8
Stimulants	8.5	7.7	8.8	8.7	9.9	12.1	15.8	10.7	8.9	8.3
Crystal Meth. (Ice)	—	—	—	—	—	—	—	—	—	—
Sedatives	5.4	4.5	5.1	4.2	4.4	4.8	4.6	3.4	3.0	2.3
Barbiturates	4.7	3.9	4.3	3.2	3.2	2.9	2.6	2.0	2.1	1.7
Methaqualone	2.1	1.6	2.3	1.9	2.3	3.3	3.1	2.4	1.8	1.1
Tranquilizers	4.1	4.0	4.6	3.4	3.7	3.1	2.7	2.4	2.5	2.1
Alcohol	68.2	68.3	71.2	72.1	71.8	72.0	70.7	69.7	69.4	67.2
Been Drunk	—	—	—	—	—	—	—	—	—	—
Cigarettes	36.7	38.8	38.4	36.7	34.4	30.5	29.4	30.0	30.3	29.3
Smokeless Tobacco	—	—	—	—	—	—	—	—	—	—
Steroids	—	—	—	—	—	—	—	—	—	—

NOTES: Level of significance of difference between the two most recent classes: s = .05, ss = .01, sss = .001. '—' indicates data not available.

Source: Johnston, O'Malley & Bachman (1996: 89).

Table 6.2 *(continued)*

	Class of 1985	Class of 1986	Class of 1987	Class of 1988	Class of 1989	Class of 1990	Class of 1991	Class of 1992	Class of 1993	Class of 1994	Class of 1995	'92-'93 change
Percent who used in last thirty days												
16,000	*15,200*	*16,300*	*16,300*	*16,700*	*15,200*	*15,000*	*15,800*	*16,300*	*15,400*	*15,400*	
29.7	27.1	24.7	21.3	19.7	17.2	16.4	14.4	18.3	21.9	23.8	+1.9
14.9	13.2	11.6	10.0	9.1	8.0	7.1	6.3	7.9	8.8	10.0	+1.2s
25.7	23.4	21.0	18.0	16.7	14.0	13.8	11.9	15.5	19.0	21.2	+2.2s
2.2	2.5	2.8	2.6	2.3	2.7	2.4	2.3	2.5	2.7	3.2	+0.5
3.0	3.2	3.5	3.0	2.7	2.9	2.6	2.5	2.8	2.9	3.5	+0.6
1.6	1.3	1.3	0.6	0.6	0.6	0.4	0.3	0.6	0.4	0.4	0.0
2.5	2.5	2.5	2.2	2.2	2.2	2.2	2.1	2.7	3.1	4.4	+1.3sss
3.8	3.5	2.8	2.3	2.9	2.3	2.4	2.3	3.3	3.2	4.6	+1.4sss
1.6	1.7	1.8	1.8	1.8	1.9	1.9	2.0	2.4	2.6	4.0	+1.4sss
1.6	1.3	0.6	0.3	1.4	0.4	0.5	0.6	1.0	0.7	0.6	−0.1
6.7	6.2	4.3	3.4	2.8	1.9	1.4	1.3	1.3	1.5	1.8	+0.3
—	—	1.3	1.6	1.4	0.7	0.7	0.6	0.7	0.8	1.0	+0.2
—	—	4.1	3.2	1.9	1.7	1.2	1.0	1.2	1.3	1.3	0.0
0.3	0.2	0.2	0.2	0.3	0.2	0.2	0.3	0.2	0.3	0.6	+0.3sss
2.3	2.0	1.8	1.6	1.6	1.5	1.1	1.2	1.3	1.5	1.8	+0.3
6.8	5.5	5.2	4.6	4.2	3.7	3.2	2.8	3.7	4.0	4.0	0.0
—	—	—	—	—	0.6	0.6	0.5	0.6	0.7	1.1	+0.4
2.4	2.2	1.7	1.4	1.6	1.4	1.5	1.2	1.3	1.8	2.3	+0.5s
2.0	1.8	1.4	1.2	1.4	1.3	1.4	1.1	1.3	1.7	2.2	+0.5ss
1.0	0.8	0.6	0.5	0.6	0.2	0.2	0.4	0.1	0.4	0.4	0.0
2.1	2.1	2.0	1.5	1.3	1.2	1.4	1.0	1.2	1.4	1.8	+0.4s
65.9	65.3	66.4	63.9	60.0	57.1	54.0	51.3	51.0	—	—	—
								48.6	50.1	51.3	+1.2
—	—	—	—	—	—	31.6	29.9	28.9	30.8	33.2	+2.4
30.1	29.6	29.4	28.7	28.6	29.4	28.3	27.8	29.9	31.2	33.5	+2.3s
—	11.5	11.3	10.3	8.4	—	—	11.4	10.7	11.1	12.2	+1.1
—	—	—	—	0.8	1.0	0.8	0.6	0.7	0.9	0.7	−0.2

society" [p. 50; see also Glassner & Loughlin (1987) and Macdonald (1984)]. In other words, when attention is focused on a more accurate indicator of serious abuse (such as daily use within the last 30 days, instead of on *any* use within the last year or even 30 days) the percentages of adolescents reporting frequent use are much lower and much less alarming.

These self-report figures, however, must be considered cautiously due to the question of respondent representativeness in the MTF. Specifically, MTF data represent the responses from individuals who were attending high school at the time of the survey. This ignores the fact that many youths drop out of school. Dropping out is especially great in the inner city, where the drug trade appears to be most concentrated. Johnston et al. (1987) point out that roughly 15 to 20 percent of students drop out and are not included in the senior survey each year; moreover, they contend that dropouts tend to use drugs more often than those who remain in school. This suggests that the data underreports the level of drug use in the population. Given this caveat, the MTF data are useful from the point of view that the survey is conducted annually and provides a standardized set of data that can be compared over time.

Table 6.3   **1996 Teen Drug Use According to Two Surveys: National Household Survey on Drug Abuse and Monitoring the Future Study**
(percentages of respondents reporting use in three time periods)

1. National Household Survey (Youths aged 12 to 17):

Drug	Ever Used	Past Year	Past Month
Any illicit drug	22.1	16.7	9
Marijuana	16.8	13	7.1
Cocaine	1.9	1.4	0.6
Crack	0.7	0.4	0.2
Heroin	0.5	0.3	na
Any psycho- therapeutic use	6.8	4.7	1.9
Alcohol	38.8	32.7	18.8
Cigarettes	36.3	24.2	18.3
Smokeless Tobacco	10	4.6	1.9

Source: Substance Abuse and Mental Health Services Administration, 1997

2. Monitoring the Future Study (High School Seniors):

Drug	Lifetime	Past Year	Past Month
Any illicit drug	50.8	40.2	24.6
Marijuana	44.9	35.8	21.9
Cocaine	7.1	4.9	2.0
Crack	3.3	2.1	1.0
Heroin	1.8	1.0	0.5
Alcohol	79.2	72.5	50.8
Been drunk	61.8		
Cigarettes	63.5	na	34.0
Smokeless tobacco	29.8	na	9.8

Source: Monitoring the Future Study Website: *http://www.isr.umich.edu/src/mtf/*

Table 6.3 presents the 1996 update for the Monitoring the Future Study and similar information from the National Household Survey on Drug Abuse. The figures from the National Household Survey are lower because they reflect drug use among a sample of youths age 12 to 17 years, whereas we have included only the data on high school seniors from the Monitoring the Future Survey. (The complete Monitoring the Future Survey includes data for eighth- and tenth-graders, as well as college students and young adults. It can be accessed at *http://www.isr.umich.edu/src/mtf/*. The website includes a press release of the 1997 data indicating that 42.4 percent of seniors used an illicit drug some time in the past year and 26.2 percent used one in the past month.)

Various researchers have argued that the level of drug use is much greater if one considers more representative samples of youths and samples of inner-city residents. Fagan and Pabon (1990) report much higher levels of drug use among inner-city youths, especially school dropouts. Based on the use of any illicit drug, they note that 30 percent of school students and 54 percent of high school dropouts report drug use in the past year. Similarly high numbers (12% and 31%, respectively) are reported for cocaine, heroin and phencyclidine (PCP) use. Altschuler and Brounstein (1991), in a study of minority youths in Washington, DC, note that while 6 percent of in-school respondents claim drug use in the past year, 31 percent of the out-of-school respondents make the same claim. Finally, Inciardi, Horowitz and Pottieger (1993) note that among inner-city Miami youths, 64 percent use cocaine daily and 82 percent use marijuana daily. Studies such as these illustrate the biased nature of the MTF results, which exclude dropouts. At the same time, however, dropout samples are similarly biased toward portraying drug use in its most negative light. Summary data for the Denver, Rochester and Pittsburgh youth studies, which are not based exclusively on school samples but are focused on large cities, reveal that by age 16 more than one-half of the youths regularly use alcohol and one-fourth regularly use marijuana (Huizinga, Loeber & Thornberry, 1994). Conversely, less than 10 percent of the youths regularly use any other drug.

Self-report figures, even those based on samples from high-crime areas, suggest that the drug problem has been blown out of proportion. The data show that the use of illicit drugs is not rampant in society. Relatively few individuals use illicit drugs with even the grossest measure of regularity (within 30 days). Figures for daily use fall to almost zero for most illicit drugs. This does not mean that adolescent drug use is not a problem. Indeed, any use of an illicit drug by juveniles is a problem. What is noteworthy is the fact that the drug problem has been exaggerated. Relatively few youths use drugs on a regular basis, although many may experiment at some point in their lives. A more important question may be: To what extent does drug use cause further deviance? Alternative sources of data are needed to shed light on this question.

The Extent of Drug Use Among Offenders

While information on the general population suggests that drug use is not a major problem and that relatively few youths use drugs on a regular basis, data based on offenders presents a different picture. Various data sources suggest that drug use is a critical problem for offenders, including adolescents. One source for information on drug use among offenders is the **Drug Use Forecasting (DUF) program**.

The DUF program collects drug use data through a combination of self-reports and urinalyses from arrested subjects. The program began in New York City in 1987 and there were 23 cities participating in the program as of 1996. Arrestees voluntarily agree to be interviewed and give a urine sample for testing. The urinalysis tests for 10 different drugs (cocaine, opiates, marijuana, PCP, methadone, benzodiazepine [Valium], methaqualone, propoxyphene [Darvon], barbiturates and amphetamines). All interviews and tests are anonymous. While the DUF program did not originally target youths, 12 sites have expanded their procedures to include data on youthful offenders. Table 6.4 presents 1996 data for male and female arrestees age nine through 18 in the juvenile DUF sites.

Table 6.4   **Drug Use among Juvenile Arrestees in 12 Sites (Percentages)**

Site	Any Drug	Cocaine	Marijuana
Birmingham	55	9	53
Cleveland	63	12	62
Denver	61	7	60
Indianapolis	44	6	43
Los Angeles	57	13	51
Phoenix	56	13	52
Portland	38	3	36
St. Louis	56	4	56
San Antonio	50	10	48
San Diego	53	5	48
San Jose	46	4	41
Washington, DC	67	4	65

Source: National Institute of Justice (1997).

These DUF results show that drug use is very common among youthful arrestees. Urinalysis reveals that about one-half of all male juvenile arrestees test positive for recent use of any drug (24 to 48 hours for all drugs except marijuana, which has a 30-day test period). For any drug, positive tests range from 38 percent in Portland to 67 percent in Washington, DC. For cocaine, positive tests range from 3 percent in Portland to 13 percent in both Los Angeles and Phoenix. For marijuana, positive tests range from 36 percent in Portland to 65 percent in Washington, D.C. Marijuana is the most prevalent individual drug in almost every city according to test results. DUF data also show that drug use is highest among members of minority groups (National Institute of Justice, 1997).

Marijuana use increased sharply and cocaine use increased slightly in 1996. The median rate of testing positive on a marijuana urinalysis for juvenile males was 52 percent in 1996, versus 41 percent in 1995 (National Institute of Justice, 1997).

Besides information from the DUF program, drug use among adolescent offenders also can be gauged through self-reports of incarcerated individuals. Table 6.5 presents drug use information for youths in public institutions. Of the offenders sent to state training schools, about 55 percent drank alcohol regularly (once a week or more for at least a month) and 60 percent report that they used an illegal drug on a regular basis prior to the commitment offense (Beck, Kline & Greenfeld, 1988: 7). More than 20 percent said they had been using cocaine regularly, 12 percent had been using LSD regularly and 5 percent had been using heroin regularly. Likewise, almost one-half of the juveniles were under the influence of alcohol or drugs at the time of the offense that resulted in their commitment to a state training school (Beck, Kline & Greenfeld, 1988: 8).

Table 6.5   **Use of Illegal Drugs by Youth in Long-Term, State-Operated Juvenile Institutions (Percentages)**

Type of drug	Ever used drugs	Used regularly	Under influence at time of offense
Any drug	83	63	39
Marijuana	81	59	30
Cocaine	46	22	13
Amphetamines	36	16	6
LSD	29	12	7
Barbiturates	27	9	3
PCP	23	9	5
Quaaludes	15	3	1
Heroin	13	5	3

Source: Beck, Kline & Greenfeld (1988).

Drug use and abuse appear to start early among institutionalized youths. One-third of the incarcerated juveniles and young adults surveyed began use between the ages of 12 and 13. Regular use (at least once a week for at least a month) began during the same ages. First use of a *major* drug, however, most often took place between the ages of 14 and 15 (Beck, Kline & Greenfeld, 1988).

The use of illicit drugs by incarcerated youths also can be looked at from the point of view of the commitment offense. That is, for what reason has the youth been incarcerated? Based on a national one-day count of juvenile facilities in 1995, 9 percent of the youths in public facilities and 13 percent of those in private facilities were there due to drug-related offenses. [This excludes alcohol, which accounted for an additional 1 percent of the youths in public facilities and an additional 2 percent of those in private facilities (Sickmund, Snyder

& Poe-Yamagata, 1997).] Data from six states participating in the testing of a new data collection effort found that the rate of incarceration for drug offenses ranged from a low of 5 percent in Illinois to a high of 31 percent in New Jersey (Krisberg & DeComo, 1993). Thus, data on commitment offenses provides support to the argument that youthful drug use is highly related to contact with the juvenile justice system.

Similar high rates of drug use are found for incarcerated adult populations. Innes (1988), studying state correctional inmates, reports that 43 percent claim daily or near daily use of a drug in the month preceding the incarceration offense. Roughly one-fifth report using heroin, methadone, cocaine, PCP or LSD. Perhaps more illuminating is the fact that more than one-third of the inmates were under the influence of a drug at the time of their offense. Innes (1988) also points out that the number of prior convictions is directly related to the use of major illicit drugs.

It must be remembered that statistics on institutionalized delinquents represent a worst-case scenario. These youths are not indicative of the majority of juveniles in the population and, therefore, the drug use figures are not applicable to noninstitutionalized youths. Indeed, this information reflects only those individuals who are caught by the system. It is possible that the use of drugs increases the risk of apprehension. In addition, the figures for incarcerated youths deal only with use at some point in the past; they do not consider current use. Additionally, the type of drug used is an important fact to consider. Although 39 percent of institutionalized youths are reportedly under the influence of a drug at the time of their offense, the overwhelming proportion of these are under the influence of marijuana rather than a "major drug" (Beck, Kline & Greenfeld, 1988). Thus, even the statistics for institutionalized youths do not support the claim that delinquents are addicted to major drugs at the time of their offenses.

Teenage boys smoking cigarettes. Status offenses, such as smoking cigarettes and drinking alcohol, make up a large part of the work of the juvenile justice system. *Photo: Jennie Woodcock; Reflections Photolibrary/Corbis*

To put offender drug use statistics in perspective, it is helpful to compare offender and nonoffender use. Using the most recent available data on use in the past month (the month prior to commitment offense, for incarcerated juveniles), 9 percent of youths age 12 to 17, 25 percent of high school seniors and 58 percent of incarcerated offenders report use of any illicit drug. Almost 30 percent of incarcerated offenders report use of a major drug (heroin, cocaine, LSD or PCP). This is much higher than the rate of nonoffenders. While the drug problem is not limited to incarcerated offenders, it is clearly greater for those individuals.

A Summary of Youthful Drug Use

The fact that relatively few youths use drugs, particularly on a regular basis, does not mean that adolescent drug use is not a problem. At the same time, high levels of drug use by offending youths do not mean that use is a rampant problem in society. Rather, these figures point out that drugs are used by a small but significant number of youths, particularly by offenders, and that the problem needs to be addressed. The problem of illicit drug use includes two recent concerns. First, illicit drug use by high school students in the United States is more extensive than in other industrialized countries (Johnston, O'Malley & Bachman, 1996). Second, drug use has been increasing in the last few years. Clearly, any use of illicit drugs by juveniles is a concern. Such use becomes a greater issue if it engenders further delinquent behavior. The degree to which drug use causes delinquency, however, has been the subject of much debate.

The Drugs-Delinquency Connection

Statistics showing drug use among delinquent youths (particularly incarcerated individuals) are often pointed to as proof that drug use causes delinquency. The evidence on the drugs-delinquency connection, however, is unclear. A variety of studies note that there is a high degree of correspondence between drug use and delinquent/criminal behavior (Anglin & Speckart, 1986; Ball, Shaffer & Nurco, 1983; Bennett & Wright, 1984b; Fagan, Weis & Cheng, 1990; Greenbaum, 1994; Huizinga, Menard & Elliott, 1989; Inciardi, Horowitz & Pottieger, 1993; Johnson et al., 1991; McBride, 1981; Newcomb & Bentler, 1988). What is not clear is which one causes which, or whether they are both the result of something else.

Possible Relationships

The actual relationship between drug use and delinquency can take a variety of forms. White (1990) outlines four possible relationships. First, *drug use may cause delinquent activity*. This argument typically focuses on the high cost of drugs and the need for youths to commit property crimes in order to secure the funds needed to buy drugs. Indeed, various authors point out that drug users often are involved in property offenses (Anglin & Speckart, 1988; Chaiken & Chaiken, 1982; Collins, Hubbard & Rachal, 1985; Johnson et al.,

1985; National Institute of Justice, 1990). Such an "economic need" argument, however, is only one reason why drug use would cause other forms of deviance. Goldstein (1989) suggests that drugs also may cause crime through their psychopharmacological effects and through systemic violence inherent in the drug market. **Psychopharmacological explanations** suggest that drugs have a direct effect, either physically or psychologically, that impel the user to act in a certain way. **Systemic violence** refers to violence due to factors such as competition between dealers, retaliation for the sale of bad drugs, the simple need to obtain a drug or other factors related to the sale and marketing of drugs.

A second approach to the drugs-delinquency relationship is the view of *delinquent activity as the cause of drug use* (White, 1990). This line of reasoning argues that delinquency leads to association with deviant peers and that it is within these peer groups that drug use appears (Akers et al., 1979; Elliott, Huizinga & Ageton, 1985; Johnston, O'Malley & Eveland, 1978; Kandel, 1973). This explanation views drug use as a form of deviance just like other delinquent acts. As youths associate with others who are involved in deviant behavior, they will participate in the same activities as the other youths. If the group is using drugs, the individual will be more prone to use drugs.

A third possible relationship views drug use and delinquency feeding one another in a **reciprocal relationship**. This approach is a combination of the first two. The final possibility is that *the relationship between drug use and delinquency may be spurious*. If a relationship is **spurious**, there would be other factors that cause both drug use and delinquency. In essence, the theoretical explanations for why a youth becomes involved in delinquency would also apply to the reasons for drug use. Drug use and delinquency are simply two manifestations of the same basic problems. Identifying which of the four possible relationships between drug use and delinquency is correct is not an easy task. Most attempts have focused on uncovering the time-order between the two variables. That is, which came first, drug use or delinquency?

Research on the Drugs-Delinquency Relationship

DELINQUENCY CAUSES DRUG USE

Research on the temporal (time) order of drug use and delinquency reveals a complex relationship. A variety of studies suggest that the dominant direction in the relationship is from delinquent activity to drug use. Based on a study using longitudinal data on almost 2,000 high school graduates, Johnston and associates (1978) claim that general delinquency predates most drug use. They argue that youthful drug use is an extension of other deviant behavior. This same pattern of drug use following delinquency is uncovered by Inciardi, Horowitz and Pottieger (1993) in a study of the behavior of serious inner-city delinquents. They claim that drug use most often appears after youths have become involved in minor delinquency. Other authors (Huba & Bentler, 1983; Johnston, O'Malley & Eveland, 1986; Kandel, Simcha-Fagan & Davies, 1986; Speckart & Anglin, 1985) also note that delinquent behavior predates actual drug use. That is, the youths commit delinquent acts, join up with other delinquent peers and enter into drug use along with their peers.

Data from the National Youth Survey (NYS) support this basic argument. Launched in 1976, the NYS is a longitudinal panel study of youths. Information on delinquency, drug use and demographic factors is collected on a yearly basis from the same youths. The use of a panel design allows for the inspection of changes in behavior over time and the identification of the temporal order in the data. Elliott, Huizinga and Ageton (1985) note that minor delinquency and tobacco use typically precede the use of alcohol and other drugs. Similarly, Huizinga, Menard and Elliott (1989) show a general progression from minor delinquency to alcohol use, Index offending, marijuana use and polydrug use, in that order. With the exception of alcohol, the data show that drug use temporally follows more general delinquent behavior. From these studies, drug use is a product rather than a cause of deviant behavior.

DRUG USE CAUSES DELINQUENCY

Other studies argue that there is an opposite direction in the relationship—that drug use precedes and causes delinquency or crime. Ball and associates (1983) report that heroin addicts commit four to six times as many offenses when they are actively using drugs than when they are not using drugs. Based on subjects in public drug treatment programs, Collins, Hubbard and Rachal (1985) point out that daily heroin/cocaine users tend to commit substantially more property offenses than nonusers or weekly users. Anglin and Hser (1987) and Anglin and Speckart (1988) note that both official and self-reported criminal activity, particularly property offenses and drug possession/sales, increase with narcotics use. Other studies report a similar trend of elevated criminality during periods of heavy drug use (Nurco et al., 1988; Watts & Wright, 1990).

Two recent analyses also provide support for the argument that drug use precedes delinquency. Huizinga, Loeber and Thornberry (1994), in a summary of the Denver, Pittsburgh and Rochester youth studies, note that changes in the type and level of substance abuse typically precede significant changes in the level of other delinquent activity. This relationship was found for males and females as well as for different age and ethnic groups. This analysis is especially important because of the longitudinal nature of the data and the use of more than a single research site. Inciardi and associates (1993) arrive at similar conclusions in their study of serious delinquents in Miami, Florida. They point out that regular drug use (and often drug sales) precede other forms of delinquent behavior. Further, they note that the mean age of onset for drug use is younger than the mean age of onset for offending. The early onset of drug use also predicts early participation in serious delinquency (Inciardi, Horowitz & Pottieger, 1993).

RECIPROCITY AND SPURIOUSNESS

The fact that no consensus has emerged on the correct causal direction between drug use and delinquency suggests that the more plausible explanation is that the relationship is reciprocal. That is, criminal activity leads to drug use *and* drug use leads to criminal activity. Support for a reciprocal relationship can be found in many of the same studies presented above. A number of authors note that increased drug use by already delinquent or criminal individuals leads to higher delinquency levels or more serious offending, not to a first offense (Anglin & Hser, 1987; Anglin & Speckart, 1988; Collins et al., 1985; Huizinga et al., 1994; Inciardi et al., 1993; Nurco et al., 1988). Similarly, Elliott et al. (1989) point out that while delinquency precedes drug use, polydrug use is a typical precursor of serious persistent delinquency. Van Kammen and Loeber's (1994) analysis of the Pittsburgh youth study data reports that property offending predicted the onset of drug use. At the same time, however, the initiation of drug use was related to escalating participation in personal offenses. From these studies, it would appear that, regardless of which came first, drug use and delinquency contribute to each other. It appears that drug use leads to crime and crime leads to drug use.

Similar to the argument for a reciprocal relationship is the view that posits a spurious relationship between drug use and delinquency. This simply means that drug use and crime are contemporaneous—they exist at the same time and vary in a similar fashion and neither is the ultimate cause of the other. Rather, they are caused by either the same common factors or by different factors. Various authors (Huba & Bentler, 1983; Kandel, Simcha-Fagan & Davies, 1986; White, Pandina & LaGrange, 1987) argue that there are common causal factors, such as peer and school influences, that underlie both delinquency and drug use. Carpenter, et al. (1988) claim that the spurious nature of the drugs-delinquency relationship is evident in the fact that few youths routinely use drugs and commit delinquent acts. They further note that the majority of drug use and delinquent actions occur in the absence of the other behavior. The more plausible argument, therefore, is for a spurious relationship. Similarly, the same analysis of the National Youth Survey data that points out a sequence of behavior beginning with minor offending and ending with polydrug use concludes that the actual cause of the behaviors probably lies with a common set of spurious influences (Huizinga et al., 1989). Other research leads to the same conclusion (Collins, 1989; Elliott, Huizinga & Ageton, 1985; Fagan & Weis, 1990; Fagan, Weis & Cheng, 1990; Loeber, 1988; White, 1990).

SUMMARIZING THE RELATIONSHIP

The fact that drug use is related to delinquency cannot be disputed. While the causal relationship is unclear, a strong correlation between the two behaviors means that drug use can be used as a predictor of other delinquent behavior (Elliott & Huizinga, 1984; Kandel et al., 1986; Newcomb & Bentler, 1988). The research also suggests that each behavior contributes to the other, thereby providing insight for intervention and treatment. It may be possible to attack delinquency by attacking drug use. Drug use in itself is a delinquent act that can bring about action by the juvenile justice system. By acting on it the system is intervening in the lives of youths who are at a higher risk of participating in other delinquent activities.

Interventions

Interventions aimed at drug use and abuse can take a variety of forms and fall under the general categories of treatment and prevention. Treatment programs typically are aimed at those individuals who already have established a pattern of continued drug use. In essence, treatment programs are geared toward addicted individuals. Four general types of treatment programs can be outlined: (1) maintenance programs, (2) detoxification programs, (3) therapeutic communities, and (4) outpatient drug-free programs. Prevention programs are geared more at keeping individuals from initial involvement with drugs or, at the least, deterring casual users from more frequent and varied drug use. Drug prevention programs for juveniles often include a variety of approaches, such as information dissemination, affective education, and resistance and social skills training. Each of the various treatment and prevention approaches will be examined below.

Treatment Approaches

What is known about the impact of drug treatment programs comes mainly from the study of programs focusing primarily on adults. This is because there have been relatively few studies of treatment programs for youths and because most juvenile interventions take a more preventive approach. While each form of treatment (maintenance programs, therapeutic communities, outpatient drug-free programs and detoxification programs) has a different emphasis, many similarities and common features appear across the programs. For example, counseling and therapy of one sort or another appear in virtually all of the programs.

MAINTENANCE AND DETOXIFICATION PROGRAMS
Maintenance programs seek to establish a steady state in which the individual does not experience withdrawal symptoms when the drug begins to wear off. Consequently, the user will be able to function more normally and participate in everyday activities without the constant need for the drug (Stephens, 1987). The most common maintenance program involves the use of methadone, an oral substitute for heroin. Besides periodic checks (usually urinalysis) to establish abstinence from other drugs, maintenance programs rely heavily on individual and group counseling and the establishment of behavioral guidelines (Anglin & Hser, 1990). Some programs attempt to detoxify patients slowly by reducing the drug dosage and weaning the subjects from the need for the drug. Evaluations of maintenance programs generally report reduced drug usage and

the commission of fewer crimes by patients when they are in the program (Anglin & McGlothlin, 1985; Ball et al., 1987; Hser, Anglin & Chou, 1988). Unfortunately, the impact of these programs tends not to survive beyond program participation. That is, patients return to preprogram levels of drug use and criminal activity if they leave the program (Anglin et al., 1989; McGlothlin & Anglin, 1981).

Often closely aligned with maintenance programs are programs that emphasize **detoxification**. This approach attempts to remove an individual from an addiction by weaning him or her off drugs. Drugs are used over a short period to minimize the pain and discomfort of withdrawal. Detoxification programs target a wide range of drugs, from alcohol to heroin, and can be found in many hospitals and facilities throughout the country. Anglin and Hser (1990) point out that while short-term follow-ups show that detoxification is successful at eliminating drug use, detoxification has not been adequately evaluated over the long-term. Unfortunately, some drug users rely on detoxification to reduce the need for massive amounts of drugs to get high. They then return to more normal drug use until they again reach a point at which small amounts are no longer sufficient to serve their needs (Bellis, 1981).

Evaluations of both maintenance and detoxification programs are somewhat mixed. Sells and Simpson (1979) note that they are effective at lowering arrests and illegal activities among juvenile drug abusers. Other positive support is found in the fact that criminal activity is lower among drug users in treatment than among those receiving no intervention (Kaplan 1983; Wish, Toborg & Bellassai 1988). Critics, however, allege that these programs are crutches that do not solve the problem, but instead lead to a nonproductive lifestyle of methadone, alcohol, other drugs and petty crime (Stephens, 1987). An additional problem is that many maintenance drugs become simple substitutes for the original drug. A prime example of this is the fact that heroin was developed to solve morphine addiction. Today, instead of curing heroin addiction, methadone addiction has itself become an issue.

THERAPUETIC COMMUNITIES AND OUTPATIENT PROGRAMS

Another major form of treatment, **therapeutic communities**, emphasizes the provision of a supportive, highly structured, family-like atmosphere within which individuals can be helped to alter their personality and develop social relationships conducive to conforming behavior (Anglin & Hser, 1990). Group sessions, called "games," often involve attention on one member because he or she is a new member of the therapeutic community, is suspected of violating a house rule or is suspected of using drugs. Pressure is exerted to induce the person to admit the particular problem and the need for support from the group (Stephens, 1987). Group counseling is used to explore the reasons for drug use and to suggest alternative methods for dealing with the factors that lead to substance abuse. Therapeutic communities, such as Synanon, Daytop Village and Phoenix House, boast positive results—including lower levels of drug use and criminal activity (Anglin & Hser, 1990; Coombs, 1981; DeLeon, 1984; DeLeon & Rosenthal, 1989). Encouraging for criminal justice audiences is

Lipton's conclusion that prison-based therapeutic communities "can produce significant reductions in recidivism rates . . . and to show consistency of such results over time" (Lipton, 1995: 51). It is important to note, however, that even successful programs do not prevent all crime, eliminate all drugs or graduate all of their initial clients. In a successful program in Delaware, for example, of the group that received 12 to 15 months of in-prison treatment followed by six months of aftercare drug treatment and job training, 76 percent were drug-free and 71 percent were arrest-free (Inciardi, 1996). This means that approximately one-quarter of the offenders who completed treatment had problems. In a California program, only 28 percent of the offenders completed the program *and* aftercare, and 22 percent dropped out prior to completing the program (Lipton, 1995).

The final treatment modality, **outpatient drug-free programs**, often follows the same basic approach as that found in therapeutic communities. The greatest difference is the lack of a residential component. Individual and group counseling form the cornerstone of these programs, though treatment professionals may participate with the clients. Programs such as Alcoholics Anonymous bring together current and former addicts to help one another stay off drugs. At meetings, members recount their drug histories and how the group is supporting them in their efforts to abstain from drug use. Other components of outpatient programs may include social skills training, vocational programming, social interaction, referral to other sources of assistance and possibly short-term drug maintenance (Anglin & Hser, 1990). Evaluating these programs is difficult due to the fact that these programs are more likely to suffer from client mortality than other interventions (Anglin & Hser, 1990). Hubbard and associates (1984) note that the results of evaluations based only on those individuals who remain in a treatment may have artificially high success rates.

TREATMENT SUMMARY

There are several problems with the various treatment approaches. First, it is often difficult to motivate addicts and abusers to enter a treatment program. Convincing addicts that they have a problem is often half the battle against the problem. Besides getting drug users into programs, it is also difficult to retain them. Studies of therapeutic communities, for example, have indicated that up to 70 percent of those entering such communities drop out before completing the program (Stephens, 1987; see also Lipton, 1995). One solution to the participation problem may entail mandatory participation as an outcome of either criminal or civil litigation. While research suggests that coerced treatment is less effective than voluntary participation (Anglin, 1988; DeLong, 1972; Maddux, 1988), there is evidence that mandatory treatment does lead to reduced drug use (Anglin & McGlothlin, 1984; Hubbard et al., 1989; Leukefeld & Tims, 1988; Visher, 1990). This may be due to the fact that such clients receive more extensive treatment.

Despite various qualifications, all four forms of treatment appear to be effective at reducing the use of and need for drugs (Visher, 1990). In one summary evaluation of all four treatment types, Simpson and Sells (1982) report lower drug use, lower criminal behavior and improved employment status for clients as long as six years after the end of treatment. Nontreatment control clients fared significantly worse. Stephens (1987), however, argues that the proof of treatment's impact is limited. Research on the effectiveness of drug treatment programs suggests that program type may not be all that important (different types of programs may be producing about the same effects) and that treatment programs may be only slightly more effective than no treatment. Thus, Stephens (1987) concludes that maturing out of the addiction cycle may be the most frequent way out of the drug problem. As addicts age, it is simply more difficult physically to be a drug addict. As a result, some addicts find it easier to give up drugs than to continue addiction. Walker is also cautious about the ability of treatment to have much impact on the drug problem. He concludes that treatment is quite effective for those individuals who have decided to quit drugs, but treatment "as a primary strategy, will not reduce the national drug problem" (Walker, 1998: 261).

Prevention Approaches

Numerous interventions try to prevent and control juvenile drug use and abuse. Among the varied approaches are "Just Say No" campaigns, knowledge/education programs, affective education and skills training programs. In many cases interventions tend to employ a range of techniques that tap into more than a single prevention approach.

THE "JUST SAY NO" CAMPAIGN AND SIMILAR PROGRAMS

Former President Ronald Reagan and First Lady Nancy Reagan, many parents and several well-known drug treatment programs share a common belief: drugs are inherently evil and must be avoided at all costs. Thus, both the formal **"Just Say No" campaign** and the informal efforts of many parents are directed at convincing youths of the harmful effects of drugs and the need to abstain from them. A key component of this approach is the emphasis on dealing with peer relationships and interpersonal involvement. Indeed, many authors refer to these approaches as "peer programs."

The "Just Say No" and other peer campaigns are very simple. Primary assumptions are that juvenile drug use develops out of peer interaction and that use occurs mainly in group situations. Children, therefore, are encouraged to make a personal decision in the face of peer influences to refuse any offer to use illicit drugs. Included in this approach is the basic message that drugs are harmful. Many of the media and school efforts convey this message without relying on specific information about the physical, psychological and legal aspects of drug use (Tobler, 1986). Some programs couple this approach with basic information about drugs. The emphasis in the "Just Say No" campaign, however, is on total avoidance of drugs.

The total avoidance of illegal drugs in light of peer pressure through a simple "no" response is somewhat shortsighted. Trebach (1987) compares such a prevention approach to related efforts to tell kids to abstain from any premarital sexual activity. As some children are going to use drugs or engage in sex no matter what adult society says, there is an unrealistic naïveté involved in "Just Say No" and similar campaigns. In addition, there may be a certain amount of hypocrisy associated with a total abstinence crusade. Youths recognize drug use by adults and are influ-

Nancy Reagan greets local members of the "Just Say No" club at the White House. The slogan urges young people to "just say no" when peers pressure them to use drugs. *Photo: UPI/Corbis-Bettman*

enced by the advertising aimed at adults. Some "Just Say No" advocates recognize that kids will use drugs anyway, but justify the approach as a way to convey a message against drugs.

KNOWLEDGE/EDUCATION PROGRAMS

A related approach to "Just Say No" programs is the provision of factual knowledge about drugs and their effects. The **knowledge approach** entails providing youths with information on different types of drugs, such as the physical and psychological effects of the drugs, as well as the extent, impact and possible legal consequences of drug use. In many instances these programs are offered as a part of the normal school curriculum. The basic assumption is that such knowledge will allow the individual to make an informed choice about drug use. It is further assumed that informed youths will opt against using drugs.

Interestingly, evaluations of knowledge/education approaches often suggest that the programs *increase* drug use by participants. What appears to be happening is that the increased knowledge leads to enhanced curiosity and experimentation by youths in a kind of "I want to find out for myself" attitude (Abadinsky, 1989; Botvin, 1990; Botvin & Dusenbury, 1989; Eiser & Eiser, 1988; Hanson, 1980; Kinder, Pape & Walfish, 1980; Swadi & Zeitlin, 1987; Weisheit, 1983). Based on information from 143 prevention programs, Tobler (1986) concluded that knowledge programs fail to show any reductions in drug use behavior. The single point on which these programs can demonstrate success is in their ability to increase subject's knowledge about drugs (Botvin, 1990).

AFFECTIVE APPROACHES

Affective approaches shift attention away from drugs and toward the individual. Rather than provide information about different substances and issues related directly to drug use, affective interventions focus attention on the individual. The assumption is that by building self-esteem, self-awareness and feelings of self-worth, the youth will be able to make wise choices and resist pressures to use drugs. Few programs, however, rely solely on affective education elements. Programs such as Here's Looking at You 2000 (HLAY 2000), which purports to use an affective approach, typically also include drug information and social skills training. Consequently, it becomes difficult to isolate the impact of affective elements such as self-esteem on subsequent drug involvement. Existing evaluations of affective interventions have failed to find any significant impact on substance use (Hansen et al., 1988; Kim, 1988; Kim, McLeod & Shantzis, 1993; Newcomb & Bentler, 1988; Tobler, 1986).

SKILLS TRAINING APPROACHES

Skills training includes a variety of elements, ranging from basic personal and social skills (which deal with general life situations and how to deal with them) to the provision of specific resistance skills aimed directly at substance abuse issues. This approach assumes that individuals who use drugs are poorly prepared to address the issues and pressures involved in daily decisionmaking. For example, individuals who find themselves left out of the societal mainstream due to the lack of education and/or job training need to be taught the skills necessary to obtain a job and succeed in an acceptable manner. Individuals who get into trouble because they simply follow the group need to be taught how to be independent, make decisions for themselves and resist following others into unwise situations. Key resistance skills taught include how to recognize a problematic situation and what alternatives are available to the individual, how to resist outside pressures (such as peers or advertising), how to identify help, how to cope with stress and how to make wise choices.

Research on resistance skills training has shown positive results. Perhaps the best example of this impact comes from a series of studies by Botvin and associates dealing with tobacco, alcohol and marijuana use (Botvin & Dusenbury, 1989; Botvin & Eng, 1980, 1982; Botvin, Eng & Williams, 1980; Botvin et al., 1984; Botvin, Renick & Baker, 1983). In these studies, "life skills training" was successful at reducing the number of youths using all three drugs, particularly tobacco. The only lingering question from the analyses is the impact of skills training over a long period of time. Positive results also appear in an evaluation of an aftercare program for youthful offenders in Washington state (Hawkins et al., 1991). Most of the analyses focused on relatively short-term effects (e.g., six-month follow-up) and there is no evidence that the changes would persist over time without continued intervention.

THE DARE PROGRAM

Perhaps the best-known drug prevention program in existence today is the **Drug Abuse Resistance Education (DARE) program**, which incorporates elements of all the previously discussed approaches to prevention. DARE is a police-taught, school-based program that began in the Los Angeles United School District in 1983. The program is aimed at elementary students in the fifth and sixth grades, although there are companion programs for youths in junior high school and for the parents of participating students (see, e.g., Bureau of Justice Assistance, 1993). Officers participating in the program receive training in the DARE curriculum, in teaching and in adolescent development. The curriculum is set up for delivery as part of the normal school year and is taught in the classroom over 17 weeks. The topics covered in the program (see Box 6.1) reflect aspects of affective training, "Just Say No" approaches, peer resistance and social skills training. The primary focus of the program is on enhancing the social skills of the individual.

Box 6.1   Components of the DARE Curriculum

Personal Safety
Drug Use and Misuse
Consequences of Using or Not Using Drugs
Resisting Pressures to Use Drugs
Resistance Techniques
Building Self-Esteem
Assertiveness Skills
Managing Stress without Drugs
Media Influences on Drug Use
Decisionmaking and Risk-Taking
Alternatives to Drug Use
Role Modeling
Forming Support Systems
Dealing with Gang Pressures
DARE Summary
Taking a Stand
Assembly and Graduation

Based on its widespread adoption by schools in every state, one would assume that the program has proved successful at combating youthful substance use. Indeed, one early evaluation indicated that participation in the DARE program was related to lower levels of subsequent drug use (DeJong, 1987). However, there was no evidence of changes in knowledge, attitudes or expectations about future use. This evaluation, however, suffered from serious methodological problems, including the lack of randomized assignment of subjects to treatment and control groups, the absence of a pretest and the fact that the posttest was conducted immediately after completion of the program.

More methodologically rigorous studies fail to find any significant changes in drug use behavior after participation in DARE. Ringwalt, Ennett and Holt (1991), in a randomized experiment in 20 North Carolina schools, report finding no impact on drug use or the intent to use drugs. Clayton, Catterello and Walden (1991), using data from schools in Lexington, Kentucky, also failed to uncover any impact on participant drug use. Perhaps the one promising outcome of these projects is that both evaluations did uncover changes in attitudes toward drug use and peers that corresponded with the intent of the program. In another evaluation, Rosenbaum and associates (1994) examined data from 36 schools in Illinois that were randomly assigned either to receive the DARE program or to serve as a control. The outcome of their tests show no significant difference in substance use between the experimental and control groups after a one-year follow-up. There is also no change in attitudes or beliefs as a result of program participation (Rosenbaum et al., 1994).

Based on these analyses, it appears that DARE has little or no impact on subsequent drug use. Why then does DARE enjoy such a good reputation, and why should it continue in our schools? The first part of the question can be answered by pointing out that DARE is a relatively nonintrusive intervention that has good intentions and has shown no negative impacts. By using the schools, no specific individuals are singled out or identified. Everyone participates in the program. As part of the educational curriculum, it also gains an immediate legitimacy among students, parents and the public. Perhaps the best reason why DARE should continue in schools is the potential it has for engendering positive changes in attitudes and beliefs among youths toward the school, the police and societal rules. The presence of a police officer in the school for a nonarrest situation opens the door for greater familiarity and understanding between juveniles and the police. It may also produce positive changes in the school environment by promoting other appropriate activities. While the program may not, in itself, bring about major changes in drug use, DARE can contribute to a more general positive school environment that may engender more broad-based changes in attitudes and actions.

A suggestion for modifying DARE comes from Tobler's (1997) meta-analysis of 120 prevention programs. She found that interactive programs were effective, with a mean effect size of .25. Noninteractive programs, such as DARE, however, which used a lecture approach, were ineffective.

A DARE officer stands by her vehicle. While research on the DARE program indicates little change in drug use behavior on the part of participants, the program remains popular—perhaps because it contributes to a more general positive school environment. *Photo: Ellen S. Boyne*

So the content of interactive and noninteractive programs was similar, but the manner of presentation appears to be critical. Perhaps police officers involved in DARE need training in how to use a more participatory style of presentation. Perhaps these programs need to be team-taught by a police officer and a teacher who knows participatory teaching techniques.

PREVENTION SUMMARY

The evidence on prevention programs suggests that drug use can be impacted by certain types of programs. Resistance skills training appears to be the most promising at reducing the level of drug use, although more rigorous and extensive testing needs to be completed. On the other hand, programs based on knowledge provision may result in increased curiosity and experimentation with illicit drugs. Programs that stress self-esteem, self-awareness and interpersonal growth in the absence of specific strategies for dealing with drugs (typically referred to as affective education programs) also fail to exhibit any influence on drug use (Botvin, 1990; Schaps et al., 1986; Tobler, 1986). Interactive programs are more effective than noninteractive programs (Tobler, 1997). In general, most prevention programs are still rather new and need to be evaluated with longer follow-up periods and better research designs (particularly using adequate comparison groups).

Alternative Responses to Drug Use

Responses to drug use do not always reflect treatment or prevention. The persistence of drug use in society over time, particularly coupled with the relative failure of most intervention approaches, has prompted some individuals and groups to propose novel responses. Two controversial responses are Toughlove programs and the legalization or decriminalization of drugs.

TOUGHLOVE

The need for more forceful interventions within the peer approach has inspired **Toughlove** programs. In this approach, parents of youths suspected of drug use are encouraged to employ strong measures. One such program encourages parents to file criminal charges against their children, to lie to their children and/or to force them into residential treatment programs that use dubious methods. In one case, parents told their son that they were taking him to visit his brother who was in a drug treatment program. The family stopped at the reception area of the treatment center and, before the unsuspecting brother knew it, he had "volunteered" himself into the drug treatment program. He was verbally harassed, called an addict (even though he had only participated in some minor experimentation with drugs), was not permitted to use restroom facilities and arguably was brainwashed. He eventually managed to escape from this treatment and find his way home, but his parents had been advised to imprison the adolescent in their home by installing locks on his windows and door. His resistance was met with firm threats to cut off funding for college and by criminal charges (for complete details on this example of the possible abuses of Toughlove approaches, see Trebach, 1987).

Toughlove-type approaches to the drug problem are analogous to the Scared Straight program. They are a search for a panacea: an inexpensive and easy intervention for a more complex problem. The problem of drugs among delinquents and law-abiding youths often represents a personal adaptation to the everyday pressures in American society. Simply avoiding drugs does not eliminate hopelessness for youths in big-city slums, nor does it remove the obsessed craze for material success in the middle and upper classes. Like Scared Straight, however, Toughlove and similar campaigns are appealing because they are cheap and based on traditional American values. Even though it is too early to examine scientific evidence on the effectiveness of such simplistic drug abuse prevention efforts, past experience with Scared Straight–type programs strongly suggests that such programming will have little or no effect on the drug problem.

READY AVAILABILITY OF DRUGS

A proposal at the other end of the political spectrum is the call for the free (or inexpensive) availability of psychoactive drugs. This is a call to legalize or at least to decriminalize the possession of drugs such as heroin and marijuana. Nadelman (1997), for example, argues that drugs should be available on a mail-order basis.

Proponents argue that such action would have several benefits. First, drug addicts would be less likely to suffer adverse health consequences from adulterated drugs or contaminated needles. Second, it could reduce street crime because addicts would not have to steal to obtain the funds to purchase drugs (Goldstein, 1989). Third, it would reduce the possibility of society alienating adolescents. "Youth may generally lose respect for a society that defines them as criminal because they use marijuana" (Stephens, 1987: 119). Fourth, legalization would reduce our law enforcement war on drugs, including the disturbing rates of arrest and incarceration of African-Americans [see comments about Miller (1996) in Chapters 7 and 14].

A major concern with the proposal to legalize drugs is the expectation that drug use would escalate at an alarming rate. Nadelman argues that this is not a problem because most Americans already resist drugs for reasons other than their status as illegal substances. He notes that 70 percent of Americans resist cigarettes and 90 percent either do not use drugs at all or use them in moderation. Nadelman concludes that these percentages suggest that Americans "do not really need drug laws to prevent them from entering into destructive relationships with drugs" (Nadelman, 1997: 287).

Although legalization may be practical for marijuana, it does not seem to be a realistic possibility for many other psychoactive substances. Current attitudes simply do not favor such a liberal approach. For example, even among high school seniors, 72 percent favor current laws against taking heroin in private and

44 percent think that smoking marijuana in private should be prohibited (Johnston, O'Malley & Bachman, 1996). Thus "our value system, rooted in the Protestant ethic, simply will not permit lawmakers to make freely available such powerful mind-altering and euphoria-producing drugs" (Stephens, 1987: 120).

The President's 1997 National Drug Control Strategy reflects the reluctance of political leaders to reduce law enforcement efforts. As shown in Box 6.2, the strategy continues to call for zero tolerance for illicit drug use by youths and for strengthening law enforcement efforts against drugs (Office of National Drug Control Policy, 1997).

Box 6.2 Strategic Goals and Objectives of the 1997 National Drug Control Strategy

Goal 1: Educate and enable America's youth to reject illegal drugs as well as alcohol and tobacco.

Objective 1: Educate parents or other caregivers, teachers, coaches, clergy, health professionals, and business and community leaders to help youth reject illegal drugs and underage alcohol and tobacco use.

Objective 2: Pursue a vigorous advertising and public communications program dealing with the dangers of drug, alcohol, and tobacco use by youth.

Objective 3: Promote zero tolerance policies for youth regarding the use of illegal drugs, alcohol, and tobacco within the family, school, workplace, and community.

Objective 4: Provide students in grades K–12 with alcohol, tobacco, and drug prevention programs and policies that have been evaluated and tested and are based on sound practices and procedures.

Objective 5: Support parents and adult mentors in encouraging youth to engage in positive, healthy lifestyles and modeling behavior to be emulated by young people.

Objective 6: Encourage and assist the development of community coalitions and programs in preventing drug abuse and underage alcohol and tobacco use.

Objective 7: Create a partnership with the media, entertainment industry, and professional sports organizations to avoid the glamorization of illegal drugs and the use of alcohol and tobacco by youth.

Objective 8: Support and disseminate scientific research and data on the consequences of legalizing drugs.

Objective 9: Develop and implement a set of principles upon which prevention programming can be based.

Objective 10: Support and highlight research, including the development of scientific information, to inform drug, alcohol, and tobacco prevention programs targeting young Americans.

Box 6.2, *continued*

Goal 2:   Increase the safety of America's citizens by substantially reducing drug-related crime and violence.

Objective 1: Strengthen law enforcement—including federal, state, and local drug task forces—to combat drug-related violence, disrupt criminal organizations, and arrest the leaders of illegal drug syndicates.

Objective 2: Improve the ability of High Intensity Drug Trafficking Areas (HIDTAs) to counter drug trafficking.

Objective 3: Help law enforcement to disrupt money laundering and seize criminal assets.

Objective 4: Develop, refine, and implement effective rehabilitative programs—including graduated sanctions, supervised release, and treatment for drug-abusing offenders and accused persons—at all stages within the criminal justice system.

Objective 5: Break the cycle of drug abuse and crime.

Objective 6: Support and highlight research, including the development of scientific information and data, to inform law enforcement, prosecution, incarceration, and treatment of offenders involved with illegal drugs.

Goal 3:   Reduce health and social costs to the public of illegal drug use.

Objective 1: Support and promote effective, efficient, and accessible drug treatment, ensuring the development of a system that is responsive to emerging trends in drug abuse.

Objective 2: Reduce drug-related health problems, with an emphasis on infectious diseases.

Objective 3: Promote national adoption of drug-free workplace programs that emphasize drug testing as a key component of a comprehensive program that includes education, prevention, and intervention.

Objective 4: Support and promote the education, training, and credentialing of professionals who work with substance abusers.

Objective 5: Support research into the development of medications and treatment protocols to prevent or reduce drug dependence and abuse.

Objective 6: Support and highlight research and technology, including the acquisition and analysis of scientific data, to reduce the health and social costs of illegal drug use.

Goal 4:   Shield America's air, land, and sea frontiers from the drug threat.

Objective 1: Conduct flexible operations to detect, disrupt, deter, and seize illegal drugs in transit to the United States and at U.S. borders.

Box 6.2, *continued*

Objective 2: Improve the coordination and effectiveness of U.S. drug law enforcement programs with particular emphasis on the southwest border, Puerto Rico, and the U.S. Virgin Islands.

Objective 3: Improve bilateral and regional cooperation with Mexico as well as other cocaine and heroin transit zone countries in order to reduce the flow of illegal drugs into the United States.

Objective 4: Support and highlight research and technology—including the development of scientific information and data—to detect, disrupt, deter, and seize illegal drugs in transit to the United States and at U.S. borders.

Goal 5:   Break foreign and domestic drug sources of supply.

Objective 1: Produce a net reduction in the worldwide cultivation of coca, opium, and marijuana and in the production of other illegal drugs, especially methamphetamine.

Objective 2: Disrupt and dismantle major international drug trafficking organizations and arrest, prosecute, and incarcerate their leaders.

Objective 3: Support and complement source country drug control efforts and strengthen source country political will and drug control capabilities.

Objective 4: Develop and support bilateral, regional, and multilateral initiatives and mobilize international organizational efforts against all aspects of illegal drug production, trafficking, and abuse.

Objective 5: Promote international policies and laws that deter money laundering and facilitate anti–money laundering investigations as well as seizure of associated assets.

Objective 6: Support and highlight research and technology, including the development of scientific data, to reduce the worldwide supply of illegal drugs.

Summary:
The Response of the Juvenile Justice System

The juvenile justice system must face several issues concerning drugs and juvenile offenders. First, many of the delinquents committing the worst and the most frequent crimes have drug problems. Statistics clearly demonstrate that incarcerated offenders tend to have drug problems. It is unclear whether drug use leads to delinquency, delinquency causes drug use, or something else causes both drug use and delinquency. What is clear is that something needs to be done. If state training schools do nothing about the drug problems of their wards, a very likely result is increased drug use and more crime.

The literature on drug treatment and prevention does offer some suggestions for action. As noted above, interactive prevention programs fare better than noninteractive programs. Therapeutic communities have had some success in prison settings, especially when followed by aftercare. Other evaluations, however, find little impact on drug use. It seems that training school officials must continue to search the drug treatment literature for promising avenues to pursue.

The juvenile justice system often attempts to deal with less serious drug users by diverting those youth to other programs. In the past,

> the rehabilitation-oriented juvenile justice system did not deal with the great majority of drug and alcohol users and . . . it handled them with greater leniency than any other category including status offenses (Schneider, 1988: 121).

The problem with diverting drug and alcohol users to voluntary programs is that such actions may lead to net-widening (see Chapter 10). That is, more youths are sent to private programs than really need to be sent. In reaction to this problem, some states, such as Washington, simply opt to divest the juvenile court of its jurisdiction over alcohol and drug users. Unfortunately, such a decision can result in complaints "from disgruntled parents who believed that social control—mandated by the court—was essential for straightening out their children" (Schneider, 1988: 123-124).

From another perspective, a lenient approach to drug use in juvenile court may have some very positive results. Carpenter and her colleagues (1988), for example, think that the New York state youths they studied were fairly typical in terms of experimenting with drugs between the ages of 12 and 15. Thus, their study supports the argument that adolescence is a period of trying out various behaviors, including drug use. Both the adult criminal justice system in New York and the juveniles themselves recognize that at age 16 things change: penalties become harsher. Deterrence appears to work; the adult penalties appear to influence many youths to cease experimentation at age 16. Thus, the conclusion was that "a well-advertised difference in kind and severity between juvenile and adult criminal justice agencies is an effective deterrent to crime for an important segment of the youth population" (Carpenter et al., 1988: 218).

Beyond the problems directly faced by the juvenile justice system, there is the fact that society has failed to take a consistent approach toward drug use. For example, while many drugs are illegal, they are still favored by both youths and adults. This puts parents and drug counselors in a bind. Warnings to avoid drugs completely may fall on unreceptive ears. On the other hand, if a parent or counselor condones some sort of "reasonable" drug use, then this position pits him or her against the prevailing laws and drug policies of the community, even though this option might be the preferred treatment strategy for some youths. Either the advisor takes an authoritarian position that is unrealistically prohibitive, or else the advice offered aids and abets illegal activity (Mandel & Feldman, 1986: 39).

There is also a long-standing effort in American society to label some drugs as dangerous and criminal and others as socially acceptable. Heroin, marijuana, cocaine and other drugs fit the first category. Alcohol, tobacco and some prescription drugs represent the latter. Thus, adults can buy and use alcohol and tobacco with little or no restraint but have to break the law to obtain even extremely small amounts of controlled substances. This societal "schizophrenia" (Hills, 1980) leads to conflicts in attitudes and hypocrisy in enforcement. Many interventions focus on certain drugs (such as heroin, cocaine and marijuana) and ignore the serious problems of alcohol and tobacco abuse. Such slighting occurs even though alcohol and tobacco cause harm to more people than any of the so-called dangerous drugs.

In summary, there are no easy answers to the question of how the juvenile justice system should deal with drug offenders.

> Rather, there are choices among several policies—some of which might produce "too much" social control and others that might result in too little attention to an important and widespread problem among juveniles (Schneider, 1988: 123).

Clear, Clear and Braga (1993) conclude that the criminal and juvenile justice systems must be realistic in their efforts. They take the position that any search for a drug-free society is unrealistic. A more realistic vision is the following:

> The purpose of correctional intervention is to prevent crimes where possible, reduce harms to families and communities where feasible, and take reasonable steps to encourage and assist offenders to forego drug use and related criminal activity. The aim is to reduce, in small measures, the pain experienced by all citizens, offenders and others alike, resulting from drugs in America (Clear, Clear & Braga, 1993: 196).

DISCUSSION QUESTIONS

1. You are asked whether drug use causes delinquency. Discuss the possible relationships between drug use and delinquency and take a position on which one is correct. Justify your position.

2. The state legislature has just appointed you to oversee all treatment and pre-vention programs dealing with drug use. What programs will you keep or institute to fight the drug problem? Why have you selected these programs?

3. Legislation has been proposed to decriminalize drug use in your state. Assuming that this legislation passes, what would you expect to happen to drug use and delinquency? What impact would this have on the juvenile justice system? What other impacts will this have in the state? Provide support for your position.

4. Discuss the goals and objectives of the National Drug Control Strategy (Box 6.2). Which goals and objectives are reasonable? Which are problematic? What was left out of the policy?

5. The local police department seeks to continue its DARE program. Having just completed a degree in criminal justice, you are called upon for advice. What advice would you offer about this issue?

CHAPTER 7

The Police and Juveniles

One of the most important aspects of the juvenile justice system is the interaction between police and juvenile offenders. Often it is the police officer who decides whether a particular juvenile will or will not continue further into the system. In other words, the police are the gatekeepers of the system. They decide whether a juvenile enters the juvenile justice system.

Because the interaction of police and juveniles is so important, this chapter will focus on these two parties. Specifically, it will discuss the police role, police attitudes toward juveniles, youth attitudes toward the police, police discretion, the organization of police work with juveniles, and police use of excessive force with juveniles.

The Police Role

Research and literature on the police have clearly demonstrated that law enforcement and crime fighting make up only part (and often the least frequent part) of the police task. Contrary to the portrayal in many television shows and movies, the police do much more than enforce laws and "fight crime." A typical weekend night in many police departments involves such activities such as warning teenagers not to drag race, assisting drunks in getting home, taking accident reports, handling complaints about loud parties, making traffic stops and assisting sick or injured persons.

One way of categorizing police work is to divide it into three functions: (1) law enforcement, (2) service, and (3) order maintenance tasks. **Law enforcement** refers to enforcing all laws, including traffic, juvenile and criminal laws. Law enforcement includes police actions specifically related to crime prevention or apprehension, such as routine patrol, chasing suspects, arresting suspects and transporting criminal suspects to jail. **Service** functions include the assistance that police provide to citizens in various situations. Examples of service activities include: starting stalled vehicles, calling or escorting ambulances for victims of heart attacks or other critical injuries or illnesses, fetching stray cats out of trees, and many other tasks that citizens expect the police to perform. The simple truth is that police and firefighters are the only civil servants on duty 24 hours per day, seven days per week (President's Commission, 1967a). They are available—or the public thinks they should be availabe—for any and all sorts of predicaments, ranging from the very serious (death) to the almost ridiculous (stray cats) "for the price of a phone call" (Sparrow, Moore & Kennedy, 1990).

The service category, however, is sometimes confused with another major aspect of the police task: order maintenance. **Order maintenance** is James Q. Wilson's term for police intervention in

> behavior that either disturbs or threatens to disturb the public peace or that involves face-to-face conflict among two or more persons. Disorder, in short, involves a dispute over what is "right" or "seemly" conduct or over who is to blame for conduct that is agreed to be wrong or unseemly. A noisy drunk, a rowdy teenager shouting or racing his car in the middle of the night, a loud radio in the apartment next door, a panhandler soliciting money from passersby, persons wearing eccentric clothes and unusual hair styles loitering in public places—all these are examples of behavior which "the public" (an onlooker, a neighbor, the community at large) may disapprove of and ask the patrolman to "put a stop to" (Wilson, 1978: 16).

Wilson used the term **watchman style** to describe a police officer or a department emphasizing order maintenance activities. He used the term **legalistic style** to describe officers or departments emphasizing law enforcement (Wilson, 1978).

One recent textbook on policing concluded that "order maintenance is the primary goal or purpose of policing" (Langworthy & Travis, 1994: 309). Order maintenance functions in policing are of critical concern for several reasons. First, such situations arise frequently, usually more frequently than crime prevention or control situations. Studies point out that order maintenance and service functions account for as much as 80 percent of police activity (Lab, 1984b;

Wilson, 1968). Second, these situations have the potential to erupt into criminal activity. Disputes over everyday matters can very easily eventuate in assaults or even homicides. Third, police exercise a great deal of discretion in handling such situations. To put it bluntly, order maintenance situations involve employees at the lowest level of the police organization—patrol officers—acting in critical situations with disputants who often do not trust or particularly like the police (Wilson, 1978).

In recent years many observers have begun to view the police role as one of **problem-solving** (Goldstein, 1990; Sparrow, Moore & Kennedy, 1990; Toch & Grant, 1991). Such observers argue that, rather than react to situations, the police can and should try to take proactive steps to solve the problems they encounter. In other words, these observers contend that the police must do more than simply arrest suspects. Arresting offenders is a "Band-Aid" approach to symptoms of urban problems that does nothing to address the underlying causes. If the police, however, focus on **problem-oriented policing**, addressing social problems such as delinquency, domestic violence, vagrancy and drugs, their actions may

> mean the difference between a city in which neighborhoods are lost to drugs and one in which they are not; between a city in which the streets look and feel secure and one in which they do not; between a city in which domestic disputes are quelled before wives are killed, and runaways housed before pimps reel them in, and one in which both are lost to violence and degradation. As the crack epidemic has shown . . . it can even mean the difference between the rule of law and vigilante violence (Sparrow, Moore & Kennedy, 1990: 6).

A variation of problem-oriented policing is **community policing**. Langworthy and Travis describe community policing as problem-oriented policing "with a twist" (1994: 257). They see both problem-oriented policing and community policing as addressing underlying causes of problems related to crime. In problem-oriented policing, the police define the problems; in community policing, "the police rely on the community to define problems and establish police policy" (Langworthy & Travis, 1994: 257). Box 7.1 lists tasks considered appropriate under the traditional (professional) model of policing and tasks considered appropriate under the newer community policing model. Note that a community policing model adds many tasks.

Policing Juveniles

For the purposes of this book, it is important to note that much of police work with juveniles involves either order maintenance or service activities rather than the enforcement of criminal behavior. For example, Werthman and Piliavin's (1967) classic study of one police juvenile bureau found that 90 percent of the offenses for which juveniles were arrested were *minor* offenses and

Box 7.1   Traditional (Professional) Policing versus Community Policing

Traditional Tasks:

• Patrolling

• Responding to calls [Example: talking to a woman who said that the boys renting the house next door had loud parties, threw garbage on their lawn and urinated out the windows (Livermore, 1971)]

• Field interrogations

• Traffic stops [stopping drivers suspected of breaking motor vehicle laws including Driving While Intoxicated laws]

• Accident investigations

• Assisting ambulance/emergency medical service calls

• Delinquency prevention [Example: operation of police athletic leagues that provide sports and recreation for at-risk teens]

Community Policing/Problem-Oriented Policing Tasks:

• Solving problems [Example: studying convenience store robberies and determining that staffing (only one cashier), lighting and blocked windows contribute to the problem (Trojanowicz et al., 1998)]

• Interacting with other agencies to solve underlying problems [Example: in Kansas City, starting a food delivery service to bring pizza and other types of food to neighborhoods where well-known national chains refuse to do so (Geller, 1998)]

• Dealing with signs of urban decay ("broken windows") [Example: dispersing groups of teenagers because they cause others to be fearful of crime. In New York City the police opted for zero tolerance of quality-of-life problems such as "squeegee boys" who would clean your windshield and demand payment]

• Interacting with residents [establishing rapport in the hope that citizens will share information about potential trouble spots]

• Chairing community meetings [Block Clubs, Neighborhood Watch Groups, etc.]

• Advocating concerns of neighborhoods [see Bazemore & Senjo, 1997]

• Enforcing city ordinances such as Public Health Codes to eliminate crack houses

• Playing basketball with delinquent youths in a neighborhood residential facility (Bazemore & Senjo, 1997)

Box 7.1, *continued*

- Gang prevention [Example: a Scared Straight program in Pennsylvania (Hsia, 1997)]

- Identifying hot spots of gang-related violence and then targeting the area with enforcement (Decker, Pennell & Caldwell, 1997)

- Picking up truants and taking them to truancy centers that contact the parents and provide counseling (Garry, 1996)

- Establishing a curfew during school hours so that police can question suspected truants and parents may be fined up to $100 (Garry, 1996)

- Knocking on doors and asking for permission to search juvenile's rooms for weapons (St. Louis)

that much of the juvenile bureau's job involved order maintenance. In 1996, juveniles were involved in 19 percent of violent crime index arrests, 35 percent of property crime index arrests, but 44 percent of vandalism arrests, 26 percent of disorderly conduct arrests and 23 percent of liquor law arrests. Juveniles accounted for 13 percent of violent crime clearances and 23 percent of property crime clearances (Snyder, 1997). Thus, a police officer who comes in contact with a juvenile may be dealing with violent or property crime but is often trying to disperse a group of rowdy teenagers (a "gang," in the eyes of some adult observers) or to quiet down a party in response to an adult's complaint of "too much noise." However, this attempt to handle the situation or maintain order (in Wilson's terminology) can result in very serious consequences for teens (e.g., being taken into custody, petitioned to court, adjudicated delinquent, and incarcerated in a state training school).

To show how a problem-oriented solution might work in policing juveniles, Eck and Spelman (1987) cite the example of juveniles being rowdy when leaving a skating rink at closing time on weekends. Traditional police practice would entail sending officers to the rink at closing time to warn the juveniles to stop on threat of arrest. A problem-solving approach, however, would entail the police taking time to explore the problem and find that there is a transportation problem at closing time. Discussions with the owner could lead to leasing more buses so that the youths can get home at closing time. With this approach police analyze and solve a problem instead of wasting resources every weekend on a temporary, "Band-Aid" approach. Although problem solving has not yet received adequate empirical support, it does seem to be a promising strategy (Sherman, 1995).

Community policing proponents envision a broad role for the police in dealing with juveniles. Trojanowicz et al. (1998) state that the police first must combat child abuse by looking for it, investigating it and linking families to

Much police work with juveniles involves service activities. In problem-oriented policing, the police attempt to take proactive steps to solve any problems they encounter. *Photo: Mark C. Ide*

agencies who can help. Second, the police must conduct surveys to determine where high levels of violence exist and then use enforcement, education and community mobilization to fight it. Third, the police must be active in community efforts to provide adequate recreational and cultural activities to area juveniles. Fourth, the police must work with schools to reduce school crime and violence and problems of drug abuse. One specific suggestion is greater police investigation of school incidents compared to school officials making insufficient investigations. Fifth, the police need to make accurate identification of gangs and gang members and then implement both enforcement and prevention activities.

Administrative Tasks in Policing

Another comment about the police role is that part of policing involves administrative tasks. Police officers must fill out reports, appear in court, attend meetings and participate in a variety of other tasks. These actions can take up a considerable portion of an officer's time and can subtract some of the time available for crime control and prevention, service, order maintenance and problem solving.

Attitudes and the Police

It is important to understand police attitudes toward the public (especially juveniles) as well as citizen attitudes (especially *juvenile* citizen attitudes) toward the police.

Police Attitudes Toward the Public

It appears that the police often harbor negative or suspicious attitudes toward both adult and juvenile citizens. Wilson, for example, offers the following description of police attitudes toward various classes of victims:

> Middle-class victims who have suffered a street attack (a mugging, for example) are generally considered most legitimate; middle-class victims of burglary are seen as somewhat less legitimate (it *could* be an effort to make a fraudulent insurance claim); lower-class victims of theft are still less legitimate (they may have stolen the item in the first place); lower-class victims of assaults are the least legitimate (they probably brought it on themselves) (Wilson, 1978: 27).

Such attitudes demonstrate that the police are suspicious and cynical about many victims.

Similarly, Kroes, Margolis and Hurrell (1974) found that more than one-third of the police officers they interviewed reported problems with perceived lack of citizen support or a negative image of police among citizens. A significant proportion of the officers felt that many citizens were apathetic or antagonistic toward the police. Moreover, these perceptions of negative citizen attitudes toward the police were more stressful to police than danger, isolation or boredom on the job. The following quotation from an Atlanta police officer serves as a concrete example of what Kroes, Margolis and Hurrell mean:

> Sometimes I get tired of the public for being so stupid and for having no reason to call the police. They should solve their problems themselves. Should use their own heads (Remington, 1981: 149).

Yet another writer, John van Maanen (1982), argues that police have great disdain for many citizens. He gives the following typical interchange between an officer and such a citizen:

> Policeman to motorist stopped for speeding: "May I see your driver's license, please?"
>
> Motorist: "Why the hell are you picking on me and not somewhere else looking for some real criminals?"
>
> Policeman: "Cause you're an asshole, that's why . . . but I didn't know that until you opened your mouth" (van Maanen, 1982: 47).

Although there has been considerable debate concerning the degree to which attitudes affect behavior, Wilson makes the argument that officer attitudes—especially toward minorities—lead to officer suspicion and harassment of African-Americans and other minorities. He argues that police believe that teens, African-Americans and lower-income individuals are responsible for many reported offenses and, thus, officers think it is reasonable to be suspicious of these individuals. If an individual belongs to one of these categories and also exhibits unusual behavior, he or she becomes doubly suspect. In fact, "[p]atrolmen believe they would be derelict in their duty if they did not treat such persons with suspicion, routinely question them on the street, and detain them for longer questioning if a crime has occurred in the area" (Wilson, 1978: 41). In anthropologist Elijah Anderson's (1990) terms, police color-code youths:

"the anonymous black male is usually an ambiguous figure who arouses the utmost caution and is generally considered dangerous until he proves he is not" (Anderson, 1990: 190).

Citizen Attitudes Toward Police

Paradoxically, citizens actually hold rather positive attitudes toward the police. For example, a 1996 Gallup Poll reported that 49 percent of those polled rated the honesty and ethical standards of police either very high or high. Respondents rated police below druggists, clergy, college teachers, doctors, dentists and engineers, but above bankers, funeral directors, journalists, television reporters, lawyers, business executives and others (Maguire & Pastore, 1997). Similarly, the same survey showed that 50 percent of those polled stated that they had "a great deal" or "quite a lot" of confidence in the ability of the police to protect them from violent crime (Maguire & Pastore, 1997). Almost 60 percent (exactly 59%) of the respondents said that they had a great deal of confidence or quite a lot of confidence in the police as one of the institutions in American society (Maguire & Pastore, 1997).

Citizens vary considerably, however, in their approval of the police. For example, 76 percent of whites but only 60 percent of African-Americans stated that they had "a great deal" or "some" confidence in the ability of the police to solve crime. Further, 32 percent of young respondents (18-29 years of age) stated they had little or no confidence at all in the ability of the police to solve crime, while only 17 percent of senior citizens (60 and over) gave police a rating that low (Maguire & Pastore, 1997). Similarly, fewer African-Americans than whites gave the police a high rating on their honesty and ethical standards (Maguire & Pastore, 1997). Thus, citizen attitudes toward the police are not uniform. Some citizens are more positive, while others are more negative.

Of great relevance to the police and juvenile justice is the fact that lower-class youths comprise one group holding negative attitudes toward the police. Anderson (1994) argues that lower-class youths have little faith in the police and subscribe to a street code whereby the "police are most often seen as representing the dominant white society and not caring to protect inner-city residents" (Anderson, 1994: 82). As a result of the perception and/or the reality that police do not respond when called, the inner-city youth often relies on self-protection: "taking care of himself" (Anderson, 1994: 82) is a critical part of this street code.

Variation in attitudes toward the police helps to explain the paradox that police often hold negative or cynical views of citizens while citizen attitudes toward the police are actually rather positive. Part of the explanation for this apparent contradiction is that the police are much more likely to come in contact with citizens with less positive views—that is, minority and younger citizens—than with older citizens who hold more positive views. A second explanation for the paradox is that the police often come into contact with citizens at inopportune times—in instances in which citizens have broken the law (even if only a traffic law), been victimized or witnessed a crime. At such times, citizens are likely to be under stress. They may react with frustration at receiving a speeding ticket or at hearing an officer say that there is little hope of recovering their $400 video cassette recorder that has just been stolen. Citizens may lash out at the available target (i.e., the police officer) much like a frustrated customer reacts to a customer service representative who is not responsible for the problem but has the unpleasant job of trying to rectify it. Repeated contacts with citizens in times of crisis can lead the police to job burnout (Maslach & Jackson, 1979), cynicism (Niederhoffer, 1967), suspicion (Skolnick, 1966) and/or stress (Crank & Caldero, 1991; Kroes, Hurrell & Margolis, 1974).

One final observation on this matter concerns the fact that victims of crime view their situation as unique, while the police view the same situation as routine. The victim often is a first-time victim who is frightened, stunned and excited about something that is entirely new to him or her. The officer is simply experiencing the third burglary report that night, the twentieth that week or the thousandth in his or her career. Additionally, the officer's realistic judgment that little or nothing can be done to "solve" the crime leads him or her to rush through the encounter with the citizen in order to write up a report so the victim can file an insurance claim. Based on television or movie stereotypes, the naïve citizen expects the officer to drop everything, spend as much time as possible on the case, and solve the crime. Realizing that the officer has a very different definition of the situation, the citizen becomes upset and reacts accordingly—possibly accusing the officer of incompetence or laziness. Such negative encounters reinforce officer perceptions of citizens as being negative toward the police, even though the public opinion poll research shows the contrary.

Implications of the Attitudinal Research

Several conclusions can be drawn from this discussion of police attitudes toward citizens and citizen attitudes toward the police. First, both sides could benefit from clarification. The police might benefit from becoming aware that citizens generally are positive about the police. Citizens, on the other hand, need to know why police may be somewhat cynical toward them. Citizens should be aware that it is likely that police officers have seen their problem before and have had contact with some victims who precipitated the crime or were otherwise tainted. More importantly, citizens must be realistic in their expectations of what the police can do. For example, the police often can do little or nothing to recover a stolen television or car. Second, police need to be careful in their dealings with citizens who hold less positive attitudes—namely, youths and minorities. Because these groups may be less favorable in their attitudes toward the police, the police need to target them for more positive treatment. Otherwise, these groups may interpret police indifference and cynicism as evidence of prejudicial attitudes and discriminatory behavior. Furthermore, police sensitivity to the attitudes of youthful and minority citizens can lead to improved police-community relations.

There has been recent emphasis on the police as problem solvers. Some police experts think that traditional policing can do little more than take reports for many problems. If policing were restructured, however, perhaps more could be done about many of the concerns that citizens have. If police spent less time running from call to call and more time exploring the causes and solutions of various problems, then the police could be more effective and have greater impact (see, e.g., Trojanowicz et al., 1998).

Police Discretion

Police discretion is a topic that has generated a great deal of debate and research. Here we will define what police discretion means, how extensive it is and how discretion can be abused.

Defining Discretion

Police discretion refers to police authority to deal with various offenses and offenders in different ways. Quite simply, the police do not arrest every lawbreaker they encounter, nor do they even pursue all types of crime with equal energy. Such discretionary decisions can be made at the departmental level or at the officer level. Box 7.2 presents some examples of police officer discretion.

Box 7.2   Examples of Police Discretion

The following hypothetical situations indicate some examples of police officer discretion:

A police officer stops a motorist for speeding on a deserted road at 2:00 A.M. The driver is not intoxicated but just "in a hurry" to get home. The police officer simply issues a warning.

Five teenagers are standing on a street corner talking and listening to a portable radio. A resident complains that a "gang" is disrupting the neighborhood. The police simply tell the youths to go home.

A youth shoplifts $10 worth of merchandise. It is a first offense and the storeowner does not insist on police action. Nevertheless, the officer takes the boy into custody (the juvenile justice system equivalent of "arrest") and refers the boy to juvenile court.

In the three instances described in Box 7.2 the police exercise discretion. They choose a course of action in a situation in which they could do otherwise. They either do or do not take a youthful suspect into custody.

Is Discretion Appropriate?

Several issues need to be considered in a discussion of police discretion. The first is whether discretion is appropriate. Herman Goldstein (1977) argues that discretion is both a fact of and a justifiable part of policing. Discretion is necessary, he believes, given the limited resources and the nature of policing. If discretion did not exist, both the police and the courts would be overwhelmed with cases—many of them not important enough for consideration. Joseph Goldstein (1988), on the other hand, argues against police discretion because he believes that such exercise of discretion infringes on the legislative function. Specifically, he argues that it is the job of state legislators to make the laws that the police should enforce. Enforcement of the laws will reveal where (if anywhere) problems may exist. Then the state legislature can modify the laws that need to be changed. If the police exercise discretion, according to Joseph Goldstein, they prevent the legislature from seeing the problems with certain laws and the need for change.

Because sentiment often favors discretion with juveniles, the problem of whether discretion should even exist is somewhat resolved in reference to juveniles. This support of discretion is based on labeling theory propositions holding that official reaction leads to further delinquency (see Chapter 4 for a discussion of labeling theory). Research indicates that this view has some (though not universal) empirical support (Palamara, Cullen & Gersten, 1986). State law may even authorize police discretion with youths. For example, the Alabama code (12-15-58) specifically authorizes police officer discretion with juvenile offenders. Similarly, the American Bar Association has recommended that in matters involving minor criminal conduct the police should have the discretion to select the least restrictive alternative—ranging from nonintervention through mandatory referral to a mental health or public health intervention program (Institute of Judicial Aministration–American Bar Association, 1980b). Likewise, the Model Juvenile Delinquency Act of the Rose Institute of State and Local Government and the American Legislative Exchange Council would authorize police to issue a "warning notice" to a juvenile instead of taking the youth into custody under certain conditions (Rossum, Koller & Manfredi, 1987: 32). Thus, unlike adult criminal codes, which (at least on paper) stipulate that the police shall enforce all laws, codes for juveniles often endorse police discretion with juveniles—either in the interest of rehabilitation, in consideration of the age of the juvenile, or for some other reason.

The problem of discretion with juveniles, therefore, turns not on the fact that it exists, but on its proper use. For example, are the police discriminatory in their dealings with juvenile suspects? Are they choosing to arrest certain youths and not arrest certain other offenders based on factors such as race, ethnicity, gender, attitude and appearance, instead of on the basis of the nature of the crime, the seriousness of the crime and the prior record of the individual?

Research on Police Discretion

There has been a great deal of research on the topic of police discretion. The research suggests the following conclusions.

OFFENSE SERIOUSNESS

First, many encounters between the police and juveniles are not instances of serious criminal violations; that is, they are not felonies (Lundman, 1996). Police discretion is more frequent in misdemeanor cases than in felonies. It is much less frequent in very serious incidents (Black & Reiss, 1970; Lundman, Sykes & Clark, 1978; Piliavin & Briar, 1964; Werthman & Piliavin, 1967).

COMPLAINANT WISHES

The police often abdicate their discretion to the complainant, following complainant preference to arrest the offender or let him or her go (Black & Reiss, 1970; Lundman, Sykes & Clark, 1978). Such citizen influence is important because many police juvenile encounters (50% or more) involve situations with a complainant.

SUBJECT DEMEANOR

Demeanor (i.e., the attitude of the juvenile toward the police officer) can affect the arrest decision. If a juvenile is either very deferential (polite) or very antagonistic, he or she is more likely to be arrested. If a youth is moderately respectful, on the other hand, he or she is less likely to be arrested (Black & Reiss, 1970; Lundman, 1996; Worden & Shepard, 1996; for a recent debate of this issue, see Klinger, 1994, 1996; Lundman, 1994, 1996a & b). Of course, attitude can be misleading. A hostile attitude may simply be a youth's reaction to perceived police prejudice or lack of concern (National Advisory Commission on Criminal Justice Standards and Goals, 1973). Thus, police could be making a very serious mistake by concluding that a negative attitude is a sign of guilt (see also Institute of Judicial Administration–American Bar Association, 1980b).

RACE

Race appears to be related to the arrest decision in a complex manner. First, some evidence suggests that African-American youths are involved disproportionately in alleged felonies, while crime severity (as noted) is clearly related to the arrest decision. Second, black complainants seem to lobby more for the arrest of black suspects than white complainants do for the arrest of white suspects. Third, police officers appear to consider the race of both the suspect and the complainant. For example, a white officer is more likely to arrest a black suspect when there is a white complainant than when the complainant and the suspect are both black (Black, 1980). In summary, race appears to affect the arrest decision (Pope & Feyerherm, 1993), but race is not the most important factor (Smith & Visher, 1981). Thus, some conclude that evidence for the claim that the police are racist is "sparse, inconsistent, and contradictory . . ." (Wilbanks, 1987: 80). (For divergent views on this issue, see Box 7.3.)

DEPARTMENTAL EFFECT

The particular department in which a police officer works also can affect decisions regarding arrest. How a department structures its hiring decisions and deployment of officers can affect discretion. A department that hires locals and uses a decentralized approach to juvenile crime may be more conducive to patrol officer discretion than a department that hires individuals from all over the country and centralizes its juvenile operations. The latter department is likely to be more uniform in its arrest policies—with a policy of arresting most youths (Wilson, 1968). Similarly, the department's emphasis on either the law enforcement role or the crime prevention role can influence the amount of discretion officers employ in their decisions to take juveniles into custody. The law enforcement role calls for arrests all or most of the time, while crime prevention emphasizes informal handling of cases (Walker, 1983).

SOCIOECONOMIC STATUS

Although legal variables such as offense severity and prior record generally outweigh the impact of the social class of the suspect (Cohen & Kluegel, 1978; Tittle, 1980), the socioeconomic class of the neighborhood can influence police arrest decisions such that "the probability of police-suspect encounters ending in arrest declines substantially with increasing neighborhood socioeconomic status" (Sampson, 1986: 884). The influence of socioeconomic status is much more noticeable in reference to minor offenses such as larceny, burglary and vandalism, and these crimes constitute "the bulk of offenses typically committed by juveniles" (Sampson, 1986: 884). The neighborhood crime rate also can affect police activity such as police being more lenient in low-crime neighborhoods that fall in high-crime patrol districts but very vigorous in low-crime neighborhoods that fall in low-crime districts (Klinger, 1997).

POLICE TRAINING

Police may not be as aware of juvenile justice procedures as they are of procedures for handling adult suspects. Thus, rather than take a juvenile suspect into custody, the easiest course of action may be to let the youth go.

GENDER

Finally, there has been some evidence of differential treatment of female youths compared to male youths. This gender differential, termed the **chivalry hypothesis,** refers to allegedly protective interaction with female offenders that in practice includes either harsher or more lenient treatment of female youthful

Box 7.3   Conflicting Viewpoints on Police Discretion and Race

Several authors have examined the issue of the impact of race on police discretion to arrest or not. Here are just a few examples of opinions on the effect of race in this area.

Donald Black originally claimed that "[N]o evidence exists in this analysis [his 1960s research] to show that the police discriminate on the basis of race" (Black, 1980: 105). Later he wrote that the matter is complex and "depends upon the characteristics of all of the participants in a legal event, including the complainant and the third parties as well as the alleged offender" (Black, 1980: 108). In other words, a different decision may well result if the suspect, the police officer and the victim are all white, all black or some combination of white and black.

Others argue that race, if not discrimination, is very much a part of police officer discretion. Although more than 20 years old, the research of Piliavin and Briar (1964) is often cited in support of this viewpoint. Those researchers reported that police were more likely to engage in surveillance of black areas and that African-American youths "were accosted more often than others by officers on patrol simply because their skin color identified them as potential troublemakers" (Piliavin & Briar, 1964: 213). In summary, Piliavin and Briar (1964: 214) described police interactions with juveniles as "prejudicial practices."

In support of Piliavin and Briar (1964), Huizinga and Elliott (1987) examined racial differences in self-report measures of delinquency and found "few if any substantial and consistent differences between the delinquency involvement of different racial groups" (p. 215). Preliminary analyses, however, did find differences in police arrest practices: "an overall arrest rate for serious offenses among minority groups that is approximately two to three times that of Whites" (Huizinga & Elliott, 1987: 219). This may be part of the explanation for differential incarceration rates between African-Americans and whites.

As noted in the text, however, one review of the research on the impact of race on arrest decisions found the alleged evidence of police discrimination to be "sparse, inconsistent, and contradictory" (Wilbanks, 1987: 80). More specifically, Wilbanks (1987: 69) found that "[T]here is little evidence that white police officers make different decisions with respect to arrest than black ones."

Several have criticized Wilbanks, however, for methodological errors or for using a definition of racisim as intentional. Defining racism as a conscious process makes it hard to prove or disprove because it is almost impossible to determine the intentions of police, judges and parole boards (Lynch, 1990).

Krisberg and Austin (1993) note that there are three possibilities:

(a) minority youth being more involved in delinquent behaviors;
(b) a juvenile justice system that treats minority and white youth differentially in its decisions to arrest, detain, adjudicate, or sentence;
or (c) a combination of these and other external factors" (Krisberg & Austin, 1993: 117).

Box 7.3, *continued*

Krisberg and Austin do think that racial stereotypes affect the decision-making of juvenile justice personnel. One such stereotype is that "African-Americans are expected to act violently." Another is that "black males are seen as less controllable and with limited family support if returned to the community," whereas white and Asian youths are seen "as having more family and institutional resources" than blacks. Such stereotypes lead "to selective over-arrest and over-incarceration of minority youth and especially black youth" (Krisberg & Austin, 1993: 129).

Miller (1996) contends that the criminal justice system, adult and juvenile, is racist. He argues that policing is different in black areas because there the police look for action and assume that young black males between the ages of 12 and 30 who hang around corners or are out driving are worthy of suspicion. Thus, for blacks, "the experience of arrest and jailing seems to have become something of a puberty rite, a transition to manhood (Miller, 1996: 99).

Thus, the debate continues about the impact of race on police practices. Hopefully both society and the criminal justice system will move closer toward the day when everyone agrees that race is not a factor.

offenders. On the one hand, the chivalry hypothesis claims that police are more severe with girls who commit status offenses (such as running away) than they are with boys who commit such offenses (Chesney-Lind, 1977). Stemming from traditional stereotypes of girls as future mothers and wives, police are chauvinistic and will arrest female status offenders to protect their virtue, while they assume that boys who commit such offenses are simply "sowing their wild oats." Conversely, according to the hypothesis, police are *less* likely to arrest girls (and adult women, for that matter) for *criminal* violations because they do not want female offenders to suffer the indignities of arrest, confinement and adjudication.

Recent evidence suggests that the first half of the chivalry hypothesis continues to be true: police continue to arrest girls for noncriminal misbehavior (status offenses) at a higher rate than boys. However, the second part of the chivalry hypothesis seems to

Police detain a young female suspect. According to the chivalry hypothesis, police will sometimes arrest female status offenders to "protect their virtue," although they may be less likely to subject girls to justice system involvement for *criminal* violations. *Photo: Mark C. Ide*

be changing. That is, police are becoming less likely to ignore the criminal offenses of female youths (Chesney-Lind & Shelden, 1992; Krohn, Curry & Nelson-Kilger, 1983).

Discretion: A Summary

The research indicates that police discretion exists. Several model juvenile codes even authorize police discretion, and many experts think that the police should not arrest every juvenile offender. Factors affecting police discretion include the seriousness of the offense, the prior record of the youth, the complainant's preference, as well as race and gender. The impact of demeanor is currently in dispute (see Klinger, 1996; Lundman, 1996). Police training and organization also can affect discretion. One observer has suggested that many of the problems associated with police discretion could be prevented if departments adopted written policies to guide officer discretion. Such guidelines could state whether arrest or nonarrest was preferred and stipulate criteria to be followed in making such decisions (Walker, 1993).

Police Effectiveness

Instead of analyzing the specific issue of police effectiveness in preventing and controlling juvenile delinquency, the research has examined police effectiveness in preventing and controlling crime in general, without any mention of the age of the offender. This is not the place for a thorough discussion of the topic of **police effectiveness** (for such a discussion, see Sherman, 1992, 1995; Walker, 1998), but a few points need to be mentioned. First, many police practices that were assumed to be related to police effectiveness have been shown to be very important. For example, investigations of the effectiveness of car patrol (Kelling et al., 1974), foot patrol (Police Foundation, 1981), fast response time (Caron, 1980), and so on have indicated that none of these measures really have much impact (if any) on crime. Thus, the sobering conclusion of much of the research on policing is that many innovations do not result in crime reduction. Contrary to common sense and deterrence theory, putting more police cars or officers on the street does not appear to decrease crime. However, some recent developments offer suggestions for improving effectiveness. For example, there is some evidence that increased patrol of hot spots—specific locations with very high levels of criminal activity—can be effective in reducing crime and not displacing it to other locations (Bayley, 1998).

Second, the ineffectiveness of many traditional police practices has led several experts to call for new approaches to policing, such as community policing (Rosenbaum, 1994; Trojanowicz et al., 1998) or problem-oriented policing

(Goldstein, 1990; Sparrow, Moore & Kennedy, 1990). These approaches see the police as involved in more than merely crime prevention or crisis management:

> Officers are encouraged to think in terms of *problems* rather than *incidents*. . . . The officer is encouraged to recognize related and recurring incidents as symptomatic of problems begging for solutions and to search for the solutions. . . . Officers at all ranks are encouraged to group similar incidents that may constitute the same type of problem and then to concentrate on thinking through the agency's response to the problem (Goldstein, 1987: 16).

Specifically, officers using this new orientation may conduct house-to-house surveys, lobby government agencies to carry out their responsibilities, or advocate new legislation. For example, to control panhandling in Madison, Wisconsin, the police department proposed a new ordinance that outlawed begging but not street musicians (Goldstein, 1987). To control convenience store robberies, the police recommended changes by owners such as requiring more than one employee in the store at night, improving lighting, installing security cameras and banning window advertising (Trojanowicz et al., 1998). In summary, many are advocating that the police become "problem-busters" instead of merely "crime-busters" (Eck & Spelman, 1987). One danger of this type of approach is that citizens will place unrealistic expectations on police to solve problems that defy solutions. Another danger is that officers may come to think they are attacking causes of problems when in fact they are merely battling symptoms (Buerger, 1994).

Curfew Laws

One recent development in police activity vis-à-vis juveniles involves the establishment of curfew laws. The intent of such legislation is to limit the opportunity of youths to commit crime. The effectiveness of such actions, however, is questionable.

The popularity of **curfews** is evident in the fact that as of February 1996, 158 of the 200 American cities with a population of 100,000 or more had curfew statutes in effect (Maguire & Pastore, 1997). In addition, arrests of juveniles for curfews increased 21 percent between 1995 and 1996 and more than 100 percent between 1992 and 1996 (Snyder, 1997). Such curfews are legal if they are "reasonably related to some legitimate state purpose" (Davis & Schwartz, 1987: 112) and are neither overbroad nor vague (Sontheimer & Volenik, 1995) (see Chapter 9 for a discussion of the constitutionality of curfew laws). Their effectiveness, however, has not been systematically evaluated. San Antonio adopted both curfews and evening youth programs in 1991 and "[b]y 1993, crimes against juveniles had dropped by 77 percent, and arrests of juveniles had declined 5 percent, during the curfew hours of midnight to 6:00 A.M. (Sherman, 1995: 343). In keeping with the **"broken windows" hypothesis** (which holds that signs of urban decay serve to make a neighborhood more conducive to crime), the experiences of cities such as San Antonio suggest that curfews may be advantageous. However, it is important to emphasize that San Antonio's inclusion of evening youth programs in addition to a curfew suggests that curfews alone may be ineffective.

The current popularity of curfews is not suprising. For many years, experts such as James Q. Wilson have advocated that police clear the streets of rowdy teenagers and other social "broken windows" in order to make (adult) citizens feel safer. Wilson praised the Chicago police for chasing "known gang members" out of a public housing project:

> In the words of one officer, "We kick ass." Project residents both know and approve of this. The tacit police-citizen alliance in the project is reinforced by the police view that the cops and gangs are the two rival sources of power in the area, and that the gangs are not going to win (Wilson, 1983: 85).

Beyond the question of whether such police activity (aggressive foot patrol) has an impact on crime, the question of the youths' civil liberties arises. Do teenagers have a right to stand on street corners despite the fact that such activity frightens many adults? Unfortunately, many police and legislative initiatives fail to consider more than the very narrow view of a problem and ignore the related issues. Police expert Lawrence Sherman (1995) argues that chasing or keeping youths off the street is only part of the picture. He refers to such tactics as a "security guard approach" to policing that focuses on immediate goals.

Perhaps a more appropriate approach is a problem-solving or public health approach to crime prevention that takes a long-term perspective. However, police efforts to solve long-term crime problems often meet resistance from third parties (including other governmental agencies) responsible for implementing long-term solutions. A related issue is whether every jurisdiction in the country is entitled to its "fair share" of help from the federal government or whether federal assistance should be targeted to locales with special needs, such as inner-city areas in large cities. If the government passes a crime bill and authorizes thousands of new police officers, does every town get one officer or do the high-crime cities get many officers? Choices need to be made and "whether we admit it or not, we cannot have it all" (Sherman, 1995: 348). Despite these attitudes, some innovative programming is emerging in policing (such as DARE programs discussed in Chapter 6).

Women in Policing

Historical Background

Women in policing have often been assigned to juvenile bureaus, based on the assumption that they are better at dealing with juveniles than are male officers. In fact, working with juveniles was the justification used to bring women into police departments between 1910 and 1930. Women officers were relegated to women's bureaus, which served to keep them out of the mainstream of policing. The Depression also prevented growth of the policewomen's movement: "[f]or the next forty years women on urban police forces worked with juveniles, prisoners, and typewriters, without significant changes in their status or duties" (Martin, 1980: 24). Beginning in about 1970, changes in laws (prohibitions against discrimination in hiring) and society (the women's movement and related phenomena) led to increased representation for women in police departments and to greater variety in the roles women officers could take (especially patrol duties). Despite such changes, however, "opposition to policewomen remains strong . . . [because of] the view of most policemen of all ranks that women are inherently unfit for police work" (Martin, 1980: 49).

The view that women are best suited for work with juveniles is based on gender stereotypes of women as being "naturally" maternal and nurturant individuals who are better at teaching, understanding and counseling children than are males. Because specific research on women as juvenile bureau officers has not been conducted, it is impossible to determine whether the gender stereotype is accurate. However, research on other aspects of women in policing provides some clues about their effectiveness in general and their specific effectiveness with juveniles.

Research on Women Police

Martin (1980) and Remington (1981) conducted participant observation studies of women police officers in Washington, DC, and Atlanta, Georgia, respectively, and found that women were not really accepted by the male police officers or by the public. One male officer commented that

> Most of the ones [female police officers] I've met honestly and sincerely try to do a good job but they just don't belong on the street. Most, because of their emotional background, are too unstable in high pressure situations . . . (Remington, 1981: 169).

Furthermore, male officers often made the following comment about the women officers:

> You're not really a police until you get your butt beat . . . and beat one in return. And the women in this department make sure that they don't ever get into a good fight (Remington, 1981: 196).

This perception was not simply the result of gender stereotyping, however, because many of the women in Remington's (1981) study *did* avoid dangerous situations on patrol. Remington attributes much of the avoidance behavior to lack of appropriate self-defense training in the police academy and to male overprotectiveness during field training. Both problems could be ameliorated or prevented. Martin (1980), for example, contends that assigning women officers to female trainers and partners encourages them to be more independent and assertive.

More recent research found that women officers "did not express concerns about a generally more hostile work environment than did male officers" (Winfree, Guiterman & Mays, 1997). This could mean that acceptance of female officers has increased or it could reflect the small size of the departments that were studied. Winfree, Guiterman and Mays (1997) contend that such smaller departments afford women more of an opportunity "to overcome the stereotypes and have a real input into the workplace, due to the tighter-knit working environment" (p. 436).

It appears that female police officers could make some positive contributions in areas of policing such as juvenile work. Research indicates that women are very effective in the interpersonal aspects of policing, such as dealing with domestic disputes. Battered women who call the police and are called on by women police officers hold more positive views of police in general and policewomen in particular than do battered women who interact with male police officers (Kennedy & Homant, 1983). Additionally, policewomen score higher than policemen on scales measuring involvement or professional concern about family fights. Finally, female police officers view themselves as more patient and understanding than male police officers and as less likely to escalate a conflict (Homant & Kennedy, 1985). Such findings about domestic violence situations are important because they stand in marked contrast to the traditional police policy of non-mobilization—"a police mentality which holds that calls for domestic assaults are not 'real police work'—that the assaulted women are not legitimate victims and that law enforcement is not apropos" (Brown, 1984: 279).

In other words, many police regard domestic situations, as well as situations involving juveniles, as not "real police work" because they do not involve "real crime." In view of such perceptions on the part of male officers, some think that it may be worthwhile to use women in these situations because women seem to be more concerned about such interpersonal disputes and more effective in handling them (Homant & Kennedy, 1985). Another study of police attitudes, however, found that "women were not significantly more likely than men to define their role in broad terms that legitimate involvement in personal problems and domestic disturbances" (Worden, 1993: 228). The study found

> little support for the thesis that female officers define their role, or see their clientele, differently than do males, and one must therefore remain skeptical (albeit not disbelieving) about claims that women bring to their beats a distinctive perspective on policing (Worden, 1993: 229).

The claims that women may be particularly effective with juveniles and in domestic disputes are not intended to reinforce traditional stereotypes that would relegate women officers exclusively to such roles or preclude them from traditional patrol or detective assignments. As Martin (1980) has pointed out, the need for physical strength in policing is greatly exaggerated by some male officers who see the entrance of women into policing as a threat. Given proper opportunity and organizational support, women can be equally effective in routine patrol and detective assignments (Martin, 1980).

Although there now appears to be less tendency to assign women officers to work exclusively with juvenile and female offenders, women are often assigned to administrative duties rather than to traffic or detective work. There also appears to be some leveling off in the number of women who become police officers. Few departments exceed 20 percent women (Natarajan, 1996).

The Question of Juvenile Bureaus

An issue pertaining to police interaction with juveniles concerns whether police departments should have specialized and centralized juvenile bureaus or decentralized juvenile detectives. It is important to note that such organizational structuring options can have important consequences at the street level. For example, Wilson (1968) compared two police departments on this dimension and found that there were important consequences on police officer discretion and discrimination. Wilson (1968) compared "Western City," which had a centralized juvenile bureau, to "Eastern City," which had a decentralized approach (one juvenile officer in each precinct). In Western City, patrol officers took arrested youths down to headquarters for transfer to the juvenile bureau detectives, while in Eastern City officers took youthful arrestees to their precinct (neighborhood) station house and turned the suspects over to the particular detective assigned to that precinct. Wilson found that Western City officers were more severe overall toward all juvenile suspects, but less discriminatory toward minority youths than were Eastern City police. Western City officers were more likely to arrest all youths, minorities included, whereas Eastern City officers were more likely to simply reprimand youths and "pass" them on to their parents for discipline at home (Wilson termed this the "pass system"). Such decisions were, at least in part, a consequence of the differing organizational structure of the two police departments.

The pass system in Eastern City was related to the fact that juvenile detectives were stationed in each neighborhood precinct (decentralization) rather than in one centralized office (downtown headquarters), as was the case in Western City. The presence of the detectives in the precincts in Eastern City discouraged Eastern City patrol officers from making arrests because the arresting officer had to bring in the arrested youth to the station house. When an arresting officer brought in a youth, the other officers were likely to make sarcastic, demeaning remarks about a "tough" officer bringing in a "dangerous" child. To avoid such ridicule, many police officers chose to pass delinquent youngsters back to their parents. Western City, on the other hand, had a centralized juvenile bureau in which officers who arrested youths did not have to face the ridicule of fellow officers at the station house. Instead, they could drive the arrested youth to the central juvenile bureau and proceed with their regular tasks without their fellow street officers even knowing that they had just arrested a delinquent. This study indicates that a centralized juvenile bureau may result in both greater fairness and greater severity. All youths may be treated the same, but equal treatment may mean severe treatment for all.

Police Brutality and Deadly Force

It is difficult to determine the nature of police interaction with juveniles with regard to the use of force in general as well as with respect to the use of deadly force. News reports and television newsmagazine shows indicate that improper uses of force continue. Because the use of force (deadly or otherwise) is a sensitive topic, it is more difficult to research than police effectiveness or police discretion. For obvious reasons, police are not as willing to talk about force as they are about less sensitive problems. Nevertheless, there is some information available.

Police Brutality

Concerning police use of excessive force, Albert Reiss reported that teens were the most likely targets of the least damaging type of **police brutality**, namely, abusive language and commands to "move on." According to Reiss, such commands were particularly frequent in the summer when black youths from the ghetto were more likely to spend more time on the streets. However, police told both black youths and white youths to leave or go home (Reiss, 1980). Recent research shows that such problems continue, especially for African-American youths. A 1991 survey of more than 300 Cincinnati youths revealed that almost one-half (46.6%) of the black youths reported having been personally hassled by police, compared to only about 10 percent of white youths. Also, approximately two-thirds of the blacks said that they knew some-one who had been hassled (Browning et al., 1994).

Although Reiss's analysis of the excessive use of physical force in 37 cases made no mention of age as a variable, Friedrich's (1983) reanalysis of the data on brutality showed a curvilinear relationship between the age of the suspect and police use of force. In a study in which the ages of the suspects varied from between 10 and 18 years of age to more than 60 years of age, "[t]he use of force increases and then decreases as the age of the offender increases, with those 18 to 25 years old most likely to receive excessive force" (Friedrich, 1983: 306). The impact of age, however, was not large enough to be statistically significant. Attitude, however, was a significant factor; antagonistic offenders were more likely to be recipients of excessive force. Thus, if youths are more likely to be antagonistic toward the police, then age has an indirect effect on the likelihood of receiving excessive force by increasing the likelihood of being antagonistic.

Geller and Toch (1996) argue that the process of stereotyping can be an important factor leading to the use of force against juveniles. A police officer can stereotype a youth as a "typical gang member" and a youth can stereotype a police officer as a "typical white cop." This stereotyping very easily leads to a process of arrest, resistance (or actions interpreted as resistance) and excessive force (or actions so interpreted) so that a series of self-fulfilling prophecies are set in motion. The problem is to stop the start of such a cycle.

A hopeful note is that a recent review of research on force concluded that "physical force is infrequently used by the police and that improper force is used even less" (Worden, 1996: 46). One problem with this research conclusion is that reality may not be the same as perceptions on the street, especially perceptions in some of the trouble spots of inner-city areas of cities such as New York and Los Angeles. In such locations, contrary perceptions help to trigger the stereotyping process and often lead to tragic results.

Deadly Force

In a review of the literature on **deadly force**, William Geller (1983) describes the typical victim of police shooting as between the ages of 17 and 30. This means that not many juveniles—only the 17-year-olds—are likely to be shot by police officers. All police shootings, however, are not typical; some do involve younger victims. In fact, a test case on the use of deadly force involved the shooting of a 15-year-old youth in Memphis, Tennessee. A Memphis police officer shot and killed Edward Garner, a 15-year-old eighth-grade student, under Tennessee's common law "fleeing felon" rule, which authorized police to shoot any fleeing felon—even nondangerous ones. Garner had been prowling inside an empty house and refused to halt in the yard when the police officer warned him to stop. Consequently, the officer shot the youth as he tried to climb a fence to escape. After this incident, the U.S. Supreme Court ruled that police may not institute a policy to shoot any and all fleeing suspects; rather, they may shoot only those escaping felons who pose a threat to the officer or to others. Box 7.4 presents excerpts from the decision. This critical case (**Tennessee v. Garner et al.**) ordered police to be much more selective in using deadly force. Research has shown that as a result of the case there has been a decrease both in shooting overall and in the appearance of discrimination in deadly force (Sparger & Giacopassi, 1992). What has happened is that police departments have been forced to devise guidelines for the use of deadly force, and the enforcement of those guidelines has been successful in decreasing police shootings (Locke, 1996).

Box 7.4   The U.S. Supreme Court on Deadly Force

In *Tennessee v. Garner et al.*, the U.S. Supreme Court set down guidelines for the constitutional use of deadly force by police officers. Here are some excerpts from the majority opinion written by Justice White:

The use of deadly force to prevent the escape of all felony suspects, whatever the circumstances, is constitutionally unreasonable. It is not better that all felony suspects die than that they escape. Where the suspect poses no immediate threat to the officer and no threat to others, the harm resulting from failing to apprehend him does not justify the use of deadly force to do so. It is no doubt unfortunate when a suspect who is in sight escapes, but the fact that the police arrive a little late or are a little slower afoot does not always justify killing the suspect. A police officer may not seize an unarmed, nondangerous suspect by shooting him dead. . . .

. . . Where the officer has probable cause to believe that the suspect poses a threat of serious physical harm, either to the officer or to others, it is not constitutionally unreasonable to prevent escape by using deadly force. Thus, if the suspect threatens the officer with a weapon or there is probable cause to believe that he has committed a crime involving the infliction or threatened infliction of serious physical harm, deadly force may be used if necessary to prevent escape, and if, where feasible, some warning has been given (*Tennessee v. Garner et al.*, 1985).

Summary

This chapter has examined the police role, police attitudes, discretion, police effectiveness, the deployment of female police officers, and police use of excessive force. We have seen that police order maintenance activity can be very important and quite controversial. James Q. Wilson (1985) argues that police should do more order maintenance work because it will reduce citizen fear of crime and also decrease crime. Others are concerned that such police activity can lead to abuses. We also have learned that police discretion is a reality and that it is influenced by a number of factors. The potential contributions of female officers were also considered. Finally, although the research is scanty, we have found that police do sometimes abuse their powers, even with juvenile suspects.

Some of the issues discussed in this chapter will reappear in the next chapter on the juvenile courts. For example, a key question in the research on juvenile courts has been a consideration of what variables are used by intake probation officers and judges in deciding who gets petitioned to court and who gets adjudicated delinquent. This question is important because court officials, like police officers, are gatekeepers who decide which juveniles penetrate further into the juvenile justice system and which simply go home.

DISCUSSION QUESTIONS

1. Problem-oriented policing and community policing approaches suggest that the job of the police is to solve the problems that lead to crime. Do you agree or disagree with this position? To what extent can society hold the police responsible for the problems that cause crime?

2. How important are police attitudes toward citizens? How important are citizen attitudes about police honesty, ethical standards and effectiveness? What can be done to improve attitudes on both sides?

3. Is police discretion good or bad? Should the police be forced to arrest everyone who breaks the law? What are the limits on police discretion? Which juvenile offenders "must" be taken into custody and which ones should never be taken into custody?

4. Would you consider a career in policing? Would you consider a job as a juvenile officer?

5. How might a police chief eliminate and prevent racial discrimination in his or her department?

6. Is there any justifiable basis for the so-called chivalry hypothesis? Should boys and girls be treated exactly the same?

7. The literature on police effectiveness suggests that many innovations in policing do not dramatically improve effectiveness; crime and delinquency stay about the same. Without losing your job as chief, how might you communicate this "truth" to the public?

CHAPTER 8

The Juvenile Court Process

Key Terms and Phrases

adjudication
blended sentencing
"boob tube" therapy
day-evening centers
detention decision
disposition
false negative
false positive
home detention
informal adjustment
intake decision

legislative waiver
nonsecure detention
petition
plea bargaining
preventive detention
secure detention
statutory exclusion
token economy programs
transfer
waiver

Once a police officer takes a youth into custody, it is fairly likely that the police will then refer that youngster to juvenile court. In 1996, 69 percent of youths taken into custody were referred to juvenile court and 6 percent of juvenile arrests were sent directly to adult criminal court. The other arrests were referred to a social welfare agency or another police agency (Snyder, 1997). When police refer a youth to juvenile court, the court personnel must then make one or more critical decisions: whether to detain (jail) the youth, whether to actually file a **petition** (charges) against the youth, whether to find (adjudicate) the youth a delinquent, and how to dispose of the petition. These decisions correspond to the adult court decisions of bail versus jail, formal charge versus dismissal, determination of guilt by plea or by trial, and sentencing. Several juvenile court actors—probation officers, defense attorneys, prosecutors and judges—are involved in these important decisions. While the judge is the primary decisionmaker, other court personnel play important roles in deciding the fate of juvenile suspects.

This chapter will examine the critical decision points in the juvenile court process: detention, intake, transfer (waiver), adjudication and disposition. We will look at the roles the various court personnel play and should play in the court process. We will describe what happens when a juvenile suspect goes through the juvenile court process and will compare the ideal with the reality. Finally, we will examine some of the controversial issues facing juvenile court today, such as the question of the impact of race on decisionmaking and whether juveniles should have the right to a jury trial.

In 1995 (the latest year for which figures were available) juvenile courts processed more than 1.7 million delinquency cases and more than 146,000 petitioned status offense cases (see Figures 8.1 and 8.2). More than one-half (55%) of the delinquency cases were petitioned and approximately 9,700 cases were transferred to adult court via judicial waiver. More than one-half million youths were adjudicated delinquent in juvenile court and 73,000 were adjudicated as status offenders (Sickmund, 1997).

Figure 8.1   Juvenile Court Processing of Delinquency Cases, 1995

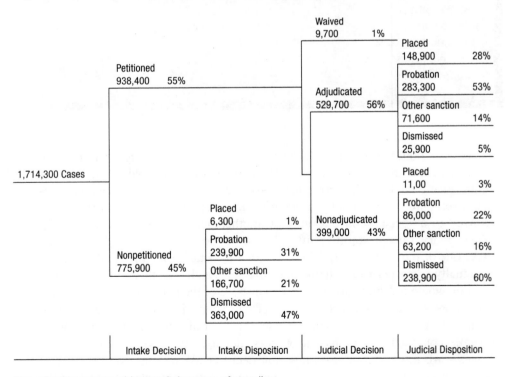

Note: Detail may not add to totals because of rounding.

Source: Sickmund (1997).

Figure 8.2   **Juvenile Court Processing of Petitioned Status Offense Cases, 1995**

			Placed	11,500	16%
	Adjudicated	73,000 50%	Probation	41,200	56%
			Other sanction	17,300	24%
146,400 Petitioned cases			Dismissed	2,900	4%
			Placed	300	<1%
	Nonadjudicated	73,400 50%	Probation	9,200	13%
			Other sanction	16,400	22%
			Dismissed	47,400	65%
Intake Decision		Judicial Decision		Judicial Disposition	

Note: Detail may not add to totals because of rounding.

Source: Sickmund (1997).

Detention

The first decision that juvenile court personnel must make is the detention decision. It must be decided whether to keep a juvenile in custody or to allow the youth to go home with his or her parents while awaiting further court action. The **detention decision** is the juvenile court counterpart of the bail decision in adult court. It is very important because it concerns the freedom of the child and, therefore, resembles the disposition decision. In fact, children sent to detention may stay there for an extensive period of time—perhaps even for a longer time than children sent to state training schools (youth prisons for juveniles determined to be delinquent). In 1995 youths were detained in approximately 20 percent of delinquency cases and in 7 percent of petitioned status offense cases. The number of detained petitioned status offense cases increased from 7,900 in 1990 to 9,900 in 1995. This was a decrease, however, from the number for 1985: 13,500 cases (Sickmund, 1997).

Detention workers or probation officers usually make the initial detention decision. State law may stipulate that a detention hearing be held within a specified period of time so that a judge can rule on the continued need for detention. The Model Juvenile Delinquency Act, a guideline for state codes, stipulates that the detention hearing be held within 36 hours and that certain criteria be used to decide whether or not to detain a particular youngster (Rossum, Koller & Manfredi, 1987: 34. See Box 8.1 for the relevant section of the Model Juvenile Delinquency Act.)

Box 8.1   Model Juvenile Delinquency Act

Section 26.   [*Grounds for Pre-Hearing Detention*] A youth taken into custody may be detained if there is probable cause to believe that
   (A) The juvenile is a fugitive from justice;
   (B) The juvenile has committed a felony while another case was pending;
   (C) The juvenile has committed a delinquent act and
      (1) The juvenile will likely fail to appear for further proceedings,
      (2) Detention is required to protect the juvenile from himself or herself,
      (3) The juvenile is a threat to the person or property of others,
      (4) The juvenile will intimidate witnesses or otherwise unlawfully interfere with the administration of justice, or
      (5) There is no person available or capable of caring for the juvenile.

Source: Rossum, Koller & Manfredi (1987:33). Reprinted with permission.

Detention Options

Court personnel have several options at the detention decision point. Releasing a child to his or her parents is the most frequently used option; this is the preferred decision in most states (e.g., Alabama Code 12-15-59). **Secure detention**—placing a child in the juvenile equivalent of a local jail—is another alternative. It involves placement in a locked facility for 10, 20 or more youths who are awaiting further court action or are awaiting transfer to a state correctional facility. In some places, **nonsecure detention** is another option for youths involved in less serious crimes and for those who do not pose much threat to the community or themselves. Such youngsters may be placed in small group homes that are not locked or not locked as comprehensively as a secure detention facility—hence the term "nonsecure." Youngsters housed in nonsecure detention centers might even go to regular public school classes during the day. Alternatives to detention (e.g., home detention) have developed in the last few years. These alternatives are important in light of extensive overuse of detention in the past (McCarthy, 1987b). They will be discussed later in this chapter.

Detention Decisionmaking

Some research on detention decisionmaking has indicated that while race is not a significant factor influencing the detention decision, gender is important (see McCarthy, 1987c, for a review of the research). In 1995, however, the likelihood of detention in delinquency cases for white juveniles was 15 percent but 27 percent for black juveniles (Sickmund, 1997). Raising further disturbing questions, one of the best studies on factors affecting the detention decision used a sample of 55,000 cases from one state and found that neither relevant legal variables (offense severity and prior record) nor sociodemographic characteristics had much impact on detention decisions. One possible conclusion of this research is that the decision "process is idiosyncratic, causing some juveniles to suffer significant deprivations of liberty based on considerations that are irrelevant to the approved purposes of detention" (Frazier & Bishop, 1985: 1151). Another study that reviewed the literature, however, concluded that race *is* a factor in the detention decision (Wordes, Bynum & Corley, 1994).

Preventive Detention

An important question that comes up in any discussion of the detention decision is the question of what court personnel should do about repeat/chronic property offenders who pose little or no threat to the physical safety of themselves or others. For example, should a frequent car thief be held in secure detention or not? That is, should detention be used primarily for youths who appear to present a high risk of not appearing for future court hearings and for youths who are a danger to themselves or others, or should detention also be used for youths who appear to be at high risk of committing more—but not necessarily violent—crime? The U.S. Supreme Court has clarified this issue to some extent by ruling that **preventive detention**—detention to prevent further delinquency while awaiting court action on an earlier charge—is constitutional (*Schall v. Martin*, 1984) (see Chapter 9 for further discussion of this case).

This ruling on the constitutionality of preventive detention, however, does not resolve all of the questions surrounding the practice. For example, the use of preventive detention means that *some* youths will be detained unnecessarily. Some of the youths whom the court considers to be at high risk of committing additional crimes will actually *not* commit any more crimes. This is an example of the so-called **false positive** problem, a major criticism of using selective incapacitation as a possible guiding philosophy for juvenile court in the future (for a discussion of chronic-violent delinquents, see Chapter 14). Past research on the false positive problem suggests that as many as 50 percent or more of the youngsters who would be held for the purpose of preventive detention really do not need to be detained. Instead, they could go home with no threat to the community (Cohen, 1983; Monahan, 1981; von Hirsch, 1984).

On the other side of the coin, studies of pretrial release in the adult courts indicate that approximately 10 to 15 percent of the offenders considered safe enough to go home actually do commit new crimes while awaiting their court hearings (Rhodes, 1985). This is the so-called **false negative** problem whereby offenders who are predicted to present little risk of committing new crimes *do* commit new crimes contrary to the prediction. Although the false negative problem is less of a problem than false positives in terms of the sheer numbers of mistakes made, it is more threatening to the community. More citizens are concerned about the youths predicted to be safe who commit crimes while on release than are concerned about youths considered dangerous and kept in detention when they could safely be sent home. In fact, part of the reason for the relatively low incidence of the false negative problem is that judges and other juvenile justice system officials tend to be concerned about public outcry when a released offender commits a new crime. Consequently, court officials are careful to release only the "best" children—the youths they consider to present the least risk of committing any further crimes.

Detention Statistics

In 1995, detention was used in 320,000 delinquency cases and almost 10,000 status offense cases. The likelihood of detention was highest for black youths (27%), then other nonwhite races (20%) and then whites (15%). Detention was more likely in delinquency cases involving males (20%) than females (14%) (Sickmund, 1997).

States vary in their use of detention. Although one might logically hypothesize that states with higher rates of detention also have higher crime or arrest rates than states with lower detention rates, that is simply not true. On the contrary, Krisberg and Schwartz (1983) found that detention admission rates were relatively unaffected by arrest rates. There was, however, a statistical relationship between detention rates and the number of beds available. In other words, if a state has X number of detention beds, those beds are usually filled, even though that state's juvenile crime problem may be much less serious than the juvenile crime problem in other states with fewer beds (and lower detention rates). Krisberg and Schwartz's findings parallel the situation in the adult criminal justice system in which state imprisonment rates do not always parallel state index crime rates or violent crime rates. That is, states that use prison the most do not necessarily have the worst violent crime problems.

Detention Programming

Detention programs can range from very inadequate to rather complex programs. About 20 years ago, Charles Silberman (1978) toured several detention centers across the country in preparation for writing a book on criminal violence and criminal justice. He found that **"boob tube" therapy** was often the normal programming. By this he meant that staff often allowed the children to watch television for hours on end. As many parents at home have found, parking children in front of the television set serves to occupy the children as well as free the supervising adults (detention houseparents or workers) from the challenging task of finding more constructive activities for the detainees.

Besides "boob tube" therapy, the psychological technique of behavior modification has inspired many detention centers to use **token economy programs**. With this approach, staff members use points or dollar values to reward detained youths for appropriate behavior and withhold or subtract points for inappropriate behavior. Youths earn credits when they follow the rules and they lose credits when they disobey the rules. If they have more credits than losses, they can "purchase" rewards such as snacks, table games and room privacy at the end of the day and/or on the weekend. (See Boxes 8.2 and 8.3 for examples of rewards, punishments and costs.) This type of program is based on psychological principles of conditioning that contend that human behavior is learned through reinforcements.

Detention officials justify the use of token economies as a way to teach appropriate behavior, in the hope that the positive behaviors will carry over to the home environments of the youths on release. Additionally, the technique is useful in controlling the youngsters while they are being detained. Critics (e.g., Russell, 1982), however, charge that there is little or no evidence that the effects of behavior modification programs actually carry over positive effects into the home environment. Rather, they are used only to control detained youths and make institutional life more comfortable for staff members. As partial support for this criticism, Silberman (1978) notes that he observed many detention per-

---

Box 8.2   Detention Rewards and Fines

How Dollars May Be Earned

1.	School Attendance	$10
2.	YMCA Activities	$10
3.	Cleaning Room (make beds, sweep, mop, etc.)	$5
4.	Extra Work (per hour)	$5
5.	Good Hygiene	$5
6.	Attending Church, etc.	$5
7.	Cleaning Unit	$10
8.	Good Behavior	$5

Fines for Inappropriate Behaviors

1.	Body Contact (slapping, etc.)	$20
2.	Disrespect (sarcastic or abusive speech, not following rules)	$30
3.	Profanity	$10
4.	Instigating (influencing others to break rules)	$30
5.	Arguing (other youth or staff)	$30
6.	Lying	$40
7.	Complaining (irritating staff with complaints about program, food, other staff, dollars, etc.)	$25
12.	Contraband	$50
18.	Fighting (another resident)	$100
20.	Attempted Escape	$150

Source: Handbook of Procedures, Rules, and Regulations (Jefferson County Detention Center, Birmingham, Alabama). Reprinted with permission.

Box 8.3   Detention Dollar Price List

Item	Price
Soft Drinks	$10
Envelopes and 2 Sheets of Paper	$5
Chips	$5
Popcorn	$10
Second Comb	$15
Second Toothbrush	$15
Extra Shampoo	$5
Hair Cuts	$10
Alcohol	$5
Vaseline	$5
Coffee	$10
Pencils	$5

Source: Handbook of Procedures, Rules, and Regulations (Jefferson County Detention Center, Birmingham, Alabama). Reprinted with permission.

sonnel simply sitting around and doing little or nothing. Critics also argue that token economies can turn detention centers into oppressive regimes that are justified on the basis of scientific intervention. The list of fines and earnings from the Birmingham, Alabama, detention center (Boxes 8.2 and 8.3), for example, lists some rather hefty fines (up to $150 per infraction of the rules), whereas rewards are much lower ($5 to $10 per instance of appropriate behavior). Since it can take a considerable amount of time to pay off some of the fines, one wonders if this example of a token economy is really the result of sound psychological theory or just a disguise for a repressive detention facility. One also may wonder whether calling "time out" in one's own room is really a scientifically justified reinforcer (Carbone, 1983) or whether it is just a modern cover-up for the very old practice of solitary confinement. In other words, scientific terminology does not erase the fact that token economies can be administered harshly, perhaps as harshly as the houses of refuge came to be administered in the mid-nineteenth century (see Chapter 2 for a description of the horror stories from those earlier institutions).

H. Ted Rubin (1985) has voiced the additional criticism that behavior modification programs are a violation of the rights of the detainees because most of the youths in detention have *not* been adjudicated of a delinquent act. Thus, to force such (presumably innocent) children to abide by the rules of a token economy system in the name of treatment is to subject them to an intervention when they have not yet been proven to have committed a crime that would justify such an intervention. Rubin has taken a civil libertarian position that the government (juvenile court and detention officials) cannot force anyone to undergo coercive programming without sufficient cause (proof of delinquency).

Interestingly, it appears that adult jails do not force such behavior modification programs on adult detainees. This is another example of a situation in which juveniles face unequal treatment because of their age or status.

Positive Programs

While some detention centers use either "boob tube" therapy inspired by token economies or behavior modification (or both), at least some detention facilities are trying to implement meaningful detention programming, especially educational programming. Several states have implemented literacy programs using intensive systematic phonics. In Mississippi, students improved their reading comprehension scores in a period from seven months to one year. In a detention center in the state of Washington, the average gain in reading was two grade levels. In a phonics program in Ohio, the average gain in reading was 1.5 grade levels one year and 2.5 grade levels the next year (Hodges, Giulotti & Porpotage, 1994). These results show that well-designed educational programs can have a postive impact in detention centers.

More generally, research on educational programs in correctional settings, programs such as Job Corps (a federal program that provides vocational training in camp settings) and effective schools has indicated that correctional facilities can provide effective education if attention is paid to proven principles. Such research has shown that correctional educational programs have often emphasized remediation, discipline and control when they need to be emphasizing the following principles:

> The academic curriculum features comprehension and complex problem-solving tasks, allowing students to develop their cognitive skills.

> The curriculum integrates basic skills into more challenging tasks that allow students to apply these skills to real-life situtaitons.

> Teachers model cognitive processes through a variety of instructional strategies, including externalizing thought processes, encouraging multiple approaches to problem solving and focusing on dialog and reciprocal learning (Gemignani, 1994: 3).

Positive progamming can have several benefits. In response to a lawsuit, the Broward Detention Center in Florida cut its population from 166 in 1988-89 to 53 in 1992 and added educational programs, a new exercise area and refurbished sleeping areas. Detainee uniforms were relaxed (changed to a "golf style" shirt) and additional child care and specialized staff (recreation, nursing and mental health workers) were hired. Such changes were associated with fewer behavioral incidents; both disciplinary confinements (isolation) and room confinement decreased. Such changes were also associated with less punitive attitudes for the staff (Bazemore, Dicker & Nyhan, 1994).

Detention Workers

A study of workers in two detention centers in Florida found that the workers strongly supported a treatment or rehabilitation orientation. More than 80 percent reported that they took their job "to help and rehabilitate youth" and "to provide care and services for youth" and that detained youths "should receive treatment and rehabilitative services" (Bazemore & Dicker, 1994: 304). On the other hand, a punishment or control orientation was also prevalent. Sixty-nine percent of the workers overall agreed that "youth in detention primarily need firm discipline" and 41 percent agreed that "most youth in detention only respond to physical intervention or the threat of physical intervention" (Bazemore & Dicker, 1994: 304). Younger employees and males were more likely to agree with such punitive statements, suggesting that maturity may produce greater tolerance (Bazemore & Dicker, 1994). As noted above, the center that had adopted a number of program improvements—the Broward Detention Center—had staff with less punitive attitudes than the other center. Still, significant numbers of the staff at Broward professed punitive attitudes. This research suggests that detention workers do favor rehabilitation but that a considerable percentage report punitive attitudes, including attitudes that are contrary to detention policy. This suggests that detention administrators need to monitor detention policies and to attempt to improve detention workers' salaries and occupational prestige, which are low compared to other juvenile justice and human service occupations (Bazemore, Dicker & Nyhan, 1994).

Detention Alternatives

Because of criticisms of detention programming and because of the high costs of detaining youngsters in secure detention facilities, many jurisdictions have sought alternatives to traditional detention facilities. For example, a few years ago, New York City found that secure detention cost about $58,000 per year per child and that nonsecure detention (foster care and boarding homes) cost about $20,000 per year. Hence, they began using converted stores or lofts as **day-evening centers**. In such centers, mornings involved formal educational programs, early afternoons were devoted to remedial and tutorial work, and late afternoons were reserved for recreational programs (e.g., weekly swimming at YMCA facilities). Two of the four New York City centers also offered evening hours twice a week for children considered to need extra supervision and for those on a waiting list for admission into the day program (Lindner, 1981).

Home Detention

Another popular alternative to traditional detention is **home detention**. This is the juvenile court counterpart of supervised pretrial release for adult criminal defendants. In home detention, the youth awaiting further juvenile court action is allowed to live at home but is also under the supervision of a detention worker who ensures that the youth is attending school (or working on a job) and maintaining a curfew. The detention worker may check on the home detention youngster up to four times a day if the worker suspects that the child is getting into new trouble (delinquency). Success rates vary from 80 to 90 percent. Some failures reflect new crimes committed, but others involve youths who either run away or break curfew or school attendance rules and thus are not criminal violators (McCarthy & McCarthy, 1984).

A vintage photo of three boys sitting in Judge Ben Lindsey's juvenile court chambers in Denver, Colorado. The juvenile court process has undergone many changes since its inception, including a general change from a *parens patriae* to a punishment perspective. *Photo: Library of Congress/Corbis*

A home detention program in New Orleans uses fax-like technology to check on juveniles. Five times a day computer-generated calls go to the juvenile's home. The juvenile must stand in front of a fax-like unit that transmits his or her picture to the Youth Study Center. The programs costs only $2.10 per day compared to about $60 a day for regular detention. Program officials claim that 86 percent of the juveniles in this home detention program have been adjudicated without a new arrest (Sontheimer & Volenik, 1995).

Bail

Bail is not universally available in juvenile court (Rossum et al., 1987: 109), but bail for juveniles appears to be an option that is receiving greater attention. New Mexico, for example, recently authorized bail for serious youthful offenders detained before trial in an adult facility (National Conference of State Legislatures, 1993). This is a reflection of the changing philosophy of juvenile court, from *parens patriae* to punishment. That is, bail is considered inappropriate in the traditional juvenile court, in which the judge acts like a concerned parent in deciding to detain or release juveniles awaiting further court action. With the changing views of juvenile crime and juvenile court, however, states are beginning to see bail as a reasonable option. The current view that the juvenile is a responsible criminal rather than an immature youth in need of help is quite consistent with the use of bail as a means to guarantee continued appearance for court hearings.

The Intake Decision

The second major decision point in juvenile court is the **intake decision**, analogous to the filing decision in adult court. At intake, a court official—either a probation officer or a prosecutor (or both)—decides whether to file a court petition of delinquency, status offense, neglect, abuse or dependency in a particular case. Traditionally, a probation officer has made the intake decision. The *parens patriae* philosophy of the court dictated this approach because its treatment orientation indicated that the probation officer (ideally a trained social worker) should consider the best interests of the child as well as the legal apsects of the case (as an adult court prosecutor might). That is, an intake probation officer is supposed to resolve every case in light of the considerations of the welfare of the child and the legal demands of the police and victim.

Informal Adjustment

One frequent decision of the intake officer is not to file a petition alleging delinquency or a status offense, but instead to try to resolve the matter without resorting to a formal petition against the child. As noted above, almost one-half (45%) of the 1.7 million delinquency cases coming to juvenile court in 1995 were not petitioned (Sickmund, 1997). (Statistics on the number of status offense cases not petitioned are not available.) Many of the nonpetitioned cases were dismissed; others were handled informally. Informal handling is usually called adjustment at intake or **informal adjustment**. Examples would include requiring a first-time shoplifter to pay restitution to the store or ordering a vandal to paint the public building he or she has defaced. Similarly, intake probation officers often try to counsel troubled family members on a short-term basis or to refer them to counseling services in the community. As a result, a youth involved in runaway behavior, chronic disobedience ("incorrigibility") or repeated truancy will not be immediately petitioned to court as a status offender. Instead, the youth receives help in dealing with the problem that brought him or her to the attention of court officials.

It is important to note that such informal adjustment practices occur as frequently as 25 percent of the time (Butts, 1994; McCarthy, 1987a) and have been part of juvenile court since its inception. With the emphasis on diversion (see Chapter 10) in the 1970s, informal adjustment practices by intake officers took on added dimensions. For example, in an attempt to prevent the filing of formal petitions, some probation departments started their own diversion units staffed by probation officers. Many community agencies not under the direction of juvenile court started diversion programs intended to be drastically distinct from juvenile court. Thus, starting about 20 years ago, intake probation officers had multiple options when dealing with troublesome youths. Alternatives include the filing of a petition, informal adjustment, referral to a probation department (or police department) diversion program without formal court action, or referral to a diversion program completely distinct from the juvenile court sytem. What can be confusing is that some writers speak of all such actions as examples of diversion from the juvenile justice system, while others consider diversion to occur only if a youngster is just sent home or is sent to a diversion program run by a noncourt agency. They think that any probation- or police-operated diversion program is not independent enough from the system and does not really deserve the title "diversion."

The Prosecutor's Role

If an intake probation officer decides to file a petition against a child, often that decision requires the approval of an attorney, normally the prosecutor. The prosecutor's approval of the probation officer's decision to file a petition ensures that a legally trained official has reviewed the legal criteria for a properly authorized petition. The prosecutor checks the legal wording of the petition, determines that enough evidence is available for establishing the petition (finding the delinquent or status offender "guilty") and makes sure that the offense occured in the court's jurisdiction and that the child was of proper age at the time of the offense.

Because of the importance of such legal criteria and because of the growing emphasis on more punitive juvenile models, some jurisdictions have turned away from the traditional probation-officer model of intake to models in which the prosecutor is either the first or the sole intake decisionmaker. Such models are more consistent with more legalistic views of juvenile court in which the state has abandoned the traditional *parens patriae* philosophy. For example, the state of Washington has switched responsibility for the intake decision to the prosecutor for all felony charges and most misdemeanors. Prosecutors make such decisions on the basis of explicit criteria: offense seriousness, prior record and the age of the youth. Furthermore, informal adjustments are no longer permitted at intake, although police agencies can still "exercise their traditional discretion regarding whether to refer or adjust incidents involving juveniles" (Schneider & Schram, 1986: 214). In place of informal adjustments at intake, minor offenses are supposed to be diverted to restitution programs. This action by the state of Washington represents a radical break with traditional juvenile court thinking and practice; it is a close approximation of adult processing with its retributive emphasis. (For a diagrammatic comparison of traditional intake and the Washington state practice, see Box 8.4.) Like Washington state, the Model Juvenile Delinquency Act also stipulates that the prosecutor shall "[d]irectly supervise all matters relating to intake," although the probation officer may continue to make the file-divert decision in misdemeanor cases if the prosecutor so delegates (Rossum et al., 1987: 40). Similarly, the National District Attorneys' Association stipulates a very active role for the prosecutor (Shine & Price, 1992) and Louisiana has given the prosecutor greater authority over the intake process (National Conference of State Legislatures, 1993).

Box 8.4   The Intake Process

Traditional Intake:

Police, parents, school officials, or victims bring youth to attention of Intake	Intake officer files petition	Juvenile Court Hearing
	OR makes an informal adjustment	
	OR diverts to a treatment program	

Prosecutorial Model (e.g., Washington State)

Police, parents, school officials, or victims bring youth to attention of Intake	Prosecutor files a petition	Juvenile Court Hearing
	OR declines to file a petition	
	OR diverts to a restitution program	

A further development is that the prosecutor is now taking on increased responsibility in juvenile cases as more and more states are allowing prosecutors to file cases directly in adult criminal court. In addition to traditional waiver (transfer), several mechanisms allow prosecutors to proceed against juveniles in criminal court: concurrent jurisdiction, statutory exclusion, presumptive waiver, reverse waiver and "once an adult/always an adult" statutes. Unfortunately, national statistics on the numbers of youths so processed in criminal court are not yet being collected on a systematic basis (DeFrances & Strom, 1997). Furthermore, because this is a new phenomenon, research studies on such processing (e.g., whether nonlegal factors such as race affect prosecutor decisionmaking) are not yet available.

Research on Intake Decisionmaking

As was the case with police discretion (see Chapter 7), many researchers and analysts have been concerned about the discretion of intake decisionmakers regarding whether to file petitions. Of particular concern has been the question of whether race is an important factor in the intake decision and whether racial discrimination occurs at intake. Several conclusions can be drawn from the studies that have been conducted on intake decisionmaking. First, seriousness of the alleged offense clearly influences the decision to file a petition, though it is not necessarily the prime factor. Thus, youths accused of more serious offenses are more likely to be petitioned to court than youths accused of less serious offenses (Bell & Lang, 1985; Cohen & Kluegel, 1978; Fenwick, 1982; McCarthy & Smith, 1986; Minor, Hartmann & Terry, 1997; Thornberry, 1973). Second, prior record is a factor. Youths with prior records are more likely to be referred (Cohen & Kluegel, 1978; Fenwick, 1982; McCarthy & Smith, 1986; Thornberry, 1973). Third, demeanor often has an effect; uncooperative youths are more likely to be petitioned than cooperative youths (Bell & Lang, 1985; Fenwick, 1982). However, demeanor often is not measured because many researchers rely on official records that do not include any record of the attitude of the child when he or she is interviewed by the court official making the intake decision. Finally, variables such as age, race, class and gender have produced mixed results. As a result there is considerable controversy surrounding the impact of each of these variables on the intake decision (Bell & Lang, 1985; Cohen & Kluegel, 1978; McCarthy & Smith, 1986; Pope & Feyerherm, 1993; Thornberry, 1973).

The methodology used in many previous studies was deficient. Specifically, many early studies looked at small, nonrepresentative samples that made it impossible to generalize to courts nationwide. Other studies used only bivariate rather than multivariate statistical analyses of their data. This means that they examined the independent effects of individual variables, such as race, on intake decisions but did not consider the effects on decisions of several variables at once. Also, many of the studies were conducted years ago, prior to the introduction of due process guarantees in juvenile court and to the relatively recent civil rights movement focusing on eliminating various forms of discrimination.

Furthermore, at least some researchers (e.g., McCarthy & Smith, 1986; Sampson & Laub, 1993b) contend that it is misleading to isolate the intake decision from the detention, adjudication and dispositional decisions. They argue that those decisions are basically parts of one complex whole that must be studied together to avoid possible distortions. An analogy would be studying decisions of college football coaches about what play to call on first down but ignoring strategy decisions on the second, third and fourth downs. Research on first-down strategy is interesting but incomplete. First-down decisions make the most sense when understood in the context of the other downs.

Going even further, Conley (1994) argues that too many studies have been quantitative rather than qualitative and have thus neglected critical factors. Conley argues that observational studies of both court decisionmaking processes and police decisions are needed.

Two Important Studies

Given the problems with many of the earlier studies, it seems appropriate to focus on two studies that used large, representative samples and that also used multivariate statistics to best determine the relative effects of several factors at once on the intake decision.

Concerning race, McCarthy and Smith (1986) analyzed data on 649 juveniles referred to a juvenile court in a southeastern metropolitan area with a population of about one million people. Looking first at the intake decision, they found that offense, prior record, and race had both direct and indirect effects on the decision to petition, while sex and the number of days detained had only indirect effects. The impact of race, however, was even greater at the adjudication and dispositional stages. McCarthy and Smith interpreted these results to mean that racial discrimination did *not* occur at the intake screening and detention decisions but it may have occurred at adjudication and disposition. They could not draw the firm conclusion of discrimination at adjudication and disposition, however, because it could be that other unmeasured factors (such as offense type, presence or absence of a weapon, extent of harm, or the nature of the crime) explain the decision (McCarthy & Smith, 1986).

Another recent study, by Bell and Lang (1985), looked at the treatment of youths at intake and found that the matter was complex:

> . . . race . . . did not display a simple pattern . . . . However, contrary to the predictions of a naive version of conflict theory, whites are not treated consistently more leniently than other offenders. Our estimates indicate that whites are less likely to receive both the most severe and the least severe dispositions. However, because relatively few persons who are arrested for the crimes covered by this study receive counsel and release [adjustment at intake], the overall treatment of whites is probably generally more lenient, as predicted by both conflict and labeling theory (Bell & Lang, 1985: 324).

In summary, race appears to have some effect on the intake decision. The research of McCarthy and Smith (1986) indicated some disadvantage for blacks (e.g., greater chance of being petitioned), but Bell and Lang (1985) found a more complex situation.

Sampson and Laub (1993) have placed the discussion of the impact of race on juvenile court decisionmaking in a theoretical context. They see race as linked to structural changes in American society, such as the deindustrialization of central cities and the concomitant rise of the underclass. Their research found that "structural contexts of 'underclass' poverty and racial inequality are significantly related to increased juvenile justice processing" (Sampson & Laub, 1993: 305). In simple terms, counties with greater poverty and racial inequality showed higher rates of detention and out-of-home placement of juveniles. Their findings are consistent with the notion that "underclass black males are viewed as a threatening group to middle-class populations and thus will be subjected to increased formal social control by the juvenile justice system" (Sampson & Laub, 1993: 306).

Pope (1995) concludes that race is a factor. He suggests that some changes need to be added to the traditional intake process to ensure that race is not a consideration. One suggestion is training. A second suggestion to have two intake officers decide each case. A third suggestion is to have a review board examine all the decisions to look for any impact of race.

If attention is given to such suggestions to improve court processing and if attention is also given to social and economic factors associated with race problems in the United States, race could cease to be a factor in juvenile court decisionmaking.

The Transfer (Waiver) Decision

For some youths petitioned to juvenile court, the most critical decision point is the **waiver** or **transfer** decision. Many states allow the court to waive or transfer certain offenders (generally older offenders who commit serious crimes) to adult court. This is a crucial decision because the transfer to adult court makes the transferred youth subject to adult penalties such as lengthy incarceration in an adult prison as opposed to a relatively short period of incarceration in a juvenile training school. Such a decision also results in the creation of an adult criminal record that is public and may hinder future opportunities for employment in certain occupations. A juvenile court record, on the other hand, may be confidential, and, therefore, should not harm the child in any way.

In 1995, approximately 9,700 juveniles were waived to adult court. This represents a 33 percent increase over the number of juveniles waived in 1986 but a 10 percent decrease compared to 1991. About one-half (47%) of the cases waived inolved personal offenses, approximately one-third (34%) were property offenses, 12 percent were drug offenses and 7 percent were public order offenses (Sickmund, 1997). An additional number of juveniles were handled in adult criminal court because of statutory exclusion or prosecutor discretion that made judicial waiver unnecessary. (For further discussion of such additional means to process juveniles as adults, see the section on the increasing punitiveness in juvenile court below.) **Statutory exclusion**, also called **legislative waiver**, means that state legislatures rule that certain offenses, such as murder, automatically go to adult court. Prosecutorial discretion occurs in those states where the prosecutor has the authority to file certain cases in juvenile court or in the adult criminal court (Sickmund, 1994).

The waiver decision is made at a hearing that is analogous to the preliminary hearing in adult court. At a waiver hearing, the prosecutor must only show probable cause that an offense occurred and that the juvenile committed the offense. The prosecutor does not have to prove guilt beyond a reasonable doubt. Proof of guilt is reserved for the trial in adult court (if waiver is successful) or for the adjudication stage in juvenile court (if the waiver motion fails). The juvenile transfer hearing differs from an adult court preliminary hearing in that the prosecutor must go further and establish that the juvenile is not amenable to juvenile court intervention or that the juvenile is a threat to public safety. An example of nonamenability would be the case of a youth who is already on parole from a state training school for an earlier delinquent act who then commits another serious offense (e.g., armed robbery). If probable cause were established that the youth committed the robbery, then the judge would have to find that the juvenile court had a history of contacts with the youth dating back several years and that one more juvenile court effort to deal with the youth's problems—either through probation or a training school—placement would be futile. An example of a case involving a threat to public safety would be a murder case or an offender with a history of violent offenses.

The Effectiveness of Transfer

Research on transfer effectiveness has produced mixed results. Bortner (1986) looked at 214 cases of juveniles remanded to adult court in a western metropolitan court between 1980 and 1981. He concluded that waiver was neither protecting the public nor identifying the most dangerous and most intractable delinquents. Specifically, only 31 percent of the remanded youths (those waived to adult court) received prison as their primary sentence and only 55 percent were charged with felonies against persons. The adult court that received the transferred juveniles, therefore, was not imprisoning all the children and it was handling a high percentage of (presumably nondangerous) property offenders.

Part of the reason why only about 30 percent of the transferred youths were sent to prison may be the "punishment gap," which seems to benefit many youth waived to adult court. The term "punishment gap" refers to the finding that "[w]hen juvenile offenders appear in adult court for the first time as adult offenders, they are typically accorded the leniency given to adult first offenders" (Feld, 1987b: 501). That is, because judges appear to view the offenses of transferred juveniles as less serious than the offenses of adult offenders, and because the prior records of the transferred juveniles often are not available to the judges, the judges tend to hand out lenient sentences.

Rudman et al. (1986), on the other hand, looked at 138 violent youths considered for transfer between 1981 and 1984 in Boston, Newark and Phoenix. They found that 94 percent of the transferred youths were convicted of crimes of violence in adult court and 90 percent of the convicted youths were incarcerated. Furthermore, youths convicted and sentenced to incarceration in adult criminal court received substantially longer sentences (about five times longer) than youths who were not transferred but received a sentence of incarceration in juvenile court. Rudman and his colleagues concluded that transfer of violent juveniles was indeed a punitive response and that it resulted "in longer terms of more secure confinement" (Rudman et al., 1986: 93).

Donna Bishop and her colleagues have done extensive research on transfer in the state of Florida. They constructed a matched sample of 2,738 youths transferred in 1987 and nontransferred youths. On the one hand, the transferred youths were more likely to receive longer sentences in the adult system than their juvenile system matches. They were also more likely actually to be incarcerated for longer periods (they actually served longer sentences) than nontransferred youths. Their recidivism, however, was higher than the nontransferred youths, which cancelled out any deterrent or incapacitative effects of transfer (Bishop et al., 1996).

When Bishop and her colleagues used a longer follow-up period, however, the nontransferred youth had a similar prevalence of recidivism. In other words, similar percentages of both transferred and nontransferred youths committed new crimes. There were still disadvantages to transfer, however, because the transferred youths who committed new crimes were arrested more frequently and more quickly than nontransferred youths (Winner et al., 1997).

Fagan examined robbery and burglary cases handled in New York criminal courts and New Jersey juvenile courts for identical offenders in matched communities. Incarceration rates were considerably higher in the adult court than in juvenile court. Approximately six out of 10 (60%) of the juvenile robbers and burglars received probation, but in criminal court, 46 percent of both types of offenders were incarcerated. Fagan also found that rearrest rates were higher for the robbery offenders processed in criminal court and that there were no differences in recidivism for the burglary offenders. Robbery offenders processed in criminal court offended more often and more quickly than their juvenile court counterparts. Fagan concluded that "public safety was, in fact, compromised by adjudication in the criminal court" (Fagan, 1995).

A study of waiver in Texas found that sentences handed down in adult court were longer than those in juvenile court but that the waived youths were often released before the length of time they could have been kept in the juvenile system. That is, the average sentence handed out in adult court was 12.8 years, but the average time served until parole was 3.5 years. So the actual sentence (time served) could have been carried out in the juvenile justice system (Fritsch, Caeti & Hemmens, 1996).

The research suggests that transfer is not a magic solution to some of the perceived problems in the juvenile court. There is conflicting evidence regarding whether transferred youths are more likely to be sentenced to incarceration or are more likely to serve longer time in incarceration. Recidivism statistics do not indicate any advantage for transferred youths. In several instances the transferred youths do worse than nontransferred youths. Nevertheless, the current climate favoring punishment suggests that transfer and other mechanisms to get juveniles into adult court will continue. This probably will occur even though some research evidence questions whether this trend is actually protecting the public more than juvenile court processing could. (For a contrasting view on what the public wants, see Box 8.5.)

Box 8.5   Attitudes Toward Early Intervention Programs

Although the "get tough" movement seems to be based on what the public wants, there is impressive evidence that the public still wants help for troubled youths. In a recent survey of residents of a southern state (Tennessee), on average, 86 percent of the respondents endorsed providing human services to at-risk children. Specifically, respondents endorsed preschool programs, treatment for troubled children in neglecting or abusing households, parent education programs, psychological services for identified youths, after-school programs, drug education, and rehabilitation programs for first offender youths. Even among a subsample of conservative men, two-thirds favored early intervention rather than incarceration (Cullen et al., 1998).

Factors Influencing Transfer

One study of the factors influencing the transfer decision found that age and offense were important factors used by judges in deciding to transfer a case to adult criminal court. Suprisingly, however, prior record was not an important factor and race had only indirect effects:

> Although more minority than Anglo youth were transferred, race effects disappeared when other variables were controlled. Instead, minority youth were more often charged with murder, and murder was a significant predictor in multivariate models. Similarly, the age of onset (that is, first arrest and length of career) was earlier for minority youth, an age-related variable predictive of transfer. Thus it appears that the effects of race are indirect, but visible nonetheless (Fagan, Forst & Vivona, 1987: 276).

In general, Feld's review of the research concluded that discretion is rampant in the waiver decision:

> The empirical reality is that judges cannot administer these discretionary statutes on a consistent, evenhanded basis. Within a single jurisdiction, waiver statutes are inconsistently interpreted and applied-from county to county and from court to court (Feld, 1987b: 492).

A study comparing 364 juveniles transferred in Virginia between 1988 and 1990 compared to a similar number of youths not transferred showed that significant correlates of transfer were current offense information, prior record and commitment record, mental health history, education and age. In addition, youths in nonmetropolitan areas were more likely to be transferred than youths in metropolitan areas. Judges may be more accustomed to serious crime in metropolitan areas or judges in metropolitan areas may have more sentencing options (programs) available for youths. Youths with a history of mental health treatment were less likely to be transferred than youths who had not received any such treatment (Poulos & Orchowsky, 1994). Still another study found that prior waiver was the critical variable affecting judicial decisions to waiver (Lee, 1994).

Alternatives to Transfer

Because attitudes toward juvenile delinquents seem to be becoming more punitive, waiver will probably continue to be used for a significant proportion of juveniles. Also, as noted above, other methods to put delinquents into adult court and/or into incarcerative facilities for lengthier sentences will also be important. Such methods include the institution of sentencing guidelines, statutory exclusion of certain offenses from juvenile court jurisdiction, a lowering of the age of criminal court jurisdiction (Fagan, Forst & Vivone, 1987) and an increase in prosecutorial discretion to file in either juvenile or adult court.

Feld (1981) has argued that statutory exclusion of certain offenders from juvenile court jurisdiction is preferable to waiver mechanisms. Waiver involves judges making individualized decisions that can very easily slip into mistakes and discrimination. Statutory exclusion of certain juveniles from juvenile court jurisdiction ("legislative waiver" in Feld's terms), on the other hand, makes it "possible to exclude on a rational and legally defensible basis (present offense and prior record) from the jurisdiction of the juvenile court those relatively few juveniles who deserve to be treated as adults" (Feld, 1981: 518). This emphasis on objective factors (current charge and prior record) prevents possible abuses of discretion and discrimination by judges.

In his advocacy of the statutory exclusion of certain offenders from juvenile court jurisdiction, however, Feld glosses over the issue of bias amplification (Dannefer & Schutt, 1982; Sampson, 1986). That is, his assumption that reliance on offense and prior record would make the practice "relatively objective" is not without criticism. Some think that police discretion contributes to the creation of the current offense and the offender's prior record. Thus, to rely on these so-called legal variables can introduce subtly subjective (if not discriminatory) factors into the exclusion decision. Sanborn (1994a) criticizes legislative waiver as an abdication of the individualization that is supposed to lie at the heart of juvenile court.

Studies of legislative waiver in two states, New York and Idaho, have indicated that there was no deterrent impact. Juvenile crime did not decrease as a result of the laws that made certain youths of specific ages automatically subject to adult court handling in the two states (Jensen & Metsger, 1994; Singer & McDowall, 1988).

Worker Attitudes

A recent survey of court worker attitudes on transfer produced some interesting results. Workers did not see transfer as necessary for protecting society from extremely dangerous or violent youthful predators. Instead, juvenile court staff claimed that transfer

> prevented juvenile courts having to address youths who had problems that were beyond the rehabilitative capacities of the system and who threatened to contaminate others' chances of rehabilitation. The workers considered transfer as simply the inability of juvenile court to service all youths, rather than as acting like a safety valve or a form of societal retribution. Most respondents rejected numerous opportunities to adopt get tough measures in certification policies; even prosecutors advised against expanding their waiver powers (Sanborn, 1994a: 275).

In other words, although the public and politicians may favor transfer as a way to "get tough" on juvenile crime, the workers do not agree. Many see transfer as a way to direct some youths out of juvenile court, thinking that adult court may be better able to handle those youths.

Adjudication and Disposition

For children not waived to adult criminal court, the next steps after the filing of a petition are **adjudication** and **disposition**. In these decisions, a judge determines whether there is enough evidence to establish the petition and then decides what to do if there is enough evidence. These decisions are comparable to the plea, trial and sentencing decisions in adult court.

Ideally, the determination of the truth of the petition occurs in a rational fashion, with the prosecutor, defense attorney and judge using their abilities and training to seek justice. In reality, juvenile court sessions often are hectic and hurried, and may reflect the self interests of the parties involved rather than justice or the best interests of the child. For example, Peter Prescott has described one day in the operations of the Bronx (NY) Family Court as a

> flow of incompetence and indifference. One court officer perpetually frowns, shaking his head in mute consternation at so much exposure to human fallibility. The court clerk, arrogant and disdainful, speaks as little as possible as if in fear of contamination. When he must speak, his tone is dry and contemptuous, his words chopped short: the burden of dealing with these people and their problems! "I've been here two years," a court officer remarks. "Two years too long. But once you're assigned to Family Court, you're stuck because no one wants to come here" (Prescott, 1981: 85-86).

An account of the Los Angeles juvenile court system (Humes, 1996) indicates that numerous problems continue to plague juvenile court, an institution marked by both frustration and heroism.

Attorneys in Juvenile Court

In a discussion of adult criminal court, Abraham Blumberg (1967) suggested that the defense attorneys he studied were really con artists who were more concerned with their fees than with proving the innocence of their clients. Blumberg observed that private defense attorneys were just as quick to attempt to talk their clients into pleading guilty as public defenders and that the ideal of an attorney fighting for the defendant in a lengthy jury trial was just a romanticized myth (Blumberg, 1967). People may watch celebrity cases or television courtroom dramas and conclude that defense attorneys work round the clock to free their client but the day-to-day truth is often less dramatic.

The situation in juvenile court is somewhat different, although the outcome has often been very similar to what Blumberg found in adult court: pressure on the defendant to admit to the petition. What is different in juvenile court is that there is probably less emphasis on the attorney's fee because most of the youths and families who go through juvenile court are not very well off financially (see, for example, Fabricant, 1983; Mahoney, 1987). Second, many lawyers have an aversion or distaste for helping juveniles to "beat a case," that is, to go free on a legal technicality. Attorneys may fear that skillful courtroom techniques that allow a factually guilty youngster to "beat the rap" only teach disrespect for the law and possibly contribute to future criminality. Therefore, some attorneys advise their youthful clients to plead guilty out of the sincere belief that the youngsters need help and that the traditional juvenile court can provide that help. Third, many lawyers may not be clear whether they are representing the parent(s) or the child. Such confusion can stem from the fact that the parent is paying the attorney's fee or from the attorney's belief that the child is not mature enough to make key decisions without parental advice. If attorneys believe that they are representing the parent(s), then they may follow parental wishes that the child confess and tell the truth. Finally, the lawyer may bow to judicial or court pressure to take a therapeutic approach rather than an adversarial stance. That is, an individual judge or an entire juvenile court system may emphasize a therapeutic or *parens patriae* approach, discouraging zealous advocacy in favor of doing what is in the best interests of the child (for an example of this, see Stapleton & Teitelbaum, 1972).

In summary, many attorneys in juvenile court are reluctant to utilize the zealous advocate approach that is, at least theoretically, the norm in adult criminal court. Attorneys in adult criminal courts justify such zealous advocacy (where the attorney fights as hard as possible for all defendants, even defendants who have admitted that they are factually guilty) on the grounds that the system is adversarial and that the adversarial process is best for bringing out the truth. In juvenile court, some attorneys, parents and judges feel that the adult criminal court norm of zealous advocacy is inappropriate. They may worry that strong advocacy can result in an outcome in which a child who "needs help" will not get it because failure to establish the petition leaves the court with no jurisdiction over the child. As a result, at least some attorneys act more like a concerned adult than a zealous advocate, encouraging youths to admit to petitions in cases in which an adversarial approach may have resulted in a dismissal of the petition.

Recent research shows that there continue to be problems in juvenile court. In a survey of 100 court workers in three juvenile courts, Sanborn (1994b) found that 79 percent of the workers thought that attorneys gave inadequate representation. One-third were of the opinion that attorneys engaged in behaviors that undermined a fair trial for their juvenile defendants. In addition, about 25 percent of the respondents thought that defense attorneys would not vigorously represent their youthful clients, and 29 percent claimed that attorneys acted like guardians rather than zealous advocates. Because of this, Sanborn (1994b) suggests that juveniles be given the right to trial by jury to counteract "judicial contamination by learning the defendant's record from countless sources and sloppy performances by judges and defense attorneys perpetrated within a private, laissez-faire atmosphere" (Sanborn, 1994b: 613).

Plea Bargaining

Because of the pressure on youths to plead guilty (admit the allegations in the petition) and because of the problems with **plea bargaining** (see, e.g., Newman, 1986), the American Bar Association has recommended that plea bargaining either be made visible or eliminated entirely (Institute of Judicial Administration–American Bar Association, 1980). The Bar Association maintains that if plea bargaining is retained, the judge should not participate in the process. However, the judge "should require disclosure of the agreement reached and explicitly indicate the conditions under which he or she is willing to honor it" (Institute of Judicial Administration–American Bar Association, 1980: 39). If the judge will not accept the plea agreement, he or she should give the juvenile a chance to withdraw his or her plea. Finally, the judge should consult with the juvenile's parents before accepting a plea (Institute of Judicial Administration–American Bar Association, 1980: 47). These regulations (or alternatively, the abolition of plea bargaining) would eliminate many of the traditional abuses of the practice.

Attorney Effectiveness

Research has shown some interesting results concerning the effectiveness of defense attorneys in juvenile court. First, Michael Fabricant's (1983) study of juvenile court public defenders in Brooklyn and the Bronx (NY) found that, contrary to stereotypes, public defenders were more effective (or at least as effective) as private attorneys in defending their juvenile clients. Specifically, the public defenders were very effective in obtaining adjournments, avoiding detention and gaining dismissals. Such indicators of adversarial effectiveness led Fabricant (1983) to conclude that New York City public defenders were not inadequate. This is an impressive finding because they were representing roughly 75 percent of the delinquency and status offense cases in New York City at the time of the study.

Stevens Clarke and Gary Koch (1980), however, found conflicting evidence. Specifically, data from two North Carolina juvenile courts in the mid-1970s indicated that "the assistance of an attorney was on the whole not helpful—and may have actually been detrimental—with respect to reducing the child's chance of being adjudicated delinquent and committed" (Clarke & Koch, 1980: 307). The attorneys may have been more concerned with "helping" the youths receive treatment than in simply "beating the rap." It should be noted that an alternative interpretation of the findings from North Carolina is that the attorneys studied were receiving the toughest cases, cases that judges had essentially decided were going to wind up in youth prisons anyway. Finally, it is important to remember that juvenile court is often a low-prestige assignment for both new public defenders and new prosecutors. Many of these attorneys "try to stay as briefly as possible" (Mahoney, 1987: 10) in these jobs. The resultant lack of experience may influence the effectiveness of both prosecutors and public defenders in juvenile court.

In an analysis of six states, Feld (1988) found results very similar to North Carolina. In three states many children did not have attorneys. In all six states, however, "unrepresented juveniles seem to fare better than those with lawyers" (Feld, 1988: 418). Juveniles with attorneys were more likely to receive placement outside the home or secure confinement than juveniles without attorneys.

Thus, the situation in America's juvenile courts appears to be that some attorneys are adversarial, some are still traditional and act as concerned adults, and some are in between the two extremes. Furthermore, in some states, many juveniles are not represented by attorneys (Feld, 1993). This state of affairs raises the issue of which is the best approach: zealous advocate, concerned adult or some compromise between the two alternatives? The chief advantage of the zealous advocate model is that it is probably the best insurance that only truly guilty youths will come under court jurisdiction. Since the attorney does not pressure the child to admit to the petition (plead guilty), there is less danger that the court will attempt some type of intervention program with youths who are not really guilty. An added advantage is that this approach may well generate the most respect from juveniles for the court system. Fewer youths will feel that they have been betrayed or tricked into something that some adult thought was best for them, despite their own wishes. The biggest danger of the zealous advocate approach is that it may contribute to what Fabricant (1983) calls the contemporary version of benign neglect. That is, since many youths appearing in juvenile court come from families racked with problems, such as low income, public assistance and/or broken homes, they do need assistance. An adversarial approach may prevent these children from being railroaded into juvenile prisons or other types of intervention due to insufficient legal defense. That adversarial approach, however, does nothing about the real problems faced by these children in their homes and their neighborhoods:

> It must be presumed that these youngsters' fundamental problems will neither be addressed nor resolved through a faithful adherence to process. Just as important, their troubles are likely to be compounded by social indifference. Therefore, a policy of calculated nonintervention may, over time, cause severe and/or increased anti-social behavior from troubled youths who initially are ignored by the court or state (Fabricant, 1983: 140).

The advantage of the concerned adult model is that it seeks to address the problems of the child that presumably led the child into delinquency. The problem is that this helping philosophy has been the rationale of the juvenile court since 1899 and, as David Rothman has so aptly phrased it, the rhetoric of individualized attention has always far outstripped the reality of ineffective if not abusive programs (Rothman, 1980).

Jury Trials for Juveniles

Since the U.S. Supreme Court has not mandated the right to a jury trial for all juveniles (see Chapter 9), only about a dozen states offer juveniles this right (Rossum et al., 1987: 112). Some contend that it is critical for juveniles to have the right to a jury trial. For example, Barry Feld (1987b) has argued that judges require less proof than juries and, therefore, it is easier to convict a youth in front of a judge than in front of a jury. The American Bar Association agrees that judges may be biased and further states:

> A jury trial gives enhanced visibility to the adjudicative process. A jury trial requires the trial court judge to articulate his or her views of the applicable law in the case through jury instructions, thereby facilitating appellate court review of the legal issues involved. Without the focus on legal issues that such an exercise entails, the danger is great that the applicable law may be misperceived or misapplied and that the error will go uncorrected on appeal (Institute of Judicial Administration–American Bar Association, 1980: 53).

Having the right to a jury trial, however, may not make that much difference in juvenile court. In her study of a suburban juvenile court, Mahoney (1985) found that only seven cases out of the 650 actually went to trial. For those seven youths, and for 87 other youths who initially requested a jury trial but later settled without a jury trial, there was no impact of setting (scheduling) a case for trial on outcomes. Thus, "in a handful of serious cases in which a child denies charges, it [a jury trial] may be essential to the cause of justice, but it is unclear how much a jury trial benefits a youth or the community in the great majority of cases" (Mahoney, 1985: 564).

The Recent Emphasis on Punitiveness

Traditionally, the disposition stage of juvenile court has been the epitome of the *parens patriae* philosophy. With the advice of probation officers, social workers, psychologists and psychiatrists, the judge has tried to act in the best interests of the child. Recently, however, disposition (sentencing) in juvenile justice has taken on an increasingly punitive character.

One indicator of this increasingly explicit focus on punishment is the revision of the purpose clauses of state juvenile codes. Forty-two states have such purpose clauses, and virtually all have some mention of what amounts to a focus on the best interests of the child. However, since the early 1980s, approximately one-third of the states have amended their juvenile code purpose clauses to include such goals as punishment, the protection of society, or accountability among the purposes of the code (Feld, 1987a, 1993a & b; National Conference of State Legislatures, 1993).

Parallel to the amendment of the purpose clauses, the states have taken more concrete measures to emphasize punishment. Three states (Washington, New Jersey and Texas) have adopted determinate sentencing statutes with an emphasis on proportionality. The law in such states limits the discretion of judges at disposition and attempts to set penalties that are proportionate to the seriousness of the offense. Some states have enacted mandatory minimum provisions. This means that if the judge commits a child to the state youth authority, the law dictates that the youth must serve a certain minimum amount of time. Some states have adopted dispositional guidelines or suggested sentences for most adjudicated delinquents. Unless a case has some unusual factors, judges are supposed to sentence within the ranges stipulated in the guidelines. Finally, there is the fear that the conditions of confinement have become more negative or soon will become so. This fear is based on the experience of the adult prison system, where determinate sentencing has led to overcrowding and other negative consequences in the institutions (Feld, 1987a).

A prime indicator of the trend toward punitiveness is the move by many states to expand provisions for processing juveniles in adult criminal court rather than juvenile court. Concerning traditional judicial waiver (transfer), between 1992 and 1995, 11 states lowered the age limit for one or more crimes, 10 states added offenses and two states expanded prior record provisions. Since 1992, nine more states added presumptive waiver laws. As of 1995, 36 states and the District of Columbia had statutory exclusion provisions for certain classes of juveniles. In other words, the covered offenses/offenders automatically went to adult court. Eighteen states have "once waived/always waived" exclusion clauses so that once a youth is processed in adult criminal court, he or she will always be processed in criminal court (Torbet, 1996).

Still another development in this direction is **blended sentencing**. In blended sentencing, either the juvenile court or the adult court imposes a sentence that can involve either the juvenile or the adult correctional system or both correctional systems. The adult sentence may be suspended pending either a violation or the commission of a new crime.

One example of the use of blended sentencing is in New Mexico. That state's "exclusive blend" of sentencing applies to 15-year-olds charged with first-degree murder or 15- to 17-year-olds charged with serious offenses or 15- to 17-year-olds charged with a felony and with three prior separate felony adjudications in a two-year period. The juvenile court has jurisdiction and can sentence the youth to a juvenile *or* an adult sentence. In juvenile-inclusive blend sentencing, the juvenile court has jurisdiction and can sentence to a sanction including both the juvenile correctional system *and* the adult correctional system. Usually (e.g., in Connecticut, Minnesota and Montana), the adult sanction is suspended unless the youth violates the juvenile sanction. Two other options are criminal-exclusive (e.g., in California and Florida) and criminal-inclusive blended sentencing (e.g., in Arkansas and Missouri), in which the criminal court tries and sentences the youth. In criminal-exclusive systems, the sentence can be to juvenile *or* adult corrections; in criminal-inclusive states, the sentence can be to both systems. The other type of blended sentencing is juvenile-contiguous, in which the juvenile court has authority to impose a sanction that goes beyond the age of its jurisdiction. Differing procedures are used to decide whether the remainder of the sentence is imposed in the adult corrections system (Torbet et al., 1996).

Still another sign of increasing punitiveness is the passing of statutes concerning the confidentiality of juvenile court records and proceedings. Traditionally, such records and court proceedings were closed to the public. The *parens patriae* rationale dictated that this would protect the juvenile from publicity so that a delinquent act would not stigmatize him or her permanently. In the last few years, however, critics have called for publicity to assure community protection and legislatures have responded. As of 1995, 22 states allow or require open court hearings for juveniles and 39 states allow releasing the juvenile offender's name or picture to the media or public under specified conditions (Torbet et al., 1996).

A possible consequence of these punitive developments is that the involved states create two ways of processing juveniles. If a youth is older, commits a serious offense and/or has a prior record, he or she will be treated as an adult or similar to an adult. If a younger youth commits a less serious offense and lacks a prior record, he or she will be handled in a traditional juvenile court. Much of the rationale behind this division of juveniles into quasi-adults and children is the belief that youths have changed. Youths who commit what appear to be willful violent crimes are considered mature and responsible adults who should be held accountable for their actions. Younger youths who commit less serious offenses are still looked on as wayward youths who can be salvaged by the traditional *parens patriae* juvenile court.

Dispositional Decisionmaking

A major issue in juvenile justice is the question of which factors influence judges in their dispositional (sentencing) decisions. Research indicates several general conclusions. Legal variables such as seriousness of the offense and prior record have a strong influence on dispositions (e.g., Clarke & Koch, 1980; Cohen & Kluegel, 1978; Dannefer & Schutt, 1982; McCarthy & Smith, 1986; Staples, 1987; Thomas & Cage, 1977; Thornberry, 1973). The impact of prior record on dispositions, however, may reflect bias amplification (Dannefer & Schutt, 1982; Sampson, 1986). In other words, prior record may mask the influence of race or social class in police decisionmaking. The impact of offender characteristics such as age, race, social class and gender has mixed results (see McCarthy & Smith, 1986 for a review of prior research in this area, especially prior research on the impact of race; see also Krisberg & Austin, 1993; Pope, 1994). Usually, the impact of these variables is weaker than the impact of legal variables. One study, however, indicated that "measures of social class and race become increasingly important as direct influences on the final disposition as youths are selected into the system for further processing" (McCarthy & Smith, 1986: 58).

A number of studies report that females receive more severe dispositions than males for minor offenses, especially status offenses. This is an example of the chivalry hypothesis mentioned in Chapter 7. It seems to reflect a paternalistic attitude toward female misbehavior compared to a condonation of boys "sowing their wild oats" (Chesney-Lind, 1977; Chesney-Lind & Shelden, 1992; Cohen & Kluegel, 1979). Although more egalitarian attitudes and practices may eventually mean the end of chivalry in juvenile justice, Chesney-Lind (1987) argues that patriarchal authority in juvenile justice is not yet dead.

Prior case processing decisions exert some influence on dispostions. For example, detained youths receive harsher dispositions (Bailey & Peterson, 1981; Chused, 1973; Clarke & Koch, 1980) or are more likely to be formally processed (Frazier & Bishop, 1985; McCarthy, 1987) than youths who are not detained. Moreover, prior case dispositions can affect subsequent dispositions (Henretta, Frazier & Bishop, 1985, 1986; Thornberry & Christenson, 1984). Finally, some authors report that dispositions vary from one jurisdiction to the next (e.g., Belknap, 1984, Dannefer & Schutt, 1982), while others fail to find such differences (e.g., Staples, 1987).

Research on the issue of factors affecting court dispositions should be better able to answer such questions in the future because the quality of the research is improving. Whereas earlier studies often looked at only one jurisdiction and may have used only simple statistical procedures, more recent studies have used large samples from several jurisdictions and have employed sophisticated multivariate analyses.

A recent review of all the decisionmaking in juvenile justice concluded with an assessment of "a discouraging picture":

> Juvenile laws are vaguely worded and inconsistently applied, permitting extensive abuses in the handling of children by social control agencies whose discretion is largely unchecked. Instead of protecting children from injustices and unwarranted state intervention, the opposite effect frequently occurs. The practices and procedures of juvenile justice agents mirror our society's class and racial prejudices and fall disproportionately on African-American, Latino, and poor people (Krisberg & Austin, 1993: 109).

Feld's (1993b) research on dispositional decisions in Minnesota is similarly pessimistic. He argues that one interpretation of his findings is that

> there is no rationale to dispositional decision making; it consists of little more than hunch, guesswork, and hopes, constrained marginally by the youth's present offense, prior record, and previous dispositions (Feld, 1993b: 232).

Another recent review concluded that race is still an important factor in juvenile justice decisionmaking:

> Minority youth, especially black youth, are often treated more severely when compared with comparable white youths. Depending upon the jurisdiction, it is not uncommon to find that minority youth are more likely to be held at intake, detained prior to adjudication, have petitions filed, be adjudicated delinquent, placed in secure confinement facilities, and transferred to adult court (Pope, 1994: 7).

These appraisals do not see discretion and individualization as positive aspects of concern; they see them as evidence of a lack of sufficient attention to legal variables such as seriousness of offense and the extent of the juvenile's prior record.

Krisberg and Austin (1993) argue that problems in juvenile court dispositions, especially any findings of possible racial disproportionality, cannot be resolved in isolation but are "tied inextricably to the pursuit of social justice. Reforms will continue to fail, as they have in the past, if they do not address the maldistribution of wealth, power and resources throughout society" (Krisberg & Austin, 1993: 110). (For a discussion of other changes intended to improve juvenile court dispositions, see Boxes 8.6 and 8.7.)

Box 8.6   The Silverton, Oregon, Reform of Juvenile Court

Silverton, Oregon, passed a law in 1995 making parents liable for juvenile offenses, including status offenses such as truancy and delinquency. Parents may be fined up to $1,000 dollars, ordered to pay damages and/or ordered to attend parenting classes.

One school official claimed that the new law has been quite effective in combating truancy. After passage of the law, parents are now calling the principal to check that their children are in school, whereas prior to the law the principal had to call parents of truant children.

Critics of the law say that it punishes parents when children break the law despite honest efforts of parents to instill good discipline. Another criticism is that the law does not send the message that children are responsible for their own conduct ("Good Morning America," June 1, 1995).

What do you think? To what extent should parents be held accountable for their children's misdeeds? Are critics right that this law might send a message that children themselves are not responsible for their actions?

Box 8.7   Some Suggestions for Reducing the Effect of Race on Court Dispositions

Frazier and Bishop (1995) studied 137,028 cases referred to juvenile justice intake units in Florida between 1985 and 1987.

They found significant race effects in dispositions even after controlling for the possible effects of other variables such as seriousness of the offense.

They offer several suggestions to reduce the impact of race in juvenile court. First, states should establish policies for reporting, investigating and responding to individual instances of suspected racial bias. A second suggestion is diversity training for employees. Third, lack of parental cooperation should not be a ban for admission to more informal juvenile justice system options. Fourth, if persons with economic resources can utilize private care instead of harsher system dispositions, then "precisely the same treatment services should be made availabe at state expense to serve the poor—whether minority or majority race youths" (Frazier & Bishop, 1995: 45).

Summary

This chapter has examined the critical decision points in juvenile court: intake, detention, waiver, adjudication and disposition. This review has shown that the ideal of a beneficent court system has not always been reached. Sometimes, for example, detention facilities have been deteriorating physical facilities concealing punitive practices. Even though 30 years have elapsed since the *In re Gault* decision established due process protections for juveniles, attorneys in juvenile court are confused about their role. Despite the history of civil rights legislation and concern, sometimes race appears to be a factor in juvenile court decisionmaking. Most recently, critics have become concerned about juvenile crime and the adequacy of the juvenile justice system to handle the serious offender. Thus, increased use of waiver and of other more punitive measures such as blended sentencing has begun to characterize many juvenile court systems. This trend will probably continue.

In light of the ferment in juvenile court and the growing emphasis on harsher measures, concern for the due process rights of juvenile offenders is more critical than ever. In the next chapter, we will discuss due process issues and the rights of juveniles in general.

DISCUSSION QUESTIONS

1. H. Ted Rubin argues that token economies and other detention programs are violations of juvenile detainees' rights because most of the youths have not been adjudicated delinquent. Do you agree or do you feel that such programs can be justified since they establish order and thereby protect the detainees? Are such practices similar to what "free" youngsters experience every day in a typical school setting?

2. Much of the research described in this chapter concerns the decisions to detain, petition and dispose of alleged delinquents. One of the basic issues in all of these decisions is whether the decisionmakers should or should not consider social factors in their decisionmaking. For example, should the attitude of the youth or the quality of parental care influence whether he or she is formally processed or allowed to go home with a warning or a much less severe consequence? Do such social factors have a place in these decisions or are such social factors so liable to ethnic bias that the decisions should be based *solely* on legal factors?

3. Do you favor the use of bail in juvenile court? If so, for what sorts of offenders and under what circumstances?

4. Would you consider a career in juvenile detention as an administrator, counselor, teacher or attendant (guard)?

5. Consider the following: A juvenile is accused of raping a 24-year-old high school teacher. You are a defense attorney and the defendant has asked you to represent him. You are convinced that you could "get the juvenile off" on a technicality. However, several members of your extended family are teachers and feel very strongly about this case. Would you accept the case? Would you pursue the technical defense that would exonerate the defendant or would you encourage the youth to plead guilty and accept the psychiatric help that an expert feels is needed for the young man?

6. What do you think about the trend toward increased punitiveness (increased criminal court processing of youths, blended sentences, changes in purpose clauses to include punishment and incapacitation as juvenile court objectives, and changes in confidentiality)? Do you favor this trend or does it represent an abandoning of the ideals of juvenile court?

7. Suppose that a 13-year-old youth became extremely agitated and angry. He went to his parents' bedroom and got a pistol that was kept there in case an intruder broke in. He then murdered a family member. If this youth had no prior record but also no evidence of psychiatric disturbance, would you favor or oppose processing this youth as an adult in criminal court? How would the factor of a prior record influence your decision? What details of a prior record would most affect your decision? What are your reasons for your position?

8. The use of blended sentences and the increased processing of juveniles in adult court will probably result in an increase in the number of youths being incarcerated in adult prisons or in new youthful offender prisons instead of traditional training schools? What might be some positive and negative consequences of this?

CHAPTER 9

Due Process and Juveniles

Key Terms and Phrases

Breed v. Jones
consent search
corporal punishment
curfew laws
Fare v. Michael C.
freedom of speech
graduated licensing
In re Gault
In re Winship
Ingraham v. Wright

Kent v. United States
legal drinking age
McKeiver v. Pennsylvania
New Jersey v. T.L.O.
reasonable doubt
Schall v. Martin
school prayer
search and seizure
student search

Juveniles share some—but not all—of the same constitutional rights as adults. While a comprehensive analysis of juvenile rights would require an entire book and is, therefore, beyond the scope of this text, it is important to examine some of the rights pertaining to juveniles. This chapter will first examine the landmark juvenile Supreme Court cases of the 1960s and 1970s (such as *In re Gault*) because those cases fundamentally altered the contours of the juvenile justice system. Then we will examine the Fourth Amendment rights of juveniles in terms of search and seizure by the police. Finally, we will analyze some other important rights of juveniles, such as rights in school and rights at home.

The Landmark Supreme Court Cases

Between the founding of the juvenile court in 1899 and the *Kent v. United States* case in 1966, the U.S. Supreme Court basically left the juvenile court alone. In other words, the Supreme Court respected the intentions of juvenile court officials to seek the best interests of the child by allowing juvenile court judges and related personnel a great deal of discretion in attempting to achieve those objectives. In the mid-1960s, however, the Supreme Court was confronted with several cases that indicated that such a hands-off approach was no longer appropriate.

Kent v. United States

In **Kent v. United States** (1966), the Supreme Court was faced with a waiver case appeal wherein a 16-year-old, Morris Kent, had been waived (transferred) to adult criminal court without a hearing, without the assistance of counsel and without any statement of the reasons for the judge's decision to transfer the matter to the adult court. A judge had decided to transfer Kent, who had been charged with rape, simply on the basis of a review of the youth's social service and probation files. The judge did not allow Kent's privately retained attorney to review any of the files, nor did the judge conduct any hearing on the matter or state the reasons that convinced him to transfer the case. Thus, the waiver decision, a very critical decision that results in the possibility of an adult criminal record and adult penalties, had been made by the judge acting alone, without any concern for Morris Kent's rights.

The Supreme Court justices decided that due process of law entitles a defendant like Morris Kent to certain minimum safeguards, including a hearing, the right to the assistance of an attorney and a statement of the reasons for transfer if the judge decides to transfer the case to adult court. The Supreme Court reasoned that the juvenile court judge denied Kent his right to the assistance of an attorney. Without a hearing, Kent's attorney had no opportunity to represent the youth. The denial of the assistance of counsel, a Sixth Amendment right, was compounded by the judge's denial of access to the case files. That denial prevented the attorney from raising any challenges to possible errors in social service or probation staff reports about the defendant.

The *Kent* case is important not so much because it corrected the wrongs done to one individual or because it put some order into the waiver (transfer) procedure, but because it marks the U.S. Supreme Court's first major examination of juvenile court processing. This examination found serious shortcomings in both the particular juvenile court that had handled Morris Kent and juvenile courts in general:

> While there can be no doubt of the original laudable purpose of juvenile courts, studies and critiques in recent years raise serious questions as to whether actual performance measures well enough against theoretical purpose to make tolerable the immunity of the process from the reach of constitutional guaranties applicable to adults. There is much evidence that some juvenile courts, including that of the District of Columbia, lack the personnel, facilities and techniques to perform adequately as representatives of the State in a *parens patriae* capacity, at least with respect to children charged with law violation.

There is evidence, in fact, that there may be grounds for concern that the child receives the worst of both worlds: that he gets neither the protections accorded to adults nor the solicitous care and regenerative treatment postulated for children (*Kent v. United States*, 1966).

In Re Gault

The case of *In re Gault* was even more significant. Gerald Gault was a 15-year-old Arizona youth who was arrested for allegedly making obscene phone calls to an adult woman. He was adjudicated a delinquent in a court proceeding that resembled a kangaroo court or a dictatorial tribunal rather than a court of law, and was sentenced to the state training school for a possible six-year sentence. The maximum penalty for an adult committing the same offense was a $50 fine and two months in jail.

Gault, after being accused, was taken into police custody and detained. Within about a week, Gerald was adjudicated a delinquent and committed to the state training school until he was discharged or turned 21 years of age, whichever came first. All of this occurred without the complainant (the target of the obscene phone calls) ever appearing in court to testify, without any detailed and specific charges being filed (Gerald was simply *accused* of being a "delinquent"), without the assistance of an attorney for Gerald (his probation officer "represented" him) and without any transcript of the proceedings. The end result was the possibility of a six-year sentence for, what was at worst, a nuisance offense.

In reviewing the case, Supreme Court Justice Abe Fortas traced the history of the juvenile court and of the *parens patriae* philosophy and found some fundamental problems. Supposedly, due process guarantees such as the assistance of an attorney were to be relaxed in juvenile court so that youths would receive the treatment benefits promised by both the founders and current advocates of the juvenile court. Instead, as the Court observed in the *Kent* case, the child often received the worst of both worlds: lack of procedural fairness and substandard treatment.

Interestingly, the Supreme Court did not go on to discard the juvenile court philosophy of *parens patriae*. Instead, Justice Fortas observed that due process rights would not hinder juvenile court judges from seeking the best interests of the child but actually would assist them in that effort:

> But recent studies . . . suggest that the appearance as well as the actuality of fairness, impartiality and orderliness—in short, the essentials of due process—may be a more impressive and more therapeutic attitude so far as the juvenile is concerned (*In re Gault*, 1967).

Judge Fortas went on to rule that juveniles do have certain due process rights in delinquency proceedings in which there is the possibility of confinement in a locked facility. Specifically, such juveniles have the Fifth Amendment privilege against self-incrimination (the right to remain silent) and Sixth Amendment rights to adequate notice of the charges against them, to confront and cross-examine their accusers and to the assistance of counsel.

In Re Winship

In 1970, the U.S. Supreme Court went a step further. In the case of *In re Winship*, an appeal of a New York case involving a 12-year-old boy who had stolen $112 from a woman's purse from a locker, the Supreme Court turned its attention to the issue of the standard of proof (how strong a case must be to prove delinquency) in juvenile court. The Court made two rulings. First, the Court ruled that the U.S. Constitution requires that adult criminals be convicted only by the standard of guilty beyond a reasonable doubt (the **reasonable doubt** standard of proof). This had been standard practice in adult courts; the Court simply stated that the Constitution mandated what the states had been doing all along. Second, the Court extended the reasonable doubt standard of proof to juvenile delinquency proceedings in which there was the possibility of commitment to a locked facility. As was the case in *In re Gault*, the Court reasoned that this safeguard of the reasonable doubt standard would not detract in any way from the noble intentions of the *parens patriae* philosophy. It also suggested that, rhetoric aside, juvenile training schools were the functional equivalents of adult prisons because both resulted in deprivation of liberty—and any such deprivation of liberty requires due process protections. Finally, the Supreme Court noted that New York State's standard of proof in juvenile proceedings (e.g., guilty by a preponderance of the evidence) was open to inaccurate findings. There was a real possibility that youths could be found delinquent when in fact there was insufficient evidence for such findings.

McKeiver v. Pensylvania

A year later, in 1971, the U.S. Supreme Court took up the issue of a juvenile's right to a jury trial in the case of **McKeiver v. Pennsylvania**. In *McKeiver*, the Supreme Court declined to go so far in extending adult rights as to grant juveniles the right to trial by jury. The Supreme Court decided not to grant juveniles the right to jury trials for several reasons. First, the Court did not want to turn the juvenile court process into a fully adversarial process and end "the idealistic prospect of an intimate, informal protective proceeding" (*McKeiver v. Pennsylvania*, 1971). Second, the Court noted that because bench trials (trials decided by a judge rather than by a jury) for adults often result in accurate determinations of guilt, jury trials are not an absolute necessity for accurate determinations of delinquency. The Court also indicated that it was reluctant to impose a federal requirement of jury trials because such a mandate could prevent individual states from experimenting with different methods. Finally, the Court noted that it had not reached such total disillusionment with the juvenile justice system that it sought to abandon it.

Barry Feld (1987b) contends that the denial of the right of a jury trial to juveniles was an important decision because judges and juries view cases differently. The result of the denial of the right to a jury trial is that it is "easier to convict a youth appearing before a judge in juvenile court than to convict a youth, on the basis of the same evidence, before a jury of detached citizens in a criminal proceeding" (Feld, 1987b: 530). In other words, Feld believes that judges need less evidence to convict than do juries and that delinquents would fare better before juries.

These cases of *Kent, Gault, Winship* and *McKeiver* constituted a philosophical revolution in juvenile court. Together, they forced juvenile courts to at least pay lip service to the notion that juveniles deserve many of the due process safeguards available to adults. Although the *McKeiver* case ruled against extending the right of trial by jury to juveniles, even this case indicated that the Supreme Court would not tolerate the wholesale denial of rights to juveniles. The *McKeiver* case implied that if accurate fact-finding were not available to juveniles, then the Supreme Court might have to impose additional limits on juvenile court discretion.

Still, it must be remembered that a philosophical revolution is not always a revolution in practice. Just because the Supreme Court has ruled that juveniles should be entitled to certain rights, such a pronouncement alone does not guarantee the actual provision of those rights. There is evidence, for example, that "less than 50% of the juveniles adjudicated delinquent receive the assistance of counsel to which they are entitled" (Feld, 1987b: 531; see also, Feld, 1993). Thus, judicial policies and juvenile court judges' "continuing hostility toward lawyers" (Feld, 1987b: 532) can prevent juveniles from actually benefiting from Supreme Court rulings.

More Recent Supreme Court Rulings

Since the landmark cases just discussed, the U.S. Supreme Court has decided several cases concerning delinquency proceedings in juvenile court.

Breed v. Jones: A Ruling on Waiver

In **Breed v. Jones** (1975), the Court made the waiver process more explicit by ruling that states cannot first adjudicate a juvenile a delinquent and then waive or transfer the youth to adult court. The Court ruled that by doing this in a particular case, the state of California violated the youth's Fifth Amendment protection against double jeopardy (being tried twice for the same crime). The state of California had claimed that double jeopardy was not at issue because the juvenile was only punished once, but the Supreme Court ruled that being tried both in juvenile court and then again in adult court did indeed constitute a violation of the double jeopardy provision.

In a sense, the case of *Breed v. Jones* was not much of a victory for juvenile rights. Prior to the case, juveniles were tried in juvenile court, adjudicated delinquent and then transferred to adult criminal court where they were tried as adults and sentenced. All that the U.S. Supreme Court ruling accomplished was a procedural change by which the juvenile court would now conduct a waiver or transfer hearing to determine if there was probable cause to believe that the juvenile committed the delinquent act. If the juvenile court finds probable cause and also determines that the juvenile is not amenable to juvenile system intervention (for example, the youth is getting too old for juvenile programs or has been in juvenile programs previously without much success), the juvenile court simply transfers the juvenile to the adult system without any final determination of the charge. A few years ago, one of the authors of this text observed such a waiver hearing that equaled a full trial on the delinquency petition in every respect except that the judge declared a finding of "probable cause" rather than "delinquent" at the end of the hearing. The practical result of such waivers (transfers) to adult criminal court is the same as if the child had been adjudicated a delinquent. *Breed v. Jones* may be more a case of window dressing rather than an influential juvenile justice case.

Fare v. Michael C.: A Ruling on Interrogation

As noted above, two of the provisions of the *Gault* case were its explicit endorsements of the Fifth Amendment privilege against self-incrimination and of the Sixth Amendment right to the assistance of counsel for juveniles. *Gault* applied to juvenile delinquency suspects the *Miranda* rights granted to adult criminal suspects. Like adults, juveniles may waive these two rights and consent to police interrogation without any attorney being present. A voluntary confession can then be used against the juvenile in court.

Gault left it unclear if a juvenile could waive these so-called *Miranda* rights without first speaking with at least one parent or with an attorney. Several state juvenile law codes stipulate that the police must contact a parent prior to interrogating a juvenile suspect. The American Bar Association has gone so far as to recommend mandatory consultation with an attorney prior to any confession to the police (Institute of Judicial Administration–American Bar Association, 1982). Most states, however, simply stipulate that the police give *Miranda* warnings in language that is understandable to juveniles (see Holtz, 1987).

The Supreme Court clarified this issue in the case of **Fare v. Michael C.** (1979). In this case a juvenile murder suspect consented to an interrogation after he was denied the opportunity to consult with his probation officer. The Court ruled that there is no constitutional mandate to allow a suspect to speak with his or her probation officer. The rationale of the Court was that the Sixth Amendment specifies the right to the assistance of counsel, while a probation officer is basically on the side of the police in seeking to prosecute any juvenile who has violated his probation. More importantly, the Court ruled that a child can voluntarily waive his or her privilege against self-incrimination without first speaking to his or her parents and consulting an attorney. In such a situation the trial court judge must evaluate the voluntariness of any confession based on the totality of the circumstances rather than on any ironclad rule (called a *per se* rule) mandating the police to bring in at least one parent or an attorney to advise the child about the wisdom of waiving his or her rights. In evaluating the totality of the circumstances of the waiver, the trial court must consider such factors as the age, maturity, experience and intelligence of the youth. Thus, judges might allow as admissible the waiver of rights by a 17-year-old high school student with a prior record but probably not the waiver of rights by a 13-year-old first offender of below-average intelligence.

It is important to note that there is some controversy about the Supreme Court's wisdom in not requiring more explicit or extensive warnings for juvenile suspects prior to interrogation. First, some research indicates that not all juveniles clearly understand their rights when arrested. In one study, about one-third of a sample of institutionalized delinquents thought (erroneously) that they were required to talk to the police (Robin, 1982). Other research has indicated that more than one-half of the youths tested lacked full understanding of all the *Miranda* warnings and only about one-fifth adequately understood all of the warnings (Holtz, 1987: 550). Second, parents tend not to be the best protectors of juvenile rights. One study showed that about one-third of the parents would advise their own children to confess criminal involvement to the police (Robin, 1982). Due to considerations such as these, some model juvenile law codes stipulate that police must have juvenile suspects consult with an attorney prior to police interrogation (Institute of Judicial Administration–American Bar Association, 1982). Others argue that it would be sufficient if the police used a simplified version of the warnings (Holtz, 1987).

Police detain a group of youths in the inner city. Juveniles share some but not all of the same constitutional rights as adults. *Photo: Mark C. Ide*

Schall v. Martin: A Ruling on Preventive Detention

In *Schall v. Martin* (1984), the U.S. Supreme Court ruled that a juvenile who is awaiting court action can be held in preventive detention if there is adequate concern that the juvenile would commit additional crimes while the primary case is pending further court action. The juvenile, however, does have the right to a hearing on the preventive detention decision and a statement of the reasons for which he or she is being detained. The Court justified its decision on the basis that evey state permits such preventive detention for juveniles and on the rationale that such detention protects "both the juvenile and society from the hazards of pretrial crime" (*Schall v. Martin*, 1984). Furthermore, the Court majority reasoned that "juveniles, unlike adults, are always in some form of custody" (*Schall v. Martin*, 1984). The three dissenting justices, on the other hand, noted the impossibility of predicting which juveniles will engage in future crime (this is the false positive issue discussed in Chapter 14) and considered the punitive nature of many detention facilities.

Search and Seizure

Consideration of these landmark U.S. Supreme Court cases demonstrates that juveniles do indeed have basic rights at important stages of the juvenile justice process, especially the waiver (transfer) hearing and the adjudication (trial) stages. Very important are the Fourth Amendment rights of juveniles during investigation or arrest.

The issue of **search and seizure** is a complex one involving a myriad of U.S. Supreme Court interpretations of the Fourth Amendment. This amendment reads:

> The right of the people to be secure in their persons, houses, papers, and effects, against unreasonable searches and seizures, shall not be violated, and no Warrants shall issue, but upon probable cause, supported by Oath or affirmation, and particularly describing the place to be searched, and the persons or things to be seized.

The Fourth Amendment indicates a preference for warrants before the police can search or arrest suspects, but this preference for warrants is riddled with numerous exceptions. This is not the place to describe those exceptions (but see, e.g., O'Brien, 1997). Here it is important to examine one situation that does affect juveniles: the **consent search** in which a defendant voluntarily allows the police to search someone or someone's effects without a search warrant.

Since *Schneckloth v. Bustamonte* (1973), the U.S. Supreme Court's ruling on adult consent searches has been that the police may simply ask a person for consent to search the person or his or her house, car or effects. Unlike the

Miranda situation, in which the police must advise a person of the right to refuse interrogation, the police do not have to specifically advise an adult suspect that he or she has the right to refuse a search. The police may simply ask an adult, "Do you mind if we take a look around your house?" If the person agrees, then—aware of it or not—the individual has agreed to a consent search. This would be a reasonable search in terms of Fourth Amendment guarantees.

In the case of juveniles, the issue arises whether a juvenile is mature enough to withstand police pressure and intelligent enough to understand his or her rights. The American Bar Association has recommended that juveniles be advised of their right to refuse a consent search and that juveniles also be advised of an opportunity to consult an attorney (Institute of Judicial Administration–American Bar Association, 1982). The Bar Association felt that these two safeguards would compensate for any youthful susceptibility to police coercion and any lack of sophistication needed to understand fully one's rights. Another set of standards, the American Law Institute Model Code of Pre-arraignment Procedure, stipulates that if a person about to be asked to consent to a search is under 16 years of age, then a parent should be the one who gives consent. The Model Code further advocates that in *any* consent search situation, involving juveniles or adults, the police should advise the individual that he or she "is under no obligation to give such consent and that anything found may be taken and used in evidence" (Wadlington, Whitebread & Davis, 1983: 301). In other words, the Model Code drafters advocated warnings for consent searches that were similar to the *Miranda* warnings used in interrogation situations. They felt that it should not be assumed that juvenile offenders are aware of their right to refuse a consent search without a clear warning of their right to do so.

A recent California case suggests that today's courts are probably inclined to rule on the side of law enforcement rather than to extend juvenile rights. In *In re Tyrell* (1994), a California court ruled that a search of a juvenile on probation (which found marijuana in his pants) did not violate the Fourth Amendment. Police made a pat-down search of the youth when they saw a knife on one of two other youths with him. Even though the police did not have probable cause to conduct the search and even though the youth did not consent to the search, the Court felt the police did not violate the juvenile's expectation of privacy because the boy had been placed on probation, which stipulated the condition that he submit to searches by police, probation officers or school officials. This probation condition erased any reasonable expectation of privacy (*Juvenile Justice Update*, 1995).

Rights in School

Because juveniles spend much of their time in school, many questions about juvenile rights have arisen within the context of school policies and procedures.

Corporal Punishment

In *Ingraham v. Wright*, the U.S. Supreme Court ruled that **corporal punishment** (e.g., paddling) of students is permissible so long as it is reasonable. The reasonableness decision depends on

> the seriousness of the offense, the attitude and past behavior of the child, the nature and severity of the punishment, the age and strength of the child, and the availability of less severe but equally effective means of discipline (*Ingraham v. Wright*, 1977).

The Court noted that corporal punishment could be abused, but observed that common law remedies were effective deterrents to any such abuse of the practice. The Court reasoned that students and their parents could sue school officials or charge them with criminal assault if they went too far in paddling any particular student.

As is often the case, dissenting opinions in Supreme Court cases raise very interesting issues. In fact, dissents sometimes are more noteworthy than the majority or plurality opinions of the Justices. Box 9.1 presents excerpts from the dissenting opinion of Justice White in the case of *Ingraham v. Wright*. This

---

Box 9.1   Excerpts from Justice White's Dissent in *Ingraham v. Wright*

If there are some punishments that are so barbaric that they may not be imposed for the commission of crimes, designated by our social system as the most thoroughly reprehensible acts an individual can commit, then, *a fortiori*, similar punishments may not be imposed on persons for less culpable acts, such as breaches of school discipline. Thus, if it is constitutionally impermissible to cut off someone's ear for the commission of murder, it must be unconstitutional to cut off a child's ear for being late to class. Although there were no ears cut off in this case, the record reveals beatings so severe that if they were inflicted on a hardened criminal for the commission of a serious crime, they might not pass constitutional muster.

. . .

The essence of the majority's argument is that school children do not need Eighth Amendment protection because corporal punishment is less subject to abuse in the public schools than it is in the prison system. However, it cannot be reasonably suggested that just because cruel and unusual punishments may occur less frequently under public scrutiny, they will not occur at all. The mere fact that a public flogging or a public execution would be available for all to see would not render the punishment constitutional if it were otherwise impermissible. Similarly, the majority would not suggest that a prisoner who is placed in a minimum-security prison and permitted to go home to his family on the weekends should be any less entitled to Eighth Amendment

Box 9.1, *continued*

protections than his counterpart in a maximum-security prison. In short, if a punishment is so barbaric and inhumane that it goes beyond the tolerance of a civilized society, its openness to public scrutiny should have nothing to do with its constitutionality.

. . .

By holding that the Eighth Amendment protects only criminals, the majority adopts the view that one is entitled to the protections afforded by the Eighth Amendment only if he is punished for acts that are sufficiently opprobrious for society to make them "criminal." This is a curious holding in view of the fact that the more culpable the offender the more likely it is that the punishment will not be disproportionate to the offense, consequently, the less likely it is that the punishment will be cruel and unusual. Conversely, a public school student who is spanked for a mere breach of discipline may sometimes have a strong argument that the punishment does not fit the offense, depending upon the severity of the beating, and therefore that it is cruel and unusual. Yet the majority would afford the student no protection no matter how inhumane and barbaric the punishment inflicted on him might be.

. . .

This tort action [student lawsuits against teachers who abuse corporal punishment] is utterly inadequate to protect against erroneous infliction of punishment for two reasons. First, under Florida law, a student punished for an act he did not commit cannot recover damages from a teacher "proceeding in utmost good faith . . . on the reports and advice of others"; the student has no remedy at all for punishment imposed on the basis of mistaken facts, at least as long as the punishment was reasonable from the point of view of the disciplinarian, uninformed by any prior hearing. The "traditional common-law remedies" on which the majority relies, thus do nothing to protect the student from the danger that concerned the Court in *Goss* [*v. Lopez*]—the risk of reasonable, good-faith mistakes in the school disciplinary process (*Ingraham v. Wright*, 1977).

shows that there are other sides to the issue of the constitutionality of corporal punishment in schools. The American Bar Association has followed Justice White's dissent, recommending that "[c]orporal punishment should not be inflicted upon a student. . . ." (Institute for Judicial Administration–American Bar Association, 1982: 136). Finally, a recent review of the research on corporal punishment concluded that it should be banned because children who receive corporal punishment are more prone as adults to various deviant acts. Among the later problems are depression, suicide, physical abuse of children and spouses, commission of violent crime, drinking problems, attraction to masochistic sex, and problems attaining a prestigious occupation (Straus, 1994).

In a recent Ninth Circuit case, the judges ruled that "no reasonable principal could think it constitutional to intentionally punch, slap, grab, and slam students into lockers" (*P.B. v. Koch*, 1996).

Freedom of Speech for Students

Another school rights issue is the First Amendment right to **freedom of speech**. Here the U.S. Supreme Court has upheld the basic principle that students have at least some degree of constitutional protection in that they do not "shed their constitutional rights to freedom of speech or expression at the schoolhouse gate" (*Tinker v. Des Moines Independent Community School District*, 1969). This does not mean that students can say or express anything they wish in whatever manner they wish. What it means is that the right of free speech is to be balanced with the school's interest in education and discipline. Students are entitled to express themselves as long as their expression does not materially and substantially interfere with school discipline or the educational process.

In the *Tinker* case, for example, at issue was the wearing of black armbands by students to protest United States involvement in the Vietnam conflict. The students doing so were suspended and sent home. When the case reached the U.S. Supreme Court, the majority of the justices ruled that the students' First Amendment rights had been violated, noting that the students had expressed themselves without creating any disturbance or interfering with school discipline. Furthermore, the school system had been inconsistent in that it had allowed some students to wear political campaign buttons and others to wear the traditional symbol of Nazism (the swastika). Writing for the majority, Justice Fortas took serious issue with school system prohibition of student expression of only one particular type:

> In our system, state-operated schools may not be enclaves of totalitarianism. School officials do not possess absolute authority over their students. Students in school as well as out of school are "persons" under our Constitution. They are possessed of fundamental rights which the State must respect, just as they themselves must respect their obligations to the State. In our system, students may not be regarded as closed-circuit recipients of only that which the State chooses to communicate. They may not be confined to the expression of those sentiments that are officially approved. In the absence of a specific showing of constitutionally valid reasons to regulate their speech, students are entitled to freedom of expression of their views . . . (*Tinker v. Des Moines Independent Community School District*, 1969).

This case can be misinterpreted as an outstanding victory for children's rights if some cautions are not noted. First, the Court was probably more concerned with the issue of free speech in general rather than with free speech for

children. That is, the ruling in favor of the pupils can probably be traced to the Supreme Court's "long tradition of zealous protection of first amendment rights" (Davis & Schwartz, 1987: 58). Second, the case may be interpreted not so much as a children's rights case as a parents' rights case, because the children in this case shared the same views as their parents on governmental involvement in Vietnam (Davis & Schwartz, 1987). If the views of the students and their parents had not been the same, the ruling may have been otherwise.

Mary Beth Tinker and John Tinker display two black armbands, the objects of the U.S. Supreme Court's consideration of how far public schools can go in limiting the wearing of political symbols. The Court ruled that the students' First Amendment rights were violated when their school suspended them for wearing black armbands to protest the Vietnam War. *Photo: UPI/Corbis-Bettman*

Finally, the case distinguished between passive expression and disruptive expression of views. Passive speech (e.g., wearing armbands) is less disruptive than disturbances or other types of expression. The Court is more likely to uphold such passive speech rather than more rowdy forms of speech.

In other First Amendment cases, the Supreme Court has addressed the issue of whether school officials can discipline a student for giving a lascivious speech and who holds editorial control over student publications. In *Bethel School District No. 403 v. Fraser* (1986), the Court addressed the issue of "whether the First Amendment prevents a school district from disciplining a high school student for giving a lewd speech at a school assembly." Matthew Fraser nominated a fellow student for a student office by using "an elaborate, graphic, and sexual metaphor." His obscene language violated a school rule, so he was suspended from school for two days. Both the District Court and the Court of Appeals ruled that the school had violated Fraser's First Amendment right to free speech. They reasoned that the speech was basically the same sort of action as the wearing of the protest armbands in the *Tinker* case. The U.S. Supreme Court, however, reversed the lower courts' decision and determined that the school does have a right to ban sexually explicit language, even if it is couched within a political speech, because it is counter to the basic educational mission of the school (see Box 9.2). The Court also limited the degree of freedom students have in expressing themselves in student publications, again justifying this by pointing out the educational mission of the schools (see Box 9.3).

Box 9.2   Lewd Speeches in School

In the *Bethel School District No. 403 v. Fraser* (1986) case, the U.S. Supreme Court argued that students do not have an absolute right to free speech under the First Amendment. They refused to equate lewd language given as part of a political statement with the wearing of protest armbands in the *Tinker* case. The justices distinguished the *Fraser* case from *Tinker* in that in the *Tinker* case the speech involved political expression and therefore merited greater protection, whereas

> the penalties imposed in this case were unrelated to any political viewpoint. The First Amendement does not prevent the school officials from determining that to permit a vulgar and lewd speech such as respondent's would undermine the school's basic educational mission. A high school assembly or classroom is no place for a sexually explicit monologue directed towards an unsuspecting audience of teenage students. Accordingly, it was perfectly appropriate for the school to disassociate itself to make the point to the pupils that vulgar speech and lewd conduct is wholly inconsistent with the "fundamental values" of public education (*Bethel School District Number 403 v. Fraser*, 1986).

Further, the Court noted that schools play an important role in preparing students for adult citizenship:

> The process of educating our youth for citizenship in public schools is not confined to books, the curriculum, and the civics class; schools must teach by example the shared values of a civilized social order. Consciously or otherwise, teachers—and indeed the older students— demonstrate the appropriate form of civil discourse and political expression by their conduct and deportment in and out of class. Inescapably, like parents, they are role models. The schools, as instruments of the state, may determine that the essential lessons of civil, mature conduct cannot be conveyed in a school that tolerates lewd, indecent, or offensive speech and conduct such as that indulged in by this confused boy.

> The pervasive sexual innuendo in Fraser's speech was plainly offensive to both teachers and students—indeed to any mature person. By glorifying male sexuality, and in its verbal content, the speech was acutely insulting to teenage girl students. The speech could well be seriously damaging to its less mature audience, many of whom were only 14 years old and on the threshold of awareness of human sexuality. Some students were reported as bewildered by the speech and the reaction of mimicry it provoked (*Bethel School District Number 403 v. Fraser*, 1986).

Box 9.3   Censorship of Student Publications

In an important First Amendment school case, the Supreme Court ruled that school officials can exercise broad editorial control over student publications:

> Instead, we hold that educators do not offend the First Amendment by exercising editorial control over the style and content of student speech in school-sponsored expressive activities so long as their actions are reasonably related to legitimate pedagogical concerns (*Hazelwood School District v. Kuhlmeier*, 1988).

The case involved a principal's censorship of a high school newspaper. The principal prevented publication of an article describing three students' experiences during pregnancy and of another article describing student reactions to parental divorce. Writing for the majority, Justice White distinguished the speech in the *Tinker* case as "a student's personal expression that happens to occur on the school premises" from "school-sponsored publications, theatrical productions, and other expressive activities" that are "part of the school curriculum" and "are supervised by faculty members and designed to impart particular knowledge or skills" (*Hazelwood School District v. Kuhlmeier*, 1988). For educational reasons, schools have "greater control" over the latter type of speech.

In his dissent, Justice Brennan castigated the majority viewpoint as approving "thought police" and the violation of "the First Amendment's prohibitions against censorship of any student expression that neither disrupts classwork nor invades the rights of others, and against any censorship that is not narrowly tailored to serve its purpose" (*Hazelwood School District v. Kuhlmeier*, 1988). Justice Brennan concluded that "[t]he mere fact of school sponsorship does not . . . license such thought control in the high school, whether through school suppression of disfavored viewpoints or through official assessment of topic sensitivity. . . ." (*Hazelwood School District v. Kuhlmeier*, 1988).

In November of 1995, the U.S. Supreme Court declined to hear a case (denied *certiorari*) involving the right of a Tennessee junior high school teacher to refuse to accept a research paper on the life of Jesus. In 1991, Britanny Settle, a junior high school student in Dickson County, submitted an outline on the life of Jesus for her research paper assignment. The original assignment noted that the topic must be "interesting, researchable, and decent." The teacher rejected Brittany's outline because, among other factors, she failed to get permission for the topic, the teacher thought that Brittany's strong belief would interfere with objectivity in a research assignment, and the assignment required four sources but Brittany used only one source: the Bible. In the U.S. District Court case, Brittany relied on *Tinker* for the right of free speech. The Court, however, relied on *Hazelwood School District v. Kuhlmeier*:

> The free speech rights of students in the classroom must be limited because effective education depends not only on controlling boisterous conduct, but also on maintaining the focus of the class on the assignment in question . . . Teachers therefore must be given broad discretion to give grades and conduct class discussion based on the content of speech . . . *Settle v. Dickson County School Board*, 53 F.3d 152, 100 EDUC. L. REP. 32 (6th Cir. 1995) at 155.

Two additional areas in which freedom of speech in schools has been questioned involve compulsory community service and school prayer. At first glance, the issue of compulsory community service would not appear to be a First Amendment issue. With the advent of programs that require service for high school graduation in several places (such as Dodge City, Kansas; Boston, Massachusetts; and the state of Maryland), opponents have argued that such service forces a student to engage in "expressive conduct." That is, the activity serves as an expresssion of support for the agency receiving the service. For example, a student might object that doing community service at the Girl Scouts sends the message that the student believes in what the Girl Scouts organization represents. This issue was argued in *Steirer v. Bethlehem Area School District*. On appeal, the Supreme Court denied *certiorari* (i.e., the Court declined to consider the case, letting the lower court ruling stand). The Court stated that there was no First Amendment free speech issue because expressive conduct was not clearly at stake. The Court noted that engaging in community service is not the same thing as wearing a black armband or burning a draft card, acts that clearly do express a viewpoint. Despite this ruling, Charters (1994) argues that community service can be seen as fostering an ideological viewpoint and that "students have no civic duty to perform acts of altruism and self-sacrifice the omission of which would justify a school district's withholding a student's diploma" (Charters, 1994: 613).

School prayer has become a topic of much debate in recent years. The key to the debate is the issue of whether school prayer represents the promotion of religion by the school. The Supreme Court, in *Lee v. Weisman* (1992), ruled that school officials erred in permitting and providing guidelines for prayer at a high school graduation ceremony. However, the U.S. Fifth Circuit Court upheld the right of students to plan and lead prayer at school functions (*Jones v. Clear Creek Independent School District*, 1992). The degree to which prayer in school will be permitted has yet to be determined. Box 9.4 provides some insight into this issue.

In May of 1997, the U.S. Court of Appeals for the Eleventh Circuit affirmed the decision of a federal district court that upheld a 1994 Georgia statute authorizing a "moment of quiet reflection" to begin the school day. The statute noted that this moment of quiet reflection "shall not be conducted as a religious service or exercise but shall be considered as an opportunity for a moment of silent reflection on the anticipated activities of the day" [O.C.G.A 20-2-1050 (1996)]. The judges noted that there was no coercion in the statute:

> All that students must do under this Act is remain silent for 60 sec-
> onds; they are not encouraged to pray or forced to remain silent
> while listening to others' prayers (*Bown v. Gwinnett County School
> District*, 112 F.3d 1464 (11th Cir. 1997) at 1473.

The court also noted that there was no endorsement of religion in the law and
no authorization of any prayer.

Student Searches

Another issue involving students is the right of school officials to conduct
searches of students versus the students' right of privacy. This issue was high-
lighted in the Supreme Court case of *New Jersey v. T.L.O.* (1985), which
involved the search of a student's purse by an assistant vice principal based on a
teacher's suspicion that the student had been smoking in the lavatory in violation
of school rules. The Court ruled that such a **student search** was legitimate if it
was reasonable in its justification and its extent. By this, the Court meant that:

> Under ordinary circumstances, a search of a student by a teacher or
> other school official will be "justified at its inception" when there
> are reasonable grounds for suspecting that the search will turn up
> evidence that the student has violated or is violating either the law or
> the rules of the school. Such a search will be permissible in its
> scope when the measures adopted are reasonably related to the
> objectives of the search and not excessively intrusive in light of the
> age and sex of the student and the nature of the infraction (*New Jer-
> sey v. T.L.O.*, 1985).

It is important to realize that the Supreme Court explicitly noted that it was not
ruling about a student's right to privacy in lockers or desks, about whether it
would make a difference if the school was acting in cooperation with or at the
suggestion of a police department, or about whether "individualized suspicion"
is such an essential element of the reasonableness standard for school searches
so as to preclude general searches of students or lockers (*New Jersey v. T.L.O.*,
1985). Thus, the U.S. Supreme Court left open many of the troubling issues surrounding searches on school premises, but it did grant school officials considerable latitude to conduct warrantless searches of students. It gave school officials
greater authority to search students than other governmental officials have to
search adults.

In the case of *New Jersey v. T.L.O.*, Justices Brennan and Marshall con-
curred in part but also dissented in part. Box 9.5 indicates some of their concerns about the majority opinion.

Box 9.4   Prayer at Graduation

"God of the Free, Hope of the Brave:

For the legacy of America where diversity is celebrated and the rights of minorities are protected, we thank You. May these young men and women grow up to enrich it.

For the liberty of America, we thank You. May these new graduates grow up to guard it.

For the political process of America in which all its citizens may participate, for its court system where all may seek justice we thank You. May those we honor this morning always turn to it in trust.

For the destiny of America we thank You. May the graduates of Nathan Bishop Middle School so live that they might help to share it.

May our aspirations for our country and for these young people, who are our hope for the future, be richly fulfilled."

Lee v. Weisman, 112 S.Ct. 2649 (1992) at 2652-2653.

A rabbi gave the above invocation at graduation for a middle school and a high school in Providence (RI) in June of 1989. The middle school principal had given the rabbi a guideline for nonsectarian prayers at civic ceremonies and recommended that the invocation and benediction be nonsectarian. One of the students' fathers unsuccessfully attempted to get a restraining order prohibiting any invocation or benediction. The District Court held that the actions of the school violated the Establishment Clause of the First Amendment banning governmental advancement of religion. The United States Court of Appeals for the First Circuit affirmed the judgment of the District Court. The case was then appealed to the Supreme Court.

Judge Kennedy's opinion for the court affirmed the lower court decision against the school's actions. Justice Kennedy was concerned about the principal's participation in the composition of the prayer: ". . . our precedents do not permit school officials to assist in composing prayers as an incident to a formal exercise for their students" (at 2657). He was also concerned "with protecting freedom of conscience from subtle coercive pressure in the elementary and secondary public schools" (at 2658). He distinguished a graduation ceremony from prayer at the opening of a legislative session "where adults are free to enter and leave with little comment" (at 2660). He concluded that "the prayer exercises in this case are especially improper because the State has in every practical sense compelled attendance and participation in an explicit religious exercise at an event of singular importance to every student, one the objecting student had no real alternative to avoid" (at 2661). Thus, "the State, in a school setting, in effect required participation in a religious exercise" (at 2659).

Box 9.4, *continued*

Writing for the dissent, Justice Scalia argued that standing silently during a prayer does not automatically imply that the person is joining in the prayer but may simply signify "respect for the prayers of others" (at 2682). Justice Scalia ridiculed the argument of subtle coercion, noting that the opinion treats students "as though they were first-graders" instead of individuals "old enough to vote" (at 2682). Theoretically, Justice Scalia lambasted the decision as "the bulldozer of its social engineering" for ignoring historical precedent and laying "waste a tradition that is as old as public-school graduation ceremonies themselves, and that is a component of an even more longstanding American tradition of nonsectarian prayer to God at public celebrations generally" (at 2679). Justice Scalia's reading of history showed that the "history and tradition of our Nation are replete with public ceremonies featuring prayers of thanksgiving and petition" (at 2679).

Shortly after the Supreme Court decision, the Fifth Circuit Court ruled that a graduation prayer did not violate the First Amendment because students voted on the prayer, participation was voluntary and students themselves, rather than a religious official, led the prayer (*Jones v. Clear Creek Independent School District*, 977 F.2d [5th Cir. 1992]). Shortly thereafter, several state legislatures introduced bills authorizing student-initiated prayer in the schools (Rossow & Parkinson, 1994a). In the spring of 1994, Congress passed an education act that would prevent funds from going to schools adopting "policies designed to prevent students from engaging in constitutionally protected prayer or silent reflection" (cited in Underwood, 1994: 1040).

What do you think? Should prayers such as this one be permitted at graduation ceremonies? Is such a prayer at graduation improper governmental intrusion into religion?

A 1981 action of the Supreme Court sheds additional light on the Court's attitude toward student searches. Specifically, the Court (*Doe v. Renfrow*, 1981) that year refused to consider an Indiana case in which school officials and police used dogs to sniff students and their possessions for marijuana, searched pockets and purses, and even went so far as to conduct nude body searches of a few students. By refusing to hear the case, the Supreme Court let stand the lower court ruling that the school could use a canine team to conduct a general search of classrooms and could legally search pockets and purses, but went too far in requiring nude body searches (*Doe v. Renfrow*, 1979).

Since the Supreme Court ruling in *New Jersey v. T.L.O.*, two Circuit Court decisions have ruled that strip searches are constitutional. In one of those cases, a 16-year-old student was strip-searched for drugs suspected to be hidden in his crotch area (none were found). The Seventh Circuit Court found no violation of *T.L.O.* (*Cornfield By Lewis v. Consolidated High School District No. 230*, 1993). Two observers conclude that the courts are trying to assist schools in combating drugs and violence in our country's schools by authorizing strip searches. These commentators are fearful that the courts may be taking the wrong approach: "unfortunately, students appear to be paying the price with the loss of their privacy and, apparently now, their clothes" (Rossow & Parkinson, 1994a: 1).

Box 9.5   Excerpts from the Brennan-Marshall Partial Concurrence-Dissent in *New Jersey v. T.L.O.*

In this case, Mr. Choplick [the assistant vice-principal who conducted the search] overreacted to what appeared to be nothing more than a minor infraction—a rule prohibiting smoking in the bathroom of the freshmen's and sophomores' building. It is, of course, true that he actually found evidence of serious wrongdoing by T.L.O., but no one claims that the prior search may be justified by his unexpected discovery. As far as the smoking infraction is concerned, the search for cigarettes merely tended to corroborate a teacher's eye-witness account of T.L.O.'s violation of a minor regulation designed to channel student smoking behavior into designated locations. Because this conduct was neither unlawful nor significantly disruptive of school order or the educational process, the invasion of privacy associated with the forcible opening of T.L.O.'s purse was entirely unjustified at its inception.

. . .

The schoolroom is the first opportunity most citizens have to experience the power of government. Through it passes every citizen and public official, from schoolteachers to policemen and prison guards. The values they learn there, they take with them in life. One of our most cherished ideals is the one contained in the Fourth Amendment: that the Government may not intrude on the personal privacy of its citizens without a warrant or compelling circumstance. The Court's decision today is a curious moral for the Nation's youth. Although the search of T.L.O.'s purse does not trouble today's majority, I submit that we are not dealing with "matters relatively trivial to the welfare of the Nation. There are village tyrants as well as village Hampdens, but none who acts under color of law is beyond the reach of the Constitution. . . ." (*New Jersey v. T.L.O.*, 1985).

The stretching of the right to search students has continued to advance. In 1995, the Supreme Court ruled that public schools could make student athletes undergo random drug testing as a condition for playing on school sports teams (*Vernonia School District v. Acton*, 1995). In *Todd v. Rush County Schools* (1998), the Seventh Circuit relied on *Vernonia* to uphold the actions of an Indiana school district that required students to undergo random, unannounced drug tests (urinalysis) before participating in *any* extracurricular programs or being able to drive to and from school. In a November 1997 case, the U.S. Court of

Appeals for the Seventh Circuit upheld a "medical assessment" of a high school student suspected of having smoked marijuana. The "assessment" involved a school nurse taking the student's blood pressure and pulse. In 1996, the Eighth Circuit upheld a search of all male sixth- through twelfth-graders. The students had to remove their jackets, shoes and socks, empty their pockets, and be given a metal detector test after a school bus driver informed the principal that there were fresh cuts on the seats of the bus (*Thompson v. Carthage School District*, 87 F. 3d 979, 110 Educ. L. Rep. 602 (8th Cir. 1996). Rossow and Parkinson (1996) argued that this decision would be welcomed by schools using metal detectors at school entrances.

Rights at Home and in the Community

Not all questions of juvenile rights have emerged in the context of school. Several issues and cases arise in the home and community.

The Constitutionality of Curfews

Chapter 7 noted that **curfew laws** have mushroomed in the United States. Cities have enacted curfews to decrease juvenile crime and to protect juveniles from victimization (Davis et al., 1997). Courts have upheld some curfew laws and struck down others. The recent trend seems to be to uphold the laws if they are narrowly drawn and if they provide exceptions for reasonable activities.

A good example of a recent case involving a curfew law that was challenged and ruled to be constitutional is *Qutb v. Strauss* (1993). This was a case that concerned the Dallas, Texas, curfew law that prohibited juveniles under age 17 from being on the streets from 11:00 P.M. until 6:00 A.M. on weeknights and from midnight until 6:00 A.M. on weekends. Exceptions included being accompanied by a parent, doing an errand for a parent, and attending school, religious or civic activities. The ordinance also allowed interstate travel or playing on one's own sidewalk or a neighbor's sidewalk.

The U.S. Court of Appeals ruled that the law did not violate either equal protection or free association grounds and therefore was not unconstitutional. The Court ruled that the law did serve a compelling state interest, namely, "to reduce juvenile crime and victimization, while promoting juvenile safety and well-being" (*Qutb v. Strauss*, 1993). Here the Court noted that the City of Dallas presented statistics on juvenile crime and victimization during the hours covered by the curfew to substantiate the argument of reducing crime and victimization. Concerning a juvenile's right to free association (a First Amendment right), the Court noted that the law had sufficient exceptions in it so that impositions on association were minor. For example, contrary to arguments that the law prohibited playing midnight basketball, the Court noted that the juvenile could play in such a game as long as it was sponsored by some organization or as long as a parent accompanied the youth to the game.

Similarly drawn curfew laws have stood appeals court challenges, while overly broad laws without exceptions have been struck down. For example, a 1981 case, *Johnson v. City of Opelousas*, was struck down because its only exception was for "emergency errands." Here the judges noted that there was no exception for such associational activities "as religious or school meetings, organized dances, and theater and sporting events, when reasonable and direct travel to or from these activities has to be made during the curfew period" (*Johnson v. City of Opelousas*).

Thus, clearly drawn curfew laws are standing constitutional challenge as long as they allow reasonable exceptions.

The Legal Drinking Age

An important children's rights issue is the question of the appropriate age for adolescents to drink alcoholic beverages. In fact, because of the actions of groups such as Mothers Against Drunk Driving (MADD) and because of the threat of reduced federal highway funds, all states prohibit the purchase of alcohol by persons under 21 years of age (Maguire & Pastore, 1997).

Interestingly, raising the **legal drinking age** to 21 is the flip side of the previous historical trend to *lower* the drinking age. Only a few years ago, lowering the drinking age was very much the norm and it was part of a more general trend in both the United States and Canada of lowering the age of privilege and responsibility, including lowering the voting age to 18. In Canada, the rationale behind this movement was that since "youths paid taxes, could quit school and work, join the military, vote federally, and drive cars, it was felt that they should be allowed to drink" (Vingilis & DeGenova, 1984: 163). In the United States, the military draft provided the added argument that if "boys were old enough to be sent to Viet Nam, . . . they were old enough to drink" (Vingilis & DeGenova, 1984: 163). Finally, there was some feeling that if "youth had to use substances, alcohol was society's preferred drug" (Vingilis & DeGenova, 1984: 163).

Proponents of a high minimum drinking age argue that it reduces automobile accidents and fatalities, especially for adolescents themselves. They reason that teens need to be protected from their immaturity and impulsiveness because they are inexperienced at both driving and drinking alcohol.

It appears that these arguments make good sense because the research suggests that lowering the drinking age has indeed been associated with increases in alcohol-related collisions and with higher fatality rates for night-time and single-vehicle crashes involving young drivers. Conversely, raising the drinking age has been associated with a reduced number of collisions (Vingilis & DeGenova, 1984: 166-169). The National Highway Traffic Safety Administration estimates that the higher drinking age has saved more than 16,500 lives (*USA Today*, 1997).

The issue, however, is not simple. First, "the research indicates that the minimum legal drinking age laws do not deter the majority of teenagers from drinking" (Vingilis & DeGenova, 1984: 170). Thus, a reasonable inference from the research on the impact of lowering and raising the drinking age seems to be that it would have some impact but it would not eliminate the problem:

> Teen-age drinkers are indeed a problem and they are undoubtedly the worst of the drunk drivers. Whether or not raising the drinking age a year or two would in fact keep alcohol out of their hands is another matter. After all, teen-agers below even the current drinking age have little difficulty getting drunk. The efficiency of this proposal [of raising the drinking age] is open to serious question (Walker, 1985: 88).

In other words, some persons under the legal age would continue to obtain intoxicating beverages, just as they have done in the past, and then drive.

A second problem with raising the drinking age is the question of fairness. That is, the specific issue of raising the drinking age raises the more general issue of the fairness of prohibiting 18-, 19- and 20-year-olds from drinking, thereby, in effect, treating them as children when the law treats them as adults for other purposes. We have seen, for example, that all states consider 18-year-olds as adults in terms of their responsibility for criminal actions. In fact, one trend in juvenile justice is toward more liberal waiver and related provisions that allow increasingly younger juveniles to be tried as adult criminal suspects (subjecting them to the possibility of imprisonment in adult facilities and even capital punishment). The question arises whether it is fair to subject teens to adult criminal court sanctions while at the same time treating them as immature children in terms of their legal ability to drink. Additional arguments against a high minimum drinking age are the "forbidden fruit" argument, which maintains that it increases the attraction of alcohol, and the "teach them to do it right" argument, which contends that parents can use a lower minimum age as an educational device (*USA Today*, 1997: 9a)

Franklin Zimring (1982) argues that it is fair to prohibit 18-year-olds from drinking, but he does not necessarily agree that it is fair to submit adolescents to criminal court sanctions, especially the death penalty. He states several reasons for his view that age 21 is a fair minimum drinking age. First, he believes that 18-year-olds are not mature but that they are in the process of becoming mature adults. Second, he is opposed to a young minimum drinking age because of the leakage problem. Leakage means, for example, that if 18-year-olds can legally purchase alcoholic beverages, then their 16-year-old dates may also drink and be subject to auto accidents and fatalities. Finally, he argues that there are three different aspects to adulthood: liberty, entitlement and responsibility. Liberty refers to the freedom of choice that adults possess in matters such as making decisions about medical care. An entitlement is a benefit or program offered by government, such as the Job Corps, that provides free job training for young persons. Responsibility means "paying the full price for misdeeds and being responsible, as are adults, for self support" (Zimring, 1982: 111). It is Zimring's position that it is better to keep the ages for these three aspects of adulthood separate rather than to lump them together. Thus, he sees no inconsistency in permitting adolescents to drive at 16, vote and be drafted at 18 and be able to purchase alcoholic beverages at 21.

Zimring also raises the intriguing issue of raising the drinking age to 25. Based on evidence that single male drivers under 25—not just under 21—are a serious driving risk, he contends that these actuarial facts and logic would argue for an even higher drinking age than 21 to prevent many accidents and fatalities. He notes that there is some precedent for this in that the Constitution does require Senators and the President to be older than 21 years of age. However, Zimring rejects raising the minimum drinking age to 25 because:

> That kind of law is not merely politically implausible and socially divisive, it is also unjust. I have argued elsewhere that our current deferral of liberties can be justified because adolescence merely *seems* like forever. But using age-grading to defer common liberty into the mid-20's is exploitation in almost every case. Adding four or seven years onto an already long wait is simply too much of a burden. The twenty-first birthday has a long history of serving as the outer boundary for legal disability based on age. There is no good reason to risk the legal incoherence and social division that pushing beyond this limit impose (Zimring, 1982: 124).

Zimring was writing just before the recent push to waive younger and younger juveniles to adult court, so he did not explicitly address the issues of the age of criminal responsibility and the appropriate age for capital punishment. There are strong indications, however, that he would not favor such actions. For example, he clearly believes that even 19- and 20-year-olds are not fully mature, and may need some protection from their youthful mistakes. Thus, Zimring is convinced that our legal policy should be one that "preserves the life chances for those who make serious mistakes, as well as preserving choices for their more fortunate (and more virtuous) contemporaries" (Zimring, 1982: 91-92).

Zimring's position is worth considering as we begin a new century. Contrary to many contemporary voices, he does not advocate a policy that on the one hand would prohibit drinking until 21, but on the other hand would allow waiver to criminal court at 14. Instead, he takes the more consistent view that persons under 21 are not fully mature and responsible, but that certain aspects of adulthood may be more appropriately begun at 18.

In connection with this issue, Barnum (1987) argues that it is false to justify the existence of a separate juvenile court system on the claim that children are less mature and less responsible for their behavior than adults. Rather, "normal intrinsic cognitive development is sufficient for this capacity [to appreciate what they are doing or what effect it will have] by age two or three" (Barnum, 1987: 72). Nevertheless, many think there are developmental differences between children and adults that do justify a separate court for juveniles:

. . . children are less able to be responsible for themselves, . . . adolescents normally experience transient irresponsibility, and . . . even poorly socialized children may have a better prognosis for rehabilitation than do poorly socialized adults (Barnum, 1987: 78).

In other words, most children do know right from wrong, just as do most adults. However, there are other differences between children and adults that may justify a separate juvenile court system. (For discussion of **graduated licensing**, see Box 9.6.)

Box 9.6   Graduated Licensing Laws

Graduated driver's licensing laws are new licensing laws under which teens gradually earn the privilege to drive. For example, they may have to drive with adults for at least six months and cannot drive after dark until they learn advanced skills. In Michigan, parents have to certify that they have provided 50 hours of supervised driving for their child, including 10 hours at night. A Level II license in Michigan allows unsupervised driving for 16-year-olds but no driving between midnight and 5:00 A.M. Level III requires age 17 plus six months at Level II. Also, teen drivers must be accident- and violation-free for 12 consecutive months to earn a Level III license.

What do you think? Is graduated licensing a necessary reform or does it represent a needless incursion into the lives of adolescents?

Source: Curley (1997).

Perhaps a fitting conclusion to this discussion is Davis and Schwartz's observation that there is a fundamental tension in the law between paternalism (protecting children) and autonomy (granting them responsibility) that will not disappear:

The law is protective of children, for example, in the areas of contracts, employment, and to a great extent, medical decision making in life-threatening cases. The law grants a measure of autonomy to children or their parents in other areas—for example, abortion decision making (but only to a limited extent), torts (but more as a result of a policy favoring compensation of victims than of a desire to grant children greater responsibility), non-life threatening medical decision making, and emancipation decision making. These disparate results stem from an inherent conflict in the law—a kind of schizophrenia—between the desire to accord children a greater degree of control over their lives and freedom of choice, and the need, on the other hand, to protect them from others, their surroundings, and, sometimes, from their own folly (Davis & Schwartz, 1987: 201).

It is interesting that, at present, society is lowering the age of criminal responsibility but at the same time insists on making 21 the age of eligibility to purchase alcohol (as well as pushing for graduated licensing). Davis and Schwartz's description of this as "a kind of schizophrenia" seems most fitting.

Summary

This chapter has examined the landmark U.S. Supreme Court cases involving juveniles. The Fourth Amendment rights of juveniles and some of the controversial rights issues in school and in the home were examined. There is no perfectly consistent treatment of juveniles and their rights. Sometimes the law treats them as children and sometimes it treats them as adults. As Zimring (1982) has pointed out, however, because the issue of juveniles' rights is so complex, perhaps a refusal to come up with one magical age for all children's rights issues is the best solution. Finally, as was noted in the discussion of the landmark Supreme Court cases, the mere stipulation of a right by the Court does not guarantee that police or courts will actually or fully protect that right. Practice is not always the same as philosophy.

DISCUSSION QUESTIONS

1. Has the Supreme Court gone too far or not far enough in protecting the rights of juvenile delinquency suspects? If you were on the Supreme Court, what would you seek to change concerning those rights?

2. Your 15-year-old brother has been arrested for the robbery of a video cassette rental store. He is of average intelligence but is immature and impulsive. This is his first arrest. Do you think that he should be allowed to waive his privilege against self-incrimination and his right to confer with an attorney or do you feel that state law should mandate that an attorney be brought in before the police can conduct any interrogation?

3. Assume that you are the editor of the high school newspaper and that one of your best reporters has just completed a lengthy article on drug use in your school. No names are mentioned in the article; in fact, your reporter has gone to great lengths to protect confidentiality. The principal has read the article and has said that she does not want it published in the school paper. What would you do?

4. Do you agree with the Supreme Court's position that corporal punishment is permissible as a school discipline technique? If you become a teacher or principal, will you use corporal punishment? If so, when and under what circumstances? How would you feel about your own children being subjected to corporal punishment?

5. If you were a high school principal, what would your policy on student searches be?

6. What is your opinion about compulsory community service? Do you think high schools should be allowed to force students to perform community service as a condition for graduation? Why or why not?

7. What is your opinion about school prayer? Should a school be allowed to invite a priest, minister, rabbi or other religious leader to graduation to offer a nonsectarian invocation? Should the students be allowed to compose and lead their own invocation at graduation? What do you think about a moment of silence to begin (or end) the school day?

8. What age do you favor as the minimum legal drinking age? How would you feel about the age being set at 25? What do you think about graduated licensing laws? Do you favor or oppose them?

Diversion

Increasing levels of crime and delinquency in the 1960s, accompanied by criticisms of the juvenile justice system, the development of the labeling perspective, and the work of the **1967 President's Commission on Law Enforcement and the Administration of Justice**, led to a wide array of ideas and innovations in the criminal and juvenile justice systems. One of the most prominent ideas to emerge was that of diversion. **Diversion** represents an attempt to find alternative forms of dealing with problem youth outside of normal system processing. Subsumed under the heading of diversion are a wide range of activities that are determined as much by the orientation of the providing agencies as by the needs of the juveniles. Where many programs in the 1970s and 1980s included the term "diversion" in their names, fewer named "diversion" programs appear today. This does not mean that diversion is no longer practiced. Rather, while the ideas persist, the name has simply lost favor. This chapter will look at the history of diversion, its basic assumptions and practices, and its impact on juvenile delinquency and juvenile justice.

A History of Diversion

While the term "diversion" came into widespread use after the work of the 1967 President's Commission on Law Enforcement and the Administration of

Justice, the idea of diversion with juveniles was not a new one. Indeed, just about every change and innovation that has been made in dealing with juveniles throughout history has been diversionary. The establishment of houses of refuge in the early 1800s represented diversion from adult institutions and poor houses. Cottage reformatories of the mid-1800s allowed for the diversion of youths from the houses of refuge. The formation of a separate juvenile court in 1899 meant diverting juveniles from the traditional adult courts to the new system. Many innovative programs in the early and mid-1900s, such as child guidance clinics, juvenile probation, nonresidential counseling, vocational education and job placement, represented varying means of diverting youths out of residential correctional facilities. The only difference between these earlier changes in dealing with youths and the diversion suggestions of the President's Commission (1967b) was the explicit use of the term "diversion."

The modern era of diversion within juvenile justice can be attributed directly to the 1967 President's Commission. This Commission critically evaluated the state of criminal justice in the United States and gave a great deal of attention to the juvenile justice system. The Commission saw formal sanctioning and system involvement as a last resort for dealing with delinquency. Instead, it called for alternative methods for dealing with problem youth.

> In place of the formal system, dispositional alternatives to adjudication must be developed for dealing with juveniles, including agencies to provide and coordinate services and procedures to achieve necessary control without unnecessary stigma (President's Commission, 1967b: 2).

The intent of the Commission was to eliminate the ineffective practices of the formal juvenile justice system and substitute methods for handling children with problems. These alternative methods would channel youths away from the formal system in order to minimize the crime-producing effects of system intervention and to provide services appropriate for helping the youth avoid future trouble. The aim was to initiate the alternative interventions after youths had come to the attention of the juvenile justice system but before they had been processed to or through the juvenile court stage. The Commission envisioned this activity as taking place at the "pre-judicial" stage of handling youths.

> [A] great deal of juvenile misbehavior should be dealt with through alternatives to adjudication, in accordance with an explicit policy to *divert* juvenile offenders away from formal adjudication and authoritative disposition and to nonjudicial institutions for guidance and other services. Employment agencies, schools, welfare agencies, and groups with programs for acting-out youths all are examples of the resources that should be used. The preference for nonjudicial disposition should be enunciated, publicized, and consistently espoused by the several social institutions responsible for controlling and preventing delinquency (President's Commission, 1967b: 16).

The move was away from the traditional handling of youths in the formal juvenile court to involving youths in a variety of helpful programs.

The Rationale for Diversion

The rationale behind the call for diversion in the late 1960s was found in the daily workings of the existing system of justice. The juvenile justice system was faced with a wide array of problems. First, the country was experiencing increased numbers of youths being arrested and brought to the juvenile court. At the same time, the juvenile system faced strong criticisms that it was ineffective at eliminating delinquency or reducing recidivism. The Commission noted that simply increasing the level of funding and support for the existing system of juvenile justice would not be a fruitful exercise. Rather, the problem

> . . . stems in important measure from the over optimistic view of what is known about the phenomenon of juvenile criminality and of what even a fully equipped juvenile court could do about it (President's Commission, 1967b: 8).

Indeed, as was seen in Chapters 3 and 4, there is little consensus among criminologists about the cause(s) of delinquency.

The failures of the juvenile system could also be attributed to the vast number of status offenders who populated the system. Status offenders comprised better than 25 percent of the juveniles in court and system institutions (President's Commission, 1967b). In California, more than 30 percent of all intake cases and more than 40 percent of all incarcerated youths in 1969 were status offenders (Baron, Feeney & Thornton, 1976). These youths took time and resources away from more serious offenders and contributed to overburdened caseloads in both juvenile courts and corrections.

A further factor favoring the establishment of diversion was the growth of the **labeling perspective** in criminological theory. Labeling theory shifted the emphasis in explanations of deviance away from the individual actor to the formal system of justice. System contact was viewed as stigmatizing and leading to increased deviance on the part of the individual. Because contact with the system was seen as criminogenic, proponents of this view believed the system should deal with only a few hard-core individuals. More problematically, intervention with status offenders and other pre-delinquents represented activity that would encourage further deviance. Recognizing the potential of labeling, the Commission recommended the use of dispositional alternatives, a narrowing of the purview of the juvenile court, the funding of community agencies, and reserving formal system intervention as a last resort (President's Commission, 1967b). These things were expected to bring about a drastic reduction in recidivism and the number of youths handled by the juvenile court.

Defining Diversion

Perhaps the greatest problem encountered in discussions of diversion was the failure of the President's Commission to delineate exactly what it meant when it promoted diversion. The clearest indication of what diversion should be appeared in discussions of the overburdened juvenile system. Diversion was seen as a means of limiting the number of cases brought before the juvenile court (Blomberg, 1979). How that was to be accomplished and exactly what was meant by diversion was left open to debate.

Box 10.1   The Definitional Problem of Diversion

The President's Commission never provided a definition of diversion. Consequently, a wide range of definitions emerged as diversion programs were implemented and research on the topic grew. Below are four definitions that have appeared. You will note that each one proposes different activities for diversion.

True Diversion (Lemert, 1981)	Informal referral to some agency/program by law enforcement officers. The child is not brought to intake or adjudicated, there is no follow-up, and there is no way to check whether the juvenile/family act on the referral.
Referral, Service and Follow-up (Dunford, 1977)	Referral before adjudication to a *non-system* source of treatment, with follow-up. Treatment must be totally separate from official agencies with no coercion. Follow-up means making sure the youth does not "fall through the cracks."
Minimization of Penetration (Vorenberg & Vorenberg, 1973; Klein, 1976)	Limiting the extent of system processing that could be imposed on a youth. Could be by the police officer on the street, at intake before a court hearing, at a court hearing, or after adjudication.
Channeling to Non-Court Institutions (Nejelski, 1976)	Moving cases that would normally go to court adjudication to some other form of intervention.

Definitions of diversion eventually represented the ideas of the institutions that used diversion and the researchers who studied the new programs. Following the idea of keeping kids out of the juvenile justice system, Lemert (1981) defined **true diversion** as "direct informal referral" of juveniles by law enforcement officers. In a strict sense, this meant the outright release of the juvenile by the police. The assumption was that the police officer would make suggestions to the youth and/or his or her parents concerning where help could be found for dealing with problems. There would be no follow-up as to whether the youths complied with the suggestions. Dunford (1977) argued that this amounted to little more than the simple screening of cases by police officers. The lack of follow-up made "true" diversion the same as doing nothing.

Most other diversion definitions assumed some degree of intervention beyond contact and release by law enforcement officers. Dunford (1977) saw diversion as the substitution of a new, nonjuvenile justice system program in place of formal system processing and adjudication. Klein (1976), Vorenberg and Vorenberg (1973) and Palmer and Lewis (1980) referred to a **minimization of penetration**. This minimization could take place at various stages or points in the juvenile justice process. Palmer and Lewis (1980) identified four such points. The first occurred at screening and entailed the idea of "true" diversion discussed above. The second point was after an arrest but before any further system involvement. Diversion at this point would be initiated by the police and typically include referral to a non–justice-system agency for help. Diversion at intake but before adjudication represents the third point, while diversion after adjudication but before the imposition of a sentence would be the fourth. Diversion at this point would usually take the form of deinstitutionalization (see Chapter 11). In essence, "minimization of penetration" could occur whenever full processing was interrupted in favor of some alternative action.

Diversion Programming

Despite the definitional problem, diversion programs exploded on the scene after the recommendations of the President's Commission. For example, from 1968 to 1974 the number of youths referred by the Los Angeles County Sheriff's Department to various social service agencies rose from 119 to 1,646 (Klein et al., 1976). Likewise, the number of diversion programs also grew. **Youth Service Bureaus**, another name for diversion programs, increased in number from zero to more than 150 in the United States between 1967 and 1971 (Howlett, 1973).

Reasons behind this sudden and great growth are easily identified. The theoretical rationale of labeling was gaining great prominence. Diversion provided a logical response and test of the theory. A second reason revolved around the capacity of the system to handle all of the youths it is sent. Diversion provided an alternative source of intervention to which problem youths could be referred. Perhaps the most important factor in the growth of diversion was the availability of federal funds for such programs (Klein et al., 1976).

The great growth of diversion programs does not mean that new and innovative programs and interventions were being initiated. Many new diversion programs differed from existing programs only in the use of the term "diversion" or "youth service bureau" in its title. Besides these new names, the programs provided many of the same services traditionally provided by the formal justice system agencies.

A number of well-known diversion programs utilized the same intervention techniques as past programs. The Sacramento 601 Diversion Project, so named because of its focus on youths who fell under Section 601 of the Welfare Code, handled youths referred by the police, families or schools and provided immediate full-family counseling (Nejelski, 1976). The Hamilton-Wentworth Diversion Project emphasized individual counseling with pre-delinquent youths (Osborne, 1979). The Van Dyke Youth Service Bureau handled court-referred girls and provided counseling and a temporary place to stay. The girls were free to leave at any time without any threat of being referred back to the court (Nejelski, 1976). Many diversion programs simply refer youths to other sources of help. The program itself serves as nothing but a source of information and follow-up. One example of this type of program is the Memphis-Metro Youth Diversion Project (MMYDP), which "places youths with established service providers, at which point its role becomes that of maintaining . . . and monitoring the progress of assigned youths" (Severy & Whitaker, 1984: 272). In this type of program, diversion is truly nothing new. It is solely a reorganization of existing resources.

Palmer and Lewis's (1980) evaluation of 15 California diversion projects illustrates the similarity of diversion programs to activities provided throughout the juvenile justice system prior to the initiation of diversion (see Box 10.2). Counseling and referral appear in the bulk of the program methods of intervention. Indeed, family and individual counseling are the most prevalent forms of intervention used in the programs they studied (72% and 52%, respectively). There is a clear tendency to provide traditional modes of intervention in diversion programs.

Some would argue that having programs that are not different from earlier interventions is not a problem. Rather, the important factor is that the programs are no longer being offered by the formal justice system. This avoids the stigma of system contact. Unfortunately, many of the diversion programs have been established and run by the police, prosecutors, probation and the court. Diversion, therefore, has become another component of the formal justice system. The name of the program is changed but the potential of labeling as a result of system contact continues to exist.

The preceding discussion does not mean that all programs are a part of the formal system or that no new ideas have been advocated or initiated since the introduction of diversion. There have been a variety of innovative programs established for their diversionary and corrective capabilities. **Juvenile awareness projects** represent one unique approach to diverting youths. These interventions are more commonly known as "Scared Straight" programs, based on a well-known program at Rahway State Prison in New Jersey. These programs seek to expose troubled youths to the realities of life as criminals and prisoners. Most programs are run by prison inmates and involve bringing youths into the prison for frank, and often confrontational, presentations on prison life. The hope is that this contact and exposure will deter the youth from further deviant behavior.

Box 10.2 Diversion Programs and Practices

Program	Intervention Methods
Compton Area Juvenile Diversion Project	Intake, evaluation of needs, referral
Imperial County Delinquency Intervention/Diversion	Counseling, recreation
Fremont Youth Service Center	Counseling, tutoring, employment counseling
Fresno County Probation Department Diversion Project	Unspecified handling of family disorganization
Pre-trial Intervention and Diversion Project	Contingency contracting, parent-child communication, coping skills, community involvement
La Colonia Youth Services Project	Counseling, tutoring, recreation
Mendocino Lake Youth Project	Counseling, tutoring, referral
Project Interface	Counseling—drug-related
New Directions	Family therapy
Vacaville Youth Service Diversion Unit	Counseling, tutoring, recreation, drug education, referral
Vallejo Youth Service Bureau	Counseling
Mid-Valley Juvenile Delinquency Prevention Project	Counseling
Pomona Valley Juvenile Diversion Project	Referral, counseling, monitoring
Curbstone Youth Service Center	Counseling, tutoring, recreation
Siskiyou County Juvenile Diversion Project	Intensive crisis counseling

Source: Palmer and Lewis (1980). Constructed from text by authors.

A second innovative approach focuses on **wilderness experience** programs. These programs place problem youths into situations in which they must learn self-reliance, interdependence and self-worth. Among the well-known wilderness programs are Vision Quest, Homeward Bound and Ocean Quest. Both Vision Quest and Homeward Bound involve outdoor programs that variably include hiking, camping, cooking, rock climbing, living off the land, and work projects. Ocean Quest takes the outdoor experience onto the open seas for similar purposes. Although innovative in comparison to other interventions,

Rahway State Prison in New Jersey was home to the well-known and controversial "Scared Straight" program, designed to deter delinquency by exposing youths to the realities of life as criminals and prisoners. *Photo: UPI/Corbis-Bettman*

the idea of taking youths out of the city for the rehabilitative effect of hard work and self-reliance dates back to the early days of the juvenile court and the work of the Chicago Area Project.

Another interesting form of intervention that has been implemented since the inception of diversion is the use of **dispute resolution** in juvenile matters. Dispute resolution entails bringing adversarial parties together in an attempt to arrive at a mutually agreeable solution to the dispute. Other names for these programs are conflict resolution and peer mediation. One of the earliest dispute resolution programs for juveniles was the New Jersey Conference Committees. These committees consisted of community volunteers who worked with minor juvenile offenders to arrive at meaningful dispositions. The dispositions included a wide range of practices such as restitution, community service and informal probation (Nejelski, 1976). Although the dispositions were typical of formal processing, the setting of the program was new. The most recent incarnation of dispute resolution involves the establishment of these programs in schools and can deal with everything from minor disputes to criminal offenses.

Not all diversion programs are treatment-oriented. The state of Washington established a program that relies on the just deserts model (see Chapter 13), which is more punitive in approach. The Washington state diversion movement relies heavily on restitution and community service for less serious offenders (Schneider, 1984; Schneider & Schram, 1982). While referred to as diversion, such an approach places emphasis on the offense and diminishes attention on the needs of the child. In a similar vein, the San Diego County Interagency Agreement emphasizes holding youths accountable for their actions while also providing services to the juveniles (Pennell, Curtis & Scheck, 1990). Various alternatives, including counseling and referral to another agency, are to be accompanied with restitutive activities. These just deserts–based diversion programs contradict most views of what constitutes diversion and are counter to the prevailing philosophy of the juvenile justice system.

Clearly, diversion takes a variety of forms and appears under varying names. The programs, whether new and innovative or traditional, are expected to bring about a variety of improvements for juvenile justice. The extent to which diversion has succeeded is considered in the next section.

The Impact of Diversion

Diversion was expected to bring about a number of changes and improvements in the way juveniles were treated. Based on its underlying rationales, diversion should:

- Reduce delinquency and recidivism.

- Reduce the numbers of juveniles handled by the court.

- Reduce the amount of stigma attached to intervention.

- Reduce the amount of money spent on dealing with problem youths.

- Reduce the level of coercion found in juvenile justice.

The success of diversion at achieving these goals has been uneven. While some evaluations have found positive outcomes, others question whether diversion fares any better than traditional processing. Much of the conflict, however, revolves around which goal one wishes to consider. Information on each of these outcome measures is found below.

Reduced Delinquency and Recidivism

POSITIVE RESULTS

The primary goal of diversion was to reduce delinquency and recidivism. Unfortunately, research has uncovered mixed findings regarding this goal. Several studies purport to have found reduced recidivism among diversion clients, particularly compared to youths undergoing normal system processing. In one of the earliest evaluations, Duxbury (1973) claimed that diversion led to fewer juvenile arrests. This observation rested on aggregated arrest figures for areas with and without functioning diversion programs. Unfortunately, there was no evidence that youths who participated in diversion programs were less likely to be arrested. Quay and Love (1977) randomly assigned youths to diversion treatment and a control group. The diversion clients received various services, including vocational assistance, education and counseling. After a one-year follow-up, the authors reported a 32 percent recidivism rate for diversion clients and 45 percent recidivism rate for the control subjects. Further, the program reduced both the number of youths who were rearrested and the average number of arrests. Examining six diversion programs in the Denver, Colorado, area, Regoli, Wilderman and Pogrebin (1985) compared recidivism for diverted youths to that for a random sample of youths subjected to normal system processing. The resultant recidivism rate for the diversion clients was lower than that for the control youths. Various other studies also have reported that diversion programs brought about lower recidivism rates (Klein, 1975; Lipsey, Cordray & Berger, 1981; McPherson, McDonald & Ryer, 1983; Pogrebin, Poole & Regoli, 1984; Whitaker & Severy, 1984). Interestingly, many of these same studies also found instances in which diversion programs exacerbated delinquency or did nothing at all.

EQUIVOCAL SUPPORT

Three good examples of qualified support for diversion are studies by Klein (1979), Palmer and Lewis (1980) and Pennell and associates (1990). Klein (1979) evaluated 13 diversion programs and found a mix of results. In three of the programs the delinquency rate decreased. For two programs, however, delinquency increased, and there was no change in delinquency for the remaining eight programs (Klein, 1979). Palmer and Lewis (1980), in an in-depth study of 15 California diversion programs, found lower recidivism in only three of the projects. There was no difference in recidivism between clients and control youths in eight of the programs (Palmer & Lewis, 1980). The remaining four programs could not be adequately evaluated for their effect on recidivism. Finally, in their evaluation of the San Diego Interagency Agreement diversion program, Pennell and associates (1990) report that "the rate of increase in arrests" decreased. At the same time, however, there was no change in crime seriousness. They conclude that the project "had limited impact on recidivism" (p. 270).

One evaluation of the research literature published from 1975 to 1984 illustrates these disparate diversion results (Lab & Whitehead, 1988). The authors found 31 programs that claimed a positive impact from diversion and an additional 24 that showed negative results or no impact. When the authors focused only on those differences that reached statistical significance, however, only 12 programs showed positive results, 14 exhibited no effect of diversion and two resulted in higher levels of delinquency (Lab & Whitehead, 1988). Similar mixed results appeared in a meta-analysis of this same data (Whitehead & Lab, 1989). In a **meta-analysis**, the reported data from each study are reanalyzed and a common statistical measure is computed. This allows for direct comparison of the results across studies and eliminates the need to compare different statistical techniques.

NEGATIVE RESULTS

Findings of no effect on recidivism permeate the literature on diversion. Most evaluations cannot demonstrate any reductions in subsequent delinquency as a result of participation in diversionary programs. A national evaluation of diversion programs (Dunford, Osgood & Weichselbaum, 1982) failed to uncover any positive impact on delinquency. Using both self-report and official measures of delinquent activity, Dunford et al. (1982) could find no differences in the behavior of youths randomly assigned to diversion programs, normal court processing or outright release from system processing. The authors also probed for differences based on varying levels of involvement in different types of diversion programs. The analysis, however, failed to identify effective diversion programs (Dunford et al., 1982). A follow-up evaluation of these data in terms of prior offense history of youths on diversion similarly failed to find any reduction in recidivism for diverted youths (Osgood, 1983).

Similar findings have appeared in other reports. Rausch (1983) compared three different diversion treatments and a pre-program control group. The three diversion projects included a community-based, minimum-intervention program; a court-based, minimum-intervention program; and a court-based, maximum-intervention program. A comparison of recidivism rates after six months found no difference even after controlling for subject demographic characteristics (Rausch, 1983). Normal court processing was as effective as any of the diversion programs. Evaluations of diversion programs in Wisconsin, Florida and Tennessee also failed to uncover any significant impact on recidivism for diversion clients compared to individuals handled through traditional interventions (Florida, 1981; Severy & Whitaker, 1982; Venezia & Anthony, 1978). In another meta-analysis, Gensheimer et al. (1986) report that "diversion interventions produce no effect on youths" (p. 51).

Adding to the claims that diversion is ineffective are those studies that find increased recidivism as an outcome of participation in diversion programs. The reports of both Lincoln (1976) and Elliott, Dunford and Knowles (1978) show that diversion aggravates the level of delinquent activity for study subjects. As noted earlier, studies that include more than one diversion program often find that some of the target programs lead to increased delinquency (see Klein, 1979; Palmer & Lewis, 1980; Regoli, Wilderman & Pogrebin, 1985).

ALTERNATE CONSIDERATIONS

An attempt to outline the "typical" successful diversion program is doomed to fail due to overgeneralizing the findings of different studies. While counseling (particularly individual counseling) appears to be a key element of many successful programs, there are evaluations that show that counseling has little or no impact. This discrepancy may be due to the variety of counseling techniques available and the general uncertainty about what causes delinquency and what to do about it. Diversion programs claiming success also tend to deal most often with first-time offenders and youths contacted for status offenses. The success, therefore, could be a result of natural desistance from further offending and not an impact of program participation. Diversion, in whatever form, has so far been unable to establish itself as a clear success in terms of reducing delinquency and recidivism with any large group of clients.

Perhaps one alternative way to assess diversion is to look at the youths who are helped. Palmer and Lewis (1980) note that although diversion may not be effective across the board, some youths benefit from some programs. This same argument has been made by Martinson (1979), Andrews and associates (1990) and others in relationship to any correctional treatment. The key problem entails matching the proper client with the proper program. Indeed, Andrews and associates (1990; Andrews & Bonta, 1998) argue that proper attention paid to assessment of risk, need and responsivity will lead to the correct matching of clients to service. Evaluations, therefore, should not be concerned with overall changes in the crime rate. Instead, emphasis should be placed on qualitative improvements in behavior, even if for just a few youths. Typical outcomes that receive attention in diversion studies include educational achievement, family adjustment, employment and evaluations by program providers. Most diversion evaluations can show improvements in these and other areas. Unfortunately, the studies often cannot show a direct relationship between these outcomes and the problems of delinquency and recidivism. While these changes may be important, they do not address the central issue of diversion—the reduction of delinquency.

Reducing the Number of Youths with System Contact

A second major goal of diversion is to reduce the number of youths coming into contact with the juvenile justice system. This goal reflects the perceived labeling and criminogenic effects of processing in the formal justice system and the fact that the formal system is overburdened with cases. Ideally, diversion clients should come from that group of youths who normally would have been dealt with in the formal system. In essence, diverted youths are to be minor offenders who are funneled away from formal processing. Reviews of the evidence, however, show that diversion has resulted in net-widening.

Net-widening refers to the practice of handling youths who normally would have been left alone in the absence of the new program. Instead of dealing with youths who normally would have experienced formal system contact, diversion often handles minor, status offenders who usually are ignored or quickly funneled out of the formal system (Klein et al., 1976; Lemert, 1981). Where in the past these individuals would have been screened out of the formal system and simply sent home, they are now being subjected to diversion (Cohen, 1979). In addition, diversion programs tend to handle more females with minor problems than are typically found in the formal system (Adler, 1984; Polk, 1981).

Estimates of the number of new youths under social control as a result of diversion often reach 50 percent. Klein (1979) notes programs in which less than 45 percent of the clients are actually diverted from the formal juvenile justice system. The other youths in the diversion programs would have been left alone prior to the advent of the new programs. Palmer and Lewis's (1980) evaluation of diversion in California produces similar results. They find that 49 percent of the diversion clients are directly attributable to net-widening. Blomberg (1979) reveals that diversion results in at least a 33 percent increase in the number of persons subjected to social control. Part of this increase is due to the forced inclusion of family members—in addition to the diverted youth—in diversion programs. Other researchers also point out that diversion increases the number of people under social control (Bohnstedt, 1978; Decker, 1985; Pogrebin, Poole & Regoli, 1984; Saul & Davidson, 1983).

Rojek (1982) views the problem of net-widening as a form of agency "self-aggrandizement." He notes that diversion is often adopted as a means of intervening in the lives of additional youths. Such increased numbers of youths under intervention provide "proof" that the agency is doing its job. "Slots left unfilled [are] viewed as programmatic failure. Clients appearing for services [become] a valued commodity for future funding" (Rojek, 1982). Little attention is paid to the effectiveness (in terms of recidivism) of these programs. Rojek's (1982) examination of the Pima County, Arizona, diversion program finds that 17 percent of the clients are nonstatus offenders, despite the fact that the program is aimed exclusively at status offenders. Additionally, 80 percent of the youths referred to education programs (set up for truants) are nontruants (Rojek, 1982). Fuller and Norton (1993) note that net-widening is related to a program's underlying philosophy. That is, interventions based on crime-control and punishment involve less net-widening than those relying on a treatment-based philosophy. Thus, the basic premise of diversion leads to a wider net.

It is clear that diversion has not lived up to the idea of reducing the number of people under social control. Some would argue, however, that the number of youths handled by diversion programs is not a problem. They would claim that the goal is the reduction of youths in contact with the formal system and not an absolute reduction in the number of youths who receive some form of intervention. Therefore, diversion could be considered a success if there are fewer youth being handled by the formal system of justice. Unfortunately, at the same time that diversion is processing new youths, the formal system is also finding new juveniles to fill the empty spaces left by those youths who are sent to diversion. For example, if diversion is handling 100 youths, 50 of those are from the formal system and the other 50 are new clients. The 50 taken from the formal system, however, do not represent a decrease in the load of the formal system. Instead, the formal system finds 50 new clients of its own to handle. The net result of diversion is an increase of 100 juveniles under some form of social control (50 new clients in diversion and 50 new clients in the formal system). There is little question that diversion has failed to reduce the number of youths being subjected to some form of intervention. This is further exacerbated by the fact that many diversion programs are run by the formal system and, thus, can be considered to be little different from past interventions.

Reducing Stigma and Labeling

One of the strongest arguments supporting diversion is the argument that system contact stigmatizes the youth and leads to greater amounts of deviant activity. The problem youth, by virtue of being apprehended and handled by the justice system, becomes identified as a delinquent by the system and society. This label then overshadows all other aspects of the youth's life and behavior. He or she is expected to be deviant and is not believed when he or she acts in an acceptable fashion. As a result, the youth finds that it is easier to act according to the deviant label (see Chapter 4 for more information on labeling).

Assuming that the labeling argument is valid, the effectiveness of diversion in eliminating the stigmatizing effect of system intervention has not been demonstrated. Research suggests that diversion can be equally stigmatizing and leads to labeling just as in formal intervention. Many diversion programs are operated by the formal system and do little more than change the label attached to youths. In place of delinquent, youths become CHINS, PINS or other euphemistic terms (Klein, 1979; Morris, 1978). In a study of the self-concept of diverted and incarcerated juveniles, Paternoster and associates are unable to find any differences in the level of perceived stigma. The two groups of youths give similar responses despite their different forms of intervention (Paternoster et al., 1979). Similarly, Rausch (1983) finds no support for labeling theory when comparing three types of diversion to normal court processing. Other researchers uncover the same lack of support for a labeling argument in diversion (Dunford et al., 1982; Elliott et al., 1978).

These results are not surprising given the fact that many diversion programs are simple extensions of the formal justice system. Youths should not be expected to differentiate, to any great extent, between processing through traditional system channels and new diversion programs. Additionally, even if a diversion program is administratively separate from the formal system, most youths still enter diversion through contact with the police or intake office. Entrance to diversion, therefore, is controlled by the very system that diversion is attempting to avoid. Juveniles still see diversion as an extension of the formal system and not as a distinct, individual entity. Indeed, Polk (1981), examining the similarity in treatment between diverted youths and those handled by traditional processing, claims that the two groups should be stigmatized equally.

Reducing Coercion

Underlying the assumption that diversion programs should be less stigmatizing is the idea that such programs should be voluntary. Problem youths and their families should be referred to diversion and it should be up to them whether they participate. In fact, the President's Commission (1967b) expressly called for participation in diversion programs to be totally voluntary. Most diversion programs, however, have been clearly coercive.

Many diversion programs coerce participation from both juvenile clients and the families of the clients. Blomberg (1979) notes that diversion programs often require the families of diverted youths to participate. Failure of the families to take part can result in the child being sent back for formal system processing. A large number of other studies also find coercion (Blomberg & Carabelo, 1979; Couch, 1974; Dunford, 1977; Nejelski, 1976; Palmer & Lewis, 1980).

Not all studies, however, find equal levels of coercion in diversion programs and traditional interventions. A national evaluation of diversion programs reports that diversion personnel are less coercive than their counterparts in other programs (Dunford et al., 1982). Similarly, Osgood and Weischelbaum (1984) find that clients view formal justice system programs as more coercive and more control-oriented than diversion interventions. Gottheil (1979) also disputes the research that notes a general air of coercion in diversion programs. The author supports her claim by pointing to a program that does not refer individuals back to the juvenile court, regardless of whether the juvenile successfully completes the program. Gottheil (1979) fails to recognize, however, that if diversion clients do not voluntarily enter the program in the first place, they will be subjected to normal system processing. This is often the case in diversion programs, particularly where the police or intake officers do the referral. Claims that coercion is not a factor in diversion, therefore, are resting on a narrow idea of what constitutes coercion.

Reducing the Costs of Intervention

The President's Commission (1967b) pointed to the great costs of formal processing as a prime reason for the development of alternative interventions. The assumption was that services could be provided at a cheaper cost by other programs. In addition, the youths in these new programs would be coming from traditional system processing. As a result, lower-cost programs would be substituted for higher-cost programs.

Research on the cost-effectiveness of diversion provides contradictory evidence. Many diversion programs can show lower costs compared to traditional system interventions. Alternatively, some diversion programs spend more money per client than formal processing. Both the Dunford et al. (1982) and Palmer and Lewis (1980) studies report wide cost ranges for diversion projects. Some have higher costs and some have lower costs. Palmer and Lewis (1980), aggregating the programs into a single analysis, claim that the overall result is a slight per-client savings (approximately $29) in the diversion programs. Despite the savings in this program, the overall conclusion seems to be that diversion seems to cost roughly the same as normal system processing. The goal of saving money does not appear to have been realized.

Additional Considerations

While most of the above results have not painted a rosy picture of diversion, neither have they been devastating to diversionary approaches. Proponents of diversion would point to the dismal record of formal system intervention throughout history, the potential of diversion to avoid many of the same problems, and results that show equal, if not better, impacts on clients. Taken in isolation from one another, the results of diversion evaluations would appear to give qualified support for this contention. Consideration of the various findings as a group, however, leads to different conclusions.

The largest concerns appear when one couples the finding of net-widening with the problems of possible stigma, the costs of the system, and recidivism. In terms of stigma, the revelation that diversion can be just as stigmatizing as usual processing is not problematic. If it were *more* stigmatizing, it would be a prime concern. However, assuming that some labeling does take place, if the diversion program is working with youths who would normally be left alone, these youths are being stigmatized and labeled solely due to the existence of diversion. Such activity may be creating problems (and delinquents) where none existed before. Diversion, at this point, becomes a new problem instead of a new solution.

A second issue arises when costs must be expended handling new clients. Although diversion may be processing youths at a lower per-client cost, the addition of totally new clients (those not diverted from the formal system) actually represents increased costs. The problem is further exacerbated if the formal system also widens the net by locating new clients to replace those juveniles who are sent to a diversion program. Not only are these new clients for the system, they are being provided with services at the same cost level as before diversion was initiated. Box 10.3 illustrates that instead of reducing the costs of dealing with youths, diversion and net-widening have actually increased the overall expenses for society.

Another major concern appears in attempts to determine which clients are recidivating. Proponents staunchly point out that, at the very least, diversion does no worse than system intervention in terms of recidivism. It is not known, however, if the youths who are recidivating are those who were always subject to system intervention. If this is true, any youths who are in diversion because of net-widening are not being harmed. Unfortunately, some of the recidivating youths may be new clients who normally would be left alone. The diversion program, through its intrusion into the youth's life and possible stigmatizing effects, may be creating a deviant where one did not already exist. At this point in time, there has been no evaluation that compares the recidivism rate of those youths who are truly diverted to that of youths who are new, net-widening clients. In the absence of evidence that the new clients are *not* among the recidivists, the most logical assumption is that the new clients do add to the recidivism figures. If this is true, diversion is a potential candidate for the cause of the recidivism and a greater threat than most persons realize.

A final concern with diversion is the lack of attention paid to due process considerations. Many persons subjected to diversionary intervention have not committed a delinquent or criminal act. A prime example of this is the forced participation of parents and siblings in diversion programs. There is no opportunity for the participants to dispute the facts (or lack thereof) or the need for their participation in the forced intervention. Persons under diversion also have little control over the actions and demands of the diversion agency. Indeed, the programs are rarely subject to oversight or held accountable by any other agency. As a result, the agencies can demand compliance with various procedures and the clients have little or no recourse to contest the intervention. There is a clear assumption of guilt and a lack of due process in many diversion programs.

Box 10.3 Illustrative Costs of Diversion

Assessing the costs of diversion vis-à-vis normal system processing can be deceiving if the impact of net-widening is not considered. The top two panels illustrate the costs of formal processing alone and formal processing plus diversion processing with *no* net-widening. The final panel shows what happens when net-widening occurs and there is an increase in the total number of youths under some form of social control. While diversion may cost less per person than formal processing, any increase in numbers served results in greater overall costs.

Panel 1—Costs of Formal Processing:

Formal System	**Diversion**
100 clients	0 clients
$100 per client	
$10,000 total cost	

Panel 2—Ideal View of Diversion Costs:

50 formal clients	50 diverted clients
$100 per client	$50 per client
$5,000 total cost	$2,500 total cost

Total cost of handling youths	=	$7,500
Savings from formal system alone	=	$2,500

Panel 3—Realistic View of Diversion Costs:

50 original formal clients	50 diverted clients
50 new formal clients	50 new diverted clients
100 total formal clients	100 clients in diversion
$100 per client	$50 per client
$10,000 total cost	$5,000 total cost

Total cost of handling youths	=	$15,000
Additional costs from diversion and net-widening	=	$ 5,000

Summary: The Future of Diversion in Juvenile Justice

Despite the failure of diversion to live up to the great expectations placed on it, diversionary programming continues to be a major movement in juvenile justice. Support for diversion does not appear to be waning. This would appear questionable in light of the many negative evaluations of diversion's impact. There are a number of reasons behind the continued support for diversion.

Sources of Support for Diversion

One major source of support comes from the operation of the formal juvenile justice system. While diversion has been unable to reduce delinquency and recidivism appreciably, the juvenile court has faced the same failures. The formal system has not become any more successful since the inception of diversion than it was prior to the development of diversion programs. Coupled with the facts that formal processing may have a greater chance of labeling a youth, may lead to incarceration and generally has a higher per-client cost, arguments to abolish diversion and return to the exclusive use of the formal justice system find little support.

Continued support for diversion is also found in the very philosophy of the juvenile justice system. The doctrine of *parens patriae*, which promotes a paternalistic system of intervention, allows for the use of a wide range of options and alternatives in processing youths. The primary limitation on *parens patriae* is that whatever intervention is implemented, it must be in the best interests of the child. Diversion, by the very nature of its multidimensional definitions and programs, closely fits the malleable ideal of juvenile justice. It is certainly more open to change and alternatives than is the formal juvenile system.

Additional support for diversion comes from the very data that condemn the programs. While most evaluations opt to interpret the study results in a negative light, it is possible to find positive impacts in the results. In terms of recidivism, diversion appears to do no worse than formal kinds of intervention. Some programs even find reduced delinquency and recidivism among diverted clients. Palmer and Lewis (1980) note that diversion should not be evaluated in terms of its aggregate effects on youths. Rather, diversion clearly helps some youths in some situations. This is aptly illustrated by the finding of effective diversion programs in different studies (Dunford et al., 1982; Klein, 1979; Palmer & Lewis, 1980). Often, the effective programs are able to provide more services or are able to better select the types of clients for which their services are most suited.

Some would argue that net-widening is not a great problem. These comments revolve around the idea that the new clients have always needed help but the system was simply not in a position to provide assistance prior to diversion. Diversion, therefore, fills a gap that had existed in the past. The programs can now handle minor status offenders before they enter the formal system. By so doing, there may be a reduction in stigma. It also is not known whether these new clients would have completely avoided system contact in the absence of diversion. The advent of diversion may simply have accelerated the juveniles' insertion into some type of intervention. Diversion simply supplies an opportunity to assist the youths at an earlier point in their lives.

Future Directions

Where does diversion go from here? Despite the questionable evidence on its effectiveness, it is evident that diversionary programs will persist. There are, however, a number of fruitful directions it could take and problems it should address. First, diversion needs to recognize its limitations. It cannot be everything to all juveniles. It has fallen into the same trap of overextending itself as has the traditional system. Each diversion program needs to identify its strong points, identify those youths most likely to benefit from those practices, and limit itself to those individuals and interventions.

A second suggestion addresses the problems of stigma and labeling. Although there remain questions about the impact of labeling, diversion should attempt to separate itself as much as possible from the formal justice system. This may mean identifying clients from sources other than the police, or simply eliminating any coercion in participation. If the police refer a juvenile, there must be no strings attached to the juvenile's choice of whether to follow through with the referral. An additional consideration would be the identification of the stigmatizing aspects of diversion programs and initiating processes to eliminate those factors. This may be possible through the comparison of programs that engender different levels of stigma.

A final suggestion mimics the comments made in any analysis of social interventions. The suggestion is the call for continued evaluation of such programs. Until such a time that diversion is proved to have only positive impacts, it is imperative that research be undertaken. This will help isolate the problem areas and identify solutions to the problems. For example, there is an immediate need to assess the impact of diversion on those clients who are in programs as the result of net-widening. At the present time it is not known whether those youths are being forced into greater amounts and types of delinquency, or whether they are simply adding to the costs of intervention. These kinds of questions can be resolved only through further research.

DISCUSSION QUESTIONS

1. You have been asked to head up a drive to establish a juvenile diversion program. The first thing you have to do is define diversion. Next, outline your program—what will it do? Finally, justify how the program differs from existing practice and, if it does not, why your program should be instituted anyway.

2. The diversion program under your guidance has been charged with solving the problem of net-widening. What is net-widening? Is the problem one to be concerned about? Why or why not? Does or could net-widening harm the juveniles in your charge?

3. Diversion has been both honored and criticized. Outline the positive and negative findings concerning diversion. Should diversion be continued or discontinued—or should it be altered (and in what way)? What factors are available to support your position?

CHAPTER 11

Institutional/Residential Interventions

Key Terms and Phrases

boot camps
creaming
deinstitutionalization
eclectic programming
guided group interaction
inmate code
job burnout
"make-believe family" role

maturation effect
Provo Experiment
regression toward the mean
shock incarceration
Silverlake Experiment
suppression effect
training schools
victimization

On February 15, 1995, 108,746 youths were in detention, correctional or shelter facilites. Just over 69,000 of these youths were in public facilities (Moore, 1997b). Two-thirds of these youths were committed and one-third were being detained prior to adjudication or were awaiting diposition or placement. The private facility custody population included a high percentage (41%) of nonoffenders, including youths referred for abuse, neglect, emotional problems or mental retardation (Sickmund, Snyder & Poe-Yamagata, 1997). The latest information available indicated that average length of stay was 225 days and average yearly cost of custody in a public institution was more than $30,000 (Cohen, 1994).

Although probation handles many more youths, institutions involve a significant minority of the offenders who go through the juvenile justice system. These facilities constitute the costliest part of the system. One public facility in New York was reported to cost more than $80,000 a year (Singer, 1996).

Correctional managers contend that these facilities seek to serve the "best interests of the child," which means that they attempt to provide educational, therapeutic and recreational programs staffed by concerned caregivers. Critics argue that, at best, the facilities are warehouses or holding tanks in which little, if any, positive change takes place. Past critics have contended that juvenile facilities harbor as many horror stories as they do children: tales of neglect, abuse and even death (Wooden, 1976).

This chapter examines various types of institutional and residential interventions with juveniles, including state training schools, youth camps, private placements and group homes. After describing these various placements, we will examine some of the current issues about their operation, such as the determination of appropriate targets for intervention, effectiveness in reducing recidivism, and client and worker adaptations to the pressures of institutional life. The chapter concludes with information on innovative trends in this area, such as deinstitutionalization and wilderness programs.

State Training Schools

State **training schools** are the juvenile justice system's equivalent of the adult prison; they house the delinquents whom juvenile court judges consider unfit for probation or some other lesser punishment. Some training schools actually resemble adult prisons in terms of their architecture: high walls or fences, locked cell blocks, self-sufficiency (they have their own laundry, hospital and maintenance facilities) and solitary confinement for the recalcitrant. Other training schools have the so-called cottage system of architectural design. The cottage system

> was introduced in 1856 to give children the closest thing to some form of home life. Those in charge are "house parents" rather than "guards." The outside area is usually quiet and pleasant and bears little semblance to a penal facility. The cottages are usually small, aesthetically pleasing, dormlike structures. Unfortunately, those I have seen have no back or side doors, or if they do, the doors are always chained and locked. The windows are also secured with heavy wire and in the event of emergencies such as fire, escape would be impossible except through the front door (Wooden, 1976: 28-29).

As one can readily tell from Wooden's comments, the cottage system is often a far cry from the homelike atmosphere intended by its founders. Cottages are often deteriorating dormitories with decrepit plumbing, heating and lighting and an accompanying host of sociocultural problems as well. Thus, Giallombardo's (1974) description of three institutions for girls applies to many training schools, including ones for males:

> the inescapable fact is that a cottage that houses twenty, forty, or more inmates can never be homelike, no matter how many "homelike touches" are added. No home that a youngster came from was so lacking in privacy as were the facilities at Eastern, Central, and Western. The sense of constraint, inherent in mass living under regulated authority permeates the institutions (Giallombardo, 1974: 240).

A tour of one southeastern training school by one of the authors showed a marked contrast in youth prison architecture. Several cottages dating from the founding of the school more than 50 years ago were still in operation. These cottages were two-story brick dormitories with a television room and pool table on the first floor. An interesting aspect of the television room was the presence of a bookcase with four shelves. During this visit, two shelves held bibles and two were empty. The implication seemed to be that religion and television were considered worthwhile activities for the delinquents, but other reading materials were either unnecessary or unaffordable. This same institution also had state-of-the-art residence halls, boasting individual rooms and a design permitting easy viewing of all areas of the facility by staff. So contemporary was the design that the buildings were built partially into the ground to be more energy efficient in all four seasons.

Box 11.1　Sample of One Training School's Rules

Below is an actual set of rules and a list of minor rule violations from a southeastern training school:

Rules:
1. There will be no misuse of any property.
2. There is to be no use of vulgar or profane language.
3. There will be no gambling.
4. There will be no tampering with fire and safety equipment.
5. Students will remain in their assigned areas.
6. Students may not borrow, sell, lend or trade their property.
7. Students are expected to always be courteous.
8. Students are expected to respect privacy and property of others.
9. Students are expected to follow all dress codes.
10. Students are expected to follow instructions of staff.

Minor Rule Violations:
1. Disruptive behavior
2. Failure to follow institutional rules
3. Horseplay
4. Out of assigned area
5. Racial slurs
6. Refusal of a direct order
7. Self-mutilation
8. Sexual slurs
9. Use of obscene language

Source: Student handbook from a southeastern state training school.

Programs for Training School Residents

The programming at state training schools is often a combination of academic and vocational education and behavior modification. Residents attend school much of the day just like their noninstitutionalized counterparts, but the school run by the prison teaches youths who are usually two to three years below their appropriate grade level in both reading and mathematics. (For a list of the school rules in one training school, see Box 11.1; for a typical daily schedule, see Box 11.2.)

Box 11.2 Typical Weekday Schedule at a Residential Placement for Delinquents

6:30 AM	Wake up: dress and clean room
7:00 AM	Calisthenics
7:30 AM	Hygiene (showers, etc.)
8:00 AM	Clean dormitories
8:30 AM	Breakfast
9:00 AM	Start school
10:30 AM	"Rap" half-hour
11:00 AM	Return to school
12:00	Lunch
12:30 PM	"Rap" half-hour
1:00 PM	School
3:30 PM	Group therapy
5:00 PM	Dinner
5:30 PM	Work details (kitchen clean-up and dormitory clean-up)
6:00-7:00 PM	TV news
7:00-9:00 PM	Activities (vary by day—Example: values clarification; occupational therapy; recreational therapy, etc.)
9:00 PM	Bedtime for Phase 1 (9:30 PM in the summer)
10:00 PM	Bedtime for Phase 2 and above.

Source: Manual from a midwestern residential facility. Note: In this context, to "rap" is to talk freely and frankly.

The behavior modification system usually involves the grading of children at one of several levels. The system includes the daily awarding of points for almost every possible action of the child's day, from getting up on time to getting to bed quietly and on time. The points earned each day can be spent on various privileges, ranging from games, television time and telephone calls home to off-campus group outings and visits home. The higher the child's level, the more extensive the privileges available. (Box 11.3 gives an actual list of opportunities for earning and spending points at a southeastern training school.) In addition to qualifying for daily privileges, such as television, the points earned also count toward movement from one level to another with additional privilege possibilities. One training school employee characterized the point system as working both as a behavioral control device and as a device to monitor progress within the institution.

Box 11.3 Typical Institutional Point System

Responsibilities	Points	
1. Get self up on time (6:00 A.M.)	+25	−50
2. Locker neat, orderly, clean room or area with bed made	+50	−100
3. Appropriately dressed	+25	−50
4. Brush teeth and comb hair	+25	−50
5. Daily bath and use deodorant	+25	−100
6. Exercise	+25	−50
7. Act appropriately: a: Breakfast	+10	−20
b: Lunch	+10	−20
c. Dinner	+10	−20
8. School	+40 per hour	
9. Study hour or watching news	+25 per hour	
10. Daily chores	+50	−100
11. Volunteer work	+60 per hour (120 maximum per day)	
13. See counselor	+25 per hour	
14. Attend group	+50	−100 per hour
15. Attend church or Sunday school services	+25	
16. Bonus points	+100 maximum per day	

Note: A +25 indicates that a resident can earn up to 25 points for performing the specified behavior. A −100 indicates that a resident can have as many as 100 points deducted if the behavior is not performed or not performed properly.

Spending Opportunities

1. Swimming	25 points
2. Recreation room	25 points
3. Parlor games (checkers, cards, etc.)	25 points
4. Telephone calls	20 points
5. Use of television room	25 points
6. Play outside	25 points
7. Group outing off campus	300 points
8. Group outing on campus	200 points
9. Living room	25 points
10. Movies in dorm	100 points
11. Home pass	350 points

Source: Student manual from a southeastern training school.

Another training school awards zero to five points for each student for each shift. Teachers/workers grade behavior in these areas:

1. Respecting others by not assaulting verbally or physically.

2. Respecting property by not stealing or damaging.

3. Staying in your assigned areas.

4. Following staff instructions.

(Source: A student handbook from a southeastern state).

In addition to education and behavior modification, programming can include such efforts as individual, group or family counseling, watching television, activities in the surrounding or nearby community (movies, sports and shopping), vocational counseling and job placement. Finckenauer (1984) characterizes such diverse efforts as **eclectic programming**, meaning that "there are multiple treatment approaches, representing different strategies with different theoretical bases—all being used simultaneously" (Finckenauer, 1984: 210). Unfortunately, such a "shotgun approach" can cause problems, such as the careless combining of several strategies into one common approach for all "groups of offenders as if these offenders all had the same needs and problems" (Finckenauer, 1984: 211). Thus, the end results of eclectic programming are often "ineffective and may even be counterproductive" (Finckenauer, 1984: 211).

In contrast to eclectic programs, whole institutions or individual cottages can be organized around a specific ideology, emphasizing custody or treatment or some combination of the two (Feld, 1981). Historically, many training schools used guided group interaction as their primary technique to change residents from delinquents to conforming youths. **Guided group interaction** involves group sessions that confront delinquents with the fact that past delinquency has led to their present status of prisoner. The technique attempts to convince the youths that if they continue in delinquency, they will continue to be caught and incarcerated. Guided group interaction attempts to show that there are law-abiding alternatives available (Bartollas, 1985). One way to do this is by adding a work program to the group sessions. The Provo Experiment (Empey & Erickson, 1972) tested the effectiveness of a guided group interaction program in Utah. The results of that research will be discussed later in the chapter. Other programs have used reality therapy (see Glasser, 1965; Masters, 1994) as their basic intervention strategy (see Chapter 12 for an explanation of reality therapy). Still other programs focus on specific offender types. A program in Wisconsin, for example, uses confrontational and supportive group therapy with adolescent rapists in an effort to impart the message that the crime was wrong but the offender is still a worthwhile individual (Hagan, King & Patros, 1994). (For details, see Box 11.4.)

Box 11.4   Program for Adolescent Rapists

The program for adolescent rapists in Wisconsin uses a confrontational yet supportive group process. The Entry Phase is an orientation phase. Phase II uses intensive group therapy to focus on sexual assaults. One part of Phase II forces the rapist to write a letter to his victim but not send it. The letter answers questions the victim might have. Phase II continues intensive group therapy and involves an in-depth examination of the offender's sexual attitudes and beliefs such as sexual fantasies and ideas on dating and marriage. Phase IV focuses on the offender's family background, patterns of thinking, drug/alcohol uses and abuse, and self-concept. One activity is the writing of an autobiography about one's life and history. The final phase of treatment attempts an integration of the group process and planning for the future.

An evaluation of this program that lacked a control group showed that during a two-year follow-up only five youths were involved in a new sexual assault but 29 youths altogether were convicted of or reported involvement in some type of crime (Hagan, King & Patros, 1994).

Other Options for Housing Delinquents

Traditional training schools are not the only means that states use for housing delinquents. In some years, almost 10,000 youths are held in long-term open facilities that allow greater freedom for residents within the facilities and more contacts with the community. The open facilities category of placements includes shelters, halfway houses, group homes and a few ranches. Group homes are residential facilities for relatively small numbers of youths (perhaps one or two dozen youngsters). The residents often attend regular public schools but participate in group counseling sessions and recreational activities at the group home. The Silverlake Experiment (Empey & Lubeck, 1971) was an important test of the effectiveness of such a group home; the results of that study will be discussed later in this chapter.

Juvenile court judges also have been known to commit juvenile delinquents to detention centers for a short period of time. Youths are placed on probation and one condition of probation is a short stay in the local detention facility. In 1982 there were slightly over 21,000 such commitments and the average length of stay for youths committed to detention was 28 days (Schwartz et al., 1987).

States also utilize private residential placements to house delinquents and some status offenders. In 1995, private facilities held almost 40,000 youths (Moone, 1997a). Private facilities, like state facilities, range from relatively large institutions to small group homes and even wilderness programs at which juveniles camp out. Many were originally started by churches as charitable institutions but have evolved into nonsectarian operations that charge the state thousands of dollars each year for each child they handle. Many private placements have a rigorous selection process that results in only the "better" delinquents being admitted. That is, many private institutions screen clients to exclude extremely violent youths, children with severe psychiatric disturbances, homosexual youths or children considered arson risks. One result of such selectivity (or **creaming**) is that only the more intelligent and better adjusted children tend to wind up in private placements, forcing state institutions to handle all of the remaining hard-to-manage children.

Some private institutions have taken children with severe problems but sometimes the motivation has been solely economic—it is questionable what level of care was actually provided for the children.

Boot Camps

A continuing trend is the use of **boot camps** (also called **shock incarceration**). Boot camps are short-term facilities (90-day/120-day/six-month) that are intended to resemble basic training facilities for the military. There is considerable emphasis on discipline and physical training, such as marching, running, calisthenics and other types of conditioning. Usually a "drill instructor" is assigned to each group of offenders. Many boot camp programs also involve aftercare supervision for program graduates. Box 11.5 shows the daily schedule at one boot camp.

Box 11.5   Daily Schedule for Offenders in a New York Boot Camp

A.M.

5:30	Wake up and standing count
5:45-6:30	Calisthenics and drill
6:30-7:00	Run
7:00-8:00	Mandatory breakfast/cleanup
8:15	Standing count and company formation
8:30-11:55	Work/school schedules

P.M.

12:00-12:30	Mandatory lunch and standing count
12:30-3:30	Afternoon work/school schedule
3:30-4:00	Shower
4:00-4:45	Network community meeting
4:45-5:45	Mandatory dinner, prepare for evening
6:00-9:00	School, group counseling, drug counseling, prerelease counseling, decisionmaking classes
8:00	Count while in programs
9:15-9:30	Squad bay, prepare for bed
9:30	Standing count, lights out

Source: Clark, Aziz & MacKenzie (1994).

The rationale behind boot camps is multifaceted. It is claimed that boot camps can protect the public, reduce prison crowding, reduce costs, punish offenders, hold offenders accountable, deter additional crime, and rehabilitate (Cronin, 1994). It is interesting that "there is considerable emphasis on rehabilitative activities in boot camps for juveniles" (Cronin, 1994: 38), including counseling and education.

The evidence regarding the effectiveness of boot camps for both adult and juvenile offenders is mixed. There is some indication that boot camps can reduce state correctional costs and that participants rate their experience in camp as positive, but the evidence shows that boot camps have little or no effect on recidivism (new crimes) (Cronin, 1994). It does appear clear, however, that "the military atmosphere alone does not reduce recidivism and increase positive activities during community supervision" (MacKenzie, 1994: 66). Ironically, many politicians like boot camps because they appear to be "tough," but it appears that the educational and rehabilitative programming is what helps the offenders.

A recent evaluation of three boot camps in Cleveland, Mobile and Denver offers insights about their advantages and disadvantages. Eligible youth for these camps were youths ages 13 to 17 who had been adjudicated by the juvenile court and were awaiting disposition. Youths considered eligible could not have any history of mental illness or involvement in violent crime but were rated at "high risk" of chronic delinquency and minimal risk of escape.

The graduation rates were positive, ranging from a low of 65 percent at Denver to 87 percent at Mobile and 93 percent at Cleveland. There was significant academic progress at Cleveland and Mobile: From one-half to two-thirds of the youths at Cleveland improved at least one grade level in various academic skills. In Mobile, about 80 percent of the youths improved at least one grade level.

The findings on recidivism, however, were discouraging. There were no significant differences in recidivism between boot camp offenders and the control group offenders at Denver or Mobile. In Cleveland, the experimentals did worse than the controls. Moreover, at all three sites, survival times—the amount of time until the commission of a new offense—were shorter for the youths who went through the boot camps than control cases (Peters, Thomas & Zamberlan, 1997).

Concerning cost-effectiveness, the costs per day of the boot camps were similar to one day of institutionalization but more expensive than a day of probation. Costs per offender were lower than controls because boot camp offenders spent less time in the boot camps. The data on costs per offender were: Cleveland: $14,021 versus $25,549 for the Ohio Department of Youth Services; Denver: $8,141 versus $23,425 for a state facility; Mobile, $6,241 versus $11,616 for a state facility (Peters, Thomas & Zamberlan, 1997: 24-25).

Peters and his colleagues conclude that boot camps are not a panacea but they do offer some advantages:

As an intermediate sanction, boot camps are a useful alternative for offenders for whom probation would be insufficiently punitive, yet for whom long-term incarceration would be excessive. As such, under certain conditions, boot camps can free bed space for more hardened offenders, thereby reducing the financial burden on correctional budgets (Peters, Thomas & Zamberlan, 1997).

A final word on boot camps is that they are part of a more general trend in society to "get tough" on crime. One author (Clear, 1994) calls this trend the "penal harm movement"; another team of authors calls it "the punishment paradigm" (Cullen & Wright, 1995). These authors contend that since 1980 the United States has operated on the premise that more punishment is needed to deter crime and incapacitate offenders. Boot camps are one component of the movement, which includes increased use of prisons and jails, lengthier sentences, determinate sentences, career criminal sentencing provisions, increased use of capital punishment, and harsher community sanctions (intensive supervision, house arrest and electronic monitoring). For juveniles, the punishment paradigm has translated into greater prosecution of juveniles in adult court and blended sentences involving the adult correctional system (see again, Chapter 8). Thus, boot camps are not an isolated phenomenon but are part of a broader trend in criminal justice focusing on retribution, deterrence and incapacitation.

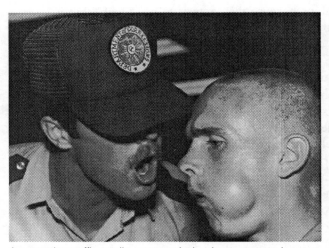

A corrections officer tells a new arrival at boot camp to hurry up with lunch. Boot camps are part of a more general trend to get tough on crime. *Photo: UPI/Corbis-Bettman*

Program Effectiveness

One of the most critical issues facing residential interventions is the effectiveness issue: Do the interventions have any impact on the criminal behavior of their charges? Although most of what follows pertains most directly to publicly run placements, the problems also affect private placements.

The Provo Experiment

Like the issue of correctional effectiveness in general, the question of the effectiveness of institutional programs for juveniles is a complex one. However, there have been some informative studies of juvenile facility effectiveness that provide ammunition for both defenders and detractors of these interventions.

One of these studies is the **Provo Experiment**, which compared the success of boys placed in the Utah State Training School to boys placed in an experimental community program using guided group interaction. The boys in the experimental community program were allowed to stay home and attend their regular school. Afternoons and weekends were reserved for group sessions using the guided group interaction technique. Summer vacations were available for work programs. As noted, guided group interaction is a group intervention strategy in which youths are encouraged to recognize the consequences of their actions and to learn legitimate opportunities to use in place of illegal ones. In Provo, the youths were pressured to admit their involvement in delinquency. They were shown that continued delinquency would lead to confinement in the state training school. However, there were opportunities to go "straight."

Measuring recidivism (returning to crime) by one new arrest after release, it was found that about 80 percent of the traditional training school inmates had at least one arrest during a four-year follow-up period, whereas only about 50 percent of the youths in the community program had one new arrest during an equivalent four-year follow-up. Another measure of recidivism—the comparison of the average number of arrests after release from the programs to the average number of arrests prior to program entry—showed that the improvement (i.e., the decline) for the training school youths was only about 25 percent compared to about 60 percent for the community program youths. The researchers concluded that their findings indicated "that efforts to improve correctional programs might be far more fruitful if they concentrated upon the improvement of community rather than institutional designs" (Empey & Erickson, 1972: 261).

Unfortunately, the experimental design of the Provo evaluation broke down early in the study. Most importantly, there were not enough boys going through the juvenile court in Provo to assign randomly one-half to the state training school and one-half to the community program. The researchers compromised by assigning all of the boys eligible for the training school to the community program and by selecting a comparison group (rather than a true control group) from the training school population (i.e., delinquents from other parts of the state). Because there was no random assignment, the researchers could not be sure that their findings of lower recidivism for the Provo community program youths (compared to the training school youths) were due to the different interventions or to differential selection of youths into the programs. In other words, the boys in Provo may have been at lower risk of committing new crimes than the training school boys from other parts of the state.

Another factor that suggests a cautious interpretation of the Provo results is the more negative findings from a similar study. In the **Silverlake Experiment**, Empey and Lubeck (1971) compared a traditional training school (Boys Republic) to an innovative residential group home that used guided group inter-action (Silverlake). The Silverlake boys lived together in the group home, went to school in the local public school and participated in group sessions every afternoon. Empey and Lubeck (1971) found basically no difference in the recidivism rates of the boys in the two interventions. This suggests that the breakdown of random assignment in the Provo Experiment may have been the reason for the more positive findings for the boys in the Provo setting. It must be remembered, however, that because Provo was not a residential progam, it differed considerably from the Silverlake project.

The Controversial Claims of Murray and Cox

One intriguing report on training school effectiveness is the Murray and Cox (1979) report of the allegedly dramatic effects of two training schools in Illinois. Apparently, the specific programming used in the training schools was a traditional program of schooling, counseling and regimentation. Murray and Cox contend that the two training schools suppressed crime by 68 percent for their dischargees. More specifically, the average number of arrests during the 12 months prior to placement was 6.3 arrests per youth but only 2.0 during the year after release. The researchers concluded that regular training schools are effective in achieving specific deterrence. These schools are perceived as such punitive and unpleasant places that the boys who go through them do not want to return; therefore, they are frightened out of committing as many new crimes as they had been committing prior to placement. According to Murray and Cox, a **suppression effect** occurred.

Murray and Cox's conclusion that training schools can be effective instru-ments of deterrence stirred considerable controversy. First, Lundman (1993) noted that the decrease in the average number of arrests per youth may simply have been an instance of the statistical artifact of **regression toward the mean**, which means that "when a particular group has been selected on the basis of an unusually high mean (average) score, simple probability dictates that the group's high mean score will eventually lower" (Lundman, 1993: 229). In sports, for example, even a last-place team may go on a winning streak and be playing .800 ball (winning percentage), but eventually that team will revert to its true average of below .500 performance. In terms of delinquency research, if a child has been committing crime frequently (above his or her true average), after release from *any* program—training school, probation or whatever—he or she most likely will revert back to his or her true average, which is much lower than the rate at which he or she was committing crime immediately prior to arrest and commitment to a training school. Such a drop is simply a drop to the youth's true average and not the result of any intervention effort.

Another criticism of the Murray and Cox (1979) conclusion is that the drop in crime may be at least partially attributable to a **maturation effect**. That is, the time the youths spent in the training school was a time of maturation and growth, which may have accounted for the subsequent drop in delinquent activity. In simple terms, they grew out of their delinquency and they would have grown out of it even if they had not spent any time in the training school. Moreover, even if the decrease in delinquent activity was true, it might have been the result of rehabilitation rather than deterrence, because the Illinois training schools offered rehabilitative programs such as education and counseling (Lundman, 1993). Thus, perhaps they were "corrected straight" rather than "scared straight."

Finally, the Murray and Cox conclusion has been accused of ignoring many of the negative aspects of training schools, such as peer norms that alienate inmates from staff and foster an exploitative view of both staff and other inmates (Sieverdes & Bartollas, 1986). In summary, Murray and Cox's conclusion that deterrence was at work may have overlooked the rehabilitative components and the negative aspects of the two training schools they studied. (For a discussion of studies showing the ineffectiveness of traditional training schools, see Krisberg & Howell, 1998.)

Reviews of Multiple Studies

While the research discussed above focused on specific programs, other researchers have tried to summarize individual program research into a global conclusion on effectiveness. Most of these studies have used the technique of meta-analysis. Meta-analysis is a technique that allows researchers to re-analyze individual studies and arrive at a summary statistic of effectiveness for each individual study that can then be compared to the summary statistics from the other studies.

Carol Garrett (1985) reported the results of her meta-analysis of 111 studies of the effects of residential treatment on adjudicated delinquents. The studies she examined were conducted between 1960 and 1983, used either a comparison group or pretest-posttest design, and concerned institutional or community residential setting programs. Garrett found positive results:

> The major finding of this quantitative integration of primary research results is that, yes, treatment of adjudicated delinquents in residential settings does work. Even the more rigorous studies showed treated youths performing at the 59th percentile relative to the comparison youths. . . . It does show that there is positive change (Garrett, 1985: 304).

The most frequent measure of success, however, was psychological and institutional adjustment. Most of the studies examined only whether the child improved on measures of personality or measures of behavior in the institution.

Less than 20 percent of the studies used recidivism as a measure of effectiveness. Concerning recidivism, the average effect size was only .13, which means that the programs that did report recidivism results had only "modest" impact on the criminal activity of the youths who went through the programs (Garrett, 1985: 305).

A meta-analysis of 443 studies published between 1970 and 1987 focused on formal contact with the juvenile justice system as an outcome measure and reported that approximately two-thirds of the study outcomes favored the treatment group over the control group. Behavioral, skill and multimodal treatment programs resulted in greater effects than other approaches. Deterrence-based programs were not effective (Lipsey, 1992).

Lipsey and Wilson (1998) conducted a meta-analysis of 83 studies of institutional programs for serious offenders and found that there were many instances of programs that had positive effects. The most effective treatment types had an impact on recidivism that was equivalent to reducing a control group baseline recidivism rate of 50 percent to around 30 or 35 percent. If the recidivism rate for these juveniles would have been 50 percent without treatment, the most effective programs reduced it to between 30 and 35 percent. They concluded that this represents a "considerable decrease, especially in light of the fact that it applies to institutionalized offenders, who can be assumed to be relatively serious delinquents" (Lipsey & Wilson, 1998: 336). Successful interventions included aggression replacement training, behavior modification and a stress innoculation program that helped youths to define anger, analyze recent anger episodes, review self-monitoring data and construct an individualized six-item anger hierarchy.

Conclusions About Program Effectiveness

Several cautious conclusions about the effectiveness of institutional programs for delinquents are in order. First, the Provo program and considerable supporting evidence indicate that community programs are at least as effective as traditional training schools. Second, Silverlake suggests that an innovative and less repressive residential program can be at least as effective as a traditional training school (Gottfredson, 1987; Lundman, 1984). Third, even training schools may have an effect in suppressing the average number of crimes committed by youths after release, but such institutions may not be able to deter their charges from committing *any* crimes after release. Fourth, this alleged suppression effect may be the result of such factors as regression toward the mean, simple maturation or the rehabilitation programs in the training schools, instead of the deterrent effect of a punitive regime in the training school. Finally, the effectiveness literature suggests that certain interventions can be effective in reducing recidivism from about 50 percent to 30 or 35 percent. It is imperative, however, that these interventions follow the principles that research has identified as effective (Lipsey & Wilson, 1998). (See Chapter 12 for further discussion of principles of effective treatment.)

Before proceeding to discuss other current issues in juvenile institutions, it is important to note that the measurement of the effectiveness of treatment programs in such settings assumes that the programs are in fact carried out as originally intended. Unfortunately, that is not always true. Although Wooden did his research years ago, his observations on this matter apply today. Specifically, Wooden contended that institutions were using behavior modification techniques "to manipulate and control the child for the convenience of the custodians" (Wooden, 1976: 101). Similarly, he alleged that some institutions were using another technique, Positive Peer Culture, with inappropriately selected children (normal children were verbally assaulting disturbed and slow youngsters) and were punishing the disobedient children in very traditional and questionable ways: "Inmates at Boonville who don't cooperate during group sessions are thrown in some of the worst solitary confinement cells I have seen in the entire country" (Wooden, 1976: 103). In one New York facility, "education" actually meant watching movies on the video cassette player, especially on Friday (Singer, 1996). Thus, impressive terms like "behavior modification," "Positive Peer Culture" or even "education" do not necessarily translate into humane and progressive interventions. Furthermore, if such interventions are implemented as Wooden noted they were, it is hardly possible to know what results an evaluation study will find or what sort of confidence can be placed in the results.

The Target Issue

The effectiveness research raises a second issue: the question of the appropriate targets of residential placements. The conclusion that many youngsters probably can do just as well in less drastic placement settings raises the issue of which offenders should be placed in which types of residential situations.

Deinstitutionalization of Status Offenders

Since the mid-1970s, there has been a movement away from placing status offenders and delinquents in the same state-operated institutions. It is felt that any mixing of status offenders and delinquents can have harmful consequences on the status offenders. In fact, much of this movement has been one of **deinstitutionalization**, that is, trying to avoid any involuntary placements of status offenders. (The practice of some states to deinstitutionalize delinquents as well as status offenders will be discussed later in this chapter.) The strength of this movement is indicated by the fact that nearly 96 percent of the juveniles in public custody on February 1, 1995 were delinquents and only 2.6 percent were status offenders. This is a considerable decrease from the 7 percent figure in 1985 (Moone, 1997a; Sickmund & Baunach, 1986).

Statistics on the number of status offenders in publicly operated institutions, however, may be misleading. Schwartz, Jackson-Beeck and Anderson (1984), for example, have argued that as it has become increasingly difficult to institutionalize status offenders in training schools, parents have resorted to "voluntary" psychiatric hospitalization and voluntary drug programs as a means of controlling unruly teenagers. Two problems with this trend are that the hospital commitments are not really voluntary (parents trick or force their children into "volunteering") and may be unnecessary (psychiatrists or insurance auditors find that the youths spend more time in the hospital than is warranted medically). (Box 11.6 gives an example of an unnecesary placement.)

Box 11.6 An Unnecessary Placement

The following case illustrates one such unnecessary placement of a young girl in a psychiatric facility:

> An adolescent Caucasian female was hospitalized for 37 days after she ran away and was found living with a Black male adolescent. The parents reported that she was out of control at home, engaged in socially inappropriate behavior, was using drugs, and was in acute danger to herself. They blamed her for a sister's suicide two years previous. She was admitted with the diagnosis "behavioral disturbance, adolescence." The patient's psychiatrist noted grief-laden depression manifested in impulsive behavior. No family counseling or previous outpatient therapy was attempted before the inpatient admission. Peer review of this case found inadequate information to justify the last 14 days of the adolescent's stay. Reviewers found no evidence of serious delinquent behavior or prostitution, but some use of drugs (Schwartz, Jackson-Beeck and Anderson, 1984: 378).

Thus, although statistics on the number of status offenders in publicly run institutions for delinquents indicate that status offenders are less likely to be locked up today than they were 20 years ago, it appears that at least some of those youngsters merely have been shunted to different forms of institutional placement, private psychiatric placements and privately run drug treatment programs. In short, the question of whether the deinsitutionalization of status offenders has been beneficial has not been clearly answered:

> If the increase [in commitments to private institutions] reflects the availability of resources, utilized on a voluntary basis by status offenders and their families, then most would agree the increase is appropriate. If it simply represents a shift from one type of secure and involuntary confinement to another, or inappropriately relabeling behavior for such purposes, then the goals of deinstitutionalization are being thwarted by shifts to the private sector (Schneider, 1985: 19).

Reserving Training Schools for Chronic-Violent Delinquents

Another aspect of the target issue is the question of which types of delinquents need to be placed in residential settings. Citing the effectiveness literature examined above, some authorities argue that very few delinquents need to be placed in secure placements such as training schools. They contend that training schools should be reserved for the chronic and/or the violent offender, and argue for institutionalizing fewer—but more serious—juvenile offenders. This rationale is also based on the cohort study research (discussed in Chapter 14) that has found that a small percentage of youths account for a disproportionate share of juvenile delinquency (e.g., Tracy, Wolfgang & Figlio, 1985, 1990). If training schools were reserved for such chronic and violent offenders, then they could offer a more appropriate program for them—including a lengthier stay. This would forestall the criticism that the violent juvenile offender gets both too easy a sentence and too short a sentence (Collier & Horowitz, 1985). (Later in the chapter we will discuss alternative programs for nonchronic and less serious delinquents.)

As noted in Chapter 8, current trends in juvenile justice include increased use of transfer to adult court and blended sentencing. Because of these trends, it appears that both adult and juvenile correctional systems are receiving additional "older, more violent juveniles who are deeply committed to criminal lifestyles" (Torbet et al., 1996:25). Some of these youths are going straight to the adult correctional system, some are being held as juveniles until a certain age and then are transferred to an adult facility, some are being designated as youthful offenders and some are staying in the juvenile system.

Institutional Life

An important area of continuing concern in juvenile justice is the effect of institutional life on youths. The theory of institutional placements is that they will provide a caring and nurturing environment that will allow the delinquents to change to prosocial behavior in the institution. This will then will carry over into future behavior after release. As we shall see, however, the practice often falls far short of the theoretical ideal.

Victimization

Probably the most dramatic example of a negative effect of the institution on incarcerated youths is the problem of **victimization**, which ranges from the relatively insignificant act of taking a youth's dessert to forcing an incarcerated boy to perform oral sodomy. Such victimization knows no geographic boundaries. In one northern training school, 53 percent of the boys exploited others and 65 percent were exploited at least on occasion (Bowker, 1980: 47). In a study of six southeastern training schools, more than one-third of the whites, but less than 25 percent of the blacks, reported frequent victimization. In addition, 61 percent of the whites, but less than 50 percent of the blacks, reported that other residents "took advantage of them" in the institution (Bartollas & Sieverdes, 1981: 538). Moreover, it appears that institutionalized girls are less subject to forceful sexual attacks but that "attacks sometimes occur, usually involving adolescent inmates who have expressed an unwillingness to participate in homosexuality and who are zealous in ridiculing inmates who engage in this behavior" (Giallombardo, 1974: 160). In one New York facility, some guards formed a "wake-up club" that administered regular beatings to misbehaving or disrespectful youths (Singer, 1996). Based on statistics such as these, Bowker's review of victimization in juvenile institutions concludes that "juvenile victimization is rampant in a wide variety of institutions across the country" (Bowker, 1980: 49). At the very least, the institutionalized youngster is deprived of the security that teenagers in positive home environments take for granted. (See Box 11.7 for a discussion of how one institution dealt with a specific instance of sexual aggression.)

Box 11.7 A Case Illustration Concerning Sexual Aggression

George H. Weber, a former head of Minnesota's youth prisons, describes a rape in a state training school where the officals knew the two perpetrators but punished the rapists only with restriction and verbal reprimand ("a real dressing-down"). Additionally, the two rapists were seen by the prison psychiatrist but "the interviewing never got off the ground. The best that can be said is that I tried to get the boys to talk, and when they didn't, I left the door open for them to come back" (Weber, 1979: 121). Weber does not specify whether this rape really happened or whether the account is only reality-based, which means that it is an account drawn "from facts that are dealt with in ways that transpose the literal truth without fundamental accuracy being altered" (Weber, 1979: 14). At the very least, Weber is claiming that the rape and the administrative response very well could have occurred, if it did not really happen. Regardless of the historical accuracy of this account, however, the account raises the question of how institutional officials should respond to actual rapes. Is it enough for a cottage supervisor to "really dress down" the boys (verbally reprimand them) and for a staff psychiatrist to *try* to counsel them? Or should training school officials take stronger action? For example, should officials file new court charges against sexual aggressors and thus push for either a new adjudication of delinquency or a waiver of the guilty parties to adult court? On the other hand, would such official action merely be a waste of time because the court would just send such youths back to the same youth prison?

Table 11.1   Incident Rates per 100 Juveniles and Annualized Estimates of Incidents in Juvenile Facilities

Type of Incident	Rate per 100 juveniles (last 30 days)	Estimated incidents (per year)
Injuries		
Juvenile-on-juvenile	3.1	24,200
Juvenile-on-staff	1.7	6,900
Staff-on-juvenile	0.2	106
Escapes		
Completed	1.2	9,700
Unsuccessful attempts	1.2	9,800
Acts of suicidal behavior	2.4	17,600
Incident requiring emergency health care	3.0	18,600
Isolation incidents		
Short-term (1-24 hrs.)	57.0	435,800
Longer-term (more than 24 hours)	11.0	88,900

Source: Abt Associates (1994: E-7).

Statistics on incident rates in juvenile facilities from one report are summarized in Table 11.1. As the table shows, it is estimated that about 24,200 juvenile-on-juvenile injuries and approximately 7,000 juvenile-on-staff injuries take place every year. Every year there are about 17,600 acts of suicidal behavior and more than 18,000 incidents requiring emergency health care (Abt Associates, 1994). Subjectively, approximately 20 percent of confined youths report not feeling safe when in custody (Abt Associates, 1994: 111). This may be a conservative estimate, however, because youths tend to compare their safety within an institution with their safety on the outside. For some youths, life in the institution may be perceived as safer than life on the streets. For example, one institutionalized youth reported that he only had to fear a punch or being hit with furniture in the institution. On the outside he had to fear being shot. Thus, in the institution "he felt perfectly safe" (Abt Associates, 1994: 111). (For further discussion of living conditions in juvenile prison, see Box 11.8.)

Racial Tension

The statistics on victimization also suggest that racial tension is a problem in juvenile institutions. For example, Bartollas and Sieverdes (1981) found African-American youths to be both more dominant and more aggressive than white inmates. "Twice as many black as white residents were classified by staff members as highly aggressive toward others; over 40 percent of whites were

Box 11.8   Making Juvenile Prisons Spartan

Many state legislatures have passed laws to make adult prisons as spartan as possible. Responding to alleged citizen displeasure with "soft" prisons, politicians have passed laws forbidding cable television and physical training equipment (weight-lifting and other body building equipment) in adult prisons.

To date this movement has only affected institutions for juveniles placed in adult facilities via transfer, direct file or blended sentencing. But the call for amenity-free prisons raises the issue of what level of "comfort" is appropriate for offenders—adult and juvenile? Is television all right but premium cable services such as Home Box Office (HBO) inappropriate? Is weight-lifting equipment inappropriate because inmates can use the equipment to get in better shape and assault other inmates or staff?

Years before this controversy erupted, prison authority John Conrad (1982) addressed this question of "What do the undeserving deserve?" His answer was that there are four essentials needed in prison: safety, lawfulness, industriousness and hope (Conrad, 1982).

What do you think? Can prisons be too soft? Can they be too tough? Are Conrad's four essential ingredients a good guideline? Why? Why not? What are your suggestions for juvenile prisons? For adult prisons?

defined by staff as passive" (Bartollas & Sieverdes, 1981: 538). Bartollas and Sieverdes attributed this situation to role reversal in the institution, where white Southern youths found themselves in the novel position of being in the minority. White inmates were outnumbered by black inmates (about 60% of the inmates were black) and about one-half of the staff members were black. The white youths felt threatened because they were in an environment very different from "the southern culture, [where] whites are used to a position of greater superiority in the free society relative to minority groups than are youth elsewhere in the United States" (Bartollas & Sieverdes, 1981: 541).

Such racial tension in youth prisons is by no means unique. Irwin (1980) has reported much the same problem in adult male prisons. Lockwood (1980) similarly found blacks much more likely to be the aggressors and whites the targets in instances of adult prison sexual violence. Some attribute the current tension to black resentment over years of white prejudice and discrimination As one black put it, "You guys been cutting our balls off ever since we been in this country. Now we're just getting even" (as quoted in Carroll, 1974: 184). Others relate the problem to the perception of racism in the criminal justice system. Others, however, see the problem a little differently. Krisberg and Austin (1993) are very concerned about the disproportionate representation of minority youths (especially African-Americans) in juvenile correctional facilities.

They are also concerned because the percentage of minorities has been increasing. Krisberg and Austin attribute this overrepresentation of African-American youths in juvenile institutions to various factors: racism, poverty, joblessness, differing family and cultural values, lack of understanding of the juvenile justice system, lack of resources, failure of the schools to provide adequate education, and drug involvement.

The fact that training schools continue to be places with significant proportions of several ethnic groups suggests that racial/ethnic tensions will continue into the foreseeable future. In 1991, for example, training schools were 37 percent white, 47 percent African-American and 13 percent Hispanic. Ranches were 41 percent white, 32 percent African-American and 23 percent Hispanic (Abt Associates, 1994). Hopefully, such tension will decrease as the next century begins, but the painful truth is that even 50 years after the Supreme Court ruled against segregated schools, race is still problematic in the juvenile justice system.

The Inmate Code

Another negative effect of institutions is that youths may develop or maintain allegiance to peer norms that run counter to staff efforts to rehabilitate the youngsters. This is the problem of the **inmate code**, which can stress such maxims as "exploit whomever you can," "don't play up to staff," "don't rat on your peers . . .," "be cool," and so on (Sieverdes & Bartollas, 1986: 137). In other words, juvenile inmates develop feelings of distrust and resentment toward staff. These feelings operate in opposition to staff efforts to build trust and openness. There has been some indication that the inmate code is moving away from minding one's own business ("do your own time") to greater exploitation of others:

> In other words, the "old con" who did his/her own time has disappeared from the juvenile correctional system and from most adult correctional systems. Inmates are now more likely to show certain allegiances to other prisoners, especially those in the same racial group or social organization. But, at the same time, this inmate is scheming to manipulate staff and to take advantage of weaker peers (Sieverdes & Bartollas, 1986: 143).

As might be expected, research indicates that organizational structure affects the norms and behavior of youthful prisoners. In other words, "[t]he more custodial and punitive settings had inmate cultures that were more violent, more hostile, and more oppositional than those in the treatment-oriented settings" (Feld, 1981: 336). This finding on the impact of organizational structure on inmate culture suggests that it is possible for administrators to reduce the negative environments in juvenile prisons by opting for an organizational structure that emphasizes treatment over custody. One specific option that administrators can take is to limit the size of juvenile residential placements. Larger populations are more susceptible to custodial climates than smaller populations. Another option is to facilitate communication between treatment staff and custodial staff so that staff members do not exacerbate potential treatment-custody conflicts.

Deprivation of Heterosexual Contact

Another negative effect of institutions is that incarcerated youths are deprived of heterosexual relationships at a time when such relationships are critical in helping the teenager to define himself or herself as a mature sexual adult. Although written about incarcerated girls, Giallombardo's comments on this matter apply equally well (with the appropriate adjustments) to imprisoned boys:

> They are developing images of themselves as adult women, and they are beset with many anxieties concerning their sexuality and acceptance by males. The exclusion of males in their own age group is a source of confusion for adolescent girls. . . . Their confusion is compounded by virtue of the fact that during incarceration they are socialized to view other women as legitimate sex objects (Giallombardo, 1974: 244).

In response to this deprivation, many of the girls adjust by participating in kinship role systems and/or homosexual alliances. In the training schools Giallombardo studied, for example, the girls had affectionate nicknames for one another, wrote love letters to other girls, picked their own special songs, "went steady" and even got married in formal ceremonies (out of staff view). Another study reported that only about 17 percent of the institutionalized girls reported at least one homosexual experience (ranging from kissing to intimate sexual contact) but that about one-half of the girls reported taking a **"make-believe family" role** (Propper, 1982). Such behavior was clearly not intended by the authorities and has been labeled a "secondary adjustment" (Goffman, 1961: 199). The problem with secondary adjustments is that they divert the youths' attention away from the main aspects of the supposedly rehabilitative programs such as education and counseling, and direct that attention to making life within the training school as pleasant as possible. (For further information on the attitudes and concerns of delinquent girls, see Box 11.9.)

Other problems faced by incarcerated youths include loss of liberty, loss of autonomy in making decisions, deprivation of goods and services, and boredom. Particularly important in terms of goods is the loss of clothing goods. This is important because it entails a loss of the opportunity to explore various clothing styles. According to Giallombardo, such exploratory behavior is very directly related to a youth's sense of identity and also his or her popularity (Giallombardo, 1974: 242).

> ## Box 11.9   What Girls Think About the System: Results from a Focus Study
>
> Belknap, Holsinger and Dunn (1997) did a focus group study of 58 delinquent girls in Ohio. The girls had been placed in group homes, probation, detention, house arrest and diversion. Their comments offer some important insights and implications for their care in correctional settings.
>
> A key finding was that the girls felt that professionals followed stereotypes about girls and boys. "In general, the girls perceived the boys as getting more privileges, more space, more equipment, more programs, and better treatment. For example, girls believe boys have more educational, recreational, and occupational opportunities" (Belknap, Holsinger & Dunn, 1997: 393). Second, the girls, especially the girls who had been placed for a long term, had serious concerns about leaving the institutional setting. They were anxious about lack of support after release and about making mistakes similar to those that got them into trouble in the first place. A consistent theme in the focus group research was "recognizing and fearing that nobody was going to be responsible for them when they left the very controlling and regimented system they currently resented" (Belknap et al., 1997: 395). A third finding was that many of the girls had been neglected or abused.
>
> Belknap and her colleagues recommend gender-specific programs and services for such girls including supportive mentoring (Belknap et al., 1997).

Effects on Workers

The institution can be a problem for the worker as well as for the youthful inmate. For example, Howard Polsky, an early participant researcher of juvenile training schools, reported that he was attacked physically and manipulated and that he might have suffered a worse fate were it not for his height (6 feet, 6 inches) (Polsky, 1962). Dembo and Dertke (1986) found that one-third of the staff in a detention facility were experiencing stress from fear of group attack.

Probably more pervasive is the role conflict between custody and treatment concerns experienced by many staff members. That is, staff are expected to be both counselors/confidants and police officers. On the one hand, staff encourage youth to confide in them and trust them almost as parents. On the other hand, staff have the authority to punish or discipline the inmates. Such roles do not always mesh well. Like probation and parole officers, staff adapt to the conflict by either emphasizing one role over the other, trying to emphasize both roles, or emphasizing neither. Such role conflict is often interpreted by the youths to mean that custody concerns clearly win out over treatment concerns. Alternatively (and perhaps worse), kids often feel that staff convenience is the primary concern (Giallombardo, 1974).

Box 11.10 Worker Burnout

Charles Shireman and Frederic Reamer offer a summary description of the burned out worker. They feel that the frequent situation is that

> relatively young, eager faces, fresh with idealism, are attracted to correctional programs because of a sincere belief that what misguided youths need is a fair shake in life and decent, respectful, and empathic care. With refreshing enthusiasm that the naïveté of inexperience fosters, these young professionals charge into a system rife with stagnation, punitiveness, indifference, cynicism, inconsistency, and disingenuousness. . . . Those who do not flee the field quickly become "realists," whose . . . zeal is diluted (Shireman & Reamer, 1986: 168).

Fortunately, research attention on this problem (Maslach, 1982; Whitehead, 1985) has suggested concrete steps to prevent or reduce job burnout for correctional employees.

Job burnout also can be a problem for staff in youth institutions. The pressures of working with delinquent and troubled youth can cause the workers to feel emotionally drained and even unsympathetic about their charges. (For a vivid description of this problem, see Box 11.10.) Such workers face the problems of frequent contact with troubled and troublesome clients, role conflict, low salaries, deficient institutional budgets, and recidivism rates that suggest failure. In Maslach's (1982) terms, it is not surprising that some staff members may become emotionally exhausted, cynical, impersonal and feel that they simply are not accomplishing all that much in their everyday work. While much of the research on job burnout has focused on either probation officers (Whitehead, 1989) or correctional officers (Whitehead & Lindquist, 1986), it is safe to say that job burnout is probably just as problematic for staff in juvenile institutions—especially in detention centers and training schools that house a very difficult population. For example, Dembo and Dertke (1986) interviewed 53 staff members in a modern regional detenion center and found that about 40 percent of the staff reported stress stemming from such concerns as possible inmate suicides, inmate sexual assaults on other inmates and inmate group attacks on staff. Furthermore, many felt that staff had fewer rights than the inmates, and 91 percent felt that their salaries were too low for the type of work they were doing. Staff are also concerned about HIV infections and AIDS. Both initial and follow-up training are needed to inform staff accurately of risks and of measures to prevent transmission (Durham, 1994). More research is needed on this topic—both to assist troubled staff and also to prevent the depersonalization stage of burnout, which has obvious negative effects on the incarcerated delinquents.

An important national study on living conditions in juvenile facilities found "substantial and widespread deficiencies" in four matters: living space, security, control of suicidal behavior, and health care (Abt Associates, 1994). Many institutions experience problems concerning crowding, safety and prevention of escapes, suicidal behavior, and health screening. That same report also felt that there was a need to collect systematic data on confined youths' educational and treatment needs. Further evidence that problems continue to exist in juvenile institutions is the publication of a recent American Bar Association manual that offers suggestions for litigation strategies to contest problematic conditions (Puritz & Scali, 1998).

New Directions in Institutional Interventions

Deinstitutionalization

Several states, including Massachusetts, Maryland, Pennsylvania and Utah, have dramatically decreased their use of training schools by closing some of these facilities. In Massachusetts, for example, only about 15 percent of the approximately 800 youths committed to the State Department of Youth services each year are first placed in a locked treatment program. The other 85 percent of the committed youths are placed in community-based programs such as group homes, forestry camps, day treatment programs, outreach-tracking programs or foster care (Krisberg & Austin, 1993). Most of the programs have been privatized; private agencies run the programs on a contract basis with the state. In addition, the residential programs are small in size, with no more than 30 youths housed in a facility (Krisberg & Austin, 1993). What this means for most youths is that they spend only about four weeks in secure placement and then are placed in nonsecure treatment programs. In states with heavy reliance on traditional training schools, most youths spend about nine months in secure confinement and then are placed on aftercare (parole).

The National Council on Crime and Delinquency evaluated the Massachusetts reform and found it to be successful. Compared to recidivism rates in other states still relying on traditional training schools, recidivism rates for Massachusetts were

> equivalent to, and in some cases lower than, youths from the other states . . . At a minimum these comparisons lend further evidence that the limited use of secure confinement in Massachusetts as compared to other states does not endanger public safety (Krisberg & Austin, 1993: 155-156).

The evaluation also found the Massachusetts effort to be cost-effective, whereas "expanded youth incarceration would require a large investment in public funds, but would achieve little expected reduction in crime rates" (Krisberg &

Austin, 1993: 163). More specifically, depending on how long Massachusetts would incarcerate youths in traditional training schools, it would have to spend $10 to $16.8 million more per year than it was spending in its deinstitutionalization mode (Krisberg & Austin, 1989).

An evaluation of the closing of one institution in Maryland, however, found contrary results. Almost three-quarters (72%) of the youths committed to the State Department of Juvenile Services after the institution's closing were rearrested during the one-year follow-up period, whereas only about 45 percent of the youths who had been institutionalized at the training school prior to its closing were rearrested. In a two-and-one-half year follow-up period, 83 percent of the post-closing group were rearrested, compared to 66 percent and 69 percent of the two groups that had been incarcerated at the training school under study. The authors concluded that "the alternatives available when Montrose [the state training school] was closed were less effective in reducing crime than institutionalization would have been" (Gottfredson & Barton, 1993: 604). The authors suggest that their findings support the conclusion that "neither institutional nor community-based programs are uniformly effective or ineffective. The *design* [emphasis in original] of the intervention rather than its location appears important" (Gottfredson & Barton, 1993: 605). In other words, simply closing traditional training schools is only one-half of a strategy. The other half is to devise effective programs for the youths who would have been committed to the training schools. It appears that Massachusetts was able to devise such effective alternative programming for its delinquent commitments. Maryland apparently did not come up with effective alternative programming, so the recidivism rates for the group not sent to the training school were disappointing.

Blended Sentencing

As noted in Chapter 8, the creation of blended sentencing allows either the juvenile court or the adult court to impose a sentence that can involve either the juvenile or the adult correctional system or both. The adult sentence may be suspended pending either a violation or the commission of a new crime. One result of blended sentencing will be a growing number of youthful offenders in adult prisons.

A study on victimization among youthful inmates in adult prisons is important in light of the development of blended sentencing. Maitland and Sluder (1998) interviewed 111 inmates aged 17 to 25. They found that less than 1 percent reported that they had been forced to engage in sexual activity, 3 percent had been forced to give up their money and 5.5 percent had had a weapon used on them. Less serious victimization experiences, however, were much more frequent. Fifty-nine percent had been verbally harassed, approximately 50 percent had had their property stolen, and 38 percent had been hit, kicked, punched or slapped. The authors concluded that "young, medium-security prison inmates are most likely to be subjected to less serious forms of victimization by peers during their terms of incarceration" (Maitland & Sluder, 1998: 68). Thus, any trend toward putting delinquents in adult prisons when they are 17 or 18 can be expected to produce such victimization results for the youthful offenders so incarcerated.

Wilderness Programs

Another new direction in residential placements is the use of various types of wilderness experiences, ranging from relatively short stays in outdoor settings to rather long wagon train or ocean ship trips. Both private operators and some states are using this type of programming, which places delinquents in situations where they learn survival skills, limits and self-esteem. The youths are put in natural settings where they must learn to cook, obtain shelter from the elements, tell directions (read a compass), start fires, and so forth. In the process of accomplishing such tasks, the youths learn to depend on both others and themselves. The theory is that a successful survival experience in a natural setting will then transfer to the youth's normal environment and he or she will turn to more constructive activities than delinquency.

Some studies have shown wilderness programs to be effective in reducing recidivism but the research has not been encouraging. In their meta-analysis of effective treatments, Lipsey and Wilson (1998) conclude that wilderness programs generally have shown to have weak effects or no effects on the recidivism rates of the youths who have gone through the programs compared to control groups.

Summary

This chapter has examined state and private residential placements, ranging from training schools to wilderness experience programs. An examination of the effectiveness of institutional placements indicates that many children do not really need to be in training schools. Instead, they can be handled in less restrictive settings without any increase in recidivism. The chapter also examined several problematic factors in residential placements, such as victimization, homosexual behavior and worker stress. Unfortunately, residential placements often translate into horror stories for the children rather than therapeutic havens. Sexual assaults and racial tension have been well-documented components of placements in the past and they are unlikely to disappear completely. Because of these and related problems, states such as Massachusetts, Maryland, Pennsylvania and Utah turned to noninstitutional approaches to delinquency, by which fewer youngsters are placed in state training schools. Blended sentencing and increased processing of juvenile offenders in adult court, however, may translate into significant numbers of youthful offenders being incarcerated in adult prisons.

In the next chapter, we will examine community interventions such as traditional probation and innovations such as intensive supervision. As will be shown, there are important developments taking place in this often neglected component of the juvenile justice system.

DISCUSSION QUESTIONS

1. What might be done to reduce the racial tension in youth prisons?

2. How can juvenile institutions be made safer? That is, what can be done to keep victimization at a minimum?

3. Given the fact that the average cost of housing a juvenile for one year in a public facility is more than $30,000, should we place more or fewer juveniles in such facilities? Are taxpayers getting their money's worth from the use of these facilities?

4. Wilfrid has just been adjudicated a delinquent for armed robbery. He is 15. This is his first violent offense. Previously he had been on probation for shoplifting, at which time he adjusted well. Is he an appropriate candidate for deinstitutionalization? If so, under what conditions could he be placed in the community?

5. Would you consider a career in institutional corrections? What type of youth prison (training school) would you want to work in?

6. Should youth prisons go co-ed (mix males and females)?

7. Do you favor or oppose the trend toward placing more juveniles in adult prisons (via blended sentencing or direct file provisions)?

CHAPTER 12

Community Interventions

Even before the founding of the first juvenile court in Illinois at the turn of the century, community interventions had been a central weapon of those seeking to fight delinquency. This chapter will examine both traditional and nontraditional community interventions and focus on some of the key problems with these approaches to the delinquency problem. Accordingly, the chapter will first describe probation and aftercare for juveniles, highlight some of the current trends in community interventions, and then look at some of the controversies and concerns in the field. One of the key issues examined in the chapter is the effectiveness issue: Do community interventions have any impact on recidivism? In other words, do community interventions help to reduce the number of offenses committed by the juveniles exposed to the programs or are the programs ineffective in reducing delinquent activity? As will be shown, the answer to this question is mixed. Although many efforts have been unsuccessful, knowledge about effective intervention principles has developed to a promising extent.

Probation

Statistics demonstrate that probation continues as a critical part of the juvenile justice system. In 1995, 283,300 youths who were adjudicated delinquent in juvenile court were placed on probation. This represents more than one-half (53%) of the more than 500,000 youths who were adjudicated delinquent. Another 86,000 youths who were not adjudicated delinquent agreed to some form of probation. Another 239,900 youths who were not petitioned agreed to some form of voluntary probation. Further, 41,200 youths were adjudicated status offenders and placed on probation, and another 9,200 petitioned but non-adjudicated status offenders were placed on probation. Altogether, probation handled well over one-half million youths who were processed in some way for delinquency or a status offense by the juvenile court in 1995 (Sickmund, 1997). (Box 12.1 shows the offenses for which delinquents and status offenders were placed on probation.) In light of all this, it is fair to call probation the workhorse of the juvenile court (Torbet, 1996).

Box 12.1 Adjudication Offenses for Juvenile Probationers

Delinquency Probationers:

Person Offenses	22%
Property Offenses	51%
Drug Offenses	9%
Public Order Offenses	19%

Status Offense Probationers:

Runaway	13%
Truancy	40%
Ungovernable	15%
Liquor Law Violations	22%
Miscellaneous	10%

Note: Delinquency list exceeds 100% due to rounding.

Source: Butts et al. (1996).

Handling this workload are about 18,000 juvenile probation professionals, 85 percent of whom are line officers. The median caseload is 41 offenders and more than one-half of officers were earning less than $30,000 per year in 1992. Officers reported that they thought optimum caseload size would be 30 cases per officer (Torbet, 1996).

As the above statistics demonstrate, most of the youths who are referred to juvenile court experience either informal or formal probation. At the very least, many youths are investigated by a probation officer so that he or she can offer a social history (presentence) investigation and disposition recommendation to the court. Officers are also important figures in violation of probation proceedings because they recommend whether juvenile probationers who have not abided by the conditions of their court sentence will be sent to institutions.

One form of probation supervision is **informal probation**. As noted in Chapter 8, at intake, probation officers often have the authority to settle delinquent and status offenses informally, including brief supervision of youths with or without formal court action. Either with or without a judge's authorization (depending on the state), an officer can require a youngster to report for a brief period of time (e.g., two to three months) in the hope that such supervision will solve the problem.

Social History (Predisposition) Investigations

When a child has been adjudicated as either a delinquent or a status offender, usually a probation officer conducts a social history investigation (**predisposition report**) of the youngster and his or her family. Similar to the presentence investigation report in adult courts, social history reports offer judges legal and social information. Legal information includes descriptive material about the delinquency or status offense, including the child's, the victim's and the police officer's (if a delinquent act) version of the offense, as well as verified data on the child's prior contacts, if any, with the juvenile court and with the police department's juvenile bureau. Social history information includes verification of the child's age (a critical legal condition for court action) and information on the child's development, family, education and possible problems such as alcohol or other drug abuse.

Probation officers gather such information by interviewing the youth, the youth's family, teachers and other school personnel, the victim and the police, and by checking various police, court and school records. They usually collect information on previous arrests from police and court files. Likewise, they may obtain a copy of the child's cumulative school record, which contains information on the child's grades, attendance, disciplinary history and intelligence testing. If necessary, in probation departments that have the resources, the officer may also see to it that a psychologist and/or a psychiatrist examine the child for any suspected emotional problems and to determine the child's intelligence quotient (IQ) more accurately (by an individual IQ test rather than a group test). The probation officer then summarizes all of this information in a report that provides the judge with a more informed basis for the disposition decision. (See Box 12.2 for a list of the types of information included in the typical social history investigation.)

Box 12.2   Information Included in a Typical Social History (Predisposition) Report

I.   Age Verification

II.   Legal History
    A.   Court appearance: description of current case
    B.   Others involved in present delinquency
    C.   Previous police record
    D.   Previous court record

III. Social History
    A.   Development: physical and mental health
    B.   Education
    C.   Leisure-time activities
    D.   Vocational interests and work record
    E.   Religion
    F.   Community adjustment
    E.   Family history: information on family members, including court record
    F.   Home, neighborhood conditions and economic status

IV.   Summary of Clinic Reports: medical, psychological, and psychiatric reports

Source: A probation department manual.

Critics have faulted presentence or social investigations for several deficiencies. Blumberg (1979) has portrayed probation officers as social voyeurs who delight in digging up "dirt" on people (offenders) who lead lives that are more interesting than the middle-class regimens of officers. Rosecrance (1988) has argued that officers emphasize the present offense and the prior record of the offender, and actually place little attention on the social history aspects of these reports. Jacobs (1990) contends that probation reports are "tragic narratives" that excuse the inevitable failure of the juvenile court system ahead of time. He means that probation officers slant probation reports so that if a child does fail it will appear that the court did all that it could do in the face of awesome odds against success.

One suggestion for improving the presentence or social history report is to privatize it so that private agencies would contract to conduct social investigations. The argument is that probation officers often become part of the courthouse team and drift away from their supposedly impartial role in collecting data on delinquent defendants. Los Angeles County used private presentence reports for juveniles for about three years in the mid-1980s. Greenwood and Turner (1993b) found that such reports "resulted in considerably less restrictive placements and shorter terms for about one-quarter of the sample," but that there were conflicts between private agency staff and court officials "which led to its demise" (p. 241).

Probation Supervision

Youngsters who are placed on **formal probation** supervision in court must follow various conditions, such as reporting regularly to a probation officer, obeying the law, attending school and remaining within the geographical jurisdiction of the court. Judges may also order specific conditions, such as restitution to the vicitm(s) of the delinquent act or community service restitution (e.g., performing cleanup work at the local park or playground). Another special condition might be to attend counseling sessions with a social worker, psychologist or psychiatrist, or require the parents to attend the counseling sessions. As noted in Chapter 11, a judge might also order a short stay (about one month) in detention as a condition of probation (Schwartz et al., 1987).

If a juvenile follows the conditions of the probation disposition and is adjusting favorably at home, in school and in the community, then the probation officer can request an early discharge from supervision. If a youngster is not abiding by the conditions and is not adjusting well, then the probation officer may request that the judge order that the youth is in violation of the probation agreement. In that case, the judge can either order the probation to continue (perhaps with additional conditions such as more frequent reporting to the probation officer) or can terminate the probation and place the youth under the supervision of the state youth correctional authority for placement in a public facility or place the youth in a private residential setting.

Aftercare

Many states also have aftercare or parole programs for youths released from state training schools, group homes or forestry camp placements. **Aftercare supervision** is very similar to probation supervision. In fact, in some states, probation officers also perform aftercare supervision duties. Just as with probation, youths on aftercare status must follow specific conditions and report on a regular basis to a parole officer. If they do not, parole can be revoked and they can be sent back to an institutional placement.

The federal Office of Juvenile Justice and Delinquency Prevention (OJJDP) has undertaken an extensive assessment and evaluation of aftercare in the United States. A report suggests that five areas are critical to intensive aftercare case management:

1. a process of disposition, confinement, and parole that consists of clearly defined steps that are closely coordinated, consistent, mutually reinforcing, and continuous;

2. some form of behavioral, contingency, or social contracting throughout the process;

3. a comprehensible and predictable pathway for client progress from disposition to the end of parole;

4. each step or phase of reentry directly related to all successive steps;

5. a rating or reporting system to monitor a youth's behavior and measure progress (Altschuler & Armstrong, 1994).

Supervision and Counseling

Probation and parole officers working with juveniles use various combinations of assistance and control (Glaser, 1964) to help youthful offenders avoid further trouble. Some officers act like social workers or counselors as they try to understand the youth and his or her problems and assist the youngster in gaining greater self-insight and self-esteem. Such officers also might attempt some family therapy to help parents better understand the family interaction patterns that have contributed to the child's misbehavior. Other officers assume a tougher role: a quasi-police officer who first threatens the youth with punishment and then monitors the compliance of the child to the court conditions. This "surveillance" (Studt, 1973) type of officer typically believes that deterrence and incapacitation are more important goals than rehabilitation.

Whether oriented toward assistance or control, probation and parole officers tend to use one of several counseling techniques—including reality therapy, client-centered therapy (nondirective therapy), rational emotive therapy and behaviorism. Assistance-oriented officers utilize these counseling techniques to a greater extent than control-oriented officers, but even the latter use some of the basic principles of these approaches to interview probationers and to establish some rapport. Given the importance of these counseling approaches, it is important to outline each technique and discuss how they are applied in community supervision (for a more in-depth analysis, see Van Voorhis, Braswell & Lester, 1997).

Reality Therapy

William Glasser's (1965) **reality therapy** has been particularly popular with probation and parole officers, partially because Glasser himself has worked with delinquents and, thus, based his theory to some extent on that work experience. Moreover, the theory emphasizes responsibility and a focus on the present. These are concerns shared by many probation officers. The goal of reality therapy is deceptively simple. After therapy, the client should be able to fulfill his or her needs in a responsible way, that is, in a manner that does not interfere with the ability of others to pursue their needs. To achieve this goal, the therapist gets involved with the client, rejects unrealistic behavior and teaches the client responsible ways to fulfill personal needs. The therapist avoids any excuses or prolonged inquiry into past and/or unconscious experiences and focuses instead on realistic behavior in the present—including present plans for future behavior. Glasser (1965) emphasizes that many troubled clients have not had an interested party ask them what their plans are. This is extremely important because it helps clients take their attention off their troubles and to begin constructive planning for future realistic and responsible goal-seeking.

Person-Centered Therapy

The late Carl Rogers's (1951) **person-centered therapy** (or **nondirective therapy**) is probably not as popular as it was a few years ago, but it is still worth noting because it emphasizes some principles that are critical to probation work in particular and human service work in general. Simply put, Rogers's counseling approach contends that empathic understanding, unconditional positive regard and congruence on the part of the therapist will set in motion a change process in the individual client that will lead to self-actualization and a fully-functioning person. Empathic understanding refers to the therapist's understanding of the client, especially the client's feelings, to the extent that the therapist has attempted to put himself or herself in the position of the client. Unconditional positive regard refers to a caring acceptance of the client, even for delinquents who have committed horrible crimes. Thus, a therapist should not reject or condemn a person who comes for counseling due to the fact that the client has commited some shocking crime. Congruence means that the therapist is genuine in his or her dealing with the client. For example, the therapist expresses his or her honest reactions to the client, even though some of those reactions may be less than positive. A concrete example of this is the therapist telling the client that the client is upsetting the therapist by talking about a trivial matter such as last night's football game when the client could be using this valuable time to discuss important issues in his or her life. If the therapist can communicate empathic understanding, positive regard and congruence, then the client should be able to be more aware of his or her own feelings and experiences. He or she should be less defensive, more open to his or her experience and should feel better about himself or herself and others.

Although many probation officers prefer a more directive approach than Rogers's nondirective approach, many incorporate the principles of empathic understanding, unconditional positive regard and congruence in their work with delinquents. In fact, one text on correctional counseling suggests that because person-centered therapy limits the advising/challenging/confronting role of the counselor, "it may be more suited for non-offender clients who are experiencing life adjustment problems" (Lester, Braswell & Van Voorhis, 1992: 116). Similarly, the research on the effectiveness of correctional treatment indicates that nondirective therapy is ineffective with most criminal justice clients (Gendreau, Cullen & Bonta, 1994).

Rational-Emotive Therapy

Albert Ellis's (1973) **rational-emotive therapy** is similar to a modern version of the Greek philosophy of stoicism. Simply put, rational emotive therapy attempts to substitute appropriate emotions for inappropriate emotions so that the individual can move on to appropriate behavior. An example illustrates. If a woman in a relationship tells a boyfriend that she wishes to end the relationship, one reaction for the male is to become extremely depressed, stop all activity (including eating) and feel that he will never find another relationship. Thus an irrational belief—that there can be only one other person who will make one happy and fulfilled—leads the rejected party to irrational consequences such as self-pity and inactivity. Ellis argues that the therapist has to dispute such irrational beliefs by pointing out that there are other desirable persons out there who would make excellent candidates for dating and marriage. Ellis also suggests "homework" assignments such as going to a singles club or a social activity and striking up a conversation with at least one person before the next counseling session. It is reasonable to be sad when a relationship ends, but extreme depression and complete inactivity are not rational responses to life problems. In probation settings, the officer can use this approach to deal with the irrational beliefs of many delinquents (e.g., "Work is for suckers" or "The world owes me a living").

In fact, one correctional counseling book lists many "thinking errors" on which offenders tend to rely. These thinking errors include blaming others for their criminal behavior, saying that they cannot accept responsibilities, failing to consider the point of view of their victims, believing in overnight success, failing to accept criticism, and others (Van Voorhis, Braswell & Lester, 1997). Like Ellis does with a general clientele, corrections workers need to help offenders identify and correct these thinking errors. Thus, it is important not to accept excuses for irresponsible actions but to show the offender how he or she hurts others, to help the offender to take on the role and perspective of others, to teach anger management and to teach competent decisionmaking (Van Voorhis, Braswell & Lester, 1997). Using such a cognitive strategy is one way to reduce delinquency, as shown in several jurisdictions that have adopted such cognitive programming (Chavaria, 1997).

The danger of rational-emotive therapy is just the opposite of person-centered therapy. Whereas person-centered therapy may be too gentle for correctional clients, rational emotive therapy may be too harsh or too dogmatic. The question may very well become who decides what is irrational or irresponsible. (Lester, Braswell & Van Voorhis, 1992). In short, there is the danger that the probation officer may impose his or her own code of morality on the correctional client.

Behavior Modification

Behavior modification is based on the work of psychologists such as B.F. Skinner (1971) and Hans J. Eysenck (1977), who argue that behavior is determined by consequences. More specifically, reinforcements increase the probability of desired behaviors, while lack of reinforcement, or punishing stimuli, decrease the probability of undesirable behaviors. Behavioristic probation officers would use techniques such as contingency contracting, in which the officer and the delinquent would contract the terms of probation. Both the desired behaviors (such as attending school, adhering to a curfew and cooperating with parents) as well as the consequent reinforcers (such as permission to go out on Saturday night and money to buy a particular item of clothing) would be clearly spelled out. The rationale is that many children experience problems because parents do not adequately or properly reinforce positive behavior in them as well as that youths will pursue appropriate behaviors if there are rewards following the desired behaviors.

Behavior modification can be effective in community interventions with juveniles (Gendreau, Cullen & Bonta, 1994), especially if the parents can be educated and motivated to carry out appropriate reinforcement practices at home. For example, research on a behavioral program in Oregon found that it was effective "in reducing aversive behavior and subsequent delinquency but that the outcome is critically dependent on the skill of the therapists and the cooperation of the parents" (Greenwood, 1987: 96). Unfortunately, parents may be resistant to changing their own patterns of inappropriate or inconsistent reinforcement. Parents may find it difficult to change past practices that were ineffective, such as inadvertently giving greater attention to misbehavior than to positive behavior or failing to be consistent in discipline.

Some people object to behavioral approaches on the grounds that they seem like bribery or because they contradict the notion of the free will of the individual. Eysenck (1977) contends that all of us are very concerned with rewards as evidenced by the importance we attach to our report cards and paychecks. In addition, many religions hold in theory that persons are free and are not biologically determined to commit violence or other types of evil. Eysenck notes, however, that these same religions that emphasize the dignity and freedom of humans are very careful not to allow freedom of choice when it comes to choosing which religion to believe in or what ethical choices to follow in sexual matters. In conclusion, he argues that even many of the world's great religions do not practically believe in the freedom they claim they support. (It should be noted in response to Eysenck that many of the major religions hold that there is no inconsistency between upholding the doctrine of free will and insisting that a certain course of action is the proper one.)

A Caution

Although knowledge of these counseling techniques and philosophies is important, one must avoid the danger of assuming that familiarity with these techniques makes one qualified to act as a full-fledged therapist in probation or parole work. As Shelle Dietrich (1979) has pointed out, true counseling in probation work is difficult for several reasons. First, extensive training in counseling approaches and techniques is needed in order to avoid harming a client by the inappropriate use of the techniques. Just as reading a book on plumbing does not make one a plumber, so also reading about counseling does not make one a counselor. A probation officer who starts to explore a probationer's childhood relationship with his or her mother may be stirring up memories of past experiences that may cause serious adjustment problems in the present. Second, correctional work entails some degree of coercion, whereas most counseling approaches assume that the client has come voluntarily to the counselor. Thus, the probationer or parolee is not free to avoid the probation or parole officer the way he or she could freely refuse the advice of a psychiatrist or psychologist.

Furthermore, the officer cannot promise the confidentiality to probationers or parolees that a counselor in a private agency can promise to clients. The courts expect the probation officer to report important information on probation (such as new crimes or inadequate progress) so that the judge can reevaluate the case and decide if perhaps a more drastic action (incarceration) is necessary. For example, if a probationer reverts to drug usage or sales while on probation and informs the officer of such activity, it may be necessary for the officer to report that information to the court. A psychologist or psychiatrist, on the other hand, might judge that such behavior is just a temporary setback on the probationer's road to recovery, and choose just to encourage the probationer to cease such activity. In summary, it is important for probation and parole officers to be aware of counseling techniques and to use some of the general principles in interviewing, but it is also important that officers not go beyond their competency and try to accomplish something they are not qualified to do.

Current Trends in Community Supervision

Several developments are taking place in community corrections. Many are calling for tougher community corrections with greater attention on punishment and controlling offender risk. Other voices, however, continue to insist that probation and other community interventions need to entail more than just strict punishment for crime.

Attack (Tough) Probation

A popular and pervasive trend is **attack probation**, a move to make probation more punitive and more incapacitative than it has been in the past. In response to criticisms that probation is too lenient and that not locking up offenders allows them to commit new crimes, the last decade has seen the growth of measures designed to make probation both punitive and incapacitative. Such measures have included intensive supervision, electronic monitoring of probationers, house arrest and even requirements to put a sign on one's house or car that one is a drunk driver, child molester or other type of offender. Proponents of these measures argue that probationers deserve greater punishment and need restrictions on their freedom to curb their opportunities to commit new crimes.

One version of this argument is that intermediate sanctions are critical. Society still needs prison and probation, but it also needs something in between these two extremes for those offenders who are not hardened enough for prison and who need something more punitive and restrictive than traditional probation (Morris & Tonry, 1990).

Miller argues that the toughening of probation has gone too far. He contends that probation has lost much of its original mission of helping the offender. He argues that probation officers have abandoned any pretense at a social work role and have become "ersatz" (imitation) cops. He says that in this new "attack probation" style (a term developed by British criminologist Andrew Rutherford) officers see "their role as one in which to search out any means possible to get the probationer into prison. The motto of this practice was mounted on the office wall of one of California's chief probation officers: "Trail 'em, Surveil 'em, Nail 'em, and Jail 'em." (Miller, 1996: 131).

A critical question about getting tough is whether such tactics are effective in reducing recidivism. That issue is discussed in the next major section of this chapter. Another interesting question posed by this get tough movement is whether it is appropriate to use **shame tactics** in probation. (For a discussion of shame tactics, see Box 12.3.) Another important issue is what citizens want from probation. (For a discussion of this issue, see Box 12.4.)

Budgetary Cutbacks

In a number of probation agencies, budgetary cutbacks are occurring and forcing the agencies to reduce their crime control and treatment services. A recent national survey of probation agencies found that budgetary constraints were named as the second major concern about fieldwork. One administrator noted that he had lost 20 percent of his staff in the previous 18 months. Another respondent reported that his agency had 5,000 cases that were unsupervised due to staff cuts. Another respondent wrote that 40 percent of the supervision

Box 12.3   Shame Tactics in Probation and Community Corrections

Shame strategies take several forms. One form of shame penalties is apology. For example, one school vandalizer was forced to apologize in front of the student bodies at the 13 schools he vandalized. Some shame penalties, however, are much more negative, and objections arise that they are stigmatizing rather than reintegrative. For example, some offenders have been required to wear T-shirts or display signs on their car or residence proclaiming their offense ("I am a convicted shoplifter" or "Convicted Drunk Driver"). Karp (1998) contends that such dramatic strategies are ineffective or worse: "Shame penalties that emphasize humiliation are likely to be counterproductive as they drive a wedge between offenders and conventional society" (p. 291). Thus, shame penalties can isolate the offender rather than assist him or her in rejoining the community. He also questions whether shame penalties are effective in a modern society with an anonymous aspect compared to the potentially more effective informal small group setting (Karp, 1998). In other words, modern America is so big that we do not know our neighbors and, thus, we do not really experience shame when others who are strangers learn that we have done wrong. Shame only has meaning in a small community where people know one another.

Andrew von Hirsch argues against shaming tactics based on an ethical position that such tactics violate the respect that the offender as a human deserves. Von Hirsch argues that punishments should not demean the dignity of the offender. If they destroy the dignity of the offender, they are unacceptable:

Acceptable penal content, then, is the idea that a sanction should be devised so that its intended penal deprivations are those that can be administered in a manner that is clearly consistent with the offender's dignity. If the penal deprivation includes a given imposition, X, then one must ask whether that can be undergone by offenders in a reasonably self-possessed fashion. Unless one is confident that it can, it should not be a part of the sanction (von Hirsch, 1990: 167).

Thus von Hirsch is opposed to T-shirts for offenders or bumper stickers that make convicted drunk drivers advertise their offense because there "is no way a person can, with dignity, go about in public with a sign admitting himself or herself to be a moral pariah" (1990: 168).

Proponents of identifying labels for offenders would argue that they enhance the punishment value of community corrections. Such marks make probation or parole tougher rather than a lenient "slap on the wrist." Supporters would also argue that there may be deterrent value in the measures. It is embarrassing to wear such markings and this could serve to deter others from drunk driving or whatever offense results in the added penalty.

What do you think? What kinds of shaming might be effective for juvenile offenders? What are the limits of acceptable strategies?

cases in her agency were "banked," that is, unsupervised unless a violation or other problem developed. Such fiscal constraints mean that whether a particular probation agency is interested in assistance or control, budget limitations make it nearly impossible to achieve the agency's goals (Lindner & Bonn, 1996).

Box 12.4   Attitudes Toward Community Supervision

Turner and his colleagues recently conducted research on public attitudes toward community supervision. They presented vignettes of offenders and their crimes to a sample of respondents. Then they asked the respondents to select their most acceptable and least acceptable sentences based on the vignettes. One of the clearest findings was that citizens will prefer or at least tolerate community sentences if they perceive such sentences to be meaningful. One thing citizens clearly do not want is offenders roaming the streets unsupervised. Instead, citizens want "community-based sanctions that intervene sufficiently in offenders' lives to exact a measure of retribution, to reduce the risk offenders pose, and to increase the chances that offenders will not recidivate" (Turner et al., 1997: 22).

The New Penology

The **new penology** (Feeley & Simon, 1992) takes a less strident stance than the punitive model and argues that probation and parole officers should be efficient monitors of the conditions of supervision. If an offender fails to follow the conditions of supervision, then the officer would be swift to report the failure to the court or the parole board. Sufficiently serious or frequent violations would land the offender in prison. Ironically, failure becomes success in this model. Whereas old-fashioned officers who aimed for the rehabilitation of offenders would consider recidivism (new crimes) a failure of supervision, new penology officers would consider a new crime a success as long as it is noted and used to get the offender back into prison. Here the officer claims that one is doing one's job because signs of continuing criminal tendencies are used to get the offender off the street. The objective is to classify offenders into various categories of risk and to place them into the proper risk-management response. There is no pretense of trying to rehabilitate or cure the offender.

Although the new penology has been applied to the adult criminal justice system rather than the juvenile system, it is possible that some proponents would also argue its value for juvenile offenders.

Renewed Emphasis on Status Offenses

It appears that emphasis on status offenses such as truancy is making a comeback in some circles (for further discussion of this issue, see Chapter 14). Kern County, California, for example has instituted a truancy program that uses two deputy probation officers to work with students and families. If initial efforts to resolve truancy fail, the truant youth is referred to one of the deputy probation officers who then meets with the family at least four times. The officer also makes unannounced home visits, monitors attendance, counsels the youth and his or her parents, and refers the family to appropriate service providers. Tracking continues for one year. If unsuccessful, the case is referred back to the school for possible referral to the district attorney for court action (Garry, 1996). What makes this emphasis on status offenses new is that status offenses like truancy are receiving increased attention due to research that indicates that they are risk factors for serious and violent delinquency. There is a fear that if these troublesome behaviors are not dealt with, then there is a definite possibility of much worse behavior in the future.

Privatization of Probation

As noted in Chapters 11, privatization is a current trend in institutional corrections. Although the usual development is private construction or operation of prisons, privatization also applies to community corrections. One type of privatization is for a private agency to contract with a state to operate a probation-like agency for certain offenders. As noted in Chapter 11, a major argument for such contracting is an economic one. The private agency argues that it can provide such supervision at less cost than a state probation agency.

A different form of privatization is for private agencies to contract to provide specific services for offenders on probation or aftercare. In Florida, private vendors have been contracting with the Department of Corrections to provide treatment services for probationers. In 1995, Florida spent about $25 million for mental health and substance abuse programs. For example, one agency would provide eight hours of anger management training at $40 per offender. Sex offender treatment cost between $780 and $2,082 for two years of treatment (Lucken, 1997). There seems to be little proof of effectiveness other than testimonials from offenders. (For further discussion of privatization, see Chapter 14.)

Restorative Justice

Bazemore and Maloney (1994) argue that **restorative justice** should be the theme in a new paradigm for criminal justice and juvenile justice in general— and probation in particular. In contrast to retributive justice, which focuses on vengeance, deterrence and punishment, restorative justice "is concerned with repairing the damage or harm done to victims and the community through a process of negotiation, mediation, victim empowerment, and reparation" (Bazemore & Maloney, 1994: 28). Contrary to much of the community service at present, which is unsupervised, unplanned and performed individually, Bazemore and Maloney argue that community service should be creatively planned, well supervised and group-oriented. It should be relevant to the offense, such as requiring teen vandals to clean up or repair a vandalized school. The service obligations should contribute to the offender's sense of competency. In other words, the service assignments should offer "positive, productive roles in the community which allow them [offenders] to experience, practice, and demonstrate ability to do something well that others value" (Bazemore & Maloney, 1994: 29). This focus on competence is related to a concern for rehabilitation that is seen not in any kind of medical model but as "the development and application of productive skills or 'competencies' that provide the basis for conventional ties or 'bonds' with community institutions" (Bazemore & Maloney, 1994: 29).

This model is very attractive because it offers a plausible alternative to the "get tough" paranoia that is currently popular. It focuses on the victim as well as the offender and the community. It seeks to make the offender more competent and productive in an effort to bond the offender more closely to the community.

Several jurisdictions have implemented the restorative justice model. For example, Allegheny County, Pennsylvania, has received federal government training and assistance to start such a program emphasizing offender accountability, community protection and competency development. Part of the program involves youths growing a garden in their neighborhood and using the crops to cook and deliver meals to homeless people. This is an example of meaningful community service. Some of the youths have learned gardening skills that have enabled them to get jobs (Hsia, 1997).

Peacemaking

Like restorative justice, **peacemaking** is a positive philosophy that seeks to go beyond simply criticizing the status quo and beyond a simple focus on recidivism reduction. Peacemaking is a perspective that supports efforts of corrections workers, whether prison counselors or probation officers, to help offenders find greater meaning in their lives. Specifically, Bo Lozoff and Michael Braswell contend that all great religions teach four classic virtues: honesty, courage, kindness and a sense of humor. In this perspective, reductions in recidivism and programs like counseling or vocational training are still important but they are more external. The deeper goal is internal personal change: "The primary goal is to help build a happier, peaceful person right there in the prison [if working with prisoners], a person whose newfound self-honesty and courage can steer him or her to adjust to the biases and shortcomings of a society which does not feel comfortable with ex-offenders" (Lozoff & Braswell, 1989: 2).

In a peacemaking perspective, personal change is the basis of social change. It is critical to begin with yourself. It is also a lifetime task that needs constant work.

Current Trends: What Does the Future Hold?

It is difficult to predict where community corrections will go from here. One possible path is to continue down the "get tough" road. A grim reality is that further financial cutbacks will force probation to do less and less. Another path is to attempt to return probation to a more traditional focus on trying to rehabilitate offenders. An important issue in deciding on which direction to take is the effectiveness of community corrections. The next two sections will discuss some important findings from the effectiveness literature. The first section will review major findings on the effectiveness of community sanctions such as probation. The second section will review the research on effective treatments. Together these findings give some assistance in thinking about the most appropriate direction for community corrections to take.

Effectiveness of Juvenile Probation and Related Sanctions

Although national recidivism statistics on juvenile probationers are not readily available, and although the research on juvenile probation has not been as extensive as the research on adult probation, there are considerable research findings available to illuminate the effectiveness issue for juvenile probation. Based on research on both juveniles and adults, several conclusions about the effectiveness of community correctional interventions for juveniles seem sound.

One implication of the research is that simply making probation tougher does not work (Altschuler, 1998; Cullen, Wright & Applegate, 1996). The cumulative research on such "get tough" measures as Scared Straight programs, boot camps and intensive supervision has demonstrated that harsher measures, without additional features, do not reduce recidivism. Experimental evaluations of such programs have randomly assigned subjects to the "get tough" measure or to a control group. Follow-up measures of new arrests (recidivism) have shown that these tough measures do not reduce recidivism (recall the information on boot camps in Chapter 11).

Related to this is the finding that often community supervision may be no worse than incarceration—that is, at least as effective as incarceration (for a list of the most well-known studies attesting to this, see Krisberg & Howell, 1998: 361). Furthermore, Lipsey and Wilson (1998) found that among programs that produced consistent evidence of positive effects for serious offenders, noninstitutional programs showed greater reductions in recidivism than institutional programs. This is important. Although offenders released to community supervision commit some new crimes, the fact that they do no worse (and may do better) than offenders sentenced to training schools and then released on traditional aftercare suggests that society can use community supervision knowing that it is not more harmful than incarceration.

Another clear lesson is that the effectiveness of probation varies from place to place. An initial report on the effectiveness of adult felony probation found that the failure rate (new arrests) was 65 percent (Petersilia et al., 1985). Subsequent studies found some rates as low as 20 percent and others in between those two rates. There are several explanations for such variation. As previously noted, some locations may be under budgetary pressures and may not have the financial resources to provide much treatment or much surveillance of offenders. Some locations may be implementing treatment programs that have proven to be effective (for a discussion of such principles, see the next section). Thus, juvenile probation may be quite effective in some locations but experience serious problems in other locations.

Still another lesson is that intensive supervision can lead to easier detection of technical violations (Petersilia, 1997). In other words, officers are more likely to detect intensive supervision offenders violating the rules of probation (e.g., not reporting to the probation officer, leaving the jurisdiction without permission, breaking curfew, testing positive on a urine drug test, skipping school). This explains why intensive supervision can be ineffective if the goal is to reduce prison or training school populations. Detection of technical violations often results in revocations of probation. Then the offender is incarcerated as punishment for breaking the conditions of probation. Therefore, a sanction (intensive supervision) intended to reduce the number of persons being institutionalized, can in fact increase the number being institutionalized. This problem can be avoided, however, if a court and correctional agency put in place a system of graduated penalties for technical violations (Altschuler, 1998).

Another finding is that officers can influence some of the statistics on probation success and failure. In the famous California Community Treatment Project, for example, experimental offenders on reduced caseloads committed about the same number of new crimes as offenders on regular caseloads, but the officers were more likely to revoke the regular offenders. This occurred because the officers with reduced caseloads wanted their efforts to appear successful (Lundman, 1993). Therefore, it is important to recognize that officer reactions to offender behavior can vary and can have important consequences on how effective a program appears to be.

A discouraging finding is that some studies have shown that simply being on probation supervision without any officer contacts sometimes is just as effective as being on probation and being seen by an officer (National Council on Crime and Delinquency, 1987). This finding questions whether probation officers have much impact on their clients. One explanation is that perhaps officers are not doing much for their clients. Another explanation is that some offenders do not need much supervision. Being caught and being placed on probation sent a clear message to these probationers; they have learned their lesson and will not reoffend.

Perhaps the most encouraging finding in recent research is that intensive supervision that includes treatment components can reduce recidivism (Petersilia, 1997). This suggests that addressing offender needs can make a difference. [Contrary to this claim, a recent study of aftercare with treatment did not show any effectiveness. The study, however, involved a sample of all substance abusing offenders (Sealock, Gottfredson & Gallagher, 1997)].

Because research indicates that treatment is critical, the next section will review the treatment research to show which types of treatment appear to offer promise and which seem to be ineffective.

Effective and Ineffective Treatment Interventions with Offenders

Although several well publicized reports claimed that little seemed to be effective in changing offenders and reducing recidivism, there now appears to be considerable consensus that there is knowledge about effective interventions and ineffective interventions. This section will discuss both types of interventions.

Gendreau and his colleagues have spearheaded much of the treatment research. They have concluded that there are several principles of effective interventions. First, interventions need to be intensive and behavioral. Intensive means that the intervention takes up at least 40 percent of the offender's time and goes on for three to nine months. Behavioral interventions are based on the principles of operant conditioning, especially reinforcement. Simply stated, the principles hold that there need to be rewards for desirable behaviors. Some examples are token economies, modeling and cognitive behavioral interventions such as problem solving, reasoning, self-control and self-instructional training. Successful programs target criminogenic needs such as antisocial attitudes, peer associations, substance abuse problems and self-control issues rather than noncriminogenic needs such as low self-esteem, anxiety or depression. The responsivity principle means that attention needs to be paid to matching offenders, therapists and programs. For example, offenders who prefer structure do better in a more structured program such as a token economy. More anxious offenders do better with therapists who show more interpersonal sensitivity. Programs need to enforce their rules in a firm but fair manner and positive reinforcers should outnumber punishers by a ratio of at least four to one. Therapists need to be sensitive and to be adequately trained and supervised. Relapse prevention and advocacy as well as brokerage with other community agencies are necessary (Gendreau, 1996). This is only a brief summary of the effectiveness literature but it gives an outline of effective intervention principles.

It is also important to note what has been found to be ineffective. Freudian psychodynamic therapy is ineffective with offenders as is Rogerian nondirective (person-centered) therapy (Gendreau, 1996). Freudian therapy seeks to uncover and resolve unconscious conflicts stemming from the failure to resolve critical developmental crises adequately in childhood. It is probably something of a blessing that it is not appropriate for offenders because it is both expensive and time-consuming. Nondirective counseling assumes that clients have the potential to change and can do so if the therapist offers unconditional positive regard and a listening forum so that the client can explore options and achieve his or her full potential. It is probably more appropriate for other populations such as college student populations in which the clients are more mature and independent. As noted above, however, principles of nondirective therapy such as positive regard and empathy still apply in other counseling strategies.

Factors Related to Effectiveness

The **effectiveness research** is critical because it informs as to what works and what does not work. It is also important, however, to recall some other factors about successful intervention with offenders. One point to note is that often programs are simply not available for offenders. For example, in 1990 the estimate was that 26 percent of all probationers needed drug abuse treatment. At the same time, the average wait for entry into outpatient programs was 22 days (Duffee & Carlson, 1996). Therefore, although research indicates that resolving criminogenic needs such as substance abuse problems is critical in changing offenders and reducing recidivism, the programs to change such offenders are not always readily available. Another problem is that the public and politicians are reluctant to increase government spending even for worthy projects.

Another factor to consider is that interventions that would appear to offer benefits for offenders do not always do so. For example, many people assume that part-time employment for teens would reduce their chances of committing delinquent acts. Some recent research, however, shows that employment is not always beneficial. Wright and his colleagues found that the "number of hours employed had an indirect effect in increasing delinquency across the sample" (Wright, Cullen & Williams, 1997: 215). It may not always be productive for probation officers to help teenage probationers get part-time jobs. Instead, it may be productive to provide teens with "modest" cash incentives to graduate. In one study, such incentives prevented approximately the same amount of crime as a three-strikes law at one-tenth the cost (Wright, Cullen & Williams, 1997). (For similar findings that youth employment is positively correlated with delinquency, especially alcohol and drug use, see Ploeger, 1997.)

This issue is complex, however. Several programs for older adolescents that included an emphasis on employment or advanced skills training had very positive effects. Thus, Krisberg et al. (1995) argue that such programs are effective for older teens.

A recent study confirmed the oft-repeated observation that workers perceive working with delinquent girls to be more difficult than working with delinquent boys. Baines and Alder (1996) interviewed youth workers in Victoria, Australia, and found that perceptions of girls were that they were "more 'devious,' 'full of bullshit,' and 'dramatic,'" contrasted with their understanding of young men as 'open' and 'honest' and therefore easier to engage" (p. 481). A distressing implication of this study is that workers disdain working with girls. Thus, female offenders, who have very real and serious needs, are not getting the attention and treatment they need. This is especially distressing given that this "may be a last chance opportunity for many of the young women who are clients of these services" (Baines & Alder, 1996: 483).

Many also thought that alternative education programs that have distinct school schedules intended for students who were not doing well in traditional classrooms would be beneficial for delinquents. A recent meta-analysis of alternative schools found that they could have positive effects on school performance and attitude but that they did not reduce delinquent behavior (Cox, Davidson & Bynum, 1995).

Perhaps the most important cautionary note in any discussion of effectiveness is that financial cutbacks often make any debate about effectiveness moot. When state legislators reduce probation budgets, it is simply impossible for probation officers to implement research findings on effective interventions. In California, for example, a recent report indicated that cutbacks caused caseloads to mushroom to 200 probationers per officer. In response, some offices resorted to computer monitoring of probationers. As a result, the probationers were not receiving any personal contacts or supervision. When there are no funds for probation supervision, all the research on effective interventions becomes meaningless. As one youth told Humes, "Probation isn't worth ____" (Humes, 1996: 360). As noted above, a recent national survey of probation agencies (Lindner & Bonn, 1996) confirmed that declining budgets are a reality for many agencies. On the positive side, the state of Ohio has had success in using financial incentives to encourage counties to send only the most serious offenders to state training schools and to treat less serious youths without committing them to state training schools (Moon, Applegate & Latessa, 1997).

Continuing Controversies in Community Corrections

As juvenile court and probation enter into their second century of formal existence since the historic founding of the Illinois juvenile court in 1899, several controversies continue. This section will discuss four such controversies: (1) goal confusion, (2) line officer job issues, (3) the no-fault society, and (4) role conflict.

Goal Confusion

Goal confusion means that judges, probation and aftercare officers, probation directors, state legislators and juvenile justice experts disagree about the purposes and objectives of juvenile court and community supervision. As noted in Chapter 2, what was once a rather clear institution for supplementing parental concern by means of adult advice and psychological/social work skills has become a matter of controversy. Some courts, officers and experts still advocate a *parens patriae* and rehabilitation philosophy. In Glaser's (1964) terminology, the emphasis is on assistance to the probationer rather than on controlling the offender. In such assistance-oriented juvenile court systems, the ideal officer is a professional social worker or psychologist who has been educated and licensed to work with troubled youths. Here the major assumption about juvenile offenders is that they are experiencing one or more problems, such as emotional distress, conflicts with other family members, difficulties in school, inferior social skills or lack of job training. In a strict rehabilitation model, the probation officer would counsel the youth directly to relieve emotional distress or would intervene to reduce interpersonal conflicts at home or in school or would try to find a job for the probationer.

In a variation of this assistance-oriented philosophy, called the **reintegration model**, the probation officer would concentrate on referring the juvenile probationer to an agency in the community that provides the services that are needed. For example, the probation officer would refer a youngster with family problems to an outside agency that engages in family therapy and would refer a youth who needs a job to an employment agency or to the local summer job program. In such a reintegration model of probation, the officer believes that the community has the resources needed to help probationers and finds it more effective to refer juveniles to appropriate service providers than to try to provide such services directly. Direct provision of services is viewed as inefficient—as needless duplication of what is already available in the community. Both the rehabilitation and reintegration models of probation assume that the probationer has needs or deficits and that assistance in meeting those needs will prevent him or her from committing more delinquency in the future.

In response to the problem of goal confusion, the American Probation and Parole Association (APPA) recently came up with a vision statement. This vision statement tries to solve the problem of goal confusion by setting forth a clear and concise statement of what probation is trying to achieve. (See Box 12.5 for the APPA Vision Statement.)

Box 12.5 APPA Vision Statement

We see a fair, just, and safe society where community partnerships are restoring hope by embracing a balance of prevention, intervention, and advocacy.
We seek to create a system of Community Justice where:
A full range of sanctions and services provides public safety by insuring humane, effective, and individualized sentences for offenders and support and protection for victims;
Primary intervention initiatives are cultivated through our leadership and guidance;
Our communities are empowered to own and participate in solutions;
Results are measured and direct our service delivery;
Dignity and respect describe how each person is treated;
Staff are empowered and supported in an environment of honesty, inclusion, and respect for differences;
Partnerships with stakeholders lead to shared ownership of our vision.

Source: American Probation and Parole Association, c/o The Council of State Governments, P.O. Box 11910, Lexington, Ky 40579-1910. http://www-appa-net.org/aboutappa. htm # Mission. Reprinted with permission.

Line Officer Issues

Another continuing concern involves the probation/parole officer. Research indicates that "a sizable minority of the officers reported that they were experiencing negative feelings about their jobs" (Whitehead, 1985: 105), for example, job burnout and job dissatisfaction. Specifically, 20 percent reported frequent feelings of emotional exhaustion, 7 percent reported frequent impersonal treatment of probationers and 47 percent reported infrequent feelings of personal accomplishment (Whitehead, 1985: 103). The presence of such negative feelings can lead dedicated workers to quit their jobs or to become disgruntled and ineffective. Neither result has positive effects on probationers. The recidivism literature indicates that one of the positive results of probation supervision comes "from contact with one of the 'good people' who are frequently in such short supply" (Martinson, 1974: 46). One cause for optimism in this area is that researchers are paying more attention to it and, therefore, at the very least, are alerting officers and would-be officers to the problem so that they in turn will at least be aware of it. Box 12.6 shows some of the problems a typical officer experiences that might lead to burnout, but it also describes the joys of the job.

Box 12.6   A Probation Officer's Reflections

In response to a request to describe the joys and satisfactions and also the disappointments and frustrations in being a probation officer, one officer wrote the following shortly after he left probation to pursue a different career in criminal justice:

Probably the greatest joy was in the job itself. It was interesting, varied and fascinating. Each new day presented new and different challenges, and each case had its own special "wrinkle" to it. I also particularly liked the investigative aspects involved in preparing the social summary [presentence report] and finding out about what was happening with the child. For me, the courtroom aspect was also satisfying; this involved dealing with the judges and attorneys, testifying, etc. Certainly another joy and satisfaction was when I knew a child had turned around, whether through my action or not. The former probationer who continued to call, the parents who reported a turnaround, other kids who knew the child and told me he had changed. I also liked the law enforcement aspect to juvenile probation work. My partner often told me I liked that the most; maybe she was right.

The greatest disappointment for me was the child that could not be reached. I am not talking about the child who would probably be an adult criminal, but rather the child who had enormous potential, but for a variety of reasons I just couldn't get to. Correlated with this was the inability of the court to force parents to get involved, particularly with regard to therapy. We could force the child, and many times he would go, but we didn't seem to be able to do much with the parents.

Box 12.6, *continued*

This also led to a frustration with parents who didn't seem to care, or wanted miracles. "Fix my kid" was so often what they would tell me, and they typically didn't want to get involved. Some had really tried and were just "burned out" but most hadn't, and wouldn't. Another frustration involved the system itself. I mean the entire child welfare system and the many agencies who dealt with the child. There seemed to be a lot of shuffling of the child back and forth between one agency and another. Many of the agencies, it appeared, looked for ways to get rid of the child, and of course, we were the last resort; we had to take most of them. It was also frustrating because the probation officer seemed to get everything. If no one knew who was supposed to do it, or could do it, we got it. There also seemed to be a lack of input from the probation officers. Many interagency organizations, councils, etc. always seemed to involve the chief probation officer, or a supervisor, not someone "in the trenches." Then they would make these recommendations, and we would have to implement them, whether they would work or not. They wanted us to be professional, yet it didn't seem we were treated like professionals.

Contrasted to this are the recent reflections of an officer who thinks that probation has become depersonalized. This officer contends that the current trends in juvenile justice, such as the increased use of adult court, are disturbing:

We are at war with our teenage children. The public attitude in the 1990s does not recognize the clients [the children and adults on probation] as members of the community or understand the impact of high caseloads and the need for investment in the resources necessary to provide meaingful intervention and services. We have not clearly defined when a child is a child, a youthful offender, or an adult offender and are discussing execution or prison for children as young as 13 years of age. This public policy debate is very confusing to me when we continually express the cliche, "Our children are our future."(Johnson, 1998: 119)

Sources: Personal communication to the authors; Johnson (1998).

An ethnographic study of probation in a suburban court offers additional information on this issue. Jacobs (1990) found that officers were making diligent efforts to save children who had two-and-one-half strikes against them. In one case, for example, an officer devoted extraordinary time and effort to work with a youth for whom many had given up hope. The officer and his court system managed what appeared to be a dream solution: placement of this very troubled youth at Boys' Town in Nebraska (the famous home for troubled youth). Unfortunately, the boy absconded from Boys' Town and collaborated in an armed robbery, abduction and attempted rape.

Jacobs concludes that **job burnout** is a normal phase of the probation career. During the initial phase of a probation career, it is very possible to be "hooked" by kids who need help—to become very involved with likable youths who have many needs. Such involvement can be costly. Surviving on the job beyond the phase of job burnout "requires learning to separate clients' troubles from one's own, to moderate expectations of achievement, and to leave case-work problems at the office" (Jacobs, 1990: 123).

The No-Fault Society

Jacobs (1990) argues that the ineffectiveness of probation supervision is a manifestation of the "no-fault society." He contends that delinquency is a social problem; its causes lie in such social problems as family, unemployment, education, and the like.

> The prevention and treatment of delinquency are quintessentially *public* matters. . . . Yet lacking the means to attack delinquency at its root—by strengthening the social ecology binding the family to community, workplace, and nation—probation officers can do no more than construe those weak ecological bonds as private patholo-gies of families and individuals (Jacobs, 1990: 269).

Jacobs is probably correct that the sources of delinquency are social, economic and political as well as individual, psychological and familial. The climate of the times, however, is not very conducive to this point of view. Much of the current political rhetoric is focused on "getting tough" on crime. As noted in Chapter 11, Clear (1994) calls this trend the "penal harm movement" and another team of authors calls it "the punishment paradigm" (Cullen & Wright, 1995). Viewpoints such as that of Jacobs are considered soft on crime and irrelevant. As an earlier section of the chapter showed, the "get tough" movement is one current response to the cry for a more punitive and more incapacitative form of community supervision.

The Problem of Role Conflict

Another problem in probation is the problem of **role conflict** for the individual probation officer (Ohlin, Piven & Pappenfort, 1956). This is similar to the previously noted goal confusion that can be a problem for the probation department. Some departments emphasize assistance to the probationer, some focus on controlling the probationer, and some try to do both. Since many departments have traditionally operated without necessarily clarifying the mission or goals of the department, the individual officer has often had to decide how he or she as an individual officer will pursue the job. As noted, some officers choose to follow a social worker role, counseling probationers and refer-ring them to various community agencies for assistance with job training, job hunting, remedial education, and so forth. Other probation officers choose a law enforcement adaptation, which emphasizes compliance to the conditions of probation and swift filing of violation charges if the probationer breaks any of the court rules of supervision. Several possible types of role conflict arise for the individual officer. First, the officer may be in conflict with his or her department, especially if the department changes its philosophy. Second, the officer may be in conflict with what the judge seeks. Third, the officer may differ from what the probationer wants. Any type of role conflict, however, can result in job stress for the officer—and for less-than-ideal interactions with probationers.

Continuing Concerns

As probation and other types of community corrections enter the new century, several concerns or issues continue to merit discussion. This section will consider three such concerns: restitution, community service, and volunteer programs.

Restitution

Restitution occurs when juvenile offenders pay for all or part of the damage inflicted on crime victims or property. Restitution can take the form of either the payment of money or the performance of work (chores) for the victim. The latter is sometimes called victim-offender reconciliation (Umbreit, 1986). In some cases, probation officers or restitution officers help juveniles find jobs so that they can afford to make restitution payments.

The costs of victimization show the importance of restitution to victims. The average loss per crime in 1992 was $524; the average loss for personal crimes was $218 and the average loss for household crimes was $914 (Klaus, 1994).

Although restitution has many positive features, especially concern for the victim, there are some problems. Some critics think that it is unfair to law-abiding juveniles to help law-breaking youths find jobs. From this viewpoint, job assistance seems like a reward for delinquency. Second, the claims made about the amounts of money paid back to victims are often exaggerated. Victims may be told that all of their losses will be recouped, but actual restitution often falls short. One study, for example, found that the percentage of youths paying all of the restitution ordered by the judge varied from 40 percent to 88 percent and that judges did not always order full restitution (Schneider & Schneider, 1984). Third, restitution advocates often neglect to consider all of the costs involved in administering a restitution program, such as the salaries of those who oversee the program. In other words, restitution advocates offer statistics on the amount of money paid back to victims and claim that that amount of money is the social benefit of the program, but restitution critics point out that such statistics are only the *gross* benefits. To calculate the *net* or actual benefits, you have to subtract the costs of running the restitution program (e.g., the salaries of the counselors) from the gross benefits. Such net figures are far less dramatic than the gross benefits.

Fourth, some critics (e.g., Klein, 1980) argue that the offender is often treated unfairly in determining the amount of the restitution order. Little consideration is given to the depreciated value of damaged or stolen property, the victim may not have to verify the value of the damaged or stolen property, and the contribution of the victim to the crime (e.g., leaving keys in a parked car) is ignored. For example, if a delinquent steals a three-year-old video cassette recorder (VCR), is it fair to order the delinquent to pay back the original cost of equipment, the current replacement cost or the depreciated cost? The decision a judge makes in such a case can change a restitution order by hundreds of dollars. Klein (1980) argues that criminal court judges are rather cavalier in their restitution dollar value decisions. They often take the word of the victim at face value and, thus, order the probationer to pay more than the victim may actually deserve. Klein thinks that civil court procedures and judges are better suited for determining cash values than many criminal court judges. Many people may not have as much sympathy for the criminal when it comes to determining restitution, but Klein does at least raise the issue that determining the actual amount of restitution to be paid to a victim is not as simple as some might think.

If a court initiates a restitution program, it should take the time and effort to develop a comprehensive program. If the court merely pays lip service to restitution and does not emphasize the importance of the restitution program to offenders, officers and victims, the program will probably not be very successful in terms of either the amount of money actually collected or in terms of keeping recidivism rates as low as possible for the youths ordered to pay restitution (Schneider & Schneider, 1984).

Community service includes the performance of unpaid work for government and private agencies as payment for crimes without personal victims. Advocates argue that community service helps delinquents realize the extent of the damage they have done. *Photo: Robert Franz/Corbis*

Evaluation research on restitution has been promising. In one study, at two of four sites, about 10 percent fewer offenders sentenced to restitution recidivated than offenders not ordered to pay restitution (Schneider, 1986). Restitution also resulted in clear suppression effects. Those juveniles ordered to pay restitution had lower arrest rates in the year after their sentences compared to the year prior to their sentences (Schneider, 1990). A study in Utah of more than 7,000 cases handled informally and more than 6,000 cases involving formal probation showed that "the use of restitution is associated with significant reductions in recidivism among certain juvenile offenders" (Butts & Snyder, 1992: 4). Finally, in a New Hampshire program cited as a model program by the Office of Juvenile Justice and Delinquency Prevention, more than 80 percent of the offenders completed their community service and restitution obligations. The recidivism rate was below 30 percent (Allen, 1994).

Community Service

Community service is similar to restitution. It means that offenders perform unpaid work for government or private agencies as payment for crimes without personal victims (e.g., vandalism of public property). Community service could include cutting grass at local parks, doing volunteer work in hospitals or painting the clubhouse of a Boys Club. Advocates argue that community service helps delinquents realize the extent of the damage they have done and feel that they have paid their debt to society. Proponents also argue that cost benefits result from the "free" labor of the youths. Critics argue that extensive use of community service could take away jobs from law-abiding citizens and that the actual cost benefits of community service are not as impressive as claimed. More specifically, critics contend that the work done is not always necessary (e.g., the clubhouse did not really need a new coat of paint) and that many of the hours of community service labor include such nonproductive activities as learning the job, work breaks and dawdling if an adult supervisor is not in constant watch over the work. These criticisms do not mean that restitution or community service is worthless but that claims about their worth should be realistic rather than exaggerated. (See Box 12.7 for further discussion of this issue.)

As noted in the earlier discussion of restorative justice, an important question is whether the community service is simply busywork or has some relationship to the delinquent's offense. If a delinquent can see the connection between his or her community service order and the harm done, or can see that the community service is a meaningful contribution to the community in which he or she lives, he or she is then more likely to see the importance of such service. As a result, the delinquent is more likely to learn something positive from the community service assignment rather than see it as a boring burden to finish as quickly as possible. Community service needs to be taken seriously by both the juvenile justice system and the juvenile so that it is a teaching tool and not just something to keep a youth busy for a few hours a week.

Use of Volunteers in Probation

Because of financial difficulties, many probation departments are utilizing volunteers to counsel, tutor and act as mentors to juvenile probationers. As noted in the chapter on the history of juvenile justice, volunteers in probation are not really new. After all, the "father of probation," John Augustus, was doing such volunteer work in 1841. As was true with Augustus, many people today think that volunteers can do the things that overworked officers simply do not have the time to do, such as establishing closer rapport with juveniles, acting as role models of constructive behavior and providing services such as tutoring.

Box 12.7   An Illustration of Exaggerated Claims for Community Service

Proponents of community service might claim that a specific program resulted in savings of thousands of dollars. For example, they might claim that 500 juvenile offenders participated in various community service projects ("clean up, paint up, and fix up" at the local Boys Club or in city parks) with the following hypothetical savings:

$$\begin{array}{r} 500 \text{ offenders} \\ \times\ 20 \text{ hours per offender} \\ \hline \end{array}$$

= 10,000 total hours of free labor

In turn, 10,000 hours × $5.00 per hour (current minimum wage of $5.15 rounded off for ease of illustration; change proposed in amount at time of publication) = $50,000 in "savings" to the community.

However, proponents often neglect to mention several factors. For example, if one probation officer or community service officer is hired to make all the community service arrangements and is paid $25,000 in total salary and benefits, the financial benefit of $50,000 is reduced by $25,000 to $25,000. Second, if each offender wastes just two hours (e.g., learning to do assignments, loafing on the job, etc.), then 1,000 hours (500 offenders times two hours) are lost at a financial loss of $5,000. Finally, if the work really did not need to be done in the first place (e.g., the Boys Club or the park benches did not need a new coat of paint), then there is no financial benefit from the program.

This is not to conclude that community service has no benefits, but to argue that the claims of community service can be exaggerated.

The evidence on the effectiveness of volunteers in probation is mixed. In a review of several volunteer programs for both juveniles and adults, Sigler and Leenhouts (1982) concluded that all of the studies they reviewed showed positive results, but many of the studies did not have adequate research designs. Others found that volunteer programs had no impact on the delinquent behavior of the probationers involved and may have even made the delinquents worse (e.g., Berger & Gold, 1978). Berger and Gold (1978) also argue that probation departments should not directly run volunteer programs because this tends to create a coercive climate that works against the rehabilitative intent of the program.

A further concern about volunteers is simply finding enough volunteers to assist a probation or community corrections agency. As people work longer hours to support themselves and their families, sometimes there is not much time left for volunteer activities and community service organizations. Many service organizations are reporting that it is more difficult to find new members. Without new members, these service organizations cannot engage in all of the volunteer projects that they have conducted on an annual basis. Although several presidents of the United States have endorsed volunteerism, it may become harder and harder to find people who have the time and commitment to be volunteers.

Summary

Both probation and parole date back to at least the middle of the nineteenth century. Most of the juveniles who go through juvenile court experience probation or other types of community supervision (e.g., restitution), whereas relatively few juveniles are sentenced to institutions. This chapter has shown, however, that there are problems with community interventions. There is confusion about the goals that probation departments should pursue, especially about the relative emphasis that should be placed on control versus assistance. Similarly, individual officers often experience role conflict as a result of the goal confusion in their department or because of conflicting demands from judges, clients and the public.

The effectiveness research has often found mixed results. There is no simple answer to the treatment and control of delinquents in the community. Even the initial enthusiasm generated by Scared Straight–type programs, boot camps and similar programs across the country has given way to a more sober assessment that these programs are not a panacea (Finckenauer, 1984), though they may have some limited beneficial results. Likewise, restitution does not automatically mean that victims get fully compensated for their losses or that the youths in the programs never commit another crime. On the positive side, research to date on community corrections and the effectiveness of rehabilitation in general suggests that programs that pay attention to principles that have been found to be critical can assist offenders with their needs and help lower recidivism (Gendreau, 1996; Gendreau, Cullen & Bonta, 1994).

As we move into the first decade of the new century and new millenium, the future of community supervision is very much in question. In light of current trends to prosecute more juveniles in adult court and to incarcerate more offenders, the noble ideals of the first juvenile courts are under attack. As Jerome Miller (1996) has pointed out, even many probation officers and officials have joined their critics and changed what used to be an effort to rehabilitate juvenile delinquents to an "attack" form of probation that "jails 'em and nails 'em."

The next chapter shifts our focus from the juvenile delinquent to the juvenile victim. The final chapter then revisits some of the themes developed in this chapter within the general context of the future of juvenile justice. The discussion will show that just as some are calling for radical changes in probation practice and philosophy, others are calling for the elimination of juvenile court or substantial changes in court philosophy and practice.

DISCUSSION QUESTIONS

1. Assume that a 15-year-old young man has been taken into custody for the armed robbery of a liquor store. The clerk was not injured and this was the offender's first offense. If you were the probation officer, would you recommend probation as the disposition. Why or why not?

2. Assume that the juvenile offender described in Question 1 is your brother. Does that affect your recommendation?

3. If you were a probation officer, what style would you adopt in your day-to-day dealings with juvenile probationers? Would you adopt more of a law enforcement or social work orientation?

4. The local probation department reports that budget cutbacks mean that there is not enough money to support supervision of all probationers. The chief suggests two courses of action. One is to put 20 percent of the caseload (the least serious 20 percent) on administrative supervision. This means no supervision, just computer monitoring for new crimes. The other solution is for the county to raise taxes by a small amount to fund supervision. Which option do you favor?

5. Would you consider a career as a probation officer?

6. Your stereo system has just been stolen, but the police caught the juvenile thief. Unfortunately, he already sold your stereo and has spent the money. Your stereo cost $600 new, but it was three years old and worth about $150 used. How much restitution should the judge order?

7. As noted in the box on shaming, some experts support shame tactics such as wearing T-shirts that proclaim one's status as an offender to the public. Do you favor any shame tactics? Which particular shame tactics do you favor or oppose? Discuss.

CHAPTER 13

The Victimization of Juveniles

Key Terms and Phrases

avoidance
child abuse and neglect
child protective services
Court Appointed Special
  Advocate (CASA)
cycle of violence
dispute resolution
domestic relations court
family courts
guardian ad litem
in camera testimony
intraindividual theories
lifestyle
mentoring programs

National Crime Victimization
  Survey (NCVS)
peer mediation
restitution
routine activities theory
social learning approaches
sociocultural explanations
vicarious victimization
victim-blaming
victim compensation
victim-offender reconciliation
  programs (VORPs)
victim precipitation

Throughout this text, the emphasis has been on delinquent juveniles and the procedures for dealing with those youths. Largely ignored in the discussion has been the problem of juveniles as victims of various forms of crime. The only form of victimization that appears in the earlier chapters entails issues of inappropriate handling of youths by the juvenile and/or criminal justice system, or juveniles being victimized by their social, economic or historical place in society, which leads them into delinquent activity. Certainly, in a text on juvenile delinquency and justice, such an orientation is both proper and customary. Unfortunately, it presents only one side of the equation and fails to consider the juvenile as a victim and the role of the justice system in assisting youthful victims.

The present chapter will attempt to do several things. First, it will present evidence on the extent and types of juvenile victimization. Included under this topic is information on the victimization of juveniles in general, victimization in the school, and data on **child abuse and neglect**. Second, the chapter will discuss various explanations for the different forms of victimization. What will become apparent is that there is no single explanation for victimization, just as there is no single explanation for delinquency. Third, we will look at how individuals respond to victimization. Finally, the chapter will address the role of the juvenile and criminal justice systems in dealing with youthful victims.

The Extent of Victimization

Gauging the extent of victimization can be accomplished through the use of various data collection techniques. Official records, such as the Uniform Crime Reports, provide some indication of the overall extent of victimization in society through counts of offenses brought to the attention of social control agencies. In discussions of victimization, however, most attention turns to surveys that ask respondents about their experiences as a victim of crime. Victim surveys are only about 30 years old. They were developed in response to criticisms that official measures underreport the level of crime in society. Consequently, most victim surveys tend to address offenses similar to those found in the Uniform Crime Reports. Victim surveys, however, have been used to address crimes occurring in specific locations, such as schools and at work, as well as other types of activities, such as abuse and neglect. Beyond victim surveys, organizations such as the American Humane Association and various medical groups also collect information on specific types of victimization.

General Victimization

The most well-known source of victimization data is the **National Crime Victimization Survey (NCVS)**. The current version of the NCVS is the direct descendant of early work in the 1960s and 1970s, which explored both the extent of self-reported victimization and the best ways to survey the public. Among the earliest victimization surveys were those commissioned by the 1967 President's Commission on Law Enforcement and Administration of Justice. Those early surveys indicated that, on the average, there was twice as much crime occurring as reflected in police records. The NCVS (originally called the National Crime Survey and begun in 1972) provides a great deal of information about the extent of victimization; characteristics of the victim; known information about the offender; data on the time, place and circumstances of the offense; the economic and physical impact of the crimes; responses by victims; and contact with the criminal justice system.

One important piece of information provided by the NCVS is the breakdown of crimes by victim age and demographic characteristics. Table 13.1 presents estimated victimization rates for youths ages 12 to 15 and ages 16 to 19. For both age groups, the estimated rate of all personal crime victimizations is roughly 120 per 1,000 youths. This means that roughly 12 percent of all youths are victims of a personal crime in a single year. Note that almost all of these offenses entail physical confrontations with an assailant.

Table 13.1   **Estimated Victimization Rates for Youthful Age Groups (per 1,000), 1994**

Victimization	Total		White		Black		Male		Female	
	12-15	16-19	12-15	16-19	12-15	16-19	12-15	16-19	12-15	16-19
All Personal Crimes	117.4	125.9	115.2	129.4	137.8	120.0	137.9	147.2	96.0	103.7
Violence	114.8	121.7	112.5	124.7	135.7	117.2	134.6	141.3	94.2	101.2
Rape/Sex Assault	3.1	5.1	3.1	4.8	3.8	7.8	0.5	0.0	5.7	10.3
Robbery	12.0	11.8	10.2	10.0	3.4	1.4	16.3	16.2	7.5	7.2
Aggravated Assault	22.2	33.7	21.7	31.9	27.0	46.4	29.1	43.9	15.0	23.2
Simple Assault	77.6	71.1	77.4	78.1	84.1	42.9	88.7	81.3	66.0	60.5
Purse Snatching/ Pocket Picking	2.6	4.2	2.7	4.7	2.1	2.8	3.3	5.9	1.8	2.5

Source: Compiled from U.S. Department of Justice (1997).

Compared to victimization figures for persons age 20 and older, youths are victimized at much higher rates. Youths are twice as likely to be violent crime victims than are those between ages 25 and 34, three times more likely than those aged 35-49, and more than seven times more likely to be victimized than those aged 50 and over. What these data show is that youths contribute disproportionately to the ranks of crime victims. Whitaker and Bastian (1991) point out that while teens make up 30 percent of the violent crime victims and 24 percent of the theft crime victims, they make up less than 15 percent of the United States population. Breakdowns by race and sex (Table 13.1) show that males are consistently more victimized than females for violent crimes (except for rape), white youths are more often robbery victims than are blacks, and black youths are victimized by aggravated assault more often than are white youths.

These NCVS figures demonstrate that a significant number of youths are victims of crimes ranging from simple larceny to aggravated assault and robbery. A number of other facts are also apparent from the NCVS. First, youths are more likely to be victimized by offenders with similar demographic characteristics. That is, the offenders tend to be of the same age, race and sex as the victims, more so than found with adult victims and their offenders (Whitaker & Bastian, 1991). Second, youths also know the offender more often than do adults. Third, juveniles are less likely to report their victimization experience to the police. Many youths report the offense to someone other than the police. Finally, Whitaker and Bastian (1991) note that many youths are victimized at school. More than one-third of the violent crimes and 81 percent of the theft offenses against 12-15 year olds were committed at school. The fact that youths are required to attend school makes these victimization figures even more problematic and has given rise to a growing emphasis on studying victimization in schools.

Victimization in Schools

Because youths spend more than one-third of their waking hours at school, it should not be surprising that they experience victimization at school. Unfortunately, victimization at school has only recently become a major concern, mostly due to media portrayals of violence and weapon use on school grounds. According to the NCVS, 13 percent of all crimes of violence occur in school or on school grounds (U.S. Department of Justice, 1997).

The NCVS has conducted two supplements focusing on school victimization, one in 1989 and one in 1995. Both supplements included approximately 10,000 students ages 12 to 19 and asked respondents about victimizations in the six months previous to the interview. The overall level of victimization in 1995 was 14.6 percent (almost identical to the 1989 figure of 14.5 percent). Four percent (4.2% exactly) of students reported a violent victimization (compared to 3.4 percent in 1989) and 11.6 percent reported a property victimization (compared to 12.2 percent in 1989). Males were more likely to report a violent victimization than females and students who reported gang presence at school were much more likely to report a violent victimization (7.5 percent) than those who reported no gang presence (2.7 percent). Public school students and students who reported that drugs were available at school reported more violent victimization than private school students and students not reporting that drugs were available, respectively (Chandler et al., 1998). (For information on school homicides and bullying, see Box 13.1.)

One source of data on victimization that has been collected for several years is the Monitoring the Future (MTF) project. This project surveys high school seniors each year on a variety of subjects, including their victimization experiences at school. Victimization data for seven offenses appears in Table 13.2.

According to the MTF results, roughly one-third of the high school seniors report being the victim of a theft worth under $50 at school during the preceding 12 months. One-fifth report a theft of more than $50 and one-fourth claim to have had personal property damaged. While only a small percentage (4.9%) claim to have been injured with a weapon, 13 percent were threatened with a weapon and 12 percent suffered an injury without the presence of weapon. The male-female comparison shows consistently higher victimization for males. In terms of race, blacks and whites report similar levels of victimization. Only for theft over $50 do the two groups differ by greater than 10 percentage points.

Box 13.1   School Violence: A Recent Report

Media attention has focused on dramatic instances of school violence, especially school homicides. For example, in Jonesboro, Arkansas, in March of 1998, two boys, aged 11 and 13, were accused of shooting four classmates and a teacher to death. In Springfield, Oregon, a few weeks later, Kip Kinkel, age 15, allegedly killed two fellow high school students when he fired 51 rounds from a rifle in the high school cafeteria. Several other killings attracted similar attention.

A recent report notes that between 1992 and 1994 there were a total of 105 school-associated violent deaths but 20 of these were self-inflicted. The most frequent motive was an interpersonal dispute (one-third of the deaths) followed by gang-related activities (31% of the deaths). Random victim events accounted for 18 percent of the school-associated deaths studied.

The report noted that lesser forms of violence, especially bullying, are much more prevalent than homicide. The report suggested that schools publicize rules against bullying and be consistent in imposing sanctions for bullying. The report also suggested that mentors work with bullies and that a buddy system be initiated for students considered at risk to become victims of bullying. Other suggestions included a parents' center on campus, education in conflict resolution and close monitoring of possible target areas such as cafeterias and playgrounds (Arnette & Walsleben, 1998).

Debate continues on the causes of school violence, especially school murders. Some stress the availability of weapons and the presence of gangs while others emphasize the experience of violence in the home. Thus, some experts suggest more screening of guns and gang intervention while others suggest reducing violence in the home.

While many politicians rush to enact laws to treat school murderers as adults and to make penalties harsher, it is important to call for caution and additional research about the causes of school homicide. In her book on adolescent parricide (teens killing parents), for example, Heide (1995) notes that adolescence is a troubled period in the life cycle and that child abuse, mental illness or a conduct disorder can be important causal factors in that type of homicide. Further research on school homicide is necessary to determine what factors contribute to such dramatic outbursts and what can be done to prevent such murders.

Table 13.2   **Victimization of High School Seniors at School, 1996 (percentages)**

Victimization	Total	Male	Female	White	Black
Theft < $50	33.7	38.0	30.0	23.0	27.8
Theft > $50	18.1	21.6	14.9	15.9	29.1
Property Damaged	25.9	32.4	20.1	25.2	26.0
Injured with Weapon	4.9	6.7	3.1	3.7	9.8
Threatened with Weapon	13.2	17.3	9.5	12.3	17.1
Injured without Weapon	11.8	13.2	10.8	11.2	15.7
Threatened without Weapon	21.6	26.4	17.3	21.9	21.9

Source: Compiled from Maguire & Pastore (1997).

Not shown in Table 13.2 is the trend in victimization from year to year. An inspection of MTF results since 1984 reveals that all seven forms of victimization have remained relatively stable. The greatest change has been a slight, but steady, decrease in thefts valued at more than $50 from 88.2 percent in 1984 to 81.9 percent in 1996 (Maguire & Pastore, 1997). This same stability in reports appear in both sex and race breakdowns.

Unfortunately, the MTF provides only a broad overview of the problem of in-school victimization. Certainly, much of the concern over school crime is focused on large cities and urban areas. An alternative way to examine in-school victimization would be to conduct an in-depth analysis in a select group of schools. One recent study has undertaken such an intensive analysis of the school crime problem. Evaluating data for one large county in the midwest, Lab and Clark (1994) uncovered more in-school victimization than found in the NCVS: School Crime Supplement. Based on responses from more than 11,000 junior and senior high school students in 45 different schools, the authors found that roughly 12 percent admitted to at least one robbery victimization at school over a six-month time period, 13 percent reported being an assault victim, almost 40 percent claimed to be the victim of a theft, and approximately 60 percent reported being harassed at school (see Table 13.3). While these percentages represent a significant level of in-school victimization, an extrapolation of the percentages to raw numbers paints an even bleaker picture. Multiplying the number of respondents (11,085) by the percent reporting each level of offending, and multiplying that figure by the midpoint of the correspondent category (i.e., 2.5 for 2-3 times) reveals more than 3,000 robberies, 9,500 thefts and 3,000 assaults at schools over a six-month period of time. Since the survey reached approximately one-third of all students in the schools, these victimization numbers could be further increased threefold to estimate the level of in-school crime for all students.

Table 13.3   In-school Victimization (percents)

# of times	Robbery	Theft	Assault	Harassment
Never	88.2	60.8	87.1	40.4
Once	5.6	20.6	6.9	13.6
2-3 times	2.6	12.2	3.2	17.7
4-5 times	1.0	2.6	0.8	5.7
6+ times	2.6	4.0	2.0	22.6

Source: Lab & Clark (1994).

Besides simply asking about the extent of victimization, Lab and Clark (1994) probed the extent of loss/injury sustained in the different events. More than one-half of the robbery victims and almost 40 percent of the theft victims report losing more than $10 at least once. Likewise, one-third of the assault victims required some degree of medical care for at least one of their victimiza-

tions. These figures point out that a significant proportion of in-school victimizations involve more than a small degree or loss or pain.

The extent of in-school victimization appears even higher when research
focuses on large city, inner-city or selected schools. Lockwood (1997) reports
on interviews with 110 middle and high-school youths in two large cities.
Youths attended either a middle school with a high rate of delinquency or an
alternative high school for problem youths. These 110 respondents reported 250
instances involving physical force or violence (mostly over a one-year time
period). Table 13.4 presents a breakdown of the type and frequency of violence. The most common forms of violence were being "kicked/bit/hit with a
fist" and being "pushed, grabbed, or shoved" (Lockwood, 1997). Aggravated
assaults (those with some form of a weapon) fall into five categories totaling 39
percent of the violent activities. Roughly one-half of the reported actions took
place in or began in school.

Table 13.4   **Type and Frequency of Violent Incidents
among Selected School Students**

	N	%
Threw Something	36	14
Pushed, grabbed, shoved	138	55
Slapped	42	17
Kicked/bit/hit with fist	168	67
Hit with something	35	14
Beat up	52	21
Threatened with gun	25	10
Threatened with knife	19	8
Used knife	6	2
Used gun	13	5

Note: Percents do not equal 100% due to multiple responses.

Source: Lockwood (1997).

Beyond being directly victimized, students may also experience **vicarious
victimization**, that is, they recognize and respond to victimizations of others.
In their survey, Lab and Clark (1994) found that 50 percent of the respondents
report both assaults and thefts occurring against others at least one to two times
per month. Additionally, more than 30 percent report robberies against others
at least one to two times per month (Lab & Clark, 1994). What these figures
show is that students perceive a large problem with victimization against others
at school.

Victimization at school raises a number of perplexing problems. The most
direct concern is the victimization itself. These youths are suffering losses and
injuries. A second concern is that when the victimization takes place at school,
the schools are failing to protect the youths under their care. This raises potential issues of liability. Third, the level of victimization at school may have a

direct impact on the quality of education received by the students. This may result from students missing days of school because of the offense or fear of being victimized. It also may occur because the school must spend time trying to establish discipline and control, or because the level of crime makes the staff feel that the students are not interested in receiving an education. Crime and victimization, therefore, may replace educating as the primary concern of the school. Consequently, victimization has both immediate and long-term impacts on students.

Child Abuse and Neglect

Yet another arena of youthful victimization is that concerning child abuse and neglect. What makes this type of victimization especially noteworthy is the fact that the offender is typically a parent or other relative. Abuse and neglect can take a variety of forms ranging from sexual assaults and physical beatings to the denial of food and daily necessities to simply ignoring the child. While not a new phenomenon, it is only since the 1960s that child abuse and neglect have been seen as a social problem. Prior to that time, these types of actions were primarily considered family problems that were best dealt with by the family.

Measuring child abuse and neglect is difficult due to the nature of the actions and the victim-offender relationship. First, abuse and neglect typically do not take place in public. Instead, they occur at home where there are no witnesses besides the victim, offender and other family members. Second, in many cases, the victim may not recognize the action by the parent as wrong. The child is either too immature to understand the nature of what is happening, cannot adequately verbalize the events or does not know who to tell about the abuse or neglect. Third, despite the abuse, children often still express love and affection for the parent/relative and may not want to do something that will get the offender into trouble. As a result, the child will not report, and may even deny, the existence of maltreatment.

Due to these problems, no firm figures on abuse and neglect are available. What is known is that the problem of child maltreatment is widespread. The National Committee to Prevent Child Abuse, in its yearly survey of child protection agencies, notes that there were more than three million cases of alleged abuse reported in 1996 (Wang & Daro, 1997). Of these, roughly one-third (one million) were substantiated, meaning that there was enough evidence to confirm the report. Most substantiated cases involve neglect (60%) and almost one-quarter are physical abuse claims (see Table 13.5). Sickmund et al. (1997) note that abuse and neglect of kids increased by almost 100 percent from 1986 to 1993.

Table 13.5   **Percent of Substantiated Child Maltreatment Cases by Type of Case**

Type of Case	%
Neglect	60%
Physical Abuse	23
Sexual Abuse	9
Emotional Abuse	4
Other	5

Source: Wang & Daro (1997).

Unfortunately, child maltreatment often leads to the death of the victim. According to the Uniform Crime Reports, 249 infants were killed in 1995, 411 murder victims were aged one to four, and an additional 103 murder victims were between the ages of five and eight (Federal Bureau of Investigation, 1996). A total of 1,819 juveniles under age 17 were murdered in 1995. There are two caveats concerning these figures. First, not all juvenile homicides are committed by parents or other family members. However, 40 percent of juvenile murder victims were killed by family members, and it is reasonable to assume that this percentage increases as the age of the victim decreases. Second, it must be kept in mind that these figures reflect only those cases in which the death of a child has been determined to be due to criminal homicide. It is possible that many more children die due to neglect or abuse but the cases are not so classified. Indeed, McCurdy and Daro (1994) estimate that three children die every day as the result of child maltreatment in the United States.

These figures for the extent of abuse and neglect are only estimates. There is no accurate count for this type of victimization. The fact that most such acts occur behind closed doors between relatives means that we may never have a complete picture of the problem. What can be concluded from the figures presented here is that these are baseline figures and that the real extent of abuse and neglect is probably much higher.

Explaining Juvenile Victimization

Attempts to explain why an individual is a victim can take a variety of forms. Certainly, one way to explain victimization is to turn the equation over and focus on the offender. The various theories addressed earlier in this text (Chapters 3 and 4) follow this more traditional approach to understanding unacceptable behavior. Since the perpetrator is the one who has violated the law, it is natural to focus attention on that individual rather than the victim. There must be something about the offender that led to the victimization. The realm of victimology, however, does not rely exclusively on the theories already presented in this text. Rather, attempts to explain juvenile victimization range from those that attempt to blame the victim for the action to others targeted at specific forms of victimization.

From Victim-Blaming to a Lifestyle Approach

Early research on victims paid considerable attention to who the victims were and the circumstances surrounding the events. Throughout these works was an underlying theme that individuals became victims because of something they did, did not do or could not do. For example, von Hentig (1941) outlined 13 categories of victims, including the young, females, the old, minorities, and mentally defective individuals. What made these people victims was the fact that they were somehow vulnerable. Some people cannot physically ward off an attack, others do not recognize they are being victimized, and others see themselves outside the societal mainstream and accept the victimization. Mendelsohn (1956) takes this argument one step further in a classification relying on the culpability of the victim. "Victims with minor guilt" place themselves into a position in which victimization is possible. The "victim more guilty than the offender" actively initiates the event that causes the victimization. Similarly, the "most guilty victim" started out as an offender and ends up the victim.

This **victim precipitation** line of reasoning reached its apex with the work of Wolfgang (1958) and Amir (1971). Both of these authors argued that substantial numbers of offenses are victim-precipitated. That is, the victim is actively involved in the offense. Wolfgang (1958) stated that

> victim-precipitated [homicide] cases are those in which the victim was the first to show and use a deadly weapon, to strike a blow in an altercation—in short, the first to commence the interplay of resort to physical violence (p. 252).

The victim, therefore, holds some responsibility for his or her own status due to his or her actions or inactions. Amir (1971) extended this argument to rape offenses by claiming that how the victim acted, where she was, how she dressed, and similar factors placed the victim in the role of contributing to her own victimization. While these early ideas of victim culpability have been referred to as **victim-blaming** and subjected to much criticism (see, Curtis, 1974; Franklin & Franklin, 1976; Weis & Borges, 1973), the idea that the actions of individuals may contribute to their victimization has not been completely discounted.

Today, consideration is given to **lifestyle** as an explanation of how victims contribute to their situation. Hindelang et al. (1978) argue that the choices individuals make about what to do, where to go, who to go with, and when to go all define their lifestyle and their chances of victimization. This is directly analogous to **routine activities theory** (see Chapter 4), in which the convergence of motivated offenders, suitable targets and an absence of guardians allows for the commission of crime (Cohen & Felson, 1979). If one's lifestyle places him or her in an area where crime is common, at a time when there is no one to provide protection, then the chances for victimization are enhanced. That person's lifestyle, therefore, contributes to becoming a victim.

Examples and support for a lifestyle explanation of juvenile victimization are plentiful. The fact that juveniles are disproportionately represented among offenders would suggest that juveniles would also be the victims for a variety of reasons. First, other youths are available to victimize—at school, out-of-doors in the neighborhood, in play groups, and as acquaintances. Second, juvenile offenders will view other youths as more physically vulnerable than most adults. Third, interaction with other youths provides knowledge and opportunities for offending. Fourth, individuals who engage in deviant behavior are themselves at higher risk of being a victim. In essence, the juvenile lifestyle includes more youths to victimize than adults.

Recent research uncovers a strong relationship between offending and victimization. Using data from the National Youth Survey, Lauritsen and associates (1991) note that delinquents are four times as likely to be victims of assault, robbery and vandalism than are nondelinquents. The most consistent predictor of victimization for most youths is their delinquent lifestyle. Similarly, Esbensen and Huizinga (1991) report that victimization is strongly related to both the commission and frequency of delinquent behavior. This relationship between delinquent/criminal lifestyle and victimization has been found in numerous other studies of both juveniles and adults (Clark & Lab, 1995; Hindelang, Gottfredson & Garofalo, 1978; Jensen & Brownfield, 1986; Sampson & Lauritsen, 1990; Sparks, 1982; Thornberry & Figlio, 1974). Clearly, as youths either find themselves or place themselves in situations where delinquency is more likely, they will invariably be victimized.

Explanations of Child Abuse and Neglect

Where the lifestyle approach emphasizes the behavior and choices of the victim as contributors to victimization, explanations of child maltreatment focus exclusively on the offender and society. The victim is not considered culpable. In general, explanations for child maltreatment can be divided into three categories: intraindividual theories, sociocultural explanations and social learning theories (Doerner & Lab, 1998). **Intraindividual theories** view child maltreatment as an internal flaw or defect of the abuser. The key is to identify the flaw and intervene to avoid future abusive behavior (Belsky, 1978). Abusers are considered to exhibit some form of psychopathological condition (Steele & Pollock, 1974), such as role reversal. Under role reversal, the abuser/parent expects the child to provide nurturance and love to the parent, rather than having to supply those things to the victim/child. Intraindividual theories have been used to absolve society of any responsibility for child abuse and lay the blame on a few "sick" individuals.

Sociocultural explanations shift the emphasis from the individual to society and the environment. The abuser is stressed by any number of factors, such as unemployment, conflicts at work or home, family size, social isolation and economic problems (Belsky, 1978; Garbarino & Gilliam, 1980; Gelles, 1980; Gil, 1971). This stress leads the individual to strike out against someone or something that cannot retaliate. Where a spouse, other adults, or an employer will not tolerate inappropriate action, a child has neither the physical stature nor the social standing to resist maltreatment. A child, therefore, becomes the recipient of abuse as a proxy outlet for stress.

Social learning approaches to child maltreatment rest on the assumption that an individual has learned to be abusive by observing past abusive behavior. This observation includes the possibility that the abuser was himself or herself abused as a child. The idea that a child who is abused or who witnesses abuse will grow up to be an abuser is often referred to as the **cycle of violence** (Schwartz, 1989; Straus, 1983). Following basic social learning tenets, a child who observes abusive behavior that is not sanctioned, particularly if it is perpetrated by a respected significant adult, is more likely to model his or her future behavior accordingly. This same argument has been used as an explanation of spousal abuse (U.S. Attorney General's Task Force, 1984). Widom (1989; 1995), following abused/neglected youths and a control group into adulthood, reports a significant relationship between abuse/neglect as a child and deviant behavior of various types later in life. Researchers of the cycle of violence theory point out a variety of methodological problems and issues and call for further research before the theory is accepted as a causal factor in abuse and deviant behavior (see, Gelles & Cornell, 1990; Pagelow, 1984; Simons et al., 1995).

Explanations for child abuse and neglect are still in their infancy. Indeed, scholarly interest in this form of victimization is relatively new, with most work dating since the 1960s. Consequently, little consensus exists on the scope of the problem, explanations for maltreatment or how to best attack the problem. This state of affairs will persist until further research is completed.

Responses to Victimization

Victimization, whether direct or vicarious, has the potential of eliciting a number of responses from the victim. Indeed, a good deal of research focuses on how different people respond to victimization. Responses can range from taking direct action at the time of an offense to raised levels of fear of crime to various actions aimed at reducing the risk of initial or further victimization.

Immediate Responses

One response to victimization is for the victim to take action at the time of the offense. Surprisingly, according to the National Crime Victimization Survey (NCVS), a large percentage of all victims invoke some self-protective action (see Table 13.6). More than 70 percent of those under age 65 take some action, with 46 percent of those age 65 and older taking precautions. Where the NCVS breaks down self-protective action by age group, it does not do so for the individual forms of response. Using information for all respondents on type of self-protective behavior, it is apparent that most measures are not confrontational in nature. The most common responses are to resist or capture the offender (20.8%), run away or hide from the offender (16.3%) and try to persuade or appease the offender (13.2%). Only 14 percent of victims directly attack or threaten an offender.

Table 13.6   **Percent of Victims Taking Self-Protective Measures and Type of Measures Taken**

Ages		Measures	
12-19	69.6%	Attacked offender with weapon	0.6%
20-34	74.5	Attacked offender without weapon	10.3
35-49	73.2	Threatened offender with weapon	1.7
50-64	75.7	Threatened offender without weapon	1.5
65+	46.2	Resisted or captured offender	20.8
		Scared or warned offender	8.9
		Persuaded or appeased offender	13.2
		Ran away or hid	16.3
		Got help or gave alarm	8.6
		Screamed from pain or fear	2.4
		Took another method	15.7

Source: U.S. Department of Justice (1997).

Fear of Crime as a Response

Whether a victim takes an action or not at the time of an offense, there will probably be some changes in beliefs or behavior subsequent to the victimization experience. Many people believe that fear of crime is directly related to victimization. While most studies show that roughly 40 to 50 percent of the population are fearful of crime (Hindelang, 1975; Skogan & Maxfield, 1981; Toseland, 1982), there is evidence that fear far exceeds the actual level of victimization (Flanagan & Maguire, 1990; Skogan & Maxfield, 1981). Further, there is some debate regarding to what extent fear is influenced by victimization, whether direct or indirect (see Ferraro & LaGrange, 1987; Gomme, 1988; Lab, 1992).

Interestingly, despite the fact that youths are among the most victimized, various studies have found them to be the least fearful of all age groups (Clemente & Kleiman, 1976; Lewis & Salem, 1986; Maguire & Pastore, 1994; Ortega & Myles, 1987; Skogan & Maxfield, 1981). Not all research, however, is in agreement on this age finding. Other authors have found that fear is greater among the young (Ferraro, 1995; Ferraro & LaGrange, 1987; LaGrange & Ferraro, 1989). Ferraro (1995) suggests that the discrepancy in the research is a result of different definitions of fear, methods of data collection, and a focus on individual crimes. There is also a tendency for greater fear among youths in more recent analyses, perhaps indicating a change over time. One drawback to most studies is the fact that they compare older youths (e.g., ages 18-20) to adults and omit any discussion of younger individuals.

When research looks exclusively at youths, fear does not appear to be minor. For example, Lab and Clark (1994) report that 30 percent of their junior and senior high school respondents claim to fear being attacked at school, independent of whether they had ever been victimized in the past. Interestingly, fear was higher for younger respondents. Similarly, the 1989 NCVS School Crime Supplement found that 22 percent of youths were fearful of being attacked at school, and 53 percent of those who had been victimized feared further attacks (Bastian & Taylor, 1991).

Beyond being a concern in itself, fear may contribute to other actions that youths take in response to actual or potential victimization. Fear does not have to be a direct result of victimization or vary with changes in victimization to be a problem for fearful individuals. Fear can be debilitating in and of itself. It can lead some people to avoid other persons and places, others may decide to carry a weapon for protection, and still others may join groups to fight crime. The very fact that fear can cause people to change their normal routine is evidence that it is something to be studied. This is not to suggest that fear is always a bad thing. Indeed, to the extent that fear alters a person's behavior and chances of being victimized, fear can be a useful tool.

Avoidance

One common reaction to actual or potential victimization is **avoidance** of certain places or people. A number of authors suggest that avoidance is perhaps the leading response to fear of victimization (DuBow, McCabe & Kaplan, 1979; Gates & Rohe, 1987; Lavrakas et al., 1981; Skogan, 1981). Two analyses that identified citizen responses to fear and victimization (Lab, 1990; Lavrakas & Lewis, 1981) found that avoidance behavior is common in the data. Reasonable avoidance behavior for a youth may include staying away from a playground where gang members are known to hang out, or refraining from walking alone at night in an area with a high crime rate.

Unfortunately, there are some instances in which avoidance is not a viable alternative due to requirements placed on an individual by a job or other function. For youths, victimization at school raises the option of staying home from school or avoiding certain places at school. Avoidance at school, however, means that school work is missed, the student is distracted from work while at school and/or there is discomfort and inconvenience involved in avoiding important parts of the school (such as a restroom or the cafeteria). In their study of in-school victimization, Lab and Clark (1994) report that 9 percent of the students stayed home at least once over a six-month time period due to fear of being assaulted at school and 5 percent avoided school for fear of having something stolen. Table 13.7 shows that, while the majority of students do not avoid school or places at school, there is a small but significant percent of students who feel they must stay away from important parts of the school. Using NCVS School Crime Supplement data to identify the predictors of avoidance behavior by students, Lab and Whitehead (1994) report that fear is by far the most important consideration, even surpassing actual victimization experiences.

Table 13.7   Percent of Junior and Senior High School Students Avoiding School and School Locations

School	
Stayed Home from Fear of Attack	9.0%
Stayed Home from Fear of Theft	4.9
Specific Aspects of School	
Buses	6.3
Shortest Route to School	4.9
Certain School Entrances	4.3
Certain Stairways	6.8
Cafeteria	6.9
Restrooms	8.1
Other Places in the Building	7.2
School Parking Lot	6.4
Other Areas on School Grounds	7.9
Extracurricular Activities	7.7

Source: Lab & Clark (1994).

Resorting to Weapons

An inescapable fact about youths in recent years is their ability to obtain and use weapons. As noted in Chapter 1, the number of youths committing homicides using a gun has drastically increased since the mid-1980s. A simple extension of this finding is that youths are also arming themselves as a self-protection measure. Nationally, more than one-fourth of the population claims to carry (or have carried) a weapon for protection, with approximately one-third of those ages 18 to 49 making this claim (Gallup, 1993). It should not be surprising to find significant numbers of youths carrying weapons for protection. Surveys of students support the conclusion that weapons are becoming an everyday occurrence in and around schools. One survey of New York City high school students reveals that, in schools without metal detectors, almost 14 percent of the students carried a weapon inside school at least once within a 30-day period ("Violence-related Attitudes," 1993). Similarly, Lab and Clark (1994) report that 24 percent of their respondents carried a weapon for protection at school at least once during the preceding six months. Both studies note, however, that the most frequent weapon being carried is a knife or razor. Guns are not the most prevalent weapon.

The carrying of weapons for self-protection is problematic for a number of reasons. First, most of these items are illegal for youths to possess. Second, possession of weapons by any individual on school grounds is illegal in most juris-dictions. Third, the presence of a weapon has the potential of escalating any confrontation to much higher levels and mitigates the possibility of defusing a situation. Fourth, a weapon may result in the victim being hurt more than if no weapon was available. Finally, accepting the premise that you meet force with force portends a mind-set wherein force becomes the solution of choice, rather than a solution of last resorts.

Grouping Together to Respond

In times of crisis or turmoil, it is natural for people to seek out support from those around them. Most victims will turn to family members for such assistance. Another source of support is close friends and peers. Yet another alternative may be to join an organized group, such as a neighborhood watch organization or a "victims of crime" group. Not all of these options, however, are equally available or feasible for everyone. Some victims may not have any family members nearby or the family members are not supportive. Others may not be aware of support organizations or none may be available. Consequently, an individual may see little choice in support groups.

For youths, particularly those in large inner cities, the available peer sup-port groups may consist of juvenile gangs. The response to victimization, there-fore, may entail joining a gang for protection. This possibility is extremely salient given the reasons why youths join gangs. As noted in Chapter 5, gangs provide a sense of belonging, status, support and control. All of these things are missing in a victimization experience. Some youths may see joining a gang as a means of restoring a feeling of security. If a youth is victimized by gang members, either directly or by mistake, joining a gang further becomes a self-defense mechanism.

Joining gangs as a response to victimization, however, is a double-edged sword. While the gang may supply some sense of protection, it typically demands participation in illegal behavior and conflict with other gangs and indi-viduals. These demands often result in further victimization of the individual, rather than protection from victimization. At the same time that gang member-ship may alleviate victimization, joining a gang can also contribute to ongoing victimization, albeit as a member of a group and not just as an individual.

Peer Mediation and Other Responses to Victimization

In recent years there has been increased attention paid to the youthful vic-tim. Most of this interest is a simple extension of more general efforts to improve the standing of victims in the criminal justice system. **Peer mediation** programs represent one area in which juvenile victims have been provided a means of responding to the offense and offender. Under peer mediation, the disputants in a matter are brought together with a third-party peer mediator in an effort to resolve the dispute to the satisfaction of both parties. Not all disputes in mediation have a clear victim and offender. Rather, both parties may have a grievance with one another. The goal is to defuse the situation and keep it from recurring. Under these programs the victim has the possibility of correcting the harm done.

Peer mediation takes a variety of forms and appears under various names. **Dispute resolution** typically deals with cases in which the disputants have not yet had their grievance decided by the courts. Most of these cases involve relatively minor disputes between individuals who know one another and there is no clear-cut offender and victim. In many instances the disputing parties may be referred to mediation by the police, a prosecutor or the criminal court. Mediation programs tend to follow very informal procedures and rules, and rely on the voluntary participation of both parties (Garofalo & Connelly, 1980).

Victim-offender reconciliation programs (VORPs) represent the newest version of mediation programs. In these cases the victim and offender are clearly identified by the fact that one party has been adjudicated as a delinquent or criminal in court (Wright & Galaway, 1989). Compared to other forms of mediation, VORP is a more formal process and the participation of the offender is often a requirement set by the court. Victim participation, however, is still voluntary. A common outcome of a VORP meeting is a determination of the degree of harm done to the victim and an agreement for the offender to make restitution to the victim. An additional goal of VORP is to provide the offender with insight into the harm caused and hopefully aid in the rehabilitative process.

Many schools have implemented conflict resolution/management programs or courses. These programs typically include a strong teaching component. Key to the programs is peer mediation in which students serve as the mediators. Educators are turning to conflict resolution as a means of not only solving the immediate dispute, but also a method for teaching students alternative methods for handling confrontation. There is a recognition that staff cannot simply impose order. Rather, the students must be involved in the process of defusing situations that can lead to crime and victimization. New York City's Resolving Conflict Creatively Program (RCCP) is one well-known example of these programs. Begun in 1985, the program operates in both primary and secondary schools and deals with issues of communication, cooperation, feelings, diversity and conflict resolution (DeJong, 1993). The state of Ohio has initiated a number of similar projects (Ohio Commission, 1993). Both the RCCP and Ohio programs report success at reducing the level of fights and improving students' ability to resolve disputes. Bynum (1996), however, reports little impact from school-level conflict resolution programs. Unfortunately, most peer mediation programs with youths are in need of rigorous evaluation. The impact of these programs, therefore, is still not adequately known.

Summary of Victimization Responses

Juveniles can respond to victimization in a variety of ways. At the same time, many of the potential responses have negative aspects to them that can exacerbate problems for the youth. Fear, which may serve as a protective measure, can lead to withdrawal from other people and the community. It can also prompt a youth to stay home from school or avoid certain places at school. Still other victims may purchase and carry weapons for protection. Victimization also may drive a youth to join a gang as a means of feeling safe. While each of these may appear reasonable, they can lead to further victimization, more serious situations and, certainly, a deterioration in the general quality of life.

The Role of Formal Social Control Agencies

Various social control agencies can become involved in youthful victimization. Most of the social control agencies, however, focus on juvenile victims of abuse and neglect and ignore the victim status as it emerges from other forms of offending. Clearly, a juvenile who loses money due to a theft or is hurt from an assault tends to be considered a witness more so than a victim by the justice system. Assistance to these victims is relatively limited to mediation and similar programs already discussed. On the other hand, victims of abuse and neglect receive a great deal of attention by various formal control agencies, particularly child protective services and the different court systems.

Perhaps the only agency that will have contact with all forms of youthful victims will be the police. This is because they are typically the ones called whenever someone is in need of help. The police, however, are geared toward identifying offenders, making arrests and preparing cases for prosecution. Except for initial contacts, providing immediate protection, providing referrals to other sources of assistance, and working with prevention programs, law enforcement officers spend little time dealing with the victim. This is true whether the victim is an adult or a juvenile. Consequently, the balance of this section looks at how other system components deal with youthful victims.

Child Protective Services

A point of system entry (alternative to the police) that has been established for the purposes of protecting youths is **child protective services**. Child protective services are mandated in every state as a direct result of the Child Abuse Prevention and Treatment Act of 1974 (Wiehe, 1992). This federal act required states to set up rules for the reporting and handling of abused children. States not conforming to the Act are denied various forms of federal funding. Since the exact nature of how a state would provide protective services was left to the state, these services appear under various state agencies such as Social Services and Departments of Human Services.

Child protective service agencies fill a variety of roles and have diverse powers in different states. First, in virtually all jurisdictions, these agencies are responsible for accepting reports of abuse and neglect cases and undertaking or coordinating the investigation of such allegations. While many investigations are done by employees of the child protective service, others may be assigned to other agencies, such as the police or prosecutor's office. A second common function of child protective services is the removal of children from suspected (or documented) abusive situations. This removal may last for only a short time or can last for an extended period, depending on the facts of the case. The protection of the child from further possible harm is the goal of any decision to remove a child from his or her parents. Child protective services often provide oversight to foster care, adoption and other forms of custodial arrangements for the state.

Finally, child protective services focus on the preservation of the family unit. Underlying this approach is the belief that the family setting is the most appropriate for raising a child. Stabilizing the family situation, removing the problematic elements in the home and improving the quality of life for the child are factors guiding the decisions made by the agency. Given this preoccupation with family preservation, most child protective agencies do not need court orders or sanctions to work with families. Much like diversion programs or informal probation, child protective services will work with families to solve problems without resorting to formal court procedures if all parties agree. In some cases the agency will actually provide the recommended intervention and in others the agency may act as more of a referral source than service provider.

Child protective services, by whatever name or form, works very closely with different courts. While it often generates cases for the criminal and juvenile courts, the courts also call on these services for assistance as cases work their way through the system. This referral from the courts to protective services can range from taking custody of children when parents are incarcerated for a crime to investigating allegations of abuse and neglect that emerge in the course of divorce proceedings.

The Juvenile Court

The juvenile court deals with a wide variety of issues related to youths. As seen earlier, the juvenile court is faced with an entire set of issues and concerns when faced with delinquent individuals. Another set of issues face the court in cases of dependency, abuse and neglect. Rather than search for reasons why the youth acted inappropriately, in these cases the court must consider the protection and needs of the juvenile victim, the needs of the entire family unit and the possible sanctioning and needs of the (typically adult) offender.

Cases of abuse and neglect force the juvenile court to assume more of a conflict orientation than presumed under the *parens patriae* philosophy. Because of the diverse issues in abuse and neglect cases, many juvenile courts are affiliated with (or even part of) what are more generally known as **family courts**. Larger family courts may designate certain judges to handle delinquency matters and others to deal with abuse and neglect cases. These latter cases typically follow a more rigorous set of procedural guidelines, including evidentiary safeguards, the presence of attorneys, and formal examination and cross-examination of witnesses. This is required because of the due process rights of the accused.

In every case of abuse and neglect, the primary concern of the juvenile court is the well-being of the juvenile and the family unit. Other youths in the home become a focal point along with the individual victim, based on the assumption that they are potential victims. Because abuse and neglect cases place the interests of the child in conflict with that of an accused parent, the court typically appoints someone to be an advocate for the needs and interests of the child. Two common names for such an advocate would be a **Court Appointed Special Advocate (CASA)** or a *guardian ad litem*. The CASA program began in Seattle in the late 1970s and has since spread to all states (Office of Juvenile Justice and Delinquency Prevention, 1987). These advocates usually serve in a voluntary capacity, although some courts provide office space, supplies and travel expenses. While the exact role and responsibility of a CASA volunteer and a guardian ad litem varies across jurisdictions, they generally receive training in the functioning of the juvenile court, the needs of youths, the availability of resources and how to investigate the circumstances of the case.

Court-appointed advocates often fulfill some of the same functions as other actors in the criminal and juvenile justice systems. These individuals, because of their focus on youths, can undertake a more thorough investigation of a case than can an overburdened police force. They also can spend the time to identify potential sources of treatment for the child, offender and family (which is not a role of law enforcement investigators). In some places, these individuals also serve in the place of an attorney on the child's behalf. One key difference, however, between attorneys and CASA volunteers or *guardians ad litem* involves their orientation toward the case. Where an attorney argues in accordance with the client's wishes, a court-appointed advocate is supposed to argue in the best interests of the child, even if that conflicts with the desires of the child (Sagatun & Edwards, 1995). These court volunteers, therefore, provide a service that may not be available in their absence.

The juvenile court can impose a variety of conditions on the child victim and the family. Among these are emergency temporary custody orders, permanent custody decisions (including adoption), individual and family counseling, mandatory treatment programs and the incarceration of offenders. In making these decisions, the juvenile court judge must rely on information from a variety of sources. Court-appointed advocates are one source of vital information and recommendations. As in adjudication decisions in which the judge relies on probation personnel for an appropriate disposition, the judge typically follows the recommendation of court-appointed advocates in cases of abuse and neglect.

Beyond the traditional role of looking out for a youthful victim's needs, juvenile courts are beginning to be proactive in their efforts to work with youths in other settings. The ideas of conflict resolution and peer mediation are examples of programs that often receive help and guidance from the court. Another movement appearing in some courts is the attempt to build **mentoring programs** for at-risk kids. These programs are designed to couple youths who are not receiving the proper familial support (i.e., neglected children) with adults from the community who will help nur-

A volunteer in a mentoring program watches as a youth aims an arrow during a session of archery. Some courts are beginning to utilize mentoring programs in which youths in need of support are matched with adults who will help nurture them. *Photo: Ted Spiegel/Corbis*

ture the youths. Many courts, partly due to the overcrowding, are searching for programs and solutions that will keep youths from becoming victims or offenders in the first place.

The Criminal Court

The criminal court holds a difficult position when faced with youthful victims, particularly abuse and neglect victims. This is because of its orientation toward determining guilt or innocence of the accused and imposing sentences on the convicted. The victim in the criminal court holds no more stature than does any witness. It is the state that is the aggrieved party and the state that is pursuing the prosecution of the offender (Doerner & Lab, 1998). As a consequence of this situation, the criminal court focuses on providing the accused with his or her due process rights. Besides the witness role, the court's only other concern for a victim is to protect him or her from further harm.

A juvenile victim in the criminal court is especially problematic due to his or her lack of maturity. The process can be very traumatic for a child, particularly if the accused is an abusive or neglectful parent. In the past, many cases never reached trial or the prosecution was unsuccessful due to problems with youthful victims/witnesses. Criminal courts in recent years, however, have started to make accommodations for youthful victims. For example, some jurisdictions provide victim counselors as a means of minimizing the trauma of a court appearance and assist youths with recall problems (Burgess & Laszlo, 1976; Geiselman, Bornstein & Saywitz, 1992). These counselors can serve in a fashion and capacity similar to CASA workers and guardians ad litem. Other courts have relaxed the hearsay rule (Levine & Battistoni, 1991) or allowed *in camera* **testimony** (Bjerregaard, 1989; Melton, 1980) as means of entering testimony while protecting the victim. The relaxed hearsay rule allows third-party testimony, such as from a counselor or psychiatrist. *In camera* testimony entails testimony outside the courtroom, such as in a judge's chambers or by means of closed-circuit television or on tape. While these efforts are not allowed in all jurisdictions, they are gaining acceptance as a way to protect the youthful victim while still prosecuting the accused.

Two efforts to assist crime victims, both adult and juvenile, are **victim compensation** and **restitution** programs. Both of these programs primarily address victims of offenses besides abuse and neglect. Victim compensation programs are found in 49 states and federal courts (Parent, Auerbach & Carlson, 1992). Victim compensation is a program in which the state makes monetary payments to the victims of (primarily) violent crimes. These payments are meant to offset the monetary and medical losses incurred in the criminal act (Doerner & Lab, 1998). Youthful victims can be compensated the same as adult victims, providing the juvenile's guardian makes application. The relationship between compensation and the court rests on the fact that victims must cooperate with any prosecution of an offender, and the fact that prosecutors and the police are common avenues for alerting victims about the availability of compensation. Restitution also seeks to restore a victim to a pre-crime state. Restitution, however, requires the offender to make payment to the victim. The role of the court in restitution is obvious. That is, you must convict the offender before restitution can be imposed. The problem with both victim compensation and restitution for juvenile victims is the fact that in many cases the loss is very small and may not qualify for repayment. It is also possible that a juvenile's loss will not be seen as important enough to warrant compensation or restitution.

On a final note, both juvenile and adult victims hold few rights in the criminal court. As noted earlier, there have been some accommodations made for juveniles as witnesses. Other inroads to the court appear in legislation that provides victims rights such as the right to be informed about court proceedings, the right to protection from intimidation, and the right to address the court at the time of sentencing (Doerner & Lab, 1998). Unfortunately, there is little discussion of youthful victims in any of the arguments for these changes or in the enacting legislation.

Domestic Relations Court

A final court in which juvenile victims may find themselves is a **domestic relations court**. These are civil courts devoted to the issues involved in divorce, child support and related matters. As with juvenile courts, domestic relations may be configured as a special court within a larger family court setting in some jurisdictions. Youthful victims appear in these courts primarily in cases in which allegations of abuse or neglect are made by one parent against another. The child does not have a separate standing in the court, despite the possibility of abuse or neglect. When such allegations are made, the court will order an investigation (often by protective services agencies) for the purpose of making a determination in the question before the court (i.e., divorce, support payments, etc.). It is possible that the court will provide a CASA worker or a *guardian ad litem* to the child when such allegations are made. If evidence of abuse or neglect is uncovered in the case, those issues are turned over to the criminal or juvenile courts for action. Therefore, while youthful victimization may emerge in domestic relations courts, those problems are outside of the court's jurisdiction and will be turned over to another court.

Summary: The Need to Recognize the Victim

Addressing children as victims of crime has long been a component of the juvenile justice system and (to a minimal extent) other courts, but this fails to garner much attention in discussions of juvenile justice. This is unfortunate because most youthful offenders prey on other youths, and significant numbers of youths are victims of abuse and neglect. While the juvenile court has long standing in the areas of abuse and neglect, youthful victims have few coping mechanisms available for dealing with other forms of victimization. This is especially true outside the juvenile justice system. To what can this anonymity of juvenile victimization be attributed? One major source of blame has to be the fact that too often the emphasis on juvenile offenders ignores the other half of the offense dyad—the juvenile victim. We have attempted to begin to rectify this shortcoming in this chapter. It is also important, however, that more emphasis be placed on research and programming for juvenile victims. Without those efforts, juvenile victims will continue to receive little attention.

DISCUSSION QUESTIONS

1.   You have recently been hired to work for an agency that deals with abused and neglected youths. Research your state statutes and report on the legal definitions of abuse and neglect, and what is mandated in terms of dealing with these victims (such as mandatory reporting, treatment, etc.). What gaps do you see in the statutes? What changes would you make?

2. You have been asked to draw up new legislation dealing with child abuse and neglect. Do the following: define the terms, outline the issues you would include in the legislation, and discuss the role you see for the juvenile court and how, if at all, it would alter the court's philosophy.

3. Discuss the responses youths take when victimized. What are the positive and negative consequences of the various responses? What types of services are available to handle victimized juveniles (not including abuse and neglect)? What services are in your town? What services would you like to see initiated?

CHAPTER 14

Future Directions in Juvenile Justice

Key Terms and Phrases

capital punishment
chronic-violent offenders
divestiture
elimination of juvenile court
extension of juvenile court

privatization
reinventing juvenile court
restorative justice model
role of the family
victim-offender reconciliation

There is widespread dissatisfaction with the juvenile court. Most agree that it had noble ideals but hardly anyone thinks that it has put those ideals into everyday practice. There are numerous suggestions for the reform of the juvenile court. In this chapter we will examine several reform proposals for the court. We will also consider some other issues concerning juveniles: violent offenders, privatization, capital punishment, status offenders, and the role of the family in delinquency.

Juvenile Court Reform Proposals

Calls for the Elimination of Juvenile Court

The most drastic reform option is the call for the **elimination of juvenile court**. Under this proposal, the adult criminal courts would assume jurisdiction over juveniles, and adult departments of correction would supervise juveniles after sentencing. This move would appease critics who argue that because juveniles are committing serious crimes such as murder in alarming numbers, they deserve to be handled as adults.

Feld (1993a & b) argues, however, that the adult criminal court would have to be modified in order to handle juveniles. He believes that youths are less culpable than adults and therefore deserve less punishment. To achieve this, juveniles could be given a "youth discount":

> Criminal courts can provide shorter sentences for reduced culpability with fractional reductions of adult sentences in the form of an explicit "youth discount." For example, a 14-year-old might receive 33% of the adult penalty, a 16-year-old 66% and an 18-year-old the adult penalty, as is presently the case (Feld, 1993a: 418).

Such a youth discount would eliminate inconsistencies and injustices, such as a youth who is one day short of his or her eighteenth birthday being tried as a juvenile while a youth who just turned 18 is tried in adult court. It would also eliminate juvenile waiver hearings, which consume an excessive degree of juvenile court time and resources (Feld, 1993a).

Feld (1993a & b) also believes that juveniles deserve special protection of their procedural rights. For example, he argues that the right to counsel for juveniles should begin "when a youth is taken into custody, that it is self-invoking and does not require an affirmative request as is the case for adults, and that youths must consult with counsel prior to waiving counsel or at interrogation" (Feld, 1993a: 420).

Feld's suggestions are logical and coherent but may not satisfy emotional demands for harsher punishment of juveniles—especially 16- and 17-year-old offenders who commit violent crimes, especially murder. As shown in earlier chapters, the increasing use of transfer to adult court and the development of blended sentencing may turn out to be steps along the path to the elimination of juvenile court.

The Extension of Juvenile Court

An intriguing alternative is the **extension of juvenile court** model to adult criminal offenders. Hirschi and Gottfredson (1993) argue that the crimes of adult and juvenile offenders are not all that different in seriousness, that both types of offenders lack self-control and that youths are not more reformable than adults. They claim that "individual differences are established before the age of intervention by the juvenile court (apparently by ages 8-10 . . .) and that these differences remain remarkably stable over long periods of time" (1993: 266). In other words, they believe that juvenile development is completed well before most youths appear in juvenile court. Despite the similarities between children over age 10 and adults, the juvenile court incarceration rate is only a fraction of that found in adult criminal courts. One logical inference is that adult offenders do not need to be incarcerated as frequently as they are:

Distinctions based on age are thus arbitrary, and probably cause more trouble than they are worth. Special treatment of juveniles is based on an erroneous image of developmental sequences, and misrepresents differences between juvenile and adult crime. We argue that one justice system would be better than two, and that of the models currently available, the juvenile system seems preferable to the adult (Hirschi & Gottfredson, 1993: 262).

As was true of Feld's suggestions, the recommendations of Hirschi and Gottfredson are logical and reasonable. Emotional and political demands for harsher punishment for both adults and juveniles, however, suggest that the Hirschi and Gottfredson proposal to make the adult system more similar to the traditional juvenile system would be difficult to implement in today's political climate.

A Restitution-Reparation Model

Some observers (Bazemore & Umbreit, 1994; Moore, 1993; Umbreit, 1993) follow a peacemaking approach (Lozoff & Braswell, 1989) and argue that new avenues should be pursued. They suggest that **victim-offender reconciliation** is possible in many juvenile cases because many involve nonviolent property crimes and because victims are often willing to meet the offender to work out a restitution agreement. Such meetings allow the victim a chance to show the offender how much harm the offender caused and establish viable plans for restitution.

Moore (1993) notes that family group conferences are being used successfully in New Zealand and parts of Australia. What differentiates the family group conferences from typical American victim-offender reconciliation meetings is that both sides "are accompanied by family members, guardians, peers, or other people with a significant relationship to the offender or the victim" (Moore, 1993: 4). Such "supporters" assist in the search for restitution and reparation agreements between victim and offender.

Moore sees several advanatages in these family group conferences:

> The model takes very seriously the resentment of the victims of crime; it offers a forum for victims to overcome this resentment by achieving symbolic (and material) reparation. The model acknowledges that any crime affects a number of "indirect victims" who will feel a general indignation at a breach of social norms; it offers a forum for the reaffirmation of social norms. The model is premised on the knowledge that most young offenders lack sufficient empathy for their victims (Moore, 1993: 22).

Moore cautions that this approach is not applicable to serious (indictable) offenses but that even such an exclusion still leaves room for a significant proportion of juvenile offenses. Most importantly, the family group conferences model "offers something other than the relentless policy pendulum swing between rehabilitation and punishment" (Moore, 1993: 23). Research on restitution in the United States has found that "the use of restitution is associated with significant reductions in recidivism among certain juvenile offenders" (Butts & Snyder, 1992: 4).

Bazemore and Umbreit (1994) call for a **restorative justice model** that emphasizes accountability, competency development and community protection. The emphasis on accountability means that the offender, the juvenile justice system and the community all strive to restore the victim's losses. Therefore, restitution is critical. Competency development refers to addressing the needs of offenders so that offenders "leave the juvenile justice system more capable of productive participation in conventional society than when they entered" (Bazemore & Umbreit, 1994: 4). Community protection refers to supervision that ensures public safety.

Reinventing Juvenile Court

Krisberg and Austin (1993) argue that juvenile justice needs to be reinvented and that society needs to reinvest in children. In a nutshell, they argue that **reinventing juvenile court** would entail doing more, not less, for today's delinquents and for all children. Specifically, they propose that there should be more emphasis on prevention and that "[g]reater attention must be placed on the harmful impact of the easy availability of guns and drugs as well as on the mass media's commercialization of violence" (Krisberg & Austin, 1993: 182). Like Feld (1993a & b), Krisberg and Austin contend that the due process rights of juveniles need careful protection. Most importantly, reinventing juvenile justice means confronting the social and economic changes that contribute to deviance. They call for a "new generation of 'child savers'" to reconstruct society.

> Now more than ever the redemptive vision that helped create the juvenile court must be rediscovered. Although the present political milieu may not be ideal for a crusade to rescue our children, there is no choice but to continue the struggle for a humane and progressive system of juvenile justice (Krisberg & Austin, 1993: 187).

In summary, Krisberg and Austin call for a renewed dedication to the original goal of the juvenile court: comprehensive assistance for juveniles. Such assistance would occur on the individual, family and societal levels. As they are well aware, however, the political climate is far from receptive to this proposal. When politicians have already reformed welfare so that there are time limits for benefits and no benefits for additional children born to single mothers on public assistance, it is hard to imagine that they will have much empathy for juvenile delinquents.

Miller's Call for an End to Racism

Jerome Miller (1996), a former commissioner of juvenile corrections in two states, calls for a radical re-examination of the system and (like Krisberg and Austin) a plea for a recommitment to the original goals of helping youths. He argues first that the adult and juvenile justice systems are racist. Like some criminologists, he argues that police target black youths who hang around street corners or are seen driving on city streets. He criticizes "the silly new breed" of "attack probation officers" who are quasi-police officers checking to see if offenders are violating curfew or using drugs (by conducting urine tests in the home or office). Instead, Miller argues that probation officers should return to their original function of being advocates for juvenile defendants. They should assist defense attorneys in finding the least restrictive alternative for such youthful offenders.

Miller is critical of a popular tool, boot camps, arguing that they are ineffective. More importantly, however, he alleges that they are racist because they convey the message "of the black man in need of taming—one whose 'reform' rests in his keepers' ability to make him run, jump about "double time," and, on command, to spout back "Yes, sir!" and "No, sir!" as ersatz "drill instructors" heap abuse on their charges" (Miller, 1996: 175).

A major part of his suggested reform is to deal with the root causes of crime and delinquency, which he thinks would be self-evident if American society were not as racist as it is:

> The work to be done in the cities will require massive infusions of funding to rebuild the infrastructure, programs directed at Head Start, family support systems, nutrition, improved education, employment opportunities, housing, and adequate family income. Rather than withdrawing aid from single mothers, we should increase it, tying it to support services that encourage and support fathers to stay in the home, as is done in Sweden—a country with a significantly higher rate of single-mother births than the United States and with little crime and violence to show for it (Miller, 1996: 237).

Miller's reform plan is twofold. First, eliminate racism. Second, return to an emphasis on rehabilitation instead of a focus on punishment. A concrete suggestion is to legislate a new assistance program that would guarantee inner-city youths either a college education or a job training program. Miller admits that this would be expensive, but he argues that it would be cheaper than going to prison, which is the fate of many black males in America today.

As noted concerning Krisberg and Austin, a major problem with Miller's suggestions is that they are contrary to the prevailing political climate. In the current agenda of cutting taxes, reducing welfare assistance and perhaps even privatizing some of Social Security, it is dubious that political leaders could garner sufficient votes to address the root causes of delinquency. Both Miller and Krisberg and Austin are correct that there is a problem, but whether support could be pooled for their proposed suggestions is questionable.

The Department of Justice Vision

The Office of Juvenile Justice and Delinquency Prevention of the United State Department of Justice has been funding considerable research on the causes of delinquency and on appropriate responses to juvenile crime. As a result of such research, it has proposed a comprehensive system of graduated sanctions. Such a system has three objectives: (1) holding youths accountable for their actions; (2) building competent, capable youths; and (3) promoting community safety (Bilchik, 1998; Wilson & Howell, 1995). Such a system would incorporate comprehensive assessment of risk and needs, treatment services and increasingly severe sanctions. The first level of intervention would involve community service, restitution and diversion. Then intermediate sanctions, residential or nonresidential, would be used for first-time violent offenders or repeat nonviolent offenders. The third level of intervention would be secure corrections for serious, violent and chronic offenders. Here "the best hope" would be "small community-based facilities providing intensive treatment services and special programming in a secure environment" (Bilchik, 1998: 93). If a youth is particularly serious, violent or chronic, he or she would be transferred to adult criminal court. This model also considers both prevention strategies and intensive aftercare to be essential in any comprehensive assault on delinquency (Bilchik, 1998).

A Call for a Reconsideration of Punishment

Logan and Gaes (1993) argue that punishment should be the primary goal of the criminal justice system. They believe that rehabilitation has been automatically judged as enobling and that rehabilitation advocates have unfairly disparaged punishment:

> If some people think that punishment is evil (perhaps a necessary evil but an evil nonetheless); that mercy is a higher value than justice; that compassion is more praiseworthy than fairness; that permissiveness and lenience are the marks of a kind and loving society, while accountability implies callousness; that forgiveness is divine, while judgment and enforcement are unpleasant human necessities; that the discretionary exercise of power and authority is trustworthy when the intent is benevolent and paternalistic but suspect when the purpose is disciplinary; or that teaching, helping, and treating offenders are laudable and prestigious activities while confining and managing them is a dirty job (though someone has to do it)—in short, that only a spirit of benevolence can give the criminal sanction any redemeeming value—then perhaps those people have false values and need to be enlightened (Logan & Gaes, 1993: 253).

Logan and Gaes contend that punishment is a positive end in and of itself:

> . . . punishment is a significant aspect of culture, with meaning and merit in itself. It is a symbol and an expression of cultural and moral values. Punishment constructs and communicates some of the most important shared meanings, values, and beliefs that define the character of a culture (Logan & Gaes, 1993: 253-254).

So conceptualized, punishment ennobles the workers who attempt to achieve it in prisons and other correctional enterprises:

> [P]rison officials and officers must accept without apology the fact that they are among society's "ministers of justice." Think about it: isn't that a more admirable mission than being a "correctional officer"? (Logan & Gaes, 1993: 254)

One problem with embracing punishment as a positive goal is that punishment is not necessarily effective. Box 14.1 examines the effectiveness of New York state's effort to reduce juvenile homicide and serious crime by making such offenses eligible for criminal court jurisdiction. Punishment can also appeal to baser instincts. Box 14.2 examines the issues of caning and corporal punishment.

Box 14.1 New York's Juvenile Offender Law

In 1978 New York recriminalized several offenses. It made 13-year-olds eligible for criminal court processing for the offense of murder. It made 14-year-olds eligible for such processing for other violent offenses.

Like the highly publicized school shootings in 1997-1998 in which young teenagers killed, the New York law change was in response to a juvenile murderer. In March of 1978, Willie Bosket, age 15, murdered two New York City subway passengers. Under New York law at the time, a 15-year-old could not be transferred to adult court. So Bosket would be subject to the comparatively lenient and treatment-oriented provisions of juvenile court (called Family Court in New York). This prospect, along with the fact that Bosket had been in trouble before, generated outrage and momentum to change the law.

Simon Singer studied the effects of the new law allowing criminal court processing of such young offenders. In New York City, homicides committed by 13- to 15-year-olds decreased by 26 percent after the law went into effect. In Philadelphia, however, they increased even more (by 58 percent). There was no change in assaults in New York City, but they decreased 20 percent in Philadelphia. Singer concludes that there was an "apparent failure of the JO [Juvenile Offender] law to reduce juvenile crime in New York" (Singer, 1996: 163).

Thus, one state's experience suggests that prosecuting juveniles accused of serious crimes such as murder as adults is not a panacea. Putting these youths through criminal court does not guarantee a decrease in the targeted crimes.

Box 14.2 Corporal Punishment at Home

Michael Fay is the American teenager who several years ago received four strokes in a caning in Singapore for allegedly vandalizing a car. He was accused of spray-painting the car, was interrogated, and pleaded guilty to the vandalism. Caning is one type of corporal punishment. Corporal punishment in general used to be a staple of family discipline. Folk wisdom used to argue that "to spare the rod was to spoil the child." Recent research shows that it is still a staple for parents. Strauss and Donnelly (1993) have defined corporal punishment as "the use of physical force with the intention of causing a child to experience pain but not injury, for purposes of correction or control of the child's behavior" (p. 420). Their survey research in 1985 found that "half or more of [American] adolescents are hit by their parents, and that when this happens, it tends to happen frequently; a median of four times during a twelve-month period and a mean of six to eight times" (p. 437).

A number of states have prohibited corporal punishment in schools, but so far no state has prohibited parents from using corporal punishment at home. Some other countries, such as Sweden, have prohibited the use of corporal punishment by parents (Straus & Donnelly, 1993).

Straus (1995) has summarized the research on corporal punishment and argues that the practice is harmful, leading to child abuse, wife abuse, delinquency and even lowered economic achievement. It is not even an effective discipline strategy. He argues that corporal punishment should be outlawed.

What do you think? Should corporal punishment continue to be permissible in the home? Do parents need this method of discipline to be effective parents? Is corporal punishment a delinquency prevention technique? Or is corporal punishment outdated, unnecessary, ineffective and brutal? Is it really child abuse masquerading under a socially acceptable label?

Summary: The Goals of the Juvenile Justice System

Perhaps the most fitting conclusion to this discussion of reform proposals for the juvenile justice system is that lofty objectives, whether punishment or rehabilitation or some other end, often lose their clarity and purity in the day-to-day demands of practice. Whatever legislators or academics propound, the realities of working with incarcerated or probationed offenders translate philosophical goals into something quite different.

Thus, Feeley and Simon (1992) make a strong case that current corrections is quite mundane. It is simply about control and system management:

> The new penology is neither about punishing nor about rehabilitating individuals. It is about identifying and managing unruly groups. It is concerned with the rationality not of individual behavior or even community organization, but of managerial processes. Its goal is not to eliminate crime but to make it tolerable through systemic coordination (Feeley & Simon, 1992: 455).

The Question of the Chronic-Violent Offender

Chronic-violent offenders have attracted a great deal of attention over the years. Researchers have had a long-standing interest in identifying those individuals who pose the most serious threat to society. Closely following that problem is the question of what to do with chronic-violent offenders.

The Suggestions of Tracy, Wolfgang and Figlio

Based on their studies of two birth cohorts, Tracy, Wolfgang and Figlio (1985) offer several suggestions for dealing with another critical issue confronting the juvenile justice system: the chronic offender (defined as a delinquent with at least five police contacts). First, contrary to the juvenile court's tendency to be lenient, Tracy and his colleagues recommend "close probation supervision for perhaps first-time and certainly for second-time violent Index offenders" (Tracy, Wolfgang & Figlio, 1985: 24). They contend that a tougher than usual approach may have either a deterrent or a rehabilitative effect whereas "[f]ailure to impose sanctions—failure to impose necessary controls early—can encourage further delinquency" (Tracy, Wolfgang & Figlio, 1985: 24). Second, they think that if probation or similar community interventions do not work, then secure confinement (possibly after the third violent offense) is necessary for incapacitation. This can be achieved either by building more secure facilities or by reserving secure space for chronic offenders. Third, they recommend habitual offender or career criminal programs "to help the juvenile justice system identify, prosecute, and punish/rehabilitate the chronic offender" (Tracy, Wolfgang & Figlio, 1985: 25). Interestingly, Tracy and his colleagues (1985) concede that the success of such programs is unknown.

Contrary to much contemporary thinking, Tracy and his associates think that even chronic offenders should remain in the juvenile justice system rather than be waived to the adult system for several reasons (refer back to Chapter 8 for a discussion of waiver). First, adult courts often sentence juveniles more leniently than juvenile courts would have treated them (Tracy, Wolfgang & Figlio, 1985: 25). Second, waiver presumes that factors such as age, current offense and prior record are sound criteria for predicting dangerousness. Tracy and his colleagues, however, argue that these factors are not good predictors of overall or violent recidivism. In fact, both false positive errors (i.e., when recidivism was predicted but none occurred) and false negative errors (i.e., when desistance from delinquency was predicted but recidivism did occur) are commonly found in research studies in this area (Tracy, Wolfgang & Figlio, 1985). Finally, Tracy et al. argue that waiver represents a premature abandoning of juvenile court without trying to modify the system to deal with chronic offenders. The flexibility of the juvenile court can lead to innovative and workable solutions.

Peter Greenwood (1987) agrees that mere incarceration is not the solution to chronic delinquency. Based on notions of social justice, Greenwood argues that genuine efforts should be made to help youths who "are most likely to become chronic offenders" because they are the ones who "have in some sense been failed by their families, their communities and their schools" (Greenwood, 1987: 93).

Another View: Hamparian's Answer

Donna Hamparian and her colleagues (Hamparian et al., 1985) also have been concerned about the issue of the chronic-violent offender. They studied delinquency in a Columbus, Ohio, birth cohort and expanded the analysis to focus on the adult criminal activity of more than 1,000 persons who had been arrested for at least one violent or assaultive juvenile offense. Like Tracy, Wolfgang and Figlio, Hamparian and her colleagues think that leniency is not the answer for chronic offenders. Instead, there is a need for "strategies that let chronic offenders know that there are predictable consequences for their antisocial behavior" (Hamparian et al., 1985: 22). Second, given their findings that chronics continue committing offenses into early adulthood, Hamparian and her colleagues argue for some integration of juvenile and adult systems to deal with 16- to 19-year-olds in a coherent manner. They specifically do *not* argue for simply "tossing" (i.e., waiving) 16- and 17-year-olds up to adult court. Rather, they contend that 16- and 17-year-olds are probably much more like 18- and 19-year-olds than 14- and 15-year-olds and thus should be treated in young adult programs designed to meet their needs. They argue for programs with an emphasis on work readiness, job training and work experience. Contrary to Tracy, Wolfgang and Figlio, Hamparian and her colleagues contend that incarceration is not the answer: ". . . it is clear that few of our juvenile cohort members desisted after their day in court or a stay in a juvenile training school" (Hamparian et al., 1985: 23). Instead, they suggest early intervention and intervention that has some meaning, not just orders "for 'supervision' without supervisory contact" (Hamparian et al., 1985: 24). The authors, however, recognize that "some juvenile offenders cannot be kept out of trouble by any programs in operation today—or by initiatives envisioned in the foreseeable future" (Hamparian et al., 1985: 24).

The attention paid to chronic-violent juvenile offenders is part of a more general trend away from rehabilitation and toward a more punitive philosophy (see, e.g., Cullen & Gilbert, 1982). However, critics argue that policies calling for transfer of violent juveniles to adult court or harsher punishment for violent offenders in the juvenile system are not panaceas. One problem is that as the adult criminal justice system and the juvenile justice system remove high-risk offenders from the population, "each year a new cohort of children moves into the high-risk age groups" (Jones & Krisberg, 1994: 35). Second, "[h]igh-risk juvenile offenders do not remain high-risk" (Jones & Krisberg, 1994: 35).

What this means is that participation in serious violent crimes reaches a peak between 16 and 17 years of age and drops dramatically after age 20. If the system incarcerates young high-risk offenders for lengthy sentences, the system will be incarcerating individuals well past their high-risk years into low-risk years. The system will be using scarce prison resources for now low-risk offenders (Jones & Krisberg, 1994). Other problems include that targeting supposed high-risk offenders does not always actually result in the incarceration of serious offenders, that race can affect the targeting decisions and that prison populations can mushroom. Many of these problems occurred when Florida implemented a new habitual offender sentencing law (Austin, 1993).

The federal government's position on the issue of serious, violent and chronic delinquents is that some such offenders may be appropriate for juvenile justice system handling in secure facilities that hold the youths accountable for their offenses and also offer a sense of security to the community (Bilchik, 1998). Depending on age, offense and prior record, other serious, violent or chronic offenders are appropriate candidates for transfer to adult court. Rather than question the tendency to make increased use of criminal court processing, the federal government (Bilchik is the administrator of the Office of Juvenile Justice and Delinquency Prevention of the Department of Justice) notes that more frequent use of transfer mechanisms "should strengthen our resolve to prevent delinquency and intervene at the earliest possible time to decrease the risk of future delinquent and criminal activity" (Bilchik, 1998: 94).

The Privatization Issue

Another issue facing the juvenile justice system is whether to continue traditional publicly funded interventions for juvenile delinquents or to turn increasingly more to privately run programs. **Privatization** could extend only to selected programs, like wilderness programs, which traditionally have not been utilized by state juvenile systems, or it could include training schools, detention centers, and probation and parole services. That is, privatization could mean a wholesale turning to the private sector.

Privatization has been advancing steadily. At year-end 1995, 95 adult prisons in the United States were privatized, with a rated capacity of just under 58,000 prisoners. While this is still only a fraction of the total prison population, privatization appears to be well beyond any experimental stage (Harding, 1997). As far as juveniles are concerned, the latest one-day census, taken on February 15, 1995, showed that almost 18,000 youths were in custody in privately operated juvenile facilities (Sickmund, Snyder & Poe-Yamagata, 1997). Privately operated correctional institutions, both nonprofit and profit, have a long history. For example, the Eckerd Foundation took over a 400+ bed facility in Florida in 1982 (Mullen, Chabotar & Carrow, 1985) and private institutions accounted for 63 percent of all commitments of delinquents to institutions in Pennsylvania over a decade ago—in 1985 (Sontheimer, 1986).

Arguments in Favor of Privatization

As with the status offense issue, there are arguments for and against privatization. Contrary to the argument presented below that punishment is a function only the state should do, privatization proponents distinguish between the allocation of punishment and the delivery of punishment (Harding, 1997). Proponents argue that the state should continue to allocate punishment; for example, judges should be the ones to decide if a juvenile receives a sentence to incarceration or probation. However, how that sentence is administered or carried out can be a legitimate activity of a private corporation (Harding, 1997).

An important argument in favor of privatization is that it can reduce the costs of juvenile programs because private operators can often run programs more efficiently, or at least more cheaply, than public programs. According to a recent conservative estimate, the cost of incarcerating a juvenile for one year is $34,000 (Cohen, 1994). In a recent review of the privatization issue, Shichor came to somewhat of a confused conclusion about the cost benefits of privatization. On the one hand, he summarized existing evaluation studies as showing "a somewhat lower cost," but he then concurred with a 1991 General Accounting Office study conclusion that, "so far, empirical studies in toto have not shown a clear advantage of private prisons over publicly operated prisons and, therefore, a clear-cut recommendation favoring them cannot be made" (Shichor, 1995: 231).

Part of the reason for alleged lower costs for private vendors is that competition for contracts forces operators to be cost-conscious. Also, private operators do not have to pay civil service wages and benefits such as retirement plans.

Another argument for privatization is that it is easier to end a contract with a private vendor than it is to close a state-run training school or probation department. Contracts can be signed for any length of time and simply not renewed, whereas once a government-operated institution is built and opened, employees and area residents lobby for continued existence to protect jobs and to support the local economy. Privatization supporters also argue that innovation is easier in the private sector than in governmental agencies that must deal with civil service regulations, legislative constraints and mandates, and bureaucratic entrenchment. Private agencies are freer to experiment. Also, if one private program is not experimental enough, then the state can simply not renew its contract and seek out a more innovative provider. A related argument is the argument of cross-fertilization. This means that if some portion of a state correctional system is private and some is public, innovations discovered by either side can then be shared ("cross-fertilized") with the other side because both are overseen by the state (Harding, 1997).

Arguments Against Privatization

Opponents see disadvantages in privatization. The strongest argument against privatization is a philosphical one, namely, that it just does not seem right for the state to relinquish its role as agent of punishment in a free society. DiIulio states:

> The badge of the arresting police officer, the robes of the judge, and the state patch of the corrections officer are symbols of the inherently public nature of crime and punishment (quoted in Harding, 1997: 21).

Second, private operators must be monitored by the state to ensure that the contract is being carried out (Albrecht, 1980). Any system subject to monitoring is subject to abuse. Third, the history of corrections, both in the last century and more recently, clearly shows that greed can lead private vendors into questionable, if not abusive, practices. Fourth, private vendors prefer the most amenable offenders and seek to avoid dealing with chronic, hard-core offenders who are much less likely candidates for success and are more expensive to treat. Wheeler calls this practice of "selecting the most socially attractive 'low-risk' problem youngster" the "child-welfare effect" (Wheeler, 1978: 69) and Sontheimer (1986) calls it "skimming." Wheeler also notes that a consequence of this policy is that the less serious offenders with family and school problems often end up serving more time in institutions than felony delinquents. Fifth, "savings" achieved by contracting out services to private vendors can be illusory if such savings are gained at the cost of either clients or employees, or both. That is, savings achieved by true gains in efficiency are preferable to savings achieved by providing fewer or lower quality services to clients (juvenile delinquents) or by paying employees unfair wages. As John Irwin (1980) has pointed out with regard to adult community correctional efforts, meaningful services such as job training and education are not cheap. Thus, if private vendors are only concerned with cost-cutting without adequate concern for service provision, then they are perpetrating a sham: corrections in name only without any substantive help being offered to the offender (for more detailed discussion, see Harding, 1997; Logan, 1990; Shichor, 1995).

A RAND Corporation evaluation of a privatized institution near Cincinnati, Ohio, sheds some light on the privatization debate. The evaluators found that there was little or no difference in outcomes between the youths who went to the private facility and a control group in a regular state training school. In a one-year follow-up, there were no significant differences in arrests or self-reported delinquency between the two groups of youths (Greenwood & Turner, 1993a). These findings lead to two possible interpretations:

> For the defenders of traditional training schools, it suggests that even overcrowded ones in systems plagued by antiquated facilities, low morale, and frequent turnovers in management are not as ineffective or harmful as many would argue, at least not in terms of the outcomes we were able to measure here. . . . For the proponents of small, open programs like PCYC [Paint Creek Youth Center], this evaluation

should lend support to the argument that such programs can be run as cost-effectively as training schools and with no undue risk to the public, and that such programs will be perceived as superior to training schools by many judges, academicians and outside observers, regardless of their actual impact (Greenwood & Turner, 1993a: 277).

Privatization will continue to be an issue, especially as cost concerns merit the attention of state legislators.

Capital Punishment for Juveniles

Considerable discussion has taken place about the appropriateness of **capital punishment** (the death penalty) for juveniles. The increase in juvenile homicide in the late 1980s and early 1990s makes this debate more critical than ever. In 1996, approximately 2,900 juveniles were arrested for murder, an increase of 50 percent over 1987 (Snyder, 1997). Although the 1996 statistics represent a continuing decline since 1993, juvenile involvement in murder is still alarming and prevalent enough that we will see increasing numbers of juveniles on the nation's death rows. Also, highly publicized juvenile homicides, especially shootings at schools, generate calls for either criminal court processing or capital punishment or both for youthful murderers.

At year-end 1996, there were 64 death row inmates (out of a total of 2,849 death row inmates) who were younger than 18 at the time of their arrest for a capital offense (Snell, 1997). Another 295 death row inmates were either 18 or 19 at the time of their arrest for a capital offense. Twelve states that have death penalty statutes set 16 or less as the minimum age for eligibility for execution and four states set a minimum age of 17 years. In 1996, Ohio added a provision to its death penalty law that defendants younger than 18 at the time of the offense would be sentenced to life rather than capital punishment (Snell, 1997).

The Supreme Court has ruled on the death penalty for minors, but not without ambiguity. In 1989, the Court ruled that it was constitutional (not a violation of the cruel and unusual punishment provision of the Eighth Amendment) for a state to execute someone who was 16 or 17 at the time of their crime (*Stanford v. Kentucky*, 492 U.S. 361 [1989]). In 1988, the Supreme Court vacated the death sentence of William Wayne Thompson, who had been convicted of first-degree murder and sentenced to death for his active participation in a brutal murder when he was 15 years of age (*Thompson v. Oklahoma*, 487 U.S. 815 [1988]). The ruling in the *Thompson* case hinged on the fact that Oklahoma did not specify any minimum age for death eligibility. One commentator argues that it is unclear, however, whether "the holding in Thompson established a constitutional bar against executing anyone under the age of 16 at the time of their crime" (Seis & Elbe, 1991: 484). Another commentator argues that "[t]hese cases [*Thompson* and *Stanford*] say this: executing a juvenile who committed a crime at 15 years of age or younger is cruel and unusual punishment and therefore unconstitutional" (del Carmen, Parker & Reddington, 1998).

Box 14.3   Some Arguments Against Capital Punishment

Two voices against capital punishment are Mark Costanzo and Donald Cabana.

One of Costanzo's arguments is that if society considers killing to be wrong, then it is just as wrong for the state to kill as it is for an individual to kill. The only exceptions are "self-defense, imminent danger, or the protection of society" (Costanzo, 1997: 135). None of these exceptions apply to the capital offender because he "has already been captured and waits in a prison cell safely isolated from the community (Costanzo, 1997: 136).

Costanzo is very empathetic to the victim's family but he argues that an execution will not bring back the victim for the family. Furthermore, an execution is "a state-sanctioned killing [that] will debase us all and create a new set of victims: the murderer's family" (Costanzo, 1997: 143). This is to be avoided because, for one, the murderer's family members are innocent of wrongdoing.

An interesting suggestion of Costanzo's is to stop trying to abolish the death penalty, at least for a period of time. Instead, opponents should try a "detour" strategy of trying to get state lawmakers to limit the death penalty to multiple or serial murder cases. There are several advantages to this strategy. First, because it would reduce the number of capital punishment cases, it would save both court trial time and appellate time. Second, it would reduce the possibility of mistakes because the evidence in multiple murder cases is "often overwhelming" (Costanzo, 1997: 155). Third, it would reduce racial bias because most serial killers are white. The overall result would be that "[w]e could finally claim that only the worst of the worst are executed" (Costanzo, 1997: 155).

Finally, Costanzo aptly expresses the argument of many that killing a murderer seems an extremely illogical way for society to convey the message that killing is wrong:

> Killing is an odd way to show that killing is wrong, an odd way to show that society is just and humane. . . . we also send the message that killing is an acceptable way of solving the problem of violence, that a life should be extinguished if we have the power to take it and the offender has taken a life. We lend legal authority to the dangerous idea that if someone has committed a depraved crime, we should treat him or her as a nonhuman who can be killed without remorse (Costanzo, 1997: 166-167).

Donald Cabana is a former warden who carried out a number of executions in the state of Mississippi. He has written about the execution of one man, Connie Evans, whom he executed and had come to know was a changed individual:

Box 14.3, *continued*

This was not the same cold-blooded murderer who had arrived on death row six years before. His tears were not just those of a young man fearful of what lay beyond death's door; I was convinced they were also tears of genuine sorrow and pain for the tragic hurt and sadness he had caused so many people.

Cabana argued to the governor for a stay but there were no legal grounds to do so. Cabana had to carry out the exectuion even though he felt that ". . . as a society we were supposed to be better than the Connie Ray Evanses of the world" (Cabana, 1996: 15). Cabana eventually resigned his warden's position and went on to become a college professor.

For adult murderers, capital punishment has been debated for years (see, e.g., van den Haag & Conrad, 1983, and Costanzo, 1997, for further discussion). The questions in the debate have been both philosophical and empirical. Some of the philosophical questions involve the moral issue of the state taking a human life (for viewpoints on this issue, see Boxes 14.3 and 14.4) and the morality of capital punishment in the face of the possibility of mistakes (i.e., executing someone who has been mistakenly convicted). The empirical questions include the deterrent impact of capital punishment (does it prevent individuals from committing murder because they fear being sentenced to die?) and the issue of racial or class bias (is the death penalty more likely to be imposed on minorities than on whites?). These same issues apply to the question of the appropriateness of the death penalty for juveniles.

Box 14.4   An Argument in Favor of Capital Punishment

Ernest van den Haag is one of the leading proponents of the death penalty. Here are some of his arguments in favor of the death penalty.

First, he thinks that many critics of the death penalty are cowards who are afraid to impose the penalty:

Aware of human frailty they shudder at the gravity of the decision and refuse to make it. The irrevocability of a verdict of death is contrary to the modern spirit that likes to pretend that nothing ever is definitive, that everything is open-ended, that doubts must always be entertained and revisions made. Such an attitude may be proper for inquiring philosophers and scientists. But not for courts. They can evade decisions on life and death only by giving up their paramount duties: to do justice, to secure the lives of the citizens, and to vindicate the norms society holds inviolable (van den Haag, 1978: 67-68).

Box 14.4, *continued*

Second, van den Haag argues that murder—the most serious crime—cries out for the most serious penalty: execution. Otherwise, society is failing to carry out the proper affirmation of common values:

> In all societies, the degree of social disapproval of wicked acts is expressed in the degree of punishment threatened. Thus, punishments both proclaim and enforce social values according to the importance given to them. There is no other way for society to affirm its values. To refuse to punish any crime with death, then, is to avow that the negative weight of a crime can never exceed the positive value of the life of the person who committed it. I find that proposition implausible (van den Haag, 1978: 68).

Third, van den Haag is not persuaded by arguments that the death penalty is wrong because it is carried out in a discriminatory fashion. If discriminatory use of the death penalty is a problem, eliminate the discrimination, not the death penalty. Furthermore, van den Haag cautions against any unfounded cries of discrimination:

> It is true that most of those currently under sentence of death are poor and a disproportionate number are black. But most murderers (indeed, most criminals) are poor and a disproportionate number are black. (So too are a disproportionate number of murder victims.) One must expect therefore that most of our prison population, including those on death row, are poor and a disproportionate number black (van den Haag & Conrad, 1983: 206-7).

Finally, van den Haag thinks that the average person favors capital punishment while the average college-educated judge opposes it. There are two reasons for this:

> First, the college-educated, including judges, usually do not move in circles in which violence, including murder, is a daily threat. Not feeling threatened by murder, they can afford to treat it leniently. . . . Second, . . . [S]tudents tend to absorb and to be victimized by the intellectual fashions of their college days. Uneducated people more often accept tradition and their own experience. . . . The idea of the criminal as a sick victim of society thrives among intellectuals. The fashion in intellectual cricles for the last fifty years has been to regard criminals as victims of society, sick people who should be treated and rehabilitated. People who are executed cannot be rehabilitated (van den Haag & Conrad, 1983: 159).

Victor Streib (1987) offers several additional concerns about imposing the death penalty on juveniles. First, based on legal history and psychology, he argues that juveniles are not mature enough to be subject to capital punishment. Second, he thinks that American and international "standards of decency reject the death penalty for juveniles and demand that we relegate the practice to our less civilized past" (Streib, 1987: 34). Third, opinion polls indicate that the majority of American citizens oppose the death penalty for juveniles, although not for adults. Fourth, the selection process for deciding which juvenile murderers have been sentenced to the death penalty has been "arbitrary and capricious" (Streib, 1987: 39). Finally, society has little to fear from sending juvenile murderers to prison and even paroling them eventually because "we know that juvenile murderers tend to be model prisoners and have a very low rate of recidivism when released" (Streib, 1987: 37). Thus, Streib concludes that no person who committed murder when under age 18 should be subject to the death penalty.

Feld (1987b) agrees with Streib about prohibiting the death penalty for offenders who committed their crimes under age 18. He provides two additional reasons for this opinion. First, he asserts that adolescents are much more susceptible to peer pressure than are adults. Second, he claims that society is partially responsible for juvenile crime because juveniles are not afforded enough opportunities to become mature. Thus, "the dependent status of juveniles systematically deprives them of opportunities to learn to be responsible (Feld, 1987b: 526).

Feld's position clearly suggests that the use of capital punishment with juveniles ignores the causal factors underlying the youth's behavior. Factors such as exposure to domestic violence (Ewing, 1990), violence in the media, the lack of parental supervision, and a host of other factors may contribute to juvenile homicide. Another factor that contributes to juvenile homicide is the ready availability of guns in the United States (see Box 14.5).

Box 14.5 Guns, Kids and Homicide

Recent research indicates that juveniles own and carry guns at an alarming rate. Wright, Sheley and Smith (1992) surveyed a sample of youthful prisoners and also 1,653 students in 10 inner-city public high schools in five large cities. They found that guns were very available and that many juveniles did own and carry guns. Eighty-three percent (83%) of the inmates stated that they owned a gun just prior to their confinement and 22 percent of the students owned a gun at the time of the survey. More alarmingly, 55 percent of the inmate sample reported actually carrying a gun at least most of the time in the year or two prior to incarceration and 35 percent of the students reported carrying guns regularly or occasionally (Sheley & Wright, 1993).

Box 14.5, *continued*

Distressingly, the youths did more than carry guns. Almost two-thirds (63%) of the inmate sample had committed crimes with their guns, close to three-quarters (74%) had obtained a gun for protection and three-quarters had fired at someone at least once (Sheley & Wright, 1993). In summary, there appears to be a "youthful willingness to pull the trigger" (Wright, Sheley & Smith, 1992: 88).

It is thus no surprise that

[t]eenagers and young adults face especially high risks of being murdered with a firearm . . . Eighty-two percent (82%) of all murder victims aged 15 to 19 . . . were killed with guns. The risk was particularly high for black males. . . . The firearm murder rate was 105.3 per 100,000 black males aged 15 to 19, compared to 9.7 for white males in the same age group (Roth, 1994: 1).

There is no simple solution to this problem. Gun control is much like closing the barn door after all the horses have already left. There are so many guns already available to our nation's youth that control would probably have little effect for decades. Wright, Sheley and Smith argue that the real need is to convince these inner-city juveniles that they do not need guns,

that they can survive in their neighborhoods without being armed, that they can come and go in peace, that their unarmed condition will not cause them to be victimized, intimidated, or slain. In brief, it requires a demonstration that the customary agents of social control can be relied upon to provide for personal security. So long as this is believed not to be the case, gun ownership and carrying in the inner city will remain widespread (Wright, Sheley & Smith, 1992: 89).

Improvements in both policing and in social conditions have to take place:

Center-city minority and underclass neighborhoods have become remarkably unsafe because decades of indifference to the social and economic problems of the cities has bred an entire class of people, especially young people, who no longer have much stake in their future. Isolation, hopelessness, and fatalism, coupled with the steady deterioration of stabilizing social institutions in the inner city and the inherent difficulties of maintaining security through normal agents of social control, have fostered an environment where "success" implies predation and survival depends on one's ability to defend against it (Wright, Sheley & Smith, 1992: 89).

Contrary to these scholarly criticisms of the death penalty for juveniles, some voices still call for capital punishment for youthful offenders, particularly in multiple-murder cases. For example, a recent survey of policymakers in a southern state found that 55 percent disagreed that the death penalty should not be imposed on a juvenile (Whitehead, 1998). Similarly, multiple murders like the 1998 case in Jonesboro, Arkansas, in which two children, ages 11 and 13, killed four students and a teacher and wounded 11 others (*USA Today*, 1998) make some people demand the death penalty for such apparently hardened youths. This issue will continue to inspire debate as the twenty-first century begins.

Jurisdiction Over Status Offenses

Also related to the fundamental issue of the philosophy and continued existence of juvenile court is the issue of **divestiture**, or eliminating juvenile court jurisdiction over status offenders. That is, assuming that a state chooses not to completely eliminate juvenile court, should it continue to exercise control over disobedient, runaway and truant adolescents? As noted, the state of Washington has opted to continue juvenile court but to eliminate jurisdiction over status offenses. Maine also has written full divestiture into law. Most states have retained jurisdiction but implemented policies of deinstitutionalization (that is, they have stopped confining status offenders in state institutions). Additionally, they have established diversion programs to handle status offenders instead of relying on the juvenile justice system (Schneider, 1985).

Despite such efforts, status offenses and status offenders continue to take up a considerable portion of juvenile court time and effort. In 1995 juvenile courts handled 146,400 petitioned status offense cases, an increase of 77 percent over 1986. Runaway, truancy and liquor law violation cases increased more than 50 percent, while ungovernable cases increased only 14 percent. Despite more than a decade of discussion about ending juvenile court jurisdiction over status offenses, approximately 11,500 youths were adjudicated status offenders and placed in out-of-home placements in 1995 (Sickmund, 1997). On February 15, 1995, almost 6,000 youths were in custody for a status offense (Sickmund, Snyder & Poe-Yamagata, 1997).

Arguments for Ending Jurisdiction

There are several arguments in favor of complete divestiture. First, it allows the juvenile court more time and resources to deal with juvenile delinquents— especially violent and chronic delinquents. Because the court does not have to process or supervise status offenders, probation officers, prosecutors, public defenders, judges and correctional program employees are able to focus on more serious delinquents. Second, the elimination of status offense jurisdiction prevents any possible violations of the due process rights of status offenders, such as being prosecuted for very vague charges. For example, how disobedient does a child have to be before he or she is "incorrigible" or how truant before he or she is eligible for a truancy petition? Status offense statutes typically are unclear and vague. Third, elimination of this jurisdiction recognizes the reality that juvenile courts are not adequately staffed and equipped to deal with status offenders. Most probation officers often have only bachelor's degrees and are not qualified to do the social work and psychological counseling necessary to assist troubled teenagers and their families. Thus, status offenders should be diverted to private agencies with trained social workers and counselors who are better equipped to handle the complex problems of these youths and their families. Furthermore, eliminating juvenile court jurisdiction would force any intervention to be voluntary, which some argue is the proper way to deal with status offenders.

Another argument for elimination is that jurisdiction over status offenses has "weakened the responsibility of schools and agencies to arrange out-of-court interventive services and solutions" (Rubin, 1985: 63). What Rubin means is that status offense laws have allowed schools to run inadequate and boring programs that promote truancy and, in turn, blame parents and children for the problem. Instead of petitioning youths to juvenile court, schools should be improving instructional programs or offering innovative approaches such as alternative schools where children attend school half a day and then work half a day for pay. In other words, prosecuting status offenders often is a blame-the-victim approach that ignores the real causes of the problems: inferior schools, ineffective parents and insensitive communities (see Rubin, 1985, and Schur, 1973, for further discussion of this issue). (For a viewpoint of child welfare caseworkers on this issue, see Box 14.6.)

Finally, Chesney-Lind (1987) believes that status offenses are intricately intertwined with the place of women in American society. She questions whether the concern over maintaining jurisdiction is one of concern or control.

> What is really at stake here is not "protection" of youth so much as it is the right of young women to defy patriarchy. Such defiance by male youth is winked at, both today and in the past, but from girls such behavior is totally unacceptable (Chesney-Lind, 1987: 21).

Much of the concern, therefore, about status offenders is not so much for the children as for maintaining a patriarchal society. Thus, like the critics of the "child savers" discussed in Chapter 2, Chesney-Lind questions the intentions of those concerned with the protection of status offenders.

Arguments for Continuing Jurisdiction

Some still think, however, that juvenile court jurisdiction over status offenses is both desirable and necessary. Proponents of continued jurisdiction contend that parents and schools need the court backing to impress adolescents

Box 14.6   Caseworker Views on the Status Offender Issue

A recent survey of more than 100 caseworkers and more than 100 residential program child care staff members in Nebraska produced some findings related to the issue of juvenile court jurisdiction over status offenders. On the one hand, the respondents felt that juvenile court was not effective with status offenders. On the other hand, "the case workers did not want responsibility for these cases" (Russel & Sedlak, 1993: 23). The authors of the research report attributed workers' reluctance to take on status offense cases to high caseloads (for such problems as child abuse and neglect cases) and lack of community resources. The caseworkers also believed that dysfunctional families and problematic schools contributed to the status offense problems.

One solution would be for juvenile courts to have more power over parents, such as the authority to order treatment for parents. One specific suggestion is that juvenile courts not accept status offense cases until the family first made an attempt to undergo family therapy (Russel & Sedlak, 1993).

with the need to obey their parents, attend school and not run away from home. Concerning truancy, Rubin argues that repeal of status offense jurisdiction would "effectively eradicate compulsory education" and that "children will be free to roam the streets with impunity" (Rubin, 1985: 65). Furthermore, such total freedom would "deny children the necessary preparation for achievement in a complex technological society (Rubin, 1985: 65). Second, proponents of court jurisdiction argue that private agencies in the community will not handle (or will not be able to handle) all of the status offense cases if the juvenile court cannot intervene. Private agencies intervene only with willing clients, and many status offenders taken to such agencies simply refuse assistance. Moreover, some agencies do not provide the services they claim to provide (Schneider, 1985).

Proponents also contend that status offenders often escalate into delinquent activity. Therefore, they claim, early intervention can prevent future delinquency. However, the escalation hypothesis is controversial. Some proportion of status offenders do indeed escalate or progress, but most do not (Lab, 1984; Rojek & Erickson, 1982; Shannon, 1982). Hence, it is questionable whether all status offenders should be subject to juvenile court jurisdiction. A similar argument is that many status offenders become involved in very dangerous situations that can cause serious harm to the child. For example, one study of runaways found that more than 50 percent dealt drugs and about 20 percent (including 19% of the male runaways) engaged in acts of prostitution to support themselves (Miller et al., 1980). Research on street children has shown that many turn to theft, prostituting oneself, "rolling johns" and selling drugs to survive (Hagan

& McCarthy, 1997). Proponents of court jurisdiction argue that court jurisdiction might prevent some children from running away and becoming involved in associated dangerous behaviors. A related argument is that because states intervene "to protect adults from their own harmful conduct" (Ryan, 1987: 64), they should protect juveniles from the harmful consequences of their actions.

Another argument in favor of continued jurisdiction is that it prevents status offenders from being processed as delinquents. That is, where divestiture has occurred, there is some evidence of treating status offenders as minor delinquents (Schneider, 1985). Finally, there is concern that total removal of status offense jurisdiction from juvenile court "changes the character of the court and may substantially weaken attempts to consider the child status of delinquent" (Mahoney, 1987: 29). In other words, Mahoney fears that removal of status offense jurisdiction, with a concen-

Michael Carneal is escorted out of the McCracken County Courthouse after his arraignment in Paducah, Kentucky. The 14-year-old Carneal opened fire inside a Paducah high school, killing three and wounding five others. He was tried as an adult. *Photo: AP Photo/Courier Journal, Sam Upshaw Jr.*

tration on delinquency only, may lead to a view of the juvenile court as concerned with crime only and, hence, a belief that adult criminal courts can exercise that function. Thus, removal of status offense jurisdiction may very well be the beginning of the end of the juvenile court.

At present, the debate over divestiture has changed. In the Justice Department's research and writing on delinquency, there is little mention of status offenses as such. Instead of debate over divestiture, the Office of Juvenile Justice and Delinquency Prevention emphasizes prevention strategies that help youngsters at risk of becoming delinquent by building up protective factors. Such protective factors include caring parents who supervise their children, personal attributes such as conventional beliefs and conflict resolution skills, and schools that have caring teachers and help youth succeed in school (Coordinating Council on Juvenile Justice and Delinquency Prevention, 1996). Concretely, the Coordinating Council is concerned with such programs as truancy reduction programs that have the police round up truants so that parents can be notified and come pick up their children. Also mentioned are mentoring programs such as Bigs in Blue, which matches high-risk youth with police officer mentors who try to help youths cope with peer pressure and also do well in school. Also noted are conflict resolution programs in schools and community efforts such as community policing cooperative arrangements that attack community risk factors such as easy availability of drugs and firearms (Coordinating Council on Juvenile Justice and Delinquency Prevention, 1996).

Unlike a decade ago, the emphasis is not so much on the status offender as a distinct problem, but on those risk factors that can lead to serious, violent or chronic delinquency. Attention to reducing risk factors and enhancing protective factors is considered to be the way to prevent such problematic delinquency.

The Role of the Family

The final topic to be considered in this chapter is the **role of the family**. Saving and strengthening the family has become a rallying cry for almost every politician. Several major investigations of delinquency written in the last few years have confirmed that the family is critical in preventing delinquency. Sampson and Laub's (1993) reanalysis of data collected by Glueck and Glueck found that "[l]ow levels of parental supervision, erratic, threatening, and harsh discipline, and weak parental attachment were strongly and directly related to delinquency" (Sampson & Laub, 1993: 247). Three related longitudinal investigations of delinquency in Rochester, Pittsburgh and Denver found that poor family attachment, communication and supervision are correlated with both delinquency and drug use (Huizinga, Loeber & Thornberry, 1994). A monograph on families and delinquency reported that a "healthy home environment" is the most important factor in combating delinquency and that parental rejection and inadequate parental supervision are major risk factors for delinquency (Wright & Wright, 1994:32).

The research clearly indicates that strong family life is necessary to prevent delinquency. However, what can be done to improve family life in the United States? There is currently a great deal of debate about how to foster positive family environments in American households.

One of the most extreme positions is Charles Murray's argument that welfare allotments for children of single mothers actually exacerbate problems by encouraging women on welfare to have more children and thus increase the numbers of children in poverty. Murray argues that reducing benefits would discourage women, especially unwed mothers, from having additional children and thus would improve the problem in the long run.

> Illegitimacy is the single most important social problem of our time—more important than crime, drugs, poverty, illiteracy, welfare or homelessness—because it drives everything else. Reversing the current trend should be at the top of the American policy agenda. . . . Except for children's medical coverage, society's signal to a single woman should be unmistakable: to have a baby that you cannot care for is irresponsible, and the government will no longer subsidize it (Murray, 1994: 51-52).

According to Murray, the government can take a stand by cutting off all welfare payments for single mothers. He suggests that perhaps society could reinvest in orphanages.

The government has elected to follow Murray's suggested course of action by imposing time limits such as two to five years on welfare benefits. The effects of welfare reform on the family are still under investigation. Because the economy has been so robust (at the time this chapter is being written, the stock market is at record high levels and unemployment is at extremely low levels), it is difficult to determine whether welfare reform has had any negative impact on families. The true test will come when the economy enters a recession and unemployment reaches a much higher level than the current level.

Less drastic but similarly conservative is Horn's position that government spending programs in general do not foster family and childhood well-being. "No government program, no social worker, and no economic transfer policy has ever provided a child with a happy childhood—parents do" (Horn, 1994: 228-229). Horn argues that direct spending on children and families is wasteful. Instead, he suggests that tax credits can assist parents in carrying out their role of child rearing.

Others argue that American society does not spend enough on children. Ozawa (1993), for example, notes that the percentage of children in poverty increased to 20.6 percent in 1990; the infant mortality rate remained higher than in 19 other countries; the three leading causes of death for young people ages 15-24 were accidents, homicide and suicide; and almost one-quarter of all children live in one-parent families.

Edelman (1994) agrees that single-parent families are on the rise and that they are problematic. She argues, however, that much of the problem stems from our consumer society, which extols competition, consumption and individualism. She sees a trend toward greater disregard of the needy. Instead, she suggests that all of us need to

> struggle to begin to live our lives in less selfish and more purposeful ways, redefining success by national and individual character and service rather than by national consumption and the superficial barriers of race and class (Edelman, 1994: 245).

Thus, according to Edelman, individual service, private charity, collective mobilization and political action are the appropriate steps for society to take.

Edelman's comments echo the emerging criminological school of peacemaking (see, for example, Lozoff & Braswell, 1989). A number of criminal justice scholars have been taking a larger view of social trends and ills and have suggested steps similar to those of Edelman. Peacemaking contends that rehabilitation is not a flawed concept.

> [I]t just needs to be perceived as a process working from the inside out rather than a process to be foisted upon the participants. . . . The primary goal is to help build a happier, peaceful person right there in the prison, a person whose newfound self-honesty and courage can steer him or her to the most appropriate programs and training, a person whose kindness and sense of humor will help him or her to adjust to the biases and shortcomings of a society which does not feel comfortable with ex-offenders (Lozoff & Braswell, 1989: 1-2).

Can the juvenile justice system engender and build the type of family necessary for raising nondelinquent, productive members of society? Huizinga, Loeber and Thornberry (1994: 24) suggest that it is highly unlikely. Instead:

> improving training in parenting skills and providing support services to empower parents to monitor and supervise their children more effectively is certainly within its scope. Also, attempting to ensure that youth in "treatment for delinquency" return to more efffective and caring homes may in some cases be possible. These types of programs need to be developed, implemented, and evaluated so that strengthened families can help reduce the involvement of youth in delinquency (Huizinga, Loeber & Thornberry, 1994: 24).

In summary, researchers agree that the family is a key factor in preventing delinquency. Disagreement arises, however, concerning the best strategies to strengthen families and what to do when a family has proven to be deficient.

One family-enhancing strategy directly related to the juvenile justice system is Moore and Wakeling's (1997) suggestion to change the juvenile court into a family court system that would deal with divorce matters, child dependency related matters including abuse and neglect, delinquency and traffic cases including driving under the influence and status offenses, and adult and juvenile guardianships and conservatorships. Part of this family court model would entail expanded social services for children supervised by the family court. They argue that even enlightened self-interest calls for increased services: "If society does not act now to deal with the plight of families and children, there will be a huge price to pay later on in terms of increased criminality and other social ills" (Moore & Wakeling, 1997: 285). More generally, they argue that the current emphasis on the family has shown its importance in many areas of American society, including concern about crime and delinquency:

> society's stakes in ensuring the quality of child rearing are very large even if largely unacknowledged. A society that neglects its children cannot hope to succeed. Nor can it claim to be either just or virtuous. And a society that has given up trying to succeed, and to be just and virtuous, is a society that is headed for bankruptcy itself (Moore & Wakeling, 1997: 294).

Summary

This chapter has examined juvenile court philosophy, the question of what to do with violent juveniles, privatization, the death penalty for juveniles, the status offender issue, and the importance of the family in preventing delinquency. Many of the current suggestions for reforming the juvenile justice system are both novel and harsh. Some critics have suggested such drastic changes as caning and orphanages for delinquents. Such suggestions, unheard of only a decade ago, are debated today with sincerity and enthusiasm.

Thus, the future of juvenile justice is very much under debate at the close of the twentieth century. One hundred years after the founding of the juvenile court in Illinois, many are seriously questioning the very existence of a separate system for juveniles. Transfer and blended sentences are a reality for many juvenile offenders. One decade from now a book such as this may be moot; it is possible that no juvenile justice system will exist. Some, however, insist that all that is needed is greater effort to revitalize the original vision of the founders of the juvenile court. Time will tell who wins this very important debate.

DISCUSSION QUESTIONS

1. What is your philosophy of juvenile court? Should juvenile court attempt to pursue rehabilitation, justice or punishment, or should juvenile court be abandoned as an anachronism?

2. Do you favor or oppose capital punishment for juveniles? If you do favor capital punishment for juveniles, what should the minimum eligibility age be—10, 12 or some other age?

3. Do you think that juvenile court should have jurisdiction over status offenders? If so, should there be any limits on such jurisdiction? Specifically, assume that your 15-year-old sister is running away from home and skipping school. Do you think that your parents should have the option of requesting juvenile court intervention?

4. Assume that Sam is a chronic car thief; he has stolen 10 autos and been on probation. What should juvenile court do when he steals car number 11?

5. Assume that Company X wants to start a residential treatment program for violent delinquents in your area. Would you favor the proposal or would you prefer that the State Department of Youth Corrections continue to supervise such youths?

6. Everyone seems to agree that stable and supportive families are important in preventing delinquency, but people disagree on how to make family life as supportive as it can be. What can be done to improve families? What is the role of government in promoting positive family environments? If a woman on public assistance gets pregnant, does the state have an obligation to increase her benefits at the birth of that child?

REFERENCES

Abadinsky, H. (1989). *Drug Abuse: An Introduction*. Chicago: Nelson-Hall.

Abrahamsen, D. (1944). *Crisis and the Human Mind*. New York: Columbia University Press.

Abt Associates (1994). *Conditions of Confinement: Juvenile Detention and Corrections Facilities: Research Report*. Washington, DC: U.S. Department of Justice.

Adams, L.R. (1974). "The adequacy of differential association theory." *Journal of Research in Crime & Delinquency* 11:1-8.

Adler, C. (1984). "Gender bias in juvenile diversion." *Crime & Delinquency* 30:400-414.

Ageton, S. and D.S. Elliott (1973). "The effects of legal processing on self-concept." Mimeograph. Boulder, CO: Institute of Behavioral Science, University of Colorado.

Agnew, R. (1984). "Goal achievement and delinquency." *Sociology and Social Research* 68:435-451.

Agnew, R. (1992). "Foundation for a general strain theory of crime and delinquency." *Criminology* 30:47-87.

Agnew, R. (1994). "The techniques of neutralization and violence." *Criminology* 32:555-580.

Agnew, R. (1997). "Stability and change in crime over the life course: A strain theory explanation." In T.P. Thornberry (ed.), *Developmental Theories of Crime and Delinquency* (pp.). New Brunswick, NJ: Transaction.

Agnew, R. and A.A.R. Peters (1986). "The techniques of neutralization: An analysis of predisposing and situational factors." *Criminal Justice and Behavior* 13:81-97.

Agnew, R. and H.R. White (1992). "An empirical test of general strain theory." *Criminology* 30:475-499.

Aichhorn, A. (1963). *Wayward Youth*. New York: Viking.

Akers, R.L. (1990). "Rational choice, deterrence and social learning theory in criminology: The path not taken." *Journal of Criminal Law and Criminology* 81:653-676.

Akers, R. (1991). "Self-control as a general theory of crime." *Journal of Quantitative Criminology* 7:201-211.

Akers, R.L., M.K. Krohn, L. Lonza-Kaduce and M. Radosevich (1979). "Social learning and deviant behavior: A specific test of a general theory." *American Sociological Review* 44:636-655.

Albrecht, G.L. (1980). "Subcontracting of youth services: An organizational strategy." In H.T. Rubin (ed.), *Juveniles in Justice: A Book of Readings* (pp. 317-331). Santa Monica, CA: Goodyear.

Allen, P. (1994). *OJJDP Model Programs 1993*. Washington, DC: U.S. Department of Justice.

Altschuler, D.M. (1998). "Intermediate sanctions and community treatment for serious and violent juvenile offenders." In R. Loeber and Farrington, D.P. (eds.), *Serious & Violent Juvenile Offenders: Risk Factors and Succssful Interventions* (pp. 367-385). Thousand Oaks, CA: Sage.

Altschuler, D.M. and T.L. Armstrong (1994). *Intensive Aftercare for High-risk Juveniles: Policies and Procedures*. Washington, DC: Office of Juvenile Justice and Delinquency Prevention.

Altschuler, D. and P.J. Brounstein (1991). "Patterns of drug use, drug trafficking and other delinquency among inner city adolescent males in Washington, DC." *Criminology* 29:589-622.

American Dietetics Association (1984). "Position paper of the American Dietetics Association on diet and criminal behavior." *Journal of the American Dietetics Association* 85:361-362.

Amir, M. (1971). *Patterns in Forcible Rape*. Chicago: University of Chicago Press.

Anderson, E. (1990). *Street Wise: Race, Class, and Change in an Urban Community*. Chicago: University of Chicago Press.

Anderson, E. (1994). "The code of the streets." *Atlantic Monthly* 273(5):81-94.

Andrews, D.A. and J. Bonta (1998). *The Psychology of Criminal Conduct*, 2nd ed. Cincinnati: Anderson.

Andrews, D.A., I. Zinger, R.D. Hoge, J. Bonta, P. Gendreau and F.T. Cullen (1990). "Does correctional treatment work? A clinically relevant and psychologically informed meta-analysis." *Criminology* 28:369-404.

Anglin, M.D. (1988). "The efficacy of civil commitment in treating narcotics addiction." *Journal of Drug Issues* 18:527-547.

Anglin, M.D. and Y. Hser (1990). "Treatment of drug abuse." In Tonry, M. and J.Q. Wilson (eds.) *Drugs and Crime* (pp. 393-460). Chicago: University of Chicago Press.

Anglin, M.D. and Y. Hser (1987). "Addicted women and crime." *Criminology* 25:359-397.

Anglin, M.D. and W.H. McGlothlin (1984). "Outcome of narcotic addict treatment in California." In Tims, F.M. and J.P. Ludford (eds.) *Drug Abuse Treatment Evaluation: Strategies, Progress and Prospects* (pp. 106-128). Washington, DC: National Institute on Drug Abuse.

Anglin, M.D. and W.H. McGlothlin (1985). "Methadone maintenance in California: A decade's experience." In Brill, L. and C. Winnick (eds.), *Yearbook of Substance Use and Abuse* (pp. 219-280). New York: Human Sciences Press.

Anglin, M.D. and G. Speckart (1986). "Narcotics use, property crime, and dealing: Structural dynamics across the addiction career." *Journal of Quantitative Criminology* 2:355-375.

Anglin, M.D. and G. Speckart (1988). "Narcotics use and crime: A multisample, multimethod analysis." *Criminology* 26:197-233.

Anglin, M.D., G.R. Speckart, M.W. Booth and T.M. Ryan (1989). "Consequences and costs of shutting off methadone." *Addictive Behaviors* 14:307-326.

Aries, P. (1962). *Centuries of Childhood*. New York: Knopf.

Arizona Prevention Resource Center (1994). *G.R.E.A.T. Pre/Post Testing and Focus Groups Evaluation Report*. Washington, DC: National Institute of Justice.

Arnette, J.L. and M.C. Walsleben (1998). "Combating fear and restoring safety in schools." *Juvenile Justice Bulletin*. Washington, DC: Office of Juvenile Justice and Delinquency Prevention.

Austin, J. (1993). *Reforming Florida's Unjust, Costly and Ineffective Sentencing Laws*. San Francisco: National Council on Crime and Delinquency.

Austin, J., B. Krisberg, R. DeComo, S. Rudenstine and D. DelRosario (1995). "Juveniles taken into custody: Fiscal year 1993." *OJJDP Statistics Report*. Washington, DC: Office of Juvenile Justice and Delinquency Prevention.

Bailey, W.C. and R.D. Peterson (1981). "Legal versus extra-legal determinants of juvenile court dispositions." *Juvenile and Family Court Journal* 32:41-59.

Baines, M. and C. Alder (1996). "Are girls more difficult to work with? Youth workers' perspectives in juvenile justice and related areas." *Crime & Delinquency* 42:467-485.

Ball, J.C., E. Corty, R. Bond and A. Tommasello (1987). "The reduction of intravenous heroin use, nonopiate abuse and crime during methadone maintenance treatment—Further findings." Paper presented at the annual meeting of the Committee on Problems on Drug Dependency, Philadelphia, PA.

Ball, J.C., J.W. Shaffer and D.N. Nurco (1983). "The day-to-day criminality of heroin addicts in Baltimore: A study in the continuity of offense rates." *Drug and Alcohol Dependence* 12:119-142.

Bandura, A. and R.H. Walters (1963). *Social Learning and Personality Development*. New York: Holt, Rinehart and Winston.

Barnum, R. (1987). "The development of responsibility: Implications for juvenile justice." In F.X. Hartmann (ed.), *From Children to Citizens: Volume II: The Role of the Juvenile Court* (pp. 67-79). New York: Springer-Verlag.

Baron, R., F. Feeney and W. Thornton. (1976). "Preventing delinquency through diversion." In R.M. Carter and M.W. Klein (eds.), *Back on the Street: The Diversion of Juvenile Offenders* (pp. 329-338). Englewood Cliffs, NJ: Prentice Hall.

Bartollas, C. (1985). *Correctional Treatment: Theory and Practice*. Englewood Cliffs, NJ: Prentice Hall.

Bartollas, C. and C.M. Sieverdes (1981). "The victimized white in a juvenile correctional system." *Crime & Delinquency* 27: 534-543.

Bastian, L.D. and B.M. Taylor (1991). *School Crime: A National Crime Victimization Survey Report*. Washington, DC: Bureau of Justice Statistics.

Bayley, David H. (1998). *What Works in Policing*. New York: Oxford University Press.

Bazemore, G. and T.J. Dicker (1994). "Explaining detention worker orientation: Individual characteristics, occupational conditions, and organizational environment." *Journal of Criminal Justice* 22:297-312.

Bazemore, G., T.J. Dicker and R. Nyhan (1994). "Juvenile justice reform and the difference it makes: An exploratory study of the impact of policy change on detention worker attitudes." *Crime & Delinquency* 40:37-53.

Bazemore, G. and D. Maloney (1994). "Rehabilitating community service: Toward restorative service sanctions in a balanced justice system." *Federal Probation* 58(1):24-35.

Bazemore, G. and S. Senjo (1997). "Police encounters with juveniles revisited." *Policing* 20:60-82.

Bazemore, G. and M.S. Umbreit, M.S. (1994). *Balanced and Restorative Justice: Program Summary*. Washington, DC: Office of Juvenile Justice and Delinquency Prevention.

Beck, A.J., S.A. Kline and L.A. Greenfeld (1988). "Survey of youth in custody, 1987." *Bureau of Justice Statistics Special Report.* Washington, DC: U.S. Department of Justice.

Beldon, E. (1920). *Courts in the U.S. Hearing Children's Cases.* Washington, DC: U.S. Children's Bureau.

Belknap, J. (1984). "The effect of local policy on the sentencing patterns of state wards." *Justice Quarterly* 1: 549-561.

Belknap, J. (1987). "Routine activity theory and the risk of rape: Analyzing ten years of National Crime Survey data." *Criminal Justice Policy Review* 2:337-356.

Belknap, J., K. Holsinger and M. Dunn (1997). "Understanding incarcerated girls: The results of a focus group study." *Prison Journal* 77:381-404.

Bell, D. and K. Lang (1985). "The intake dispositions of juvenile offenders." *Journal of Research in Crime and Delinquency* 22:309-328.

Bellis, D.J. (1981). *Heroin and Politicians: The Failure of Public Policy to Control Addiction in America.* Westport, CT: Greenwood.

Belsky, J. (1978). "Three theoretical models of child abuse: A critical review." *Child Abuse & Neglect* 2:37-49.

Bennett, T. (1986). "Situational crime prevention from the offender's perspective." In K. Heal and G. Laycock (eds.), *Situational Crime Prevention: From Theory to Practice.* London: Her Majesty's Stationery Office.

Bennett, T. and R. Wright (1984a). *Burglars on Burglary.* Brookfield, VT: Gower.

Bennett, T. and R. Wright (1984b). "The relationship between alcohol use and burglary." *British Journal of Addiction* 79:431-437.

Bentham, J. (1948). *An Introduction to the Principles of Morals and Legislation.* New York: Hafner.

Berger, R.J. and M. Gold (1978). "An evaluation of a juvenile court volunteer program." *Journal of Community Psychology* 6:328-333.

Bilchik, S. (1998). "A juvenile justice system for the 21st century." *Crime & Delinquency* 44:89-101.

Bishop, D.M., C.E. Frazier, L. Lanza-Kaduce and L. Winner (1996). "The transfer of juveniles to criminal court: Does it make a difference?" *Crime & Delinquency* 42:171-191.

Bjerregaard, B. (1989). "Televised testimony as an alternative in child sexual abuse cases." *Criminal Law Bulletin* 25:164-175.

Bjerregaard, B. and C. Smith (1993). "Gender differences in gang participation, delinquency, and substance use." *Journal of Quantitative Criminology* 4:329-355.

Black, D. (1980). *The Manners and Customs of the Police.* New York: Academic Press. Black, D. and A. Reiss, Jr. (1970). "Police control of juveniles." *American Sociological Review* 35:63-77.

Black, D. and A. Reiss, Jr. (1970). "Police control of juveniles." *American Sociological Review* 35:63-77.

Bloch, H.A. and A. Niederhoffer (1958). *The Gang: A Study in Adolescent Behavior.* New York: Philosophical Library.

Block, C.R. and R. Block (1992). "Street gang crime in Chicago." *Research in Brief.* Washington, DC: National Institute of Justice.

Blomberg, T.G. (1979). "Diversion from juvenile court: A review of the evidence." In F.L. Faust and P.J. Brantingham (eds.), *Juvenile Justice Philosophy: Readings, Cases and Comments*, 2nd ed. (pp. 415-429). St. Paul, MN: West.

Blomberg, T.G. and S.L. Carabelo (1979). "Accelerated family intervention in juvenile justice: An exploration and a recommendation for constraint." *Crime & Delinquency* 25:497-502.

Blumberg, A. (1967). "The practice of law as a confidence game: Organizational cooptation of profession." *Law and Society Review* 1:15-39.

Blumberg, A.S. (1979). *Criminal Justice: Issues and Ironies* (2nd ed.). New York: New Viewpoints.

Bohnstedt, M. (1978). "Answers to three questions about juvenile diversion." *Journal of Research in Crime and Delinquency* 15:109-123.

Bonnett, P.L. and C.L. Pfeiffer (1978). "Biochemical diagnosis for delinquent behavior." In L.J. Hippchen (ed.), *Ecologic-Biochemical Approaches to Treatment of Delinquents and Criminals* (pp. 183-205). New York: Van Nostrand Reinhold.

Bookin-Weiner, H. and R. Horowitz (1983). "The end of the youth gang: Fad or fact?" *Criminology* 21:585-602.

Booth, A. and D.W. Osgood (1993). "The influence of testosterone on deviance in adulthood: Assessing and explaining the relationship." *Criminology* 31:93-118.

Bordua, D.J. (1958). "Juvenile delinquency and 'anomie': An attempt at replication." *Social Problems* 6:230-238.

Bortner, M.A. (1986). "Traditional rhetoric, organizational realities: Remand of juveniles to adult court." *Crime & Delinquency* 32:53-73.

Botvin, G.J. (1990). "Substance abuse prevention: Theory, practice and effectiveness." In Tonry, N. and J.Q. Wilson (eds.) *Drugs and Crime* (pp. 461-520). Chicago: University of Chicago Press.

Botvin, G.J., E. Baker, N. Renick, A.D. Filazzola and E.M. Botvin (1984). "A cognitive-behavioral approach to substance abuse prevention." *Addictive Behaviors* 9:137-147.

Botvin, G.J. and L. Dusenbury (1989). "Substance abuse prevention and the promotion of competence." In Bond, L.A. and B.E. Compas (eds.) *Primary Prevention and Promotion in the Schools* (pp. 146-178). Newbury Park, CA: Sage.

Botvin, G.J. and A. Eng (1980). "A comprehensive school-based smoking prevention program." *Journal of School Health* 50:209-213.

Botvin, G.J. and A. Eng (1982). "The efficacy of a multicomponent approach to the prevention of cigarette smoking." *Preventive Medicine* 11:199-211.

Botvin, G.J., A. Eng and C.L. Williams (1980). "Preventing the onset of cigarette smoking through life skills training." *Journal of Preventive Medicine* 9:135-143.

Botvin, G.J., N. Renick and E. Baker (1983). "The effects of scheduling format and booster sessions on a broad spectrum psychological approach to smoking prevention." *Journal of Behavioral Medicine* 6:359-379.

Bowker, L.H. (1980). *Prison Victimization*. New York: Elsevier.

Bowker, L.H. and M.W. Klein (1983). "The etiology of female juvenile delinquency and gang membership: A test of psychological and social structural explanations." *Adolescence* 18:739-751.

Braithwaite, J. (1989). *Crime, Shame and Reintegration.* Cambridge, England: Cambridge University Press.

Braswell, M. and T. Seay (1984). *Approaches to Counseling and Psychotherapy,* 2nd ed. Prospect Heights, IL: Waveland.

Brennan, P.A., S.A. Mednick and J. Volavka (1995). "Biomedical factors in crime." In J.Q. Wilson and J. Petersilia (eds.), *Crime* (pp. 65-90). San Francisco: ICS Press.

Brenzel, B.M. (1983). *Daughters of the State: A Social Portrait of the First Reform School for Girls in North America, 1856-1903.* Cambridge, MA: MIT Press.

Brown, S.E. (1984). "Police responses to wife beating: Neglect of a crime of violence." *Journal of Criminal Justice* 12:277-288.

Brown, W.K. (1978). "Black gangs as family extensions." *International Journal of Offender Therapy and Comparative Criminology* 22:39-45.

Browning, S.L., F.T. Cullen, L. Cao, R. Kopache and T.J. Stevenson (1994). "Race and getting hassled by the police: A research note." *Police Studies* 17 (1): 1-11.

Brunner, H.G. (1996). "MAOA deficiency and abnormal behavior: Perspectives on an association." In G.R. Bock and J.A. Goode (eds.), *Genetics of Criminal and Antisocial Behavior* (pp. 155-163). Chichester, England: John Wiley and Sons.

Buerger, M.E. (1994). "A tale of two targets: Limitations of community anticrime actions." *Crime & Delinquency* 40:411-436.

Bureau of Justice Assistance (1993). *An Introduction to the National DARE Parent Program.* Washington, DC: Bureau of Justice Assistance.

Burgess, A.W. and A.T. Laszlo (1976). "When the prosecutrix is a child: The victim consultant in cases of sexual assault." In E.C. Viano, *Victims & Society.* Washington, DC: Visage Press.

Burgess, E.W. (1928). "Factors influencing success or failure on parole." In Bruce, A.A., A.J. Harno, E.W. Burgess and L. Landesco (eds.), *The Workings of the Indeterminate-Sentence Law and the Parole System in Illinois.* Springfield, IL: State Board of Parole.

Burgess, E.W. (1925). "The growth of the city." In R.E. Park, E.W. Burgess and R.D. McKenzie (eds.), *The City.* Chicago: University of Chicago Press.

Burgess, R.L. and R.L. Akers (1968). "Differential association-reinforcement theory of criminal behavior." *Social Problems* 14:128-147.

Bursik, R.J. and H.G. Grasmick (1993). *Neighborhoods and Crime: The Dimensions of Effective Community Control.* New York: Lexington.

Butts, J.A. (1994). "Offenders in juvenile court, 1992." *Juvenile Justice Bulletin.* Washington, DC: U.S. Department of Justice.

Butts, J.A. (1996). "Offenders in juvenile court, 1994." *Juvenile Justice Bulletin.* Washington, DC: Office of Juvenile Justice and Delinquency Prevention.

Butts, J.A. and E. Poe, E. (1993). "Offenders in juvenile court, 1990." *Juvenile Justice Bulletin.* Washington, DC: U.S. Department of Justice.

Butts, J.A. and H.N. Snyder (1992). "Restitution and juvenile recidivism." *Juvenile Justice Bulletin: OJJDP Update on Research.* Washington, DC: U.S. Department of Justice.

Butts, J.A., H.N. Snyder, T.A. Finnegan, A.L. Aughenbaugh and R.S. Poole (1996). *Juvenile Court Statistics 1994.* Washington, DC: U.S. Department of Justice.

Butts, J.A., H.N. Snyder, T.A. Finnegan, A.L. Aughenbaugh, N.J. Tierney, D.P. Sullivan, R.S. Poole, M.S. Sickmund and E.C. Poe (1994). *Juvenile Court Statistics 1991*. Washington, DC: U.S. Department of Justice.

Bynum, T. (1996). "Reducing school violence in Detroit." Paper presented at the National Institute of Justice Crime Prevention Conference, Washington, DC.

Cabana, D.A. (1996). *Death at Midnight: The Confession of an Executioner*. Boston: Northeastern University Press.

California, State of (1972). *Annotated Welfare and Institutions Code*. St. Paul, MN: West.

Camp, C.G. and G.M. Camp (1984). *Private Sector Involvement in Prison Services and Operations*. Washington, DC: U.S. Department of Justice.

Campbell, A. (1984). "Girls' talk: The social representation of aggression by female gang members." *Criminal Justice and Behavior* 11:139-156.

Campbell, A. (1990). "Female participation in gangs." In Huff, C.R. (ed.), *Gangs in America* (pp. 163-182). Newbury Park, CA: Sage.

Carbone, V.J. (1983). "The effectiveness of short duration timeouts in a juvenile detention facility." *Juvenile and Family Court Journal* 34:75-81.

Caron, N.A. (1980). *Response Time Analysis: Synopsis*. Washington, DC: U.S. Department of Justice.

Carpenter, C., B. Glassner, B.D. Johnson and J. Loughlin (1988). *Kids, Drugs, and Crime*. Lexington, MA: Lexington Books.

Carroll, L. (1974). *Hacks, Blacks, and Cons: Race Relations in a Maximum Security Prison*. Lexington, MA: D.C. Heath.

Cavan, R.S. and T.N. Ferdinand (1981). *Juvenile Delinquency*, 4th ed. New York: Harper and Row.

Chaiken, J.M. and M.R. Chaiken (1982). *Varieties of Criminal Behavior*. Santa Monica, CA: RAND.

Chandler, K.A., C.D. Chapman, M.R. Rand and B.M. Taylor (1998). *Students' Reports of School Crime: 1989 and 1995*. Washington, DC: U.S. Department of Justice.

Charters, C.A. (1994). "Volunteer work assumes a new role in public high school: Steirer v. Bethlehem Area School District." *Journal of Law and Education* 23:607-613.

Chavaria, F.P. (1997). "Probation and cognitive skills." *Federal Probation* 61:57-60.

Cherniss, C. (1980). *Staff Burnout: Job Stress in the Human Services*. Beverly Hills, CA: Sage.

Chesney-Lind, M. (1977). "Judicial paternalism and the female status offender: Training women to know their place." *Crime & Delinquency* 23:121-130.

Chesney-Lind, M. (1978). "Young women in the arms of the law." In L.H. Bowker (ed.), *Women, Crime and the Criminal Justice System* (pp. 171-196). Lexington, MA: Lexington Books.

Chesney-Lind, M. (1987). "Girls' crime and woman's place: Toward a feminist model of female delinquency." Paper presented at the annual meeting of the American Society of Criminology, Montreal, Canada.

Chesney-Lind, M. and R.G. Shelden (1992). *Girls, Delinquency, and Juvenile Justice*. Pacific Grove, CA: Brooks/Cole.

Chilton, R.J. (1964). "Continuities in delinquency area research: A comparison of studies for Baltimore, Detroit and Indianapolis." *American Sociological Review* 29:71-83.

Chin, K. (1990). *Chinese Subculture and Criminality: Nontraditional Crime Groups in America.* Westport, CT: Greenwood.

Chin, K., J. Fagan and R.J. Kelly (1992). "Patterns of Chinese gang extortion." *Justice Quarterly* 9:625-646.

Christiansen, K.O. (1974). "Seriousness of criminality and concordance among Danish twins." In R. Hood (ed.). *Crime, Criminology, and Public Policy.* New York: Free Press.

Chused, R. (1973). "The juvenile court process: A study of three New Jersey counties." *Rutgers Law Review* 26:488-615.

Clark, C.L., D.W. Aziz and D.L. MacKenzie (1994). *Shock Incarceration in New York: Focus on Treatment.* Washington, DC: U.S. Department of Justice.

Clark, R.D. and S.P. Lab (1995). "The relationship between victimization and offending among junior and senior high school students." Paper presented at the Academy of Criminal Justice Sciences Annual Meeting, Boston, MA.

Clarke, R.V. and M. Felson (1993). *Routine Activities and Rational Choice.* New Brunswick, NJ: Transaction.

Clarke, S.H. and G.G. Koch (1980). "Juvenile court: Therapy or crime control, and do lawyers make a difference." *Law and Society Review* 14:263-308.

Clarke, J.P. and L.L. Tifft (1966). "Polygraph and interview validation of self-reported deviant behavior." *American Sociological Review* 31:516-523.

Clayton, R.R., A. Cattarello and K.P. Walden (1991). "Sensation seeking as a potential mediating variable for school-based prevention interventions: A two-year follow-up of DARE." *Journal of Health Communications* 3:229-239.

Clear, T.R. (1994). *Harm in American Penology: Offenders, Victims, and Their Communities.* Albany, NY: SUNY Press.

Clear, T.R., V.B. Clear and A.A. Braga (1997). "Correctional alternatives for drug offenders in an era of overcrowding. In M. McShane and F.P. Williams (eds.), *Criminal Justice: Contemporary Literature in Theory and Practice* (pp. 24-44). New York: Garland.

Clemente, F. and M.B. Kleiman (1977). "Fear of crime in the United States: A multivariate analysis." *Social Forces* 56:519-531.

Cloward, R. and L. Ohlin (1960). *Delinquency and Opportunity: A Theory of Delinquent Gangs.* New York: Free Press.

Cohen, A.K. (1955). *Delinquent Boys: The Culture of the Gang.* Glencoe, IL: Free Press.

Cohen, J. (1983). "Incapacitating criminals: Recent research findings." *National Institute of Justice Research in Brief.* Washington, DC: National Institute of Justice.

Cohen, L.E. and M. Felson (1979). "Social changes and crime rate trends: A routine activities approach." *American Sociological Review* 44:588-608.

Cohen, L.E. and J.R. Kluegel (1978). "Determinants of juvenile court dispositions: Ascriptive and achieved factors in two metropolitan courts." *American Sociological Review* 43:162-176.

Cohen, L.E. and J.R. Kluegel (1979). "Selecting delinquents for adjudication: An analysis of intake screening decisions in two metropolitan juvenile courts." *Journal of Research in Crime and Delinquency* 16:143-163.

Cohen, M.A. (1994). *The Monetary Value of Saving a High-Risk Youth*. Washington, DC: The Urban Institute.

Cohen, S. (1979). "Community control—A new utopia." *New Society* 15:609-611.

Collier, P. and D. Horowitz (1985). "Getting away with murder." In J.J. Sullivan and J.L. Victor (eds.), *Annual Editions: Criminal Justice 85/86* (pp. 187-195). Guilford, CN: Dushkin.

Collins, J.J. (1989). "Alcohol and interpersonal violence: Less than meets the eye." In Wiener, N.A. and M.E. Wolfgang (eds.) *Pathways to Criminal Violence* (pp. 49-67). Newbury Park, CA: Sage.

Collins, J.J., R.L. Hubbard and J.V. Rachal (1985). "Expensive drug use and illegal income: A test of explanatory hypotheses." *Criminology* 23:743-764.

Conger, R.D. and R.L. Simons (1997). "Life-course contingencies in the development of adolescent antisocial behavior: A matching law approach." In T.P. Thornberry (ed.), *Developmental Theories of Crime and Delinquency* (pp.). New Brunswick, NJ: Transaction.

Conley, D.J. (1994). "Adding color to a black and white picture: Using qualitative data to explain racial disproportionality in the juvenile justice system." *Journal of Research in Crime and Delinquency* 31:135-148.

Conrad, J.P. (1982). "Can corrections be rehabilitated." *Federal Probation* 46(2):3-8.

Cooley, C.H. (1902). *Human Nature and the Social Order*. New York: Scribner.

Coombs, R.H. (1981). "Back on the streets: Therapeutic communities' impact upon drug abusers." *American Journal of Alcohol Abuse* 8:185-201.

Cooper, C.N. (1967). "The Chicago YMCA Detached Workers: Current status of an action program." In M.W. Klein (ed.), *Juvenile Gangs in Context* (pp. 183-193). Englewood Cliffs, NJ: Prentice Hall.

Coordinating Council on Juvenile Justice and Delinquency Prevention (1996). *Combating Violence and Delinquency: The National Juvenile Justice Action Plan: Report*. Washington, DC: U.S. Department of Justice.

Corbett, R.P. (1996). "When community corrections means business: Introducing "reinventing" themes to probation and parole." *Federal Probation* 60 (1): 36-42.

Cornish, D.B. and R.V. Clarke (1986). *The Reasoning Criminal*. New York: Springer-Verlag.

Cortés, J.B. (1972). *Delinquency and Crime*. New York: Seminar Press.

Costanzo, M. (1997). *Just Revenge: Costs and Consequences of the Death Penalty*. New York: St. Martin's Press.

Couch, A.J. (1974). "Diverting the status offender from the juvenile court." *Juvenile Justice* 25:18-22.

Cox, S.M, W.S. Davidson and T.S. Bynum (1995). "A meta-analytic assessment of delinquency-related outcomes of alternative education programs." *Crime & Delinquency* 41:219-234.

Crank, J.P. and M. Caldero (1991). "The production of occupational stress in medium-sized police agencies: A survey of line officers in eight municipal departments." *Journal of Criminal Justice* 19:339-349.

Cromwell, P.F., J.N. Olson and D.W. Avary (1991). *Breaking and Entering: An Ethnographic Analysis of Burglary*. Newbury Park, CA: Sage.

Cronin, R.C. (1994). *Boot Camps for Adult and Juvenile Offenders: Overview and Update*. Washington, DC: National Institute of Justice.

Crowe, R.R. (1972). "The adopted offspring of women criminal offenders." *Archives of General Psychiatry* 27:600-603.

Cullen, F.T. and K.E. Gilbert (1982). *Reaffirming Rehabilitation*. Cincinnati: Anderson.

Cullen, F.T. and J.P. Wright (1995). "The future of corrections." In Maguire, B. and P. Radosh (eds.), *The Past, Present, and Future of American Criminal Justice* (pp. 198-219). New York: General Hall.

Cullen, F.T., J.P. Wright and B.K. Applegate (1996). "Control in the community: The limits of reform? In A.T. Harland (ed.), *Choosing Correctional Options that Work: Defining the Demand and Evaluating the Supply* (pp. 69-116). Thousand Oaks, CA: Sage.

Cullen, F.T., J.P. Wright, S. Brown, M.M. Moon, M.B. Blankenship and B.K. Applegate (1998). "Public support for early intervention programs: Implications for a progressive policy agenda." *Crime & Delinquency* 44:187-204.

Cummings, S. (1993). "Anatomy of a wilding gang." In Cummings, S. and D.J. Monti (eds.), *Gangs: The Origins and Impact of Contemporary Youth Gangs in the United States* (pp. 49-74). Albany, NY: SUNY Press.

Cummings, S. and D.J. Monti (1993). "Public policy and gangs: Social science and the urban underclass." In Cummings, S. and D.J. Monti (eds.), *Gangs: The Origins and Impact of Contemporary Youth Gangs in the United States* (pp. 305-320). Albany, NY: SUNY Press.

Curley, T. (1997, April 21). "Easing teens into the driver's seat." *USA Today* (p. 3a).

Curry, G.D. (1996). *National Gang Surveys: A Review of Methods and Findings*. Tallahassee, FL: National Youth Gang Center.

Curry, G.D., R.A. Ball and S.H. Decker (1996). "Estimating the national scope of gang crimes from law enforcement data." *National Institute of Justice Research in Brief*. Washington, DC: National Institute of Justice.

Curry, G.D., R.J. Fox, R.A. Ball and D. Stone (1993). *National Asssessment of Law Enforcement Anti-Gang Information Resources*. Washington, DC: National Institute of Justice.

Curry, G.D., R.A. Ball, R.J. Fox and D. Stone (1992). *National Assessment of Law Enforcement Anti-Gang Information Resources: Final Report*. Washington, DC: National Institute of Justice.

Curry, G.D. and S.H. Decker (1998). *Confronting Gangs: Crime and Community*. Los Angeles: Roxbury.

Curtis, L.A. (1974). *Criminal Violence: National Patterns and Behavior*. Lexington, MA: D.C. Heath and Company.

Dahrendorf, R. (1959). *Class and Conflict in Industrial Society*. Stanford: Stanford University Press.

Dalton, K. (1964). *The Premenstrual Syndrome*. Springfield, IL: Charles C Thomas.

Dannefer, D. and R.K. Schutt (1982). "Race and juvenile justice processing in court and police agencies." *American Journal of Sociology* 87:1113-1132.

Davis, S.M and M.D. Schwartz (1987). *Children's Rights and the Law.* Lexington, MA: D.C. Heath.

Davis, S.M., E.S. Scott, W. Wadlington and C.H. Whitebread (1997). *Children in the Legal System: Cases and Materials,* 2nd ed. Westbury, NY: Foundation Press.

Decker, S. (1985). "A systematic analysis of diversion: Net-widening and beyond." *Journal of Criminal Justice* 13:207-216.

Decker, S.H., S. Pennell and A. Caldwell (1997). *Illegal Firearms: Access and Use by Arrestees.* Washington, DC: U.S. Department of Justice.

Decker, S.H. and B. Van Winkle (1994). "'Slinging dope': The role of gangs and gang members in drug sales." *Justice Quarterly* 11:583-604.

Decker, S.H. and B. Van Winkle (1996). *Life in the Gang: Family, Friends, and Violence.* New York: Cambridge University Press.

Decker, S., R. Wright and R. Logie (1993). "Perceptual deterrence among active residential burglars: A research note." *Criminology* 31:135-147.

DeFleur, M.L. and R. Quinney (1966). "A reformulation of Sutherland's differential association theory and a strategy for empirical verification." *Journal of Research in Crime and Delinquency* 3:1-22.

DeFrances, C.J. and K.J. Strom (1997). *Juveniles Prosecuted in State Criminal Courts.* Washington, DC: U.S. Department of Justice.

DeJong, W. (1987). "A short-term evaluation of project DARE (Drug Abuse Resistance Education): Preliminary indications of effectiveness." *Journal of Drug Education* 17:279-294.

DeJong, W. (1993). "Building the peace: The Resolving Conflicts Creatively Program (RCCP)." NIJ Program Focus. Washington, DC: Department of Justice.

del Carmen, R.V., M. Parker and F.P. Reddington (1998). *Briefs of Leading Cases in Juvenile Justice.* Cincinnati: Anderson.

DeLeon, G. (1984). "Program-based evaluation research in therapeutic communities." In Tims, F.M. and J.P. Ludford (eds.) *Drug Abuse Treatment Evaluation: Strategies, Progress and Prospects* (pp. 69-87). Washington, DC: National Institute on Drug Abuse.

DeLeon, G. and M.S. Rosenthal (1989). "Treatment in residential therapeutic communities." In Kleber, H. (ed.) *Treatment of Psychiatric Disorders: A Task Force Report of the American Psychiatric Association*, Vol. 2. Washington, DC: American Psychiatric Association.

DeLong, J.V. (1972). "Treatment and rehabilitation." *Dealing with Drug Abuse: A Report to the Ford Foundation.* New York: Praeger.

Dembo, R. and M. Dertke (1986). "Work environment correlates of staff stress in a youth detention facility." *Criminal Justice and Behavior* 13:328-344.

Denno, D.W. (1996). "Legal implications of genetics and crime research." In G.R. Bock and J.A. Goode (eds.), *Genetics of Criminal and Antisocial Behavior* (pp.248-255). Chichester, England: John Wiley and Sons.

Dentler, R.A. and L.J. Monroe (1961). "Social correlates of early adolescent theft." *American Sociological Review* 26:733-743.

Dietrich, S.G. (1979). "The probation officer as therapist." *Federal Probation* 43(2):14-19.

Dinitz, S., B. Kay and W.C. Reckless (1958). "Group gradients in delinquency potential and achievement scores of sixth graders." *American Journal of Orthopsychiatry* 28:598-556.

Doerner, W.G. (1978). "The index of southernness revisited." *Criminology* 16:47-56.

Doerner, W.G. and S.P. Lab (1998). *Victimology*, 2nd ed. Cincinnati: Anderson.

DuBow, F., E. McCabe and G. Kaplan (1979). *Reactions to Crime: A Critical Review of the Literature*. Washington, DC: U.S. Government Printing Office.

Duffee, D.E. and B.E. Carlson (1996). "Competing value premises for the provision of drug treatment to probationers." *Crime & Delinquency* 42:574-592.

Dunford, F.W. (1977). "Police diversion: An illusion?" *Criminology* 15:335-352.

Dunford, F.W., D.W. Osgood and H.F. Weichselbaum (1982). *National Evaluation of Diversion Projects*. Washington, DC: U.S. Department of Justice.

Durham, A.M. (1994). *Crisis and Reform: Current Issues in American Punishment*. Boston: Little, Brown.

Durkheim, E. (1933). *The Division of Labor in Society*. (Translated by G. Supson.) New York: Free Press.

Duxbury, E. (1973). *Evaluation of Youth Service Bureaus*. Sacramento: California Youth Authority.

Eck, J.E. and W. Spelman (1987). "Who ya gonna call?: The police as problem-busters." *Crime & Delinquency* 33:31-52.

Edelman, M.W. (1994). "If the child is safe." In Brown, R. (ed.), *Children in Crisis* (pp. 238-247). New York: H.W. Wilson.

Ehrenkranz, J., E. Bliss and M.H. Sheard (1974). "Plasma testosterone: Correlation with aggressive behavior and social dominance in man." *Psychosomatic Medicine* 36:469-475.

Eiser, C. and J.R. Eiser (1988). *Drug Education in Schools*. New York: Springer-Verlag.

Elliott, D.S. (1985). "The assumption that theories can be combined with increased explanatory power: Theoretical integrations." In R.F. Meier (ed.), *Theoretical Methods in Criminology* (pp. 123-150). Beverly Hills: Sage.

Elliott, D.S., S.S. Ageton and R.J. Canter (1979). "An integrated theoretical perspective on delinquent behavior." *Journal of Research in Crime and Delinquency* 16:3-27.

Elliott, D.S., S.S. Ageton, D. Huizinga, B.A. Knowles and R.J. Canter (1983). *The Prevalence and Incidence of Delinquent Behavior: 1976-1980*. Boulder, CO: Behavioral Research Institute.

Elliott, D.S., F.W. Dunford and B. Knowles (1978). *Diversion: A Study of Alternative Processing Practices*. Boulder, CO: Behavioral Research Institute.

Elliott, D.S. and D. Huizinga (1984). *The Relationship between Delinquent Behavior and ADM Problems*. Boulder, CO: Behavioral Research Institute.

Elliott, D.S., D. Huizinga and S.S. Ageton (1985). *Explaining Delinquency and Drug Use*. Beverly Hills: Sage.

Elliott, D.S., D.H. Huizinga and S. Menard (1989). *Multiple Problem Youth: Delinquency, Substance Use and Mental Health Problems*. New York: Springer-Verlag.

Ellis, A. (1973). *Humanistic Psychotherapy: The Rational-Emotive Approach*. New York: McGraw-Hill.

Ellis, L. (1982). "Genetics and criminal behavior: Evidence through the end of the 1970's." *Criminology* 20:43-66.

Empey, L.T. (1982). *American Delinquency: Its Meaning and Construction*. Homewood, IL: Dorsey Press.

Empey, L.T. and M.L. Erickson (1972). *The Provo Experiment: Evaluating Community Control of Delinquency*. Lexington, MA: Lexington Books.

Empey, L.T. and S.G. Lubeck (1971). *The Silverlake Experiment: Testing Delinquency Theory and Community Intervention*. Chicago: Aldine.

Ennis, P. (1967). *Criminal Victimization in the United States: A Report of a National Survey*. Washington, DC: U.S. Government Printing Office.

Erikson, E.H. (1968). *Identity, Youth and Crisis*. New York: Norton.

Erickson, M.L. (1971). "The group context of delinquent behavior." *Social Problems* 19:114-129.

Erickson, M.L.(1973). "Group violations and official delinquency: The group hazard hypothesis." *Criminology* 11:127-160.

Erickson, M.L. and G. Jensen (1977). "Delinquency is still group behavior: Toward revitalizing the group premise in the sociology of deviance." *Journal of Criminal Law and Criminology* 68:262-273.

Erlanger, H.S. (1974). "The empirical status of the subculture of violence thesis." *Social Problems* 22:280-292.

Esbensen, F. and D. Huizinga (1991). "Juvenile victimization and delinquency." *Youth and Society* 23:202-228.

Esbensen, F. and D. Huizinga (1993). "Gangs, drugs, and delinquency in a survey of urban youth." *Criminology* 31:565-590.

Esbensen, F. and D.W. Osgood (1997). "National evaluation of G.R.E.A.T." *NIJ Research in Brief*. Washington, DC: National Institute of Justice.

Estrich, S. (1994, May 5). "The wrong answer to crime." *USA Today* (p. 11A).

Ewing, C.P. (1990). *Kids Who Kill*. Lexington, MA: Lexington Books.

Eysenck, H.J. (1977). *Crime and Personality*. St. Albans: Paladin.

Fabricant, M. (1983). *Juveniles in the Family Courts*. Lexington, MA: Lexington Books

Fagan, J. (1990). "Social process of delinquency and drug use among urban gangs." In Huff, C.R. (ed.), *Gangs in America* (pp. 183-219). Newbury Park, CA: Sage.

Fagan, J. (1995). "Separating the men from the boys: The comparative advantage of juvenile versus criminal court sanctions on recidivism among adolescent felony offenders." In J.C. Howell, B. Krisberg, J.D. Hawkins and J.J. Wilson, *A Sourcebook: Serious, Violent, & Chronic Juvenile Offenders* (pp. 238-260). Thousand Oaks, CA: Sage.

Fagan, J., M. Forst and T.S. Vivona (1987). "Racial determinants of the judicial transfer decision: Prosecuting violent youth in criminal court." *Crime & Delinquency* 33:259-286.

Fagan, J. and E. Pabon (1990). "Contributions of delinquency and substance use to school dropout among inner city youths." *Youth and Society* 21:306-354.

Fagan, J. and J.G. Weis (1990). *Drug Use and Delinqeuncy among Inner City Youth*. New York: Springer-Verlag.

Fagan, J., J.G. Weis and Y. Cheng (1990). "Delinquency and substance use among inner-city students." *The Journal of Drug Issues* 20:351-402.

Farrington, D.P. (1983). "Offending from 10 to 25 years of age." In K.T. Van Dusen and S.A. Mednick (eds.), *Prospective Studies of Crime and Delinquency* (pp. 17-38). Boston: Klewer-Nijkoff.

Farrington, D.P. (1985). "Predicting self-reported and official delinquency." In D.P. Farrington and R. Tarling (eds.), *Prediction in Criminology* (pp. 150-173). Albany, NY: SUNY Press.

Fattah, E.A. (1993). "The rational choice/opportunity perspectives as a vehicle for integrating criminological and victimological theories." In Clarke, R.V. and M. Felson (eds.), *Routine Activity and Rational Choice* (pp. 225-258). New Brunswick, NJ: Transaction.

Faust, F.L. and P.J. Brantingham (1979). *Juvenile Justice Philosophy: Readings, Cases and Comments*. St. Paul, MN: West.

Federal Bureau of Investigation (1967). *Crime in the United States, 1966*. Washington, DC: U.S. Government Printing Office.

Federal Bureau of Investigation (1972). *Crime in the United States, 1971*. Washington, DC: U.S. Government Printing Office.

Federal Bureau of Investigation (1977). *Crime in the United States, 1976*. Washington, DC: U.S. Government Printing Office.

Federal Bureau of Investigation (1982). *Crime in the United States, 1981*. Washington, DC: U.S. Government Printing Office.

Federal Bureau of Investigation (1993). *Crime in the United States: Uniform Crime Reports, 1992*. Washington, DC: U.S. Department of Justice.

Federal Bureau of Investigation (1994). *Crime in the United States: Uniform Crime Reports, 1993*. Washington, DC: U.S. Department of Justice.

Federal Bureau of Investigation (1996). *Crime in the United States: Uniform Crime Reports, 1995*. Washington, DC: U.S. Department of Justice.

Federal Bureau of Investigation (1997). *Crime in the United States, 1996*. Washington, DC: U.S. Department of Justice.

Feeley, M.M. and J. Simon (1992). "The new penology: Notes on the emerging strategy of corrections and its implications." *Criminology* 30:449-474.

Feld, B.C. (1981). "Legislative policies toward the serious juvenile offender: On the virtues of automatic adulthood." *Crime & Delinquency* 27:497-521.

Feld, B.C. (1987a). "The juvenile court meets the principle of the offense: Changing juvenile justice sentencing practices." Paper presented at the 1987 Annual Meeting of the American Society of Criminology, Montreal, Quebec, Canada.

Feld, B.C. (1987b). "The juvenile court meets the principle of the offense: Legislative changes in juvenile waiver statutes." *Journal of Criminal Law and Criminology* 78:471-533.

Feld, B.C. (1988). *In re Gault* revisited: A cross-state comparison of the right to counsel in juvenile court. *Crime & Delinquency* 34:393-424.

Feld, B. (1993a). "Juvenile (in)justice and the criminal court alternative." *Crime & Delinquency* 39:403-424.

Feld, B. (1993b). *Justice for Children: The Right to Counsel and the Juvenile Courts.* Boston: Northeastern University Press.

Fenwick, C.R. (1982). "Juvenile court intake decision making: The importance of family affiliation." *Journal of Criminal Justice* 10:443-453.

Ferraro, K.F. (1995). *Fear of Crime: Interpreting Victimization Risk.* Albany, NY: SUNY Press.

Ferraro, K.F. and R.L. LaGrange (1987). "The measurement of fear of crime." *Sociological Inquiry* 57:70-101.

Feyerherm, W. (1980). "The group hazard hypothesis: A reexamination." *Journal of Research in Crime and Delinquency* 17:58-68.

Finckenauer, J.O. (1984). *Juvenile Delinquency and Corrections: The Gap between Theory and Practice.* New York: Academic Press.

Fishman, L.T. (1988). "The Vice Queens: An ethnographic study of black female gang behavior." Paper presented at the 1988 Annual Meeting of the American Society of Criminology, Chicago, IL.

Flanagan, T.J. and K.M. Jamieson (1988). *Sourcebook of Criminal Justice Statistics—1987.* Washington, DC: U.S. Department of Justice.

Flanagan, T.J. and K. McGuire (1990). *Sourcebook of Criminal Justice Statistics—1989.* Washington, DC: Bureau of Justice Statistics.

Florida, State of (1981). *Evaluation of the Juvenile Services Project.* Tallahassee, FL: Health and Human Services.

Foster, J.D., S. Dinitz and W.C. Reckless (1972). "Perceptions of stigma following public intervention for delinquent behavior." *Social Problems* 20:202-209.

Fox, J.A. (1993). "Teenage males are committing murder at an increasing rate." Mimeograph.

Fox, J.R. (1985). "Mission impossible? Social work practice with black urban youth gangs." *Social Work* 30:25-31.

Franklin II, C.W. and A.P. Franklin (1976). "Victimology revisited: A critique and suggestions for future direction." *Criminology* 14:177-214.

Frazier, C.E. and D.M. Bishop (1985). "The pretrial detention of juveniles and its impact on case dispositions." *Journal of Criminal Law and Criminology* 76:1132-1152.

Frazier, C.E. and D.M. Bishop, D.M. (1995). "Reflections on race effects in juvenile justice." In K.K. Leonard, C.E. Pope and W.H. Feyerherm, *Minorities in Juvenile Justice* (pp. 16-46). Thousand Oaks, CA: Sage.

Friedrich, R.J. (1983). "Police use of force: Individuals, situations, and organizations." In C.B. Klockars (ed.), *Thinking about Police: Contemporary Readings* (pp. 302-313). New York: McGraw-Hill.

Fritsch, E.J., T.J. Caeti and C. Hemmens (1996). "Spare the needle but not the punishment: The incarceration of waived youth in Texas prisons." *Crime & Delinquency* 42:593-609.

Fuller, J.R. (1998). *Criminal Justice: A Peacemaking Perspective.* Boston: Allyn & Bacon.

Fuller, J.R. and W.M. Norton (1993). "Juvenile diversion: The impact of program philosophy on net widening." *Journal of Crime and Justice* 16:29-46.

Gallup, G. (1993). *The Gallup Poll Monthly*, No. 339. Princeton, NJ: The Gallup Poll.

Garbarino, J. and G. Gilliam (1980). *Understanding Abusive Families*. Lexington, MA: Lexington Books.

Garfinkel, H. (1956). "Conditions of successful status degradation ceremonies." *American Journal of Sociology* 61:420-424.

Garofalo, J. and K.J. Connelly (1980). "Dispute resolution centers, part I: Major features and processes." *Criminal Justice Abstracts* 12:416-436.

Garrett, C.J. (1985). "Effects of residential treatment of adjudicated delinquents: A meta-analysis." *Journal of Research in Crime and Delinquency* 22:287-308.

Garry, E.M. (1996). *Truancy: First Step to a Lifetime of Problems*. Washington, DC: U.S. Department of Justice.

Gastil, R.D. (1971). "Homicide and a regional subsulture of violence." *American Sociological Review* 36:412-427.

Gates, L.B. and W.M. Rohe (1987). "Fear and reactions to crime: A revised model." *Urban Affairs Quarterly* 22:425-453.

Gay, B.W. and J.W. Marquart (1993). "Jamaican Posses: A new form of organized crime." *Journal of Crime and Justice* 16:139-170.

Geary, D.P. (1983). "Nutrition, chemicals and criminal behavior: Some psychological aspects of anti-social conduct." *Juvenile and Family Court Journal* 34:9-13.

Geiselman, R.E., G. Bornstein and K.J. Saywitz (1992). "New approach to interviewing children: A test of its effectiveness." *NIJ Research in Brief*. Washington, DC: U.S. Department of Justice.

Geller, W.A. (1983). "Deadly force: What we know." In C.B. Klockars (ed.), *Thinking about Police: Contemporary Readings* (pp. 313-331). New York: McGraw-Hill.

Geller, W.A. (1998). "As a blade of grass cuts through stone: Helping rebuild urban neighborhoods through unconventional police-community partnerships." *Crime & Delinquency* 44: 154-177.

Geller, W.A. and H. Toch (1996). "Understanding and controlling police abuse of force." In W.A. Geller & Toch, H. (eds.), *Police Violence: Understanding and Controlling Police Abuse of Force* (pp. 292-328). New Haven, CT: Yale University

Gelles, R.J. (1980). "Violence in the family: A review of research in the 70's." *Journal of Marriage and the Family* 42:873-885.

Gelles, R.J. and C. P. Cornell (1990). *Intimate Violence in Families*. Beverly Hills: Sage.

Gemma, P.B. Jr. (1994, May 5). "Bring back the switch." *USA Today* (p. 10A).

Gemignani, R.J. (1994). "Juvenile correctional education: A time for change." *Juvenile Justice Bulletin*. Washington, DC: U.S. Department of Justice.

Gendreau, P. (1996). The principles of effective intervention with offenders. In A.T. Harland (ed.), *Choosing Correctional Options that Work: Defining the Demand and Evaluating the Supply*. (pp. 117-130). Thousand Oaks, CA: Sage.

Gendreau, P., F.T. Cullen and J. Bonta (1994). "Intensive rehabilitation supervision: The next generation in community corrections?" *Federal Probation* 58(1):72-78.

Gensheimer, L.K., J.P. Mayer, R. Gottschalk and W.S. Davidson (1986). "Diverting youth from the juvenile justice system: A meta-analysis of intervention efficacy." In Apter, S.J. and A. Goldstein (eds.), *Youth Violence: Programs and Prospects* (pp. 39-57). New York: Pergamon.

Giallombardo, R. (1974). *The Social World of Imprisoned Girls*. New York: John Wiley.

Gil, D. (1971). *Violence Against Children: Physical Child Abuse in the United States*. Cambridge, MA: Harvard University Press.

Giordano, P.C. and S.A. Cernkovich (1979). "On complicating the relationship between liberation and delinquency." *Social Problems* 26:467-481.

Giordano, P.C., S.A. Cernkovich and M.D. Pugh (1986). "Friendship and delinquency." *American Journal of Sociology* 91:1170-1202.

Glaser, D. (1956). "Criminality theories and behavioral images." *American Journal of Sociology* 61:433-444.

Glaser, D. (1964). *The Effectiveness of a Prison and Parole System*. Indianapolis: Bobbs-Merrill.

Glass, S. (1997, November 17). "Anatomy of a policy fraud: The hollow Crime Bill." *New Republic* 217(20):22-25.

Glasser, W. (1965). *Reality Therapy*. New York: Harper and Row.

Glassner, B. amd J. Loughlin (1987). *Drugs in Adolescent Worlds: Burnouts to Straights*. New York: St. Martin's.

Glueck, S. and E. Glueck (1956). *Physique and Delinquency*. New York: Harper.

Goddard, H.H. (1920). *Efficiency and Levels of Intelligence*. Princeton: Princeton University Press.

Goffman, E. (1961). *Asylums: Essays on the Situation of Mental Patients and Other Inmates*. Garden City, NY: Anchor Books.

Gold, M. (1970). *Delinquent Behavior in an American City*. Belmont, CA: Brooks/Cole.

Goldman, D., J. Lappalainen and N. Ozaki (1996). "Direct analysis of candidate genes in impulsive behavior." In G.R. Bock and J.A. Goode (eds.), *Genetics of Criminal and Antisocial Behavior* (pp.). Chichester, England: John Wiley and Sons.

Goldstein, A.P. (1990). *Delinquents on Delinquency*. Champaign, IL: Research Press.

Goldstein, A.P. (1993). "Gang intervention: A historical review." In Goldstein, A.P. and C.R. Huff (eds.), *The Gang Intervention Handbook* (pp. 21-51). Champaign, IL: Research Press.

Goldstein, A.P. and B. Glick (1994). *The Prosocial Gang: Implementing Aggression Replacement Training*. Thousand Oaks, CA: Sage.

Goldstein, H. (1977). *Policing a Free Society*. Cambridge, MA: Ballinger.

Goldstein, H. (1987). "Toward community-oriented policing: Potential, basic requirements, and threshold questions." *Crime & Delinquency* 33:6-30.

Goldstein, H. (1990). *Problem-oriented Policing*. New York: McGraw-Hill.

Goldstein, J. (1988). "Police discretion not to invoke the criminal process: Low-visibility decisions in the adminstration of justice." In G.F. Cole (ed.), *Criminal Justice: Law and Politics* (5th ed.) (pp. 83-102). Pacific Grove, CA: Brooks/Cole.

Goldstein, P.J. (1989). "Drugs and violent crime." In Weiner, N.A. and M.E. Wolfgang (eds.) *Pathways to Criminal Violence* (pp. 16-48). Newbury Park, CA: Sage.

Gomme, I.M. (1988). "The role of experience in the production of fear of crime: A text of a causal model." *Canadian Journal of Criminology* 30:67-76.

Gordon, R. (1976). "Prevalence: The rare datum in delinquency measurement and its implications for the theory of delinquency." In M.W. Klein (ed.), *The Juvenile Justice System* (pp. 201-284). Beverly Hills, CA: Sage.

Goring, C. (1913). *The English Convict: A Statistical Study*. Montclair, NJ: Patterson Smith.

Gottfredson, D.C. and W.H. Barton (1993). "Deinstitutionalization of juvenile offenders." *Criminology* 31:591-611.

Gottfredson, D.M. (1987). "Prediction and classification in criminal justice decision making." In D.M. Gottfredson and M. Tonry (eds.), *Prediction and Classification: Criminal Justice Decision Making* (pp. 1-20). Chicago: University of Chicago Press.

Gottfredson, M.R. and T. Hirschi (1990). *A General Theory of Crime*. Stanford, CA: Stanford University Press.

Gottheil, D.L. (1979). "Pretrial diversion: A response to the critics." *Crime & Delinquency* 25:65-75.

Grasmick, H.G., C.R. Tittle, R.J. Bursik and B.J. Arneklev (1993). "Testing the core empirical implications of Gottfredson and Hirschi's general theory of crime." *Journal of Research in Crime and Delinquency* 30:5-29.

Gray, G.E. and L.K. Gray (1983). "Diet and juvenile delinquency." *Nutrition Today* 18:14-21.

Green, L. (1996). *Policing Places with Drug Problems*. Thousand Oaks, CA: Sage.

Greenbaum, S. (1994). "Drugs, delinquency, and other data." *Juvenile Justice* 2(1):2-8.

Greenwood, P.W. (1987). "Care and discipline: Their contribution to delinquency and regulation by the juvenile court." In F.X. Hartmann (ed.), *From Children to Citizens: Volume II: The Role of the Juvenile Court* (pp. 80-106). New York: Springer-Verlag.

Greenwood, P.W. (1994). "What works with juvenile offenders: A synthesis of the literature and experience." *Federal Probation* 58(4):63-67.

Greenwood, P.W. and S. Turner (1993a). "Evaluation of the Paint Creek Youth Center: A residential program for serious delinquents." *Criminology* 31:263-279.

Greenwood, P.W. and S. Turner (1993b). "Private presentence reports for serious juvenile offenders: Implementation issues and impacts." *Justice Quarterly* 10:229-243.

Gross, J. (1987, December 15). "Family court: Stage for suffering and crises." *New York Times* (pp. B1 & B10).

Hackney, S. (1969). "Southern violence." *American Historical Review* 74:906-925.

Hagan, M.P., R.P. King and R.L. Patros (1994). "The efficacy of a serious sex offenders program for adolescent rapists." *International Journal of Offender Therapy and Comparative Criminology* 38:141-150.

Hagan, J. and McCarthy, B. in collaboration with P. Parker and J. Climenhage (1997). *Mean Streets: Youth Crime and Homelessness*. New York: Cambridge University Press.

Hagedorn, J.M. (1994). "Homeboys, dope fiends, legits, and new jacks." *Criminology* 32:197-220.

Hagedorn, J.M. (1988). *People and Folks: Gangs, Crime and the Underclass in a Rustbelt City.* Chicago: Lakeview Press.

Hagedorn, J.M. with P. Macon (1998). *People and Folks: Gangs, Crime and the Underclass in a Rustbelt City,* 2nd ed. Chicago: Lakeview Press.

Hamparian, D.M., J.M. Davis, J.M. Jacobson and R.E. McGraw (1985). *The Young Criminal Years of the Violent Few.* Washington, DC: U.S. Department of Justice.

Hansen, W.B., C.A. Johnson, B.R. Flay, J.W. Graham and J.L. Sobel (1988). "Affective and social influences approachers to the prevention of multiple substance abuse among seventh grade students: Results from project SMART." *Preventive Medicine* 17:135-154.

Hanson, D.J. (1980). "Drug education: Does it work?" In Scarpitti, F.S. and S.K. Datesman (eds.) *Drugs and the Youth Culture* (pp. 251-282). Beverly Hills, CA: Sage.

Harding, R.W. (1993). "Gun use in crime, rational choice, and social learning theory." In Clarke, R.V. and M. Felson (eds.), *Routine Activity and Rational Choice* (pp. 85-102). New Brunswick, NJ: Transaction.

Harding, R. W. (1997). *Private Prisons and Public Accountability.* New Brunswick, NJ: Transaction.

Hardt, R.H. and S. Peterson-Hardt (1977). "On determining the quality of the delinquency self-report method." *Journal of Research in Crime and Delinquency* 14:247-261.

Hathaway, S.R. amnd E.D. Monachesi (1953). *Analyzing and Predicting Juvenile Delinquecy with the MMPI.* Minneapolis: University of Minnesota Press.

Hawkins, J.D., J.M. Jensen, R.F. Catalano and E.A. Wells (1991). "Effects of a skills training intervention with juvenile delinquents." *Research in Social Work Practice* 1:107-121.

Heide, K.M. (1995). *Why Kids Kill Parents: Child Abuse and Adolescent Homicide.* Thousand Oaks, CA: Sage.

Henretta, J.C., C.E. Frazier and D.M. Bishop (1985). "Juvenile justice decision-making: An analysis of the effects of prior case outcomes." Paper presented at the Annual Meeting of the American Society of Criminology, San Diego, CA.

Henretta, J.C., C.E. Frazier and D.M. Bishop (1986). "The effect of prior case outcomes on juvenile justice decision-making." *Social Forces* 65:554-562.

Herrnstein, R.J. and C. Murray (1994). *The Bell Curve: Intelligence and Class Structure in American Life.* New York: Free Press.

Hills, S.L. (1980). *Demystifying Social Deviance.* New York: McGraw-Hill.

Hindelang, M. (1975). *Public Opinion Regarding Crime, Criminal Justice, and Related Topics.* Washington, DC: U.S. Department of Justice.

Hindelang, M.J. (1971). "The social versus solitary nature of delinquent involvement." *British Journal of Criminology* 11:167-175.

Hindelang, M.J. (1973). "Causes of delinquency: A partial replication and extension." *Social Problems* 20:470-487.

Hindelang, M.J., M.R. Gottfredson and J. Garofalo (1978). *Victims of Personal Crime: An Empirical Foundation for a Theory of Personal Victimization.* Cambridge, MA: Ballinger.

Hindelang, M.J., T. Hirschi and J.G. Weis (1981). *Measuring Delinquency.* Beverly Hills: Sage.

Hippchen, L.J. (1978). *Ecologic-Biochemical Approaches to Treatment of Delinquents and Criminals*. New York: Van Nostrand Reinhold.

Hippchen, L.J. (1981). "Some possible biochemical aspects of criminal behavior." *International Journal of Biosocial Research* 2:37-48.

Hirschi, T. (1969). *Causes of Delinquency*. Berkeley: University of California Press.

Hirschi, T. and M. Gottfredson (1993). "Rethinking the juvenile justice system." *Crime & Delinquency* 39:262-271.

Hirschi, T. and M.J. Hindelang (1977). "Intelligence and delinquency: A revisionist review." *American Sociological Review* 42:572-587.

Hodges, J., N. Giuliotti and Porpotage, F.M. (1994). *Improving Literacy Skills of Juvenile Detainees* (NCJ No. 150707). Washington, DC: U.S. Department of Justice.

Holtz, L.E. (1987). "Miranda in a juvenile setting: A child's right to silence." *The Journal of Criminal Law and Criminology* 78:534-556.

Homant, R.J. and D.B. Kennedy (1985). "Police perceptions of spouse abuse: A comparison of male and female officers." *Journal of Criminal Justice* 13:29-47.

Hope, T. (1997). "Inequality and the future of community crime prevention." In S.P. Lab (ed.), *Crime Prevention at a Crossroads* (pp. 143-158). Cincinnati: Anderson.

Hooten, E. (1931). *Crime and Man*. Cambridge, MA: Harvard University Press.

Horn, W.F. (1994). "Government can't buy you love." In Brown, R. (ed.), *Children in Crisis* (pp. 227-237). New York: H.W. Wilson.

Horney, J. (1978). "Menstrual cycles and criminal responsibility." *Law and Human Behavior* 2:25-36.

Horowitz, R. (1983). *Honor and the American Dream: Culture and Identity in a Chicano Community*. New Brunswick, NJ: Rutgers University Press.

Howell, J.C. (1997a). 'Youth gangs." *OJJDP Fact Sheet #72*. Washington, DC: Office of Juvenile Justice and Delinquency Prevention.

Howell, J.C. (1997b). *Youth Gang Homicides and Drug Trafficking*. Washington, DC: Office of Juvenile Justice and Delinquency Prevention.

Howlett, F.W. (1973). "Is the YSB all it's cracked up to be?" *Crime & Delinquency* 19:485-492.

Hser, Y., M.D. Anglin and C. Chou (1988). "Evaluation of drug abuse treatment: A repeated measure design assessing methadone maintenance." *Evaluation Review* 12:547-570.

Hsia, H.M. (1997). *Allegheny County, PA: Mobilizing to Reduce Juvenile Crime*. Washington, DC: U.S. Department of Justice.

Huba, G.J. and P.M. Bentler (1983). "Causal models of the development of law abidance and its relationship to psychosocial factors and drug use." In W.S. Laufer and J.M. Day (eds.), *Personality Theory, Moral Development and Criminal Behavior* (pp. 165-215). Lexington: D.C. Heath.

Hubbard, R.L., M.E. Marsden, J.V. Rachal, H.J. Harwood, E.R. Cavanaugh and H.M. Ginzburg (1989). *Drug Abuse Treatment: A National Study of Effectiveness*. Chapel Hill, NC: University of North Carolina Press.

Hubbard, R.L., J.V. Rachal, S.G. Craddock and E.R. Cavanaugh (1984). "Treatment outcome prospective study (TOPS): Client characteristics and behavior before, during and after treatment." In Tims, F.M. and J.P. Ludford (eds.) *Drug Abuse Treatment Evaluation: Strategies, Progress and Prospects* (pp. 42-68). Washington, DC: National Institute on Drug Abuse.

Huff, C.R. (1989). "Youth gangs and public policy." *Crime & Delinquency* 35:524-537.

Huff, C.R. (1990). "Denial, overreaction, and misidentification: A postscript on public policy." In Huff, C.R. (ed.), *Gangs in America* (pp. 310-317). Newbury Park, CA: Sage.

Huff, C.R. (1993). "Gangs in the United States." In Goldstein, A.P. and C.R. Huff (eds.), *The Gang Intervention Handbook* (pp. 3-20). Champaign, IL: Research Press.

Huizinga, D. and D.S. Elliott (1987). "Juvenile offenders: Prevalence, offender incidence, and arrest rates by race." *Crime & Delinquency* 33:206-223.

Huizinga, D.H., R. Loeber and T. Thornberry (1994). *Urban Delinquency and Substance Abuse: Initial Findings: Research Summary*. Washington, DC: Office of Juvenile Justice and Delinquency Prevention.

Huizinga, D.H., R. Loeber and T. Thornberry (1995). *Urban Delinquency and Substance Abuse: Reseach Summary*. Washington, DC: Office of Juvenile Justice and Delinquency Prevention.

Huizinga, D., S. Menard and D. Elliott (1989). "Delinquency and drug use: Temporal and developmental patterns." *Justice Quarterly* 6:419-456.

Humes, E. (1996). *No Matter How Loud I Shout: A Year in the Life of Juvenile Court*. New York: Simon & Schuster.

Hunter, A. (1985). "Private, parochial and public school orders: The problem of crime and incivility in urban communities." In Suttles, G.D. and M.N. Zald (eds.), *The Challenge of Social Control: Citizenship and Institution Building in Modern Society* (pp). Norwood, NJ: Ablex.

Hutchings, B. and S.A. Mednick (1977). "Criminality in adoptees and their adoptive and biological parents: A pilot study." in S.A. Mednick and K.O. Christiansen (eds.), *Biosocial Bases of Criminal Behavior* (pp. 127-141). New York: Gardner Press.

Hutchinson, R. and C. Kyle (1993). "Hispanic street gangs in Chicago's public schools." In Cummings, S. and D.J. Monti (eds.), *Gangs: The Origins and Impact of Contemporary Youth Gangs in the United States* (pp. 113-136). Albany, NY: SUNY Press.

Inciardi, J.A. (1996). *A Corrections-Based Continuum of Effective Drug Abuse Treatment*. Washington, DC: U.S. Department of Justice.

Inciardi, J.A., R. Horowitz and A.E. Pottieger (1993). *Street Kids, Street Drugs, Street Crime: An Examination of Drug Use and Serious Delinquency in Miami*. Belmont, CA: Wadsworth.

Ingersoll, S. and D. LeBoeuf (1997). *Reaching Out to Youth Out of the Education Mainstream*. Washington, DC: U.S. Department of Justice.

Innes, C.A. (1988). "Drug use and crime." *Bureau of Justice Statistics Special Report*. Washington, DC: Bureau of Justice Statistics.

Institute of Judicial Administration–American Bar Association (1980a). *Juvenile Justice Standards: Standards Relating to Adjudication*. Cambridge, MA: Ballinger.

Institute of Judicial Administration–American Bar Association (1980b). *Juvenile Justice Standards: Standards Relating to Police Handling of Juvenile Probelms*. Cambridge, MA: Ballinger.

Institute of Judicial Administration–American Bar Association (1982). *Juvenile Justice Standards Project: Standards for Juvenile Justice: A Summary and Analysis*, 2nd ed. Cambridge, MA: Ballinger.

Irwin, J. (1980). *Prisons in Turmoil*. Boston: Little, Brown.

Jackson, P.G. (1983). *The Paradox of Control: Parole Supervision of Youthful Offenders*. New York: Praeger.

Jackson, P.I. (1991). "Crime, youth gangs, and urban transition: The social dislocations of post-industrial economic development." *Justice Quarterly* 8:379-397.

Jacobs, M.D. (1990). *Screwing the System and Making it Work*. Chicago: University of Chicago Press.

Jacobs, P.A., M. Brunton and M.M. Melville (1965). "Aggressive behavior, mental subnormality and the XYY male." *Nature* 208:1351-1352.

James, J. and W.E. Thornton (1980). "Women's liberation and the female delinquent." *Journal of Research in Crime and Delinquency* 17:230-244.

Jamieson, K.M. and T. Flanagan (1987). *Sourcebook of Criminal Justice Statistics—1986*. Washington, DC: U.S. Department of Justice.

Jeffery, C.R. (1965). "Criminal behavior and learning theory." *Journal of Criminal Law, Criminology and Police Science* 56:294-300.

Jensen, A.R. (1969). "How much can we boost IQ and scholastic achievement?" *Harvard Education Review* 39:1-123.

Jensen, E.L. and L.K. Metsger (1994). "A test of the deterrent effect of legislative waiver on violent juvenile crime." *Crime & Delinquency* 40:96-104.

Jensen, G.F. (1972). "Delinquent and adolescent self-conceptions: A study of the personal relevance of infractions." *Social Problems* 20:84-103.

Jensen, G.F. and D. Brownfield (1983). "Parents and drugs." *Criminology* 21:543-554.

Jensen, G.F. and D. Brownfield (1986). "Gender, lifestyles, and victimization: Beyond routine activity theory." *Violence and Victims* 1:85-99.

Joe, D. and N. Robinson (1980). "Chinatown's immigrant gangs: The new young warrior class." *Criminology* 18:337-345.

Johnson, B.D., P.J. Goldstein, E. Prebel, J. Schmeidler, D.S. Lipton, B. Sprunt and T. Miller (1985). *Taking Care of Business: The Economics of Crime by Heroin Abusers*. Lexington, MA: Lexington Books.

Johnson, B.D., E.D. Wish, J. Schmeidler and D. Huizinga (1991). "Concentration of delinquent offending: Serious drug involvement and high delinquency rates." *The Journal of Drug Issues* 21:205-229.

Johnson, S.J. (1998). "Probation, my profession, my lifetime employment, my passion." *Crime & Delinquency* 44:117-120.

Johnston, L.D., P.M. O'Malley and J.G. Bachman (1987). *National Trends in Drug Use and Related Factors among American High School Students and Young Adults, 1975-1986*. Rockville, MD: National Institute on Drug Abuse.

Johnston, L.D., P.M. O'Malley and J.G. Bachman (1996). *National Survey Results on Drug Use from the Monitoring the Future Study, 1975-1995*. Vol. 1. Washington, DC: U.S. Department of Health & Human Services.

Johnston, L.D., P.M. O'Malley and L.K. Eveland (1978). "Drugs and delinquency: A search for causal connections." In D.B. Kandel (ed.), *Longitudinal research on drug use: Empirical findings and methodological issues* (pp. 137-156). Washington, DC: Hemisphere.

Johnstone, J.W.C. (1981). "Youth gangs and black suburbs." *Pacific Sociological Review* 58:355-375.

Jones, M. and B. Krisberg (1994). *Images and Reality: Juvenile Crime, Youth Violence, and Public Policy*. San Francisco: National Council on Crime and Delinquency.

Juvenile Justice Update (1995). "Juveniles subject to warrantless search as a probation condition have no expectation of privacy." *Juvenile Justice Update* April/May 1(2):8.

Kandel, D.B. (1973). "Adolescent marijuana use: Role of parents and peers." *Science* 181:1067-1070.

Kandel, D.B., O. Simcha-Fagan and M. Davies (1986). "Risk factors for delinquency and illicit drug use from adolescence to young adulthood." *Journal of Drug Issues* 16:67-90.

Kanter, D. and W. Bennett (1968). "Orientation of street-corner workers and their effects on gangs." In S. Wheeler (ed.), *Controlling Delinquents*. New York: Wiley.

Kaplan, J. (1983). *The Hardest Drug: Heroin and Drug Policy*. Chicago: University of Chicago Press.

Kappeler, V.E., M. Blumberg and G.W. Potter (1996). *The Mythology of Crime and Criminal Justice*, 2nd ed. Prospect Heights, IL: Waveland.

Karp, D.R. (1998). "The judicial and judicious use of shame penalties." *Crime & Delinquency* 44:277-294.

Katz, J. and W.J. Chambliss (1995). "Biology and crime." In J.F. Sheley (ed.), *Criminology: A Contemporary Handbook* (pp. 275-304). Belmont, CA: Wadsworth.

Keane, C., P.S. Maxim and J.J. Teevan (1993). "Drinking and driving, self-control and gender." *Journal of Research in Crime and Delinquency* 30:30-46.

Kelling, G. (1975). "Leadership in the gang." In D.S. Cartwright, B. Tomson and H. Schwartz (eds.), *Gang Delinquency* (pp. 111-126). Monterey: Brooks/Cole.

Kelling, G., T. Pate, D. Dieckman, and C.E. Brown (1974). *The Kansas City Preventive Patrol Experiment: A Summary Report*. Washington, DC: The Police Foundation.

Kennedy, D.B. and R.J. Homant (1983). "Attitudes of abused women toward male and female police officers." *Criminal Justice and Behavior* 10:391-405.

Kennedy, L.W. and D.R. Forde (1990). "Routine activities and crime: An analysis of victimization data in Canada." *Criminology* 28:137-152.

Kim, S. (1988). "A short- and long-term evaluation of Here's Looking at You alcohol education program." *Journal of Drug Education* 18:235-242.

Kim, S., J.H. McLeod and C. Shantzis (1993). "An outcome evaluation of Here's Looking at You 2000." *Journal of Drug Education* 23:67-81.

Kinder, B.N., N.E. Pape and S. Walfish (1980). "Drug and alcohol education programs: A review of outcome studies." *International Journal of the Addictions* 15:1035-1054.

Kitsuse, J.J. and D.C. Dietrick (1959). "Delinquent boys: A critique." *American Sociological Review* 24:208-215.

Klaus, P.A. (1994). *The Costs of Crime to Victims*. Washington, DC: U.S. Department of Justice.

Klein, J.F. (1980). "Revitalizing restitution: Flogging a horse that may have been killed for just cause." In M.D. Schwartz, T.R. Clear and L.F. Travis (eds.), *Corrections: An Issues Approach* (pp. 280-299). Cincinnati: Anderson.

Klein, M.W. (1969). "Gang cohesiveness, delinquency, and a street-work program." *Journal of Research in Crime and Delinquency* 6:135-166.

Klein, M.W. (1971). *Street Gangs and Street Workers*. Englewood Cliffs, NJ: Prentice Hall.

Klein, M.W. (1975). *Alternative Dispositions for Juvenile Offenders*. Los Angeles: University of Southern California.

Klein, M.W. (1976). "Issues in police diversion of juvenile offenders." In R.M. Carter and M.W. Klein (eds.), *Back on the Street: The Diversion of Juvenile Offenders* (pp. 73-104). Englewood Cliffs, NJ: Prentice Hall.

Klein, M.W. (1979). "Deinstitutionalization and diversion of juvenile offenders: A litany of impediments." In N. Morris and M. Tonry (eds.), *Crime and Justice* (Vol. 1) (pp. 145-202). Chicago: University of Chicago Press.

Klein, M.W. (1995). *The American Street Gang: Its Nature, Prevalence and Control*. New York: Oxford University Press.

Klein, M.W. and L.Y. Crawford (1968). "Groups, gangs and cohesiveness." *Journal of Research in Crime and Delinquency* 4:63-75.

Klein, M.W., M.A. Gordon and C.L. Maxson (1986). "The impact of police investigations on police-reported rates of gang and nongang homicides." *Criminology* 24:489-512.

Klein, M.W. and C.L. Maxson (1989). "Street gang violence." In Weiner, N.A. and M.E. Wolfgang (eds.), *Violent Crime, Violent Criminals* (pp. 198-234). Newbury Park, CA: Sage.

Klein, M.W, C.L. Maxson and L.C. Cunningham (1991). "Crack, street gangs, and violence." *Criminology* 29:623-650.

Klein, M.W., C.L. Maxson and M.A. Gordon (1984). *Evaluation of an Imported Gang Violence Deterrence Program. Final Report*. Los Angeles: Social Science Research Institute.

Klein, M.W., K.S. Teilmann, J.A. Styles, S.B. Lincoln and S. Labin-Rosenweig (1976). "The explosion of police diversion programs: Evaluating the structural dimensions of a social fad." In M.W. Klein (ed.), *The Juvenile Justice System* (pp. 101-119). Beverly Hills: Sage.

Klinger, D.A. (1994). "Demeanor or crime? Why 'hostile' citizens are more likely to be arrested." *Criminology* 32:475-493.

Klinger, D.A. (1996). More on demeanor and arrest in Dade County. *Criminology* 34:61-82.

Klinger, D.A. (1997). Negotiating order in patrol work: An ecological theory of police response to deviance. *Criminology* 35:277-306.

Klockars, C.B. (1979). "The contemporary crisis of Marxist Criminology." *Criminology* 16:477-515.

Klockars, C.B. (1986). "Street justice: Some micro-moral reservations." *Justice Quarterly* 3:513-516.

Knox, G.W. (1991). *An Introduction to Gangs*. Berrien Springs, MI: Vande Vere.

Kohlberg, L. (1981). *The Philosophy of Moral Development*. San Francisco: Harper and Row.

Kopp, C.B. and A.H. Parmelee (1979). "Prenatal and perinatal influences on infant behavior." In J.D. Osofsky (ed.), *Handbook of Infant Development*. New York: Wiley.

Kornhauser, R.R. (1978). *Social Sources of Delinquency*. Chicago: University of Chicago Press.

Kowalski, G.S. and T.A. Petee (1991). "Sunbelt effects on homicide rates." *Sociology and Social Research* 75:73-79.

Kraska, P.B. and L.J. Cubellis (1997). "Militarizing Mayberry and beyond: Making sense of American paramilitary policing." *Justice Quarterly* 14:607-629.

Kretschmer, E. (1925). *Physique and Character*. London: Kegan Paul.

Kreuz, L.E. and R.M. Rose (1972). "Assessment of aggressive behavior and plasma testosterone in a young criminal population." *Psychosomatic Medicine* 34:321-332.

Krisberg, B. and J. Austin (1978). *The Children of Ishmael*. Palo Alto: Mayfield.

Krisberg, B. and J.F. Austin (1993). *Reinventing Juvenile Justice*. Newbury Park, CA: Sage.

Krisberg, B., J. Austin and P.A. Steele (1989). *Unlocking Juvenile Corrections: Evaluating the Massachusetts Department of Youth Services*. San Francisco: National Council on Crime and Delinquency.

Krisberg, B., E. Currie, D. Onek and R.G. Wiebush (1995). "Graduated sanctions for serious, violent, and chronic juvenile offenders." In J.C. Howell, B. Krisberg, J.D. Hawkins and J.J. Wilson (eds.). *A Sourcebook: Serious, Violent and Chronic Juvenile Offenders* (pp. 142-170). Thousand Oaks, CA: Sage.

Krisberg, B. and R. DeComo (1993). *Juveniles Taken Into Custody: Fiscal Year 1991 Report*. Washington, DC: U.S. Department of Justice.

Krisberg, B. and J.C. Howell (1998). "The impact of the juvenile justice system and prospects for graduated sanctions in a comprehensive strategy. In R. Loeber and D.P. Farrington (eds.) *Serious & Violent Juvenile Offenders: Risk Factors and Succssful Interventions* (pp. 313-345). Thousand Oaks, CA: Sage.

Krisberg, B. and I.M. Schwartz (1983). "Rethinking juvenile justice." *Crime & Delinquency* 29:333-364.

Kroes, W.H., B.L. Margolis and J.J. Hurrell (1974). "Job stress in policemen." *Journal of Police Science and Administration* 2:145-155.

Krohn, M.D., J.P. Curry, and S. Nelson-Kilger (1983). "Is chivalry dead?: An analysis of changes in police dispositions of males and females." *Criminology* 21:417-437.

Krohn, M. and J. Massey (1980). "Social control and delinquent behavior: An examination of the elements of the social bond." *Sociological Quarterly* 21:529-543.

Lab, S.P. (1984a). "Patterns in juvenile misbehavior." *Crime & Delinquency* 30:293-308.

Lab, S.P. (1984b). "Police productivity: The other eighty percent." *Journal of Police Science and Administration* 12:297-302.

Lab, S.P. (1990). "Citizen crime prevention: Domains and participation." *Justice Quarterly* 7:467-492.

Lab, S.P. (1992). *Crime Prevention: Approaches, Practices and Evaluations*. Cincinnati: Anderson.

Lab, S.P. (1997). *Crime Prevention: Approaches, Practices and Evaluations*, 3rd ed. Cincinnati: Anderson.

Lab, S.P. and R.B. Allen (1984). "Self-report and official measures: a further examination of the validity issue." *Journal of Criminal Justice* 12:445-456.

Lab, S.P. and R.D. Clark (1994). "Gauging crime and control in the schools." Paper presented at the 1994 Annual Meeting of the American Society of Criminology, Miami, FL.

Lab, S.P. and J.T. Whitehead (1988). "An analysis of juvenile correctional treatment." *Crime & Delinquency* 34:60-83.

Lab, S.P. and J.T. Whitehead (1994). "Avoidance behavior as a response to in-school victimization." *Journal of Security Administation* 17(2):32-45.

LaGrange, R.L. and K.F. Ferraro (1989). "Assessing age and gender differences in perceived risk and fear of crime." *Criminology* 27:697-719.

Lander, B. (1954). *Towards an Understanding of Juvenile Delinquency*. New York: Columbia University Press.

Langworthy, R.H. and L.F. Travis III (1994). *Policing in America: A Balance of Forces*. New York: Macmillan.

Lauritsen, J.L., R.J. Sampson and J.H. Laub (1991). "The link between offending and victimization among adolescents." *Criminology* 29:265-292.

Lavrakas, P.J. and D.A. Lewis (1980). "The conceptualization and measurement of citizens' crime prevention behaviors." *Journal of Research in Crime and Delinquency* 17:254-272.

Lavrakas, P.J., J. Normoyle, W.G. Skogan, E.J. Herz, G. Salem and D. Lewis (1981). *Factors Related to Citizen Involvement in Personal, Household, and Neighborhood Anti-Crime Measures: Executive Summary*. Washington, DC: National Institute of Justice.

LeBlanc, M. (1997). "A generic control theory of the criminal phenomenon: The structural dynamic statements of an integrative multilayered control theory." In T.P. Thornberry (ed.) *Developmental Theories of Crime and Delinquency*. New Brunswick, NJ: Transaction.

Lee, L. (1994). "Factors determining waiver in a juvenile court." *Journal of Criminal Justice* 22:329-339.

Lemert, E.M. (1951). *Social Pathology: A Systematic Approach to the Theory of Sociopathic Behavior*. New York: McGraw-Hill.

Lemert, E.M. (1981). "Diversion in juvenile justice: What hath been wrought?" *Journal of Research in Crime and Delinquency* 18:34-46.

Lester, D. and M. Braswell (1987). *Correctional Counseling*. Cincinnati: Anderson.

Lester, D, M. Braswell and P. Van Voorhis (1992). *Correctional Counseling*, 2nd ed. Cincinnati: Anderson.

Leukefeld, C.G. and F.M. Tims (1988). *Compulsory Treatment of Drug Abuse: Research and Clinical Practice*. Rockville, MD: National Institute on Drug Abuse.

Levine, M. and L. Battistoni (1991). "The corroboration requirement in child sex abuse cases." *Behavioral Sciences and the Law* 9:3-20.

Lewis, D.A. and G. Salem (1986). *Fear of Crime: Incivility and the Production of a Social Problem*. New Brunswick, NJ: Transaction.

Lilly, J.R., F.T. Cullen and R.A. Ball (1995). *Criminological Theory: Context and Consequences*. 2nd ed. Thousand Oaks, CA: Sage.

Lincoln, S.B. (1976). "Juvenile referral and recidivism." In R.M. Carter and M.W. Klein (eds.), *Back on the Street: Diversion of Juvenile Offenders* (pp. 321-328). Englewood Cliffs, NJ: Prentice Hall.

Lindner, C. (1981). "The utilization of day-evening centers as an alternative to secure detention of juveniles." *Journal of Probation and Parole* 13:12-18.

Lindner, C. & Bonn, R.L. (1996). "Probation officer victimization and fieldwork practices: Results of a national study." *Federal Probation* 60 (2):16-23.

Lipsett, P. (1968). "The juvenile offender's perception." *Crime & Delinquency* 14:49-62.

Lipsey, M.W. (1992). "Juvenile delinquency treatment: A meta-analytic inquiry into the viability of effects." In T. Cook, H. Cooper, D. Corday, H. Hartman, L. Hedges, R. Light, T. Louis and F. Mosteller (eds.), *Meta-analysis for explanation: A casebook* (pp. 83-127). New York: Russell Sage Foundation.

Lipsey, M.W., D.S. Cordray and D.E. Berger (1981). "Evaluation of a juvenile diversion program using multiple lines of evidence." *Evaluation Review* 5:283-306.

Lipsey, M.W. and D.B. Wilson (1998). "Effective intervention for serious juvenile offenders: A synthesis of research." In Loeber, R. and D.P. Farrington, *Serious & Violent Juvenile Offenders: Risk Factors and Successful Interventions* (pp. 313-345). Thousand Oaks, CA: Sage.

Lipton, D.L. (1995). *The Effectiveness of Treatment for Drug Abusers under Criminal Justice Supervision*. Washington, DC: U.S. Department of Justice, 1995.

Livermore, J. (1971). "Policing." *Minnesota Law Review* 55:651-665.

Locke, H.G. (1996). "The color of law and the issue of color: race and the abuse of police power." In W.A. Geller and H. Toch, *Police Violence: Understanding and Controlling Police Abuse of Force* (pp. 129-149). New Haven, CT: Yale University Press.

Lockwood, D. (1980). *Prison Sexual Violence*. New York: Elsevier.

Lockwood, D. (1997). "Violence among middle school and high school students: Analysis and implications for prevention." *NIJ Research in Brief*. Washington, DC: National Institute of Justice.

Loeber, R. (1988). "Natural histories of conduct problems, delinquency and related substance abuse." In Lahey, B.B. and A.E. Kazdin (eds.), *Advances in Clinical Child Psychology*, Vol. 11. New York: Plenum.

Loftin, C.K. and R.H. Hill (1974). "Regional subculture and homicide: An empirical examination of the Gastil-Hackney thesis." *American Sociological Review* 39:714-724.

Logan, C.H. (1990). *Private Prisons: Cons and Pros*. New York: Oxford University Press.

Logan, C.H. and G.G. Gaes (1993). "Meta-analysis and the rehabilitation of punishment." *Justice Quarterly* 10:245-264.

Lombroso, C. (1876). *On Criminal Man*. Milan, Italy: Hoepli.

Lowney, J. (1984). "The Wall Gang: A study of interpersonal process and deviance among twenty-three middle-class youths." *Adolescence* 19:527-538.

Lozoff, B. and M. Braswell (1989). *Inner Corrections: Finding Peace and Peace Making*. Cincinnati: Anderson.

Lucken, K. (1997). Privatizing discretion: "'Rehabilitating' treatment in community corrections." *Crime & Delinquency* 43:243-259.

Lundman, R.J. (1993). *Prevention and Control of Juvenile Delinquency*, 2nd ed. New York: Oxford.

Lundman, R.J. (1994). "Demeanor or crime? The Midwest City police-citizen encounters study." *Criminology* 32:631-653.

Lundman, R.J. (1996a). "Demeanor and arrest: Additional evidence from previously unpublished data." *Journal of Research in Crime and Delinquency* 33:306-323.

Lundman, R.J. (1996b). "Extralegal variables and arrest." *Journal of Research in Crime and Delinquency* 33:349-353.

Lundman, R.J., R.E. Sykes and J.P. Clark (1978). "Police control of juveniles: A replication." *Journal of Research in Crime and Delinquency* 15:74-91.

Lynch, M. (1990). "Racial bias and criminal justice: Definitional and methodological issues." *Critical Criminologist* 2(1):3-12.

Lyons, M.J. (1996). "A twin study of self-reported criminal behavior." In G.R. Bock and J.A. Goode (eds.), *Genetics of Criminal and Antisocial Behavior* (pp. 61-69). Chichester, England: John Wiley and Sons.

MacAllair, D. (1993). "Reaffirming rehabilitation in juvenile justice." *Youth and Society* 25:104-125.

Macdonald, D.I. (1984). *Drugs, Drinking, and Adolescents*. Chicago: Year Book Medical.

Mack, J.W. (1909). "The juvenile court." *Harvard Law Review* 23: 104-119.

MacKenzie, D.L. (1994). "Results of a multisite study of boot camp prisons." *Federal Probation* 58(2):60-66.

Maddux, J.F. (1988). "Clinical experience in civil commitment." In Leukefeld, C.G. and F.M. Tims (eds.) *Compulsory Treatment of Drug Abuse: Research and Clinical Practice* (pp. 35-56). Washington, DC: National Institute on Drug Abuse.

Magill, S. (1998). Adolescents: Public Enemy #1, *Crime & Delinquency* 44:121-126.

Maguire, K. and A.L. Pastore (1996). *Sourcebook of Criminal Justice Statistics 1995*. Washington, DC: Bureau of Justice Statistics.

Maguire, K. and A.L. Pastore (1997). *Sourcebook of Criminal Justice Statistics 1996*. Washington, DC: U.S. Department of Justice.

Maguire, K., A.L. Pastore and T.J. Flanagan (1993). *Sourcebook of Criminal Justice Statistics— 1992*. Washington, DC: U.S. Department of Justice.

Mahoney, A.R. (1985). "Jury trial for juveniles: Right or ritual?" *Justice Quarterly* 2:553-565.

Mahoney, A.R. (1987). *Juvenile Justice in Context*. Boston: Northeastern University Press.

Maitland, A.S. and R.D. Sluder (1998). "Victimization and youthful prison inmates: An empirical analysis." *Prison Journal* 78: 55-73.

Mandel, J. and H.W. Feldman (1986). "The social history of teenage drug use." In G. Beschner and A.S. Friedman, *Teen Drug Use* (pp. 19-42). Lexington, MA: Lexington Books.

Marcos, A.L., S.J. Bahr and R.E. Johnson (1986). "Test of a bonding/differential association theory of adolescent drug use." *Social Forces* 65:135-161.

Martin, S.E. (1980). *Breaking and Entering: Policewomen on Patrol*. Berkeley: University of California Press.

Martinson, R. (1974). "What works?— questions and answers about prison reform." *The Public Interest* 35:22-54.

Martinson, R. (1979). "New findings; new view: A note of caution regarding sentencing reform." *Hofstra Law Review* 7:243-258.

Marx, K. and F. Engels (1906). *Capital: Critique of Political Economy*. Chicago: Charles Kerr.

Maslach, C. (1982). *Burnout: The Cost of Caring*. Englewood Cliffs, NJ: Prentice Hall.

Maslach, C. and S.E. Jackson (1979). "Burned-out cops and their families." *Psychology Today* 12(12):59-62.

Massey, J.L. and M.D. Krohn (1986). "A longitudinal examination of an integrated social process model of deviant behavior." *Social Forces* 65:106-134.

Masters, R.E. (1994). *Counseling Criminal Justice Offenders*. Thousand Oaks, CA: Sage.

Matsueda, R.L. and K. Heimer (1997). "A symbolic interactionist theory of role-transitions, role-commitments, and delinquency." In T.P. Thornberry (ed.), *Developmental Theories of Crime and Delinquency* (pp.). New Brunswick, NJ: Transaction.

Matza, D. (1964). *Delinquency and Drift*. Englewood Cliffs, NJ: Prentice Hall.

Mause, L. (1974). *The History of Childhood*. New York: Psychohistory Press.

Maxson, C.L. (1995). "Street gangs and drug roles in two suburban cities." *NIJ Research in Brief*. Washington, DC: National Institute of Justice.

Maxson, C.L., M.A. Gordon and M.W. Klein (1985). "Differences between gang and nongang homicides." *Criminology* 23:209-222.

Maxson, C.L., K. Woods and M.W. Klein (1996). "Street gang migration: How big a threat?" *NIJ Journal* 230:26-31.

Mays, G.L., K. Fuller and L.T. Winfree (1994). "Gangs and gang activity in southern New Mexico: A descriptive look at a growing rural problem." *Journal of Crime and Justice* 17:25-44.

McBride, D. (1981). "Drugs and violence." In J.A. Inciardi (ed.), *The Drugs/Crime Connection* (pp. 105-124). Beverly Hills: Sage.

McCarthy, B.R. (1987a). "Case attrition in the juvenile court: An application of the crime control model." *Justice Quarterly* 4:237-255.

McCarthy, B.R. (1987b). *Intermediate Punishments: Intensive Supervision, Home Confinement, and Electronic Surveillance*. Monsey, NY: Criminal Justice Press.

McCarthy, B.R. (1987c). "Preventive detention and pretrial custody in the juvenile court." *Journal of Criminal Justice* 15:185-200.

McCarthy, B.R. and B.J. McCarthy (1984). *Community-Based Corrections*. Monterey, CA: Brooks/Cole.

McCarthy, B.R. and B.L. Smith (1986). "The conceptualization of discrimination in the juvenile justice process: The impact of administrative factors and screening decisions on juvenile court dispositions." *Criminology* 24:41-64.

McCurdy, K. and D. Daro (1994). "Child maltreatment: A national study of reports and fatalities." *Journal of Interpersonal Violence* 9:75-94.

McGlothlin, W.H. and M.D. Anglin (1981). "Shutting off methadone: Costs and benefits." *Archives of General Psychiatry* 38:885-892.

McPherson, S.J., L.E. McDonald and C.W. Ryer (1983). "Intensive counseling with families of juvenile offenders." *Juvenile and Family Court Journal* 34:27-33.

Mead, G.H. (1934). *Mind, Self and Society*. Chicago: University of Chicago Press.

Meehan, P.J. and P.W. O'Carroll (1992). "Gangs, drugs, and homicide in Los Angeles." *American Journal of Diseases of Children* 146:683-687.

Megargee, E.I. and M.J. Bohn (1979). *Classifying Criminal Offenders: A New System Based on the MMPI*. Beverly Hills: Sage.

Melton, G.B. (1980). "Psycholegal issues in child victims' interaction with the legal system." *Victimology* 5:274-284.

Menard, S. and B.J. Morse (1984). "A structuralist critique of the IQ-delinquency hypothesis: Theory and evidence." *American Journal of Sociology* 89:1347-1378.

Mendelsohn, B. (1956). "The Victimology." *Etudes Internationale de Psycho-sociologie Criminelle* (July):23-26.

Merton, R.K. (1938). "Social structure and anomie." *American Sociological Review* 3:672-682.

Miethe, T.D., M.C. Stafford and J.S. Long (1987). "Social differentiation in criminal victimization: A test of routine activities/lifestyle theories." *American Sociological Review* 52:184-194.

Miller, D., D. Miller, F. Hoffman and R. Duggan (1980). *Runaways— Illegal Aliens in their Own Land: Implications for Service*. New York: Praeger.

Miller, J.G. (1996). *Search and Destroy: African-American Males in the Criminal Justice System*. New York: Cambridge University Press.

Miller, W.B. (1958). "Lower class culture as a generating milieu of gang delinquency." *Journal of Social Issues* 15:5-19.

Miller, W.B. (1966). "Violent crime in city gangs." *Annals* 343:97-112.

Miller, W.B. (1975). *Violence by Youth Gangs and Youth Groups as a Crime Problem in Major American Cities*. Washington, DC: National Institute for Juvenile Justice and Delinquency Prevention.

Miller, W.B. (1980). "Gangs, groups and serious youth crime." In D. Shichor and D.H. Kelly (eds.), *Critical Issues in Juvenile Delinquency* (pp. 115-138). Lexington, MA: Lexington Books.

Miller, W.B. (1982). *Crime by Youth Gangs and Groups in the United States*. Washington, DC: Office of Juvenile Justice and Delinquency Prevention.

Miller, W.B., H. Gertz and H.S.G. Cutter (1961). "Aggression in a boys' street-corner group." *Psychiatry* 24:283-298.

Minor, K.I., Hartmann, D.J., & Terry, S. (1997). "Predictors of juvenile court actions and recidivism," *Crime & Delinquency* 43:328-344.

Minor, W.W. (1981). "Techniques of neutralization: A reconceptualization and empirical examination." *Journal of Research in Crime and Delinquency* 18:295-318.

Moffitt, T.E. (1997). "Adolescence-limited and life-course-persistent offending: A complementary pair of developmental theories." In T.P. Thornberry (ed.), *Developmental Theories of Crime and Delinquency*. New Brunswick, NJ: Transaction.

Moffitt, T.E., W.F. Gabrielli, S.A. Mednick and F. Schulsinger (1981). "Socioeconomic status, IQ, and delinquency." *Journal of Abnormal Psychology* 90:152-156.

Monahan, J. (1981). *The Clinical Prediction of Violent Behavior*. Rockville, MD: National Institute of Mental Health.

Monti, D.J. (1993). "Origins and problems of gang research in the United States." In Cummings, S. and D.J. Monti (eds.), *Gangs: The Origins and Impact of Contemporary Youth Gangs in the United States* (pp. 3-26). Albany, NY: SUNY Press.

Moon, M.M., Applegate, B.K. and Latessa, E.J. (1997). "RECLAIM Ohio: A politically viable alternative to treating youthful felony offenders," *Crime & Delinquency* 43:438-456.

Moone, J. (1997a). *Juveniles in Private Facilities 1991-1995*. Washington, DC: U.S. Department of Justice.

Moone, J. (1997b). *States at a Glance: Juveniles in Public Facilities, 1995*. Washington, DC: U.S. Department of Justice.

Moore, D.B. (1993). "Shame, forgiveness, and juvenile justice." *Criminal Justice Ethics* 12(1):3-25.

Moore, J. (1988). "Introduction: Gangs and the underclass a comparative perspective." In Hagedorn, J.M., *People and Folks: Gangs, Crime and the Underclass in a Rustbelt City* (pp. 3-18). Chicago: Lake View Press.

Moore, J. (1991). *Going Down to the Barrio: Homeboys and Homegirls in Change*. Philadelphia: Temple University Press.

Moore, J. (1993). "Gangs, drugs, and violence." In Cummings, S. and D.J. Monti (eds.), *Gangs: The Origins and Impact of Contemporary youth Gangs in the United States*. Albany, NY: SUNY Press.

Moore, M.H. and S. Wakeling (1997). "Juvenile Justice: Shoring up the Foundations." In *Crime and Justice: A Review of Research*. (Vol. 22) (pp. 253-301). Chicago: University of Chicago Press.

Morris, A. (1978). "Diversion of juvenile offenders from the criminal justice system." In N. Tutt (ed.), *Alternative Strategies for Coping with Crime* (pp. 45-63). Oxford, England: Basil Blackwood and Martin Robertson.

Morris, N. and M. Tonry (1990). *Between Prison and Probation: Intermediate Punishments in a Rational Sentencing System*. New York: Oxford University Press.

Morton, J.H., H. Addition, R.G. Addison, L. Hunt and J.J. Sullivan (1953). "A clinical study of premenstrual tension." *American Journal of Obstetrics and Gynecology* 65:1182-1191.

Mullen, J., K. J. Chabotar, and D.M. Carrow (1985). *The Privatization of Corrections*. Washington, DC: U.S. Department of Justice.

Murray, C.A. and L.A. Cox (1979). *Beyond Probation: Juvenile Corrections and the Chronic Offender*. Beverly Hills: Sage.

Nadelmann, E.A. (1997). "Thinking seriously about alternatives to drug prohibition." In M. McShane & F.P. Williams (eds.), *Criminal Justice: Drug Use and Drug Policy* (pp. 269-316). New York: Garland.

Nassi, A. and S.I. Abramowitz (1976). "From phrenology to psychosurgery and back again: Biological studies of criminality." *American Journal of Orthopsychiatry* 46:591-607.

Natarajan, M. (1996). "Women police units in India: A new direction." *Police Studies* 19(2):63-75.

National Advisory Commission on Criminal Justice Standards and Goals (1973). *Police*. Washington, DC: U.S. Government Printing Office.

National Conference of State Legislatures (1993). *1993 State Legislature Summary*. Washington, DC: National Conference of State Legislatures.

National Council on Crime and Delinquency (1987). *The Impact of Juvenile Court Sanctions: A Court That Works: Executive Summary*. San Francisco: National Council on Crime and Delinquency.

National Dairy Council (1985). "Diet and behavior." *Dairy Council Digest* 56:19-24.

National Institute of Justice (1990). *Drugs and Crime: 1989 Drug Use Forecasting Report*. Washington, DC: author.

National Institute of Justice (1997). *Drug Use Forecasting 1996: Annual Report on Adult and Juvenile Arrestees*. Washington, DC: U.S. Department of Justice.

Nejelski, P. (1976). "Diversion: The promise and the danger." *Crime & Delinquency* 22:393-410.

Nelson, C., J. Corzine and L. Huff-Corzine (1994). "The violent West reexamined: A research note on regional homicide rates." *Criminology* 32:149-161.

Newcomb, M.D. and P.M. Bentler (1988). *Consequences of Adolescent Drug Use*. Newbury Park: Sage.

Newman, D.J. (1986). *Introduction to Criminal Justice*, 3rd ed. New York: Random House.

Newman, H.H., F.H. Freeman and K.J. Holzinger (1937). *Twins: A Study of Heredity and Environment*. Chicago: University of Chicago Press.

Niederhoffer, A. (1967). *Behind the Shield: The Police in Urban Society*. Garden City, NY: Anchor Books.

Nimick, E.H., H.N. Snyder, D.P. Sullivan and N.J. Tierney (1987). *Juvenile Court Statistics, 1983*. Washington, DC: U.S. Department of Justice.

Nurco, D.N., T.W. Kinlock, T.E. Hanlon and J.C. Ball (1988). "Nonnarcotic drug use ove an addition career—A study of heroin addicts in Baltimore and New York City." *Comprehensive Psychiatry* 29:450-459.

O'Brien, D.M. (1997). *Constitutional Law and Politics: Volume II*, 3rd ed. New York: W.W. Norton & Co.

O'Brien, R.M. (1985). *Crime and Victimization Data*. Beverly Hills: Sage.

O'Carroll, P.W. and J.A. Mercy (1989). "Regional variation in homicide rates: Why is the west the worst?" *Violence and Victims* 4:17-25.

Office of Juvenile Justice and Delinquency Prevention (1987). *History of the CASA Program*. Washington, DC: Office of Justice Programs.

Office of Juvenile Justice and Delinquency Prevention (1997). *1995 Natonal Youth Gang Survey: Program Summary*. Washignton, DC: Office of Juvenile Justice and Delinquency Prevention.

Office of National Drug Control Strategy (1997). *The National Drug Control Strategy, 1997.* Washington, DC: U.S. Government Printing Office.

Ohio Commission on Dispute Resolution and Conflict Management (1993). *Conflict Management in Schools: Sowing Seeds for a Safer Society.* Columbus, OH: author.

Ohlin, L.E., H. Piven and D.M. Pappenfort (1956). "Major dilemmas of the social worker in probation and parole." *National Probation and Parole Officer Journal* 2:211-225.

Ortega, S.T. and J.L. Myles (1987). "Race and gender effects on fear of crime: An interactive model with age." *Criminology* 25:133-152.

Osborne, J.A. (1979). "Juvenile justice policy in Canada: The transfer of the initiative." *Canadian Journal of Family Law* 2:7-32.

Osgood, D.W. (1983). "Offense history and juvenile diversion." *Evaluation Review* 7:793-806.

Osgood, D.W. and H.F. Weichselbaum (1984). "Juvenile diversion: When practice matches theory." *Journal of Research in Crime and Delinquency* 21:33-56.

Ozawa, M.N. (1993). "America's future and her investment in children." *Child Welfare* 72:517-529.

Padilla, F. (1993). "The working gang." In Cummings, S. and D.J. Monti (eds.), *Gangs: The Origins and Impact of Contemporary Youth Gangs in the United States* (pp. 173-192). Albany, NY: SUNY Press.

Pagelow, M.D. (1984). *Family Violence.* New York: Greenwood Press.

Palamara, F., F.T. Cullen and J.C. Gersten (1986). "The effect of police and mental health intervention on juvenile deviance: Specifying contingencies in the impact of formal reaction." *Journal of Health and Social Behavior* 27:90-105.

Palmer, T. (1978). *Correctional Intervention and Research: Current Issues and Future Prospects.* Lexington, MA: Lexington Books.

Palmer, T. and R.V. Lewis (1980). *An Evaluation of Juvenile Diversion.* Cambridge, MA: Oelgeschlager, Gunn and Hain.

Parent, D.G., B. Auerbach and K.E. Carlson (1992). *Compensating Crime Victims: A Summary of Policies and Practices.* Washington, DC: U.S. Department of Justice.

Parsloe, P. (1978). *Juvenile Justice in Britain and the U.S.: The Balance of Needs and Rights.* London: Routledge and Kegan Paul.

Paternoster, R., G.P. Waldo, T.G. Chiricos and L.S. Anderson (1979). "The stigma of diversion: Labeling in the juvenile justice system." In P.L. Brantingham and T.G. Blomberg (eds.), *Courts and Diversion: Policy and Operations Studies* (pp. 127-142). Beverly Hills: Sage.

Pennell, S., C. Curtis and D.C. Scheck (1990). "Controlling juvenile delinquency: An evaluation of an interagency strategy." *Crime & Delinquency* 36:257-275.

Peters, M., D. Thomas and C. Zamberlan (1997). *Boot Camps for Juvenile Offenders: Program Summary.* Washington, DC: U.S. Department of Justice.

Petersilia, J. (1997). "Probation in the United States." In Tonry, M. (Ed.). *Crime and Justice: A Review of Research.* (Vol. 22.) (pp. 149-200). Chicago: University of Chicago Press.

Petersilia, J. and E.P. Deschenes (1994). "What punishes?: Inmates rank the severity of prison vs. intermediate sanctions." *Federal Probation* 58(1):3-8.

Petersilia, J., S. Turner, J. Kahan and J. Peterson (1985). "Executive summary of Rand's study, 'Granting felons probation: Public risks and alternatives.'" *Crime & Delinquency* 3:379-392.

Peterson, M.A., H.B. Braiker and S.M. Polich (1981). *Who Commits Crimes?* Cambridge, MA: Oelgeschlager, Gunn and Hain.

Piaget, J. (1965). *The Moral Development of the Child*. London: Routledge and Kegan Paul.

Pierce, G.L. and J.A. Fox (1992). "Recent trends in violent crime: A closer look." Mimeograph. Boston: National Crime Analysis Program, Northeastern University.

Piliavin, I. and S. Briar (1964). "Police encounters with juveniles." *The American Journal of Sociology* 70:206-214.

Piliavin, I., C. Thornton, R. Garten and R.L. Matsueda (1986). "Crime, deterrence, and rational choice." *American Sociological Review* 51:101-119.

Pinderhughes, H. (1993). "'Down with the program': Racial attitude and group violence among youth in Bensonhurst and Gravesend." In Cummings, S. and D.J. Monti (eds.), *Gangs: The Origins and Impact of Contemporary Youth Gangs in the United States* (pp. 75-94). Albany, NY: SUNY Press.

Pisciotta, A.W. (1979). *The Theory and Practice of the New York House of Refuge, 1857-1935*. Unpublished Ph.D. dissertation, Florida State University.

Pisciotta, A.W. (1982). "Saving the children: The promise and practice of parens patriae, 1838-98." *Crime & Delinquency* 28:410-425.

Pisciotta, A.W. (1983). "Race, sex and rehabilitation: A study of differential treatment in the juvenile reformatory, 1825-1900." *Crime & Delinquency* 29:254-269.

Platt, A.M. (1977). *The Child Savers: The Invention of Delinquency*. Chicago: University of Chicago Press.

Ploeger, M. (1997). "Youth employment and delinquency: Reconsidering a problematic relationship." *Criminology* 35:659-675.

Podolsky, E. (1964). "The chemistry of murder." *Pakistan Medical Journal* 15:9-14.

Pogrebin, M.R., E.D. Poole and R.M. Regoli (1984). "Constructing and implementing a model juvenile diversion program." *Youth and Society* 15:305-324.

Police Foundation (1981). *The Newark Foot Patrol Experiment*. Washington, DC: The Police Foundation.

Polk, K. (1981). "Youth Service Bureaus: The Record and Prospects." Unpublished manuscript.

Polsky, H. (1962). *Cottage Six*. New York: John Wiley.

Poole, E.D. and R.M. Regoli (1979). "Parental support, delinquent friends and delinquency." *Journal of Criminal Law and Criminology* 70:188-193.

Pope, C.E. (1994). "Racial disparities in juvenile justice system." *Overcrowded Times* 5(6):1, 5-7.

Pope, C.E. (1995). "Equity within the juvenile justice system: Directions for the future." In K.K. Leonard, C.E. Pope and W.H. Feyerherm (eds.), *Minorities in Juvenile Justice* (pp. 201-216). Thousand Oaks, CA: Sage.

Pope, C.E. and W. Feyerherm (1993). *Minorities and the Juvenile Justice System*. Washington, DC: U.S. Department of Justice.

Poulos, T.M. and S. Orchowshy (1994). "Serious juvenile offenders: Predicting the probability of transfer to criminal court." *Crime & Delinquency* 40:3-17.

Prescott, P.S. (1981). *The Child Savers: Juvenile Justice Observed*. New York: Knopf.

President's Commission on Law Enforcement and Administration of Justice (1967a). *Task Force Report: The Police*. Washington, DC: U.S. Government Printing Office.

President's Commission on Law Enforcement and Administration of Justice (1967b). *Task Force Report: Juvenile Delinquency and Youth Crime*. Washington, DC: U.S. Government Printing Office.

Propper, A.M. (1982). "Make-believe families and homosexuality among imprisoned girls." *Criminology* 20:127-138.

Puritz, P. and M.A. Scali (1998). *Beyond the Walls: Improving Conditions of Confinement for Youth in Custody*. Washington, DC: Office of Juvenile Justice and Delinquency Prevention.

Quay, H.C. (1965). "Personality and delinquency." In H.C. Quay (ed.), *Juvenile Delinquency* (pp. 139-169). New York: Litton.

Quay, H.C. and C.T. Love (1977). "The effect of a juvenile diversion program on rearrests." *Criminal Justice and Behavior* 4:377-396.

Quicker, J.C. (1974). "The effect of goal discrepancy on delinquency." *Social Problems* 22:76-86.

Quinney, R.A. (1970). *The Social Reality of Crime*. Boston: Little, Brown.

Rada, R.T., D.R. Laws and R. Kellner (1976). "Plasma testosterone levels in the rapist." *Psychosomatic Medicine* 38:257-268.

Rausch, S. (1983). "Court processing versus diversion of status offenders: A test of deterrence and labeling theories." *Journal of Research in Crime and Delinquency* 20:39-54.

Reckless, W.C. (1962). "A non-causal explanation: Containment theory." *Excerpta Criminologica* 1:131-134.

Reckless, W.C. (1967). *The Crime Problem*. New York: Appleton, Century, Crofts.

Reckless, W.C., S. Dinitz and E. Murray (1956). "Self-concept as an insulator against delinquency." *American Sociological Review* 21:744-756.

Regoli, R., E. Wilderman and M. Pogrebin (1985). "Using an alternative evaluation measure for assessing juvenile diversion programs." *Children and Youth Services Review* 7:21-38.

Reiss, A.J., Jr. (1980). "Police brutality." In R.J. Lundman (ed.), *Police Behavior: A Sociological Perspective* (pp. 274-296). New York: Oxford University Press.

Reiss, A.J. and A.L. Rhodes (1961). "The distribution of juvenile delinquency in the social class structure." *American Sociological Review* 26:720-732.

Reiss, A.J. and J.A. Roth (1993). *Understanding and Preventing Violence*. Vol. 1. Washington, DC: National Academy Press.

Remington, P.W. (1981). *Policing: The Occupation and the Introduction of Female Officers*. Washington, DC: University Press of America.

Rengert, G.F. and J. Wasilchick (1985). *Suburban Burglary: A Time and a Place for Everything*. Springfield, IL: Charles C Thomas.

Reppetto, T.A. (1974). *Residential Crime*. Cambridge, MA: Ballinger.

Rhodes, W. (1985). "Pretrial release and misconduct." *Bureau of Justice Statistics Special Report*. Washington, DC: National Institute of Justice.

Rich, J.M. and J.L. DeVitis (1985). *Theories of Moral Development*. Springfield, IL: Charles C Thomas.

Ringwalt, C.L., S.T. Ennett and K.D. Holt (1991). "An outcome evaluation of Project D.A.R.E." *Health Education Research: Theory and Practice* 6:327-337.

Robin, G.D. (1967). "Gang member delinquency in Philadelphia." In M.W. Klein (ed.), *Juvenile Gangs in Context* (pp. 15-24). Englewood Cliffs, NJ: Prentice Hall.

Robin, G.D. (1982). "Juvenile interrogations and confessions." *Journal of Police Science and Administration* 10:224-228.

Rogers, CR. (1951). *Client-Centered Therapy*. Boston: Houghton-Mifflin.

Rojek, D.G. (1982). "Juvenile diversion: A study of community cooptation." In D.G. Rojek and G.F. Jensen (eds.), *Readings in Juvenile Delinquency* (pp. 316-321). Lexington, MA: D.C. Heath.

Rojek, D.G. and M.L. Erickson (1982). "Delinquent careers: A test of the career escalation model." *Criminology* 20:5-28.

Roncek, D.W. and P.A. Maier (1991). "Bars, blocks, and crimes revisited: Linking the theory of routine activities to the empiricism of 'hot spots.'" *Criminology* 29:725-753.

Rosecrance, J. (1988). "Maintaining the myth of individualized justice: Probation presentence reports." *Justice Quarterly* 5:235-256.

Rosenbaum, D.P. (1994). *The Challenge of Community Policing: Testing the Promises*. Thousand Oaks, CA: Sage.

Rosenbaum, D.P., R.L. Flewelling, S.L. Bailey, C.L. Ringwalt and D.L. Wilkinson (1994). "Cops in the classroom: A longitudinal evaluation of Drug Abuse Resistance Education (DARE)." *Journal of Research in Crime and Delinquency* 31:3-31.

Rossow, L.F. and J.R. Parkinson (1994a). "State legislatures react to *Jones v. Clear Creek and Bishop Knox* behavior." *School Law Reporter* 36(5):1-2.

Rossow, L.F. and J.R. Parkinson (1994b). "Yet another student strip search upheld: *Cornfield By Lewis v. Consolidated High School District No. 230*." *School Law Reporter* 36(3):1-2.

Rossum, R.A., B.J. Koller and C.P. Manfredi (1987). *Juvenile Justice Reform: A Model for the States*. Claremont, CA: Rose Institute of State and Local Government and the American Legislative Exchange Council.

Roth, J.A. (1994). *Firearms and Violence: National Institute of Justice Research in Brief*. Washington, DC: U.S. Department of Justice.

Rothman, D.J. (1971). *The Discovery of the Asylum: Social Order and Disorder in the New Republic*. Boston: Little, Brown.

Rothman, D.J. (1980). *Conscience and Convenience: The Asylum and Its Alternatives in Progressive America*. Boston: Little, Brown.

Roush, D.W. (1993). "Juvenile detention programming." *Federal Probation* 57(3):20-33.

Rubin, H.T. (1985). *Juvenile Justice: Policy, Practice, and Law*, 2nd ed. New York: Random House.

Rubin, H.T. (1995). "New Mexico's revised Children's Code creates three types of offenders: 'Serious Youthful Offender,' 'Youthful Offender,' and 'Delinquent Offender.'" *Juvenile Justice Update* 1(2):1, 2, 12, 15.

Rudman, C., E. Hartstone, J. Fagan and M. Moore (1986). "Violent youth in adult court: Process and punishment." *Crime & Delinquency* 32:75-96.

Russel, R. & Sedlak, U. (1993). "Status offenders: Attitudes of child welfare practitioners toward practice and policy issues." *Child Welfare* 72:13-24.

Russell, E. (1982). "Limitations of behavior control techniques." In N. Johnston and L.D. Savitz (eds.), *Legal Process and Corrections* (pp. 288-297). New York: John Wiley & Sons.

Rutter, M. (1996). "Introduction: Concepts of antisocial behavior, of cause and of genetic influences." In G.R. Bock and J.A. Goode (eds.), *Genetics of Criminal and Antisocial Behavior* (pp. 1-14). Chichester, England: John Wiley & Sons.

Ryan, C.M. (1987). "Juvenile court jurisdiction: Intervention and intrusion." In F.X. Hartmann (ed.), *From Children to Citizens: Volume II: The Role of the Juvenile Court* (pp. 56-64). New York: Springer-Verlag.

Ryerson, E. (1978). *The Best-Laid Plans: America's Juvenile Court Experiment.* New York: Hill and Wang.

Sagarin, E. (1980). *Taboos in Criminology.* Beverly Hills: Sage.

Sagatun, I.J. and L.P. Edwards (1995). *Child Abuse and the Legal System.* Chicago: Nelson-Hall.

Sameroff, A.J. and M.J. Chandler (1975). "Reproductive risk and the continuum of caretaking causality." In F. Horowitz (ed.), *Review of Child Development Research,* Vol. 4 (pp. 187-244). Chicago: University of Chicago Press.

Sampson, R.J. (1986). "Effects of socioeconomic context on official reaction to juvenile delinquency." *American Sociological Review* 51:876-885.

Sampson, R.J. and J.H. Laub (1993a). *Crime in the Making: Pathways and Turning Points through Life.* Cambridge, MA: Harvard University Press.

Sampson, R.J. and J.H. Laub (1993b). "Structural variations in juvenile court processing: Inequality, the underclass, and social control." *Law and Society Review* 27:285-311.

Sampson, R.J. and J.H. Laub (1997). "A life-course theory of cummulative disadvantage and the stability of delinquency." In T.P. Thornberry (ed.), *Developmental Theories of Crime and Delinquency.* New Brunswick, NJ: Transaction.

Sampson, R.J. and J.L. Lauritsen (1990). "Deviant lifestyles, proximity to crime, and the offender-victim link in personal violence." *Journal of Research in Crime and Delinquency* 27:110-139.

Sanborn, J.B., Jr. (1994a). "Certification to criminal court: The important policy questions of how, when, and why." *Crime & Delinquency* 40:262-281.

Sanborn, J.B., Jr. (1994b). "Remnants of *parens patriae* in the adjudicatory hearing: Is a fair trial possible in juvenile court?" *Crime & Delinquency* 40:599-615.

Sanders, W.B. (1994). *Gangbangs and Drive-bys: Grounded Culture and Juvenile Gang Violence.* New York: Aldine de Gruyter.

Saul, J.A. and W.S. Davidson (1983). "Implementation of juvenile diversion programs: Cast your net on the other side of the boat." In J.R. Kluegel (ed.), *Evaluating Juvenile Justice* (pp. 31-46). Beverly Hills: Sage.

Scarpitti, F.R., E. Murray, S. Dinitz and W.C. Reckless (1960). "The 'Good Boy' in a high delinquency area: Four years later." *American Sociological Review* 25:555-558.

Schafer, S. (1968). *The Victim and His Criminal: A Study in Functional Responsibility*. New York: Random House.

Schaps, E., J.M. Moskowitz, J.H. Malvin and G.A. Schaeffer (1986). "Evaluation of seven school-based prevention programs: A final report of the Napa project." *International Journal of the Addictions* 21:1081-1112.

Schauss, A.G. (1980). *Diet, Crime and Delinquency*. Berkeley, CA: Parker House.

Scheff, T.J. (1967). *Mental Illness and the Social Processes*. New York: Harper and Row.

Schlossman, S.L. (1977). *Love and the American Delinquent: The Theory and Practice of "Progressive" Juvenile Justice, 1825-1920*. Chicago: University of Chicago Press.

Schlossman, S.L. and M. Sedlak (1983). *The Chicago Area Project Revisited*. Santa Monica: RAND.

Schlossman, S.L., G. Zellman and R. Shavelson (1984). *Delinquency Prevention in South Chicago: A Fifty-Year Assessment of the Chicago Area Project*. Santa Monica: RAND.

Schneider, A.L. (1984). "Sentencing guidelines and recidivism rates of juvenile offenders." *Justice Quarterly* 1:107-124.

Schneider, A.L. (1985). *The Impact of Deinstitutionalization on Recidivism and Secure Confinement of Status Offenders*. Washington, DC: U.S. Department of Justice.

Schneider, A.L. (1986). "Restitution and recidivism rates of juvenile offenders: Results from four experimental studies." *Criminology* 24:533-552.

Schneider, A.L. (1988). "A comparative analysis of juvenile court responses to drug and alcohol offenses." *Crime & Delinquency* 34:103-124.

Schneider, A.L. (1990). *Deterrence and Juvenile Crime: Results from a National Policy Experiment*. New York: Springer-Verlag.

Schneider, A.L. and P.R. Schneider (1984). "A comparison of programmatic and ad hoc restitution in juvenile courts." *Justice Quarterly* 1:529-547.

Schneider, A.L. and D.D. Schram (1982). *A Justice Philosophy for the Juvenile Court*. Salem, OR: Institute for Policy Analysis.

Schneider, A.L. and D.D. Schram (1986). "The Washington State juvenile justice system reform: A review of findings." *Criminal Justice Policy Review* 2:211-235.

Schrag, C. (1971). *Crime and Justice: American Style*. Washington, DC: U.S. Government Printing Office.

Schuessler, K.F. and D.R. Cressey (1950). "Personality characteristics of criminals." *American Journal of Sociology* 55:476-484.

Schulsinger, F. (1972). "Psychopathy: Heredity and environment." *International Journal of Mental Health* 1:190-206.

Schur, E.M. (1973). *Radical Nonintervention: Rethinking the Delinquency Problem*. Englewood Cliffs, NJ: Prentice Hall.

Schwartz, I.M., G. Fishman, R. Rawson Hatfield, B.A. Krisberg and Z. Eisikovits (1987). "Juvenile detention: The hidden closets revisited." *Justice Quarterly* 4:219-235.

Schwartz, I.M., M. Jackson-Beeck and R. Anderson (1984). "The 'hidden' system of juvenile control." *Crime & Delinquency* 30:371-385.

Schwartz, M. and S.S. Tangri (1965). "A note on self-concept an an insulator against delinquency." *American Sociological Review* 30:922-926.

Schwartz, M.D. (1989). "Family violence as a cause of crime: Rethinking our priorities." *Criminal Justice Policy Review* 3:115-132.

Schwendinger, H. and J. Schwendinger (1979). "Delinquency and social reform: A radical perspective." In L. Empey (ed.), *Juvenile Justice* (pp. 245-290). Charlottesville: University of Virginia Press.

Sealock, M.D., D.C. Gottfredson and C.A. Gallagher (1997). "Drug treatment for juvenile offenders: Some good and bad news." *Journal of Research in Crime and Delinquency* 34:210-236.

Sechrest, L. (1987). "Classification for treatment." In D.M. Gottfredson and M. Tonry (eds.), *Prediction and Classification: Criminal Justice Decision Making* (pp. 293-322). Chicago: University of Chicago Press.

Seis, M.C. and K.L. Elbe (1991). "The death penalty for juveniles: Bridging the gap between an evolving standard of decency and legislative policy." *Justice Quarterly* 8:465-488.

Sells, S.B. amd D.D. Simpson (1979). "Evaluation of treatment outcomes for youths in the drug abuse reporting program (DARP): A follow-up study." In G.M. Beschner and A.S. Friedman (eds.), *Youth Drug Abuse* (pp. 571-628). Lexington, MA: Lexington.

Severy, L.J. and J.M. Whitaker (1984). "Memphis-Metro Youth Diversion Project: Final report." *Child Welfare* 63:269-277.

Shah, S.A. and L.H. Roth (1974). "Biological and psychophysiological factors in criminality." In D. Glaser (ed.), *Handbook of Criminology* (pp. 101-173). New York: Rand McNally.

Shannon, L.W. (1982). *Assessing the Relationship of Adult Criminal Careers to Juvenile Careers.* Iowa City, IO: Iowa Urban Community Research Center.

Sharn, L. and S. Tangonan (1995). "Chain gangs back in Alabama." *USA Today* May 4:3A.

Shaw, C.R. and H.D. McKay (1942). *Juvenile Delinquency and Urban Areas.* Chicago: University of Chicago Press.

Shaw, C.R., F.M. Zorbaugh, H.D. McKay and L.S. Cottrell (1929). *Delinquency Areas.* Chicago: University of Chicago Press.

Sheldon, W.H. (1949). *Varieties of Delinquent Youth: An Introduction to Correctional Psychiatry.* New York: Harper and Brothers.

Sheley, J.F. and J.D. Wright (1993). *Gun Acquisition and Possession in Selected Juvenile Samples.* Washington, DC: Office of Juvenile Justice and Delinquency Prevention.

Sherman, L.W. (1992). "Attacking crime: Policing and crime control." In Tonry, M. and N. Morris (eds.), *Modern Policing* (pp. 159-230). Chicago: University of Chicago Press.

Sherman, L.W. (1995). "The police." In James Q. Wilson and J. Petersilia (eds.), *Crime* (pp. 327-348). San Francisco, CA: Institute for Contemporary Studies Press.

Shichor, D. (1995). *Punishment for Profit: Private Prisons/Public Concerns.* Thousand Oaks, CA: Sage.

Shine, J. and D. Price (1992). "Prosecutors and juvenile justice: New roles and perspectives." In I.M. Schwartz (ed.), *Juvenile Justice and Public Policy: Toward a National Agenda* (pp. 101-133). New York: Lexington Books.

Shireman, C.H. and F.G. Reamer (1986). *Rehabilitating Juvenile Justice.* New York: Columbia University Press.

Shockley, W. (1967). "A 'try simplest cases' approach to the heredity-poverty-crime problem." *Proceedings of the National Academy of Sciences* 57:1767-1774.

Short, J.F. (1960). "Differential association as a hypothesis: Problems of empirical testing." *Social Problems* 8:14-25.

Short, J.F. and I. Nye (1958). "Extent of unrecorded delinquency: Tentative conclusions." *Journal of Criminal Law, Criminology and Police Science* 49:296-302.

Short, J.F. and F.L. Strodbeck (1965). *Group Process and Gang Delinquency.* Chicago: University of Chicago Press.

Shover, N. S. Norland, J. James and W.E. Thornton (1979). "Gender roles and delinquency." *Social Forces* 58:162-175.

Sickmund, M. (1994). "How juveniles get to criminal court." *Juvenile Justice Bulletin.* Washington, DC: U.S. Department of Justice.

Sickmund, M. (1997). *Offenders in Juvenile Court, 1995.* Washington, DC: U.S. Department of Justice.

Sickmund, M. and P.J. Baunach (1986). "Children in custody: Public juvenile facilities, 1985." *Bureau of Justice Statistics Bulletin.* Washington, DC: U.S. Department of Justice.

Sickmund, M., H.N. Snyder and E. Poe-Yamagata (1997). *Juvenile Offenders and Victims: 1997 Update on Violence.* Washington, DC: Office of Juvenile Justice and Delinquency Prevention.

Sieverdes, C. and C. Bartollas (1986). "Security level and adjustment patterns in juvenile institutions." *Journal of Criminal Justice* 14:135-145.

Sigler, R.T. and K.J. Leenhouts (1982). "Volunteers in criminal justice: How effective?" *Federal Probation* 46(2):25-29.

Silberg,, J., J. Meyer, A. Pickles, E. Simonoff, L. Eaves, J. Hewitt, H. Maes and M. Rutter (1996). "Heterogeneity among juvenile antisocial behaviors: Findings from the Virginia Twin Study of Adolescent Behavioral Development." In G.R. Bock and J.A. Goode (eds.), *Genetics of Criminal and Antisocial Behavior* (pp. 76-85). Chichester, England: John Wiley and Sons.

Silberman, C.E. (1978). *Criminal Violence, Criminal Justice.* New York: Random House.

Simon, R.J. (1975). *Women and Crime.* Lexington: Lexington Books.

Simons, R.L., C. Wu, C. Johnson and R.D. Conger (1995). "A test of various perspectives on the intergenerational transmission of domestic violence." *Criminology* 33:141-171.

Simpson, D.D. and S.B. Sills (1982). "Effectiveness of treatment for drug abuse: An overview of the DARP research program." *Advances in Alcohol and Substance Abuse* 2:7-29.

Simpson, E.L. (1974). "Moral development research: A case study of scientific cultural bias." *Human Development* 17:81-106.

Singer, S.I. (1996). *Recriminalizing Delinquency: Violent Juvenile Crime and Juvenile Justice Reform.* New York: Cambridge University Press.

Skinner, B.F. (1953). *Science and Human Behavior*. New York: Macmillan.

Skogan, W.G. (1981). "On attitudes and behavior." In D.A. Lewis (ed.), *Reactions to Crime*. Beverly Hills, CA: Sage.

Skogan, W.G. and M.G. Maxfield (1981). *Coping with Crime: Individual and Neighborhood Reactions*. Beverly Hills, CA: Sage.

Skolnick, J. (1966). *Justice Without Trial*. New York: Wiley.

Skolnick, J.H., R. Bluthenthal and T. Correl (1993). "Gang organization and migration." In S. Cummings and D.J. Monti (eds.), *Gangs: The Origins and Impact of Contemporary Youth Gangs in the United States* (pp. 193-218). Albany, NY: SUNY Press.

Smith, M.D. and R.N. Parker (1980). "Type of homicide and variation in regional rates." *Social Forces* 59:136-147.

Snyder, H.N. (1997). "Juvenile Arrests 1996." *Juvenile Justice Bulletin*. Washington, DC: U.S. Department of Justice.

Snyder, H.N., T.A. Finnegan, E.H. Nimick, M.H. Sickmund, D.P. Sullivan and N.J. Tierney (1987). *Juvenile Court Statistics 1984*. Washington, DC: U.S. Department of Justice.

Snyder, H.N., T.A. Finnegan, E.H. Nimick, M.H. Sickmund, D.P. Sullivan and N.J. Tierney (1990). *Juvenile Court Statistics 1987*. Washington, DC: U.S. Department of Justice.

Sontheimer, H.G. (1986). "The privatization of corrections in the juvenile and adult systems of Pennsylvania." Paper presented at the annual meeting of the American Society of Criminology, Atlanta, GA.

Sontheimer, H. and A. Volenik (1995). "Fax-like technology gives home detention a boost." *Juvenile Justice Update* (February) 1(1):5.

Sparger, J.R. and D.J. Giacopassi (1992). "Memphis revisited: A reexamination of police shootings after the Garner decision." *Justice Quarterly* 9:211-225.

Sparks, R.F. (1982). *Research on Victims of Crime*. Washington, DC: U.S. Government Printing Office.

Sparrow, M.K., M.H. Moore and D.M. Kennedy (1990). *Beyond 911: A New Era for Policing*. New York: Basic Books.

Spergel, I.A. (1966). *Street Gang Work: Theory and Practice*. Reading, MA: Addison-Wesley.

Spergel, I.A. (1984). "Violent gangs in Chicago: In search of social policy." *Social Service Review* 58:199-226.

Spergel, I.A. (1986). "The violent gang problem in Chicago: A local community approach." *Social Service Review* 60:94-131.

Spergel, I.A. and G.D. Curry (1990). *Survey of Youth Gang Problems and Programs in 45 Cities and 6 Sites*. Washington, DC: Office of Juvenile Justice and Delinquency Prevention.

Spergel, I.A. and G.D. Curry (1993). "The national youth gang survey: A research and development process." In Goldstein, A.P. and C.R. Huff (eds.), *The Gang Intervention Handbook* (pp. 359-400). Champaign, IL: Research Press.

Spergel, I.A., G.D. Curry, R. Chance, C.Kane, R. Ross, A. Alexander, E. Simmons and S. Oh (1990). *National Youth Gang Suppression and Intervention Program: Executive Summary, Stage 1: Assessment*. Arlington, VA: National Youth Gang Information Center.

Staff (1994, May 5). "Condemn caning, flogging; Torture merits no applause." *USA Today* (p. 10A).

Staples, W.G. (1987). "Law and social control in juvenile justice dispositions." *Journal of Research in Crime and Delinquency* 24:7-22.

Stapleton, W.V. and L.E. Teitelbaum (1972). *In Defense of Youth: A Study of the Role of Counsel in American Juvenile Courts*. New York: Russell Sage Foundation.

Steele, B.F. and C. B. Pollock (1974). "A psychiatric study of parents who abuse infants and small children." In R.E. Helfer and C.H. Kempe (eds.), *The Battered Child*, 2nd ed. Chicago: University of Chicago Press.

Stephens, R.C. (1987). *Mind-altering Drugs: Use, Abuse, and Treatment*. Newbury Park, CA: Sage.

Straus, M.A. (1983). "Ordinary violence, child abuse, and wife-beating: What do they have in common?" In D. Finkelhor, R.J. Gelles, G.T. Hotaling and M.A. Straus (eds.), *The Dark Side of Families: Current Family Violence Research*. Beverly Hills, CA: Sage.

Straus, M.A. [with D.A. Donnelly] (1994). *Beating the Devil Out of Them: Corporal Punishment in American Families*. New York: Lexington Books.

Straus, M.A. and D.A. Donnelly (1993). "Corporal punishment of adolescents by American parents." *Youth and Society* 24:419-442.

Street, D., R.D. Vinter and C. Perrow (1966). *Organization for Treatment: A Comparative Study of Institutions for Delinquents*. New York: Free Press.

Streib, V.L. (1987). *Death Penalty for Juveniles*. Bloomington, IN: Indiana University Press.

Studt, E. (1973). *Surveillance and Service in Parole: A Report of the Parole Action Study*. Washington, DC: National Institute of Corrections.

Substance Abuse and Mental Health Services Administration (1997). *National Household Survey on Drug Abuse: Population Estimates 1996*. Washington, DC: U.S. Department of Health and Human Services.

Sullivan, C., M.Q. Grant and J.D. Grant (1957). "The development of interpersonal maturity: Applications to delinquency." *Psychiatry* 20:373-385.

Sutherland, E.H. (1939). *Principles of Criminology*, 3rd ed. Philadelphia: Lippincott.

Sutherland, E.H. and D.R. Cressey (1974). *Criminology*, 9th ed. Philadelphia: Lippincott.

Swadi, H. and H. Zeitlin (1987). "Drug education to school children: Does it really work?" *British Journal of Addiction* 82:741-746.

Sykes, G.M. (1974). "The rise of critical criminology." *Journal of Criminal Law and Criminology* 65:206-213.

Sykes, G.M. and D. Matza (1957). "Techniques of neutralization: A theory of delinquency." *American Sociological Review* 22:664-670.

Szumanski, L.A. (1994). *Waiver/Transfer/Certification of Juveniles to Criminal Court: Age Restrictions—Crime Restrictions (1993 Update)*. Pittsburgh: National Center for Juvenile Justice.

Taft Youth Center (no date). *Student Handbook*. Pikeville, TN.

Tangri, S.S. and M. Schwartz (1967). "Delinquency research and the self-concept variable." *Journal of Criminal Law, Criminology and Police Science* 58:182-190.

Tannenbaum, F. (1938). *Crime and the Community*. New York: Columbia University Press.

Taylor, C.S. (1990). "Gang imperialism." In Huff, C.R. (ed.), *Gangs in America* (pp. 103-115). Newbury Park, CA: Sage.

Taylor, I., P. Walton and J. Young (1973). *Critical Criminology*. Boston: Routledge and Kegan Paul.

Taylor, M. and C. Nee (1988). "The role of cues in simulated residential burglary." *British Journal of Criminology* 28:396-407.

Tennenbaum, D.J. (1977). "Personality and criminality: A summary and implications of the literature." *Journal of Criminal Justice* 5:225-235.

Thomas, C.W. and S. Bilchik (1985). "Prosecuting juveniles in criminal courts: A legal and empirical analysis." *The Journal of Criminal Law and Criminology* 76:439-479.

Thomas, C.W. and R. Cage (1977). "The effect of social characteristics on juvenile court dispositions." *Sociological Quarterly* 18: 237-252.

Thornberry, T.P. (1973). "Race, socioeconomic status and sentencing in the juvenile justice system." *Journal of Criminal Law and Criminology* 64:90-98.

Thornberry, T.P. (1987). "Toward an interactional theory of delinquency." *Criminology* 25:863-892.

Thornberry, T.P. and J.H. Burch (1997). *Gang Members and Delinquent Behavior*. Washington, DC: Office of Juvenile Justice and Delinquency Prevention.

Thornberry, T.P. and R.L. Christenson (1984). Unemployment and criminal involvement: An investigation of reciprocal causal structures, *American Sociological Review* 49:398-411.

Thornberry, T.P. and R.M. Figlio (1974). "Victimization and criminal behavior in a birth cohort." In Thornberry, T.P. and E. Sagarin (eds.), *Images of Crime: Offenders and Victims* (pp. 102-112). New York: Praeger.

Thornberry, T.P., M.D. Krohn, A.J. Lizotte and D. Chard-Wierschem (1993). "The role of juvenile gangs in facilitating delinquent behavior." *Journal of Research in Crime and Delinquency* 30:55-87.

Thornberry, T.P., A.J. Lizotte, M.D. Krohn, M. Farnworth and S.J. Jang (1994). "Delinquent peers, beliefs, and delinquent behavior: A longitudinal test of interactional theory." *Criminology* 32:47-84.

Thrasher, F.M. (1936). *The Gang*. Chicago: University of Chicago Press.

Thurman, Q.C. (1984). "Deviance and the neutralization of moral commitment: An empirical analysis." *Deviant Behavior* 5:291-304.

Tittle, C. (1980). "Labelling and crime: An empirical evaluation." In W. Gove (ed.), *The Labelling of Deviance* (pp. 241-263). Beverly Hills, CA: Sage.

Tittle, C., W. Villemez and D. Smith (1978). "The myth of social class and criminality: An empirical assessment of the empirical evidence." *American Sociological Review* 43:643-656.

Tobler, N.S. (1986). "Meta-analysis of 143 adolescent drug prevention programs: Quantitative outcome results of program participants compared to a control or comparison group." *Journal of Drug Issues* 16:537-567.

Tobler, N.S. (1997). Meta-analysis of adolescent drug prevention programs: Results of the 1993 meta-analysis. In W.J. Bukoski (ed.), *Meta-Analysis of Drug Abuse Prevention Programs* (pp. 5-68). Rockville, MD: National Institute on Drug Abuse.

Toch, H. and J.D. Grant (1991). *Police as Problem Solvers*. New York: Plenum.

Toennies, F. (1957). *Community and Society*. (Translated by C.P. Loomis.) East Lansing: Michigan State University Press.

Torbet, P.M. (1996). *Juvenile Probation: The Workhorse of the Juvenile Justice System*. Washington, DC: U.S. Department of Justice.

Torbet, P., R. Gable, H. Hurst, I. Montgomery, L. Szymanski and D. Thomas (1996). *State Responses to Serious and Violent Juvenile Crime*. Washington, DC: Office of Juvenile Justice and Delinquency Prevention.

Toseland, R.W. (1982). "Fear of crime: who is most vulnerable?" *Journal of Criminal Justice* 10:199-210.

Toy, C. (1992). "A short history of Asian gangs in San Francisco." *Justice Quarterly* 9:647-666.

Tracy, P.E., M.E. Wolfgang and R.M. Figlio (1985). *Delinquency in Two Birth Cohorts: Executive Summary*. Washington, DC: U.S. Department of Justice.

Tracy, P.E., M.E. Wolfgang and R.M. Figlio (1990). *Delinquency Careers in Two Birth Cohorts*. New York: Plenum.

Trasler, G. (1993). "Conscience, opportunity, rational choice, and crime." In Clarke, R.V. and M. Felson (eds.), *Routine Activity and Rational Choice* (pp. 305-322). New Brunswick, NJ: Transaction.

Trebach, A.S. (1987). *The Great Drug War: And Radical Proposals That Could Make America Safe Again*. New York: Macmillan.

Trojanowicz, R. (1983). *An Evaluation of the Neighborhood Foot Patrol Program in Flint, Michigan*. East Lansing, MI: Michigan State University.

Trojanowicz, R., V.E. Kappeler, L.K. Gaines and B. Bucqueroux (1998). *Community Policing: A Contemporary Perspective*, 2nd ed. Cincinnati: Anderson.

Tunnell, K. (1992). *Choosing Crime: The Criminal Calculus of Property Offenders*. Chicago: Nelson-Hall.

Turk, A.T. (1972). *Legal Sanctioning and Social Control*. Washington, DC: U.S. Government Printing Office.

Turk, A.T. (1980). "Analyzing official deviance: For nonpartison conflict analysis in criminology." In J.A. Inciardi (ed.), *Radical Criminology: The Coming Crisis* (pp. 78-91). Beverly Hills: Sage.

Turner, M.G., F.T. Cullen, J.L. Sundt and B.K. Applegate (1997). "Public Tolerance for Community-Based Sanctions." *Prison Journal* 77: 6-26.

Umbreit, M.S. (1986). "Victim/offender mediation: A national survey." *Federal Probation* 50(4):53-56.

Umbreit, M.S. (1994). *Victim meets offender: The impact of restorative justice and mediation*. Monsey, NY: Criminal Justice Press.

Umbreit, M.S. & Coates, R.B. (1993). Cross-site analysis of victim-offender mediation in four states. *Crime & Delinquency* 39:565-585.

Underwood, J. (1994). "Prayer in the schools." *Schools and the Courts* 20(May): 1039-1050.

U.S. Attorney General's Task Force on Family Violence (1984). *Family Violence*. Washington, DC: U.S. Government Printing Office.

U.S. Bureau of Census (1992). *Census of the Population*. Washington, DC: U.S. Department of Commerce.

U.S. Department of Justice (1995). *Criminal Victimization in the United States, 1993*. Washington, DC: U.S. Department of Justice.

U.S. Department of Justice (1997). *Criminal Victimization in the United States, 1994*. Washington, DC: U.S. Department of Justice.

USA Today (1997, December 26). "Don't swallow the hype." *USA Today* (p. 9A).

van den Haag, E. (1978). "In defense of the death penalty: A legal-practical-moral analysis." *Criminal Law Bulletin* 14:51-68.

van den Haag, E. and P. Conrad (1983). *The Death Penalty: A Debate*. New York: Plenum.

Van Kammen, W.B. and R. Loeber (1994). "Are fluctuations in delinquent activities related to the onset and offset in juvenile illegal drug use and drug dealing?" *The Journal of Drug Issues* 24:9-24.

van Maanen, J. (1982). "The disagreeable complainant." In N. Johnston and L.D. Savitz (eds.), *Legal Process and Corrections* (pp. 44-55). New York: John Wiley and Sons.

Van Voorhis, P., Braswell, M. and Lester, D. (1997). *Correctional Counseling and Rehabilitation*, 3rd ed. Cincinnati: Anderson.

Venezia, P. and D. Anthony (1978). *A Program Level Evaluation of Wisconsin's Youth Service Bureaus*. Tuscon: Association for Youth Development.

Vigil, J.D. (1988). *Barrio Gangs: Street Life and Identity in Southern California*. Austin, TX: University of Texas Press.

Vigil, J.D. (1993). "The established gang." In Cummings, S. and D.J. Monti (eds.), *Gangs: The Origins and Impact of Contemporary Youth Gangs in the United States* (pp. 95-112). Albany, NY: SUNY Press.

Vigil, J.D. (1997). "Learning from gangs: The Mexican American experience." *ERIC Digest* (February).

Vingilis, E.R. (1984). "Youth and the forbidden fruit: Experiences with changes in legal drinking age in North America." *Journal of Criminal Justice* 12:161-172.

Vingilis, E.R. and K. De Genova (1984). "Youth and the forbidden fruit: Experiences with changes in legal drinking age in North America." *Journal of Criminal Justice* 12:161-172.

"Violence-related attitudes and behaviors of high school students—New York City, 1992." (1993). *Journal of School Health* 63:438-440.

Virkkunen, M, D. Goldman and M. Linnoila (1996). "Serotonic in alcoholic violent offenders." In G.R. Bock and J.A. Goode (eds.), *Genetics of Criminal and Antisocial Behavior* (pp. 168-176). Chichester, England: John Wiley and Sons.

Visher, C.A. (1983). "Gender, police arrest decisions, and notions of chivalry." *Criminology* 21:5-28.

Visher, C.A. (1990). "Incorporating drug treatment in criminal sanctions." *NIJ Reports* 221. Washington, DC: National Institute of Justice.

Vito, G.F. (1989). "The Kentucky substance abuse program: A private program to treat probationers and parolees." *Federal Probation* 53(1):65-72.

Vold, G.B. (1958). *Theoretical Criminology*. New York: Oxford University Press.

Vold, G.B. (1979). *Theoretical Criminology*, 2nd ed. New York: Oxford University Press.

Vold, G.B. and T.J. Bernard (1986). *Theoretical Criminology*, 3rd ed. New York: Oxford University Press.

von Hentig, H. (1941). "Remarks on the interaction of perpetrator and victim." *Journal of Criminal Law, Criminology and Police Science* 31:303-309.

von Hirsch, A. (1984). "Selective incapacitation: A critique." *National Institute of Justice Reports* January 1984:5-8. Washington, DC: National Institute of Justice.

von Hirsch, A. (1990). "The ethics of community-based sanctions." *Crime & Delinquency* 36:162-173.

Vorenberg, E.W. and J. Vorenberg (1973). "Early diversion from the criminal justice system: practice in search of a theory." In L.E. Ohlin (ed.), *Prisoners in America* (pp. 151-183). Englewood Cliffs, NJ: Prentice Hall.

Wadlington, W., C.H. Whitebread and S.M. Davis (1983). *Cases and Materials on Children in the Legal System*. Mineola, NY: Foundation Press.

Waldo, G.P. and S. Dinitz (1967). "Personality attributes of the criminal: An analysis of research studies, 1950-1965." *Journal of Research in Crime and Delinquency* 4:185-202.

Walker, S. (1983). *The Police in America: An Introduction*. New York: McGraw-Hill.

Walker, S. (1985). *Sense and Nonsense about Crime: A Policy Guide*. Monterey, CA: Brooks/Cole.

Walker, S. (1998). *Sense and Nonsense about Crime and Drugs: A Policy Guide*, 4th ed. Belmont, CA: West/Wadsworth.

Walker, S. (1993). *Taming the System: The Control of Discretion in Criminal Justice*. New York: Oxford University Press.

Walters, G.D. (1992). "A meta-analysis of the gene-crime relationship." *Criminology* 30:595-613.

Wang, C.T. and D. Daro (1997). *Current Trends in Child Abuse Reporting and Fatalities: The Results of the 1996 Annual Fifty State Survey*. Chicago: National Committee to Prevent Child Abuse.

Watts, W.D. and L.S. Wright (1990). "The relationship of alcohol, tobacco, marijuana, and other illegal drug use to delinquency among Mexican-American, black, and white adolescent males." *Adolescence* 25:171-181.

Weber, G.H. (1979). *Child-Menders*. Beverly Hills, CA: Sage.

Weis, K. and S.S. Borges (1973). "Victimology and rape: The case of the legitimate victim." *Issues in Criminology* 8:71-115.

Weisheit, R.A. (1983). "The social context of alcohol and drug education: Implications for program evaluations." *Journal of Alcohol and Drug Education* 29:72-81.

Werthman, C. and I. Piliavin (1967). "Gang members and the police." In D. Bordua (ed.), *The Police: Six Sociological Essays* (pp. 72-94). New York: John Wiley.

West's Annotated Claifornia Codes (1982). St. Paul: West.

West's Annotated California Codes (1972). St. Paul: West.

Wheeler, G.R. (1978). *Counter-deterrence: A Report on Juvenile Sentencing and Effects of Prisonization*. Chicago: Nelson-Hall.

Whitaker, C.J. and L.D. Bastian (1991). *Teenage Victims: A National Crime Survey Report*. Washington, DC: Bureau of Justice Statistics.

Whitaker, J.M. and L.J. Severy (1984). "Service accountability and recidivism for diverted youth: A client- and service-comparison analysis." *Criminal Justice and Behavior* 11:47-74.

White, G.F. (1990). "The drug use-delinquency connection in adolescence." In Weisheit, R. (ed.) *Drugs, Crime and the Criminal Justice System*. Cincinnati: Anderson.

White, H.R., R.J. Pandina and R.L. LaGrange (1987). "Longitudinal predictors of serious substance use and delinquency." *Criminology* 25:715-740.

Whitehead, J.T. (1985). "Job burnout in probation and parole: Its extent and intervention implications." *Criminal Justice and Behavior* 12:91-110.

Whitehead, J.T. (1989). *Burnout in Probation and Corrections*. New York: Praeger.

Whitehead, J.T. (1998). "Good ol' boys" and the chair: Death penalty attitudes of policy makers in Tennessee." *Crime & Delinquency* 44:245-256.

Whitehead, J.T. and S.P. Lab (1989). A meta-analysis of juvenile correctional treatment." *Journal of Research in Crime and Delinquency* 26:276-295.

Whitehead, J.T. and C.A. Lindquist (1986). "Correctional officer job burnout: A path model." *Journal of Research in Crime and Delinquency* 23:23-42.

Whitehead, J.T., L.S. Miller and L.B. Myers (1995). "The diversionary effectiveness of intensive supervision and community corrections programs." In J.O. Smykla and W.L. Selke (eds.), *Intermediate Sanctions: Sentencing in the 1990s* (pp. 135-151). Cincinnati: Anderson.

Wiatrowski, M., D. Griswold and M. Roberts (1981). "Social control theory and delinquency." *American Sociological Review* 46:525-541.

Widom, C.S. (1989). "Child abuse, neglect, and violent criminal behavior." *Criminology* 27:251-271.

Widom, C.S. (1995). "Childhood victimization and violent behavior." Paper presented at the Annual Conference on Criminal Justice Research and Evaluation, Washington, DC.

Wiehe, V.R. (1992). *Working with Child Abuse and Neglect*. Itasca, IL: F.E. Peacock.

Wilbanks, W.L. (1985). "Predicting failure on parole." In D.P. Farrington and R. Tarling (eds.), *Prediction in Criminology* (pp. 78-95). Albany, NY: SUNY Press.

Wilbanks, W. (1987). *The Myth of a Racist Criminal Justice System*. Monterey, CA: Brooks/Cole.

Williams, H. and A.M. Pate (1987). "Returning to first principles: Reducing the fear of crime in Newark." *Crime & Delinquency* 33:53-70.

Williams, N. and S. Williams (1970). *The Moral Development of Children*. London: Macmillan.

Wilson, J.J. and J.C. Howell (1995). "Comprehensive strategy for serious, violent, and chronic juvenile offenders." In J.C. Howell, B. Krisberg, J.D. Hawkins and J.J. Wilson (eds.) *A Sourcebook: Serious, Violent and Chronic Juvenile Offenders* (pp. 36-46). Thousand Oaks, CA: Sage.

Wilson, J.Q. (1968). *Varieties of Police Behavior*. New York: Harvard University Press.

Wilson, J.Q. (1978). *Varieties of Police Behavior: The Management of Law and Order in Eight Communities*. Cambridge, MA: Harvard University Press.

Wilson, J.Q. (1983). *Thinking about Crime* (rev. ed.). New York: Vintage Books.

Wilson, J.Q. and R.J. Herrnstein (1985). *Crime and Human Nature*. New York: Simon & Schuster.

Wilson, J.Q. and G.L. Kelling (1982, March). "Broken windows: The police and neighborhood safety." *Atlantic Monthly* (pp. 29-38).

Winfree, L.T., Guiterman, D. & Mays, G.L. (1997). "Work assignments and police work: Exploring the work world of sworn officers in four New mexico police departments." *Policing: An International Journal of Police Stragegies and Police Departments* 20:419-441.

Winner, L., L. Lanza-Kaduce, D.M. Bishop and C.E. Frazier (1997). "The transfer of juveniles to criminal court: Re-examining recidivism over the long term." *Crime & Delinquency* 43:548-563.

Wish, E.D., M.A. Toborg and J.P Bellassai (1988). *Identifying Drug Users and Monitoring Them During Conditional Release*. Washington, DC: U.S. Department of Justice.

Witken, H.A., S.A. Mednick, F. Schulsinger, E. Bakkestrom, K.O. Christiansen, D.R. Goodenough, K. Hirschhorn, C. Lundsteen, D.R. Owen, J. Phillip, D.B. Rubin and M. Stocking (1976). "XYY and XXY men: Criminality and aggression." *Science* 193:547-555.

Wolfgang, M.E. (1958). *Patterns in Criminal Homicide*. Montclair, NJ: Patterson Smith. Reprinted 1975.

Wolfgang, M.E. and F. Ferracuti (1967). *The Subculture of Violence: Toward an Integrated Theory of Criminology*. London: Tavistock.

Wood, P.B., B. Pfefferbaum and B.J. Arneklev (1993). "Risk-taking and self-control: Social psychological correlates of delinquency." *Journal of Crime and Justice* 16:111-130.

Wooden, K. (1976). *Weeping in the Playtime of Others: America's Incarcerated Children*. New York: McGraw-Hill.

Worden, A.P. (1993). "The attitudes of women and men in policing: Testing conventional and contemporary wisdom." *Criminology* 31:203-237.

Worden, R.E. (1996). "The causes of police brutality: Theory and evidence on police use of force." In W.A. Geller, W.A. and H. Toch (eds.) *Police Violence: Understanding and Controlling Police Abuse of Force* (pp. 23-51). New Haven, CT: Yale University Press.

Worden, R.E. and R.L. Shepard (1996). "Demeanor, crime, and police behavior: A reexamination of the police services study data." *Criminology* 34:61-82.

Wordes, M., T.S. Bynum and C.J. Corley (1994). "Locking up youth: The impact of face on detention decisions." *Journal of Research in Crime and Delinquency* 31:149-165.

World Health Organization (1964). *WHO Expert Committee on Addiction Producing Drugs: 13th Report*. #23. Geneva: author.

Wright, J.D., J.F. Sheley, and M.D. Smith (1992). "Kids, guns, and killing fields." *Society* 30:84-89.

Wright, J.P., F.T. Cullen and N. Williams (1997). "Working while in school and delinquent involvement: Implications for social policy." *Crime & Delinquency* 43:203-221.

Wright, K.N. and K.E. Wright (1994). *Family Life, Delinquency, and Crime: A Policymaker's Guide: Research Summary*. Washington, DC: Office of Juvenile Justice and Delinquency Prevention.

Wright, M. and B. Galaway (1989). *Mediation and Criminal Justice: Victims, Offenders and Community*. Newbury Park, CA: Sage.

Wright, R.T. and S.H. Decker (1994). *Burglars on the Job: Streetlife and Residential Break-ins*. Boston: Northeastern University Press.

Yablonsky, L. (1962). *The Violent Gang*. New York: Macmillan.

Yin, P. (1988). *Victimization and the Aged*. Springfield, IL: Charles C Thomas.

Young, J. and R. Matthews (1992). "Questioning left realism." In Matthews, R. and J. Young (eds.), *Issues in Realist Criminology* (pp. 1-18). Newbury Park, CA: Sage.

Zastrow, C. (1993). "The social work approach to juvenile delinquency in the U.S." *International Journal of Comparative and Applied Criminal Justice* 17:251-259.

Zatz, M.S. (1985). "Los Cholos: Legal processing of Chicano gang members." *Social Problems* 33:13-30.

Zevitz, R. (1993). "Youth gangs in a small midwestern city: Insider's perspectives." *Journal of Crime and Justice* 16:149-166.

Zimring, F.E. (1982). *The Changing Legal World of Adolescence*. New York: Free Press.

Ziskin, J. (1970). *Coping with Psychiatric and Psychological Testimony*. Beverly Hills: Law and Psychology Press.

Court Cases and Statutes

Alabama Code 12-15-59

Bethel School District No. 403 v. Fraser, 478 U.S. 675, 106 S.Ct. 3159, 92 L.Ed.2d 549 (1986).

Breed v. Jones, 421 U.S. 519, 95 S.Ct. 1779, 44 L.Ed.2d 346 (1975).

Cal. Welf. & Inst. Code 602 (West 1982).

Commonwealth v. Fisher, 213 Pa. 48 (1905).

Cornfield By Lewis v. Consolidated High School District No. 230, 991 F.2d 1316 (7th Cir. 1993)

Doe v. Renfrow, 451 U.S. 1022 (1981). Denial of certiorari in Doe v. Renfrow, United States District Court, N.D. Indiana, 475 F. Supp. 1012 (1979).

Doe v. Renfrow, United States District Court, Northern District of Indiana, 1979, 475 Federal Supplement 1012).

Ex parte Crouse, 4 Wheaton (Pa.) 9 (1838).

Fare v. Michael C., 442 U.S. 707, 99 S.Ct. 2560, 61 L.Ed.2d 197 (1979).

Gonzalez v. Mailliard, Civ. No. 50424, N.D. Cal., 2/9/71. Appeal U.S. No. 70-120, 4/9/71 (1971).

Goss v. Lopez, 419 U.S. 565, 95 S.Ct. 729, 42 L.Ed.2d 725 (1975).

Hazelwood School District v. Kuhlmeier, 484 U.S. 260, 107 S.Ct., 96 L.Ed.2d 694 (1988).

H.L. v. Matheson, 450 U.S. 398, 101 S.Ct. 1164, 67 L.Ed.2d 388 (1981).

Honig v. Doe, ___ U.S. ___, 108 S.Ct. 255, 98 L.Ed 2d 213 (1988).

Ingraham v. Wright, 430 U.S. 651, 97 S.Ct. 1401, 51 L.Ed.2d 711 (1977).

In re Gault, 387 U.S. 1, 87 S.Ct. 1428, 18 L.Ed.2d 527 (1967).

In re Tyrell, 22 Cal. Rptr. 2d33 (1994).

In re Winship, 397 U.S. 358, 90 S.Ct. 1068, 25 L.Ed.2d 368 (1970).

Jones v. Clear Creek Independent School District, 977 F.2d (5th Cir. 1992).

Kent v. United States, 383 U.S. 541, 86 S.Ct. 1045, 16 L.Ed.2d 84 (1966).

Kolender v. Lawson, 461 U.S. 352, 103 S. Ct. 1855, 75 L.Ed. 2d 903 (1983).

Lee v. Weisman 112 S.Ct. 2649 (1992).

McKeiver v. Pennsylvania, 403 U.S. 528, 91 S.Ct. 1976, 29 L.Ed.2d 647 (1971).

New Jersey v. T.L.O., 469 U.S. 325, 105 S.Ct. 733, 83 L.Ed.2d 720 (1985).

P.B. v. Koch, No. 95-3506, 1996 WL 547829 (Sept. 27, 1996) at 5.

People v. Turner, 55 Ill. 280 (1870).

Schall v. Martin, 467 U.S. 253, 104 S.Ct. 2403, 81 L.Ed.2d 207 (1984).

Schneckloth v. Bustamonte, 412 U.S. 218, 93 S.Ct. 2041, 36 L.Ed.2d 854 (1973).

Steirer v. Bethlehem Area School District, 987 F2d 989 (3d Cir. 1994).

Tennessee v. Garner 83 U.S. 1035, 105 S. Ct. 1694, 85 L.Ed. 2d 1 (1985).

Thompson v. Oklahoma, 724 P.2d 780 (Oklahoma Criminal App. 1986), certiorari granted, 107 S.Ct. 1281 (1987).

Tinker v. Des Moines Independent Community School District, 393 U.S. 503, 89 S.Ct. 733, 21 L.Ed.2d 731 (1969).

Vernonia School District v. Acton, 63 LW 4653 (1995)

GLOSSARY

Selected Terms in Juvenile Justice

A

abandonment: the permanent desertion of a child; an acceptable practice from the fourth to the thirteenth centuries when a child was an economic burden to a household

abuse: any nonaccidental infliction of injury that seriously impairs a child's physical or mental health

adjudication: the process of determining whether there is enough evidence to find a youth to be a delinquent, a status offender or a dependent

affective approach: an approach to drug use prevention that focuses attention on the individual in order to build self-esteem, self-awareness and feelings of self-worth

aftercare: mandatory programming for youths after release from training schools or other placements, similar to parole in adult courts

Aggression Replacement Training (ART): a method for eliminating gang-member deficiencies in dealing with everyday situations. The three main components taught are: skillstreaming (teaching proper behavioral responses to various situations), anger control and moral education.

anomie: Emil Durkheim's concept of the a state of normlessness in society

atavistic: a term describing ape-like physical qualities of the head and body that were supposed by Cesare Lombroso to be indicative of the individual's developmental state

"attack" (tough) probation: also known as "tough probation," the trend to make probation supervision stricter (tougher) by devoting less emphasis to assistance and counseling and greater attention to monitoring the conditions of probation. Attack probation can refer to intensive supervision, electronic monitoring of offender movements, and shame tactics.

avoidance: a common reaction to actual or potential victimization in which an individual stays away from particular locations where or individuals by whom victimization is anticipated

B

behavior modification: a therapeutic approach based on the work of B.F. Skinner and Hans J. Eysenck that entails the use of reinforcements to increase the probability of desired behaviors and a lack of reinforcement, or punishment stimuli, to decrease the probability of undesirable behaviors

blended sentencing: a recent development in juvenile justice in which either the juvenile court or the adult court imposes a sentence that can involve either the juvenile or the adult correctional system or both. Blended sentencing is one example of increased punitiveness toward juvenile offenders.

bond to society (also called **social bond**):   in Travis Hirschi's control theory, the connections an individual has to the social order; the four elements of the bond are attachment, commitment, involvement and belief

"boob tube" therapy: the practice of allowing youths in detention homes or training schools to watch television as a way of occupying them and freeing up the time of supervising adults

boot camp: a short-term program that resembles basic military training by emphasizing physical training and discipline; boot camps often include educational and rehabilitative components.

"broken windows" hypothesis: the belief that signs of urban decay, such as broken windows, in a neighborhood serve to make the neighborhood more conducive to crime and more fear-inducing

burnout: See **job burnout**

C

Chancery Court: a body concerned with property matters in feudal England; responsible for overseeing the financial affairs of orphaned juveniles who were not yet capable of handling their own matters

Chicago School: a perspective explaining deviance as the natural outgrowth of the location in which it occurs; named for the work performed by social scientists at the University of Chicago

child protective services: a state's method of handling child abuse cases; usually responsible for accepting and investigating reports of abuse and neglect and for removing children from potential or actual abusive situations

child saver: Anthony Platt's term for a person involved in the development of the juvenile court

chivalry hypothesis: the allegedly protective interaction of the police and other authorities with female offenders, leading to either harsher or more lenient treatment of female youthful offenders

classicism: a school of thought that sees humankind as having free will, that is, humans calculate the pros and cons of an activity before choosing what to do (Compare to **positivism**)

community policing: problem-oriented policing that relies on input from the public to define problems and establish police policy

community service: the practice of having offenders perform unpaid work for government or private agencies as payment for crimes without personal victims

concentric zone theory: a theory of city growth as following the natural progression of ever-increasing circles around the original city center

conflict theory: a theory that addresses the making and enforcing of laws rather than the breaking of laws

confrontation session: a session between adult prisoners and juveniles to deter juveniles from delinquency (e.g., Scared Straight)

congruence: genuineness on the part of a therapist

consent search: a search in which a defendant voluntarily allows the police to search person or effects without a search warrant

containment theory: Walter Reckless's social control theory holding that behavior is controlled through outer containment (influences of family, peers, etc.) and inner containment (strengths within an individual), working in opposition to external pushes, external pressures and external pulls

corporal punishment: physical punishment

cottage system: a training school design that attempts to simulate home life more closely than would a prison-like institution; it divides the larger prison into smaller "cottages" for living

Court-Appointed Special Advocate (CASA):   a voluntary advocate for children in child abuse and neglect cases

creaming: selectivity in accepting placements in a facility, screening out the more difficult cases

culture conflict: the conflict resulting when one set of cultural or subcultural practices necessitates violating the norms of a coexisting culture

curfew: an order that prohibits juveniles from going outside after a particular hour

D

day-evening center: a detention alternative in which a center was formed to devote time to formal education and remedial and tutorial work in the day and recreational programs in the evening

deadly force: police actions that have the potential to cause the death of the offender

deinstitutionalization: the practice of avoiding any involuntary residential placements of status offenders; also, the general idea of removing any youths from institutional control

delinquency: in general, conduct that subjects a juvenile individual to the jurisdiction of the juvenile court (for more on the various definitions comprised under this term, see pp. 2-6 in Chapter 1)

detached worker program: a program designed to place system workers into the environment of the gang

detention decision: the decision whether to keep a juvenile in custody or to allow the youth to go home while awaiting further court action

detoxification: a treatment approach that attempts to remove an individual from an addiction by weaning him or her off drugs

differential association: Edwin Sutherland's theory suggesting that criminal behavior is learned when an individual encounters an excess of definitions favoring deviant definitions over those that conform to the law

differential opportunity: suggested by Cloward and Ohlin, the availability of illegitimate opportunities when legitimate opportunities are blocked

differential reinforcement: a theory that proposes that an individual can learn from a variety of sources, both social and nonsocial, and that the differing levels of reinforcement received will help shape future behavior

disposition: the process of determining what intervention to give a juvenile offender upon his or her adjudication as a delinquent

dispute resolution: bringing together adversarial parties in an attempt to arrive at a mutually agreeable solution

diversion: attempting to find alternative forms of dealing with problem youth outside of normal system processing

divestiture: elimination of juvenile court jurisdiction over status offenses

domestic relations court: a civil court devoted to issues involved in divorce, child support and related matters

double jeopardy: being tried twice for the same offense

drift: the concept that individuals are pushed and pulled toward different modes of activity at different times in their lives (that is, a person can "drift" in and out of crime)

Drug Abuse Resistance Education (DARE) program: a school-based, police-taught program aimed at elementary students that attempts to reduce drug use by focusing on enhancing the social skills of the individual

Drug Use Forecasting (DUF) Program: a program that forecasts drug use through a combination of self-reports and urinalyses from arrested subjects

E

eclectic programming: the use of multiple treatment approaches

ecological fallacy: the fallacy of attributing results based on grouped data to the individual level

elaboration model: a perspective that takes components of various theories in order to construct a single explanation that incorporates the best parts of the individual theories

entitlement: a benefit or program offered by the government

F

factor analysis: a statistical technique that isolates common dimensions on a set of variables under study

false negative prediction: a prediction in which it is claimed that something will not happen and it does

false positive prediction: a prediction in which it is claimed that something will happen and it does not

family court: a court designated to deal with family matters

focal concerns: the concerns designated by Walter Miller to represent the cultural values of the lower class; they include, trouble, toughness, smartness, excitement, fate and autonomy

foray: an attack, usually by two or three youths, upon one or more rival gang members (e.g., a drive-by shooting)

G

gang: in general, a group that exhibits characteristics that set them apart from other affiliations of juveniles, often involved in deviant activity (for more on the various definitions comprised under this term, see pp. 127-129 in Chapter 5)

ganging: the process of developing gangs

general strain theory: Robert Agnew's theory positing that the removal of valued stimuli or the presentation of negative stimuli can lead to strain and, perhaps, deviance

goal confusion: the state of affairs in which judges, probation and aftercare officers, probation directors, state legislators, juvenile justice experts and others in the system disagree about the objectives of juvenile court an community supervision

GREAT (Gang Resistance Education and Training) program: a program operated by the Bureau of Alcohol, Tobacco and Firearms in which local police officers present a curriculum to middle-school children designed to induce them to resist the pressure to join a gang

group hazard hypothesis: a contention that delinquency committed in groups has a greater chance of being detected and acted upon by the juvenile and criminal justice systems

group home: a community residential facility housing delinquent youths in relatively small numbers

guardian ad litem: an individual appointed by the court to serve as an advocate for a child in a child abuse or neglect case (Also see **Court-Appointed Special Advocate**)

guided group interaction: a technique for changing delinquents into conforming youths, involving group sessions that confront delinquents with the fact that past delinquency has led to their present status as offender

H

home detention: programs that supervise juveniles at home instead of in custody while they are awaiting further court action

houses of refuge: early institutions for children that were designed to separate the youth from the detrimental environment of the city

I

I-levels: See **interpersonal maturity levels**

in camera **testimony:**   testimony given outside the courtroom, often used for the testimony of children in abuse and neglect cases

Index offense: an offense included in Part I of the Uniform Crime Reports. The eight crimes included are murder, rape, robbery, aggravated assault, burglary, larceny, motor vehicle theft, and arson

infanticide: the deliberate killing of young children, a common practice prior to the fourth century when a child was an economic burden to a household

informal adjustment: informal handling of an offense without the filing of a petition (e.g., a probation intake officer orders the payment of restitution)

inmate code: a group of peer norms or a code of behavior among inmates that may or may not conflict with the norms expected by treatment professionals and correctional staff

intake decision: the decision whether to file a court petition of delinquent, status offense, abuse or dependency

intelligence quotient (IQ):   a test, developed by Alfred Binet. that provides a numerical representation of the mental ability of an individual [the formula is IQ = (mental age/chronological age) × 100]

intensive supervision: supervision outside of a residential faculty in which more oversight than simple probation is provided

intermediate sanction: a sentence that is more punitive than simple probation but less severe than imprisonment

interpersonal maturity levels (I-levels):   developed by Sullivan et al., the seven levels that reflect the progressive development of social and interpersonal skills

intraindividual theory: in explanations of child maltreatment, a theory that views child maltreatment as an internal defect of the abuser

involuntary servitude: selling or trading a youth to another for service

J

"Just Say No" campaign: a school- and media-based program designed to encourage children to make a personal decision to refuse any offer to use illicit drugs in the face of peer influences

job burnout: the emotional exhaustion, cynicism and depersonalization that can affect youth workers such as probation officers

justice model: a model for the criminal and juvenile justice systems in which the overriding goal is to administer fair and proportional punishment

juvenile: a minor (The precise definition of a juvenile varies from jurisdiction to jurisdiction, currently ranging from under age 16 to under age 19)

juvenile awareness project: interventions (such as the Scared Straight program) that involve bringing youths into the prison for presentations on prison life

K

knowledge approach: an approach to drug use prevention that entails providing youths with information on different types of drugs and the possible legal consequences of using them

L

labeling: the contention that the fact of being labeled deviant by society leads an individual to act in accordance with that label

legislative waiver: state laws that provide for automatic transfer of juvenile to adult court, as opposed to judicial waiver or transfer (see **waiver**)

M

maintenance program: a drug treatment program that seeks to establish a state in which the individual does not experience withdrawal systems

maturation effect: the effect when a decrease in delinquent activity can be attributed to growing older (maturation) rather than treatment or punishment

medical model: a perspective that approaches the deviant act as a symptom of a larger problem (or "disease")

mentoring program: a program for at-risk youth that is designed to bring together youths who are not receiving the proper familial support with adults in the community who will help nurture the youths

meta-analysis: a statistical technique that uses data from a number of studies to compute a common statistic in order to compare results across studies

minimization of penetration: keeping court processing of juveniles at the lowest possible level

Minnesota Multiphasic Personality Inventory (MMPI):   a 556-question inventory that serves as a standardized method for tapping personality traits in individuals.

modeling: a form of learning that entails copying the behavior of others

modes of adaptation: according to Merton, the various ways of adapting to strain; the five modes of adaptation are conformity, innovation, ritualism, retreatism and rebellion.

Monitoring the Future (MTF) survey: a self-report survey, administered annually to high school seniors, college students and young adults, that includes both serious and less serious offenses, such as robbery, aggravated assault, hitting teachers, use of weapons, group fighting and drug usage.

N

National Crime Victimization Survey (NCVS):   a victim survey administered by the U.S. Census Bureau

National Youth Gang Survey: a survey administered by Spergel and Curry (1993) that identified the five common gang-intervention strategies of suppression, social intervention, organization change and development, community organization, and opportunities provision

National Youth Survey (NYS):   a self-report survey administered to 11- to 17-year-old youths that taps information on index offenses

nature-nurture controversy: the debate as to whether intelligence is inherited (nature) or whether it is an outcome of growth in the environment (nurture)

near group: an assembly of individuals characterized by a relatively short lifetime, little formal organization, a lack of consensus between members, a small core of continuous participants, self-appointed leadership and limited cohesion

neglect: the failure to provide life's essentials (e.g., food, shelter, clothing, etc.) to a child

neoclassicism: the middle ground between classicism and positivism, the contention that humankind exercises come degree of free will, but that choices are limited by a large number of factors both within and outside of the individual (Also called **soft determinism**)

net-widening: the practice of handling youths (or other offenders) who normally would have been left alone

nondirective therapy: see **person centered therapy**

nonsecure detention: the placement of a delinquent youth in a small group home that is not as securely locked to await further court action (Compare to **secure detention**)

nullification: a refusal to enforce the law or impose a punishment

O

operant conditioning: the reinforcement of behavior through a complex system of rewards

order maintenance: police intervention into behavior that disturbs or threatens to disturb the public peace

outpatient drug-free program: a nonresidential form of drug treatment that emphasizes the provision of a supportive, highly structured, family-like atmosphere within which a patient can be helped to alter his or her personality and develop social relationships conducive to conforming behavior

P

parens patriae: a legal doctrine under which the state is seen as a parent

peer mediation: a program in which disputants in a matter are brought together with a third-party peer (youth) mediator in an effort to resolve the dispute to the satisfaction of both parties

person-centered therapy: Carl Rogers's approach contending that empathic understanding, unconditional positive regard and congruence will initiate change in the individual toward self-actualization (See p. 316 for explanations of these components.) Also called **nondirective therapy**

petition: the document filed in juvenile court alleging that a juvenile is a delinquent, status offender or dependent

phrenology: the idea that the shape of the skull and facial features are linked to levels of aggression

physiognomy: the idea that facial features are related to behavior

police brutality: police use of excessive force

police discretion: the authority of police to enforce or not enforce the law, or how to enforce the law

positivism: a school of thought based upon determinism, wherein what an individual does is determined by factors beyond the control of the individual (Compare to **classicism**)

preventive detention: detention to prevent further delinquency while awaiting court action on an earlier charge

primary deviance: those actions that are rationalized or otherwise dealt with as functions of a socially acceptable role (Compare to **secondary deviance**)

problem-oriented policing: addressing the underlying causes of problems (such as delinquency) rather than simply addressing the symptoms

program effectiveness: the question of whether programs achieve their objectives

punishment gap: the finding that when juveniles are tried in adult court for the first time they are usually given the same degree of leniency given to adult first offenders

Q

Quay typology: a typology suggested by Herbert Quay that identifies four personality types among delinquent youths; the four types include: neurotic-disturbed; unsocialized-psycopaths, "subcultural-socialized" and inadequate-immature

R

radical nonintervention: the practice of leaving youths alone as much as possible in order to avoid labeling (see **labeling**)

rational choice theory: the theory that potential offenders make choices based on various factors in the physical and social environments

rational-emotive therapy: therapy that attempts to substitute appropriate emotions for inappropriate emotions so that the individual can move on to appropriate behavior

reality therapy: William Glasser's therapeutic approach in which the youth is taught to accept responsibility and pursue needs in a responsible manner

reasonable doubt standard: the standard of proof used in both adult criminal cases and juvenile delinquency cases: doubt based on reason and that a reasonable man or women might entertain

regression toward the mean: the return of behavior toward its true average rate after an unusually high or low rate of behavior

reintegration model: a model suggesting that probation personnel refer youths with problems to outside agencies that can help with integrating the youths into law-abiding society

restitution: the practice of offenders paying for all or part of the damage inflicted on persons or property damaged by the offense

restitution program: a program in which the offender makes monetary payment to the victim(s) of the crime he or she committed

restorative justice: a model of justice that is concerned with repairing the damage or harm inflicted through processes of negotiation, mediation, empowerment and reparation

risk-control model: a model for the criminal and juvenile justice systems in which the focus is on preventing future delinquency

role-taking: the process in which an individual (a child) assumes the role of a person or character whom they have observed (see **modeling**)

routine activities perspective: a perspective that assumes that the normal, day-to-day behavior of individuals contributes to deviant events; that is, the convergence of motivated offenders, suitable targets and an absence of guardians allows for the commission of crime

rumble: a gang fight

S

Salient Factor Score: a scale that makes predictions of parole success based on items such as: no prior convictions, no prior periods of incarceration, no juvenile commitments, no commitment for auto theft, no prior parole revocation, a lack of drug dependence, a high school education, employment for at least six months over the past two years, and a place to live upon release from prison

secondary deviance: deviance that occurs when deviant behavior is used as a means of adjusting to society's reactions (Compare to **primary deviance**)

secure detention: the placement of a youth in a locked facility with other youths who are awaiting either further court action or transfer to a state correctional facility

selective incapacitation: the argument that some juveniles are high-rate offenders and as a result need special attention so as to incapacitate them from committing more delinquency

self-control theory: Gottfredson and Hirschi's theory holding that self-control, internalized by individuals early in life, is what constrains a person from involvement in deviant behavior

service: the various forms of assistance that the police provide to the public

shame tactics: measures designed to embarrass offenders in order to punish them and to deter them from further delinquency. Examples include bumper stickers proclaiming one to be a drunk driver or shirts announcing one to be a shoplifter.

skills training: an approach to drug use prevention that seeks to train youths in the personal and social skills needed to resist pressures to use drugs

social area analysis: the process of identifying geographical areas in terms of their social characteristics

social bond: see **bond to society**

social disorganization: the state of a community in which the people in that community are unable to exert control over those living there

social history investigation: an investigation performed by a probation officer into the legal and social history of a delinquent youth and his or her family, similar to a presentence investigation in adult court

social learning approach: in explanations of child maltreatment, an approach that contends that an individual learns to be abusive or neglectful by observing past behavior of that type

Social Prediction Table: an instrument created by Glueck and Glueck (1950) that scores youths according to the presence or absence of discipline by the father, supervision by the mother, affection by the father, affection by the mother and family cohesiveness

sociocultural explanation: in explanations of child maltreatment, an explanation that emphasizes the role of society and the environment in leading to deviant behavior

soft determinism: (see **neoclassicism**)

somatotypes: physiques (e.g., ectomorph, endomorph and mesomorph) supposedly corresponding to particular temperaments

status degradation ceremony: a ceremony or ritual that moves a person to a lower social status

status offense: an action illegal only for persons of a certain status (i.e., juveniles); an action for which only a juvenile can be held accountable (e.g., runaway behavior, truancy)

strain theory: Robert Merton's theory that deviance results from a disjuncture between the goals approved by a culture and the means approved for reaching those goals

subculture of violence: a value system that accepts the use of violence to solve problems

suppression effect: a decrease in the number of offenses committed after treatment or incarceration compared to the number of offense committed prior to treatment/incarceration

symbolic interaction: the process through which an individual creates his or her self-image through interaction with the outside world

systemic violence: violence due to factors related to the sale and marketing of drugs

T

techniques of neutralization: techniques outlined by Sykes and Matza that allow a juvenile to accommodate deviant behavior while maintaining a positive self-image

therapeutic community: a residential form of drug treatment that emphasizes the provision of a supportive, highly structured, family-like atmosphere within which a patient can be helped to alter their personality and develop social relationships conducive to conforming behavior

token economy: a behavior modification strategy, often used in training schools and other residential facilities, in which point or dollar values are assigned to particular behaviors and are used as a way of rewarding appropriate behavior

Toughlove: an approach to drug use prevention that encourages the use of strong measures (e.g., filing criminal charges) by parents

training school: an institution that houses delinquents considered to be unfit for probation or another lesser punishment

transfer: see **waiver**

true diversion: referral of a juvenile to a non-court agency program

V

vicarious victimization: the phenomenon in which an individual recognizes and responds to the victimization of others

victim-blaming: assigning some of the responsibility for a victimization to the victim

victim compensation program: a program in which the state makes monetary payments to the victim(s) of a crime

victim precipitation: a situation in a victimization experience in which the victim may have struck the first blow or somehow initiated the victimization

victim survey: a survey of the general population about their experiences with being the victim of deviance

victim-offender reconciliation program (VORP):   a formal mediation program in which victim and offender are clearly identified and the participation of the offender is often a requirement of the court

W

waiver: the process by which an individual who is legally a juvenile is sent to the adult criminal system for disposition and handling (Also called **judicial waiver** or **transfer**)

wannabe: a juvenile who aspires to join a gang

wilderness experience: a program in which youths undergo an outdoor experience that is designed to teach self-reliance, independence and self-worth

wilding gang: a middle-class gang that strikes out at what its members perceive to be inequalities and infringements on their rights by other ethnic groups

Y

Youth Service Bureaus: common name for diversion agencies

SUBJECT INDEX

AUTHOR INDEX

INDEX TO COURT CASES